THE ILLUSTRATED ENCYCLOPEDIA OF
ROYAL BRITAIN

THE ILLUSTRATED ENCYCLOPEDIA OF
ROYAL BRITAIN

A MAGNIFICENT STUDY OF BRITAIN'S ROYAL HERITAGE WITH A DIRECTORY
OF ROYALTY AND OVER 120 OF THE MOST IMPORTANT HISTORIC BUILDINGS

CHARLES PHILLIPS
CONSULTANTS: Dr. JOHN HAYWOOD FRHistS
AND Professor RICHARD G. WILSON FRHistS

METRO BOOKS
New York

CONTENTS

THE KINGS & QUEENS OF BRITAIN

This complete history of the royal families of Britain charts the lives and legends of her kings and queens, their consorts and children, and the pretenders, usurpers and regents. From the first Saxon king, Egbert, in AD825 to the modern House of Windsor, this authoritative chronicle features more than 100 individual biographies, including the rulers of Scotland to the time of King James I and VI. Feature boxes highlight the major events of each reign, and family trees give important information on every British dynasty and the royal lines of succession. This is the in-depth story of one of the longest-running monarchies in the world covering the colourful reigns of Tudor monarchs Henry VIII and Elizabeth I, the rise of the British Empire under Queen Victoria, and the state of the monarchy under Elizabeth II.

Left: Four medieval kings of England – William I, William Rufus II, Henry I and Stephen, c. 1250–59.
Below: Heraldic shields of William I, Henry IV, William III and Victoria.

BRITAIN'S ROYAL FAMILIES

On 2 June 1953, Elizabeth, eldest daughter of the late King George VI, rode in the golden coach of state through rain-drenched London streets, from Buckingham Palace to Westminster Abbey, to be crowned Queen Elizabeth II in a ceremony of the utmost gravity and splendour.

She made a solemn series of vows, among other things, 'To govern the Peoples of the United Kingdom of Great Britain and Northern Ireland, Canada, Australia, New Zealand, the Union of South Africa, Pakistan and Ceylon, and of [her] Possessions and other Territories to any of them belonging or pertaining, according to their respective laws and customs', to 'Cause Law and Justice, in Mercy, to be executed in all [her] judgements', and to 'Maintain and preserve inviolably the settlement of the Church of England, and the doctrine, worship, discipline and government thereof, by law established in England'. Then, dressed in a simple linen dress, having removed the ermine-

Below: William the Conqueror began building the White Tower in 1066. It became a part of the Tower of London.

trimmed crimson velvet robes in which she had arrived, she was anointed with holy oil on the palms of both hands, on the breast and on the crown of the head in commemoration of the coronation of the Biblical King Solomon of Israel. 'As Solomon was anointed king by Zadok the priest and Nathan the prophet, so be thou anointed, blessed, and consecrated Queen over the Peoples, whom the Lord thy God hath given thee to rule and govern.'

The pomp and splendour of the coronation celebrated the queen's pre-eminence and her elevation far above her subjects; throughout the order of service she was referred to as 'Her Majesty'. At the same time, the resonant liturgical language emphasized that the queen's status as God's chosen ruler laid upon her a sacred duty to be the faithful servant of her subjects.

NINE CENTURIES OF HISTORY

Elizabeth II's coronation was rich in royal history and tradition. Performed in the abbey church established at Westminster by King Edward the Confessor (1042–66), it closely followed the order for coronation in the 14th-century *Liber regalis*, which was itself

Above: Edward the Confessor's body is carried to Westminster Abbey, in a detail from the Bayeux Tapestry (1082).

derived from the rite of ordination and coronation devised by St Dunstan, Archbishop of Canterbury, for the elevation to the throne of King Edgar at Bath on 11 May 973. At Edgar's ceremony a choir sang the anthem 'Zadok the Priest'. The anthem has been used at every subsequent coronation, and since the crowning of George II, in 1727, in the celebrated setting by German-born court composer George Frideric Handel.

At the moment of her anointment, Elizabeth sat in 'King Edward's Chair', the throne built *c*.1300 by Edward I to contain the ancient Pictish-Scottish royal 'Stone of Scone', which was supposedly used for the anointing of Scottish rulers from the time of Fergus Mor (AD498–501). (In 1953 the coronation chair still contained the 'Stone of Scone', but the stone was subsequently removed. It was returned to Scotland on 15 November 1996.) By receiving the blessing of God and the acclamation of her people in the abbey, Elizabeth II took her place in a line of monarchs stretching right back to King Harold II (1066). Every king and queen since Harold has been crowned in Westminster Abbey except Edward V and Edward VIII, neither of whom found time to be crowned at all in their brief reigns.

DEFENDERS OF THE FAITH

Major changes intervened in the long years from 1066 to 1953, not least the introduction of the royal oath to preserve the Church of England. From the time of King Henry VIII, who established the Church of England in 1534, the English sovereign was 'Defender of the Faith'. Then, beginning in 1688 when the English Parliament replaced the Catholic Stuart king, James II, with James's eldest daughter, Mary, and her husband, the Protestant William of Orange, kings and queens crowned in Westminster Abbey had to vow to 'Maintain in the United Kingdom the Protestant Reformed Religion established by law'.

William and Mary came to the throne at the invitation of parliament, which interfered in the dynastic succession to remove a Catholic king

Below: Built by Edward IV in 1475, St George's Chapel, within Windsor Castle, has been the burial place of many kings.

Above: Dunstan of Canterbury (AD 924–88) was a monastic reformer as well as the creator of royal ordination–coronation rites.

and so safeguard the Protestant faith in England. At their coronation, they swore therefore to 'Rule in line with the statutes of Parliament'. They were king and queen in a 'constitutional monarchy' wherein the real power lay with elected MPs rather than with leading members of an hereditary royal family. In the 300-odd years since William and Mary took these vows, kings and queens have adapted to being

Above: Henry I (1100–35). The king's legitimate son died in 1120. Henry's nephew and daughter disputed the succession.

subject to parliament, to being figure-heads for the state, to reigning rather than ruling. Yet in the same period, and particularly from around 1850 onwards as Britain created the greatest empire known to history, the prestige of the monarchy, and the public pomp and ceremony associated with the crown, rose ever higher.

By 1953 the British Empire was being dismantled but its successor, the Commonwealth of Nations, was thriving; Elizabeth's coronation procession included state vehicles bearing heads of government from many Commonwealth countries. Subsequently, Elizabeth II had to adapt the monarchy to fast-changing times, in particular with unprecedented levels of television and press scrutiny of the queen herself and the royal family. However, she has wisely maintained the ceremony associated with earlier times, as seen in the two meticulously planned and highly successful royal occasions of the early 21st century: the funeral of Queen Elizabeth, the Queen Mother, in 2002, and the celebrations of the queen's Golden Jubilee later the same year.

THE RIGHT TO RULE

The English word 'king' derives from the Germanic *cyning/kuning*, which was imported by Anglo-Saxon raiders who sailed across the North Sea to invade Britain in the 5th and 6th centuries AD. In modern usage, the word usually means a supreme ruler, with sovereign authority over an independent state.

Britain certainly had 'kings' in the sense of supreme rulers before Anglo-Saxon times. The first known by name are those who faced the Roman invasions of 55–54BC and then AD43, tribal leaders such as Cassivellaunus and Caratacus, rulers of the Catuvellauni of southern England.

In this period and throughout the era of the early Anglo-Saxons, kings were warrior leaders who held power primarily on the basis of force. When a warrior-king died, his kingdom often died with him, as there was little, if any, belief in a hereditary right to rule.

However, very slowly the idea of an inherited right to rule began to develop: not necessarily through a dynasty of blood relations, but at least by means of a king's designation of his chosen successor. This introduced the idea of a ruler's legitimacy, so that force of arms alone was no longer all.

By the 7th century, Christianity was taking root in Britain. As the religion spread after the conversion in *c.* AD600 of King Aethelbert of Kent, the first Anglo-Saxon monarch to become Christian, so the idea developed of divine election. Kings were presented to their subjects as God's chosen instruments, with a special capacity to bring God's blessing to the kingdom and its people. As the Christian God was King of Heaven, bringing justice and showering blessings on the needy, so the king on earth brought similar if less glorious benefits to his people. Kings were, like priests, servants of the Lord: the ordination-coronation in 973 of King Edgar, in which he was anointed with holy oil, brought out this point explicitly.

Centuries later, it was still a key part of Elizabeth II's ordination ceremony in 1953. 'O Lord and heavenly Father, the exalter of the humble and the strength of thy chosen, who by anointing with Oil didst of old make and consecrate kings, priests, and prophets, to teach and govern thy people Israel: Bless and sanctify thy chosen servant Elizabeth, who by our office and ministry is now to be anointed with this Oil and consecrated Queen.'

THE FAERIE QUEEN

On 30 November 1601 Elizabeth II's revered predecessor and namesake Elizabeth I made a celebrated speech to a representative group of MPs. She was 68 years old, and had been on the throne for 43 years.

As Elizabeth drew towards the end of a reign of magnificent achievements for her country, a reign that would give its name to the 'Elizabethan age', she was popularly and officially revered as the 'Virgin Queen', 'married' to her country and tied to her people by bonds of love and gratitude. Her words that day celebrated these bonds and came to be known as her 'golden speech'. She declared, 'There is no jewel, be it of never so rich a price, which I

Above: Henry VIII (1509–47) ruled through council and other instruments of government, but his will was not to be crossed.

set before this jewel: I mean your love. For I do esteem it more than any treasure or riches … I have cause to wish nothing more than to content the subject and that is a duty which I owe.

Below: Mother to her people. Elizabeth I (1558–1603), who never married, was promoted as a Protestant 'Madonna'.

Below: Mary Queen of Scots was queen at the age of seven days in 1542, but was forced to abdicate, aged 24, in 1567.

Neither do I desire to live longer days than I may see your prosperity and that is my only desire.'

The relationship between queen and subjects celebrated in these memorable words was like that of a mother and her loyal offspring: a connection sustained by deep feelings of love and duty. The queen loved and was loved: her behaviour was bound by her sense of duty to her subjects and to God, whose chosen instrument of government she was.

The speech was, of course, propaganda: it represented an idealized image of Elizabeth's interaction with her subjects and government through parliament. Nonetheless, it captured the romance of the Elizabethan age, of years in which men such as Sir Francis Drake carried the name of England and her queen to far-flung corners of the world, and in which the poet Edmund Spenser immortalized the queen in Gloriana, heroine of his epic *The Faerie Queene*.

If the relationship of the monarch with MPs and the people could be seen as a chaste love affair at the close of Elizabeth's reign, it was one that soured quickly under the strain of attempts by Elizabeth's Stuart successors – James I and his son Charles I – to rule with absolute authority.

Below: Return of the House of Stuart. Eleven years after Charles I's execution, Charles II regained the crown in 1660.

THE AGE OF THE BARONS

From the time of England's Anglo-Saxon kingdoms, monarchs sought to establish and extend their authority through the rule of the king's law. To this end the Anglo-Saxon kings relied on the support of the king's council or Witan. This body, which consisted of leading nobles and churchmen, was summoned by the king to advise him, to approve new laws, to attest royal grants of land and to back him when confronting rebels.

The Witan legitimized the king's actions, his rule and even his accession: in theory, members of the Witan were responsible for electing the king, although in practice this was a matter of approving a *fait accompli*. Even though

Above: Divine right. In 1598 James VI of Scots (later James I of England) declared that kings were instruments of God's will.

the role and person of Anglo-Saxon monarchs remained to a large extent in the Germanic tradition of king as warrior-leader, the king's power was stabilized by the role of the Witan.

From the 11th century onwards, the Witan's successor, the *commune concilium* of Anglo-Norman kings, performed the same role: the king ruled with full authority, given the consent of his barons. These men, the principal landowners in England, were formally bound to the monarch in a subordinate position through the ties of the feudal system.

A CHARTER OF LIBERTIES

In the 13th century, the barons asserted their power in the face of abuses of royal authority, forcing the agreement of King John to the Magna Carta, a charter guaranteeing the 'liberties' of leading subjects, in 1215. Henry I, King Stephen and Henry II had all issued charters, but these had been granted by royal will. The Magna Carta was the first charter imposed upon the king by barons threatening civil war. It contained a clause empowering a baronial council of 25 men to take up arms against the king, should he fail to abide by the agreed terms.

In the reign of King John's son, Henry III, the barons were increasingly angered by the king's reliance on French advisers, following his marriage to Eleanor of Provence, and imposed significant limits on royal power by forcing Henry to agree to the Provisions of Oxford in 1258. Under this agreement, a privy council of 15 members, appointed by the barons, was established to control government.

Henry later renounced the Provisions, leading to a civil war in which he was briefly deposed and power passed into the hands of the nobleman Simon de Montfort. While in power, in 1263-5,

Below: Venetian master Antonio Canaletto (1697–1768) celebrates Westminster Abbey, scene of coronations since 1066.

Above: James Thornhill's painting at Greenwich of George I glorifies the triumph of the Protestant succession.

de Montfort called a widely representative governmental council, which in addition to clerics and barons included two knights from each shire and two burgesses from each borough. Henry III's son, Prince Edward, defeated de Montfort in 1265 at Evesham and subsequently ruled with great authority as King Edward I. Yet even he was reliant on the support of a council of advisers, principally to approve taxation to fund his ferocious military campaigns against the Scots and Welsh.

THE RISE OF PARLIAMENT

At around this time the council began to be called 'parliament' (from the Old French *parlement*, 'a talk'). Edward I summoned combined meetings of the *Magnum Concilium* ('Major Council'), which was made up mainly of churchmen and magnates and the *Curia Regis* ('Royal Court') of lay advisers. Some meetings of the *Curia Regis* began to be known as the *Concilium Regis in Parliamento* ('Royal Council in

Parliament'). To some meetings – around one in every seven – Edward called knights and burgesses. The meeting in 1295 is generally labelled the 'Model Parliament' and identified as the first representative English parliament. In addition to magnates and leading churchmen, it included representatives of lesser clergy, pairs of knights from each county, two burgesses from every borough and two citizens from every city.

Thereafter, for some 400 years, the king of England ruled through parliament. He could call it and dismiss it at will. Members of parliament were by no means independent of royal power – and individuals might be imprisoned or put to death if they overstepped the mark.

Only in the reign of Charles I, the second successive ruler of the House of Stuart to seek to rule with absolute

Above: The future George IV acted as Prince Regent for nearly a decade during the illness of his father George III (1760–1820).

power, did parliament present itself as an equal player in its relationship with the king. A 'Grand Remonstrance' passed by MPs on 22 November 1641, presented a long list of the King's failings in government – and for the first time made it clear that parliament could remove a king who was guilty of abuses of power. The scene was set for the civil war, Charles's execution, the abolition of the monarchy and England's brief experiment with republicanism.

Within 50 years came the establishment, in 1688, of the constitutional monarchy, in which the king and queen were subject to the will of MPs.

THE ROYAL COURT

From at least the time of King Henry I, when the oldest surviving account of a king's household was written, the royal court was at the centre of government. Key officials were the chamberlain (usually a leading magnate) and the treasurer (a top cleric or churchman), who took responsibility for the king's living chambers and finances. The chancellor, another man of the Church, was in

charge of the king's chapel, his scribes and the royal seal, which was used as a mark of authority on proclamations and other documents. Royal household positions included the butler (in charge of wine), cooks, grooms, keepers of tents and the bearer of the king's bed. A standing army, consisting of household cavalry and infantry, accompanied the court. In the medieval period the court was often on the move as the king maintained his visibility throughout his territories, although from as early as Henry I's reign, Westminster began to be increasingly established as the centre of government.

Merchants, noblemen, foreign dignitaries and representatives of foreign monarchies came to the royal court to seek favour or advancement. This situation pertained for centuries: it was only from the late 17th century, with the gradual establishment of a constitutional monarchy, that the court began to be eclipsed by parliament as the centre of self-advancement and political intrigue.

This process has continued and the court in the early 21st century has a ceremonial rather than a political importance. Nonetheless, even today the royal court retains a significant role in national life, not least as a setting for state receptions and formal dinners

Above: Mother of a dynasty. Victoria with her son Edward VII, grandson George V and great-grandson Edward VIII as a baby.

for visiting politicians and dignitaries, and in the honours system as the arena in which knighthoods, MBEs, OBEs and other rewards for national service are bestowed.

Below: A new beginning. Prince Charles, Camilla Parker-Bowles and family pose for an official wedding portrait by Tim Graham.

BRITAIN'S MONARCHS

This list of monarchs names the kings and queens of Britain from the time of the ancient rulers of England and Scotland to the present day.

Much of the monarchy's authority and prestige derives from its ancient roots, from the centuries of historical continuity celebrated in genealogical and dynastic tables. Yet there are countless examples of force of arms and political manoeuvring intervening in dynastic or designated succession. In 1066, Duke William of Normandy famously had to enforce his claim that he was the designated successor of King Edward the Confessor in the face of several rival claims, including that of Harold Godwine, Earl of Wessex, who had himself declared King Harold II and was crowned on the very day after Edward the Confessor's death. William's claim triumphed at the Battle of Hastings.

The great Scottish national hero Robert the Bruce killed his chief rival to the succession, John Comyn, before having himself crowned King Robert I of Scots. Richard III of England occupied the throne at the expense of his uncrowned nephew, the 12-year-old King Edward V, whom Richard almost certainly had murdered in the Tower of London. King Henry VII won the English crown in battle against King Richard III.

Throughout these and many other upheavals, the theory of dynastic succession with God's blessing was maintained and all these kings – usurpers or murderers as they might be – laid claim to a dynastic link and were anointed as God's chosen servants on the throne. Henry IV, a usurper, brought an innovation to the coronation in an attempt to legitimize his rule. His ordination was the first to use holy oil reputedly given to Saint Thomas à Becket by the Virgin Mary.

KINGS AND QUEENS OF SCOTLAND (TO 1603)

THE HOUSE OF MACALPINE
Kenneth I mac Alpin 841–859
Donald I 859–863
Constantine I 86–877
Aed Whitefoot 877–878
Eochaid 878–889 (joint)
Giric 878–889
Donald II Dasachtach 889–900
Constantine II 900–943
Malcolm I 943–954
Indulf 954–962
Dubh 962–967
Culen 967–971
Kenneth II 971–995
Constantine III 995–997
Kenneth III 997–1005
Malcolm II 1005–1034

THE HOUSE OF DUNKELD
Duncan I 1034–1040
Macbeth 1040–1057
Lulach 1057–1058
Malcolm III Canmore 1058–1093
Donald III 1093–1094
Duncan II 1094
Donald III 1094–1097 (joint)

Below: King David II of Scotland (left) makes peace with King Edward III of England, in 1357.

Above: James IV of Scotland presenting arms to his wife Queen Margaret, daughter of King Henry VII of England.

Edmund 1094–1097 (joint)
Edgar 1097–1107
Alexander I 1107–1124
David I 1124–1153
Malcolm IV the Maiden 1153–1165
William I the Lion 1165–1214
Alexander II 1214–1249
Alexander III 1249–1286
Margaret, Maid of Norway 1286–1290

THE HOUSE OF BALLIOL
John Balliol 1292–1296

THE HOUSE OF BRUCE
Robert I the Bruce 1306–1329
David II 1329–1332, 1338–1371

THE HOUSE OF BALLIOL
Edward Balliol 1332–1336

THE HOUSE OF STEWART
Robert II 1371–1390
Robert III 1390–1406
James I 1406–1437
James II 1437–1460
James III 1460–1488
James IV 1488–1513
James V 1513–1542
Mary, Queen of Scots 1542–1567
James VI 1567–1603

KINGS AND QUEENS OF ENGLAND

THE HOUSE OF WESSEX
Egbert (802–839)
Aethelwulf (839–858)
Aethelbald (858–860)
Aethelbert (860–865/6)
Aethelred I (865/6–871)
Alfred the Great (871–899)
Edward the Elder (899–924/5)
Athelstan (924/5–939)
Edmund I (939–946)
Eadred (946–955)
Eadwig (955–959)
Edgar (959–975)
Edward the Martyr (975–978)
Aethelred II the Unready (978–1013,
   1014–1016)
Edmund Ironside (1016)

THE DANISH LINE
Cnut (1016–1035)
Harald I Hardrada (1035–1040)
Harthacnut (1040–1042)

THE HOUSE OF WESSEX, RESTORED
Edward the Confessor (1042–1066)
Harold II (1066)

THE NORMANS
William I the Conqueror (1066–1087)
William II Rufus (1087–1100)
Henry I (1100–1135)
Stephen (1135–1154)

Above: King John goes riding. Hunting was the sport of kings from William I.

THE PLANTAGENETS
Henry II (1154–1189)
Richard I the Lionheart (1189–1199)
John (1199–1216)
Henry III (1216–1272)
Edward I (1272–1307)
Edward II (1307–1327)
Edward III (1327–1377)
Richard II (1377–1399)

THE HOUSE OF LANCASTER
Henry IV (1399–1413)
Henry V (1413–1422)
Henry VI (1422–1461, 1470–1471)

THE HOUSE OF YORK
Edward IV (1461–1470, 1471–1483)
Edward V (1483)
Richard III (1483–1485)

THE HOUSE OF TUDOR
Henry VII (1485–1509)
Henry VIII (1509–1547)
Edward VI (1547–1553)
Lady Jane Grey (1553)
Mary I (1553–1558)
Elizabeth I (1558–1603)

Left: The heraldic badges of Kings Edward III, Richard II and Henry IV from Writhe's Garter Book.

KINGS AND QUEENS OF GREAT BRITAIN

THE HOUSE OF STUART
James I (1603–1625)
Charles I (1625–1649)
Charles II (1660–1685)
James II (1685–1688)
William III and Mary II
   (1689–1694)
William III (1689–1702)
Anne (1702–1714)

THE HOUSE OF HANOVER
George I (1714–1727)
George II (1727–1760)
George III (1760–1820)
George IV (1820–1830)
William IV (1830–1837)
Victoria (1837–1901)

THE HOUSE OF SAXE-COBURG-GOTHA
Edward VII (1901–1910)

THE HOUSE OF WINDSOR
George V (1910–1936)
Edward VIII (1936)
George VI (1936–1952)
Elizabeth II (1952–)

Below: The Archbishop of Canterbury reverently places the crown on George V's head at the coronation in 1911.

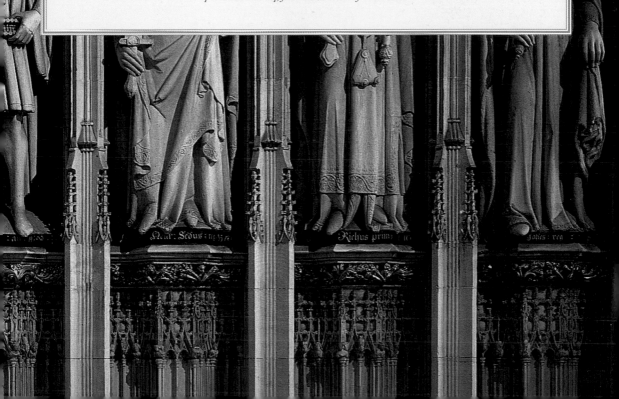

PART ONE

ANCIENT MONARCHS

The lives and legacies of the earliest British kings and queens are all but lost to verifiable history. This is the era of legendary figures such as King Arthur, famed lord of Camelot. Their successors among ancient and medieval monarchs include well-documented rulers, men of deathless renown – such as Alfred the Great, who defeated the Vikings in 871 and promoted English learning; Robert I the Bruce, hero of the 1314 Battle of Bannockburn; and Henry V of England, icon of English nationalism.

Left: Statues of the kings of England from William the Conqueror to King John, 1473–1505, by William Hindley, from the cathedral of York Minster.

CHAPTER ONE

BOUDICCA TO STEPHEN

TO 1154

The origins of the British monarchy are shrouded in legend. The 12th-century Welsh churchman and chronicler Geoffrey of Monmouth produced, in his *Historia regum Britanniae* ('History of the Kings of Britain', *c.*1135–9), a chronology of 76 kings of Britain descended from the island's supposed first settlers: Brutus, great-grandson of Aeneas of Troy and his fellow-Trojan Corineus, who gave his name to Cornwall. Geoffrey claimed that he translated his chronicle from 'a very old book in the British tongue', but in truth the *Historia* was a combination of oral history, folklore, legend and the writer's invention.

Monmouth's chronology contains many romantic tales of famous kings, such as King Leir (the original of Shakespeare's *King Lear*), King Coel ('Old King Cole', supposedly the King of the Britons in the 3rd century and the grandfather of the Roman emperor Constantine the Great), and King Lud (said to have given his name to London). Lud's tale brings us to the beginning of true royal history for, according to Geoffrey, Lud was the brother of Cassivellaunus, an historical figure who fought against Julius Caesar's invaders in 54BC. Because of their encounters with the literate Romans, who wrote about them, the kings of this time in south-east England are the first British rulers whose names we know. Among the contemporaries or near-contemporaries of Cassivellaunus were Commius, king of the Atrebates tribe of Hampshire, and Togidubnus (formerly Cogidubnus), king of the Regnenses tribe (Sussex), who built himself the splendid Roman palace at Fishbourne, near Chichester.

Left: In a scene from the Norman Bayeux Tapestry (1082), Harold Godwine is crowned King of England by Archbishop Stigand.

TRIBAL AND ROMAN RULE

TO AD449

When Roman general and dictator Julius Caesar invaded Britain from Gaul in 54BC, he encountered organized resistance under the command of Cassivellaunus, king of the Catuvellauni tribe, which occupied the territory of modern Hertfordshire. Cassivellaunus was probably the most powerful man in Celtic Britain at that time, but he was not the chosen leader of a united country. His tribal state was one of several in fierce competition: rivals in

Above: One of the coins issued in the name of Tasciovanus. His principal mint was at St Albans, the Catuvellauni capital.

what would become south-east England included the tribes of the Regnenses (occupying Sussex), the Cantiaci (Kent), the Atrebates (Hampshire) and the Trinovantes (Essex).

Caesar, who famously declared, '*Veni, vidi, vici*' ('I came, I saw, I conquered'), in fact had mixed success on his two invasion raids of Britain in 55BC and 54BC. But, on the second raid, Cassivellunus was unable to prevent his opponent from returning to Gaul with alliance agreements and hostages.

Almost everything we know about British rulers of this period comes from Roman written sources. Cassivellaunus is the first British native whose name is recorded, because Caesar wrote it down. However, coinage also provides some evidence. For example, Cassivellaunus's successor as ruler of the Catuvellauni, Tasciovanus, is the first British ruler whose face and name can be seen on a coin, which was minted *c.*10BC.

The next king of the Catuvellauni, Cunobelinus (ruled AD10–41) was described as *Rex Britannorum* ('King of

Above: Julius Caesar led two seaborne invasions of Britain in 55–54BC. Both times he landed on Deal Beach in Kent.

the Britons') by the Roman historian Suetonius, but like his predecessor Cassivellaunus he was by no means the ruler of a united land, merely the most important and powerful of several rival kings. Nevertheless, he called himself *rex* and after conquering the Essex territories of the Trinovantes ruled almost the whole of south-east England from his capital at Colchester.

INVASIONS FROM ROME

Roman emperor Claudius launched a new invasion of Britain in AD43, landing an army of 40,000–50,000 well-organized troops on the coast of Kent. Many tribes, mindful of the benefits of Roman trading links as well as the might of the invading army, accepted rule from Rome under a consular governor of Britain. The first was Aulus Plautius, who governed until AD47.

Some Britons put up resistance. Cunobelinus died in AD40, to be replaced by his sons Caratacus and Togodumnus, who both chose to fight the Romans. Togodumnus was slain in combat and Caratacus was driven to the west until AD50 when, after a defeat at

---

KING LEAR

One of the legendary British kings recorded by Geoffrey of Monmouth is King Leir, whose story, known from British and Irish folklore, was used by William Shakespeare as the basis for his great tragedy *King Lear*.

Geoffrey of Monmouth recounted that Leir ruled for 60 years and that, in the course of his reign, he founded the city of Leicester. Monmouth's narrative was reworked by 16th-century chronicler Raphael Holinshed, who wrote that Lear governed Britain for around 40 years *c.*800BC. Holinshed was one of William Shakespeare's key sources for *King Lear*.

The tale of Lear was also told by Edmund Spenser in his allegorical epic

The Faerie Queene. According to the legend, the king in his old age unwisely divided his country between his daughters on the basis of their professions of love for him. The most devoted daughter, Cordelia, refused to make profession of her love on demand, so the king cut her off from her inheritance and split the kingdom between his harsh elder daughters Goneril and Regan. They mistreated him and he lost his wits.

In the version told by Monmouth, Leir is reunited with Cordelia and comes back to the throne, but in Shakespeare's better-known version, Cordelia dies and Lear grieves for her with words of devastating simplicity.

the hands of Plautius's successor as Roman governor, Ostorius Scapula, he fled to Yorkshire. There Cartimandua, queen of the Brigantes and an ally of Rome, handed Caratacus over to the invaders. Caratacus and his family were transported to Italy. He famously made such a dignified appeal for mercy that Emperor Claudius allowed the British king and his family to live on in Rome.

ANGER OF A ROYAL WIDOW

The year AD60 saw the death of Prasutagus, king of the Iceni tribe of Norfolk. As a client king under Roman rule, he left half his estate to the Emperor Nero and half to his two daughters, but imperial officials disregarded these instructions and attempted to seize the entire inheritance, while Roman soldiers ran amok, flogging Prasutagus's widow, Boudicca and raping her daughters.

Boudicca and the Iceni rose in revolt, slaughtering as many as 70,000 Romans and their allies. However, at Mancetter (Warwickshire) her 100,000-strong army was humiliated by a Roman force barely one-tenth its size. Boudicca took poison rather than be captured.

Below: Togidubnus, king of the Regnenses tribe of Sussex, accepted Roman rule. He built a splendid palace at Fishbourne.

The occupying Roman army made steady progress in stamping out pockets of Celtic-British resistance. In the years AD77–84, Roman governor Julius Agricola won major victories in southern Scotland, northern England and Wales, more or less completing the process, although parts of Wales and northern England remained resistant and a large portion of Scotland was never incorporated into the empire. The conquest initiated over 300 years of Roman rule in Britain, when the kings of rival British states were subject to a

Above: Warrior queen. This 1902 statue celebrates Boudicca's heroic resistance against Roman tyranny. It stands by the Houses of Parliament in central London.

consular governor appointed by Rome. However, in about AD410 the Britons effectively declared independence, expelling the Roman administration. Initially the patterns of Roman life in Britain carried on. As time passed and the Romans did not return, there was increasing competition between Celtic rulers and Romanized Britons, as well as waves of invasion by Germanic peoples from the east, Irish from the west and Picts from the north.

A British ruler named Vortigern ('Great king') was pre-eminent by c.AD430. To bolster defences against the northern Picts, he hired Germanic mercenaries and rewarded them by allowing them to settle along the eastern coast of Britain.

In AD449, however, settlers led by Horsa ('Horse') and Hengest ('Stallion') began to seize land and operate independently. The scene was set for centuries of struggle between Germanic incomers and British natives, whom the incomers tended to call 'Welsh' (meaning, in this instance, 'foreigners').

ARTHUR
KING OF CAMELOT

In folklore, legend and literature, King Arthur of Camelot, lord of the Knights of the Round Table, is revered above all other kings and queens. Narratives of the golden age of chivalry in his court at Camelot are tinged with knowledge of its inevitable decay and self-destruction, an elegiac sadness rooted in the knowledge that all things – youth, physical perfection, political achievement, life itself – must pass.

THE HISTORICAL ARTHUR

Stirring legends of King Arthur grew up around the life of a relatively minor 5th- or 6th-century British or Welsh prince who fought against the advancing Saxons and who was perhaps the British leader at a famous victory over the Saxons at 'Mount Badon' c.AD500. Arthur was first mentioned by name in the *Historia Brittonum* ('History of the Britons') by the Welsh cleric Nennius c.AD830, some 300-odd years after his probable death. Nennius lists 12 battles in which Arthur took on the Saxons, including the great triumph at Mons Badonicus (Mount Badon). In the slightly later *Annales Cambriae* ('Annals of Wales', c.AD960) the anonymous chronicler records that Arthur led his people to victory at Mount Badon in AD516 but was killed in battle at 'Camlann' in AD539.

An earlier reference by the British priest Gildas in his *De excidio et conquestu Britanniae* ('The Ruin and Conquest of Britain', c.AD550) describes an

Above: Arthur and his queen Guinevere leave a banquet, from a manuscript by French poet Chrétien de Troyes (d.1183).

unnamed British war leader who triumphed at the Battle of Mount Badon (here dated to c.AD500) and who was probably Ambrosius Aurelianus, the historical prototype for Arthur. One theory contends that the name Arthur, which means 'bear man', was a nickname given to Ambrosius by his men because he was big and hairy like a bear or because he wore the bearskin cloak of late Roman officers.

Many historians locate Mount Badon near Bath in southern England, perhaps at the vast hillfort of Little Solsbury Hill, which archaeologists have shown was used by the British at the end of the 4th century. They suggest that Arthur's victory there drove back West Saxons advancing from the Thames Valley. However, other clues point to the north of England and some believe that 'Camlann' might refer to Birdoswald (Cumbria), which was known as Camboglanna in the Roman era.

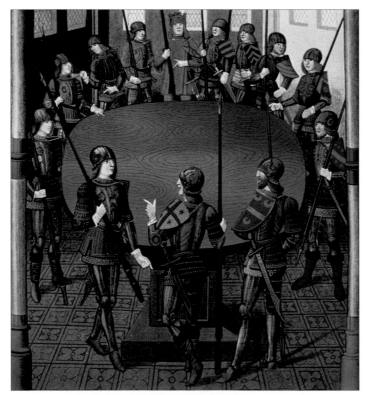

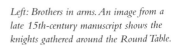

Left: Brothers in arms. An image from a late 15th-century manuscript shows the knights gathered around the Round Table.

If Arthur was active in that region in the early 6th century, then he cannot have been combating Saxons, for their advance had not reached this area.

But the search for the historical Arthur is probably beside the point: the King of Camelot is mainly a figure of legend, whose enduring importance lies in his use by successive ages as a symbol of a past golden age of knightly virtue, right government and peace.

THE LEGEND GROWS
In Welsh folklore and early literature King Arthur began to be associated with tales of wonder and magic. The 12th-century Welsh prose romance *Kulhwch and Olwen* identified Arthur with a band of heroes, an idea that would develop into the Arthurian court and the Knights of the Round Table. The legend was given life by Geoffrey of Monmouth in his *Historia regum Britanniae* ('History of the Kings of Britain', c.1135–9). His version contains many familiar elements: the magician Merlin changes Uther Pendragon, King of Britain, into the likeness of Gorloise, Duke of Cornwall, so Uther can sleep with Gorloise's ravishing wife, Ygerna. Arthur is born as a result of this union, and crowned king at a time when the

Below: The 'Arthurian' round table in the Great Hall of Winchester Castle was made in the 1270s, in Edward I's reign.

KING ARTHUR'S INFLUENCE AND LEGACY
The romance of Arthur's court at Camelot and of the company of the Knights of the Round Table, together with the popularity of the Continental tradition of courtly love, inspired the enduring cult of chivalry at the royal courts of England in the 14th–16th centuries. King Edward III and his leading barons were devoted to the practice of jousting and in 1348 Edward founded the knightly Order of the Garter based on that of Arthur and the Knights of the Round Table, whom he regarded as historical figures. At the Tudor courts of King Henry VIII and Queen Elizabeth I, the Arthurian chivalric tradition was still in full flower: Edmund Spenser used Malory's *Le Morte d'Arthur* as a key source for his poem in praise of Elizabeth, *The Faerie Queene* (c.1590).

The Arthurian tradition became very popular once more in the Victorian period, when the Pre-Raphaelite artistic movement used Arthurian themes in painting, stained glass and other forms, while English poet Alfred, Lord Tennyson wrote *The Idylls of the King* (1842) using elements of the legend.

In the 20th century, the narrative of King Arthur was the inspiration for the English novelist T.H. White's series of books *The Once and Future King*, which in turn inspired the Broadway musical *Camelot* (1960). In the English language, the word Camelot has come to be used to describe any golden age doomed to end before its time, such as the administration of US President John F. Kennedy, which was cut short by his assassination in Dallas, Texas, in 1963.

country is threatened by marauding Saxons. He trounces the Saxons, then defeats the Irish and Picts, marries Guinevere and inaugurates a golden age of chivalry. When he travels to France to defeat a Roman army, he leaves England in the care of his nephew Mordred, who seduces Guinevere and usurps the throne. Upon his return, Arthur is defeated and killed in Cornwall.

Geoffrey of Monmouth's work was translated into French in the *Roman de Brut* (1155) of the Anglo-Norman author Wace. The *Roman* was the first book to mention the round table used at Arthur's court. A group of 13th-century French romances known to scholars as the 'Vulgate' and 'post-Vulgate' cycles then developed the elements of the legend: an illicit romance between Arthur's queen, Guinevere, and his knight, Lancelot; the quest for the Holy Grail and the identification of Lancelot's son, Sir Galahad, as the only knight pure enough to succeed in the Grail quest. Another strand of the Vulgate cycle developed the theme of Arthur's childhood and the

narrative of how he proved his royal standing by drawing the magic sword Excalibur from stone. The legend of King Arthur had a new flowering in England in the 15th and 16th centuries, with Monmouth's *Historia* and Sir Thomas Malory's English prose romance, *Le Morte d'Arthur* (c.1470).

Below: The Arthurian legend developed in a series of French romances. This image is from a 15th-century Grail manuscript.

ANGLO-SAXON KINGDOMS

AD500–871

Waves of Germanic invaders swept into Britain in the 5th and 6th centuries AD. There were three main groups: the Angles, from the region of Angulus (modern Angeln district) in northern Germany on the Baltic coast; the Saxons, from the North Sea Coast between the Jutland peninsula and the River Weser; and the Jutes, probably from Jutland in Scandinavia. The Angles settled mainly in East Anglia and to the north of the river Humber, and gave their name both to England and the English language; the Saxons settled largely in southern England; and the Jutes made their home in Kent.

They spread out across south-east England, meeting only the occasional setback. Among the most notable of these was at Mount Badon, the heroic British victory *c.*AD500 celebrated in the mythology of King Arthur. By *c.*AD600, seven main Anglo-Saxon kingdoms were established: Mercia, Northumbria, East Anglia, Kent, Wessex, Sussex and Essex. The British Celts held only Wales and the south-western kingdom of Dumnonia, part of today's Somerset, Devon and Cornwall.

Below: This helmet was among the treasure buried with a king – probably Raedwald of East Anglia – at Sutton Hoo c.AD625.

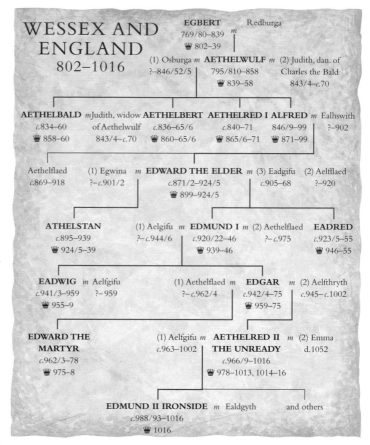

WESSEX AND ENGLAND 802–1016

EGBERT 769/80–839 ♛ 802–39	Redburga *m*	

(1) Osburga *m* **AETHELWULF** *m* (2) Judith, dau. of
?–846/52/5　795/810–858　　　Charles the Bald
♛ 839–58　　　843/4–*c.*70

AETHELBALD *m* Judith, widow **AETHELBERT** **AETHELRED I** **ALFRED** *m* Ealhswith
*c.*834–60　of Aethelwulf　*c.*836–65/6　*c.*840–71　846/9–99　?–902
♛ 858–60　843/4–*c.*70　♛ 860–65/6　♛ 865/6–71　♛ 871–99

Aethelflaed　(1) Egwina　*m* **EDWARD THE ELDER** *m* (3) Eadgifu　(2) Aelfflaed
*c.*869–918　?–*c.*901/2　　*c.*871/2–924/5　　*c.*905–68　?–920
♛ 899–924/5

ATHELSTAN　(1) Aelgifu *m* **EDMUND I** *m* (2) Aethelflaed　**EADRED**
*c.*895–939　?–*c.*944/6　*c.*920/22–46　?–*c.*975　*c.*923/5–55
♛ 924/5–39　　♛ 939–46　　♛ 946–55

EADWIG *m* Aelfgifu　　(1) Aethelflaed *m* **EDGAR** *m* (2) Aelfthryth
*c.*941/3–959　?–959　　?–*c.*962/4　*c.*942/4–75　*c.*945–*c.*1002
♛ 955–9　　　　　　♛ 959–75

EDWARD THE　　(1) Aelfgifu *m* **AETHELRED II** *m* (2) Emma
MARTYR　　*c.*963–1002　**THE UNREADY**　d.1052
*c.*962/3–78　　　　*c.*966/9–1016
♛ 975–8　　　　♛ 978–1013, 1014–16

EDMUND II IRONSIDE *m* Ealdgyth　　and others
*c.*988/93–1016
♛ 1016

KINGDOMS IN COMPETITION

The rival Anglo-Saxon realms were drawn into competition, seeking territory and wider control. Northumbria and Mercia were the dominant forces in the 7th century. Northumbria began the century as two kingdoms, those of Bernicia and Deira. These were combined by AD616.

Under Edwin (AD616–33), Oswy (AD642–70) and Ecgfrith (AD670–85), Northumbria became a power to be reckoned with, especially after Oswy defeated and killed his rival warrior-king, Penda, ruler of Mercia in AD655. Northumbria's importance began to

Below: An illuminated manuscript of the first words of Saint Luke's Gospel, from the Lindisfarne Gospels, written c.AD694.

Right: Kings of Kent. Aethelbert (left) was the first Christian Anglo-Saxon king and Eadbald (right) was his successor.

decline after Ecgfrith was killed fighting the Picts at Nechtansmere near modern Forfar on 20 May AD685.

In Mercia, King Wulfhere (AD657–70) expanded southwards as far as the River Thames. The Mercian ruler Aethelbald (AD716–57) called himself 'King of Britain' and seized London and the whole of modern Middlesex from Essex, as well taking control of large parts of Wessex and even conquering territories in Wales. However, he was assassinated by his bodyguard in AD757. His successor was the renowned Offa, who declared himself 'King of the English' and ruled most of Wessex, and all of Sussex, Kent and East Anglia as well as his Mercian heartland. His fame spread far and wide and he was addressed as 'brother' by great Charlemagne, King of the Franks, when negotiating trade terms. Offa also embarked upon the building of a vast – but not continuous – earth barrier along Mercia's border with Wales – Long sections of 'Offa's Dyke', a vast construction, 149 miles (240km) long, 11ft (3.3m) tall and 22 yards (20m) in width, still stand today.

After Offa's death in AD796, Wessex rose to become the pre-eminent Anglo-Saxon kingdom under the rule of King Egbert. Egbert annexed Sussex, Kent and Essex and also campaigned to the west, taking control of former Celtic lands in modern Devon and Cornwall. To the north, he defeated the Mercians in AD825 at the Battle of Ellendun.

From the late 8th century, all Anglo-Saxon kings faced a common foe, the marauding Vikings, whose first raid on England was at Portland in Wessex c.AD786. Egbert of Wessex defeated a Cornish and Viking army in AD838 at Hingston Down, Cornwall, but the raiders remained a major problem for Anglo-Saxon England until the reign of Egbert's grandson, Alfred the Great.

THE RISE OF CHRISTIANITY

Aethelbert, the long-lived King of Kent (r. AD560–616), was the first Anglo-Saxon monarch to adopt Christianity. Under the influence of his Frankish queen, who had already been baptized in the religion, Aethelbert allowed a Christian missionary from Rome, Augustine, to settle and begin preaching at Canterbury. Augustine, who was hugely influential and who won many converts, was made the first Archbishop of Canterbury. In AD600 King Aethelbert himself converted to Christianity.

Further north, Christian missionaries spreading south from Scotland were disseminating a distinct form of Christianity that followed Irish instead of Roman customs. Christianity had been established in Ireland since as early as c.AD400–450. The Irish monk Saint Columba founded a monastery on the island of Iona off the west coasts of Scotland in c.AD563 and Saint Aidan came from Iona to found the celebrated monastery of Lindisfarne, off the coast of Northumberland in northern England, in AD634. It was here that the beautifully illuminated Lindisfarne Gospels were made in about the year AD694.

By this date, the Roman Christian tradition had won an important victory over its Irish counterpart on the mainland. This was decided at the Synod of Whitby called by King Oswy of Northumbria in AD663–4.

KINGS OF IRELAND

From time immemorial, according to the songs of the Celtic bards, Ireland was governed by a high king, who ruled from Tara (north of modern Dublin). In the bardic tradition, the first high king was Niall Noígiallachi ('Niall, Taker of Nine Hostages'), who led military campaigns into Britain.

In fact, the Ireland they described consisted of more than 100 clan groupings (*tuatha*), each with an elected king. *Tuatha* were clustered in larger regional groups, each under one king acting as overlord. The main groups were the Cuig Cuigi ('Five Fifths'), Connacht (Connaught), Laighin (Leinster), Midhe (Meath), Mumhain (Munster) and Ulaidh (Ulster). The historical Niall was a king of Midhe (d. early 5th century). His descendants, ruling from Tara, were claiming to be kings of all Ireland by the 6th century. From AD795, all the Irish kingdoms faced an onslaught from the invading Norse Vikings, who founded the settlement that would become Dublin in AD841. The kings of Mumhain, ruling from Cashel, grew powerful enough to sack the Norse settlements at Limerick and Dublin. The acclaimed Brian Boru, ruler of Mumhain, became the first true high king of all Ireland in 1002.

ALFRED THE GREAT
AD871–899

As Alfred came to the throne of Wessex, aged 22 in AD871, his kingdom and, indeed, the whole of Anglo-Saxon England, was seemingly at the mercy of Viking invaders. Nonetheless, he managed to contain and then drive back the Viking threat and to rule with wisdom and energy for almost three decades. In his reign, learning was revived in England and the incomparable *Anglo-Saxon Chronicle* begun. He is the only monarch in English history to have been awarded the epithet 'Great'.

THE VIKING ONSLAUGHT

After the landing of a Danish Viking 'Great Army' in East Anglia in AD865, the Vikings had taken York, captured

Below: The Great King Alfred. Hamo Thorneycroft's statue of Alfred was unveiled in Winchester in 1901.

Northumbria in AD867 and taken control of East Anglia in AD869. However, in the spring of AD871, Alfred and his brother King Aethelred of Wessex led the men of Wessex in a morale-boosting victory over the Vikings on the Ridgeway at Ashdown in Berkshire, killing thousands of invaders, including five earls and a king.

A few weeks later, on 23 April AD871, Alfred came to the throne on Aethelred's death, but the Ridgeway victory brought little lasting benefit to the new king. Almost at once Alfred's army was scattered far and wide by a renewed Viking assault that hit when he was attending Aethelred's funeral at Wimborne. One of Alfred's first acts as king, therefore, was to 'buy peace' by bribing the Vikings. This brought respite for a few years, while the Vikings were occupied in conquering Mercia, but in

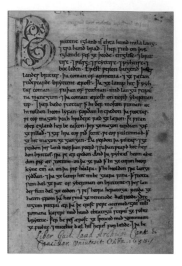

Above: The Anglo-Saxon Chronicle was unusual for the period in being written entirely in Anglo-Saxon rather than Latin.

AD877 a Viking force led by Guthrum renewed the attack and captured Exeter. The following January, when a surprise attack on Chippenham resulted in another Viking victory, Guthrum won control of most of Wessex.

Alfred was forced to retreat deep into the Somerset countryside and, from a base at Athelney in the Somerset marshes, he began to conduct a guerrilla war against the invaders. In May AD878, he led an army of men from Wiltshire, Somerset and Hampshire in a famous victory over the Vikings at Edington, at the northern limit of Salisbury Plain, and drove the remnants of the enemy all the way back to their base at Chippenham, a distance of over 15 miles (24km).

Under the peace treaty that followed, the Vikings agreed to withdraw entirely from Wessex and Guthrum accepted baptism as a Christian. Alfred showed great generosity to his former adversary, recognizing him as an adoptive son.

KING ALFRED THE GREAT,
AD871–899

Born: c.AD849, Wantage
Father: King Aethelwulf of Wessex
Mother: Queen Osburga
Accession: 23 April AD871, Dorset
Queen: Ealhswith (m. AD868; d. AD905)
Succeeded by: His son, Edward 'the Elder'
Greatest achievement: Containing the Viking threat
AD871: Leads English army to victory over Vikings at Ashdown
May AD878: Defeats Vikings at Battle of Edington
c.AD886: Captures formerly Mercian city of London
c.AD887: Learns Latin and begins translation of Pope Gregory the Great's *Cura Pastoralis* ('Pastoral Care or Rule')
Death: 26 Oct AD899, Winchester

THE KING WHO BURNT THE CAKES

At the lowest ebb of his reign, while King Alfred was forced to live incognito in deepest Somerset, he was scolded by a swineherd's wife. The story goes that Alfred was seated by the fireside in the swineherd's hut, lost in thought as he tried to plot a way of defeating the seemingly invincible Vikings. Perhaps he did not hear the woman of the house, who was leaving for a few moments, ask him to mind the cakes that she was baking, or perhaps he forgot to do as he was asked. When she returned and found that the cakes were burnt she was furious and battered the king about the head with her stick. This apocryphal story can be traced as far back as a *Life of St Neot*, written in the 10th century, and was mistakenly included in the edition of Bishop Asser's *Life of King Alfred* (AD893) which was published by Archbishop Matthew Parker in 1574. Thereafter it appeared in many modern accounts of Alfred's life and the story continues to be told into the 21st century.

Right: Sir David Wilkie painted King Alfred burning the cakes in 1806.

THE DANELAW

Guthrum and the Vikings pledged not to attack Wessex, but they remained in strength in other English kingdoms, establishing themselves in East Anglia and the lands to the north and east of Watling Street, the Roman road running from London in the south-east to Chester in the north-west. Here, in the 'Danelaw' (roughly modern Yorkshire, east Midlands and East Anglia), they flourished, establishing several prosperous settlements.

Alfred meanwhile set about strengthening the military defences of Wessex. He built several *burhs*, or fortified towns, reorganized the army so that half could be rested while the other half was on campaign and created an English navy, consisting of manoeuvrable warships of his own design, each with 60 oars. The navy proved its worth in AD896 by defeating a powerful Danish Viking raiding party off the Isle of Wight.

THE REVIVAL OF LEARNING

Alfred was able to provide stability for the people of Wessex and, in a previously lawless era, his kingdom came to be known for its just royal laws and honest administration. He collected laws from diverse sources and published an English law code. His coins recognized him as *Rex Anglorum* ('King of all the English') and he was increasingly accepted as king of all Englishmen and women not subject to the Danes.

As a young child, Alfred had visited the learned Frankish court, which had been established early in the 9th century by the great Charlemagne. This experience may have inspired him to initiate and oversee the revival of education and learning that occurred at his court in Winchester and throughout his kingdom.

Alfred himself was illiterate until his later teens but he determined that free-born English boys should have the chance to learn through reading, and established schools to this end. He also saw that those books in his words 'most necessary for all men to know' should be made available to his people in their own tongue and provided for their education.

King Alfred learned Latin at the age of 38 in order to translate the *Cura Pastoralis* ('Pastoral Care or Rule') by Pope Gregory the Great, and he subsequently sent a copy of his translation with an exquisite aestel (bookmark) to every bishop in the kingdom. A key part of his commitment to knowledge was his sponsorship of the vast *Anglo-Saxon Chronicle*, an historical record of England which went as far back as the Roman invasion.

A TEMPLATE FOR KINGSHIP

Alfred was plagued throughout his life by illness. Some scholars suggest he was an epileptic, others that he suffered from haemorrhoids or from venereal disease contracted in his bachelor days before his AD868 marriage to Ealhswith of Mercia. Yet despite the debilitating effect of his illness, the king brought energy, intelligence, and courage to all his endeavours. He was, in the words of his devoted and perspicacious biographer Bishop Asser of Sherborne, an 'immovable pillar of the people of the west, a just man, an energetic warrior, full of learning in speech, above all instructed in divine knowledge'.

Above: The exquisite 'Alfred jewel' – the head of a pointer or bookmark – is marked 'Alfred ordered me made'.

THE HOUSE OF WESSEX

AD899–978

The great King Alfred was succeeded in AD899 by his son, Edward, who performed wonders in consolidating and extending his father's achievements. Where Alfred had concentrated on defence against the Viking threat, Edward took an aggressive approach. In a series of stunning victories in AD917, he captured Essex and the East Midlands and forced the Vikings of East Anglia to submit to the rule of Wessex. Then, in AD918, he further expanded the kingdom by taking control of western (English) Mercia from its female ruler, his niece Aelfwynn, and conquered Danish Mercia (the region known as 'the Five Boroughs') and the Danish-ruled kingdom of East Anglia. Before his death, on 17 July AD924, he had also received the

Below: King Edgar, one of the first kings to be anointed with holy oil, with St Dunstan, creator of the coronation ceremony.

submission of the rulers of the Welsh kingdoms of Dyfed and Gwynnedd, while the kings of the northern Danish territory of York and the independent Anglo-Saxon earldom of Northumbria, Strathclyde and Alba (Scotland) had accepted him as 'lord'. His dominance extended across the entire island.

LINE OF SUCCESSION

Edward, usually known as 'the Elder', was briefly succeeded by his son Aelfweard, (who ruled for just 16 days and may have been assassinated) and then by another son, Athelstan, who won further victories for Wessex and was the first king to rule all of England.

Athelstan was succeeded by another of Edward's sons, Edmund I (AD939–46), who suffered a major setback when Olaf Gothfrithson, King of the Dublin Norse, captured York and parts of Mercia in AD940. Edmund won back most of the land for Wessex in

ATHELSTAN, KING OF ENGLAND, AD924–939
Birth: c.AD895
Father: Edward the Elder
Mother: Egwina
Accession: 17 July AD924
Coronation: 4 Sept AD924
Succeeded by: His half-brother, Edmund I
Death: 27 Oct AD939, Gloucester

AD942, then died an untimely death four years later, aged just 25, when he was killed in a skirmish while attempting to defend his steward from a thief named Leofa.

Yet another son of Edward the Elder, Eadred (AD946–55), defeated Erik Bloodaxe, the last Viking king of York, in AD954 and consolidated the Wessex dynasty's control of all England. His natural death at around the age of 30 created something of a succession crisis, as his two sons were just 15 and 14.

ROYAL SEX SCANDAL

The accession of Edmund's elder son Eadwig threatened all that Alfred's heirs had achieved, for Eadwig, while a good-looking young boy, lacked the seriousness his position demanded.

His reign began in scandal when he left his coronation feast and was discovered by the venerable Abbot Dunstan *in flagrante* with both a maiden named Aelfgifu and her mother.

Within two years the kingdom split when Mercia and Northumbria rejected the young king's dubious authority and chose his 14-year-old brother Edgar in his place. Fortunately for the future of England, the dissolute Eadwig died before his 20th birthday, on 1 October AD959, and the energetic, pious and astute Edgar came to the throne in his place.

Right: The lands ruled by Athelstan, King of Wessex. His power reached as far north as York and as far west as Cornwall.

THE LORD'S ANOINTED

Edgar brought to England an era of peace and reform of the kind attributed to his great predecessor Alfred. With his Archbishop of Canterbury, the renowned Dunstan, he introduced church and monastic reforms and developed the idea of the king as God's representative on Earth.

On Whit Sunday, 11 May AD973, Edgar was crowned king of England in a splendid ceremony in Bath that included an anointing: a deliberate reference to the ordination of a priest. The coronation-anointing took place 14 years into the reign because by AD973 Edgar was 30, the minimum age for a priest. Later the same year, in a celebration at Chester, Edgar was recognized as overlord by no fewer than eight kings – including King Kenneth II of Scots, King Malcolm of Strathclyde and King Iago of Gwynnedd.

The Five Boroughs
Kingdom of the English

ATHELSTAN: KING OF ALL ENGLAND

Edward the Elder's son Athelstan (AD934–9) was the first king to rule all of England. In AD927 he pushed Wessex's borders further north by conquering the Viking kingdom of York. He received

vows of submission from the Britons of Cornwall and five kings in Wales c.AD930. The *Anglo-Saxon Chronicle* praised him in ringing tones: 'Royal Athelstan, lord of warriors, giver of rings to men, with his kingly brother Edmund, won glory beyond compare with their sharp swords.'

Athelstan was the king who first sent Englishmen into military action on the European Continent. In AD939 he despatched a fleet to Flanders to back his nephew, Louis of France. He commissioned an illuminated edition of Bede's *Life of St Cuthbert* that contains a portrait of the king. This is the first contemporary image in English history of a ruling monarch.

Left: Athelstan's portrait is contained by a capital G in an illuminated edition of Bede's Life of St Cuthbert.

Edgar was a great reformer. He oversaw a realignment of county boundaries that would endure for more then 1000 years (until 1974), and also reformed weights and measures and the coinage, introducing a new currency in AD973.

Below: Athelstan's coins were inscribed 'King of all Britain', indicating that the Scots and Welsh accepted his authority.

FROM AETHELRED II TO HARTHACNUT

AD978–1042

The rule of Aethelred II (AD978–1016) began in treachery. He came to the throne at the age of just 10, when his half-brother King Edward was stabbed to death by Aethelred's retainers.

King Edward was the son of King Edgar by his beautiful first wife, Aethelflaed, while Aethelred was Edgar's son by his second wife, Aelfthryth. Naturally, Aelfthryth was opposed to Edward's accession and when the king was killed during a visit to Aelfthryth's house, suspicion inevitably fell upon her. Although no proof was ever found of the involvement of Aethelred or of Aelfthryth in the murder, the deed cast a shadow over the king's rule.

AN INHERITANCE LOST

Aethelred's reign ended with the king sidelined and his son Edmund 'Ironside' facing defeat in the struggle against Cnut's Danish forces. In just 38 years, Aethelred lost a stable and prosperous kingdom, which had been built up over 100 years by Alfred the Great and his heirs.

The king is often known as 'King Aethelred the Unready'. This derives from 'Aethelred unraed', which is a pun on his name and means 'Noble advice, evil advice'. In fact, Aethelred's reign was not a failure because he was 'unready' or unprepared, or because he took poor advice – although he did make a number of costly mistakes that had profound long-term effects. The principal reason Aethelred lost a kingdom was the sudden surge of Danish power under King Harold Bluetooth and his son Sweyn in the years after AD980.

It certainly did not help that Aethelred was an unconvincing general. He lost much of the support of his leading subjects in a series of defeats by the Danish invaders. After the Battle of Maldon, in Essex, in AD991, Aethelred initiated a doomed policy of bribing the Danes to stay away with vast sums of gold and silver. Over a period of 20 years, these bribes, known as *Danegeld*, cost England a fortune. Aethelred made

Above: Aethelred, Rex Anglorum ('King of the English'). In his reign, a few of these pennies would have bought a sheep.

another decision with damaging long-term consequences when, in 1001, he married Emma, daughter of the Duke of Normandy, as part of an Anglo-Norman alliance designed to outmanoeuvre the Danes.

Aethelred then made plans for a massacre of all the Danes in England on St Brice's Day, 13 November 1002. However, this was only partially carried out and served to provoke the Danes into fiercer military action. In 1013 King Aethelred fled to Normandy, and the Danish king, Sweyn, claimed the English throne. However, Aethelred returned the following year, and he succeeded in ousting Sweyn's son, Cnut. To win the support of his leading nobles he was forced to pledge reforms and surer government in future in the first such agreement between monarch and subjects in English history.

In 1015 Aethelred's son Edmund – known as 'Ironside' for his strength and courage – revolted against his father's rule and took control of the army. Aethelred died, powerless, in April 1016 and after a bruising series of battles Edmund Ironside and Cnut agreed to share power, with Edmund taking Wessex and Cnut ruling all the land to the north of the River Thames.

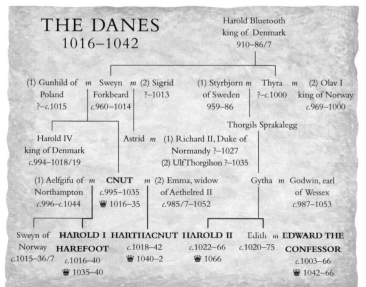

THE DANES
1016–1042

Harold Bluetooth
king of Denmark
910–86/7

(1) Gunhild of Poland ?–c.1015	*m*	Sweyn Forkbeard c.960–1014	*m* (2) Sigrid ?–1013	(1) Styrbjorn of Sweden 959–86	*m* Thyra ?–c.1000 *m*	(2) Olav I king of Norway c.969–1000

Thorgils Sprakalegg

Harold IV king of Denmark c.994–1018/19	Astrid *m*	(1) Richard II, Duke of Normandy ?–1027 (2) Ulf Thorgilson ?–1035	

(1) Aelfgifu of Northampton c.996–c.1044	*m* **CNUT** c.995–1035 ♔ 1016–35 *m*	(2) Emma, widow of Aethelred II c.985/7–1052	Gytha *m* Godwin, earl of Wessex c.987–1053

Sweyn of Norway c.1015–36/7	**HAROLD I HAREFOOT** c.1016–40 ♔ 1035–40	**HARTHACNUT** c.1018–42 ♔ 1040–2	**HAROLD II** c.1022–66 ♔ 1066	Edith *m* **EDWARD THE** c.1020–75 **CONFESSOR** c.1003–66 ♔ 1042–66

Above: The scandal that dogged Aethelred. A 15th-century manuscript depicts events surrounding the murder of King Edward.

CNUT RULES ALONE

When King Edmund Ironside also died, on 30 November 1016, his subjects in Wessex were left to the mercy of King Cnut. The new king acted swiftly to secure his position: he had Edmund Ironside's brother, Eadwig, killed; he executed the powerful earls of East Anglia and Mercia; and he married King Aethelred's widow, Emma of Normandy, hoping to consolidate his standing in the country by marrying its queen.

Cnut already had two sons by his existing English wife, Aelfgifu, but under the terms of the new marriage agreement, only his children by Emma would have a claim to the throne. In 1019 Cnut became King of Denmark

THE KING WHO COULD NOT TAME THE WAVES

The best-known story about King Cnut is the legend – of doubtful authenticity – that he taught his flattering courtiers a lesson by pretending he thought he could tell the waves to go back. With an empire including land on both sides of the North Sea, Cnut was the most powerful ruler in Europe in the early 11th century.

As an increasingly devout Christian Cnut was ever mindful of the divine power from which his own claim to rule was derived. Impatient with courtiers who flattered and praised him too much, he played along with the idea that he thought he was important enough to command the waves. He had a throne placed on the edge of the beach and ordered the waves to retreat. When they did not, and indeed rushed over his feet

and drenched his robes, he pretended to be angry and ordered them back once more. When he finally dropped the game, he told his courtiers never again to forget the extent to which his own mortal power was limited and bade them to remember how little consequence it had beside the power of God, who could command the oceans.

Right: Cnut and his queen, Emma, present a cross to the New Minster, Winchester, in an image of c.1030.

and at a stroke England became part of a Scandinavian empire. Cnut was increasingly committed to imperial expansion in Norway and wanted to maintain England as a secure, untroublesome source of wealth. Cnut

was a Christian and made pilgrimages to Rome in 1027 and 1031. According to a chronicler of the 12th century, Cnut changed from a wild warrior to 'a most Christian king'.

A TROUBLED SUCCESSION

Cnut had proved himself a very effective ruler. However, after his death in 1035, his dynasty was destroyed by infighting in just seven years. Cnut's designated successor was Harthacnut, but because he was in Norway at the time of Cnut's death, Harthacnut appointed his half-brother Harold regent. Harold then claimed the throne but he was soon dead, probably having been assassinated. Harthacnut returned to England to occupy the throne, but he died on 8 June 1042, apparently from overindulging in drink at a wedding.

Left: The Danes are coming. Aethelred's nemesis, King Sweyn, disembarks with his army and invades England.

EDWARD THE CONFESSOR AND HAROLD II

1042–1066

On the death of Harthacnut, the throne passed to Edward, son of Queen Emma by her first husband, Aethelred. His accession was manoeuvred by the ruthless Earl Harold Godwine. In 1045 Edward married Godwine's daughter, Edith. Then, in 1051, Edward attempted to assert his independence by exiling Godwine and by naming his cousin, Duke William of Normandy, as his successor – if William's later account is to be believed. Nevertheless, the following year Godwine returned stronger than ever to win the full support of the king's ruling council, the Witan. Godwine died in 1053 but his sons, Tostig, Gyrth and Harold, occupied powerful positions as the earls of Northumbria, East Anglia and Wessex.

STRUGGLE FOR SUCCESSION

In his final years, Edward was much occupied with rebuilding the abbey church of St Peter at Westminster. By

Below: Edward the Confessor celebrates Easter at a banquet in 1053. Godwine's death is depicted in the foregound.

EDWARD THE CONFESSOR, KING OF ENGLAND, 1042–1066
Birth: *c.*1003, Islip
Father: Aethelred II
Mother: Emma of Normandy
Accession: 8 June 1042
Coronation: 3 April 1043, Winchester Cathedral
Succeeded by: Harold II
Death: 5 Jan 1066, Westminster

the time it was consecrated, in December 1065, however, he was too ill to attend, and on 5 January 1066 he died. Harold Godwineson, Earl of Wessex, was crowned King of England the very next day, claiming to have been designated by Edward as his successor.

William of Normandy was enraged. He claimed both that Edward had chosen him as successor in 1051 and that Harold Godwine had pledged to support William's claim on a mission to Normandy in 1064. William also had a hereditary claim to the throne, albeit

HAROLD II, KING OF ENGLAND, 1066
Birth: *c.*1022
Father: Godwine, Earl of Wessex
Accession: 5 Jan 1066
Coronation: 6 Jan 1066, Westminster Abbey
Succeeded by: William I
Greatest achievement: Securing the throne, Battle of Stamford Bridge
Jan 1066: Marries Ealdgyth, sister of Earls of Mercia and Northumbria
25 Sept 1066: Defeats Harald Hardrada and Earl Tostig at the Battle of Stamford Bridge
14 Oct 1066: Defeated by Duke William of Normandy at the Battle of Hastings; dies during battle

a tenuous one: he was the great-nephew of King Cnut's second wife, Emma of Normandy. In addition to William, King Harold faced two other rivals for his throne: King Harald Hardrada of Norway and Edgar the Atheling (or 'prince'). Harald's claim to the throne was inherited from his nephew King Magnus the Good of Norway who had acquired the claim by treaty from Harthacnut in 1036. Edgar the Atheling had the most convincing hereditary claim as Aethelred II's great-grandson, but he was fatally handicapped by being just 14 years old and having no proof that he was a man of war or fit for power.

King Harold had the throne by virtue of acting swiftly. His two rivals prepared to invade. In addition, Harold had made an enemy of his brother, Earl Tostig, by depriving him of power in Northumbria because of his incompetence, and replacing him with the earl of Mercia's brother, Morcar.

In the summer of 1066 Harold waited for the twin invasions – but nothing happened. In September he

allowed his soldiers to return home, but then had hastily to gather an army and march north to York when news reached him that Earl Tostig and King Harald Hardrada had mounted a joint invasion. He routed their combined force at the Battle of Stamford Bridge, near York, on 25 September.

Harold now heard that William had landed a fleet 250 miles (400km) to the south. He gathered his 7000-odd troops and marched south in 11 days. He could have chosen to hold back and engage the Norman army in the course of the winter, but instead staked everything on a quick victory in battle at Hastings.

Right: The Norman cavalry take on Anglo-Saxon foot soldiers in a Bayeux Tapestry scene from the Battle of Hastings.

THE BATTLE OF HASTINGS

The battle near Hastings on 14 October 1066 lasted all day. King Harold's army of 7000, including many untrained peasants, occupied a strong position on high ground, with Duke William's smaller force of around 4000 – consisting of archers, foot soldiers and cavalry – arranged on the slope beneath them.

The Normans opened the assault with their archers and the Anglo-Saxons fought back with spears and slings. When the Norman cavalry attacked, its men and horses were cut to pieces by Harold's soldiers with their double-handed axes. Twice the Norman cavalry pretended to retreat, drawing groups of Anglo-Saxons from the high ground, and then turned to destroy them.

At one point, scholars believe, William's horse was cut from under him and the word went among his men that he was dead. However, he claimed another horse and, once in the saddle, raised his helmet to rally his troops by showing them his face, declaring, 'Look, I am alive – and by God's grace will still win the victory!'

The decisive moment in the battle came when King Harold was killed. From the evidence of the Bayeux Tapestry (made about 1077) he was either shot in the eye with an arrow or had his legs hacked from under him by a Norman foot soldier. The Anglo-Saxons fought on without a leader, but at dusk they broke and fled, leaving the field to Duke William of Normandy. Some historians believe that King Harold's corpse was chopped into many pieces by victors maddened by battle.

Left: A 13th-century manuscript depicts the moment of Harold's death.

After his triumph over Harold at Hastings, William marched his Norman army across south-east England in a show of military might. Canterbury and Winchester surrendered almost immediately and by December resistance was over and the throne was secured.

Below: Feudal power. An enthroned William I grants lands to Alain de Brittany, who swears loyalty in return.

WILLIAM I THE CONQUEROR
1066–1087

The illegitimate Norman known in his homeland as Guillaume le Bâtard was crowned King William I of England in Edward the Confessor's abbey church at Westminster by Ealdred, Archbishop of York, on Christmas Day, 1066.

His initial victory had been won by military might and it was consolidated with great ruthlessness in the ensuing six years in the face of a series of revolts. William and his army put down rebellions in Cornwall in 1068 and then repeated uprisings in the north in 1068–9, during which Norman earl Robert de Comines was burnt alive with 900 men in Durham. King Sweyn II of Denmark and Edgar the Atheling captured York briefly during this period, burning the Minster. William's brutal reprisals laid waste the countryside so that thousands of people died of starvation and disease. In 1070, Anglo-Saxon rebels in East Anglia led by Hereward the Wake joined up with Danish sailors to plunder Peterborough Abbey. William made peace with King Sweyn II in June 1070 and the Danes departed, but Hereward became a focus for Anglo-Saxon rebels who gathered to him in his hideout on the Isle of Ely. William defeated them in April 1071, but Hereward escaped to carry on the fight as an outlaw.

INVASION CONSOLIDATED

Across the country the Normans raised imposing castles to keep their peace. In 1067–8 alone, William built castles in Exeter, Warwick, Nottingham, York, Lincoln, Huntingdon and Cambridge. In the course of his reign, William raised 78 castles, including the White Tower, now the heart of the Tower of London, and the New Castle near the mouth of the river Tyne that gave its name to Newcastle. In the Welsh Marches, on

Above: A scene from the Bayeux Tapestry depicts William the Conqueror with Bishop Odo and Robert de Mortain.

the English border with Wales, William settled powerful Norman nobles who were allowed free rein so long as they kept the Welsh and English under control.

The Normans now 'invaded' the land-owning aristocracy and the Church, replacing Anglo-Saxons in a host of key positions. In 1066 there were 4,000 landowning *thegns* in King Harold's country, but by 1087 (the year of William's death) this territory had been appropriated and shared out among 200 French aristocrats; only two Anglo-Saxon landowners remained.

William made his intentions towards the Church clear in 1070, when he replaced the native Archbishop of Canterbury, Stigand, with his own man, Lanfranc, previously Abbot of St Stephen's in Caen, Normandy. Most of the country's bishops and abbots were replaced by Norman clerics.

By about 1072, England was securely conquered. William spent most of the remainder of his reign in France, campaigning against the French king, Philip I, the Counts of Flanders and Anjou and, from time to time, against his own eldest son, Robert Curthose.

THE DANES AND DOMESDAY

William returned to England in 1085, to face a threatened Danish invasion under King Cnut IV. To raise finance for an army he declared a land tax on all, but then – realizing the need for more accurate records of landholdings – he commissioned a land survey, 'The Description of All England', dubbed *The Domesday Book* by his subjects because there was no escaping it, just like the Day of Judgement. This remarkable survey was completed in less than a year and presented to William on 1 August 1086. In the end, King Cnut died and the invasion did not come.

William then returned to France, where he died in 1087 after being seriously injured in a fall from his horse during an attack on Nantes as part of a campaign against Philip I. He was buried on 12 September in St Stephen's Abbey, Caen. His unfortunate mourners left the building gagging after the king's fat and decomposing body burst its sarcophagus, emitting a stench of rotting flesh.

Before he died, William was ill for some weeks and had time to repent. He reputedly confessed his brutality with some remorse, saying, 'I am stained with the rivers of blood that I have spilled'.

WILLIAM I THE CONQUEROR, KING OF ENGLAND, 1066–1087

Birth: *c.*1027, Falaise, Normandy
Father: Robert, Duke of Normandy
Mother: Herleva
Accession: 14 Oct 1066
Coronation: 25 Dec 1066, Westminster Abbey
Queen: Matilda, daughter of Baldwin V (m. *c.* 1050–2; d. 2 Nov 1083)
Succeeded by: His son William II Rufus
Death: 9 Sept 1087, Priory of St Gervais, Rouen

WILLIAM II RUFUS
1087–1100

 On his deathbed, William I is supposed to have left the English crown to his second son, William, while giving Normandy to his eldest son, Robert Curthose, and giving his third son, Henry, no land but the compensation of £5,000. William secured the crown for himself before Robert could act. Travelling swiftly to England from Normandy, he was crowned king in Westminster Abbey on 26 September 1087.

Before a year was out, William faced rebellion. His uncle, Bishop Odo, Earl of Kent, led an uprising with the aim of replacing William with Robert. Although the rebels captured several towns, the rebellion collapsed, Odo and his supporters were exiled and William seized their land.

William spent some years fighting on and off in Normandy to seize his brother's lands and reunite their father's inheritance. In 1096 Robert Curthose joined the First Crusade and, to finance his part in the expedition, pawned his duchy to William for 10,000 marks. Before Robert returned from the Crusade, William was dead – perhaps assassinated – after what was officially a hunting accident in the New Forest.

WILLIAM II RUFUS, KING OF ENGLAND, 1087–1100
Birth: c.1056/60, Normandy
Father: William I
Mother: Matilda of Flanders
Accession: 9 Sept 1087
Coronation: 26 Sept 1087, Westminster Abbey
Succeeded by: His brother, Henry I
Death: 2 Aug 1100, New Forest, Hampshire

ROYAL WHODUNIT
King William II died in suspicious circumstances while out hunting in August 1100. The official story is that the king and his friends were taking their pleasure in the New Forest, Hampshire, the vast 95,000-acre hunting preserve created by William I, when the fateful arrow was loosed by William's friend, Walter Tirel. The arrow struck William in the chest and he died at once. However, suspicion is inevitable that William's brother Henry, who was in the party and who subsequently became king, was somehow involved in the 'accident'. Henry rode at once to Winchester, where he secured the royal treasury, then proceeded to London to have himself elected king by the ruling council.

Crucially, the 'accident' happened while the rightful heir, Duke Robert Curthose of Normandy, was away on the First Crusade and Tirel himself was never punished.

Left: William II's red hair, which won him the nickname 'Rufus' (from Latin for red), is not visible in this later portrait.

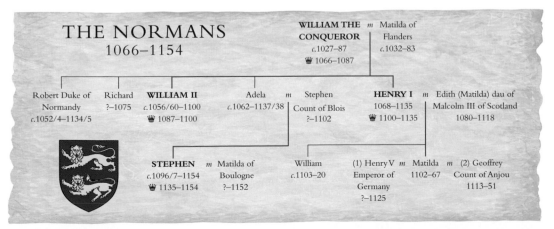

THE NORMANS 1066–1154

WILLIAM THE CONQUEROR c.1027–87 ♔ 1066–1087 m Matilda of Flanders c.1032–83

Robert Duke of Normandy c.1052/4–1134/5 | Richard ?–1075 | **WILLIAM II** c.1056/60–1100 ♔ 1087–1100 | Adela c.1062–1137/38 m Stephen Count of Blois ?–1102 | **HENRY I** 1068–1135 ♔ 1100–1135 m Edith (Matilda) dau of Malcolm III of Scotland 1080–1118

STEPHEN c.1096/7–1154 ♔ 1135–1154 m Matilda of Boulogne ?–1152 | William c.1103–20 | (1) Henry V Emperor of Germany ?–1125 m Matilda 1102–67 m (2) Geoffrey Count of Anjou 1113–51

HENRY I
1100–1135

The first years of King Henry I's reign were clouded by doubt over his succession and by revolts led by barons seeking to put Duke Robert Curthose of Normandy, William the Conqueror's eldest son, on the throne. These were effectively ended by Henry's defeat of Robert at Tinchebrai, Normandy, in September 1106.

The new king also bolstered his position by recalling and making peace with Anselm, the Archbishop of Canterbury, with whom William II had quarrelled bitterly. Anselm had been in exile overseas since 1097, but returned early in the new reign, at Henry's invitation, in October 1100.

A NEW MORALITY

One of the main points of disagreement between William II and Archbishop Anselm had been the Archbishop's disapproval of what he saw as decadence at William's court. In a Lenten sermon in 1094, Anselm had attacked effeminacy and the practice of homosexuality at the court, denouncing the men of the court for growing beards, wearing their hair long and sporting extravagant shoes.

Life at Henry's court was far more sober and clean-shaven, and Henry was a loyal patron of the Church. For example, he sponsored the rebuilding of Canterbury Cathedral choir, a project that was completed in 1130.

Left: A detail from a manuscript image of the loss of the White Ship shows Henry mourning the death of his sons.

Henry's marriage to Edith, the great-granddaughter of Edmund II 'Ironside' (who was briefly king in 1016) and sister of King Edgar of Scots, cemented a valuable alliance with the Scots and allowed Henry to reinforce his claim to the throne by marrying into the royal line of the Anglo-Saxons. After the wedding, Edith took the Norman name Matilda, perhaps in honour of Henry's mother.

LOSS OF THE WHITE SHIP

In 1120, Henry I won a diplomatic triumph by agreeing a peace treaty with King Louis VI of France, under which the long-disputed duchy of Normandy was to pass to Henry's only legitimate male heir, his son Prince William the Atheling, on Henry's death. However, as the royal court returned to England from Normandy, a ship transporting Prince William, sank in the Channel. Apparently the pilot was drunk and he had allowed the vessel, the White Ship, to run on to a rock off Barfleur. Everyone on board died, apart from one Rouen butcher.

NO MALE HEIR

Although Henry had fathered 21 children, only two of them were legitimate. The White Ship tragedy killed William the Atheling, his only legitimate male heir, leaving only a daughter, Matilda, who in 1114 had married Holy Roman Emperor Henry V. On 1 January 1127 Henry prevailed over his reluctant barons, persuading them to accept Matilda, by now a widow, as his heir. But baronial opposition to her succession only grew stronger when, the following year, she married Count Geoffrey of Anjou, who was nicknamed

Above: Henry's jester, Rahere, founded the priory church of St Bartholomew the Great in Smithfield, London, in 1123.

'Plantagenet' because he used the broom plant (Latin: *planta genista*) as his family emblem.

King Henry I died in December 1135 after overindulging in eating lampreys. Although his daughter Matilda was his official heir, many barons instead supported the claim of Henry's nephew Count Stephen of Blois.

HENRY I, KING OF ENGLAND, 1100–1135

Birth: Sept 1068, Selby, Yorkshire
Father: William I
Mother: Matilda of Flanders
Accession 3 Aug 1100
Coronation: 5/6 Aug 1100, Westminster Abbey
Queens: (1) Matilda, daughter of Malcolm III of Scotland (m. 11 Nov 1100; d. 1 May 1118); (2) Adeliza, daughter of Geoffrey VII, Count of Louvain (m. 1121; d. 1151)
Succeeded by: His nephew, Stephen of Blois, although Henry had named his daughter Matilda as his successor
Death: 1/2 Dec 1135, near Rouen, Normandy

STEPHEN

1135–1154

On learning of his uncle King Henry I's death, Count Stephen sailed to England and was crowned in Westminster Abbey on 26 December 1135. His accession, in direct contravention of the oath he and leading English barons had sworn to King Henry I to support the Empress Matilda as Queen, plunged the country into a bitter civil war.

YEARS OF CIVIL TURMOIL

In 1139, the Empress Matilda and her husband Geoffrey of Anjou, in alliance with her half-brother, the illegitimate Robert, Earl of Gloucester, landed an army in south-west England to claim the throne and set up their own royal court in Bristol. In 1140 Earl Ranulf of Chester rose in revolt and captured Lincoln. In 1141, King Stephen was defeated by Robert, Earl of Gloucester, at the battle of Lincoln, on 2 February.

Right: The coronation of King Stephen, a miniature from the Flores Historiarum *by the Benedictine monk and chronicler Matthew Paris (d. 1259).*

STEPHEN, 1135–1154

Birth: *c.*1096/7 (before 1100), Blois, France

Father: Stephen Henry, Count Palatine of Blois, Brie, Chartres and Meaux

Mother: Adela of Normandy

Accession: Usurps the throne 22 December 1135

Coronation: 26 Dec 1135, Westminster Abbey

Queen: Matilda (m. before 1125; d. 2/3 May 1152)

Succeeded by: His second cousin, Henry II

Death: 25 Oct 1154, Dover, Kent

He was imprisoned in chains in Gloucester's castle. The Empress Matilda was elected Queen at Winchester on 8 April. Stephen's wife – another Matilda – arrived with an army of mercenaries from Flanders.

When the armies of the two Matildas met at Winchester, the troops of the Empress were defeated and her key ally Gloucester was taken prisoner. The Empress Matilda's brief ascendancy was over; she was forced to exchange Stephen for Gloucester, and Stephen was crowned King of England for a second time, at Canterbury on Christmas Day 1141.

The civil war ran on for another decade or more. The key years were 1147–8, when the Earl of Gloucester died, and 1153 when Stephen lost his only heir with the death of his beloved son Eustace. However, the bruising conflict could not truly be said to be over until, on 6 November 1153, in the Treaty of Wallingford, King Stephen agreed that the Empress Matilda's son Henry Plantagenet was to be his heir and would inherit the throne. The following year, on 25 October 1154, King Stephen died and Henry inherited the throne of England as King Henry II.

CHAPTER TWO

THE PLANTAGENETS

1154–1399

When Henry, Duke of Normandy, Count of Anjou, Touraine and Maine and Duke of Aquitaine was crowned King Henry II of England in 1154, he founded England's longest-reigning dynasty, that of the Plantagenets. The House of Plantagenet ruled for 331 years, until 1485, supplying 14 English kings.

The name 'Plantagenet' came from a nickname for Henry II's father, Geoffrey, Count of Anjou. The nickname derived from *planta genista*, the Latin name for the broom plant, and was applied to Geoffrey either because he used the plant as his emblem, because he wore broom sprigs in his hat or because he planted broom on his land to provide cover when hunting. Although historians use the name Plantagenet, Count Geoffrey's descendants went without any form of surname for 250-odd years.

Some historians identify the first kings of the Plantagenet line – Henry II, Richard I and John – as 'Angevins', from their title as Count of Anjou, and reserve the title 'Plantagenet' for the succeeding kings, Edward I, Edward II and Edward III. The three Plantagenet kings who were descendants of the Duke of Lancaster are identified as the House of Lancaster (Henry IV, Henry V and Henry VI), and the final three, descendants of the Duke of York, as the House of York (Edward IV, Edward V and Richard III). Nonetheless, all were Plantagenets.

Left: In 1382, Richard II married Anne of Bohemia at Westminster. Both were aged 15. The illustration is from the Chronicles of Jean Froissart *(c. 1333-1400).*

HENRY II

1154–1189

At Christmas 1154 the newly crowned Henry II celebrated the first undisputed accession to the English throne since that of Harold II in 1066. Henry's claim to the throne was not beyond dispute: it was as the son of Empress Matilda, who had plagued Stephen I's reign with repeated assertions of her own royal pedigree as the daughter of King Henry I. However, he acceded peacefully under the terms of an 1153 agreement between Stephen and Matilda that guaranteed the crown for Matilda's son. After years of civil war in Stephen's reign, there was no appetite for a struggle against the king among the nobles and people of England.

FIRST PLANTAGENET KING

In England, Henry acted swiftly and decisively to quell opposition among the barons, destroying a number of castles that had been used as bases for

HENRY II, KING OF ENGLAND, 1154–1189:	
Birth: 5 March 1133, Le Mans	**June 1162:** Thomas à Becket
Father: Geoffrey Plantagenet, Count	appointed Archbishop of Canterbury
of Anjou	**1163:** Overlord of Wales
Mother: Empress Matilda, daughter	**1166:** Assize of Clarendon establishes
of King Henry I of England	trial by jury
Accession: 25 Oct 1154	**29 Dec 1170:** Becket killed, Canterbury
Coronation: 19 Dec 1154,	**1174:** Overlord of Scotland under
Westminster Abbey	Treaty of Falaise
Queen: Eleanor of Aquitaine	**12 July 1174:** Henry does penance
(m. 1152; d. 1204)	in Canterbury Cathedral
Succeeded by: His son, Richard I	**1175:** Overlord of Ireland under
Greatest achievement: Founding	Treaty of Windsor
Royal House of Plantagenet	**Death:** 6 July 1189, Chinon, France

Above: King and Archbishop in dispute. A manuscript of 1300 depicts Henry and Becket engaged in an intense debate.

tyrannical local rule. He also made a series of legal reforms that created the foundation of the English 'common law' that has endured for centuries. To replace the existing local courts presided over by the barons, he established royal courts with the king's officials travelling on a circuit to bring impartial justice to all parts of the realm. The law was codified in works such as the *Treatise on the Laws and Customs of England*, written by the king's justiciar, or legal officer, Ranulph Glanville. Trial by a 12-man jury was introduced in 1166.

Henry, the first Plantagenet king and ruler over western Europe's largest 'empire', was king of England by sovereign right. He held all of his French titles and lands – as Duke of Normandy, Count of Anjou, Touraine and Maine and Duke of Aquitaine – as a vassal of the king of France, and herein lies one of the causes of the Hundred Years War.

HENRY AND BECKET

For the first ten years of the reign, Henry and Thomas à Becket, England's leading prelate, were close allies: Henry appointed Becket Chancellor in one of his first acts as king in January 1155, and in June 1162 named Becket Archbishop

of Canterbury. However, in 1164 the pair argued after Becket rejected the Constitutions of Clarendon, which attempted to establish royal authority over churchmen and prevent clerics appealing on legal matters to the Pope in Rome.

Becket fled to a Cistercian monastery in France and Henry confiscated the Archbishop's English possessions. By 1170 Henry and Becket had moved towards reconciliation and, at the king's invitation, Becket returned to England. Once there, however, he defied Henry once more by suspending or excommunicating bishops who had opposed him. In a moment of exasperated rage, Henry is reported to have cried out, 'Will no one rid me of this turbulent priest?' This was the trigger for the attack that led to Becket's death. Four knights, led by Sir Reginald FitzUrse, confronted Becket in Canterbury Cathedral and violated its sanctuary by killing him with their swords.

Within 18 months and amid outrage, the Pope declared Becket a saint. Papal legates found that Henry was not responsible for the murder, and the king made a public act of penance at Becket's tomb in Canterbury Cathedral in July 1174.

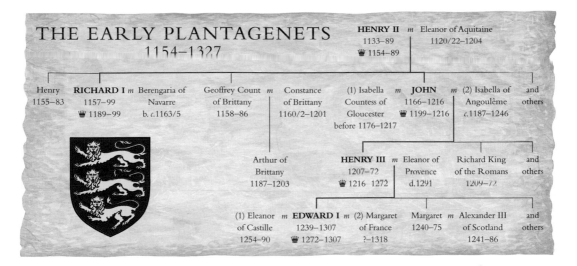

THE EARLY PLANTAGENETS
1154–1327

HENRY II *m* Eleanor of Aquitaine
1133–89   1120/22–1204
♛ 1154–89

Henry	**RICHARD I** *m* Berengaria of	Geoffrey Count *m* Constance	(1) Isabella *m* **JOHN** *m* (2) Isabella of	and
1155–83	1157–99 Navarre	of Brittany of Brittany	Countess of 1166–1216 Angoulême	others
	♛ 1189–99 b. *c.*1163/5	1158–86 1160/2–1201	Gloucester ♛ 1199–1216 *c.*1187–1246	
			before 1176–1217	

Arthur of   **HENRY III** *m* Eleanor of   Richard King   and
Brittany   1207–72   Provence   of the Romans   others
1187–1203   ♛ 1216–1272   d.1291   1209–72

(1) Eleanor *m* **EDWARD I** *m* (2) Margaret   Margaret *m* Alexander III   and
of Castille   1239–1307   of France   1240–75   of Scotland   others
1254–90   ♛ 1272–1307   ?–1318   1241–86

A FORBIDDING QUEEN: ELEANOR OF AQUITAINE

Henry's queen, Eleanor of Aquitaine, was the most powerful woman of her age, who married two kings and was the mother of two more. She encouraged her sons to revolt against their father and, according to tradition, arranged the slaughter of King Henry's beloved mistress, Rosamund Clifford.

Eleanor was the wife of King Louis VII of France before she married Henry. Just eight weeks before Eleanor wed Henry, in the summer of 1152, Louis had had their marriage annulled by mutual consent. Although she was 12 years older than the 18-year-old Henry and was capricious in character, she was a great beauty and became a patron of the arts, especially of courtly literature. She brought with her the vast territories of Aquitaine in central-southern France,

which she had inherited from her father and which, under feudal law, reverted to her on her divorce.

Henry and Eleanor had seven children, including two future kings of England: Richard I and King John. However, king and queen grew apart and an ageing Eleanor was increasingly jealous of King Henry's many younger mistresses. In 1173 she encouraged a rebellion by his sons and even tried to join the campaign, disguised as a man, but was captured by King Henry's troops. Henry survived this revolt but a second family rebellion in 1189 sent him to his deathbed.

After 1173 Henry and Eleanor were publicly estranged and the king lived with his favourite mistress, Rosamund Clifford. According to legend, Eleanor killed 'Fair Rosamund' – in one account, confronting her with a dagger and a cup of poison and forcing her to choose which way to die. She outlasted her husband and lived to see two of her sons on the throne. She died, aged 82, in 1204.

Left: After the failed rebellion of 1173, Eleanor was captured by her husband; a fresco of c.1200 from Chinon, France.

Without shirt or shoes, he walked to the cathedral and flung himself before the tomb of his former enemy and friend before submitting to a penitential flogging at the hands of monks.

ROYAL OVERLORD

In a series of treaties, Henry won recognition as feudal overlord from rulers at home and abroad. In 1163 Owain Gwynedd, king of Gwynedd, reaffirmed Henry's overlordship. Henry had power over Scotland under the Treaty of Falaise signed in 1174 with King William of Scots, and he was overlord of Ireland under the 1175 Treaty of Windsor.

FAMILY BETRAYAL

Although Henry crushed a revolt by his sons and estranged queen in 1173, he was outmanoeuvred and defeated 16 years later by his son Prince Richard in alliance with King Philip II of France. Henry was forced to pay homage to Philip for all England's territories in France and to pass England and his Plantagenet holdings to Richard. It is said that when the ageing king discovered that his favourite youngest son, John, had joined the alliance against him, it broke his heart and two days later he died. His final words were, 'Shame, shame on a vanquished king'.

RICHARD I THE LIONHEART

1189–1199

King Richard I is celebrated as the English warrior-king above all others, dubbed *Coeur de Lion* ('Lion Heart') for his chivalrous achievements on the Third Crusade (1190–92) and on the battlefields of Europe. In fact, he had limited connection to his English territories and only spent six months of his 10-year reign in England.

Above: Crusader king. The English Luttrell psalter (1340s) depicts Richard fighting his great foe, Saladin, on crusade.

KNIGHTLY AMBITION

Born in 1157 in Oxford, Richard was raised in France where his French mother, Queen Eleanor of Aquitaine, held court at Poitiers. He was schooled in the arts of knighthood and grew up with a passionate desire to prove himself a chivalric prince in the Holy Land, perhaps inspired by tales of his fearless mother's travels there during the Second Crusade (1147–49) when she was still married to her first husband Louis VII

Below: In an image from the Chronicles of England *(c. 1470) of Jean de Wavrin, Richard processes to his coronation.*

of France. Encouraged by Eleanor, Richard joined a revolt against his father King Henry II in 1173, when he was only 15 years old. In 1179 he proved himself in battle, capturing the castle of Taillebourg during a campaign in Aquitaine to put down rebel lords. At his coronation on 3 September 1189 he cut a dashing figure. Tall, blue-eyed, he was the perfect knight.

IN THE MIDDLE EAST

Richard's main interest at the start of his reign was to raise money for a new crusade. To this end, in December 1189, he cancelled the Treaty of Falaise, under

which the Scots recognized English overlordship, in return for a payment from King William of Scots of 10,000 marks. He departed for the Holy Land with Philip of France in the following year. However, the venture got off to a bad start because the kings quarreled before they even reached the Holy

RICHARD I, KING OF
ENGLAND, 1189–1199

Birth: 8 Sept 1157, Oxford
Father: King Henry II of England
Mother: Queen Eleanor of Aquitaine
Accession: 6 July 1189
Coronation: 3 Sept 1189, Westminster Abbey; recrowned 17 April 1194, Winchester
Queen: Berengaria of Navarre (m. 1191; d. 1230)
Succeeded by: His brother, John
Greatest achievement: Military victories on Third Crusade
Dec 1189: Cancels Treaty of Falaise
1191: Captures Arsuf in Holy Land
1192: Imprisoned by Holy Roman Emperor Henry VI
1193: Freed on payment of ransom of 150,000 marks
Death: 6 April 1199, Châlus, France

Above: Richard is shown imprisoned in Vienna (left) and in the moment before being shot by a crossbowman at Châlus.

Land. At a stop in Sicily, Philip and Richard argued over Richard's refusal to keep his promise to make a dynastic marriage with Philip's sister, Alice.

Philip travelled ahead. Richard captured Cyprus after a quarrel with its Greek king and there, on 12 May 1191, he married Berengaria of Navarre, who was crowned Queen of England. In the Holy Land, Richard and Philip patched up their quarrel and together captured Acre. Here Richard quarrelled bitterly with Duke Leopold of Austria over the sharing out of the gains and also alienated Philip once more.

Philip left for home in August 1191, while Richard proceeded to capture Arsuf and to march on Jerusalem. He twice came within view of the holy city but was forced to retreat because of the strength of Saladin's defending army. The crusade ended in a truce, under which Saladin remained in control of

Jerusalem, but Christian pilgrims were permitted to visit the city. Richard set sail for home in September 1192. Although he had not achieved all his goals, his victories re-established a viable Crusader kingdom in the Holy Land.

TROUBLE AT HOME

Richard had laid plans to protect his English realm while he was away. He entrusted William Longchamps, Bishop of Ely, with the position of Chief Justiciar and the power to rule the country, while making his brother Prince John promise not to travel to England from France or attempt to take control there. The plan failed. John did not keep his word and set up his own government, driving Longchamps into exile in France and plotting with Philip of France to prevent Richard returning.

CAPTURED IN AUSTRIA

Hearing of this plot while returning from the Holy Land, Richard attempted to evade capture. After he was ship-wrecked he disguised himself but he

was then recognized in Vienna and imprisoned, first by his enemy Duke Leopold of Austria and then by the Holy Roman Emperor Henry VI. His release was made subject to payment of a king's ransom of 150,000 marks, the equivalent of 35 tonnes of gold.

In England, the new Chief Justiciar Hubert Walter somehow managed to raise this vast sum. Freed in 1193, Richard returned to England the following year and was crowned for a second time by Walter, now Archbishop of Canterbury, at Winchester on 17 April 1194. The king forgave his brother for his part in the plot against him. Then, after spending a mere two months in England he returned to France to seek revenge against Philip and to fight for the return of lost territories. He died there on 6 April 1199 after the wound made in his shoulder by a crossbow bolt at Châlus became gangrenous. He was buried alongside his father – and later joined by his mother, Eleanor of Aquitaine – at Fontevrault Abbey in Normandy.

Below: Coeur de Lion. Richard's image as the crusading king par excellence has inspired artists of many eras.

JOHN
1199–1216

An unprincipled opportunist, King John made a series of bad decisions in pursuit of short-term advantage. By the end of his reign he had not only lost the vast French empire created by his father, Henry II, but had also alienated the crown's leading English supporters as well as the pope and the Church establishment.

'LACKLAND' AND LOYALTY

John was the youngest of King Henry's sons, and because his older brothers received large territorial inheritances and he was given nothing, he was nick-named 'Lackland'. In 1189 John joined Richard in revolt against their father. This betrayal is said to have left Henry a broken man, for John was his father's favourite. Then when Richard I was on

Right: John's favourite hunting lands were said to be Clipstone in Sherwood Forest, home of legendary outlaw Robin Hood.

JOHN, KING OF ENGLAND, 1199–1216

Born: 24 Dec 1167, Oxford
Father: King Henry II of England
Mother: Queen Eleanor of Aquitaine
Accession: 6 April 1199
Coronation: 27 May 1199, Westminster Abbey
Queens: (1) Isabella of Gloucester (m. 1176; divorced 1200; d. 1217); (2) Isabella of Angoulême (m. 1200; d. 1246)
Succeeded by: His son, Henry III
Greatest achievement: Defeat of Irish revolt, 1210
Nov 1209: Excommunicated by Pope Innocent III
1215: Magna Carta
Death: 18 Oct 1216, Newark

---

the Third Crusade in 1190–2, John reneged on a promise not to interfere in England. He declared himself King of England when Richard was captured and imprisoned in Austria on his way home from the Holy Land in 1192. Richard nonetheless forgave John and the pair fought in tandem to regain Richard's French lands.

On Richard's death in April 1199, John was invested Duke of Normandy in Rouen and then crowned King of England in Westminster Abbey. When John dropped the banner bearing his ducal insignia at the Rouen ceremony, many saw it as a bad omen.

John came to the throne at the age of 32. As he did so, his attention was focused on safeguarding his French lands in the face of a challenge from his nephew, Arthur of Brittany, who claimed Anjou and Touraine.

THE PRINCE OF ALL WALES

Welsh overlord Llewelyn ab Iorwerth, prince of Gwynedd, established himself as ruler without equal in Wales at the end of King John's reign, earning himself the epithet 'the Great'. Hearing of plans for a joint attack on Gwynedd by King John and Gwenwynwyn, lord of the rival Welsh kingdom of Powys, Llewelyn declared Gwenwynwyn guilty of treachery and marched into his lands to annex them. Gwenwynwyn returned from England to defend Powys, but failed, was injured and forced to retreat to Cheshire. Llewelyn's queen was Joan, an illegitimate daughter of King John. After Llewelyn's death, on 11 April 1240 at Aberconway in Gwynedd, a chronicler called him 'Prince of Wales'.

Above: A 1957 memorial marks the spot at Runnymede near Windsor at which John signed the Magna Carta.

FRENCH LOSSES

In the first year of King John's reign, after divorcing his first wife, Isabella of Gloucester, he married the 12-year-old Isabella of Angoulême, making an enemy of the French baron Hugh de Lusignan, who had been betrothed to Isabella. The de Lusignans owed John allegiance in his role as Count of Aquitaine but they appealed to his feudal overlord, King Philip of France, for justice in the case of the marriage. John refused to appear before the French king to answer the charges, and Philip dispossessed John of all the lands he held in France, on the grounds that John was a 'contumacious vassal' (since he had failed to fulfil his feudal obligation).

The dispute with the de Lusignans and other French nobles led to war in 1202. John was initially successful, capturing Arthur and the de Lusignans at Mirebeau, but when word got out that he had murdered Arthur, Brittany rose against him and John lost the support of the barons in Anjou and Normandy. He retreated to England in 1203 and by 1206 had lost all his French holdings save Aquitaine.

DISPUTE WITH ROME

When the Archbishop of Canterbury, Hubert Walter, died in 1206, John refused to accept Stephen Langton, the man nominated by the pope, as Walter's successor. The dispute led to John's excommunication by Pope Innocent III in 1209. In theory the pope had the power to order John's subjects to depose him and replace their king with a more godly man, but John backed down. He accepted Langton as archbishop in 1213 and then agreed that Ireland and England were fiefs of Rome. At Winchester on 20 July 1213, Archbishop Langton formally absolved John of his excommunication.

JOHN AND MAGNA CARTA

In 1214 John launched an ill-fated attempt to regain his French possessions that ended with the defeat of his German ally, the emperor Otto of Brunswick, at Bouvines. His campaigns had been extremely expensive and John's English subjects were restless under the weight of taxation that he imposed to finance them. In 1215 a revolt by leading barons forced John to agree to a charter of liberties, *Magna Carta* ('Great Charter') at Runnymede to the west of London.

The charter, which was reissued in 1216, 1217, 1225 and 1297, guaranteed the reform of royal abuses of power and turned out to be the first step in

THREE LIONS

John adopted three gold lions *passant*, or striding, on a red background as his coat of arms. He based the device on the emblem used by his father and brother, of two striding lions. Heraldic devices were worn by knights jousting at chivalric tournaments and in battle as an identifying mark. John's three lions were incorporated into the royal seal.

establishing constitutional government in England. It stated that the law had force independently of the will of the king. The following year, when John renounced it, the barons rebelled, imported Louis, the son of King Philip II of France, and prepared to depose John. Before this could happen John died of dysentery at Newark on 18 October 1216. The final event of his reign was a characteristically bungled manoeuvre in which he lost the crown jewels in quicksand while crossing the Wash, a tidal estuary in eastern England.

Below: John's tomb (1232) in Worcester Cathedral is carved with an effigy of the king flanked by St Wulfstan and St Oswald.

HENRY III
1216–1272

Following King John's sudden death and with London in the hands of rebel barons preparing to elevate France's Prince Louis to the English throne, nine-year-old Prince Henry was crowned in great haste at Gloucester Abbey on 28 October 1216. A bracelet belonging to his mother, Queen Isabella, was used in place of the crown because King John had lost the crown jewels. With the Archbishop of Canterbury away in Rome, the ceremony was performed by the French-born Bishop of Winchester.

John's disastrous reign had brought England to its knees and the future of the Angevin dynasty looked grim. However, thanks to an effective regency by William Marshal, Earl of Pembroke, the knight chosen on his deathbed by King John, the country and the dynasty were stabilized. Marshal defeated the rebels in 1217, bringing the civil war to an end, and on his death in 1219 was succeeded by Hubert de Burgh. Henry III took the reins of power in January 1227, aged 20.

ROYAL WEDDING
Henry married the beautiful 19-year-old Eleanor of Provence in Canterbury Cathedral on 14 January 1236. To house

Above: In this miniature of his coronation ceremony, Henry holds a model of Westminster Abbey, rebuilt in his reign.

his new queen in suitable splendour he renovated the royal palace at Westminster, installing glass in the windows and plumbing, fitting large fireplaces and commissioning fine wall-paintings for private chambers. Later the same month, on 30 January 1236, Eleanor was crowned Queen of England, in Westminster Abbey.

The marriage brought trouble, for the influx of the new queen's relatives seeking wealth and power made the English barons resentful. Trouble broke out in the mid-1250s after Henry agreed to provide financial support for Pope Innocent IV's proposed military campaign in Sicily. In June 1258 he was forced to agree to the Provisions of

HENRY III, KING OF ENGLAND, 1216–1272	
Birth: 1 Oct 1207, Winchester	**Jan 1227:** Henry takes power at the end of his minority
Father: King John of England	**May 1240:** Crowns Dafydd of Gwynedd 'paramount prince in Wales'
Mother: Queen Isabella of Angoulême	**June 1258:** Provisions of Oxford
Accession: 18 Oct 1216	**1264:** Civil war
Coronations: (1) 28 Oct 1216 Gloucester; (2) 17 May 1220, Westminster Abbey	**14 May 1264:** Captured by Simon de Montfort
Queen: Eleanor of Provence (m. 14 Jan 1236; d. 1291)	**4 Aug 1265:** Defeat of Simon de Montfort at Battle of Evesham
Succeeded by: His son, Edward I	**Death:** 16 Nov 1272, London

KING OF ANIMALS

In London Henry built a menagerie at the Tower of London, partly as a home for the first elephant ever to be brought to England. The beast was a gift to Henry from France's King Louis IX in 1255. It was carried as far as Tilbury Docks by water and then walked the remainder of the way while gaping crowds marvelled at the sight. Earlier, in 1237, Henry had built a leopard house at the Tower, and he was given a polar bear as a gift from the King of Norway in 1252. In keeping a zoo, Henry was following the example of his great grandfather, Henry I, who had kept a collection of camels, lions and leopards at Woodstock in Oxfordshire. Richard I, it is said, even brought a crocodile to England from his travels, but the creature escaped into the Thames.

Henry's brother Richard, Earl of Cornwall, and that of leading barons. Exiled as a result in 1239, he won great honour on crusade (1240–2) and during King Henry's unsuccessful invasion of France in 1242. He subsequently became convinced that Henry was unfit to govern, largely because of the king's poor decision-making after sending him to put down a baronial revolt in Gascony in 1248.

In 1264 de Montfort led an open rebellion to reinstate the Provisions of Oxford after they had been repudiated by Henry in 1262 and then annulled at an agreed arbitration by King Louis IX of France. De Montfort defeated the king's army at Lewes in 1264, captured Henry III and his son Edward, and for a year became the effective ruler of England. At this time he called a Parliament that, in addition to barons and clerics, held two burgesses from each borough and two knights from each shire. However, in the summer of 1265, Prince Edward escaped and, joining up with allies, turned on de Montfort and won a crushing victory at the Battle of Evesham in Worcestershire. In death, de Montfort was horribly mutilated by royalist soldiers. His head, hands and feet were cut off and his genitals thrown on to his face.

The king's authority had been restored – by his son. However, de Montfort had achieved a lasting legacy, because England's king would ever afterwards have to be mindful of the will of Parliament.

Above: 14th-century chroniclers stressed Henry's piety. He supported orphans and provided food for paupers. He is even said to have washed and kissed lepers' feet.

Oxford, by which a council of 15 barons was created to govern jointly with the king.

DE MONTFORT'S RISE AND FALL

Simon de Montfort, Earl of Leicester, was the driving force behind this challenge to royal authority. Born in France, he had arrived in England in 1229 and set about building a power base. In January 1238 he married the king's sister, Eleanor, thus provoking the anger of

A PRINCE FOR WALES

In May 1240, amid great ceremony at Gloucester, Henry III crowned Dafydd of Gwynedd the 'paramount prince in Wales'. Dafydd was the younger son of Llywelyn the Great of Gwynedd and his wife Joan, an illegitimate daughter of King John, and was therefore Henry's

nephew. Towards the end of Henry's reign, in 1267, the English king recognised Dafydd's nephew Llywelyn ap Gruffudd as Prince of Wales.

ROYAL PATRON

Henry was a pious and highly cultured man, whose 56-year reign was a golden age of learning, architecture and the arts. In addition to his large-scale renovation of Westminster Palace, Henry oversaw a major rebuilding of Westminster Abbey to house a shrine to the church's original royal founder, Edward the Confessor. The French-trained architect Master Henry de Reyns pulled down all of Edward's church except the nave and rebuilt it in the Gothic style on a French cathedral plan. The work took 36 years and cost £46,000. Henry's reign also saw major work on the magnificent cathedrals at St Alban's, Salisbury, Lincoln and Wells in Somerset. Learning thrived under this cultured king, and the first colleges in Oxford University – Merton, University and Balliol – were founded in the years between 1249 and 1264.

Left: Salisbury Cathedral was begun in 1220 and dedicated in 1258. The 404ft (123m) spire was added in 1330.

EDWARD I
1272–1307

Edward I came to the throne, aged 33, a proven warrior. He had already fought with distinction in Henry III's campaigns against Welsh prince Llywelyn ap Gruffudd in 1259 and in 1265 had restored royal power by crushing Simon de Montfort's rebellion at the Battle of Evesham. He was in Sicily, returning from fighting on the Eighth Crusade (1270–2) when he was declared king on 17 November 1272.

'LONGSHANKS'

Edward brought a ferocious martial vigour to his reign, forcefully imposing his authority on his realm, ending Welsh independence and waging a series of brutal wars in the north that later earned him the nickname 'Hammer of the Scots'. Standing imperiously 6ft 2in (1.9m) tall – an astonishing height for

---

EDWARD I, KING OF ENGLAND, 1272–1307

Birth: 17 June 1239, Westminster
Father: Henry III of England
Mother: Eleanor of Provence
Accession: 16 Nov 1272
Coronation: 19 Aug 1274, Westminster Abbey
Queens: (1) Eleanor of Castile (m. Oct 1254; d. 1290); (2) Margaret of France (m. 10 Sept 1299; d. 1318)
Succeeded by: His son, Edward II
March 1284: Statute of Rhuddlan
1290: Royal edict expelling Jews from England
1296: Invades Scotland, Battle of Dunbar
1301: Edward's son Edward created first English 'Prince of Wales'
1305: Captures and executes Scottish rebel William Wallace
Death: 7 July 1307 of dysentery at Burgh by Sands, near Carlisle

---

Map legend:
- Castle built/rebuilt by Edward I
- Castle captured/repaired by Edward I
- Castle built/rebuilt by owner for Edward I

North Atlantic Ocean

North Sea

○ ABERDEEN

GLASGOW ○ ○ EDINBURGH

NEWCASTLE

MIDDLEHAM

Irish Sea

RHUDDLAN
CONWY HOLT
DOLWYDDELAN FLINT
BEAUMARIS ○ CONISBROUGH
CAERNARFON HAWARDEN
CRICCIETH DEBBIGH CAERGWRLE ○ YORK
HARLECH RUTHIN CHIRK ○ DERBY
CASTELL BERE

ABERYSTWYTH LUDLOW ○ KENILWORTH
BUILTH HEDINGHAM
GOODRICH ○ ORFORD
BERKELEY TOWER OF LONDON ROCHESTER
Bristol Channel ○ BRISTOL LONDON CANTERBURY
SOUTHAMPTON LEEDS DOVER
EXETER LEWES HASTINGS
PEVENSEY *Strait of Dover*
TINTAGEL
PLYMOUTH

English Channel

Above: Realm of fortresses. The map shows the network of castles built between 1066 and the end of Edward I's reign in 1307.

the 13th century – he cut a commanding and regal figure and was admiringly known as 'Longshanks'.

At home he carried out much needed legal reforms, improved the efficiency of administration and is remembered as the king in whose reign Parliament's role in government was consolidated. The changes he oversaw in government strengthened rather than diluted royal authority, clarifying Parliament's role as an instrument of the king's rule – used in particular to levy

Above: One of Edward's forbidding Welsh castles, Harlech was built in 1283–90 by his engineer, Master James of St George.

taxes to pay for military campaigns. The legal reforms codified English law, providing a legal basis for inheritance of land and improving public order laws.

VICTORY IN WALES

Llywelyn ap Gruffydd was the first sole ruler of a united Wales. However, he grew overconfident of his position and, when he refused to pay homage to Edward I, provoked a savage 1276 invasion that within a year reduced his realm to a small region in Snowdonia. An uprising led by Llywelyn's brother Dafydd in 1282 provoked a second English invasion in which Llywelyn was killed at Builth and then Dafydd was hung, drawn and quartered as a traitor at Shrewsbury.

Under the Statute of Rhuddlan of March 1284, English officials were brought in to govern the new English-style shires that were to replace the existing Welsh kingdoms. Edward built a series of forbidding castles across Wales at Flint, Rhuddlan, Builth, Conway, Caernarfon, Criccieth, Harlech, Denbigh and Beaumaris to impose his will on what was now a subject country. In Caernarfon castle, in 1284 the king's son Edward was born. Some 17 years later

Below: Liberties confirmed. The 14th-century manuscript, Statutes of England, *shows Edward reissuing Magna Carta.*

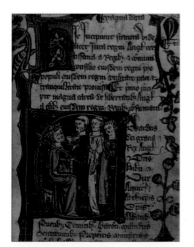

A LOYAL HUSBAND

Henry was devoted to his first wife, Eleanor of Castile. Their marriage in 1254 was a diplomatic one, made when the future king was 15 and his wife just 9, but grew to be a love match. An elegant, dark-haired woman, Eleanor travelled with her husband to Wales, Gascony and even to the Holy Land on crusade. Perhaps their bond was strengthened by a brush with death in 1287, when a lightning strike in Gascony killed two people in the very room in which the royal couple were sitting.

Queen Eleanor bore Edward 11 daughters and 4 sons, including the future Edward II. When she herself died, aged 54, on 28 November 1290, her desolate spouse wrote 'in life I dearly loved her and I will not stop loving her in death'. In her honour he erected 12 Memorial Crosses to mark the places where her funeral cortège stopped on its journey from Harby, in Nottinghamshire, where the queen died, to Westminster Abbey, where she was buried. Three of these crosses survive today – at Geddington and Hardingstone in

Nottinghamshire and Waltham Cross in Essex; a memorial at Charing Cross in London is a 19th-century replica of the original cross that stood there.

Edward married for a second time, on 10 September 1299, again making a diplomatic match when he wed Margaret, the sister of France's King Philip IV. Despite a 40-year age differential between the 60-year-old king and his 20-year-old bride, this marriage too turned out well.

Below: Eleanor's memory was celebrated by this monument at Hardingstone.

---

this boy, now heir to the throne, was created the first English Prince of Wales. This was the first time an English royal ruler officially took the title of 'prince'.

THE HAMMER OF THE SCOTS

When John Balliol was named King of Scots in 1292 after a two-year interregnum following the death of the infant Queen Margaret, he paid homage to Edward as his feudal overlord. However, in October 1295 the Scots made an alliance with France rather than join Edward in a French military campaign, and the following spring John Balliol refused to pay homage to Edward.

Edward invaded Scotland with a 25,000-strong army and overran Berwick, killing 7,000 of its population, before defeating a Scottish army at Dunbar. King John Balliol abdicated

and, in a humiliating public ceremony, was stripped of his crown and royal finery.

Edward unleashed the force of the English army and its powerful long-bowmen on the Scots again in 1298 and 1300. That year he made a calculated insult to Scottish pride by removing the Scots' ancient coronation stone from its place at Scone and installing it at Westminster as part of a new coronation throne.

Edward invaded Scotland again in 1301–2 and in 1303–5. When he finally captured the outlawed Scottish leader William Wallace, he was taken to London and executed by having his head and limbs severed from his body.

When Edward died near Carlisle, on 7 July 1307, he was travelling north in preparation for yet another of his Scottish campaigns.

EDWARD II
1307–1327

 Edward II was blessed with intelligence, bravery and good looks and inherited the throne of a secure and well-governed country. However, he exhibited a self-indulgence and lack of judgement in public and private life that made a bitter enemy of his formidable queen and of prominent barons and that led inexorably to the loss of his crown and a gruesome end in a prison cell.

A ROYAL FAVOURITE
Before he became king, Edward's close friendship – and probably homosexual relationship – with Piers Gaveston, the son of a Gascon knight, caused scandal at court. Edward I is said to have been outraged when his son asked for a gift of territory for his friend. The king exiled Gaveston and reportedly tore at his son's hair, shouting, 'You base-born whoreson! Do you want to give lands

Above: Gravity and majesty. Edward II stands between Edwards I and III in a group of statues at York Cathedral.

Below: Edward II founded Oriel College, Oxford, in 1326 as 'The House of the Blessed Mary the Virgin in Oxford'.

EDWARD II, KING OF ENGLAND, 1307–1327
Birth: 25 April 1284, Caernarfon
Father: Edward I of England
Mother: Eleanor of Castile
Accession: 8 July 1307
Coronation: 25 Feb 1308, Westminster Abbey
Queen: Isabella of France (m. 25 Jan 1308; d. 1358)
Succeeded by: His son, Edward III
Greatest achievement: English economic boom fuelled by exports to continental Europe of English wool
Sept 1311: Ordinances strengthen power of Parliament
24 June 1314: Defeated by Scots in Battle of Bannockburn
1326: Civil war
24 Jan 1327: abdicated
Death: 22 Sept 1327 murdered Berkeley Castle, Gloucestershire

away now, you who have never gained any?' However, there was nothing to stand in Edward's way when he became king and within a month of acceding to the throne he recalled Gaveston and made him Earl of Cornwall, a position normally reserved for the son of the reigning king. Shortly afterwards Edward gave his niece in marriage to Gaveston, then made his friend regent while he, Edward, travelled to France to make a diplomatic wedding match with the French king's daughter, Isabella.

Leading barons led by Thomas, Earl of Lancaster turned against the king, who in 1311 was forced to accede to a series of demands that placed limits on his power and in particular required him to strip Gaveston of his title and send him into exile. Edward did as he was required to do, but Gaveston returned the following year. The angry barons seized the royal favourite and, at Blacklow Hill in Warwickshire, they

beheaded him. Gaveston's death greatly upset Edward, but had the effect of repairing his relationship with Queen Isabella. The couple's son, who was named Edward after his father, was born on 13 November 1312.

DEFEAT AND HUMILIATION

In 1314, Edward led an English army into Scotland to relieve Stirling Castle, which was besieged by Scottish forces under King Robert I 'the Bruce'. Although they outnumbered the Scots, Edward's army was humiliated in the two-day Battle of Bannockburn, afterwards celebrated as the event that cemented Scottish independence. Edward was forced to flee for his life. In England, Thomas, Earl of Lancaster sidelined the king and established himself as the country's effective ruler.

CIVIL WAR

Edward did not change his ways. He found new favourites in two lords from the Welsh Marches, Hugh le Despenser and his father, also Hugh, to whom he gave an abundance of titles and territories in Wales. Lancaster banished the Despensers in August 1321, and the king went to war on their behalf,

Below: Gothic masterpiece. Edward III honoured his father by building this superb marble tomb in Gloucester Cathedral.

THE DEATH OF KING EDWARD II

After installing Edward III on the throne, Queen Isabella and Roger Mortimer ordered that Edward II be jailed at Berkeley Castle in Gloucestershire and starved to death. But the king, whose spirit must have remained strong, lingered painfully on. The king's minders devised a sadistic means of killing their prisoner that would leave no mark on his body: after a metal funnel was inserted into the king's anus, a red-hot soldering iron was thrust into his bowels. His screams of agony filled the air.

The king's colourful reign and brutal end inspired 16th-century English dramatist Christopher Marlowe to write *Edward II* (*c.*1592), one of the first historical plays of the Elizabethan era. This play in turn inspired the 20th-century filmmaker Derek Jarman to make the acclaimed movie *Edward II* (1991).

Below: Berkeley Castle was built by Roger de Berkeley in the 11th century.

defeating the Earl in the Battle of Boroughbridge, in Yorkshire, in March 1322. Edward then had Lancaster executed, recalled the Despensers and for a short while governed as he pleased. However, trouble was brewing.

Queen Isabella, angered at her husband's relationship with the younger Hugh le Despenser, abandoned him. She began to live openly in France with Roger Mortimer, Earl of March, an exiled opponent of the Despensers, and to plot the king's downfall. Such was the ferocity of her newfound hatred of her husband that at court in England they nicknamed her the 'she-wolf of France'. Crucially for their planned revolt, Mortimer and Isabella had the king's heir, Edward, living with them.

Backed by a mercenary army from Flanders, Isabella and Mortimer invaded in October 1326. Edward fled to Wales, while the queen's forces set themselves up at Gloucester. The following month the queen had her revenge on the younger Despenser. At Hereford, on 24 November 1326, he was cruelly executed. His genitals were sliced off because, contemporary accounts said, 'he was held to be guilty of unnatural practices with the king'. His entrails were cut from him and burned. Finally, he was decapitated and his body quartered. His head was sent to London and the pieces of his body sent to the corners of the kingdom.

Isabella and Mortimer imprisoned Edward II in Kenilworth Castle, and forced him to abdicate his throne. They declared the 14-year-old Prince Edward king. After the coronation, they kept the former King Edward II imprisoned in Berkeley Castle, Gloucestershire, where he met a death matching that of his former lover le Despenser for atrocity.

EDWARD III

1327–1377

When Edward III became king at the age of only 14, he was little more than a pawn of his power-hungry mother, Queen Isabella, and her lover Roger Mortimer, Earl of March, who had used the boy-king to depose his father Edward II. However, he grew quickly to manhood and shortly before his 18th birthday took power into his own hands. He led a night raid in Nottingham Castle that surprised Isabella and Mortimer as they prepared for bed, sent Mortimer to the Tower and exiled his mother from power and the royal court by despatching her to Castle Rising in Norfolk.

CHAUCER'S KING

Edward proved to be a forceful king, the Christian world's most celebrated warrior of the day. At home he repaired the civil ructions of his father's years and presided over a court in which chivalry, fashion and the finest literature were all celebrated, knights jousted in single combat, courtiers wore extravagant gowns and robes, and the first great English poet, Geoffrey Chaucer, found employment as a civil servant and trusted diplomat.

AT WAR WITH FRANCE

Early in Edward's reign Charles IV of France died without issue and Queen Isabella pressed Edward's claim to the French throne on the basis that Edward was Charles's nephew. The French *parlement* chose Charles's cousin to rule as Philip VI. Initially Edward paid homage to Philip for his French lands, but in 1340 he declared himself King of France. He destroyed the French fleet in July 1340, beginning a prolonged military campaign in France that would later be identified as the first phase of the Hundred Years War (1337–1453).

In 1346 Edward led an invasion of France that climaxed in a famous victory at Crécy on 26 August, when

Above: The Black Prince captured King Jean II of France in the course of the English triumph at Poitiers in 1356.

an army of professional English soldiers and Welsh longbowmen trounced a much larger French force under King Philip VI. Some 10,000 Frenchmen were killed in an encounter that led to just 42 English dead and a few dozen Welsh infantry.

A major figure in Edward's French campaigns was his son Edward, the Prince of Wales, known as the Black Prince because of his black armour. Knighted by his father at the age of 16 in France in 1346, the Black Prince fought bravely that year at Crécy, where he killed the King of Bohemia and took as his own the king's emblem of three feathers and the motto *Ich Dien* ('I serve'). He led the English to another proud victory, in 1356, at the Battle of Poitiers, where an English army of no more than 8,000 defeated a French force of 50,000, killing 13 counts and 66 barons and capturing the French king, Jean II.

From this high point, English fortunes in France declined, for King Edward and his commanders were unable to translate military victories into more lasting power.

EDWARD III, KING OF ENGLAND, 1327–1377

Birth: 13 Nov 1312, Windsor Castle
Father: Edward II of England
Mother: Queen Isabella
Accession: 24 Jan 1327
Coronation: 1 Feb 1327, Westminster Abbey
Queen: Philippa of Hainault (m. 24 Jan 1328; d. 1369)
Succeeded by: His grandson, Richard II
Greatest achievement: Victories over French in Battles of Crécy and Poitiers
26 Aug 1346: Battle of Crécy
17 Oct 1346: Battle of Neville's Cross, Durham
1348: Black Death strikes England
24 June 1348: founds the Most Noble Order of the Garter
19 Sept 1356: Battle of Poitiers
Death: 21 June 1377, Sheen Palace

Above: Regal warrior. This anonymous portrait of the king is at Hampton Court.

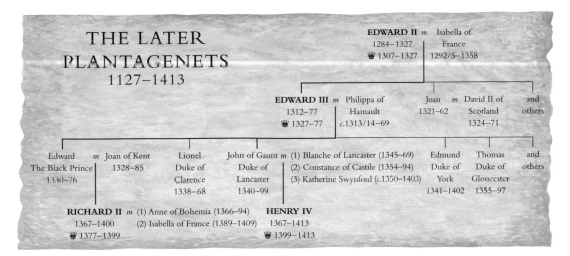

THE LATER PLANTAGENETS
1127–1413

				EDWARD II	m	Isabella of
				1284–1327		France
				♔ 1307–1327		1292/5–1358

EDWARD III	m	Philippa of		Joan	m	David II of	and
1312–77		Hainault		1321–62		Scotland	others
♔ 1327–77		c.1313/14–69				1324–71	

Edward	m	Joan of Kent	Lionel	John of Gaunt	m	(1) Blanche of Lancaster (1345–69)	Edmund	Thomas	and
The Black Prince		1328–85	Duke of	Duke of		(2) Constance of Castile (1354–94)	Duke of	Duke of	others
1330–76			Clarence	Lancaster		(3) Katherine Swynford (c.1350–1403)	York	Gloucester	
			1338–68	1340–99			1341–1402	1355–97	

RICHARD II	m	(1) Anne of Bohemia (1366–94)	HENRY IV
1367–1400		(2) Isabella of France (1389–1409)	1367–1413
♔ 1377–1399			♔ 1399–1413

In September 1360 under the Treaty of Brétigny, Jean II was returned to his countrymen – after four years in English captivity – for a ransom of three million gold crowns. Edward renounced his claim to the French throne, while the French recognized English rights in Calais, Poitou and Gascony.

In the following 20-odd years, the French won back many of these lands. Thus, despite heroic victories on French soil, the great warrior king Edward III had fewer French holdings at his death than he had had at his accession.

SCOTTISH KING IN CUSTODY

King Edward also held Scotland's King David II in captivity for almost exactly 11 years after David was captured at the battle of Neville's Cross in 1346.

Earlier in his reign, Edward had provided military backing for the claim of John Balliol's son Edward to the Scottish throne, and in 1334 King David, then just nine years old, was forced to flee to France. In 1341, David had returned to Scotland and then attempted an ill-fated invasion of northern England intended to regain land ceded to Edward III by Edward Balliol.

David was released under the Treaty of Berwick, signed on 6 November 1357, under which the Scots promised to pay a ransom of 100,000 marks for

their king and a ten-year Anglo-Scottish truce was agreed. For a short while in 1356–7, Edward had the strange distinction of holding the kings of both France and Scotland in captivity.

POWER FOR PARLIAMENT

Edward's military campaigns in France and Scotland proved extremely expensive and he needed regular levies of taxation to pay for them. Parliament was in a strong bargaining position and won a number of new powers. These included agreements in 1340 that no new taxes could be imposed without the approval of the Commons in Parliament and, the following year, that the king's ministers would be required to pledge acceptance of Magna Carta and the law in Parliament.

THE BLACK DEATH

The Black Death – a Europe-wide pandemic of bubonic and pneumonic plague – hit England in 1348. It killed the king's favourite daughter, Princess Joan, two archbishops of Canterbury and around one third to one half of the population of the country. As a result of the drastic loss of labour this entailed, the survivors were able to charge more for their labours, leading to severe wage inflation. The 1351 Statute of Labourers once more set wages at pre-1348 levels.

THE ORDER OF THE GARTER

In 1344, Edward III held a round-table tournament at Windsor and took a solemn vow to form an order of Arthurian knights. The Most Noble Order of the Garter, consisting of 26 knights – the king and the Prince of Wales, each with 12 companions – was formed at Windsor on 24 June 1348.

Legend has it that the Order's name and motto derived from a racy incident at a ball in 1347, when a lady – in some accounts the king's mistress, Joan of Kent, Countess of Salisbury – dropped her garter and the king picked it neatly up and tied it around his knee, saying gallantly, *Honi soit qui mal y pense* ('may evil come to the one who has impure thoughts'). St George was the Order's patron saint.

RICHARD II
1377–1399

Richard of Bordeaux, son of Edward, the Black Prince, acceded to the crown of England at the age of 10 in 1377. He had become heir to the throne only the previous year, on the death from dysentery of his warrior father. Richard was crowned amid great pageantry and solemn ceremony on 16 July 1377, watched by his uncle John of Gaunt, Duke of Lancaster, oldest surviving son of the late King Edward III. Until Richard came of age, power was in the hands of a ruling council.

THE PEASANTS' REVOLT
The young king proved that he had inherited his father's courage when he faced down a crowd of angry country labourers at Smithfield on 15 June 1381. The men of Kent and Essex had risen in the 'Peasants' Revolt' to protest against the inequitable poll tax that demanded one shilling from every person, whether rich or poor.

The peasants had arrived in London on 13 June and run riot, demolishing John of Gaunt's palace and the following day storming the Tower of London and executing the Chancellor, Archbishop Simon of Sudbury.

Returning from attending Mass at Westminster on the morning of 15 June, Richard met the rebels in person. When the rebel leader Wat Tyler rode forward to press their demands upon their ruler, he was stabbed to death by the Mayor of London, William Walworth. Tyler's men were about to attack when Richard silenced them with the words, 'Sirs, would you kill your king? I am your king, I am your captain and your leader.' The moment of crisis passed thanks to his bravery and he proceeded to promise sufficient concessions to make the men disperse. Subsequently he would go back on his promises, making the celebrated declaration, 'Villeins ye are, and villeins ye shall remain'.

Richard's early success may have encouraged the traits of arrogance and unwillingness to compromise that led eventually to his downfall. He clashed repeatedly with Parliament and his leading barons, notably over his favourite Robert de Vere, whom he made Duke of Ireland in 1386. Leading barons led by Richard, Duke of Gloucester took up arms in 1387 and issued an appeal to the king to rid himself of de Vere and the Earl of Suffolk, whom they accused of

RICHARD II, KING OF ENGLAND 1377–1399
Birth: 6 Jan 1367, Bordeaux
Father: Edward, Prince of Wales ('the Black Prince')
Mother: Countess Joan ('the Fair Maid of Kent')
Accession: 21 June 1377
Coronation: 16 July 1377, Westminster Abbey
Queens: (1) Anne of Bohemia (m. 1382; d. 1394); (2) Isabella of France (m. 1397; d. 1409)
Succeeded by: His cousin, Henry Bolingbroke, Duke of Lancaster
Greatest achievement: Facing down Peasants' Revolt 1381; receiving lords' submission in Ireland 1395
1381: Peasants' Revolt
1387: Uprising of 'Lords Appellant'
1397: Murder and execution of the Lords Appellant Gloucester and Arundel
1398: Exile of Henry Bolingbroke
30 Sept 1399: Deposed in Parliament
14 Feb 1400: Dies in captivity, Pontefract Castle

treason. Richard was always unwilling to compromise and called on de Vere to defend the royal cause. At the Battle of Radcot Bridge near Oxford, rebel forces under Gloucester and his nephew Henry Bolingbroke defeated de Vere and forced him to flee. The following year, Gloucester and the leading barons – known as the 'Lords Appellant' because they had issued the 1387 appeal to the king – forced Richard to renew his coronation oaths and at the 'Merciless Parliament' purged the court of Richard's intimates and favourites.

Left: A late 15th-century Flemish chronicle represents the teenage Richard surrounded by his ruling council.

The Lords condemned the exiled de Vere and Suffolk for treason and executed Sir Nichols Bembre, former London mayor, and Sir Robert Tresilian, former chief justice.

Richard waited nine years to have his revenge. In July 1397 the king arrested Gloucester and the Earl of Arundel. He sent Gloucester to Calais, where he was murdered. In September Parliament condemned all the Lords Appellant for plotting against the monarch; Arundel was executed and Warwick exiled. The following year Richard also exiled Henry Bolingbroke for ten years. However, the repercussions of this conflict would bring the king down, for in 1399 Henry Bolingbroke returned to seize the crown and Richard – now deposed – met his end in captivity, possibly at the hands of a murderer in 1400.

DIPLOMATIC SUCCESS

Before the drama of the Lords Appellant had been fully played out, Richard achieved one of the triumphs of his reign. In 1394–5 he led an army to triumph in Ireland and, after spending Christmas in Dublin, received the submission of 80 Irish chiefs, who as a result were confirmed as rulers in their inherited lands. Under the agreement, all land east of a line from Dundalk to Waterford was considered English territory and later called the 'English Pale'. In 1396, moreover, Richard negotiated a 28-year truce with France. At a meeting with Charles VI near Calais, he pledged friendship, promising to support French policy while nevertheless maintaining his claim to the throne.

RICHARD'S MARRIAGES

Richard had two queens. His first was Anne of Bohemia, married in 1382 when both were 15 years old. Although initially a diplomatic match – Anne's father was Holy Roman Emperor Charles IV – this became a close and loving relationship. When Anne died aged just 28 on 7 June 1394, Richard commissioned a truly magnificent

Westminster Abbey tomb with twin effigies of himself and his queen. At her funeral in the Abbey, on 3 August, he was enraged when the Earl of Arundel rudely arrived late, and felled him with his sceptre. In 1397 he made a second diplomatic marriage. As part of the treaty signed with France he took Charles VI's eldest daughter Isabella, aged just seven, as his wife.

Richard was a major artistic patron. He supported poet Geoffrey Chaucer, who had been a diplomat in Edward III's reign and who wrote his poem 'The Parliament of Fowls' in 1382 to celebrate Richard's marriage to Anne of Bohemia. In the 1380s Chaucer was much troubled by debt, and in 1389 he was appointed Clerk of the King's Works, a well-salaried position that brought responsibility for maintaining royal buildings. In 1391 the poet was given work as a forester on the king's lands at North Petherton, in Somerset.

To mark his coming of age Richard commissioned a royal portrait by Andre Beauneveu of Valenciennes to be placed in Westminster Abbey. This image, which represents the king crowned and splendidly robed while holding the royal sceptre, is the first royal portrait painted from life. Richard also rebuilt Westminster Hall from 1393 onwards, adding a porch

Above: In the exquisite Wilton Diptych, Richard kneels beside St Edward the Confessor, St Edmund and a pilgrim, before the Virgin Mary and Christ.

and an oak hammer-beam roof that had the broadest unsupported span in the country. In the 1390s he commissioned a beautiful but anonymous painting, the Wilton Diptych, which he may have used as a portable altarpiece when travelling from palace to palace.

Below: The great poet of Richard's age, Geoffrey Chaucer, was saved from financial troubles by royal patronage.

CHAPTER THREE

RULERS OF SCOTLAND

TO 1603

In 1306, Robert the Bruce, newly established as King of Scots, was in miserable exile in the Western Isles following defeats to English forces at Methven, near Perth, and at Dalry, close to Tyndrum in Perthshire. The old enemy, England, appeared unbeatable, and its vigorous martial ruler King Edward I seemed determined to destroy Scotland as an independent nation and bring its beautiful lands within his own realm.

According to legend, at this low ebb Robert drew comfort from watching a spider as it attempted again and again, undaunted by failure, to spin its web – and finally succeeded. Robert was inspired to fight back, and eight years later he led a Scots army to a famous victory over the English at the Battle of Bannockburn, in 1314. In 1323 he forced Edward I's successor, Edward II of England, to sue for peace. Of course the peace did not last, but Robert is remembered as probably Scotland's greatest king and national hero, 'the Bruce'.

Among the Bruce's lords at Bannockburn was Walter Stewart, scion of a famous family whose name came from their hereditary position as High Steward of Scotland. Walter married the Bruce's daughter Marjorie, and their son, who ruled as Robert II (r.1371–90), founded the great royal house of Stewart (or Stuart, in the French spelling), which was later established by his descendant Mary, Queen of Scots.

In 1603, Mary's son James Charles Stuart united the crowns of Scotland and England when he travelled south to London as King James VI of Scots (r.1567–1603). There he was finally crowned as King James I of England (r.1603–25).

Left: James V took Frenchwoman Mary of Guise as his second queen in 1538. Their daughter was Mary, Queen of Scots.

THE CREATION OF SCOTLAND

TO 1040

The lands now known as Scotland were a military battleground until the 9th century, when King Kenneth mac Alpin forged the first recognizable ancestor of the modern country of the Scots.

ANCIENT FOREBEARS

Four rival groups played an important part in the creation of this country. The first and most venerable were the Picts, present from c.AD300. Little is known about them because their culture was apparently entirely oral; and most of the evidence was destroyed when they were defeated by their rivals in the 9th century. By the 3rd century AD the dozen or so British tribes north of the Forth-Clyde isthmus had merged to form the Caledonians and the Maetae, and it was from these two tribal coalitions the Picts emerged as a recognizable ethnic group.

Celtic Britons made inroads into the south-west of what would become Scotland. The partially Romanized but still independent Britons who lived between the Forth-Clyde isthmus and Hadrian's Wall established a number of kingdoms around the time of the end of Roman rule, most notably Rheged and Gododdin. By c.AD700 they were forced back to the small kingdom of Strathclyde in south-western Scotland.

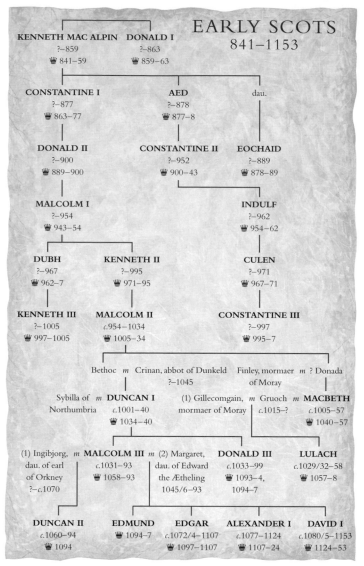

EARLY SCOTS
841–1153

KENNETH MAC ALPIN
?–859
♛ 841–59

DONALD I
?–863
♛ 859–63

CONSTANTINE I
?–877
♛ 863–77

AED
?–878
♛ 877–8

dau.

DONALD II
?–900
♛ 889–900

CONSTANTINE II
?–952
♛ 900–43

EOCHAID
?–889
♛ 878–89

MALCOLM I
?–954
♛ 943–54

INDULF
?–962
♛ 954–62

DUBH
?–967
♛ 962–7

KENNETH II
?–995
♛ 971–95

CULEN
?–971
♛ 967–71

KENNETH III
?–1005
♛ 997–1005

MALCOLM II
c.954–1034
♛ 1005–34

CONSTANTINE III
?–997
♛ 995–7

Bethoc *m* Crinan, abbot of Dunkeld
?–1045

Finley, mormaer *m* ? Donada
of Moray

Sybilla of *m* **DUNCAN I**
Northumbria   c.1001–40
♛ 1034–40

(1) Gillecomgain, *m* Gruoch *m* **MACBETH**
mormaer of Moray   c.1015–?   c.1005–57
♛ 1040–57

(1) Ingibjorg, *m* **MALCOLM III** *m* (2) Margaret,
dau. of earl   c.1031–93   dau. of Edward
of Orkney   ♛ 1058–93   the Ætheling
?–c.1070   1045/6–93

DONALD III
c.1033–99
♛ 1093–4,
1094–7

LULACH
c.1029/32–58
♛ 1057–8

DUNCAN II
c.1060–94
♛ 1094

EDMUND
♛ 1094–7

EDGAR
c.1072/4–1107
♛ 1097–1107

ALEXANDER I
c.1077–1124
♛ 1107–24

DAVID I
c.1080/5–1153
♛ 1124–53

Above: Scandinavian horseman. This Viking warrior is from a tapestry in Baldishol Church, Norway (1180).

Both Picts and Britons faced incursions into western Scotland from Irish tribes. The Irish established the kingdom of Dal Riada, traditionally under their founding king Fergus Mor (AD498–501), in the area now called Argyll. These people were later called the Scotti (Latin for 'Irish').

The fourth group were the Angles from northern Germany, who arrived as part of the influx of Germanic tribes into Britain in the 5th and 6th centuries AD. They founded the kingdom of Bernicia, which later became part of the northern Anglo-Saxon realm of Northumbria.

Left: Scotland in c.AD850, at the time when Kenneth mac Alpin took advantage of Pictish defeats by the Vikings to forge the Scottish–Pictish kingdom of Alba.

FOUNDING FATHER

Scholars often compare the Scottish founding monarch Kenneth mac Alpin to Alfred the Great. Like Alfred, Kenneth forged a united kingdom under persistent threat from Viking invaders, which was consolidated over several reigns. Kenneth's kingdom of Alba was ruled by his brother Donald I (AD859–63), by Kenneth's sons Constantine (AD863–77) and Aed (AD877–8), by their cousin Giric who ruled jointly with Eochaid (AD878–89), by Constantine's son, Donald II (AD889–900), and then by Donald II's nephew and Kenneth's grandson, Constantine II (AD900–43).

In the 9th century the Vikings created kingdoms in Shetland, the western isles and Orkney. The Scots tried to contain the expansionism of Wessex and other 'English' kingdoms in the 10th century. Claims to be overlord of Scotland by English kings began in AD918 with Edward the Elder of Wessex, who made Constantine II submit to his rule.

Above: Seaborne invaders in the north. This whalebone plaque was found in the boat burial of a Viking chieftain on Sanday, Orkney.

THE STONE OF DESTINY

In AD843 King Kenneth mac Alpin held a sacred investment ceremony on Moot Hill at Scone, ancient royal site of the Picts, using the venerable Irish-Dal Riadan royal stone, the Stone of Destiny. Traditionally the Stone was brought to Scotland from Ireland by King Fergus Mor. According to legend, the Stone originated in the Holy Land and came to Ireland by way of Egypt and Spain. It was used for the investiture of all Scottish kings until it was taken from Scone by King Edward I of England (1272–1307) and placed in Westminster Abbey, where it remained until 1996, when it was finally returned to Scotland.

Above: The Stone was incorporated into Edward I's Coronation Chair.

MACBETH

1040–1057

King Duncan I of Scots, grandson of Malcolm II and son of Crinan, the Abbot of Dunkeld, came to the throne in 1034. Six years later he was slain and his crown taken by Macbeth Macfinlay, the ruler of Moray. Shakespeare's tragedy *Macbeth* (probably first performed in 1606) made these royal names among the most resonant in British history, with King Duncan celebrated as the archetype of the wise, noble and divinely ordained ruler and Macbeth as the usurper maddened first by ambition and superstitious belief in prophecy, then by guilt.

FROM FACT TO FOLKLORE

In Shakespeare's play, Macbeth is a brave and well-respected general in King Duncan's army who encounters three witches on a heath and hears their prophecy that he will be made Thane of Cawdor and become king. When Duncan makes him Thane of Cawdor,

Below: Haunted by his misdeeds, Macbeth shies away from the ghost of his fellow general Banquo, whom he murdered.

MACBETH, KING OF SCOTLAND, 1040–1057
Birth: *c.*1005
Accession: 14 Aug 1040
Queen: Gruoch (m. after 1032)
Succeeded by: His stepson, Lulach
Death: 15 Aug 1057 at the Battle of Lumphanan

the prophecy begins to work at him and, encouraged by his wife, Lady Macbeth, he murders Duncan in his bed during the king's visit to his castle.

In fact, as *mormaer* ('ruler' in Gaelic, or high steward) of Moray, the region of northern Scotland around Inverness, Macbeth Macfinlay was a natural rival of Duncan's for power. The Moray *mormaers* were long-term opponents of the kings of Scotland. Moreover, although Macbeth probably had no hereditary claim to Duncan's throne, Macbeth's wife Gruoch and Duncan were third-generation rivals for the throne of Scotland, for Gruoch was granddaughter of King Kenneth III, who had been

Above: Engraver John Boydell (1719–1804) had a romantic vision of Macbeth's encounter with the Three Witches.

killed in battle at Monzievaird in 1005 by Duncan's grandfather, Malcolm II. The historical Duncan does not seem to have been an effective king, for he led several unsuccessful raids into Northumbria, including a failed attack on Durham in 1039. His authority was doubtless weakened by these events.

Duncan's campaign against Macbeth ended in his own death at the Battle of Pitgaveny, near Elgin, on 14 August 1040. Duncan's son Malcolm escaped into exile and stayed first with his mother's relatives at the northern court of Siward, Earl of Northumberland, and then at the court of Edward the Confessor, King of England.

DRAMATIC LICENCE

In Shakespeare's play, Macbeth is unhinged by guilt and fear. He gets drawn further and further into blood-shed as, maddened by new prophecies, he slaughters his fellow general Banquo and the wife and children of Macduff, Thane of Cawdor, against whom he has been warned. Then, in alliance with Duncan's son Malcolm, Macduff invades and kills Macbeth at Dunsinane and Malcolm is proclaimed king.

In fact, Macbeth Macfinlay enjoyed a relatively long and stable rule. He fought several campaigns against the

TANISTRY'S LEGACY OF FAMILY VIOLENCE

For the century prior to the reigns of Duncan and Macbeth, Scotland followed a form of succession known as tanistry, under which two branches of Kenneth mac Alpin's family shared the succession. The Scottish throne passed successively from one branch to the other, cousin to cousin or uncle to nephew. The system had the unfortunate effect of fostering violence.

AD943: Constantine II retires to St Andrew's monastery, Fife. He is succeeded by his cousin Malcolm I, who subjugates Moray

AD954: King Malcolm I is killed in Moray uprising and is succeeded by his cousin Indulf

AD962: Indulf is killed by Danes and succeeded by Malcolm's son Dubh

AD967: Dubh is murdered on the orders of his cousin Culen, who succeeds to the crown

AD971: Culen is assassinated in a revenge attack by Dubh's brother; Kenneth II succeeds

AD995: Kenneth II is killed by noblewoman Finvela; his cousin Constantine III succeeds

AD997: Constantine III is killed; Dubh's son Kenneth III succeeds

1005: Kenneth II's son Malcolm kills Kenneth III and takes the throne as Malcolm II

c.1018: Malcolm II acquires Strathclyde and Lothian for Scotland

1034: After a 28-year reign Malcolm II rejects the tanistry tradition and leaves the country to his grandson Duncan.

Above: Cawdor Castle, the supposed site of Macbeth's murder of Duncan, was actually built in the late 14th century.

Norse in Caithness and Sutherland, defeated a rebel force near Dunkeld (modern Tayside) in 1045, killing Malcolm's grandfather Crinan, Abbot of Dunkeld, and in 1046 was victorious over Siward, Earl of Northumbria, who was seeking to elevate Duncan's son Malcolm to the kingship.

Below: Far from being the paragon of noble kingship celebrated by Shakespeare, Duncan was a rather ineffectual ruler.

On 27 July 1054, however, he was defeated at Dunsinane, near Scone, by Siward and Malcolm and forced to cede Lothian and Strathclyde in southern Scotland to Malcolm. The invasion was supported by the English troops of Edward the Confessor, who had provided hospitality to Malcolm at his

Below: The historical Macbeth was mormaer of Moray from c.1031 and ruled all of Scotland for 17 years.

court and who envisaged him as a puppet ruler on the Scottish throne. In 1057 Macbeth was killed in battle at Lumphanan, west of Aberdeen, by Malcolm himself. Macbeth's 25-year-old stepson Lulach briefly inherited the crown, but was killed by Malcolm in an ambush in 1058. Macbeth himself was clearly not regarded as a usurper, for he was laid to rest on Iona, which was the burial ground only of lawful monarchs.

THE DEADLY APPLE

Contrary to Shakespeare's account, Duncan was not in truth a victim of treachery in Macbeth's household, but one of his royal predecessors did fall foul of deadly hospitality.

In AD995 King Kenneth II was murdered by or at the instigation of Scots noblewoman Finvela, who blamed him for the death of her only son. According to legend, she invited him to her house and treated him to a great banquet with wine. When her royal guest was drunk, Finvela led him into another chamber, where she had prepared a bizarre contraption: a statue bearing a golden apple connected to a number of hidden crossbows, which were set to fire when the apple was lifted. She invited Kenneth to take the apple as a symbol of their reconciliation and, when he lifted the golden fruit, he was shot.

MALCOLM III TO MALCOLM IV
1058–1165

Malcolm III Canmore ('big head' or 'great leader') regained the throne lost 18 years earlier by his father King Duncan, in 1058, with English backing. The 18-year rule of the lords of Moray – Macbeth Macfinlay (1040–57) and his stepson Lulach (1057–8) – was over. Malcolm had spent the first 14 of those 18 years in exile in England and after returning to Scotland remained involved in the upheavals south of the border.

ENGLISH ALLIANCES
In 1066, when Harold Godwineson became King Harold II of England, Malcolm III Canmore joined the northern invasion raised by Earl Tostig and King Harald Hardrada of Norway. Then, in 1068, following Duke William of Normandy's occupation of the English throne as King William I, Malcolm gave sanctuary in Scotland to another of William's rivals, Edgar the

Above: Might and right. A manuscript of 1588 depicts King Malcolm III of Scots and his pious second wife, Margaret.

Atheling and his mother and sisters. The next year he took one of the sisters, the pious and later sainted Margaret, as his wife. Malcolm raided Northumbria in 1070, and in 1072 William I invaded eastern Scotland with naval backup to punish him. Malcolm made peace rather than engage the formidable Norman army. In a treaty signed at Abernethy, near Perth, on 15 August 1072, Malcolm acknowledged William I's overlordship. He was also forced to send his son Duncan into exile as an English hostage and to expel his brother-in-law Edgar the Atheling from Scotland.

Despite having acknowledged English overlordship, Malcolm again raided Northumbria in 1079, 1090 and 1093. The last attack ended in Malcolm's death in an ambush. Malcolm's son and heir Edward was also killed and a succession crisis was sparked.

Four years of dynastic disputes were ended by the victory in 1097 of Edgar, one of Malcolm's sons with Queen Margaret. During his ten-year reign,

Left: Edinburgh Castle stands high on a rock above the city. It contains a Norman chapel to St Margaret, wife of Malcolm III.

Edgar restored stability. His pious character and patronage of the Church won him the nickname 'Gentle King Edgar' and one contemporary, St Aelred of Rievaulx, declared that he equalled Edward the Confessor in holiness.

Two key events of Edgar's reign were the recognition in 1098 of Norwegian rule in the Hebrides by King Magnus III 'Barefoot' of Norway and the diplomatic marriage in 1100 between England's new king, Henry I, and Edgar's sister Edith (who later took the Norman name Matilda). Edgar himself remained unmarried. At his death, aged 33, on 8 January 1107 he was succeeded by his brother, Alexander.

RISE OF KING DAVID
Alexander I followed his elder brother Edgar's instructions in allowing his younger brother, David, to govern southern Scotland while he himself controlled the north. Alexander maintained good relations with his brother-in-law King Henry I of

ROYAL INFANTICIDE

King David paid a high price for offering hospitality in 1114, when he was governing southern Scotland in his brother Alexander I's reign. David gave houseroom to a Scandinavian priest who had been blinded and had had his feet and hands amputated as a punishment for the brutal sacrifice of a colleague on a church altar in Norway. Sadly the priest proved to be insane: he used the metal hook he wore in place of a hand to cut open and kill David's infant son Malcolm. Wild with a father's grief, David ordered the priest to be tied to horses so that he would be torn apart when they were whipped and sent galloping in different directions.

England, accepted the status of Henry's feudal vassal and entered a diplomatic marriage to Sibylla, Henry's illegitimate daughter. Alexander also fought alongside the English king, leading a Scottish troop during Henry's campaigns in Wales in 1114.

On Alexander's death aged 47, on 23 April 1124, David took power over all of Scotland and ruled as King David I. He had many connections with England. He was brother-in-law to King Henry I through the late Queen Matilda (formerly 'Edith') and was himself married to Maud, daughter of Earl Waltheof of Northumbria. Furthermore, he had lived as an exile at the English court in the 1090s during the succession crisis that followed the death of his father Malcolm III.

In David's reign, Scotland and its monarchy gained a new strength and prestige. He established a central government administration, introduced royal coinage and imported an Anglo-Norman feudal system. Many notable Anglo-Norman lords settled in Scotland, receiving grants of land in return for royal service and intermarrying with the local aristocracy. Celebrated Scottish

families including Bruce, Stewart and Comyn were among the influx of Anglo-Normans that occurred during King David's reign.

David was a great church patron, founding many Cistercian and Augustinian monastic establishments. Several castles and burghs, or fortified settlements, were also raised or rebuilt under his rule, including Edinburgh, Berwick, Roxburgh and Stirling.

Under David, the country grew to its largest extent. After 1130, he succeeded in subjugating the always troublesome earldom of Moray, possession of the descendants of Macbeth Macfinlay (1040–57). In the course of the civil war in England in King Stephen's reign (1135–54), David initially backed Henry I's daughter, the Empress Matilda, but twice made peace with Stephen. He gained Cumberland, Northumberland,

Durham, Westmorland and, for a time, Lancaster for Scotland, a state of affairs recognized by Henry Plantagenet (the future Henry II) in 1149.

SWIFT DECLINE

David's territorial gains in northern England were short-lived, however. He died in Carlisle on 24 May 1153 and, because both his sons were already dead, was succeeded by his 12-year-old grandson Malcolm IV. The youthful king did succeed in subduing Galloway in 1160, and in 1164 put down a rebellion led by Somerled, 'Lord of the Western Isles', at Renfrew, but aside from that, his reign was short and largely uneventful and he died aged only 23.

Below: Growing territory. By the end of King David's reign in 1153, Scotland stretched as far south as the river Tees.

WILLIAM I THE LION
1165–1214

On the unexpected death of the quiet, pious and chaste King Malcolm IV in December 1165, his energetic, red-haired brother William came to the throne. Invested at Scone on Christmas Eve 1165, William would remain on the throne for 49 years, the longest reign of any Scots king in the medieval period. His posthumous nickname, 'the Lion', may derive from his fearlessness and strength in battle, but is more likely to have been a reference to the heraldic device he adopted, of a red lion rampant against a yellow background.

NORTHUMBERLAND CONTROL

The vexed question of Scottish control over Northumberland, gained by William's grandfather David I but lost by Malcolm IV, troubled much of William's reign. Early on, in 1174, William saw an opportunity. Henry II's sons Henry the Young King, Richard and Geoffrey were in open revolt against their father in Normandy, so

Above: In the 14th century, John of Fordun named William leo justitiae ('lion of justice') – a possible source of his nickname 'the Lion'.

William invaded Northumberland. However, the Scots king was caught unawares in mist when besieging Alnwick Castle. Unable to see clearly, he mistook a group of English cavalry for his own knights. He was surprised and, although he fought valiantly, had

---

WILLIAM I 'THE LION', KING OF SCOTLAND, 1165–1214
Birth: 1142/3
Father: Henry, Earl of Northumberland
Mother: Ada de Warenne
Accession: 9 Dec 1165
Investiture: 24 Dec, 1165, Scone
Queen: Ermengarde (m. 5 Sept 1186; d. 1233)
Succeeded by: His son Alexander
Greatest achievement: Stability of a 49-year reign
1168: Alliance with France
1174: Captured at Alnwick and imprisoned by Henry II
Dec 1174: Treaty of Falaise: William swears allegiance to Henry II
1178: Founds Arbroath Abbey
1189: Treaty of Falaise cancelled by King Richard I
Death: 4 Dec 1214, Stirling

---

his horse killed beneath him and was ultimately overpowered. The humiliation of being captured alive was made worse when he was thrown in jail and kept as a prisoner of King Henry II for five months, powerless to prevent the gleeful English troops from plundering southern Scotland.

Below: Stirling Castle. William created a royal hunting ground at Stirling and died in the castle on 4 December 1214.

ARBROATH ABBEY

King William the Lion established the Abbey of Arbroath in 1178 to honour the memory of St Thomas à Becket. Becket had been murdered eight years earlier at Canterbury by knights who were probably acting on behalf of Henry I, and he was canonized only 15 months later in 1172. The Abbey housed monks of the Tironensian order, which originated in Tiron, France, and had Kelso Abbey – founded by King David I – as its main Scottish base. However, the monks of Arbroath were independent of the 'mother house'.

Arbroath Abbey became one of the wealthiest in Scotland. William made the monks many grants of income and also allowed them to establish a fortified settlement, hold a market and construct a harbour. Following his death in 1214, King William was buried at the Abbey. A little over a century later, in 1320, Scotland's resounding statement of independence from England, the Declaration of Arbroath, was signed at the Abbey

Left: The impressive south transept still stands among the ruins of Arbroath Abbey.

Above: Alnwick Castle, Northumberland, was the site of William the Lion's catastrophic capture by English knights.

Worse still was to follow. The price of William's release was the punitive Treaty of Falaise, signed in December 1174, under which William had to pledge allegiance to Henry as his vassal, to accept that the English Church was supreme over the Scottish Church and to pay for the establishment of English garrisons in Scottish territory. Scotland had become a feudal possession of the English king.

FREEDOM FOR SALE

This state of affairs improved 15 years later when, following the death of Henry II, King Richard I 'the Lionheart' was raising money to fund his departure for the Holy Land on the Third Crusade. Richard I agreed to accept that the Treaty of Falaise had been obtained by force and reversed its terms in return for a cash payment of 10,000 marks.

A little later, the clause of the treaty that had established the supremacy of the English Church was undermined by Pope Celestine III who, in 1192, declared that the Church in Scotland owed allegiance to Rome alone and could not be forced to submit to the English Church.

Following the accession of King John in 1199, William plotted a further invasion to reassert Scotland's claim over Northumberland. According to tradition, the king – who was a pious man – received a divine warning that a major campaign in northern England would have dire consequences for Scotland. He limited himself to minor raiding, which in itself brought disastrous results. A show of English military strength forced a treaty signed at Norham, Northumberland, on 7 September 1209, in which William again had to recognize the English king as his feudal overlord and allow John to arrange marriages for his daughters.

FRENCH CONNECTION

In 1168 William made an alliance with Louis VII of France that some scholars identify as the beginning of the 'Auld Alliance', the centuries-long diplomatic 'friendship' between French and Scottish monarchs eager to strengthen their position against the English.

At home William built on David's legacy, founding burghs and consolidating a local law system of sheriffs and justices.

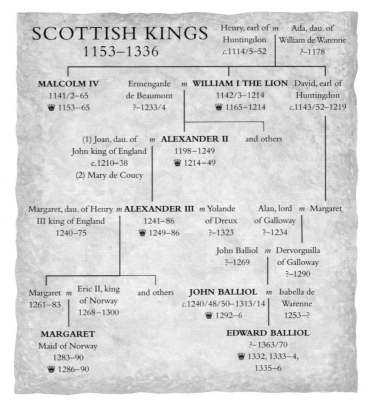

SCOTTISH KINGS
1153–1336

	Henry, earl of *m* Huntingdon *c.*1114/5–52	Ada, dau. of William de Warenne ?–1178

MALCOLM IV 1141/2–65 ♛ 1153–65 — Ermengarde de Beaumont ?–1233/4 *m* **WILLIAM I THE LION** 1142/3–1214 ♛ 1165–1214 — David, earl of Huntingdon *c.*1143/52–1219

(1) Joan, dau. of John king of England *c.*1210–38 — *m* **ALEXANDER II** 1198–1249 ♛ 1214–49 — and others
(2) Mary de Coucy

Margaret, dau. of Henry III king of England 1240–75 — *m* **ALEXANDER III** 1241–86 ♛ 1249–86 — *m* Yolande of Dreux ?–1323 — Alan, lord *m* Margaret of Galloway ?–1234

John Balliol *m* Dervorguilla ?–1269 — of Galloway ?–1290

Margaret *m* Eric II, king of Norway 1268–1300 1261–83 — and others — **JOHN BALLIOL** *c.*1240/48/50–1313/14 ♛ 1292–6 — *m* Isabella de Warenne 1253–?

MARGARET Maid of Norway 1283–90 ♛ 1286–90

EDWARD BALLIOL ?–1363/70 ♛ 1332, 1333–4, 1335–6

ALEXANDER II
1214–1249

Following the stability of William the Lion's 49-year reign, William's 16-year-old son Alexander came to the throne in 1214. The next year, sensing an opportunity to make progress towards his father's long-held dream of regaining former Scottish territory in Northumberland, Alexander sided with the barons of England when they rose up and imposed the Magna Carta on King John.

THE PEACE OF YORK

Alexander paid homage to Prince Louis, heir to the French crown, who had been offered the English throne. However, John had his revenge, launching a savage attack on Lothian designed, he declared, to 'hunt the red foxcub from his lairs', a reference to the red hair that Alexander had inherited from his father. Following the death of King John in 1216 and the collapse of the baronial rebellion in 1217, Alexander made peace with England's new king, Henry III, paying homage to him for his lands in England at Christmas 1217. Then on 19 June 1221, at York, he married Henry's sister, Joan.

Above: Alexander allied himself to the English barons who in the Magna Carta set limits on his father-in-law King John's authority.

The new harmonious Anglo-Scottish atmosphere resulted in the 1237 Peace of York, under which Alexander renounced his claim to the disputed northern territories, including Northumberland, and the border between the two countries was agreed as running north-east from the Solway to the Tweed – roughly the border that has survived to this day. The peace treaty rewarded Alexander's accommodating approach by giving him rights to a number of English estates.

PEACE AND STABILITY

Alexander II maintained peace for Scotland and his byname became 'the Peaceful'. However, he had to be tough and pragmatic. Like his predecessors, he

had his work cut out to impose his authority in the west and north-west of his realm. He put down revolts in Galloway in 1234–5 and 1247 and brutally punished rebels in Caithness, in the far north, by ordering that each captured rebel have one hand and one foot cut off. He caught a fever whilst on campaign and died aged 50 in 1249.

Left: Alexander II was warned in a dream not to try to recapture the Hebrides from Norway. He disregarded the advice – and died of a fever while on campaign.

ALEXANDER II, KING OF SCOTLAND, 1214–1249
Birth: 24 Aug 1198, Haddington, East Lothian
Father: William I the Lion
Mother: Ermengarde de Beaumont
Accession: 4 Dec 1214
Coronation: 6 Dec 1214, Scone Abbey
Queens: (1) Joan, daughter of King John of England (m. June 1221; d.1238); (2) Mary de Coucy (m. 15 May 1239)
Succeeded by: His son Alexander III
Death: 6 July 1249, on the Isle of Kerrara in the Bay of Oban

ALEXANDER III
1249–1286

Alexander II had reigned for a very respectable 34 years, but his unexpected end was not well timed, for his son and heir, who came to the throne as King Alexander III, was just eight years old.

JUNIOR ROYAL WEDDING

Within three years, at the age of just ten, Alexander III made a major diplomatic match when he was married to King Henry III's 21-year-old daughter Margaret. The ceremony took place on 26 December 1251 in York Abbey and was long remembered, not least for Henry's attempt to take advantage of Alexander's tender years and make him pay homage to the English king for all his Scottish lands. Alexander, canny and well prepared, replied that he was present to be married and 'not to answer about so difficult a matter'.

A DEAL WITH NORWAY

At peace with England, Alexander pressed on with his father's project of regaining control of the Western Isles. In 1263 he offered to buy Kintyre and the Western Isles from King Haakon IV of Norway. Haakon refused and, acting on reports that the Scots had attacked Skye, led a punitive raid along the west coast. His fleet anchored off Largs, near Ayr, but was wrecked in a storm and an invading party was driven back by Scottish troops in a beach battle at Largs on 2 October. On his return from this bungled expedition, Haakon became ill and died in Orkney.

Haakon's successor on the Norwegian throne, King Magnus V, agreed the Treaty of Perth in 1266 under which Scotland regained the Western Isles.

Right: Tradition has it that Colin Fitzgerald, first chief of Clan Mackenzie, saved Alexander III from a stag. Benjamin West imagined the scene in 1786.

In August 1274 King Alexander and Queen Margaret were guests at the coronation of Margaret's brother Edward as King Edward I of England. Alexander was pleased to maintain friendly relations with England, but he would not allow Scotland's independence to be undermined. Visiting Westminster in October 1278, he willingly paid homage for his lands in England to Edward I, but made a proud declaration of Scotland's independence when it was suggested by the Bishop of Norwich that a Scottish king should pay homage to his English counterpart for all his territories. Alexander replied in ringing tones, 'To homage for my kingdom of Scotland no one has right except God alone. Nor do I hold it except of God alone'.

Alexander's Scotland was prosperous, stable and secure, but his sudden death in March 1286 plunged the country into a succession crisis. Riding from Edinburgh to Dunfermline on 19 March 1286, Alexander and his horse fell over a cliff during a storm. With his

---

ALEXANDER III, KING OF SCOTLAND, 1249–1286

Birth: 4 Sept 1241, Roxburgh
Father: Alexander II
Mother: Mary de Coucy
Accession: 8 July 1249
Coronation: 13 July 1249, Scone Abbey
Queens: (1) Margaret, daughter of Henry III of England (m. 26 Dec 1251); (2) Yolande or Joletta, daughter of Robert IV, Count of Dreux (m. 1 Nov 1285; d. 1323)
Succeeded by: Margaret
Death: 19 March 1286

---

three children already dead, his only heir was his granddaughter Margaret, the daughter of King Eric II of Norway, and Alexander III's daughter, another Margaret. This infant girl, born only the previous year and known as the 'Maid of Norway', was therefore declared Queen of Scotland.

JOHN BALLIOL AND ROBERT I 'THE BRUCE'

1286–1329

Scotland's child-queen, Margaret the 'Maid of Norway', ruled for four years without setting foot in her realm. She died in the Orkney Islands in 1290, aged just seven, as she was travelling to Scotland for the first time. She left a power vacuum in which there were 13 rival claimants for the throne. The strongest of these were John Balliol and Robert Bruce (the grandfather of Robert I Bruce), both descendants of King David I's daughters.

AN EMPTY THRONE

Edward I of England was determined to force the Scots to recognize him as their overlord and sensed a magnificent opportunity in this succession crisis.

At Norham, near Berwick, he acted as mediator between the rivals and chose Balliol, who had the stronger legal claim and who also promised to pay homage to Edward. However, Balliol later defied Edward by choosing to ally

Below: King John Balliol is pictured with the heraldic arms that he had stripped from him by a merciless Edward I of England.

JOHN BALLIOL, KING OF SCOTLAND, 1292–1296

Birth: *c.*1240/48/50, Barnard Castle
Father: John Balliol
Mother: Devorguilla of Galloway
Accession: 17 Nov 1292
Coronation: 30 Nov 1292, Scone Abbey
Queen: Isabella, daughter of John de Warenne, 6th Earl of Surrey (m. before 7 Feb 1281)
10/11 July 1296: Abdicates at Brechin
Death: 1313/14, Normandy

with France in the 1295 Treaty of Paris rather than fight alongside Edward in a proposed war against the French. Edward's army invaded Scotland in 1296, sacked Berwick and then crushed Balliol's Scottish army at Dunbar. On 10 July, Balliol was stripped of his knightly arms, crown, sword and sceptre and then despatched to London, where he was cast into the Tower. The event won John the mocking nickname 'Toom Tabard' (vacant coat'), a reference to the removal of his heraldic arms.

For ten years the Scottish throne remained empty. In 1300 Edward I rubbed in his victory by removing the Stone of Destiny from Scotland and using it as part of a newly constructed coronation chair in Westminster Abbey.

Scottish pride was in the hands of rebel leader Sir William Wallace, who defied Edward for eight years, crushing an English army at Stirling in 1297 and later the same year taunting the English king by raiding Northumberland and Cumberland. Wallace was captured in Scotland in 1305, taken to London, condemned as a traitor and brutally executed. His name lived on, however, as an inspiration to those fighting for Scottish independence.

BRUCE TAKES POWER

Meanwhile the Scottish families of Bruce and Comyn (Cumming) were the principal claimants to the vacant Scottish throne. Robert the Bruce (grandson of the Robert Bruce who had lost the crown to Balliol in 1292) seized the initiative. On 10 February 1306 he or his followers murdered his chief rival, John Comyn, in the Franciscan Church at Dumfries. Bruce then had himself crowned King Robert I of Scots, at Scone, on 27 March. He immediately set about eliminating resistance to his rule. However, he received two major and near-immediate setbacks in the form of military defeats by English troops at Methven on 19 June and Dalry, close to Tyndrum, on 11 August. He fled into exile.

VICTORY AT BANNOCKBURN

In 1307 Robert I's prospects improved when his principal adversary, the great warrior-king Edward I, died of dysentery as he was travelling north to invade Scotland once more. Edward I's successor, the hot-headed Edward II, was far less of a threat. In Scotland, Robert I established his own rule over all of the

Above: 'We fight… for freedom alone'. Scotland's independence was declared at Arbroath by Robert I's nobles in 1320.

Right: The Holkham Bible *of 1327 has a near-contemporary representation of the Scots' 1314 victory at Bannockburn.*

country save the south-east corner and routed Edward II's army at the battle of Bannockburn, in June 1314.

Edward had led his large army into Scotland to relieve the English garrison in Stirling Castle, which was besieged by Robert I. Greatly outnumbered, the Scots were rallied by King Robert, who told them, 'Fight for your nation's honour'. First with cavalry and then with spearmen, the Scots took the battle to the English. The invading army panicked and broke when King Edward II fled for his life. Thousands of Englishmen were slain.

This remarkable victory over the Plantagenet English army made Robert the Bruce a hero in Scotland, established his claim to the throne beyond doubt, united the Scots and ended the Bruce–Comyn war.

ROBERT I THE BRUCE, KING OF SCOTLAND, 1306–1329

Birth: 11 July 1274, Turnberry Castle, Ayrshire

Father: Robert (VI) de Brus (d. 1304)

Mother: Marjory, Countess of Carrick

Accession: 10 Feb 1306

Investiture: 27 March 1306, Scone

Queen: Elizabeth (m. 1302; d. 1327)

Succeeded by: His son David

Greatest achievement: Safeguarding Scottish independence

10 Feb 1306: Murders rival John Comyn and seizes power

June–August 1306: Military defeats drive him into hiding

24 June 1314: Battle of Bannockburn

1320: Declaration of Arbroath

1328: Treaty of Edinburgh

Death: 7 June 1329, Cardross, Dumbartonshire

DECLARATION OF ARBROATH

In 1320, Robert encouraged his leading nobles to make the resonant statement of Scotland's independence known as the Declaration of Arbroath. The document, drawn up on 6 April 1320, probably by Bernard de Linton, Abbot of Arbroath Abbey and Chancellor of Scotland, was addressed to Pope John XXII at Avignon, who had excommunicated Robert I following the murder of John Comyn and who so far refused to accept Scottish independence. The Declaration stated that the Scots were bound to their King Robert, 'By law and by his strengths, so that we may continue free, and we will continue to stand by him, come what may', but it added that they would drive their king out, 'As an enemy' if he consented to make Scotland subject to England once more. The Declaration also stated that the Scots were fighting not for wealth or glory or worldy status, 'But for freedom – and for freedom only, which no honourable man will give up but with his life'.

Robert's dream was realized in 1328, following the deposition of Edward II and the accession of the youthful Edward III, in the Treaty of Edinburgh and Northampton. England recognized Scotland's independence.

Robert I, great hero of Scottish independence, suffered from illness in his later years and died, probably of leprosy, in 1329. In 1328 the Pope had lifted the writ of excommunication that he had imposed ten years earlier. On his deathbed, Robert arranged to have his heart excized after his death and made Sir James Douglas pledge to take the heart with him on crusade to the Holy Land. The king's body was buried at Dunfermline Abbey and the heart – returned to Scotland after Douglas was killed in Spain *en route* for the Holy Land – was interred at Melrose Abbey.

Below: Robert I is shown with his first wife, Isabella of Mar. Their grandson was Robert II, the founder of the House of Stewart.

DAVID II
1329–1371

Robert I's death in June 1329 plunged newly independent Scotland back into rivalry between Balliol and Bruce as dynastic feuding erupted. John Balliol's son Edward claimed the throne, invaded Scotland, defeated David II's guardian Donald of Mar on Dupplin Moor and was made king in September. In December, barons loyal to Bruce drove Balliol out and reinstated David II.

In March 1333 Balliol invaded again and, with Edward III, defeated the Scots at Halidon Hill on 19 July to regain the throne. David II fled into exile.

Balliol was little more than Edward III's puppet, to whom he paid homage as feudal overlord and ceded large parts of southern Scotland in June 1334. Balliol proved unable to impose his authority on the country. He was deposed once more

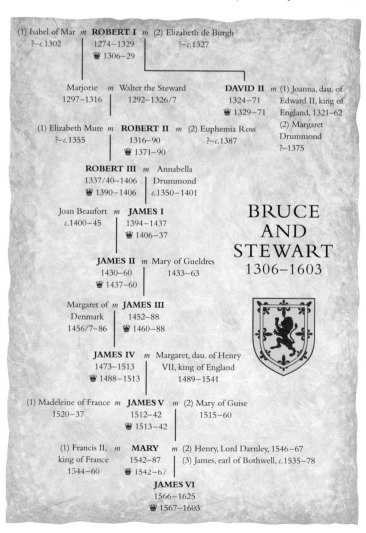

(1) Isabel of Mar *m* **ROBERT I** *m* (2) Elizabeth de Burgh
?–*c*.1302   1274–1329   ?–*c*.1327
                   ♛ 1306–29

Marjorie *m* Walter the Steward   **DAVID II** *m* (1) Joanna, dau. of
1297–1316   1292–1326/7   1324–71   Edward II, king of
                                          ♛ 1329–71   England, 1321–62
(1) Elizabeth Mure *m* **ROBERT II** *m* (2) Euphemia Ross   (2) Margaret
?–*c*.1355   1316–90   ?–*c*.1387   Drummond
                       ♛ 1371–90   ?–1375

         ROBERT III *m* Annabella
         1337/40–1406   Drummond
         ♛ 1390–1406   *c*.1350–1401

Joan Beaufort *m* **JAMES I**
c.1400–45   1394–1437
                  ♛ 1406–37

         JAMES II *m* Mary of Gueldres
         1430–60   1433–63
         ♛ 1437–60

Margaret of *m* **JAMES III**
Denmark   1452–88
1456/7–86   ♛ 1460–88

         JAMES IV *m* Margaret, dau. of Henry
         1473–1513   VII, king of England
         ♛ 1488–1513   1489–1541

(1) Madeleine of France *m* **JAMES V** *m* (2) Mary of Guise
1520–37   1512–42   1515–60
                            ♛ 1513–42

(1) Francis II, *m* **MARY** *m* (2) Henry, Lord Darnley, 1546–67
king of France   1542–87   (3) James, earl of Bothwell, *c*.1535–78
1544–60   ♛ 1542–67

         JAMES VI
         1566–1625
         ♛ 1567–1603

**BRUCE
AND
STEWART
1306–1603**

**DAVID II, KING OF
SCOTLAND, 1329–1371**
Birth: 5 March 1324, Dunfermline
Father: Robert I the Bruce
Mother: Elizabeth de Burgh
Accession: 7 June 1329
Coronation: 24 Nov 1331, Scone Abbey
Queens: (1) Joan of England (m. 17 July 1328; d. 7 Sept 1362); (2) Margaret Drummond (m. 1363/4; d. 31 Jan 1375)
Succeeded by: His nephew Robert II
Death: 22 Feb 1371, Edinburgh Castle

---

in 1334, ruled again in 1335–6 but was deposed yet again in 1336, after which he effectively abandoned his pretensions to the Scottish crown.

KING DAVID'S RETURN
After seven years' exile in France, David returned to reclaim the throne in 1341. The Scots army was crushed in 1346 by an English force at the Battle of Neville's Cross, and David took an arrow in the face before being captured and thrown in jail. He remained in English captivity until 1357.

Below: Peace reigns. In the 1357 Treaty of Berwick David II of Scots agreed terms with the powerful Edward III of England.

ROBERT II AND ROBERT III
1371–1406

 David's ill-starred reign ended in February 1371. He died without offspring and was succeeded by his nephew Robert Stewart.

THE HOUSE OF STEWART
The new king inaugurating a new and subsequently celebrated dynasty was the grandson of the great Robert I through his daughter Marjorie Bruce. Marjorie married the wealthy and powerful Walter Stewart in 1315. His surname derived from the fact that his family had held the hereditary post of Great Steward of Scotland since the reign of David I.

On accession, Robert was a mature man of 55 years, who had been the king's heir apparent for 45 years. During David II's exile and imprisonment Robert had been variously joint-regent and sole regent. In the course of his reign the Scots regained many English-held territories in southern Scotland in 1384 and then launched several raids in northern England, in 1388 winning a

Above: On accession, Robert II was a mature man of 55, who had been David II's heir apparent for 45 years.

long-celebrated victory over an English army led by Henry Percy at the Battle of Otterburn. However, Robert took no part in these heroics and, indeed, left affairs of government to his eldest son John, Earl of Carrick.

THE INEFFECTUAL ROBERT III
Robert II died in April 1390 and was succeeded by Carrick who, on his accession, took the name Robert III because after the years of John Balliol, the name 'John' was considered to be

Below: The circular Rothesay Castle, on the Isle of Bute, was a favoured dwelling of Robert II and his Stewart successors.

ROBERT II, KING OF SCOTLAND, 1371–1390
Birth: 2 March 1316, Paisley
Father: Walter the Steward
Mother: Marjorie, daughter of Robert I
Accession: 22 Feb 1371
Coronation: 22 Feb or 26 March 1371, Scone Abbey
Queens: Elizabeth Mure (m. 1336; d. before 1355); (2) Euphemia, Countess of Moray (m. after 2 May 1355; d. 1387)
Succeeded by: His son John, who took the name Robert on his accession to the throne
Death: 19 April 1390, Dundonald Castle

ROBERT III, KING OF SCOTLAND, 1390–1406
Birth: c.1337/40
Father: Robert II
Mother: Elizabeth Mure
Accession: 19 April 1390
Coronation: 14 Aug 1390, Scone Abbey
Queen: Annabella Drummond (m. c.1366/7; d. c.Oct 1401)
Succeeded by: His son James I
Death: 4 April 1406, Dundonald Castle

unlucky for a king. However, following an accident in 1388, in which he was badly kicked by a horse, Carrick became an invalid no longer fully capable of public life. When he became king, government was largely in the hands of his brother Robert, Earl of Fife and from 1398 Duke of Albany.

Under Albany's venal rule Scotland became a lawless and corrupt place. He tried to refashion the succession, in 1401 arresting and imprisoning his nephew David, Duke of Rothesay, who was heir to the throne. Rothesay died in Albany's castle, according to some accounts from starvation – although an enquiry in 1402 found that he had 'departed this life by divine providence'.

In 1406, to prevent a similar fate befalling the next in succession to the throne, Robert III sent his remaining son, the 11-year-old James Stewart, to safety in France, but James was captured by English pirates, taken to King Henry IV and cast into the Tower of London.

Robert III died later in 1406. He had become a depressive in his later years and famously declared that he could fittingly be buried in a refuse heap beneath the epitaph, 'Here lies the worst among kings and the most wretched of men in the entire country'.

JAMES I
1406–1437

On the death of King Robert III in 1406, his son James Stewart became James I of Scots at the age of 11. James had been captured that very year while travelling to France to escape potential harm at the hands of his corrupt uncle the Duke of Albany and on accession was in prison in the Tower of London. He became king in exile, but power in Scotland remained in the hands of Albany.

Above: Scots king and English rose. While forcibly exiled in England, James I married the beautiful Lady Joan Beaufort.

DEATH OF ALBANY

Secure in his position, Albany had little incentive to ransom James; by contrast he did succeed in negotiating the release of his own son, Murdoch Stewart, who was freed by King Henry V of England in 1416. Albany had been the power behind the throne since *c.*1388–90, but his long 'rule' came to an end on 3 September 1420, when he died aged 80 in Stirling Castle. Murdoch became regent in his stead.

In April 1424, James was freed to return to Scotland, following agreement of a £40,000 ransom to be paid in instalments. Once home, he moved swiftly to impose his authority. On the very day of his return, he is said to have declared, 'If God spares me...I shall see to it throughout the whole of my kingdom that the key keeps the castle and the thorn bush the cow', meaning that property would once again be safe. Within a year he had arrested several rebellious lords and had Murdoch, Duke of Albany executed at Stirling Castle, with two corrupt Stewart kinsmen.

THE POET–KING IN EXILE

James was a man of intelligence, bravery and great ability, and while in England he certainly did not merely rot in prison. He fought in the famous campaigns of King Henry V in France, and he must have won that great monarch's admiration, for in April 1421, Henry invested James as a Knight of the Garter, the prestigious order founded by King Edward III. In addition, James learned about England's developing systems of administration, taxation and government. In 1423 he fell deeply in love with one of Henry's relatives, Lady Joan Beaufort, whom he married in February 1424. Inspired by his love for Joan, James wrote the intense and complex 379-line poem *The Kingis Quair* ('The King's Book'), a work of the highest quality in the tradition of the great Geoffrey Chaucer.

A REFORMING KING

James moved to remodel the Scottish Parliament by increasing the role for lesser nobility (probably in imitation of the House of Commons in Westminster). He greatly improved local justice and instigated reforms of taxation and royal finances. He also had some success in suppressing the independent power of Highland clan leaders. However, on 21 February 1437 he was stabbed to death at Blackfriars Priory in Perth in an attack by several of his leading nobles. They were angered by the king's decision to default on his ransom payments, which had left noble hostages to die in England. James's reputation had also been damaged by his humiliating failure to recapture Roxburgh Castle from the English in a campaign the previous year. The murdered king was succeeded by his 6-year-old son, who ruled as James II.

JAMES I, KING OF SCOTLAND, 1406–1437

Birth: probably late July 1394, Dunfermline Palace
Father: Robert III
Mother: Annabella Drummond
Accession: 4 April 1406 (proclaimed in June 1406)
Coronation: 2 or 21 May 1424
Queen: Joan Beaufort (m. February 1424; d. 1445)
Succeeded by: His son James II
Death: Assassinated in the monastery of Friars Preachers, 21 Feb 1437

Left: James I was a man of many accomplishments – archer, wrestler, athlete, horserider, musician and poet.

JAMES II AND JAMES III
1437–1488

 James II came to the throne at the age of just six. The violent feuding of Scotland's lawless nobility continued throughout his minority, as three leading families – Douglas, Crichton and Livingston – competed for the prince and the crown.

A HOT-HEADED KING

James began to rule as king in 1449, (when he also married Mary of Gueldres) and he dealt severely with his foes, seizing the Livingstone lands. James was a hot-headed young man and in 1452 he murdered William, eighth Earl of Douglas, in a quarrel at Stirling Castle by stabbing him in the neck. He then took on the full might of that powerful family, winning a decisive victory at the Battle of Arkinholm in 1455 and greatly enriching the crown by confiscating the vast Douglas estates.

After 1457, largely secure at home, James turned his attention to the persistent problem of the border with England and led a number of successful military raids against English garrisons. He was killed at Roxburgh Castle, in 1460, when a cannon exploded next to him and blew him to pieces.

Above: James II of Scots had a vermilion birthmark on the left-hand side of his face, not shown in this 16th-century portrait.

JAMES III

Scotland was plunged into another minority with the accession of the eight-year-old James III on 3 August 1460. Keen to avoid further feuding, the Scottish parliament awarded custody of the boy-king to his mother, the queen dowager Mary of Gueldres, a strong and devout woman. When she died in 1463, James was under the protection of James Kennedy, Bishop of St Andrews. In 1466 he was seized by Sir Alexander Boyd, Keeper of Edinburgh Castle, who declared himself Guardian of Scotland.

In 1469, James broke free of the Boyds and began to rule in his own right. The same year he wed Margaret of Denmark. A major benefit accrued to Scotland under the marriage treaty, when Denmark agreed to cede the Shetlands and Orkney Islands to Scotland as dowry.

Trouble broke out in the 1470s, when James arrested his brothers Alexander, Duke of Albany, and John, Earl of Mar, accusing them of plotting against him. Mar was killed, while Albany escaped and then returned with

Above: This formal 18th-century portrait of James III of Scots transformed him into a posed, bewigged figure of that later age.

an English army, claiming the throne as Alexander IV. Berwick was captured, Edinburgh sacked and Albany restored to his landholdings, but James continued to reign.

James was killed during another uprising in 1488, by rebels promoting his son the Duke of Rothesay as King James IV. The throne thus passed to yet another youthful Scots king, the 15-year-old James IV.

JAMES II, KING OF SCOTLAND, 1437–1460

Birth: 16 Oct 1430, Holyrood Palace, Edinburgh
Father: James I
Mother: Joan Beaufort
Accession: 21 Feb 1437
Coronation: 25 March 1437, Holyrood Abbey, Edinburgh
Queen: Mary of Gueldres (m. 3 July 1449; d. 1463)
Succeeded by: His son James III
Death: 3 Aug 1460, killed in cannon explosion at the siege of Roxburgh

---

JAMES III, KING OF SCOTLAND, 1460–1488

Birth: May 1452
Father: James II
Mother: Mary of Gueldres
Accession: 3 Aug 1460
Coronation: 10 Aug 1460, Kelso Abbey
Queen: Margaret of Denmark (m. July 1469; d. 1486)
Succeeded by: His son James IV
Death: 11 June 1488, near Bannockburn

JAMES IV
1488–1513

James IV of Scots became involved in government from his accession, aged 15, in 1488. His efforts to extend the power of the crown into the north and west of the country met with success. In 1493 he humbled the fiercely independent John MacDonald, fourth and last Lord of the Isles, and could boast that his rule extended throughout the Northern and Western Isles.

A RENAISSANCE MAN

James lived up to the ideal of the 'Renaissance prince'. He was a firm and effective ruler who presided over a largely peaceful Scotland and greatly strengthened royal finances: in the course of the reign the king's revenue rose threefold. He was also a renowned patron of the arts and architecture: he built a royal chapel at Stirling Castle and a palace at Falkland and began work on the magnificent Holyrood Palace in Edinburgh. His court became famous throughout Europe as a centre for the arts and the most up-to-date sciences. The king himself was dedicated to medicine and education: he founded King's College, Aberdeen, in 1495, the first British university to have a chair of medicine, and a surgeons' college in Edinburgh. James was also keen on arcane subjects such as alchemy and the possibility of man-powered flight and financed the researches of an Italian

JAMES IV, KING OF SCOTLAND, 1488–1513
Birth: 17 March 1473
Father: James III
Mother: Margaret of Denmark
Accession: 11 June 1488
Coronation: 26 June 1488, Scone Abbey
Queen: Margaret Tudor (m. 8 Aug 1503; d. 1541)
Succeeded by: His son James V
Death: 9 Sept 1513 at the Battle of Flodden

scholar, John Damien, in these areas. He was a keen student of literature and devoured the works of the Scottish poets William Dunbar and Robert Henryson. He also granted a charter in 1507 to Scotland's first printing press.

RELATIONS WITH ENGLAND

In the 1490s James was drawn into the dynastic unrest in England that followed Henry Tudor's seizure of the crown as King Henry VII in 1485.

In 1495 the Scottish court at Stirling welcomed the Pretender to the English throne, Perkin Warbeck, who claimed to be Richard, Duke of York. James became friendly with the imposter, whom he addressed as 'Prince Richard', and even prepared to invade England in support of Warbeck.

In the event, the 'war' was no more than a few raids, and in late 1497 England and Scotland agreed a seven-year truce. Subsequently Warbeck was captured, confessed that his claim was false and was executed on 24 November 1499. The English truce, though, was transformed into a perpetual peace

Left: Stewart wed Tudor when James IV of Scots married Henry VII of England's daughter, Margaret, in August 1503.

Above: James IV, Scotland's first authenticated golfer. Royal accounts in the early 1500s include a record of payment for the king's 'golf clubbis and ballis'.

agreement in a treaty signed in London on 24 January 1502, which also provided for James's marriage to Margaret Tudor, daughter of King Henry VII.

James and Margaret's wedding on 8 August 1503, was celebrated with pageants, tournaments and a poem, 'The Thistle and the Rose', by William Dunbar. Although none can have known this at the time, it paved the way for the union of the crowns of Scotland and England in 1603, when James and Margaret's great-grandson, James Stuart, James VI of Scots, would accede as King James I of England.

The 'perpetual peace' was short-lived. By 1513 Scotland was once more at war with England. When England's King Henry VIII invaded France in 1513, James sent his fleet to Normandy to help Louis XII of France and himself invaded northern England with the Scottish army. The move was a disaster. At the battle of Flodden Field on 9 September 1513, James's army was routed. Around 10,000 Scots were killed, including the king himself.

JAMES V
1513–1542

 Once again Scotland's heir was an infant: James's 17-month-old son, another James, who was crowned King James V at Stirling Castle on 21 September 1513.

FRANCE OR ENGLAND?

In his minority, pro-French and pro-English factions competed for control of king and country. Initially the boy's mother, Queen Margaret, was his guardian but after her marriage to the pro-English Archibald Douglas, 6th Earl of Angus, the pro-French John Stewart, Duke of Albany, was named regent in her place in July 1515.

In 1522, Albany left for France, hoping to raise military backing for an attack on England, and there he remained after a 1524 coup brought the queen's pro-English party back to power. In 1526, Angus captured James and for the following two years kept him captive, but in 1528 James escaped, raised an army of supporters and drove Angus into exile in England.

As king, James set about enforcing his authority. A Catholic at the time of King Henry VIII's break with Rome, he pursued a strongly pro-French policy

THE 'AULD ALLIANCE'

The alliance between Scotland and France that played such an important part in the reigns of Kings James IV and V of Scots was more than two centuries old. Historians usually date the alliance from the 1295 Treaty of Paris, agreed in the reign of John Balliol by leading Scots nobles with King Philip IV of France.

However, some trace the long-standing and intermittently renewed alliance right back to the 1168 treaty between King William I 'the Lion' of Scotland and King Louis VII of France.

The alliance survived the 14th and 15th centuries, but might have been expected to die following the 1502 Treaty of Perpetual Peace with England. Yet James IV renewed the alliance in 1512 in the face of Henry VIII's aggression towards both France and Scotland, and the French alliance was important in the reign of his successor, King James V.

The Auld Alliance had two important side effects. Scots soldiers fought in the French army, particularly after Agincourt (1415). Scottish merchants had a preferential deal on French claret, and so the nobles of Scotland enjoyed finer wine.

Left: James V. In his reign, the Treaty of Rouen renewed the Auld Alliance between Scotland and France.

JAMES V, KING OF SCOTLAND, 1513–1542

Birth: 10 April 1512, Linlithgow Palace
Father: James IV
Mother: Margaret Tudor
Accession: 9 Sept 1513
Coronation: 21 Sept 1513
Queens: (1) Madeleine de Valois (m. 1 Jan 1537; d. 7 July 1537); (2) Mary of Guise (m. 12 June 1538; d. 11 June 1560)
Succeeded by: His daughter Mary
Death: 14 Dec 1542, Falkland Palace

---

and, in 1537, married Madeleine, the 16-year-old daughter of King Francis I of France. She was a frail creature who died only seven months into their marriage, but her vast dowry of 100,000 livres must have been some comfort to James, especially as he was able to negotiate a second prestigious marriage in as many years when he wed the prominent French noblewoman Mary of Guise in 1538.

War erupted with England in 1542 and initial minor successes encouraged King James to invade. At Solway Moss, near Carlisle, on 24 November 1542 the Scots army suffered another catastrophic defeat. Before the year was out the king was dead, aged only 30, devastated by the defeat and the loss the previous year of his two young sons.

Below: According to tradition, James V liked to travel his country in disguise, identified as 'The tenant of Ballengiech'.

MARY, QUEEN OF SCOTS
1542–1567

When King James V of Scots died in despair at Falkland Palace on 14 December 1542, he had only one heir, his seven-day-old daughter, Mary. She became the first Queen of Scots and the country's youngest-ever monarch. The regency was secured for the tiny queen's French-born mother, Mary of Guise.

A GLORIOUS DESTINY

Mary, Queen of Scots was sent to France at the age of five and there enjoyed a royal education and gilded youth. She grew up a staunch Catholic, speaking French while also learning Latin, Greek, Spanish and Italian, and she became a renowned dancer. As a result of her French upbringing, she changed the spelling of her family name from 'Stewart' to the French form, 'Stuart'.

At the age of 15, in 1558, she married the French heir to the throne, the Dauphin Francis, and with the accession of Queen Elizabeth I of England in November that year, Mary became next

Above: This 19th-century French portrait represents Mary mourning the death of her first husband, Francis II of France.

in line for the English throne too. For Catholics (who did not accept Henry VIII's divorce of Catherine of Aragon and 1533 marriage to Elizabeth's mother, Queen Anne Boleyn), she was the rightful Queen of England. Finally, with the death in July 1559 of Henry II of France from the effects of a hunting wound, her husband Francis became king of France. The young queen's destiny appeared to be glorious.

MISSED OPPORTUNITY

Somehow it all went wrong. Mary loved her young husband, but he died aged only 16 in 1560. She bravely returned home to Scotland and tried without success to find a middle way acceptable to competing Protestant and Catholic camps. She was unable to tame the violent power struggle among competing barons.

Four years after her return, Mary married her handsome but unpopular Tudor cousin Henry Stuart, Lord Darnley, a fellow Catholic who also had a claim to the English throne.

The events of 1566–7 sealed her fate. First her husband Darnley led a group of nobles in butchering Mary's Italian secretary David Rizzio. Next Mary gave birth to a son, James Stuart: while the 'Virgin Queen' Elizabeth I of England remained childless, this boy would be heir to the English throne as well as that of Scotland. Then Darnley was murdered in 1567, perhaps with Mary's involvement, by a group led by the Earl of Bothwell. Mary's marriage to Bothwell in May convinced Scots that she had been involved in Darnley's murder. Rebel nobles triumphed over Mary and Bothwell, and in July 1567 the queen was forced to abdicate in favour of her 13-month-old son.

In 1568 Mary fled to England, seeking sanctuary with her cousin Elizabeth. She was several times the focus of Catholic plots to oust Queen Elizabeth. Mary remained in Elizabeth's custody until her conviction for plotting against Elizabeth's life and was executed on 1 February 1587. After her flight from Scotland she never again set eyes on her only son.

Above: Mary's ill-advised third marriage to James Hepburn, the Earl of Bothwell, forced events that led to her abdication.

MARY, QUEEN OF SCOTS, 1542–1567

Birth: 8 Dec 1542, Linlithgow Palace

Father: James V

Mother: Mary of Guise

Accession: 14 Dec 1542

Coronation: 9 Sept 1543

Husbands: (1) Francis II of France (m. 24 April 1558; d. 5 Dec 1560); (2) Henry Stuart, Lord Darnley (m. 29 July 1565; d. 10 Feb 1567); (3) James Hepburn, fourth Earl of Bothwell (m 15 May 1567; d. 14 April 1578)

Abdicates: 24 July 1567

Succeeded by: Her son James I and VI

Death: Executed 8 Feb 1587

JAMES VI OF SCOTS

1567–1603

James VI of Scots was crowned aged one year on 29 July 1567 in a church by the gates of Stirling Castle, where he was being kept. In Scotland a succession of four regents – the earls of Moray, Lennox, Mar and Morton – took power. Meanwhile, James received a thorough classical and Protestant religious education, studying Latin, Greek and French under the guidance of his tutor, the learned scholar George Buchanan.

At the age of 16, in August 1582, James was kidnapped by Protestant nobles led by the first Earl of Gowrie, to prevent him falling further under the spell of his Catholic friend Esmé Stuart, the French-born Duke of Lennox and specifically to avert a rumoured plot in which Lennox would force James to convert to Catholicism and then mount an invasion of England. However, James escaped after ten months confinement, and thereafter ruled in his own name.

THE ANGLO-SCOTTISH PACT

As King of Scots, James VI set about cultivating a good relationship with England and in particular with Queen Elizabeth I, with a view to bolstering

---

THE DIVINE RIGHT OF KINGS

James VI was a highly educated intellectual as well as a largely effective, practical king. In September 1598 he published a theory of kingship in his *The Trew Law of Free Monarchies: Or the Reciprock and Mutuall Dutie Betwixt a Free King and his Naturall Subjects*. He argued that kings rule by divine right and are responsible to the Almighty for their actions: 'Kings are called gods by the prophetical King David (the Biblical Psalmist David) because they sit upon God's throne on Earth and have the account of their administration to give unto him'. Their duty is to 'minister justice', 'advance the good and punish the evil', 'establish good lawes' and 'procure the peace of the people'. It follows that subjects have no right to rebel. James urged his people to 'arme your selves with patience and humilitie', adding that since God 'hath the only power to make [a king]' he also 'hath the onely power to unmake him' and subjects' duty was 'onely to obey'. This assertion was to cause a lot of trouble for James' successors.

---

his chances of succession to the English throne after her death. In May 1585 the two monarchs agreed a defensive peace treaty under which James received £4,000 annually. Even Elizabeth's execution of James's mother, Mary, Queen of Scots two years later in 1587 did not seriously disturb the new Anglo-Scottish pact. Although James made a formal complaint about the execution, he knew that his mother's death made him next in line for the English throne.

In Scotland James maintained a strong rule, successfully managing rival Protestant and Catholic sections of the nobility, and establishing his authority as head of the Presbyterian Church.

When, as he had long planned, James acceded to the throne of England on the death of Queen Elizabeth I in 1603, he had been on the throne for 36 years; quite an achievement in the wildly unstable environment of late 16th-century Scotland; and as he told the English Parliament, he was already, 'An old and experienced king'.

Right: This portrait of James VI was sent to the Danish court during negotiations for his marriage to Anne of Denmark.

Above: The two sides of the Jacobus 6 Dei Gratia Rex Scotorum, a gold 'hat piece', worth £4, minted in Edinburgh in 1591.

JAMES VI, KING OF SCOTLAND, 1567–1603; KING OF ENGLAND AND SCOTLAND 1603–1625

Birth: 19 June 1566, Edinburgh Castle

Father: Henry Stuart, Lord Darnley

Mother: Mary, Queen of Scots

Accession: 24 July 1567

Coronation: 29 July 1567

Queen: Anne of Denmark (m. 23 Nov 1589; d. 2 March 1619)

Succeeded by: His son Charles I

Death: 27 March 1625, Theobalds Park, Herts

CHAPTER FOUR

LANCASTER
AND YORK
1399–1485

A leading baron and a warrior, Henry Bolingbroke elevated martial vigour above the right of hereditary succession to the throne in the summer and autumn of 1399. Having returned from the exile into which King Richard II had cast him, Bolingbroke led a rebel army to London and forced the king to abdicate in Parliament before claiming the throne himself. When Bolingbroke was crowned King Henry IV in Westminster Abbey on 13 October 1399, he founded the House of Lancaster, a cadet or junior line of the House of Plantagenet. Henry IV's claim to the throne was as the son of John of Gaunt, fourth son of King Edward III. John of Gaunt had married Blanche, the heiress to the duchy of Lancaster, so his son Bolingbroke was Duke of Lancaster. The king he deposed, Richard II, was his cousin.

The usurper king's dynasty lasted for the reigns of three monarchs – Henry IV himself, his son Henry V, the battle-winning hero of Agincourt, and his ineffective grandson Henry VI who ascended the English throne at the age of just nine months.

The decline of Henry VI into madness led to the elevation of the ambitious Richard, Duke of York, to the role of Protector and Defender of the Kingdom in March 1454. Richard himself had a viable claim to the throne as the great-grandson of King Edward III through the male line via Edmund of Langley, 1st Duke of York (1341–1402). The bitter Wars of the Roses in the second half of the 15th century were fought between the supporters of the rival 'Yorkist' and 'Lancastrian' claims to the throne.

Left: Henry IV was a usurper, but he made sure that his magnificent coronation stressed his majesty and divine appointment to the throne.

HENRY IV
1399–1413

Henry IV claimed the throne of England on the basis of his descent from King Edward III, but the claim was distant. Henry was the son of King Edward's fourth son, John of Gaunt, and Blanche, daughter of the Duke of Lancaster. His claim thus came through the male line. However, if a claim through the female line were allowed, as it had been before, then Edmund Mortimer, Earl of March, had a stronger claim, as the great-grandson of King Edward III's second son, Lionel Duke of Clarence through Lionel's daughter Philippa, Countess of Ulster. Also in his favour was the fact that Richard had recognized him as his heir presumptive. In fact, Henry's most compelling claim to the throne lay in his person; in 1399 he was an accomplished soldier and a man of drive, wealth and education while Edmund Mortimer was a boy of less than 10.

STRUGGLE FOR SUCCESSION

Henry could also claim to have been wronged by Richard II. Henry was one of the Lords Appellant, who had challenged Richard's rule in 1387 and forced the king to restate his coronation

Below: The English gold noble coin was inscribed with a king standing on a ship. First issued by Edward III in 1344, this one was minted for Henry IV in 1412.

HENRY IV, KING OF ENGLAND, 1399–1413	
Birth: 3 April 1367, Bolingbroke Castle	**Succeeded by:** His son Henry V
Father: John of Gaunt, Duke of Lancaster	**Greatest achievement:** Founding the House of Lancaster
Mother: Blanche of Lancaster	**30 Sept 1399:** Richard II deposed
Accession: 30 Sept 1399	**21 July 1403:** Defeats rebels at Battle of Shrewsbury
Coronation: 13 Oct 1399, Westminster Abbey	**1406:** Develops mystery illness – leprosy?
Queens: (1) Mary de Bohun (m. 5 Feb 1381; d. 1394); (2) Joan of Navarre (m. 7 Feb 1403; d. 1437)	**1409:** Captures Harlech Castle to end long-running Welsh revolt
	Death: 20 March 1413, Westminster

oath the following year. He suffered when the king revenged himself in the late 1390s. Richard exiled Henry for ten years in 1398, and in the following year seized Henry's inheritance on the death of John of Gaunt.

On 4 July 1399, while King Richard was campaigning in Ireland, Henry landed from France near Spurn Head with a force of 300 men. Initially he claimed he wanted only to regain his rightful inheritance but as he marched southwards and his army swelled with supporters his demands rose. By then Richard was in hiding in Wales, following his return from Ireland; when the king finally arrived in London, Henry cast him into the Tower.

On 30 September 1399, Richard II was deposed in parliament and the following month Henry was crowned King Henry IV in Westminster Abbey. Richard was imprisoned in Pontefract Castle. The deposed king – no longer Richard II, but merely Richard of Bordeaux – died in jail early the following year, apparently brutally put to death on the orders of Henry IV.

REBEL CHALLENGES

Henry defeated two major uprisings in his reign. His principal opponents were the Welsh prince Owain Glyndwr and the Percy family of Northumberland.

Early in the reign, Glyndwr, Lord of Glyndyfrydwy, declared himself Prince of Wales and gathered support for an uprising against English rule. Despite a largely successful attack on Wales in autumn 1403 and a series of raids led by the English Prince of Wales, the 16-year-old heir to the throne, Prince Henry, the rebellion remained a thorn in Henry's side until 1409.

The Percys were Henry's former allies. They rose in revolt because they believed that the king had failed to reward them sufficiently for their past

Below: Princely patriarch. John of Gaunt, son of Edward III, founded the House of Lancaster through his son, Henry IV.

Above: Froissart's Chronicles *depicts Henry riding into London, the English crown within his grasp.*

in 1406 Glyndwr, Sir Edmund Mortimer, the younger Edmund's uncle, and the Percys agreed to split England between them in the event that they defeated Henry. The rebels, however, suffered a decisive defeat at the Battle of Bramham Moor in February 1408, after which Hotspur's father, the Earl of Northumberland, was executed. In 1409 the king's capture of Harlech Castle effectively ended the Welsh revolt, reducing the proud prince Glyndwr to a landless rebel who had no choice but to hide in caves. His place and date of death are unknown.

TROUBLED IN OLD AGE

Victory did not bring Henry peace of mind or body. Beginning in 1406, he suffered an agonizing illness that may have been leprosy and was identified by some as the judgement of God, perhaps for the murder of Archbishop Scrope of York. Henry was also increasingly at odds with his son, Prince Henry, partly because of rumours in 1411–12 that the prince was plotting to take the throne from his father.

In these later years, the formerly ruthless and ambitious Henry Bolingbroke became careworn and tormented by guilt. As early as 1409, in his will, he declared, 'I Henry, sinful wretch,

Above: The young man who seized the crown spoke French, Latin and English. He holds the red rose of Lancaster.

ask my lords and true people forgiveness if I have misentreated them in any wise'. He died on 20 March 1413 after fainting before the Westminster Abbey shrine to his saintly predecessor on the English throne, Edward the Confessor. He was given the last rites and died in the 'Jerusalem Chamber' in the abbot's house at Westminster. His death thus fulfilled a prophecy that the king would die 'in Jerusalem'.

support, so they rallied around the claim to the throne of Edmund Mortimer, Earl of March. However, in July 1403 the king defeated a rebel army led by Henry Percy ('Hotspur'), warrior son of the Earl of Northumberland, in the Battle of Shrewsbury.

The rebellion continued. In 1405, conspirators Thomas Mowbray and Richard Scrope, Archbishop of York, were captured and put to death. Then

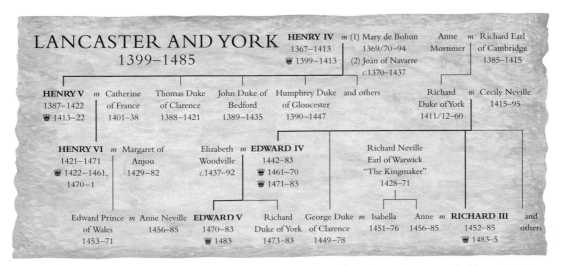

LANCASTER AND YORK
1399–1485

HENRY IV 1367–1413 ♔ 1399–1413	*m* (1) Mary de Bohun 1369/70–94 (2) Joan of Navarre *c.*1370–1437	Anne Mortimer	*m* Richard Earl of Cambridge 1385–1415

| **HENRY V** 1387–1422 ♔ 1413–22 | *m* Catherine of France 1401–38 | Thomas Duke of Clarence 1388–1421 | John Duke of Bedford 1389–1435 | Humphrey Duke of Gloucester 1390–1447 | and others | Richard Duke of York 1411/12–60 | *m* Cecily Neville 1415–95 |

| **HENRY VI** 1421–1471 ♔ 1422–1461, 1470–1 | *m* Margaret of Anjou 1429–82 | Elizabeth Woodville *c.*1437–92 | *m* **EDWARD IV** 1442–83 ♔ 1461–70 ♔ 1471–83 | Richard Neville Earl of Warwick "The Kingmaker" 1428–71 |

| Edward Prince of Wales 1453–71 | *m* Anne Neville 1456–85 | **EDWARD V** 1470–83 ♔ 1483 | Richard Duke of York 1473–83 | George Duke of Clarence 1449–78 | *m* Isabella 1451–76 | Anne 1456–85 | *m* **RICHARD III** 1452–85 ♔ 1483–5 | and others |

HENRY V
1413–1422

Henry V led a bedraggled 6,000-strong army in one of the greatest and most celebrated military exploits in English history – the defeat of a French force more than three times larger, at the Battle of Agincourt, on 25 October 1415. His victories during a whirlwind, four-month campaign in France that autumn won him an enduring place in English history and also set the scene for the remarkable treaty signed at Troyes on 21 May 1420, under which Henry was made French regent and recognized as heir to the throne of France.

Before he was king, Henry had made declaration of his martial vigour. He took the fight to Welsh rebel Owain

Glyndwr in 1400, when in his early teens, and in 1409 aged 21, he won decisive victories at Aberystwyth and Harlech. When Henry IV lay dying, young Henry took the crown from his father's head, but his father, rallying, asked him what right he had to the crown since it had been won in blood and not received through a divinely blessed hereditary line. The future Henry V told the ailing king, 'As you have kept the crown by the sword, so will I keep it while my life lasts'.

A REFORMED CHARACTER

Henry was crowned King Henry V in Westminster Abbey on Passion Sunday, 9 April 1413. A blizzard enveloped the

Above: Henry married Catherine, daughter of Charles VI of France, on 2 June 1420. James I of Scots was a wedding guest.

Right: Henry V's campaigns in France yielded memorable victories that led to the triumph of the Treaty of Troyes.

HENRY V, KING OF ENGLAND, 1413–1422

Birth: 16 Sept 1387
Father: King Henry IV of England
Mother: Mary de Bohun
Accession: 20 March 1413
Coronation: 9 April 1413, Westminster Abbey
Queen: Catherine of France (m. 2 June 1420; d. 1438)
Succeeded by: His son Henry of Windsor
Greatest achievement: Battle of Agincourt 1415, Treaty of Troyes 1420
25 Oct 1415: Wins Battle of Agincourt
c.1416: Death of Owain Glyndwr
21 May 1420: Becomes regent of France and heir to the French king Charles VI
Death: 31 Aug 1422, Castle of Bois-de-Vincennes, France

English victories
French victories

Abbey, and during the new king's coronation feast onlookers noted that he looked serious and severe and did not indulge in the splendid feast laid out on the banqueting tables before him. As Prince of Wales, Henry had been celebrated for the raucous company he kept and for their wild escapades. Famously, he was involved in a midnight brawl in an Eastcheap tavern, and he also laid ambushes for members of the royal household. Upon his coronation he decisively put his wild years behind him however, declaring that none of his former companions were permitted to come within 10 miles (16km) of him.

WAR IN FRANCE

Henry declared his intention of fighting for the throne of France in early July 1415. He laid claim to the French crown as great-grandson of Edward III, whose mother was the daughter of French king Philip IV. He saw an opportunity to be grasped in France, where the king, Charles VI, was intermittently subject to bouts of madness. Henry set sail in August, besieged and captured Harfleur, then marched for Calais. He defeated the French at Agincourt, then returned to great acclaim from his countrymen, who shouted, 'Welcome, Henry V, King of

England and France' as he rode through the city of London. In a second campaign in 1417–19, Henry captured Caen and Rouen, capital of Normandy. Under the Treaty of Troyes he then married Catherine, daughter of the French King Charles VI, and was thereby recognized as heir to the French throne and installed as regent for the French king's periods of madness. But Henry had to fight on to counter the threat presented by King Charles's son, the Dauphin Charles, who was disinherited by this treaty.

Henry's queen, Catherine of France, gave birth to a son, Henry, on 6 December 1421 at Windsor. As Henry

Above: Warrior king. Henry sported a soldier's haircut; such was his athleticism, he was said to be able to outrun a deer.

lay dying the following year of dysentery contracted during the siege of Meaux, near Paris, he appointed his brothers as regents of his domains. Humphrey, Duke of Gloucester, was appointed regent of England, and John, Duke of Bedford, became regent of France. Henry died at the age of just 35.

Below: On 25 October 1415, at the Battle of Agincourt, Henry V's army of 6,000 defeated a French force of 20,000. The victory entered English folklore.

HENRY VI
1422–1461, 1470–1471

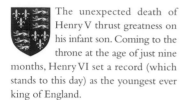

The unexpected death of Henry V thrust greatness on his infant son. Coming to the throne at the age of just nine months, Henry VI set a record (which stands to this day) as the youngest ever king of England.

At first government was in the hands of the young king's uncle, Duke Humphrey of Gloucester, who had been appointed regent by Henry V. Gloucester was soon in open conflict with Henry Beaufort, Bishop of Winchester and Chancellor of England, for control of the boy-king and of the country. Henry was unable to provide the strong rule needed to safeguard the achievements of his illustrious warrior father. Even when he came to adulthood, his character prevented him from becoming master of events and establishing authority over the squabbling barons who surrounded him. For the king was simple, pious, easily swayed and, like his maternal grandfather, King Charles VI of France, subject to bouts of madness. Henry VI's reign was a long, slow decline from the position of considerable strength he inherited.

Below: Joan of Arc said she was guided by Sts Michael, Catherine and Margaret in her campaign against the English in France.

A decline in which England lost its holdings in France and slid into the violent dynastic conflicts that came to be known as the 'Wars of the Roses'.

DISASTERS IN FRANCE

In the spring and early summer of 1429, a French peasant girl known as Joan of Arc led the French army in a string

Above: Boy among men. Even as an adult, Henry VI was never equal to the task of ruling 15th-century England.

of remarkable triumphs against the English. Then in July, the Dauphin, Charles, son of the French King Charles VI, was crowned King Charles VII of France. This coronation was in direct

HENRY VI, KING OF ENGLAND, 1422–1461, 1470–1471

Birth: 6 Dec 1421, Windsor Castle
Father: King Henry V of England
Mother: Queen Catherine of Valois
Accession: 31 Aug 1422
Coronation: 6 Nov 1429, Westminster Abbey; 16 Dec 1431 (as King of France), Notre Dame de Paris
Queen: Margaret of Anjou (m. 22 April 1445; d. 1482)
Succeeded by: Edward IV
Greatest achievement: Founding

King's College, Cambridge, and Eton College
1450: Jack Cade's rebellion
17 July 1453: English defeated at Battle of Castillon
22 May 1455: Battle of St Albans
4 March 1461: Deposed by Edward IV
3 Oct 1470: Restored to throne
11 April 1471: Deposed once more
Death: 21 May 1471, probably murdered, Tower of London

Above: In 1450, Jack Cade's rebels called for the recall of Richard, Duke of York and the dismissal of several ministers.

contravention of the 1420 Treaty of Troyes, which guaranteed the French crown to King Henry V's son and his descendants. In order to counter this, the 10-year-old Henry VI was taken to Paris and crowned as Henri II, King of France, in December 1431. By this time Joan of Arc had been captured, tried for heresy and burnt at the stake in Rouen. Despite her personal fate, Joan had done much to restore French pride.

In 1435 English hopes in France suffered a double blow. The Duke of Burgundy, previously a key ally of England, made peace with the Dauphin. Then Henry VI's uncle, the Duke of Bedford and regent of France, died in Rouen. The Dauphin's army captured Paris from the English in 1436.

In August 1443, Henry – by now 21 years old and ruling in his own right – despatched an English army to France under the command of John Beaufort, Duke of Somerset. The following year, the two countries negotiated a five-year peace and Henry VI married Margaret, daughter of the Duke of Anjou. However, England's French possessions continued to dwindle. Within six

months of the wedding, at the urging of his forceful his new queen, Henry agreed to hand over the duchy of Maine to Margaret's father, René of Anjou. War resumed in 1448-9 and the English lost Normandy in 1450 and Bordeaux and Gascony in 1451. The English sent a force to recover Gascony but the French won a decisive victory at Castillon in July 1453, finally bringing to a close the conflict of the Hundred Years War and leaving Calais England's only remaining French possession.

A PATRON OF EDUCATION

Henry's authority dwindled at home. In 1450 Jack Cade, a former soldier going under the name of 'John Mortimer', led a rebel force of labourers towards the royal court. As Henry fled to the north, the rebels ran riot in London. They were only dispersed when the intrepid Queen Margaret, who had remained in London, offered them pardons.

Henry's mild and pious character may have ill fitted him to be an effective king in late medieval England, but his devoutness inspired him to be a great educational patron, the founder of two

Below: 101 years' work. The magnificent chapel in King's College, Cambridge, was begun in 1446 and completed in 1547.

major English institutions. In 1440, he established the King's College of Our Lady of Eton, later known as Eton College, and in 1441 he laid the foundation stone for King's College, Cambridge. Generous royal funding provided free education for the 25 poor scholars and 25 paupers at Eton; they were expected to proceed to King's College to complete their education.

THE WARS OF THE ROSES
ENGLAND AT WAR, 1455–1485

The weak rule of King Henry VI made England vulnerable to power struggles and civil conflict. The king was unable to stamp his authority on the feuding barons around him, who included the ambitious Duke of York, his backer Richard Neville, the Earl of Warwick (later known as 'Warwick the kingmaker') and royal favourites the dukes of Suffolk and Somerset. The barons came into increasingly open competition. Following Suffolk's death in 1450, the struggle was between York and Somerset. The king's susceptibility to periods of madness tipped the balance and a tense standoff eventually erupted into open conflict.

Below: After a defeat for the Yorkist cause at Ludford Bridge in October 1459, the future Edward IV fled to Calais.

Above: The Wars of the Roses are named from the badges of the opposing sides: a red rose for Lancaster and a white rose for York.

THE SLIDE TO CIVIL WAR

King Henry's first attack of insanity in 1453 followed hard on the loss of England's possessions in France. Henry became incapable of making decisions or holding reasoned debate. Richard, Duke of York, was named Protector and Defender of the Kingdom in March 1454 and at once imprisoned Somerset. However, in 1455, after regaining his clarity and sense of purpose, Henry resumed royal rule and released Somerset from the Tower of London.

York rebelled against the king in an attempt to recover his lost authority. On 22 May 1455, York defeated the 'Lancastrian' forces of the king and Somerset at St Albans. As fighting raged in the town, Somerset was trapped in the Castle Inn and put to the sword by Yorkist soldiers. King Henry was shot in the neck with an arrow but managed to escape to safety in the home of a local tanner. York found him there and swore loyalty to his monarch before escorting him from the battlefield to St Albans Abbey and then to London.

The battle was no more than a skirmish, but it marked the beginning of the 33 years of dynastic and political instability and occasional civil war that would be remembered as the Wars of the Roses. In these wars, Lancastrians loyal to King Henry VI and the royal House of Lancaster fought with Yorkist supporters of Richard, Duke of York. The Duke of York had a valid claim to the throne, for he was the nephew of Edmund Mortimer, Earl of March, who had been excluded from the succession when Henry IV seized the throne.

At first the Yorkists had the upper hand. The Duke of York became Constable of England in May, following the St Albans battle, and in November was made Protector for the second time. However, the following year he was deprived of the Protectorship once more as Queen Margaret and her Lancastrian allies manoeuvred against him. In 1458 Henry enforced a reconciliation between the warring parties.

Above: King Henry VI is captured by the forces of Richard, Earl of Warwick, after the Battle of Northampton, in 1460.

Right: Major battle sites of the Wars of the Roses. The conflict was fought out over 30 years and virtually the whole of England.

North Atlantic Ocean

North Sea

Hedgely Moor 1464

Hexham 1464

Irish Sea

LANCASTER

Towton 1461

YORK

Wakefield 1460

Ferrybridge 1461

Blore Heath 1459

Stoke 1487

The Wash

Ludford Bridge 1459

Bosworth 1485

Losecote Field 1470

Tewksbury 1471

Northampton 1460

Mortimer's Cross 1461

Edgecote Moor 1469

St Albans 1455, 1461

Barnet 1471

Bristol Channel

BRISTOL

LONDON

EXETER

SOUTHAMPTON

Strait of Dover

⊗ **Lancastrian victories**
⊗ **Yorkist victories**

English Channel

On 25 March – remembered as 'Loveday' – Yorkists and Lancastrians were made to walk in procession, hand in hand, to St Paul's Cathedral in London, and the Yorkists were forced to agree to compensate the descendants of those harmed at St Albans. However, the king was not strong enough to impose peace for long and the following year battle recommenced. After an initial victory at Blore Heath on 23 September, the Yorkists suffered a devastating defeat in the Battle of Ludford Bridge on 12 October. The Duke of York fled to Ireland and in November was condemned as a traitor by Parliament.

A YEAR OF MIXED FORTUNES

In 1460 the Yorkists experienced both triumph and despair. On 10 July, at Northampton, a Yorkist army led by Richard Neville, Earl of Warwick, and the Duke of York's son, Edward, Earl of March, trounced the Lancastrian-royalist forces and captured Henry VI. This appeared to be a decisive victory: York returned from Ireland and in the Act of Accord of 24 October, was named as the heir to Henry VI. However, the ever-resourceful Queen

Margaret orchestrated a Lancastrian response and the pendulum swung in her favour before the year was out.

The queen's army, led by Somerset, defeated the Yorkists at Wakefield in December and killed Richard, Duke of York. The Lancastrians, on Margaret's orders, cut off his head and displayed it

in a paper crown on the gates of York. On 17 February 1461, back at St Albans, her army defeated Warwick and rescued Henry VI from captivity. Just two weeks later, the Yorkists gained the upper hand. Warwick and Edward of York entered London and on 4 March Edward declared himself King Edward IV.

YEARS OF CONFLICT

Edward IV ruled with a firm hand for 22 years, establishing the new dynasty of the House of York. However, the country endured two further bouts of bloody dynastic conflict as the Wars of the Roses re-ignited. In 1470–1, Edward was forced into exile and Henry VI was briefly declared king once more, before Edward returned to defeat and kill Warwick. The triumph of the House of York seemed complete.

But only 12 years later in 1483, following Edward's death, his brother Richard seized the throne as Richard III, apparently having had Edward's sons Edward V and Richard killed. Richard III's reign lasted no more than two years: the Lancastrians returned to win a final victory – in the form of Henry Tudor, the grandson of Henry V's widow, Catherine of Valois, and great-grandson of John of Gaunt, Duke of Lancaster (1340–99).

EDWARD IV

1461–1470, 1471–1483

In the eyes of his subjects, Edward proved the justice of his claim to the throne and his fitness to govern by defeating a Lancastrian army under the Duke of Somerset at the Battle of Towton, in March 1461. With the Lancastrian cause in disarray and Queen Margaret having fled to Scotland, Edward was crowned with great ceremony on 28 June in Westminster Abbey.

AN UNDIPLOMATIC MARRIAGE

A proven warrior, Edward had little of his predecessor Henry VI's profound piety, instead exhibiting a strong liking for the pleasures of the flesh. Early in his reign he won himself a reputation as a

Below: King Edward had a taste for lavish clothes, made from the finest animal furs, velvet and cloth of gold.

Above: Physical authority. Powerfully built and 6ft 4in (1.93m) tall, Edward IV was both approachable and charismatic.

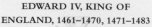

EDWARD IV, KING OF ENGLAND, 1461–1470, 1471–1483
Birth: 28 April 1442, Rouen, Normandy
Father: Richard, Duke of York
Mother: Cecily, Duchess of York
Accession: 4 March 1461
Coronation: 28 June 1461, Westminster Abbey
Queen: Elizabeth Woodville (m. 1 May 1464; d. 1492)
Succeeded by: His son Edward V
Greatest achievement: Establishment of House of York
29 March 1461: Battle of Towton
1470: Flees into exile
14 April 1471: Defeats Warwick the Kingmaker at Battle of Barnet
21 May 1471: Reclaims throne
Death: 9 April 1483, Windsor

womanizer. Indeed, Edward's weakness for beautiful women led to one of the major misjudgements of his reign: his secret marriage to Elizabeth Woodville, the widow of a Lancastrian nobleman who had been killed in the 1461 Battle of St Albans. The story goes that Edward met Elizabeth when he visited a castle during a hunting trip and was at once deeply taken with her looks. She resisted all his advances and declared that he would have to marry her in order to have what he wanted. Unable to resist her charms, Edward married Elizabeth in utmost secrecy in May 1464.

Edward's subjects felt that Elizabeth did not have the social status necessary to be queen. More importantly, the marriage angered Edward's great noble ally Warwick the Kingmaker, for Elizabeth imported her five brothers and seven sisters to the royal court and insisted that Edward shower them with favours that Warwick resented. In addition, Warwick was secretly in negotiations with King Louis of France, in which he had promised the king's hand in marriage to a French princess and these talks now came to nothing.

FORCED INTO EXILE

In 1469 Warwick inspired a revolt in Yorkshire against Edward. The rebels, fronted by 'Robin of Redesdale' (in reality close Warwick ally Sir John Conyers), defeated the king in battle. Edward was briefly imprisoned by Warwick before he was released and returned to the throne in London.

Then, in 1470, Edward was betrayed and forced into exile. Journeying to France, Warwick had allied himself with his former enemy Queen Margaret and with the king's brother, the Duke of Clarence. When Edward marched north to deal with further Warwick-inspired rebellions, Warwick and Clarence landed an army on the south coast with the intention of restoring Henry VI to the throne. Even then, Edward remained confident of his ability to see off his former mentor, but he was betrayed by the Marquis of Montagu who allied himself with Warwick and left the king so heavily outnumbered that he was forced to flee to exile in Burgundy. Warwick and Clarence took control, freed Henry VI

Below: Beguiled by beauty, Edward recklessly plunged into a secret marriage to Elizabeth Woodville in May 1464.

ENGLAND'S FIRST PRINTED BOOK

King Edward was a man of culture and taste as well as a warrior and political schemer. He financed the printing of the first dated book in English, which was also the first book printed in England.

The Dictes and Sayenges of the Phylosophers was printed by William Caxton in 1477. Caxton was a Kent-born merchant who flourished in Flanders and Holland and learned printing in Cologne in the early 1470s. He translated *The Recuyell of the Historyes of Troye* into English and printed it, but without a date, in Bruges, in 1475. The following year Caxton returned to London and set up his printing press in Westminster. He presented *The Dictes and Sayenges of the Phylosophers* to Edward in the year of its publication.

Left: This woodcut of a knight was used to illustrate Caxton's Game of the Chesse.

from the Tower of London, where he had been kept, and crowned him once more as King of England.

The revival of Henry's reign lasted no more than six months. Edward returned to England, made peace with Clarence, then defeated and killed Warwick and Montagu in battle at Barnet on 14 April 1471. Afterwards he returned Henry to imprisonment in the Tower.

In May he trounced the forces of Queen Margaret at Tewkesbury, capturing Margaret herself and beheading her prominent supporters, including the Duke of Somerset. Margaret's son Edward, the Prince of Wales, was killed as he tried to escape and shortly thereafter Henry VI died in mysterious circumstances. It is likely that he was killed, perhaps by Edward's brother Richard of Gloucester. The new king's victory seemed complete and the crown secure with the new House of York.

APPETITE FOR PLEASURE

Edward was a man of urgent appetites, who was rumoured to make himself vomit during banquets so he could continue to gorge on rich foods and who boasted that he had three mistresses, 'One the merriest, the other the wiliest, the third the holiest harlot in the

realm'. They included Elizabeth Shore, a London grocer's wife, and Elizabeth Lucy, daughter of a Hampshire nobleman and mother of a notable illegitimate son, Arthur Plantagenet.

Edward's overindulgence probably contributed to his sudden death, aged 40. In his later years he grew corpulent, and in March 1483 he was struck down by a mystery illness variously said to have been malaria, pneumonia or a stroke. He died on 9 April, 1483.

Below: Edward asserted his authority at Barnet in April 1471, killing the Marquis of Montagu and Earl of Warwick.

THE PRINCES IN THE TOWER
ROYAL MURDER, 1483

As Protector of the Kingdom in summer 1483, Richard Duke of Gloucester had the 12-year-old King Edward V and the king's brother Richard housed in the Tower Of London, which at that time was a palace as well as a jail. Shortly after Gloucester engineered his elevation to the throne, the princes disappeared and many assumed, then and since, that they had been murdered on Richard's orders. The question of what happened to the princes in the Tower is one of the most enduringly fascinating mysteries of English royal history.

THE PRINCES DISAPPEAR

Around the time of Gloucester's coronation as King Richard III on 6 July 1483, Edward and Richard were moved within the Tower of London complex from the royal apartments to the Garden Tower. They were seen playing with bows and arrows in the constable's garden close by. They were then moved again, to the White Tower, where many prison cells were situated. After this, they simply disappeared.

In the 16th century, Richard III was generally assumed to have been behind the princes' disappearance. Within weeks of their disappearance, the Venetian ambassador wrote home to say that the princes had been murdered on Richard's orders. It is certain that Richard had plenty to gain from their deaths. When he claimed the throne he justified it by declaring that the young King Edward V and his brother were illegitimate, since their father Edward IV's marriage to Queen Elizabeth Woodville had been invalid. He knew that if Edward lived

Below: Many romantic visions of the brothers were painted in the 19th century, including this one by Paul Delaroche.

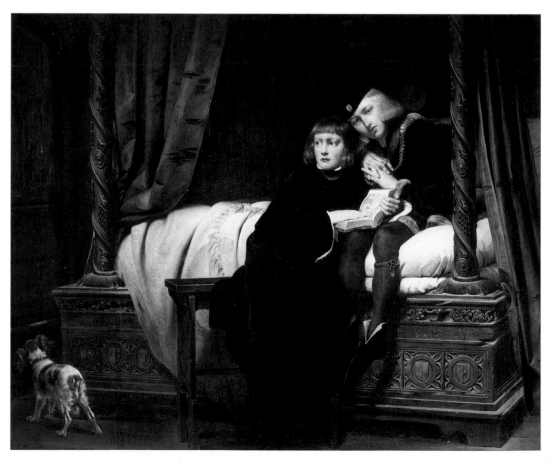

Above: In 1878, Sir John Everett Millais pictured the princes caught like innocent animals with nowhere to run.

figurehead for rebel discontent long after his deposition by Edward IV in 1461 and was even released from imprisonment to reoccupy the throne briefly in 1470. After that event, Henry VI himself met a mysterious death in May 1471, according to some reports at the hand of the future Richard III, at the time the brother of the ruling king, Edward IV.

CHARACTER ASSASSINATION?

Traditionally, Richard III has been seen as a cruel, treacherous and ruthlessly ambitious man, easily capable of dark deeds such as the murder of the boys, his life blighted by the success of his brother Edward IV and his own hunch-backed physique. However, this popular conception of the king's build and char-acter derives from propaganda issued by the Tudors after Henry Tudor had taken Richard's crown at Bosworth in August 1485. Historians know, for example, that the idea of Richard being a hunchback – so familiar from Shakespeare's play *King Richard III* – was entirely an invention, and that he was broad-shouldered and 5 ft 8in (1.72m) in height, taller than most of his contemporaries.

Henry Tudor had as much, if not more, to gain from the death of young Edward V, for his own claim to the throne did not stand if Edward lived. It was squarely in his interests for the boys to disappear and for the blame to be cast on their uncle Richard. Henry was able to rally support for his attack on Richard by casting him as a scheming usurper, a murderer of the rightful king, young Edward.

THEORIES ASSESSED

According to one theory, the princes were still alive when Richard was defeated by Henry Tudor at Bosworth Field and lived on in captivity for around two years into the reign of Henry VII. At that time Henry decided they were a threat to his own position, and they were murdered. Another theory is that Henry, Duke of Buckingham

Above: Innocence betrayed. Another 19th-century view imagines the dark hour of the boys' murder by Richard III's henchmen.

was responsible for the deed. Buckingham, a former ally of Richard III, himself had a viable claim to the throne as a descendant of King Edward III; he was also a supporter of the cause of Henry Tudor. In killing the boys he could have been seeking to open the way to the throne either for himself or for Tudor.

On balance, however, it seems most likely that King Richard was responsi-ble for the boys' deaths. Few people would claim that he killed them with his own hands. Sixteenth-century accounts indicated that Sir James Tyrell, carrying out the king's orders, hired two of the boys' keepers, Miles Forest and John Dighton, as assassins. They smoth-ered the princes as they slept in their beds and afterwards buried their lifeless bodies in the grounds of the Tower.

According to the doctor who attended the boys in the Tower before their disappearance, Edward was living in fear that he might die at any time. The doctor relates that the doomed boy declared poignantly, 'I would my uncle would let me have my life though I lose my kingdom'.

he would be a figurehead for rebellions. It was a common occurrence in the political-dynastic manoeuvrings of 14th- and 15th-century royal history for a deposed monarch to die, usually in captivity and in mysterious circum-stances, shortly after losing power. This fate had befallen Edward II, and the case of Henry VI would have cautioned Richard against allowing the princes to live. Henry had remained a

THE BONES OF THE PRINCES?

In 1674, in the reign of King Charles II, two skeletons were discovered buried at the Tower of London. Judged to be the bones of the young princes, they were reinterred at Westminster Abbey. In 1993, scientists examined the bones and determined that they were the remains of males who had died in boyhood, consistent with the possibil-ity that the skeletons were those of the young princes. However, the scientists were unable to find definitive proof that the skeletons were those of the ousted King Edward V and his brother.

EDWARD V AND RICHARD III
1483–1485

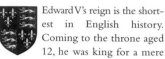

Edward V's reign is the shortest in English history. Coming to the throne aged 12, he was king for a mere two months and 17 days, from the death of his father Edward IV, on 9 April 1483, to the fateful day of 25 June, on which the boy-king's uncle Richard Duke of Gloucester accepted Parliament's request that he accede to the throne himself as King Richard III.

A ROYAL COUP
Gloucester engineered a coup. On his deathbed, Edward IV named Gloucester Protector of the Kingdom and guardian of young Prince Edward. The late king's widow, Queen Elizabeth Woodville, had other plans, however. She was determined to exclude Gloucester from power, to have her son crowned without delay and to surround him with members of the Woodville family, who were highly unpopular at court. She asked young Edward's guardian, Anthony Woodville, Earl Rivers, to

Below: The general image of King Richard is that of an ogre tormented by his sins, as presented in Shakespeare's Richard III.

EDWARD V, KING OF ENGLAND, 1483

Birth: 2 Nov 1470, the Sanctuary, Westminster Abbey
Father: Edward IV
Mother: Elizabeth Woodville
Accession: 9 April 1483
Deposed: 25 June 1483
Succeeded by: His uncle Richard III
Death: 3 Sept 1483. Probably murdered with his brother Richard, Duke of York, in the Tower

---

escort the prince from Ludlow Castle in Shropshire, where they were staying, to London for a coronation ceremony planned for 4 May. Gloucester, who was in Yorkshire at the time of Edward IV's death, travelled south to intervene.

Near Northampton on 30 April, Gloucester and his close ally Henry, Duke of Buckingham, arrested Rivers and the escort and took Prince Edward into their own care. Hearing the news, Queen Elizabeth took sanctuary in Westminster Abbey with her younger son, Richard, Duke of York.

In London, Gloucester became Protector on 6 May and rescheduled Edward's coronation for 22 June. He put Edward in the Tower of London. On 13 June he accused his former ally Lord Hastings of plotting against him and had him executed. Then he took the nine-year-old Duke of York from sanctuary in the Abbey and put him with his brother in the Tower. On 22 June he declared that the late king's secret marriage to Elizabeth Woodville was not valid and that the heir to the throne and his brother were illegitimate. On these grounds he declared himself the rightful inheritor of the crown. On 25 June Parliament backed Gloucester's claims and asked him to be king. He was crowned Richard III on 6 July.

Above: Edward V seemed destined for greatness on the throne. He was known for his charm, intelligence and good looks.

POLITICAL FALLOUT
The young princes officially remained in the Tower, but they were not seen after Richard III's coronation day. People were increasingly convinced the princes were dead, probably murdered. When Richard's former ally Henry Stafford, Duke of Buckingham, rose in revolt in October, he assumed the boys were dead and proposed that Richard be replaced on the throne by Henry Tudor, a descendant

---

THE SAINTED MEMORY OF HENRY VI

In August 1484 King Richard III had the body of his predecessor Henry VI moved from Chertsey Abbey, where it was buried in 1471 after his unexplained death in the Tower of London, to a tomb in the choir of St George's Chapel, Windsor. There it lies, directly opposite the tomb of Richard's brother King Edward IV, who was Henry's rival in life. Henry VI was increasingly revered as a saintly figure, capable of working miracles for his supporters.

RICARDO · III

RICHARD III, KING OF ENGLAND, 1483–1485

Birth: 2 Oct 1452, Fotheringhay Castle, Northamptonshire
Father: Richard Plantagenet, Duke of York
Mother: Cecily Neville
Accession: 26 June 1483
Coronation: 6 July 1483
Queen: Anne Neville (m. 12 July 1472; d. 16 March 1485)
Succeeded by: Henry VII
Death: 22 Aug 1485 at the Battle of Bosworth Field, Lincs

Above: This 16th-century portrait follows chronicle accounts, which represent Richard III as thin-lipped, haggard and nervous.

of Henry V's queen, Catherine of Valois and also a representative of the Lancastrian claim to the throne as the son of Margaret Beaufort, granddaughter of John of Gaunt. Henry prepared to invade England from exile in Brittany, but Buckingham was captured and executed on 2 November, and Henry retreated.

PERSONAL COSTS

The following year King Richard's 11-year-old son and only child, Edward, Prince of Wales, died. Richard and his queen, Anne, were maddened with grief. The prospect of a Yorkist inheritance, so dear to Richard's heart, began to look extremely vulnerable and when,

in March 1485, Queen Anne died after a prolonged illness, rumours circulated that Richard had had her killed so that he could bolster his position by marrying his niece, Elizabeth of York.

In the event, Yorkist rule only lasted a further five months. Henry Tudor won the backing of Charles VIII of France as well as of Queen Elizabeth and the Woodville camp for his claim to the throne.

BOSWORTH FIELD

Henry encountered Richard's army at Market Bosworth on 22 August. The battle was decided by the king's desperate attempt to try and bring the fighting to a quick conclusion, a manoeuvre that threw away a position of strength. As Richard watched the vanguard of his army take on the vanguard of Henry's, he had plenty of strength in reserve. However, in the

distance he saw Henry Tudor's standard defended by only a few score troops and decided to attack, in the hope of bringing the clash to an early end by killing Henry.

At first the onslaught was successful and Richard killed several of Henry's bodyguards. When his horse was slain, he fought on, on foot. At this point Sir William Stanley threw his men into an attack on the king. Richard was killed, his body stripped and slung naked across a horse. Henry Tudor left Bosworth Field wearing the crown he had won.

Richard III's body was lost for more than five centuries, but in 2012 an archaeological excavation on the site of the church of Greyfriars, Leicester, unearthed a male skeleton affected by scoliosis. In February 2013, the University of Leicester confirmed that beyond reasonable doubt this was the skeleton of Richard III.

Below: In August 1485, the succession was decided at Bosworth. Richard III fought bravely, if recklessly, in his final battle.

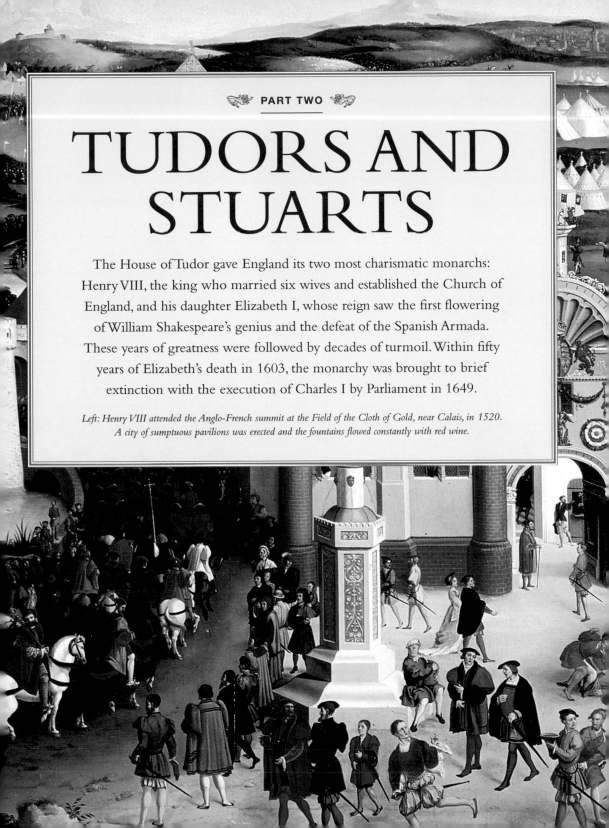

PART TWO

TUDORS AND STUARTS

The House of Tudor gave England its two most charismatic monarchs:
Henry VIII, the king who married six wives and established the Church of
England, and his daughter Elizabeth I, whose reign saw the first flowering
of William Shakespeare's genius and the defeat of the Spanish Armada.
These years of greatness were followed by decades of turmoil. Within fifty
years of Elizabeth's death in 1603, the monarchy was brought to brief
extinction with the execution of Charles I by Parliament in 1649.

*Left: Henry VIII attended the Anglo-French summit at the Field of the Cloth of Gold, near Calais, in 1520.
A city of sumptuous pavilions was erected and the fountains flowed constantly with red wine.*

CHAPTER FIVE

THE HOUSE OF TUDOR

1485–1558

In defeating Richard III and claiming the crown at Bosworth Field, Henry VII not only founded the Tudor dynasty but also won final victory for the Lancastrians in their decades-long struggle against the House of York for the English crown.

The House of Tudor encompassed the reigns of five monarchs – Henry VII, Henry VIII, Edward VI, Mary I and Elizabeth I – across 118 years, 1485–1603. The Tudors reigned during a time of religious turmoil, when the European Reformation created the new cultural and intellectual force of Protestantism. In England, Catholics and Protestants struggled for control of the country's future and hundreds of men and women were executed for holding true to new or traditional religious beliefs. These were years, too, of magnificent cultural achievement and enduring fame: when Christopher Marlowe and William Shakespeare were at work and England was beginning to look abroad to the 'New World' of North America.

In these years, the monarchy exercized a more concentrated, centralized authority than ever before, and came to be far less dependent on the support of leading nobles. Arising from the ashes of the Wars of the Roses, the Tudors claimed to give the country a secure and lasting foundation for prosperity: providing an heir and a stable succession became a Tudor obsession. Ultimately, however, the House of Tudor was undone by the lack of an heir. The crown passed out of the Tudor line on the death of Queen Elizabeth, to the first Stuart monarch: King James VI of Scots and I of England.

Left: The Tudor Succession. Henry VIII seated, with Edward VI kneeling on his left, Mary I (left, with her husband, Philip of Spain) and (right) his daughter Elizabeth I.

HENRY VII
1485–1509

Henry Tudor's defeat of Richard III at Bosworth Field was decisive. The battle ushered in the new Tudor dynasty and brought to an end 30 years of dynastic feuding in the Wars of the Roses. Over the ensuing 12 months, Henry proved himself an astute and resourceful king in consolidating a somewhat tenuous grip on the crown. For although he had invaded Richard III's kingdom as representative of the Lancastrian cause, his claim to the throne was relatively weak (he was descended through the female line from Edward III's fourth son John of Gaunt, first Duke of Lancaster).

CONSOLIDATING POWER

The new king's position had been strengthened by the death of the principal Yorkist figureheads, the 'princes in the Tower' Edward V and Richard, Duke of York. To be on the safe side, however, the day after Bosworth, Henry seized and imprisoned in the Tower the next in the Yorkist line to the throne,

Below: The imposter Perkin Warbeck who was adopted by Henry VII's Yorkist foes. He was coached in aristocratic manners by Margaret, sister of Edward IV.

Edward, Earl of Warwick, 15-year-old son of Edward IV's brother George, Duke of Clarence. It was also an advantage that many of Richard III's most important supporters had been killed with him at Bosworth Field.

Henry now determined to bolster his position by attempting to bring an end to Yorkist and Lancastrian rivalries, initially through marriage. During his exile in Brittany, he had pledged to marry Elizabeth, daughter of Edward IV and heiress of the Yorkist cause. Following his coronation as Henry VII in October 1485, he married Elizabeth in Westminster Abbey in January 1486. In March, Henry received papal dispensation for the match, which was against strict church law because the couple were first cousins. The document sent by Pope Innocent stated further that any who rebelled against Henry and his heirs would be excommunicated. As a symbol of the newfound spirit of reconciliation, Henry's personal device, the Tudor Rose, combined the white rose of York and the red rose of Lancaster.

YORKIST PRETENDERS

Henry still faced two Yorkist challenges in the first decade of his reign. The first arose in 1487, when an Oxford joiner's

Above: A watchful eye. Philosopher Sir Francis Bacon wrote of Henry, 'He was a prince sad, serious and full of thoughts.'

son named Lambert Simnel was promoted by Yorkists as Edward, Earl of Warwick, despite the fact that the real Earl of Warwick was in the Tower of London. Simnel was crowned Edward VI in Dublin, in May 1487, then landed with a Yorkist army in Lancashire on 4 June. Henry and his army marched to

---

HENRY VII, KING OF ENGLAND, 1485–1509

Birth: 28 Jan 1457, Pembroke Castle
Father: Edmund Tudor, 1st earl of Richmond
Mother: Margaret Beaufort
Accession: 22 Aug 1485
Coronation: 30 Oct 1485, Westminster Abbey
Queen: Elizabeth of York (m. 18 Jan 1486; d. 1503)
Succeeded by: His son Henry VIII
Greatest achievement: Establishing the House of Tudor

16 June 1487: Defeats and captures Pretender Lambert Simnel
Oct 1497: Captures Pretender Perkin Warbeck
1497: Cornishmen revolt over taxes and march on London
14 Nov 1501: Prince Arthur marries Catherine of Aragon
8 Aug 1503: King James IV of Scots weds Henry's daughter Margaret Tudor
Death: 21 April 1509, Richmond Palace, Surrey

QUEST FOR A 'NEW WORLD'

In 1492, Genoese adventurer Christopher Colombus made landfall in the 'New World' of the Caribbean islands with the backing of King Ferdinand of Aragon and Queen Isabella of Castile. Just a few years later, in 1497, another Italian sailor, John Cabot, captained an English voyage of exploration backed by King Henry VII. Cabot, known as Giovanni Caboto in his native land, sailed from Bristol in the *Matthew* in May 1497, made landfall on 24 June on the far side of the Atlantic Ocean and returned to Bristol on 6 August. The place where Cabot landed has never been definitively identified. Possible sites are Cape Breton Island, Newfoundland and southern Labrador. Cabot himself thought it was the north-east of Asia, which he claimed for England. Cabot reported to King Henry, who was delighted and made him a gift of £10. The explorer embarked on a second voyage, with five ships, in 1498. The fleet was lost at sea, though it is not known whether this was before or after he reached north America.

Below: Global view, Henry stands with Venetian sailor John Cabot, in a portrait from the Doges' Palace, Venice.

Above: White rose entwined with red when Elizabeth of York married the Lancastrian Henry Tudor (Henry VII) in 1486.

meet them, and at Stoke on 16 June the royalists defeated the rebel force and captured Simnel. Rebel leader John de la Pole, Earl of Lincoln, was killed. Backing for this uprising was never wholehearted among Yorkists. When Lincoln tried to raise support in Yorkshire he met with little success, and the gates of York were shut against him. King Henry felt that he could afford to be magnanimous and, rather than have Simnel executed, he gave him a job in the palace kitchens.

A second Pretender to the throne made more of an impact and proved a greater threat. Arriving in Ireland in 1491, an elegant and well-built young man from Flanders named Perkin Warbeck claimed to be Richard, Duke of York, the younger of the two princes in the Tower.

He won the support of various European rulers, including Charles VIII of France, Holy Roman Emperor Maximilian I and James IV, King of Scots, who awarded Warbeck a £1200 annual allowance and the hand of James's cousin, Lady Catherine Gordon. In 1497, Warbeck led an invasion of

England, landing in Cornwall with a small force and proclaiming himself King Richard IV. Marching inland, he did manage to gather some support but the revolt melted away in the face of an approaching royal army. Warbeck was captured and confessed himself to be an imposter. Henry cast him in the Tower alongside Edward, Earl of Warwick, but in 1499 had both men executed for plotting against the king.

Below: In Westminster Abbey a bronze tomb of 1518 by Italian Pietro Torrigiano commemorates Henry and Elizabeth.

THE TUDOR SUCCESSION
THE NEW DYNASTY, 1485–1509

The future for the Tudor dynasty began to look brighter when, after nine months of marriage to King Henry, Elizabeth of York gave birth to a son at Winchester on 19 September 1486. Henry was keen to stress his Welsh–British rather than French–Plantagenet roots and named the boy Arthur after the legendary British king of the 5th century AD. At the age of three, Arthur was created Prince of Wales at Ludlow Castle on 29 November 1489. In the ceremony his father was praised as a restorer of Welsh pride, a King of all the Britons capable of bringing order after years of chaos.

A LOST PRINCE

Arthur was raised for kingship. He had the best education in literature and philosophy under the guidance of poet and chronicler Bernard André. At the age of 15 in 1501 he took control in his capacity as Prince of Wales of the council governing Wales. He made a significant diplomatic marriage to

Below: The great Dutch New Testament scholar Erasmus, a friend of Thomas More, was a visitor at the court of Henry VII.

QUEEN ELIZABETH'S CHILDREN

Queen Elizabeth gave birth to seven (or perhaps eight) children, but four died an untimely death, as did the queen herself. She died giving birth to her fourth daughter Katherine on 2 Feb 1503. Her children were:

Arthur: Born 19 Sept 1486, died 2 April 1502
Margaret: Born 28 Nov 1489, died 18 Oct 1541
Henry: (the future King Henry VIII) Born 28 June 1491, died 28 Jan 1547
Elizabeth: Born 2 July 1492, died 14 Sept 1495
Mary: Born 18 March 1496, died 25 June 1533
Edmund: Born 21 Feb 1499, died 19 June 1500
Katherine: Born and died 2 Feb 1503

In some accounts another son named Edward was born, but most historians believe this name to be a mistaken form of Edmund.

Below: Three siblings. Arthur, Prince of Wales, with Prince Henry and Princess Margaret, aged 10, 5 and 7 in 1496.

Princess Catherine, the daughter of King Ferdinand of Aragon, on 14 November 1501, but the following year, on 2 April 1502, the prince died of consumption, leaving Catherine a widow at the age of 18 and leaving his brother Henry, Duke of York, heir to the throne.

DIPLOMATIC MARRIAGES

Henry VII had used the promise of Arthur's hand in marriage as a bargaining tool in diplomatic talks. Arthur and Catherine of Aragon had been promised to one another as early as 1488, when Arthur was 18 months old and Catherine was three. The plans for the wedding had then been reconfirmed in the Treaty of Medina del Campo, signed on 27 March 1489.

The importance of the Spanish alliance was reconfirmed when, just over a year after Arthur's death, it was agreed that Prince Henry, now aged 12, would marry Catherine of Aragon. In the event the wedding was postponed when

part of Catherine's agreed dowry was late to arrive. Prince Henry did not marry Catherine until after the death of his father Henry VII had made him King Henry VIII.

A second major diplomatic marriage was arranged with Scotland in a treaty of perpetual peace signed by English and Scottish diplomats in London, in 1502. At Holyrood House palace, Edinburgh, on 8 August 1503, King James IV of Scots married Henry VII's daughter Margaret Tudor. Scots poet William Dunbar produced a poem, 'The Thistle and the Rose', to celebrate the rapprochement between the ruling houses of Scotland and England.

A PALACE IN RICHMOND

The royal palace at Sheen in Surrey was Henry VII's favourite residence, and princes Arthur and Henry were raised there. At Christmas in 1497, however, Sheen Palace burned to the ground after a conflagration began in the king's quarters. Henry ordered the construction of a magnificent new dwelling and renamed the site Richmond after his family's earldom in Yorkshire.

Completed in 1501, Henry called the new palace, 'this earthly paradise of our realm of England'. It had four towers and a great timber-roofed hall 100ft (70m) in length.

Henry's court was a place of great culture, where leading names of European learning such as the humanists Polydore Vergil and Desiderius Erasmus were welcomed. Vergil arrived in England in 1502 and served as Archdeacon of Wells; his *Anglicae Historiae Libri XXVI* (1534–55) is a valued resource for historians studying Henry VII's reign. Erasmus was a friend and frequent guest of Thomas More – a great name of Henry VIII's reign – who was already active at court in Henry VII's time, serving as a royal envoy to

Above: In 1499 Sheen Palace burnt down; it was rebuilt by Henry VII.

Flanders. Henry rewarded acclaimed Scots poet William Dunbar for his poem in praise of London in 1501. He also began work on a magnificent new chapel at Westminster Abbey, which he hoped to dedicate to Henry VI.

A REIGN OF MANY ADVANCES

Henry died at Richmond, aged 52, after a reign of 23 years. His reign must be judged a significant success. He created stability after decades of civil dissension, thereby establishing the Tudor dynasty while, through astute diplomacy, he boosted England's standing in Europe and stabilized the country's finances.

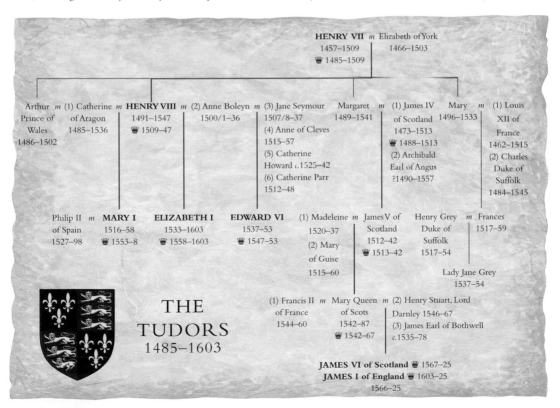

THE TUDORS 1485–1603

HENRY VII *m* Elizabeth of York
1457–1509   1466–1503
♛ 1485–1509

Arthur *m* (1) Catherine *m* **HENRY VIII** *m* (2) Anne Boleyn *m* (3) Jane Seymour   Margaret *m* (1) James IV   Mary *m* (1) Louis
Prince of   of Aragon   1491–1547   1500/1–36   1507/8–37   1489–1541   of Scotland   1496–1533   XII of
Wales   1485–1536   ♛ 1509–47   (4) Anne of Cleves   1473–1513   France
1486–1502   1515–57   ♛ 1488–1513   1462–1515
     (5) Catherine   (2) Archibald   (2) Charles
     Howard *c.*1525–42   Earl of Angus   Duke of
     (6) Catherine Parr   ?1490–1557   Suffolk
     1512–48   1484–1545

Philip II *m* **MARY I**   **ELIZABETH I**   **EDWARD VI**   (1) Madeleine *m* James V of   Henry Grey *m* Frances
of Spain   1516–58   1533–1603   1537–53   1520–37   Scotland   Duke of   1517–59
1527–98   ♛ 1553–8   ♛ 1558–1603   ♛ 1547–53   (2) Mary   1512–42   Suffolk
     of Guise   ♛ 1513–42   1517–54
     1515–60   Lady Jane Grey
         1537–54

(1) Francis II *m* Mary Queen *m* (2) Henry Stuart, Lord
of France   of Scots   Darnley 1546–67
1544–60   1542–87   (3) James Earl of Bothwell
   ♛ 1542–67   *c.*1535–78

JAMES VI of Scotland ♛ 1567–25
JAMES I of England ♛ 1603–25
1566–25

HENRY VIII

1509–1547

Henry VIII acceded to the throne aged 17, a young man of imposing build and looks, 6ft 3in (1.9m) tall, with red hair and a florid complexion, full of youthful exuberance and with a love of display and extravagant pleasures. In character and appearance, the new king presented a marked contrast to his cautious and sober-faced father, who in the last years of his reign had been stricken with tuberculosis.

HONOURING THE FATHER

In the first month of his reign, Henry honoured the memory of Henry VII, presiding over a long and splendid funeral procession and memorial service as the late king's body was carried to Westminster from Richmond, where he had died, and interred in the Abbey.

Henry VII was buried there on 11 May 1509. The magnificent chapel that the late king had begun in 1503 and hoped to dedicate to Henry VI became his own final resting place and a monument to the glories of the Tudor dynasty. A magnificent marble and gilt bronze tomb effigy of Henry VII and his beloved queen, Elizabeth, by the Florentine sculptor Pietro Torrigiano, was completed in 1518.

Within two months of his accession, Henry married his brother Arthur's widow, Catherine of Aragon, in accordance with a diplomatic agreement of 1503 and, so the young king said, in honour of his father's dying wish. The marriage in the Church of the Franciscans, at Greenwich on 11 June, was followed by a joint coronation in Westminster Abbey on 24 June. A huge

Above: Cardinal Wolsey dominated Henry VIII's government, 1515–29. He had great self-belief and enormous reserves of energy.

HENRY VIII, KING OF ENGLAND, 1509–1547

Birth: 28 June 1491, Greenwich Palace
Father: Henry VII
Mother: Elizabeth of York
Accession: 21 April 1509
Coronation: 24 June 1509, Westminster Abbey
Queens: Catherine of Aragon (m. 11 June 1509; d. 1536); Anne Boleyn (m. 24 Jan 1533; executed 19 May 1536); Jane Seymour (m. 30 May 1536; d. 24 Oct 1537); Anne of Cleves (m. 6 Jan 1540; d. 17 July 1557); Catherine Howard (m. 28 July 1540; executed 13 Feb 1542); Catherine Parr (m. 12 Jul 1543; d. 7 Sept 1548).
Succeeded by: His son, Edward VI, aged 9
Greatest achievement: Introducing the Protestant Reformation to England
16 Aug 1513: Defeats French at the Battle of the Spurs
20 Feb 1516: Birth of the future Queen Mary I

Above: With a small mouth and wide face, Henry resembled Edward IV.

1518: Treaty of London: mutual defence pact between England, Spain, France and the Holy Roman Empire

7–24 June 1520: Summit with Francis I of France at 'Field of the Cloth of Gold'
23 May 1533: Marriage to Catherine of Aragon annulled
1 June 1533: Anne Boleyn crowned Queen
7 Sept 1533: Birth of the future Queen Elizabeth I
30 Apr 1534: Act of Succession declares Princess Mary illegitimate and make Princess Elizabeth heir to throne
28 Nov 1534: Act of Supremacy makes Henry 'Supreme Head' of the Church of England
19 May 1536: Anne Boleyn executed
12 Oct 1537: Queen Jane Seymour gives birth to future Edward VI
1539: Publication of the 'Great Bible' in English
1541. Henry declares himself 'King of Ireland'
13 Feb 1542: Catherine Howard executed
Death: 28 Jan 1547, Whitehall Palace

banquet in Westminster Hall was capped by a week of ceremonial jousting to mark the occasion.

INTERNATIONAL DIPLOMACY

Henry VII had won England a significant place in Europe through marriage and diplomatic alliance and, in the first years of his reign, King Henry VIII determined to cement this international standing. His marriage to his brother's widow, Catherine, in 1509 cemented the alliance with the Spanish kingdom of Aragon against France. In 1511 the Holy Roman Emperor, Maximilian, made Henry a gift of a suit of the best armour in Europe, from Germany, in honour of the young king's prowess in jousting at tournaments.

In 1512 Henry set out to emulate his great predecessor Henry V by reconquering France. He won the support of Pope Julius II and, after forming an alliance with his father-in-law Ferdinand of Aragon and the Holy Roman Emperor Maximilian, declared war in April 1512 and sent an English army to Gascony. This expedition ended in mutiny and failure. The next year led

Below: Cardinal Wolsey began the building of Hampton Court Palace in 1515. Henry took it over when Wolsey fell from favour.

'GREAT HARRY'

At more than 1000 tons in weight, with five masts and five tiers of guns, the *Henri Grace à Dieu* – or 'Great Harry', as she was more popularly known – was the world's largest battleship when she was launched at Erith on 13 June 1514. Henry was a great believer in the need for English sea power to protect merchant vessels and back up land armies in European conflicts. Unfortunately, the 'Great Harry' only just survived its namesake: six years after Henry VIII's death in 1547, the warship was accidentally destroyed in a fire in 1553.

Above: 'Great Harry' was among the first ships to carry guns fired through side-ports.

---

to a more successful invasion of France from Calais. On 16 August 1513 Henry won the Battle of the Spurs, so called because the French fled without joining battle and suffered the indignity of the capture of several standards and important prisoners. The allied army also captured the towns of Thérouanne and Tournai. At home, meanwhile, an attempted invasion by King James IV of Scots met with disaster. His army was annihilated by an English force under the 70-year-old Earl of Surrey at Flodden, Northumberland, and James IV himself was killed.

Henry's chief adviser Thomas Wolsey pressed for peace with France, for the war there was achieving little but costing a great deal. A treaty was agreed on 6 August 1514 under which Henry VIII's 17-year-old sister, Mary Tudor, married France's 52-year-old king, Louis XII. This was the first marriage between French and English royals since Henry V's match with Catharine of Valois a century earlier. An unexpected alliance with France was complemented by the four-way Treaty of London of 1518 under which Spain, France, England and the Holy Roman Empire agreed a mutual defence pact.

Such was Henry's European standing that in 1519, with papal encouragement, he even manoeuvred to try to win election as Holy Roman Emperor following Maximilian's death. However, the electors in Frankfurt preferred the claim of King Charles of Spain.

The most extraordinary statement of England's new international standing in the early 16th century was the sumptuous three-week summit with France held near Calais in June 1520. Stage-managed by Thomas Wolsey and known as the 'Field of the Cloth of Gold', the event comprised a series of meetings between Henry and King Francis I of France accompanied by banquets, jousting, hunting and courtly entertainments.

THE SIX WIVES OF HENRY VIII
ROYAL MARRIAGES, 1509–1547

Within two months of his accession to the throne, Henry married his brother Arthur's widow, Catherine of Aragon. Catherine was certainly a suitable bride for the young prince. Although she had been married to his brother, she was only five years older than the 18-year-old Henry and was widely considered a beauty. She was the daughter of King Ferdinand of Aragon and Queen Isabella of Castile and the aunt of Europe's most powerful royal, Charles, Duke of Burgundy, King of Spain and future Holy Roman Emperor. Catherine was very well educated; she was fluent in Latin, French and her native Spanish, although she found it less easy to speak in English.

DESPERATE FOR AN HEIR

Catherine was, however, unable to provide what Henry, determined to safeguard the Tudor dynasty, was desperate to have: a healthy baby boy as his heir. She gave birth to a stillborn daughter in 1510, then in 1511 to a son,

Below: Catherine of Aragon. Highly intelligent, she was an effective regent when Henry fought in France 1512–14.

Above: Anne Boleyn. Although she failed to provide a male heir, she did give birth to the baby destined for glory as Elizabeth I.

christened Henry, who tragically died aged two months. Another son, born in November 1513, died after only a few hours' life and a third son was stillborn in December 1514. Finally on 18 February 1516 a healthy baby daughter, later christened Mary, was born. The next child, born in November 1518, was a stillborn daughter.

Henry meanwhile maintained an active sexual life with his mistresses, one of whom, Elizabeth Blount, gave birth to a healthy boy, named Henry Fitzroy, in 1519. This served to convince the king of his reproductive virility and focused his mind on the need for a legitimate male heir. Matters came to a head in 1527 when Henry, infatuated with court beauty Anne Boleyn, declared that his marriage to Catherine of Aragon had never been legitimate since she was his brother Arthur's wife before she became Henry's bride.

'ANNE OF A THOUSAND DAYS'

The daughter of Sir Thomas Boleyn, Anne was dark-haired, with beautiful features, a long graceful neck and lively

Above: Jane Seymour. She was lady in waiting to both Catherine of Aragon and Anne Boleyn before marrying the king.

manners. She was sister of one of Henry's mistresses, Mary, but despite lavish gifts of jewellery from the king, she refused to become his mistress and held out for becoming his queen. At court she was unpopular and gossip suggested she must be a witch to have driven the king to such desperation.

Henry began proceedings to have his marriage to Catherine declared invalid, but Pope Clement VII – who was under pressure from Catherine's nephew, Charles V of Spain – would not grant the annulment. After almost six years, Henry finally had his way when he secretly married Anne Boleyn on 24 January 1533.

On 23 May Thomas Cranmer, the Archbishop of Canterbury, declared the king's first marriage invalid. Anne was crowned queen on 1 June, and the following month Catherine of Aragon, who refused to renounce her own regal title, was placed under house arrest at Buckden, Cambridgeshire. On 7 September 1533, at Greenwich, Anne gave birth to a daughter, the future Queen Elizabeth I.

Above: Anne of Cleves. After accepting an annulment of her marriage to Henry, she lived on for 17 years until 1557.

Anne's elevation was short-lived. She, too, failed to provide a healthy male heir and the king's interest turned to one of Anne's ladies in waiting, Jane Seymour. After Anne had a miscarriage and then gave birth to a stillborn baby boy, Henry accused her – probably falsely – of adultery and on 2 May 1536 cast her into the Tower of London.

Anne was unanimously convicted by a court of peers under her uncle the Duke of Norfolk and beheaded on 19 May 1536. She kept her wits to the last, declaring, 'The king has been good to me. He promoted me from a simple maid to a marchioness. Then he raised me to be a queen. Now he will raise me to be a martyr'.

NO LONGER A LADY-IN-WAITING

The very next day, Henry proposed to Jane Seymour and the couple were married before the month was out, on 30 May in Whitehall Palace.

A modest woman with a child-like face, Jane was well-liked at court and finally delivered what the king and the country longed for: a legitimate male heir. Prince Edward was born on 12 October 1537 at Hampton Court Palace.

However, twelve days later Jane died suddenly, perhaps from post-natal fever, causing her royal husband apparently genuine grief.

THE 'FLANDERS MARE'

Henry's fourth wedding was a diplomatic match with Princess Anne of Cleves, sister of William, Duke of Cleves in Germany, made to cement an alliance with Protestant German princes against the Holy Roman Emperor Charles V.

Henry was not pleased when he set eyes on his rather plain-looking bride, and declared to Thomas Cromwell, 'My lord, if it were not to satisfy the world and my realm, I would not do that I must this day for none earthly thing'.

Nevertheless, the wedding went ahead at Greenwich Palace on 6 January 1540. By all accounts Henry's marriage to the woman he called his 'Flanders mare' was never consummated, and Henry was apparently humiliated and angered by his impotence.

In summer 1540 the queen agreed happily to a divorce that freed Henry to marry the woman who had become the object of his latest infatuation, the ill-fated Catherine Howard.

Below: Catherine Parr. Well educated and religious, she wrote A Lamentacion or Complaynt of a Sinner *in 1548.*

Above: Catherine Howard. A cousin of Anne Boleyn, she served as a maid of honour to Anne of Cleves.

A WOMAN OF EXPERIENCE

Beautiful, buxom and with healthy appetites, Catherine was one of ten children of the impoverished Lord Edmund Howard. She married Henry on 28 July 1540, less than three weeks after the king's fourth marriage to Anne of Cleves had been annulled on 9 July. Catherine's downfall came when Henry discovered that she had had premarital affairs and might even have been unfaithful after her marriage to the king. With the backing of a parliamentary bill declaring it treason for an 'unchaste' woman to wed a king, Catherine was beheaded at the Tower of London on 13 February 1542.

A COMPANION IN OLD AGE

Henry wed his sixth wife, Catherine Parr, at Hampton Court on 12 July 1543. She had already been twice married and twice widowed. An intelligent and well-balanced woman, she was a helpful companion for Henry in his last years. She was a good stepmother to the three surviving children of his previous marriages and oversaw their education. She survived the king and took a fourth husband, Lord Thomas Seymour.

HENRY AND THE CHURCH OF ENGLAND
DEFENDER OF THE FAITH, 1529–1547

Henry VIII's momentous religious reforms were driven by self-interest: the king's increasingly desperate desire to rid himself of Catherine of Aragon so that he could wed Anne Boleyn.

Henry instructed Thomas Wolsey, the dominant statesman of the first part of the reign, to use his influence as papal legate to persuade Pope Clement VII to grant an annulment of the marriage. Wolsey failed: a legatine court in London examining the validity of King

Below: Royal palaces, major towns and the spread of monasteries in the early years of Henry VIII's reign. The Dissolution of the Monasteries began in 1536.

Henry's case for divorce and presided over by the cardinals Wolsey and Campeggio in May–July 1529 adjourned without reaching a decision, and on 13 July the same year Pope Clement VII ordered that the case must be heard in Rome.

HEAD OF THE CHURCH

Henry turned on Wolsey. A broken man, the king's former adviser died before he could be thrown in the Tower. Henry forced the Convocations of the English clergy at York and Canterbury to submit to him on two issues. In February 1531 they recognized him as 'Supreme Head of the Church of England' and in May 1532

Above: Cranmer, the first Protestant Archbishop of Canterbury, freed Henry to wed Anne Boleyn when he declared the marriage to Catherine of Aragon invalid.

Residences
Residences & Tombs
Other orders
Cistercian
Benedictine

North Atlantic Ocean

North Sea

Falkirk
Stirling
Dunfermline
Linlithgow
Edinburgh Holyrood

CARLISLE
DURHAM

YORK

CHESTER LINCOLN
The Wash
NORWICH

Westminster Abbey
St James's Palace Tower of London
Whitehall Bridewell
Westminster Palace
Richmond Palace
Greenwich Palace
LONDON
Hampton Court Palace

0 2 4 kms
0 1 2 3 miles

HEREFORD WORCESTER
Woodstock
ST. DAVID'S
OXFORD
Windsor CANTERBURY
Winchester Nonsuch Eltham
EXETER
Strait of Dover

Bristol Channel

English Channel

they accepted that all their legislation was subject to royal approval. The king rather than the pope was the final authority on church matters.

Henry, while remaining a Catholic, was convinced of the rightness of his case, so much so that he travelled to a diplomatic summit with the King of France in October–November 1532 with Anne Boleyn as his consort.

Thomas Cranmer, appointed as Archbishop of Canterbury on 30 March 1533, won the backing of the Convocation of English clergy to the twin propositions that, first, the Bible outlawed a man's marriage to his brother's widow and, second, that the pope had no authority to allow such a union. Archbishop Cranmer declared the marriage to Catherine invalid on 23 May 1533 and Henry had Anne Boleyn crowned as Queen on 1 June. By this time Anne was already six months pregnant.

TIDE OF CHANGE

Both Cranmer and Henry's Chancellor, Thomas Cromwell, were sympathetic to what contemporaries called the 'new learning' of the Reformed (Protestant) Church, and they were happy to engineer Henry's extinction of papal authority in England.

The Act of Succession, passed by Parliament on 30 April 1534, provided legal backing to Cranmer's May 1533 declaration. Under the Act, the marriage to Catherine of Aragon was annulled, making Catherine's daughter, Mary, illegitimate, while every adult male was required to take a succession oath of allegiance to Queen Anne that recognized her daughter Elizabeth and any other possible children of the marriage as heirs to the throne.

Above: The medieval Glastonbury Abbey was one of those broken up in the Dissolution of the Monasteries.

Above: The frontispiece to the 1539 Great Bible in English shows Henry giving the 'Word of God' to Cranmer and Cromwell.

Under the Act of Supremacy, passed by Parliament on 28 November 1534, Henry VIII was declared, 'The only supreme head in earth of the Church of England'. Further legislation made it treasonable to deny his supremacy. Under this law the former Chancellor Thomas More and Bishop John Fisher of Rochester were executed in 1535.

SQUANDERED WEALTH

As the head of the Church in England, Henry now had access to its vast landholdings. The Dissolution of the Monasteries, which was implemented by Cromwell in 1536–40, brought immense wealth to the crown, most of which Henry squandered. The last monastery to be dissolved was Waltham Abbey in March 1540.

Throughout the years to 1540, Cromwell and Cranmer moved on the religious revolution in England – with a 1538 campaign in which the country's major shrines were closed down, and injunctions in 1536 and 1538 making use of the English-language Bible compulsory in all English parishes.

Below: Victim of the Reformation. This dramatic vision of Thomas More's fall is by French artist Antoine Caron (1521–99).

A DEBATE FOR SCHOLARS

The debate over whether King Henry had Biblical justification for divorcing Queen Catherine exercised scholars across Europe for a decade.

The two key Biblical texts were Leviticus Chapter 20 Verse 21: 'If a man shall take his brother's wife, it is an impurity; he hath uncovered his brother's nakedness; they shall be childless' and Deuteronomy Chapter 25 Verse 5: 'When brethren dwell together and one of them dieth without children, the wife of the deceased shall not marry to another: but his brother shall take her, and raise up seed for his brother'.

While Henry could claim, citing Leviticus, that his marriage was accursed under Biblical law and that this was the reason for the trouble Catherine had had in bearing a healthy son, Catherine's defenders could argue, with the backing of Deuteronomy, that it had been Henry's duty to marry her. Moreover, Catherine argued that her marriage to Arthur had never been consummated and so the issue did not even arise.

THE LAST YEARS OF HENRY VIII
DEATH OF A MONARCH, 1536–1547

The religious changes of the mid-1530s was to provoke the worst rebellion faced by any Tudor ruler and the most serious civil unrest since the Peasants' Revolt of 1381. A major Catholic uprising across the north of England in 1536 called on the king to make peace with the pope, to reopen the monasteries that had been closed, to restore Princess Mary as heir to the throne and to exclude low-born councillors from his inner circle; a reference to the widely unpopular Thomas Cromwell, Thomas Cranmer and Hugh Latimer. The rebels, who gathered under the badge of the 'Five Wounds of Christ' and who called themselves the 'Pilgrimage of Grace for the Commonweal', even reopened some of the monasteries that had been closed. Their leader was a Yorkshire lawyer named Robert Aske.

The crisis was averted. Henry's representative, Thomas Howard, the Duke of Norfolk, managed to disperse the uprising by promising a general amnesty and a Parliament in York within twelve months. That might have been that, but in January 1537, Yorkshire landowner Sir Francis Bigod tried to

start a separate and entirely different revolt. The leaders of the Pilgrimage of Grace, including Aske, were arrested, given an arbitrary trial and executed in a brutal show of royal authority in June 1537.

AN ENGLISH 'EMPIRE'
The year 1536 saw the first of two major Acts of Parliament under which Wales became part of the kingdom of England and Wales. The 1536 Act stated, 'Wales is and ever has been incorporated, annexed, united and subject to and under the imperial Crown of the Realm as a member of the same'. In this and a second Act of 1543, Wales was organized into 13 counties, each represented by MPs at the Westminster Parliament, and the Welsh language was banned for official use. Those who spoke only Welsh were barred from public office.

In 1541 the Irish Parliament accepted Henry as King of Ireland and Head of the Irish Church. Under the Crown of Ireland Act, the king of England became automatically the king of Ireland.

Left: Thomas Cromwell. He died in great agony on Tower Hill on 28 July 1540 because the executioner's axe was blunt.

Above: Unique glory. Henry VIII's Nonsuch Palace in Surrey was so called because there was 'none such' (none like it). He died before the palace was complete.

Henry was the first to hold this title; previous Irish rulers had been 'high kings' or 'Lord of Ireland', a title which was bestowed on Henry II by the pope. Henry VIII had no desire to rule Ireland by right of a title granted by the papacy before the Reformation.

Henry's attempt to bring Scotland into the English kingdom met with less success. The Treaty of Greenwich, in 1543, proposed a dynastic alliance in which Henry's seven-year-old heir, Prince Edward, would marry Mary, Queen of Scots, then less than one year old. However, a change of heart by Scots governor the Earl of Arran provoked Henry to unleash a military raid commanded by Edward Seymour, Earl of Hertford in 1544.

The Earl of Hertford captured Leith and Edinburgh, where he started fires that reportedly burned for four days, in a campaign dubbed 'rough wooing' because of the earlier marriage negotiations. However, the invasion had no lasting impact. In February the following year the English force was defeated by Scottish troops at the battle of Ancrum Moor.

The latter years of the reign saw England at war with Scotland, France and Ireland, These were ruinously expensive campaigns and in order to pay for them Henry was forced to sell on into private ownership the greater part of the lands he had seized from the Church in the Dissolution of the Monasteries.

THE FALL OF CROMWELL

Henry's chief minister Thomas Cromwell fell abruptly from power in the summer of 1540, when his opponents at court, notably Thomas Howard, third Duke of Norfolk and Bishop Stephen Gardiner, persuaded the king that Cromwell was guilty of heresy and of plotting treason.

Historians generally agree that Cromwell's fall from the king's grace was mainly due to the disaster of Henry's marriage to Anne of Cleves, which Cromwell had negotiated as a diplomatic match in the autumn of 1539. The wedding took place in January 1540, but the match was apparently never consummated and, although Cromwell was elevated to the earldom of Essex as late as April 1540, he never recovered the king's favour. As a result of Norfolk's machinations, Cromwell was arrested in the king's council chamber on 10 June 1540, convicted without trial and beheaded.

CORRUPTION OF THE BODY

In the mid-1540s Henry became grossly corpulent and prematurely aged. Unable to exercise after a sporting injury to his leg, he continued to indulge his vast appetite and his waistline grew to 66in (1.68m). He could no longer walk, but had to be carried by four courtiers; he began to lose his hair and was feared at court for the ease with which he lost his temper. But his sixth wife, Catherine Parr, was attentive to his needs and brought him some peace.

Nevertheless the king fell into a long illness and the end of his reign was obviously drawing near. The Conservative-Catholic faction led by the Duke of Norfolk manoeuvred against supporters of the reformed religion for influence over the country's future direction. The matter was decided by the downfall of the Duke of Norfolk's family. Norfolk's son Henry Howard, Earl of Surrey, bragged of his family's Plantagenet ancestry – as descendants of Edward III – and added the royal arms to his heraldic device. Surrey was found guilty of treason and beheaded on 19 January 1547. His father was condemned without trial as

Above: His Majesty. The words, associated with the Roman emperor, were first used of the king in 1534 as he sought to establish his authority to challenge the pope.

a traitor and was scheduled to be executed on the very day that the king happened to die.

Henry's reign – which had seen such momentous changes in State and Church – ended early in the morning of 28 January 1547. Despite six marriages and all the desperate manoeuvring to ensure a succession, the king was survived by only three legitimate children, including his sole male heir, the nine-year-old Prince Edward.

EDWARD VI
1547–1553

Edward was a small, pale, precocious boy aged nine when he acceded to the throne previously occupied by his giant of a father. The boy-king was already highly educated, having learned Latin and Greek from the age of five, and well versed in Protestant ideas after studying northern Europe's religious 'reformation'. He was serious and rather withdrawn, for he had little experience of family life until the kindness of Queen Catherine Parr brought Henry's three children together after 1544. His pastimes were solitary: viewing the night sky and playing the lute.

THE LORD PROTECTOR

On 18 February, King Edward processed from the Tower of London to Westminster Abbey. He wore a magnificent outfit of cloth of silver and white velvet and rode beneath a crimson canopy on a white charger. Much to his delight, street entertainments were laid on along the route, including a high-wire act at St Paul's, an 'angel' at Cheapside, a children's choir at Cornhill and a 'giant' at London Bridge. The following day he was crowned in the Abbey, amid solemn ceremonial.

His country was in the hands of his uncle Edward Seymour, Earl of Hertford. King Henry had stipulated in

Above: Prince precocious. Edward was known throughout Europe for his learning and intelligence, and also for his saintly piety.

his will the creation of a ruling regency council. However, Seymour had been able to delay public announcement of King Henry's death for three days until 31 January, while he manoeuvred behind the scenes to have himself declared Lord Protector. Subsequently he broke up the council of regents and assumed sole power. On 16 February he was named Duke of Somerset.

Above: The frontispiece of the 1549 Book of Common Prayer shows the young King Edward (top) sitting in council.

The Protector maintained Henry's wars against France and Scotland. After initial difficulties he won a significant victory at the Battle of Pinkie near Musselburgh, Scotland, on 10 September 1547 but was unable to build on it. The Scots aligned themselves with the French, who besieged Boulogne, which England had taken under a 1546 treaty.

Somerset was committed to the Protestant cause and under his Protectorate strict religious reforms were put in place. The 1549 Act of Uniformity outlawed the traditional Catholic Mass and made the use of the Book of Common Prayer compulsory.

ROYAL LOVE TRIANGLE

Early in 1549 one of the king's uncles, Lord Thomas Seymour, was executed after an extraordinary royal love scandal. Seymour, brother of Henry VIII's favourite wife, Jane Seymour, secretly

---

EDWARD VI, KING OF ENGLAND, 1547–1553

Birth: 12 Oct 1537, Hampton Court
Father: Henry VIII
Mother: Jane Seymour
Accession: 28 Jan 1547
Coronation: 20 Feb 1547, Westminster Abbey
Succeeded by: His cousin Lady Jane Grey, for nine days; afterwards by his sister, Mary I
Greatest achievement: Foundation of

grammar schools in several towns
10 Sept 1547: Battle of Pinkie
1549: First Book of Common Prayer. Popular protests against the new prayer book and land enclosures
Oct 1549: John Dudley, Earl of Warwick, replaces Edward Seymour, Duke of Somerset, as Lord Protector
1552: Second Book of Common Prayer
Death: 6 July 1553, London

married Henry's widow Catherine Parr in the very year of the king's death. Then reports circulated that he had been caught trying to seduce Henry's daughter, the red-haired Princess Elizabeth. Some versions indicated that a love triangle had developed involving Catherine, Thomas and Elizabeth and that he had even fathered a child with Elizabeth. Lord Thomas was charged with high treason and the fact that his brother, Edward, was Lord Protector did not save him. He was executed on 20 March 1549.

By the summer of 1549 the Duke of Somerset's hold on power was looking insecure. Catholics in the West Country rose up against the imposition of the Book of Common Prayer, while peasants in Norfolk, the Midlands and Yorkshire protested against land enclosures by local gentry. John Dudley, Earl of Warwick, led troops against the rebels at Dussindale in Norfolk on 26 August, and in the ensuing massacre at least 3,500 people were killed.

Among aristocrats at court and in London, Somerset came under concerted attack for his stated sympathy with the peasant opponents of land enclosure. Warwick saw his chance to seize power and in October had Somerset arrested and thrown in the Tower of London, while he himself was declared Lord Protector in his place.

THE KING'S SICKNESS

Warwick, created the Earl of Northumberland in 1551, oversaw the imposition of a stricter form of Protestant worship in 1552 with a second Book of Common Prayer and a new measure outlawing Catholic dress and forms of worship, including priestly vestments and prayers for the dead.

By the autumn and winter of that year it was clear that the young king was sickening unto death and the most pressing matter for Protestants such as Northumberland became finding a way of preventing a Catholic succession to the throne.

King Edward had fallen ill in summer 1552 and was diagnosed with smallpox and measles, but he did not recover and apparently developed pulmonary tuberculosis in the very cold winter that followed. He was also losing

Above: Sir Edward Seymour, Duke of Somerset and Lord Protector, was also a great military commander, victor both at Pinkie (1544) and Boulogne (1545).

his hair and, according to some accounts had inherited congenital syphilis from his father. Henry VIII's will stated that if Edward died childless, the throne would pass to Edward's sisters, first Mary then Elizabeth. Mary, next in line, was a Catholic and would not only undo hard-won Protestant reforms but also move against Northumberland himself.

As Edward VI neared death, he and Northumberland drew up a 'device' – a kind of will – that shut Mary and Elizabeth out from the succession, and named Lady Jane Grey as his heir.

Lady Jane, the 16-year-old daughter of the Duke of Suffolk, was Henry VIII's great-niece, for her mother Frances was the daughter of Henry VIII's sister Mary. Most importantly for those planning her succession, she was a devout Protestant.

The king's council and Parliament accepted the device. Edward VI died in London on 6 July 1553 and four days later Lady Jane Grey was declared Queen by the King's Council.

Left: The English painting An Allegory of the Reformation (c.1570) shows the pope and his cronies undone by Edward.

MARY I

1553–1558

The Earl of Northumberland's attempt to engineer the succession in favour of his niece, Lady Jane Grey, was nothing more than a total failure. Henry VIII's eldest daughter and his rightful heir, Mary Tudor, proclaimed herself queen on 19 July 1553 and was welcomed to the capital by cheering crowds on 3 August.

Below: The Tudor Princess. This portrait, by 'Master John', shows the future queen as a young woman of 28, in 1544.

RETURN TO CATHOLICISM

Mary was an intelligent and independent-minded woman with a fierce devotion to the Roman Catholic faith, which her father Henry VIII had sought to undermine. Now, as queen, she set about eradicating Protestantism.

By mid-September she had arrested the most important Protestant clerics, including the Archbishop of Canterbury Thomas Cranmer, principal author of the Books of Common Prayer published in 1549 and 1552 and architect of many of Edward VI's reforms.

Acts of Parliament rapidly repealed the anti-Catholic legislation introduced under Edward. On 16 November, moreover, she declared her intention of marrying the Roman Catholic Prince Philip of Spain, son of Charles V, Holy Roman Emperor and King of Spain. It was increasingly clear that Mary intended to sweep away the Church of England and return her country to full-blown European Catholicism. The proposed marriage, meanwhile, raised the unwelcome possibility that England would become no more than a satellite

ANNO DNI 1544
LADI MARI THE MOST KINGE HENRI
DOVGHTER TO VERTVOVS PRINCE THE EIGHT
THE AGE OF XXVIII YERES

MARY I, QUEEN OF ENGLAND, 1553–1558

Birth: 18 Feb 1516, Greenwich Palace

Father: Henry VIII

Mother: Catherine of Aragon

Accession: 19 July 1553

Coronation: 1 Oct 1553, Westminster Abbey

Husband: Philip II of Spain, son of Charles V, King of Spain and Holy Roman Emperor (m. 25 July 1554; d. 1598)

Succeeded by: Her sister Elizabeth I

Greatest achievement: England's first reigning queen

25 Jan 1554: Kentish rebels attack London

30 Nov 1554: Cardinal Reginald Pole absolves England following dispute with papacy

Aug 1555: King Philip abandons Mary and leaves for Netherlands

16 Oct 1555: Bishops Hugh Latimer and Nicholas Ridley martyred

21 March 1556: Archbishop of Canterbury, Thomas Cranmer, martyred

7 Jan 1558: French retake Calais

Death: 17 Nov 1558, London

The beautiful, learned, sensitive and intelligent 16-year-old Lady Jane Grey is said to have fainted when the idea was first put to her that she should become queen. In the end, she reluctantly permitted Edward VI and her uncle, the Duke of Northumberland and Lord Protector of Edward, to elevate her to the English crown. She married Northumberland's son, Lord Guildford Dudley, on 21 May 1553. Northumberland proclaimed her queen on 10 July and urged her to name his son king, but she steadfastly refused. In the event she ruled for just nine days before she was deposed by the rightful heir, Mary.

Lady Jane and her husband were thrown in the Tower of London in July 1553 and executed on 12 February 1554.

Right: In 1833 Paul Delaroche painted Lady Jane Grey as an innocent victim.

Above: A Protestant engraving illustrates the martyrdom of Hugh Latimer, Nicholas Ridley and Thomas Cranmer.

territory of Spain. Rebellion erupted: on 25 January, Sir Thomas Wyatt marched to London at the head of a troop of Kentish rebels to protest against the planned Spanish marriage.

As 7,000-odd rebels prepared to attack the City of London, Queen Mary made a passionate appeal to an assembly of Londoners declaring, 'I love you as a mother loves her child'. She won their loyalty and the rebels were crushed.

Wyatt was executed on 11 April and Mary's sister Princess Elizabeth, who was suspected of involvement in the plot, was cast into the Tower of London and only freed after a period of two months' imprisonment.

Opposition to the marriage remained strong, and broadsheets and ballads opposing the match were all the rage in London. The wedding went ahead, however. Mary, 38, married Philip – at 27, eleven years her junior – on 25 July 1554 in Winchester Cathedral. Philip was proclaimed King of England, but only in the role of king-consort. He would not succeed to the throne if the marriage were childless.

BLOODY MARY

On 20 November 1554 papal legate Cardinal Reginald Pole, exiled since 1532 in protest at Henry VIII's religious reforms, returned to England. Ten days later, Pole pronounced absolution marking England's formal peace with the pope. The following year began the execution of Protestants that earned the queen her reputation in English history as 'Bloody Mary'. In all, 287 Protestants were slain at her command.

On 16 October 1555, Bishops Hugh Latimer and Nicholas Ridley were burned at the stake while Thomas Cranmer watched from his prison cell; Latimer sounded a resounding note as he comforted his fellow victim. 'We shall this day light such a candle by God's grace in England as I trust shall never be put out'.

Mary's marriage, meanwhile, proved unhappy. The queen was deeply in love with her husband, but he did not reciprocate her feelings. In 1555 Mary suffered a phantom pregnancy, which raised and then dashed hopes that an heir might be born. The same month she was abandoned by her consort, as Philip left for the Netherlands. He did not return until July 1557, despite much anguished pleading from Mary. Even then, Philip's main motive in returning was to persuade Mary to ally England with Spain in a war against France.

Within a few months he departed once again for the Netherlands. The war with France into which he had drawn her was a disaster, resulting in the loss to French troops of Calais, England's last French possession. This deeply affected Mary, who declared, 'When I have died and am opened up, you will find Calais lying in my heart'.

On 17 November 1558 Mary died at St James's Palace, tortured by the knowledge that she had been unable to produce an heir to guarantee a Catholic succession and that her Protestant sister Elizabeth was to inherit the crown.

Below: 'Bloody Mary'. England's first reigning queen was a woman of strong convictions, iron will and ruthlessness.

CHAPTER SIX

THE AGE OF ELIZABETH

1558–1603

The 45-year reign of the last of the Tudors, Queen Elizabeth I, was a time of triumphant English achievement. The might of the Spanish Armada was repelled, adventurers such as Sir Walter Raleigh set foot fearlessly in the New World, naval heroes such as Sir Francis Drake proved England's daring and might on the high seas, and such geniuses as dramatist William Shakespeare, artist Nicholas Hilliard and composer William Byrd hit unprecedented artistic heights. In these proud years Elizabeth kept peace at home and established England as a major player on the world stage: her people recovered from the bloody religious conflict of the reigns of King Edward VI and Queen Mary and became confident in their own abilities, her country a vibrant success.

In these years, too, the English people came to love and revere their monarch as never before or, arguably, since – in the state-proclaimed mythology of the 'Virgin Queen', Elizabeth was married not to some foreign prince but to her own realm. In her final speech to Parliament, this great queen declared herself a happy instrument of God in serving and loving her people: 'For myself I was never so much enticed with the glorious name … or royal authority of a Queen as delighted that God hath made me his instrument to maintain his truth and glory and to defend his kingdom … There will never Queen sit in my seat with more zeal to my country, care to my subjects and that will sooner with willingness venture her life for your good and safety than myself.' And she declared in unforgettable terms: 'Though God has raised me high, yet this I count the glory of my crown, that I have reigned with your loves'.

Left: In the celebrated 'Armada Portrait', Elizabeth remains regally composed while English ships see off the Spanish invasion.

ELIZABETH I

1558–1603

When Elizabeth came to the throne in November 1558 the country was in crisis, virtually bankrupt and recently deprived of its last French possession in Calais. England was demoralized and conquest by a foreign power was all too likely: both France and Spain, whose king had been married to the last Queen Mary, eyed England greedily. As Elizabeth rode into London that autumn she was greeted by cheering crowds. After the bloody turmoil and ultimate failure of Queen Mary's reign, her people wanted and needed success for the flame-haired princess, whose colouring and regal manner may have reminded them comfortingly of her father, Henry VIII.

PRAGMATIC PROTESTANTISM

Religious passions were running high. In the eleven years before Princess Elizabeth's accession, England had been transformed into a militantly Protestant country by her brother Edward VI, then changed back to a staunchly Catholic

ELIZABETH I, QUEEN OF ENGLAND, 1558–1603

Birth: 7 Sept 1533, Greenwich Palace
Father: Henry VIII
Mother: Anne Boleyn
Accession: 17 Nov 1558
Coronation: 15 Jan 1559, Westminster Abbey
Succeeded by: James VI of Scots, James I of England
Greatest achievement: Defeat of the Spanish Armada, 1588
Feb 1559: House of Commons urges Queen to marry
April 1559: Acts of Supremacy and Uniformity establish Elizabeth as the supreme governor of the Church of England
23 April 1564: William Shakespeare born, Stratford upon Avon
1568: Mary, Queen of Scots imprisoned by Elizabeth
1569: Catholic uprising in northern England
Feb 1570: Elizabeth excommunicated by Pope Pius V

2 June 1572: The Duke of Norfolk executed for plot to depose Elizabeth
26 Sept 1580: Francis Drake completes circumnavigation of world
1584–9: Foundation of England's first overseas colony, 'Virginia'
1585: Sends English army to back Protestant revolts in the Netherlands
8 Feb 1587: Execution of Mary, Queen of Scots
1588: Defeats Spanish Armada
25 Feb 1601: Essex beheaded for treason
Death: 24 March 1603, Richmond Palace, Surrey

Below: Signature of a queen.

A PRINCESS LEARNED AND WITTY

As a child, Elizabeth was unusually serious, with the gravity of 40 when she was only six, according to one sycophantic account. She received an excellent education that made her fluent in Greek, Latin, French and Italian and instructed her in history, Protestant theology, moral philosophy and rhetoric. She had a shrewd mind – later, as queen, she would write her own speeches – and a capacity to inspire devotion.

In the 1550s, her Greek and Latin tutor, Roger Ascham, praised her strength of mind, her perseverance and her memory which, he said, 'Long keeps what it quickly picks up'. He was also captivated by her beautiful handwriting and her musical skills.

Above: Elizabeth's tutor Roger Ascham was a Cambridge fellow and humanist.

realm by her sister Mary. In punitive campaigns enforcing first one religious orthodoxy and then another, hundreds of English men and women had gone to their deaths as martyrs. One of Queen Elizabeth's great achievements in the early part of her reign was averting further major religious bloodshed.

Elizabeth herself was a Protestant, although a pragmatic rather than a radical or passionate one. In Mary's reign she had been willing, under pressure, to submit to Catholicism. Once she became queen, she reverted to the Protestantism espoused by her mother Anne Boleyn. At Elizabeth's magnificent coronation in Westminster Abbey on 15 January 1559, she pointedly refused to witness the Catholic ritual of Bishop Oglethorpe elevating the Host (communion bread).

Protestantism was officially reintroduced in England under the Acts of Supremacy and Uniformity of April 1559, which recognised the queen as supreme governor of the Church of England and brought Cranmer's 1552 Book of Common Prayer back into use.

The religious settlement was not harsh on Catholics. The wording of the Holy Communion sentences did not endorse transubstantiation (the Catholic doctrine that the bread turned into Christ's body), but at least was possibly compatible with the Catholic faith – communicants were encouraged to 'feed on [Christ] in thy heart by faith'. Elizabeth, who declared that she would not open windows into men's souls, was certainly not about to return to the bloody imposition of orthodoxy.

A HUSBAND FOR THE QUEEN

At her accession Elizabeth was aged 25, and the question of when and whom she would marry to provide an heir loomed large. Even as a princess, in her sister Mary's reign, Elizabeth had received many offers – including ones from Duke Emmanuel Philibert of Savoy and Prince Erik of Sweden, which were both declined. She was also

the recipient of flirtatious attention from Queen Mary's husband, King Philip of Spain, and after Elizabeth's accession Philip renewed his interest with indecent haste, making a formal offer of marriage on 10 January 1559, less than a month after Mary's burial. Elizabeth declined. The following month the House of Commons issued a 'loyal address' to the young queen, urging her to accept a husband in order to produce an heir to the throne. However, Elizabeth declared that she had no intention of marrying at present and reassured the Commons that if she changed her mind then she would choose a husband who was as committed as she to England's safety.

Left: The Pelican Portrait of Elizabeth I, c. 1574, by miniaturist Nicholas Hilliard.

Above: Contemporary accounts suggest that Elizabeth combined her mother's beauty and wit with her father's natural authority.

Meanwhile, court gossips noted that the queen was extremely close to the young and handsome Lord Robert Dudley, later the Earl of Leicester. This was not the first time that Elizabeth had been associated with handsome men at court; she was even reported to have been involved with Lord Thomas Seymour as a teenager.

While Elizabeth was celebrated as 'the Virgin Queen' she remained close to Dudley and later in her reign had similarly intense friendships with elegant noblemen including Sir Christopher Hatton, Robert Devereux, Earl of Essex, and Sir Walter Raleigh.

THE VIRGIN QUEEN
ELIZABETH AND MARRIAGE

On 28 September 1564, in a splendid ceremony at St James's Palace in London, Elizabeth elevated her long-term favourite Robert Dudley to the earldom of Leicester, a position usually reserved for the king or queen's son, which brought many great territories with it. While Elizabeth officially remained the chaste 'Virgin Queen' and was the object of many a marriage proposal from European kings and princes, at court Dudley effectively lived as her consort, with apartments next to the queen in all her main places of residence and acting as her principal host at entertainments.

CULT OF THE VIRGIN QUEEN
Meanwhile, in 1563, after Elizabeth had suffered an attack of smallpox in December 1562, both Houses of Parliament petitioned her to take heed of the potential for a disastrous renewal of dynastic conflicts should she die unexpectedly and without an heir, and the House of Lords urged her to accept a royal husband.

This approach was the second time that the queen had been asked by Parliament to consider the succession, following an earlier 'loyal address' in 1559. In responding the first time, Elizabeth had declared, 'Nothing, no wordly thing under the sun, is so dear to me as the love and goodwill of my subjects', adding, 'in the end this shall be for me sufficient, that a marble stone shall declare that a queen, having reigned such a time, lived and died a virgin'. In her response in 1563, Elizabeth asked for MPs' trust and denied suggestions that she had taken vows of celibacy.

The cult of the Virgin Queen flourished: Elizabeth needed no princely husband, for she was married to her people. The language and behaviour of Arthurian chivalry and courtly love

informed life at court, apparently easing the confusion and difficulty caused by the role reversal of a woman lording over the country's most powerful men. The queen could use her 'prerogative' as a mistress to grant and then withdraw favours or defer decisions on difficult matters. The role suited a woman whose characteristic response to challenges was to be defensive and difficult to read.

Historians are divided as to whether Elizabeth's self-proclaimed virginity was a front or was genuine. Some have suggested that the queen was physically

Above: In 1560 Elizabeth rejected a marriage proposal from Erik of Sweden, acknowledging his 'zeal and love' but adding 'we have never yet conceived a feeling of that... affection towards anyone'.

incapable of having sexual relations; indeed, this was the report of her private physician, Dr Huick, in the 1560s. Others suggest that the queen would have been highly conscious of the potential political fallout should she become pregnant with an illegitimate child. To counter Dr Huick's evidence,

FAVOURITES OF THE VIRGIN QUEEN

Robert Dudley (1532/3–88) Handsome, ambitious and a long-term intimate of the queen, Robert Dudley was created Earl of Leicester and Baron Denbigh in 1564. Dudley recovered from Elizabeth's displeasure at his secret marriage to Lettice Knollys, the widowed Countess of Essex, to become lieutenant-general of the army raised to counter the feared invasion of 1588.

Sir Christopher Hatton (1540–91) A beautiful dancer and accomplished in the traditions of 'courtly love', Hatton rose from the queen's bodyguard to become privy councillor and later Lord Chancellor 1587–91.

Robert Devereux (1567–1601) Cousin of the queen and her favourite towards the end of the reign, he inherited the earldom of Essex aged nine and was an experienced soldier. He had a fiery relationship with Elizabeth and often went against her wishes, yet retained her favour. However, in 1601 he tried to lead a revolt against her rule that led to his execution for treason.

Sir Walter Raleigh (*c.*1554–1618) Writer, soldier and adventurer, he delighted Elizabeth by asking permission to name territory he discovered in the New World after her: it was called 'Virginia' in honour of the Virgin Queen. He was knighted in 1585.

Left: Sir Christopher Hatton became a royal bodyguard after giving up legal study.

Right: Robert Devereux often provoked the queen, but stayed in favour.

historians cite the reports of two medical committees at different times in the reign that certified Elizabeth to be capable of conceiving and giving birth.

A HATRED OF MARRIAGE

Elizabeth had a very strong dislike of marriage and was enraged when favourites or courtiers were wed. In the summer of 1579, when she found out that her great favourite of the early years, Leicester, had secretly wed Lettice Knollys, Countess of Essex, she claimed she would despatch Leicester to the Tower of London. In 1592 she found out that her later favourite, Sir Walter Raleigh, had not only married but also fathered a son, she went one better and actually jailed Raleigh and his wife

Right: Robert Dudley, earl of Leicester. Elizabeth once put down his attempt to insist upon a favour with the words 'I will have here but one mistress and no master'.

Elizabeth. The queen certainly had ample evidence to suggest that marriage was a risky and probably unrewarding enterprise. Her own mother's marriage had been brief and ended with the executioner's sword, and her sister Mary's marriage to Philip of Spain had

been a humiliating disaster. Marrying an Englishman would have encouraged factionalism by favouring one noble family above others. By refusing to marry, Elizabeth was able to retain full independence and avoid expectations that a wife – even a queen – should be obedient to her husband.

As Elizabeth aged, her virginity was presented and understood increasingly as self-sacrifice. Her image shifted from that of the virginal mistress to that of the virginal mother, with connotations of the Virgin Mary. Symbols such as the crescent moon and the pearl – once associated with the Virgin Mary – now became linked to Elizabeth.

Over the years, by staying clear of the international diplomatic unions into which so many of her regal predecessors had been drawn, she maintained the independent standing of her increasingly confident country, sacrificing her dynasty to maintain internal stability.

ELIZABETH AND MARY
COUSINS AND QUEENS

Queen Elizabeth's cousin Mary Stuart posed a potential threat to the English crown from the very start of the reign. Catholics considered the Protestant Elizabeth to be illegitimate, because they did not recognize Henry's divorce of Catherine of Aragon and marriage to Elizabeth's mother, Anne Boleyn, in 1533. The Catholic Mary Stuart – reigning as Mary, Queen of Scots since 1542 – had a viable claim to the English throne as granddaughter of Henry VIII's elder sister Margaret Tudor. Mary's was the second strongest claim after Elizabeth's, and she became a figurehead to Catholics for those wanting a return to the old religion.

Above: In November 1586 MPs twice asked Elizabeth to order Mary's death. She signed the order on 1 February 1587.

COMPETING QUEENS

In England Elizabeth encountered no opposition to her claim as she was welcomed to London and crowned in Westminster Abbey on 15 January 1559. However, in France, Mary, Queen of Scots and her husband the Dauphin (heir to the French throne) began to quarter the English arms with the French arms in their emblem in a provocative gesture that could only be interpreted as a claim to the English throne either in the present or as Elizabeth's successor. It was a gesture that enraged Elizabeth.

Mary had acceded to the Scottish throne aged just seven days on the death of King James V in 1542, then been exiled to France for her own safety since 1548, early in the reign of Edward

Left: A French portrait of Mary, Queen of Scots. Her execution ended plots to kill Elizabeth and replace her with a Catholic.

VI, while her French mother Mary of Guise (James V's widow) ruled as regent. In July 1559 Mary's husband Francis became King of France on the death of his father King Henry II, but after the former's sudden death aged just 16 in late 1560, negotiations began for Mary's return to claim her throne in Scotland.

The cousins were at loggerheads. Elizabeth initially refused to grant Mary safe passage to England; Mary would not recognize the Treaty of Edinburgh that accepted Elizabeth as Queen of England. Elizabeth would not name Mary as her heir.

Mary arrived in a Scotland that had embraced Protestantism and where government was in the hands of competing groups of fractious nobles. Over the ensuing eight years she tried and failed to win control. In a long and dramatic series of events she married her handsome Tudor cousin Henry Stuart, Earl of Darnley, gave birth to an heir, James, survived Darnley's murder and then unwillingly wed the probable murderer, James Hepburn, 4th Earl of Bothwell. In 1567 she abdicated under threat of death in favour of her one-year-old son, James VI. Then in May 1568, following civil war in Scotland, she fled to England for sanctuary.

LOYALTY TO MARY

Elizabeth refused to see Mary or to provide military or political support, but equally she resisted calls from Parliament and her senior advisors for Mary's execution. She would not consent to do away with Mary, even after a Catholic uprising in late 1569 in northern England. The rebellion was led by the earls of

Right: Mary's crucifix and rosary. During her incarceration, Mary had in her retinue a Catholic priest disguised as an almoner.

Northumberland and Westmorland in support of a plot to marry Mary to the powerful Duke of Norfolk and depose the queen. A royal army under the Earl of Sussex was victorious and the rebellion melted away, but Elizabeth exacted brutal revenge, ordering the hanging of as many as 900 rebels. She was merciful to Norfolk, who was spared the death penalty, placed in custody and released within six months.

Matters became more difficult still in February 1570, when Elizabeth was excommunicated by Pope Pius V, whose papal bull *Regnans in Excelsis* denounced the queen as a heretic and freed Catholics from their allegiance to her. After this, rebels could argue that it was the duty of devout Catholics to depose Elizabeth and replace her with Mary. In reponse, increasingly fierce anti-Catholic legislation was passed by Parliament. In 1571 Mary's position became more vulnerable again with the discovery of the 'Ridolfi plot', devised by a Florentine banker named Roberto di Ridolfi. It proposed that a rebellion led by the Duke of Norfolk, arranged to coincide with a

Above: Mary pronounced forgiveness on her executioners, declaring sadly 'I hope you will make an end of my troubles'.

Spanish invasion, would depose Elizabeth and crown Mary Queen of England. In the aftermath, Norfolk was found guilty of treason and executed.

AN END TO THE MATTER

Mary remained in captivity for 19 years and on 14 October 1586 she was found guilty of being involved in a plot to assassinate Elizabeth led by Derbyshire nobleman Anthony Babington. Elizabeth prevaricated for as long as she could, hard pressed by her councillors to condemn Mary, but desperate to find a different way of dealing with her cousin. She even tried to arrange Mary's assassination to avoid the need for an execution, but Mary was finally beheaded at Fotheringhay Castle in Northamptonshire on 8 February 1587.

Elizabeth appeared at once to regret what she had done, for she was maddened with grief at the news of the death, claimed she had not meant to send the death warrant and cast Sir William Davison, the secretary of state who supervised the warrant, into the Tower of London.

Mary's death may have caused Elizabeth private grief, but it was met by public rejoicing.

EUROPE IN THE TIME OF ELIZABETH
FRANCE, THE NETHERLANDS AND IRELAND

 Elizabeth's foreign policy put defence first. Determined to avoid the large-scale foreign campaigns that devastated royal finances in the reign of Henry VIII, she preferred to use diplomacy and make low-key military interventions in furtherance of Protestant resistance to the might of Catholic France and Spain.

THE CATHOLIC THREAT
At the start of the reign, the main concern of the queen and her advisors was the threat of a Franco-Scottish Catholic alliance. The 16-year-old Mary, Queen of Scots was married to Francis, heir to the French throne; meanwhile, Mary's French mother, Mary of Guise,

Above: The slaughter of Huguenots in the St Bartholomew's Day Massacre of 1572 horrified Protestants across Europe.

Left: Europe in the reign of Elizabeth. The most important military clash was the sea battle of Gravelines against the Armada.

ruled Scotland as regent. England was officially at peace with France, having signed the treaty of Cateau-Cambrésis in April 1559. In Scotland, Elizabeth provided aid to the Protestant Lords of the Congregation, who deposed Mary of Guise and attempted to drive out the French presence. Under the Treaty of Edinburgh in July 1560, a Protestant Regency Council was established. In France, too, Elizabeth supplied aid to Protestants seeking to undermine a Catholic ruler, and under the 1562 Treaty of Hampton Court she supported the French Huguenots.

AN ENEMY OF ROME
After Elizabeth's excommunication in 1570 and the discovery of the Ridolfi plot the following year, the queen came under pressure from her Privy Council

Above: Don John, Catholic scourge of the Dutch Protestants, wanted to invade England and marry Mary, Queen of Scots.

not only to execute Mary but also to take a more active role in Continental struggles between Protestants and Catholics. In 1572 the stakes were raised by a series of violent outbursts against French Huguenots (called the 'St Bartholomew's Day Massacre') that resulted in the deaths of approximately 70,000–100,000 Protestants there. Queen Elizabeth quietly sent money and munitions to the Huguenots but publicly remained on friendly terms with the French Catholic regime.

DUTCH COURAGE

Elizabeth also backed Dutch Protestants in their rebellion against Spanish rule. In 1576 when Spain sent Austrian commander Don John to put down the revolt, Elizabeth was offered the sovereignty of the Netherlands if she would provide military force and agree an Anglo-Dutch alliance. She declined, but agreed loans and financial support totalling £120,000 to help the Protestant cause. She entered a formal alliance with the rebels in December 1577 but the following year the rebels were decisively defeated by Don John. In 1585, following the assassination of Dutch leader William of Orange and with war against Spain looming, Elizabeth agreed to send a 7,000-strong army to the Netherlands under the Earl of Leicester and to garrison the ports of

Above: The Earl of Essex. After failing to impose himself on Irish rebels, Essex was unable to regain the favour of the queen.

Flushing and Brill. Elizabeth's decision to help brought her the title 'Protector of the Netherlands'. In 1589, Elizabeth finally sent English troops into France, to back the claim of the prominent Huguenot, Henry of Navarre, to the French throne.

ELIZABETH AND IRELAND

Elizabeth's attempt to impose the Protestant religious 'settlement' of 1560 in overwhelmingly Catholic Ireland provoked a series of uprisings. The major disturbances were in the years 1569–73, 1579–83 and 1595–8.
June 1569: Military captain James Fitzmaurice Fitzgerald launches a Catholic revolt by attacking English colonists at Kerrycurihy, County Cork.
1570–2: Sir John Perrot, appointed to the new position of Lord President of Munster, wins the submission of James Fitzmaurice Fitzgerald and stamps out revolt in the province.
1579: Fitzgerald heads a new religious revolt, declaring Elizabeth a heretic, with secret support from both the pope and Philip II of Spain.

1580: English forces defeat the rebels. Lord Grey de Wilton, the queen's newly appointed deputy in Ireland, crushes an Irish garrison at Smerwick, Munster.
Nov 1583: Fitzgerald's cousin, the Earl of Desmond, is captured and killed by English forces under de Wilton.
1594: Hugh O'Neill, Earl of Tyrone, heads a new Catholic revolt, in Ulster.
May 1595: Sir John Norris is despatched to Ireland to put down the revolt, but fails.
14 Aug 1598: Tyrone wins a great victory at Yellow Ford, Ulster, over an English army led by Sir Henry Bagenal. The English commander and 830 English troops die.
April 1599: The Earl of Essex, the newly appointed Lord Lieutenant of Ireland, agrees a truce with Tyrone against Elizabeth's express instructions.

However, following accusations that Essex had made a treasonable pact with the Irish earl, he abandons his post and returns to England to explain his conduct to the Queen. He is later arrested, charged with maladministration and finally – on 25 February 1601 – beheaded for treason.
Sept 1601: The continuing Irish revolt is strengthened by the arrival of 3,400 Spanish troops.
24 Dec 1601: Charles Blount, Lord Mountjoy, defeats Irish rebels and their Spanish reinforcements in battle near Kinsale.
March 1603: Tyrone's revolt has not recovered from the 1601 defeat. He submits to Elizabeth and after her death receives a royal pardon from King James I.

THE ARMADA
A FAMOUS VICTORY, 1588

The defeat of the Spanish Armada in 1588 occupies a hallowed place in English history. Elizabeth's navy, commanded by Lord Howard of Effingham, forced the 130-galleon fleet of King Philip II of Spain to abandon plans for an invasion of England and to set sail for home. Around 15,000 Spaniards died in the encounter, compared with English losses of fewer than 100. Lord Howard afterwards declared: 'I do warrant you, all the world never saw such a force as theirs was'.

THE RUN-UP TO INVASION
The Armada invasion came after years of growing tension between England and Spain. King Philip, former husband of Elizabeth's sister Mary and a one-time suitor of Elizabeth herself, was increasingly enraged by Elizabeth's support for Protestant revolt against Spanish rule in the Netherlands and by the activities of English adventurers such as Francis Drake and John Hawkins in harrying Spanish colonial shipping.

AN INVINCIBLE FLEET
The impetus for Philip's military action was Elizabeth's 1585 despatch of an English army to the Netherlands and the 1587 execution of Mary, Queen of Scots. With the death of Mary, Philip saw that he himself could now lay claim to the English crown in the event of the restoration of Catholicism.

Philip had become king of Portugal in 1580 and so had access to the Atlantic port of Lisbon. The Spanish ships –

Above: Elizabeth gave the 'Armada Jewel' to Sir Thomas Heneage, Treasurer of War, to celebrate the triumph of 1588.

THE QUEEN'S SPEECH

In facing the threat of invasion Elizabeth was characteristically fearless, inspirational and defiant. On 9 August, before it was clear at home that the Armada was a spent force, she visited the troops assembled at Tilbury in Essex under the command of the Earl of Leicester. As her army prepared to repel a Spanish force commanded by the Duke of Parma, King Philip's regent in the Netherlands, Elizabeth rode among them, wearing a steel breastplate and seated on a grey gelding, to deliver a stirring speech that lived long in popular memory. Onlooker James Aske likened her to a 'sacred general'.

'My loving people, We have been persuaded by some that are careful of our safety to take heed how we commit ourselves to armed multitudes for fear of treachery, but I assure you I do not desire to live to distrust my faithful and loving people. Let tyrants fear…I have always so behaved myself that, under God, I have placed my chiefest strength and safeguard in the loyal hearts and good will of my subjects, and therefore I am come amongst you as you see at this time, not for my

Left: A painted 17th-century panel from St Faith's Church at Gaywood, Norfolk, shows Elizabeth arriving at Tilbury.

recreation and disport, but being resolved, in the midst and heat of the battle, to live or die amongst you all, to lay down for my God and for my kingdom, and for my people, my honour and my blood, even in the dust. I know I have the body of a weak and feeble woman, but I have the heart and stomach of a king, and of a king of England too, and think it foul scorn that Parma or Spain or any Prince of Europe should dare invade the borders of my realm, to which, rather than any dishonour shall grow by me, I myself will take up arms, I myself will be your general, judge and rewarder of every one of your virtues in the field. I know already for your forwardness you have deserved rewards and crowns; and we do assure you, on the word of a Prince, they shall be duly paid to you….By your valour in the field, we shall shortly have a famous victory over these enemies of my God, of my kingdom and of my people.'

Above: Spanish ships flounder in the teeth of a south-west wind. This image of the sea battle off Gravelines is by Nicholas Hilliard.

ironically dubbed *El Armada Invencible* ('The Invincible Fleet') – set sail from there on 30 May 1588 under the command of the Duke of Medina Sidonia.

The plan was to sail to the Netherlands and ferry 16,000 Spanish troops from there to England, where they would support a popular uprising among Catholic sympathizers in the south-west. Philip's ultimate goal was to sweep Elizabeth from the throne and restore freedom of Catholic worship in England. He sent his admiral, the Duke of Medina Sidonia, on what he saw as a sacred mission, with these words ringing in his ears. 'If you fail, you fail; but the cause being the cause of God, you will not fail.'

SPANISH SEA POWER WRECKED

The fleet of some 130 ships had a troubled voyage northwards and was forced by storms into the northern Spanish port of Coruña; it did not reach the Channel for over two months. The English watched and waited and finally sighted the Armada off the Lizard coast of Cornwall on 29 July. As news of the invasion threat was spread across southern England by messengers and hilltop beacons, Francis Drake and Lord Howard put to sea with about 120 ships. They engaged the Spanish fleet three times – off Eddystone, off Portland and near the Isle of Wight – before the Armada anchored out from Calais, the former English possession in France.

Then in a dramatic midnight mission conceived by Lord Howard's vice-admiral, none other than Sir Francis Drake, empty English fireships stocked with wood and explosives were sent in and, helped by strong winds, created a wall of fire among the Spanish ships.

Below: Drake's drum. Over the years since 1588 its ghostly roll has reputedly been heard at times of English deliverance – such as the German navy's surrender in 1918.

The Spanish galleons put to sea in a panic and, in the face of storming south-west winds were unable to regroup before the English ships attacked again off Gravelines. The chief ships of the English fleet, the 20 royal galleons, were faster than the Spanish ships, more manoeuvrable, better armed and bigger.

With his fleet in disarray and having already lost 2,000 men in a week of fighting the superior English fleet, the Duke of Medina Sidonia ordered retreat. The wind forced the Armada to sail not back down the English Channel, but north up the east coast of England and Scotland, hoping to round the Orkneys and the Hebrides and regain the relative safety of the Atlantic Ocean. They were harried by English ships as far as Scottish waters and in the Atlantic were hit by storms. By the time that the fleet arrived back home it had lost at least 63 ships and around half of its 30,000 men.

The defeat was a key event of Elizabeth's reign. As well as safeguarding Elizabeth's religious settlement and preventing a potential bloodbath in England, it boosted the reputation of the English fleet and consolidated the growing self-confidence of the English. The victory also marked a shift in power from Catholic southern Europe to Protestant northern countries.

VOYAGES OF DISCOVERY
GLOBAL EXPLORATION

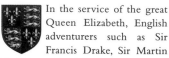 In the service of the great Queen Elizabeth, English adventurers such as Sir Francis Drake, Sir Martin Frobisher, Sir John Hawkins and Sir Walter Raleigh tamed the high seas as they made voyages of exploration, piracy and colonization around the globe.

LAND OF THE 'VIRGIN QUEEN'
Under Elizabeth, England founded its first short-lived overseas colony, named Virginia in honour of the Virgin Queen, at Roanoke Island, now North Carolina in the years 1584–9. Virginia was established by one of Elizabeth's principal favourites, Sir Walter Raleigh, who in the 1580s was employed at court and in trade in London; he did not visit the New World himself until later years. In 1584, however, he sent two men, Philip Amadas and Arthur Barlowe, to find a site for a colony, and upon their return with promising reports, he despatched 107 settlers under the command of Sir Richard Grenville in 1585. The first group, discouraged by

Below: Scourge of Spain. Sir Francis Drake was known as El Draque *('the Dragon') by his Spanish foes.*

Native American attacks, abandoned the settlement and returned to England, but Raleigh sent a second group of around 150 settlers in 1587. The settlers built houses, but their commander, John White, sailed to England for further supplies and was delayed in returning because of the Spanish Armada's threat. When he did return in 1590 he found the colony had mysteriously vanished – the only clue was the word 'Croatoan' cut in a tree trunk. The attempt to establish the colony was abandoned.

Raleigh did later lead a New World voyage: in 1595 he explored what is now Venezuela and sailed the Orinoco river in search of the legendary city of gold, Manoa, which was said to be ruled by a king named 'El Dorado'.

SIR FRANCIS DRAKE
The most celebrated of Elizabeth's roving seafarers, Francis Drake, first made his name and fortune in a voyage to South America and Panama in 1572–3. He set sail from Plymouth on 24 May 1572, with a privateering commission from the queen; essentially the permission to

Above: This contemporary engraving of the arrival of the English in Virginia was made by Theodore de Bry (1528–98).

plunder Spanish territories and riches. A militant Protestant, he saw it not only as profitable but as a religious duty to plunder Catholic Spain. In Panama he attacked the Spanish settlement of Nombre de Dios and left with great riches before exploring the Isthmus of Panama on foot and, from a tree on high ground, becoming the first Englishman to see the Pacific Ocean. He captured a Spanish caravan and took large amounts of silver to add to his plunder from attacking Spanish shipping on the high seas and returned to England with the most astonishing haul of New World riches yet seen.

Drake next departed in 1577 on a voyage to explore South America and the South Pacific, where a vast hidden continent was rumoured to exist. Before his departure he had an audience with Queen Elizabeth, who told him she hoped he could win some measure of revenge for various slights against her by

Above: England's first slave trader and a cousin of Sir Francis Drake, Sir John Hawkins explored Guinea and the Spanish West Indies.

Above: Sir Walter Raleigh was a natural philosopher as well as an adventurer. He was fascinated by potential uses of mathematics as a navigational aid.

Hind was weighed down with glittering treasures and exotic spices. On 4 April 1581, Queen Elizabeth – secretly delighted at the damage Drake had done to Spanish interests – came aboard the *Golden Hind* on the Thames at Deptford and knighted Sir Francis. The Spanish ambassador was outraged.

Sir Francis Drake was now a trusted royal servant. In 1587 Elizabeth sent him to attack Spain's empire: on this voyage he plundered Spanish settlements in the Cape Verde Islands, Colombia, Florida and Hispaniola (the Dominican Republic and Haiti).

FROBISHER AND HAWKINS

Another of Queen Elizabeth's free-ranging 'privateers' was Martin Frobisher, who led three voyages to Baffin Island and Labrador in search of gold mines in 1576–8, the second two with the queen's financial investment. He left his name in Frobisher Bay (south-eastern Baffin Island), but failed to find any gold. Like Raleigh, Frobisher also attempted to establish a New World colony, but failed. Subsequently, he sailed with Drake to the West Indies in 1585 and was knighted for his services to the queen in defeating the Armada.

Sir John Hawkins was England's first slave trader. After making a great fortune in a pioneering 1562–3 voyage financed by London merchants in which he sold Africans captured in Guinea as slaves in

the king of Spain. He set sail in the *Golden Hind* in December 1577. Reaching South America, he sailed through the Strait of Magellan and entered the Pacific, then sailed up the western coast of the continent, winning rich pickings from Spanish ships and colonial settlements, before trying and failing to find the Northwest Passage. Anchoring off the area of modern San Francisco, he claimed the land for Queen Elizabeth and dubbed it 'New Albion'. From there he sailed westwards across the Pacific, then home across the Indian Ocean and around the Cape of Good Hope to the Atlantic.

Drake landed at Plymouth on 26 September 1580 to complete his circumnavigation of the world; the first by an Englishman and only the second ever, following that by Portuguese captain Ferdinand Magellan. The *Golden*

Right: Exploration routes to the Americas and the Far East followed by some of Elizabeth's fearless naval pioneers.

the Spanish West Indies, he won the queen's backing for a second successful trip in 1564–65. A third trip with his relative, Francis Drake, nearly ended in disaster, however.

Later Hawkins was responsible for supervising the construction of the swift, well-armed ships that outgunned the galleons of the Spanish navy in 1588. He was knighted for his part in England's great victory.

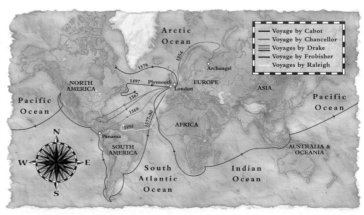

ELIZABETH'S COURT
A GLITTERING PRESENCE

In July 1575 the Earl of Leicester laid on lavish celebrations for Elizabeth and her travelling court at Kenilworth Castle, in Warwickshire, which had been a gift from the queen ten years earlier.

AN ARCADIAN FANTASY
At enormous expense, the castle and grounds were transformed into a chivalric and arcadian fantasy. Leicester gave over to Elizabeth an entire, extravagantly decorated wing of the building and flooded a field in front of the castle to make an artificial lake. As she arrived, Elizabeth was greeted by a boy dressed as a nymph on an island in the lake. He declaimed the words, 'The Lake, the Lodge, the Lord are yours for to command.' At the castle gates a scholar disguised as Hercules hailed the queen in blank verse. As she entered, the clocks were stopped – time would stand still while the queen was in residence.

The queen stayed at Kenilworth for 18 days of hunting, dancing, feasting and elaborate pageants. On one evening, a

Below: Elizabethan noblemen kept alive the traditions of knightly chivalry revived under Edward III and popular in the reign of Elizabeth's father, Henry VIII.

Above: The queen's glory. Admirers crowd close as Elizabeth, a shimmering white vision in a sedan chair, is carried past.

banquet of 300 dishes was provided, on another Elizabeth greatly enjoyed a play, *The Slaughter of the Danes at Hock Tide*, put on by the Men of Coventry.

At every turn, Leicester had laid on surprises and entertainments. When the queen complained that she could not view the castle gardens from the window of her bedchamber, Leicester secretly had a garden laid out in the course of one night so that when she awoke, she might find that her wish had been granted.

The events at Kenilworth were part of Elizabeth's majestic 'summer progress' in 1575 when, with Leicester as her guide, she made a series of visits to country houses across central England. In these 'progresses', held each year, Elizabeth descended upon her nobles and people to impress all with her glittering magnificence. She travelled with some 300 wagons and 2,000 horses, either riding on horseback or carried in a litter. Country folk lined the roads to watch this vision of regal power pass.

COURTLY FASHIONS
By the 1570s, Elizabeth's court was a place of extravagant display, whose running costs had reached several hundred pounds a week. Elizabeth had a huge

abundance of dresses, jewellery and precious stones, since she received vast numbers of jewels as gifts from ambassadors, courtiers and suitors. Each New Year's Day was a time of ceremonial gift-giving, when the Queen received dresses, jewellery, gloves, petticoats and other presents from leading courtiers. On New Year's Day 1588, Sir Christopher Hatton gave Elizabeth a gold necklace and earrings set with

Above: A celestial presence. This portrait, by Italian Taddeo Zuccari (d. 1566), is one of many from the reign showing the queen lavishly dressed and smothered in jewellery.

ENGLAND'S GODDESS

From the 1570s onward, Elizabeth's accession day, 17 November, was celebrated as a national holiday, with bonfires, the ringing of church bells, services of thanksgiving and ceremonial tilts and pageants at Whitehall Palace. It was a day of English Protestant pride that put half-remembered Catholic saints' days deep in the shade. Henry Lee, the Queen's Champion in tilting, initiated and organized the celebrations at Whitehall Palace each year until he retired aged 57 in 1590.

Above: This delicate miniature portrait of the queen by the great Nicholas Hilliard is found within the 'Armada Jewel'.

rubies and diamonds; the queen's jewellery collection was thought to be the most valuable in Europe.

Elizabeth's devotion to glittering display was, in part, a political decision to project herself as magnificence personified; a goddess on earth.

In 1575, summer progress celebrations were held in Warwick, where a vast firework display over the River Avon was backed up with the booming of cannon from the Tower of London, transported from the capital at the expense of Lord Warwick, Master of the Ordinance. The queen's encounter with town people and officials in Warwick is revealing of both her magnificence in their eyes and of her easy manner.

When the town recorder was overcome with nerves at speaking in front of her, she called him forth saying, 'Come hither, little Recorder. It was told me that you would be afraid to look upon me or to speak boldly, but you were not so afraid of me as I was of you and I now thank you for putting me in mind of my duty'. When the firework display started a fire that damaged a house, Elizabeth summoned the elderly couple who owned the dwelling and offered to right the damage.

GLORIANA
THE REALM OF THE FAERIE QUEEN

Towards the end of the reign, the poet Edmund Spenser dedicated his allegorical chivalric romance, *The Faerie Queen*, to Elizabeth, 'by the Grace of God Queen of England, France and Ireland and of Virginia, Defender of the Faith, &c'. In the work, published in 1590–6, the Queen of Fairie land, named Gloriana, represents glory both in the abstract and in the person of Elizabeth. As Spenser wrote, 'In that Faerie Queen I mean glory in my general intention, but in my particular I conceive the most excellent and glorious person of our sovereign the Queen'. The poet presented the first three manuscript books of the poem to the queen at court in 1589.

Elizabeth was an enthusiastic and discerning patron of the arts, which burst forth in an extraordinary flowering during her reign. In addition to Spenser,

Below: A Christian warrior slays a beast in an engraving from the 1590 edition of Edmund Spenser's The Faerie Queene.

Above: William Shakespeare at 34, in 1598. By this time the playwright's work was already a favourite of the queen's.

whose epic is considered one of the finest poems in English, the period produced dramatists William Shakespeare, Christopher Marlowe and Ben Jonson; musicians Thomas Tallis and William Byrd; and the renowned miniaturist artist Nicholas Hilliard.

FLOWERING OF DRAMA

London's first theatre was founded in Holywell Street, Shoreditch, by actor James Burbage in December 1576. At Christmas 1582, five plays were put on at court for the entertainment of Elizabeth and her current suitor, the

Duke of Alençon. In 1583 'the Queen's Men' were one of the companies of theatrical players formed in London. Some probably fanciful accounts of William Shakespeare's life claim that he first came to London having joined the Queen's Men as an actor in his native Stratford in 1587.

Shakespeare's plays were first performed in London in the early- to mid-1590s. His early works included the histories *Richard III* and the first part of *Henry VI*, comedies *The Taming of the Shrew* and *Two Gentlemen of Verona* and the tragedy *Romeo and Juliet*.

From 1594, he was one of the Lord Chamberlain's Men, based at the Globe Theatre in Bankside from 1598. Elizabeth so much enjoyed Shakespeare's *The History of Henry IV, with the Humorous Conceits of Sir John Falstaff* in 1597 that she asked for a new play showing Falstaff 'in love'; Shakespeare produced *The Merry Wives of Windsor*, which first played in 1600.

ELIZABETH'S PLAYWRIGHTS

Ben Jonson's dramatic genius is considered in some quarters to have been the equal of Shakespeare, but his major works were written after Elizabeth's death, when he was a favourite at the court of King James I.

The playwright Christopher Marlowe is believed also to have been an agent in Elizabeth's secret service, who was sent in 1587 to spy on Catholics in France. He also had a reputation as an atheist and blasphemer and, perhaps for this reason, the Privy Council issued an order for his arrest on

Above: This manuscript poem in praise of Elizabeth was presented to the queen in 1586 by its author Georges de la Motthe.

18 May 1593. He was killed in a tavern brawl in Deptford on 30 May 1593, probably over nothing more significant than the bill. His plays, which include *Tamburlaine the Great, The Tragical History of Doctor Faustus* and *The Jew of Malta*, were performed to great acclaim in London by the Admiral's Men and their star Edward Alleyn.

Nicholas Hilliard was the pre-eminent portrait artist of Elizabeth's day. He worked mainly in miniature – an art known to Elizabethans as 'limning'– and was also a jeweller and goldsmith. In 1572 he was appointed the queen's official limner. In 1584 he designed the queen's second great seal.

TALLIS AND BYRD

Queen Elizabeth recognized the musical genius of the great sacred composers Thomas Tallis (right, top) and William Byrd (right, bottom) by granting them, a monopoly licence to print and sell music in England in 1575. In the same year, the two composers published *Cantiones Sacrae* ('Sacred Songs'), containing 16 motets by Tallis and 18 by Byrd. The book was dedicated to Queen Elizabeth. Tallis was by this time a man of 65 and had served as a gentleman of the Chapel Royal, the queen's musical body, since *c.*1542, well before the beginning of Elizabeth's reign. Byrd, Tallis's protégé, had joined the Chapel Royal from a position as organist at Lincoln Cathedral three years earlier.

THE REALITY BEHIND THE MASK
THE LAST DAYS OF ELIZABETH

Queen Elizabeth was very conscious of her public image. As early as 1563, the production of unauthorized portraits of the queen was banned. From the 1570s onwards, the projection of Elizabeth as the Virgin Queen, an earthly goddess or Protestant Madonna, was carefully managed. However, as she aged, the image of magnificence she wished to promote was increasingly at odds with physical reality.

THE EFFECTS OF AGE

Some authorities suggest that Elizabeth manufactured a glittering, magnificently costumed, jewel-laden public image to compensate for her waning physical charms. Essayist and philosopher Sir Francis Bacon, Lord Chancellor under King James I, wrote, 'She imagined that the people, who are much influenced by externals, would be diverted by the glitter of her jewels from noticing the decay of her personal attractions'. If this was a deliberate strategy, it largely succeeded, but it became more and

Below: William Cecil, Lord Burghley. Elizabeth was devoted to her great statesman, and in his final illness she sat by his bed and fed him with a spoon.

Above: Even the Faerie Queene was subject to the ravages of ageing. This portrait of Elizabeth in old age is by Dutch artist Marcus Gheeraerts the Younger.

more difficult to operate. The effects of ageing could not be avoided, even by the Queen, and beneath the laboriously constructed public face she became an old woman in a red wig, with bad teeth. In 1596, now aged over 60, she ordered the seizure of all paintings in which she looked ill, old or weak. In public, Elizabeth's age was clearly taking its toll: at the opening of the 1601 Parliament

she found the velvet and ermine robes were too heavy and stumbled, falling into the arms of a peer alongside her. On a visit to Sir Robert Sidney around this time, she needed a walking stick to climb a staircase and appeared weary and forgetful.

CHANGE MUST COME

In the 1590s, Elizabeth was worn out and a little of the gloss had come off her reputation and achievements. Unemployment and taxation were both high, harvests failed in 1594–7, hard times led to rising crime rates and

TRUTHS IN THE MIRROR

For years Elizabeth avoided seeing herself in a looking glass, but in 1603 she commanded her courtiers to show her her true reflection, for the first time in two decades. She was devastated by the sight of the sickly, 69-year-old face she saw in the mirror. By this time the ailing queen was close to death, stubbornly refusing food and medicine, resisting sleep, sitting forlornly on a floor cushion at Richmond Palace. She had been ill since late 1602. Her dearest friends and confidants were already dead: Leicester had died long before, in 1588; Sir Christopher Hatton, in 1591; William Cecil, Lord Burghley, in 1598; and she had sent Robert Devereux, Earl of Essex, to a traitor's death in 1601. Her favourite cousin, Kate Carey, Countess of Nottingham, died in late February 1603, and this was perhaps the final blow.

Left: A symbol of death hovers behind the now weary queen in this anonymous panel from Corsham Court, Wiltshire.

Eugenia, daughter of Philip II of Spain and wife of the Governor of Flanders, Archduke Albert; Lord Beauchamp, a descendant of Lady Jane Grey's family; and the Protestant James Stuart, the son of her cousin Mary Queen of Scots, ruling as King James VI of Scots. Yet Elizabeth could not bring herself to name a successor, since this would involve accepting her own end.

THE SETTING OF THE SUN

Queen Elizabeth died at last in the early hours of 24 March 1603. According to some accounts she was unable to the last to name a successor, but did rouse herself on her deathbed to condemn the claim of Lord Beauchamp: 'I will have no rascal's son in my seat, but one worthy to be a king'. In other versions of events she was by now unable to speak and indicated by a movement of her hand that she wished the throne to pass to James Stuart. On her final evening she was visited by John Whitgift, Archbishop of Canterbury, who told the dying queen, 'Though she had been long a great queen here upon earth, yet shortly she was to yield an account of her stewardship to the King of Kings'.

Below: William Cecil's Burghley House. He entertained Elizabeth no fewer than 12 times at his various country houses.

record numbers of executions for felons, Spain remained a threat and there was a troubling uncertainty over the succession. Some began to speak out against Elizabeth's rule, and to call for change.

Yet the mythology of the Virgin Queen was sustained to the end. Sir Robert Cecil laid on an entertainment for Elizabeth in December 1602, in which he celebrated her as Astraea, virgin of Roman poet Virgil's *Eclogues*: a just and saintly figure, whose presence on Earth brought a wonderful age of eternal spring and endless peace.

Elizabeth herself maintained her stance of devotion to her people: in her celebrated 'golden speech' to representatives of the 1601 Parliament she declared, 'I do not so much rejoice that God hath made me to be a Queen, as to be a Queen over so thankful a people', adding, 'I have cause to wish nothing more than to content the subject' and, 'It is my desire to live nor reign no longer than my life and reign shall be for your good.' As before, she used the language of love in place of a language of politics, casting herself as the mistress,

wife or mother of her country, driven always by care and devotion rather than duty or self-interest.

Elizabeth's own sun was preparing to set, but as the celebrated Virgin Queen she had no child to succeed to her throne. There were as many as a dozen people with at least a potentially viable claim to the English crown, including the Catholic Infanta Isabella Clara

CHAPTER SEVEN

THE UNION OF
THE CROWNS AND
CIVIL WAR

1603–1660

The royal House of Stewart – or Stuart as it came to be spelled
in the late 16th century – had been ruling in Scotland for 232
years by the time King James VI of Scots travelled south from
Edinburgh to take possession of the English crown as King James I
of England in 1603. The first Stewart king was King Robert II
(1371–90), who acceded as the son of Robert I the Bruce's
daughter, Marjorie. Robert II's descendants ruled in a direct male
line until the death of King James V (1513–42), when James's
daughter Mary, Queen of Scots, began her troubled reign at the
age of seven days. Mary's son, another James, acceded as James VI
on his mother's abdication in July 1567.

On the Scots throne James proved himself an effective ruler, but
in England his indulgence of favourites, authoritarian approach and
apparent disdain for MPs provoked increasingly severe clashes with
Parliament that worsened to the point of breaking during the reign
of his son, Charles I. Charles had many opportunities to broker
a mutually beneficial deal with Parliament, but his refusal to
compromise was a key reason for the slide into civil war in the
1640s, which led to his conviction for treason and subsequent
execution on a wooden platform outside the Banqueting House
in Whitehall one freezing January day in 1649.

*Left: This magnificent triple portrait of Charles I is by Sir Anthony van Dyck. As king
Charles made a series of disastrous political decisions that hastened his own end and the
monarchy's temporary abolition, but he proved a discerning patron in the visual arts.*

JAMES I AND VI
1603–1625

James VI of Scotland learned of his accession to the throne of England in Edinburgh on 26 March 1603, when a horseman brought news to Holyrood Palace of the death two days earlier of Queen Elizabeth I. After an emotional farewell to his own people, James began a prolonged procession through England, reaching London a month later, on 7 May. Everywhere, vast crowds were eager to see the Stuart king come to claim the throne vacated by the Tudors. James became James I when he and his wife Anne were crowned at Westminster Abbey on 25 July 1603.

THE KING'S DIGNITY

In person and manners King James presented a stark and unwelcome contrast to the regal dignity of his illustrious predecessor. A slovenly man, with over-prominent eyes, a large tongue that tended to make him drool and an unfortunate tendency to drunkenness and laziness, he could scarcely have made a greater contrast to the carefully stage-managed public persona of the Virgin Queen. Leading nobles – already somewhat suspicious of the elevation of a Scottish king to rule over England – resented James's expression of his homosexuality in infatuations with effeminate young men such as Robert Carr and George Villiers, both of whom he raised to high office. The king also had a forthright manner of speaking that was far removed from tact. It is said that when annoyed by the large crowds dogging his every move in London, he exclaimed 'God's wounds, I will pull down my breeches and they shall see my arse'.

Yet James's self-indulgent behaviour was allied to a vast intelligence and a highly educated mind convinced of the king's dignity and his absolute right to demand obedience. He had very

Above: Scots king on the English throne. James wanted to create, in his words, 'one kingdom…one uniformity of laws'.

difficult relations with Parliament, which he treated with great tactlessness, often lecturing the Commons on their duty of obedience. Despite his appearance and behaviour, he saw himself as a man of regal bearing, dignity and authority.

'GREAT BRITAIN'

Early in his reign James attempted to combine England and Scotland in a unified kingdom of 'Great Britain'. This was the policy he presented to his first Parliament, called on 22 March 1604. The Commons was not convinced and resisted the union: one member complained that to combine the (Tudor) rose with the (Scottish) thistle might produce a monstrous result.

James defied them. On 20 October 1604 he proclaimed a new title for himself as 'King of Great Britain'. On 12 April 1606 a new Anglo-Scottish flag was introduced for shipping, combining

---

**JAMES I AND VI, KING OF ENGLAND, SCOTLAND
AND IRELAND, 1603–1625**

Birth: 19 June 1566, Edinburgh Castle

Father: Henry Stewart, Lord Darnley

Mother: Mary, Queen of Scots

Accession: 24 July 1567 (Scotland); 24 March 1603 (England)

Inauguration/Coronation: 29 July 1567 (Stirling); 25 July 1603 (Westminster)

Queen: Anne of Denmark (m. 23 Nov 1589; d. 2 March 1619)

Succeeded by: His son Charles I

Greatest achievement: Peaceful union of the crowns of England and Scotland

1603: James recognizes Shakespeare's theatre company as 'King's Men'

18 Aug 1604: England is at peace with Spain

20 Oct 1604: James declares himself 'King of Great Britain'

Nov 1604: Shakespeare's great tragedy *Othello* plays at court

5 Nov 1605: Gunpowder Plot fails

13 May 1607: English settlers found 'Jamestown' in Virginia

1611: King James Authorized Version of the Bible is published

1616: Native American princess Pocahontas meet James at court

23 April 1616: William Shakespeare dies

16 Sept 1620: Pilgrim Fathers leave Plymouth aboard the *Mayflower*

26 Dec 1620: *Mayflower* pilgrims found settlement of New Plymouth

1624: Virginia becomes King's Royal Colony

Death: 27 March 1625, at Theobalds, Hertfordshire. Buried in Westminster Abbey

THE 'KING JAMES VERSION' OF THE BIBLE

A new English translation of the Holy Bible, 'authorized' by King James, was published in 1611. James had proposed a new easily comprehensible English-language version of the Bible in 1601, before his accession in London, when he was ruling as King James VI of Scots. In January 1604, the idea was brought forward again by Oxford University's John Reynolds at a conference on the church, which was held at Hampton Court under Archbishop of Canterbury John Whitgift. James personally approved 54 scholars to work on the translation, of whom 47 were finally involved, working for seven years with the original texts as well as existing English translations. For more than three centuries the work – known as the 'Authorised version' or the 'King James version' – was the standard Bible in English churches.

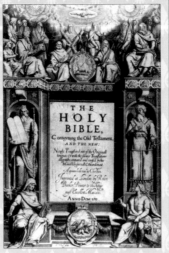

Above: The Authorised Bible, dedicated to James, 'principal mover and author'.

Above: Gunpowder, treason and plot. Victorian artist Sir John Gilbert represents Guy Fawkes kneeling before King James.

and restore Catholicism in England. It followed harsh new laws passed in 1604 against Catholics who refused to worship in Church of England services.

The plot centred on the opening of James's second session of Parliament, scheduled for 5 November 1605. Catholic lords led by Robert Catesby and Guy Fawkes planned to blow up the Palace of Westminster with gunpowder and then foment a Catholic rebellion in the Midlands. Details of the plan came out when one of the gang, Francis Tresham, warned his brother-in-law Lord Mounteagle, who would have been killed in the Lords by the explosion. Lord Mounteagle passed on the information to those in authority and the plot was foiled at the last moment.

---

the crosses of St George and St Andrew and called the 'Great Union' – or the 'Union Jack' (from 'Jacques', the French form of the king's name, which he preferred to use). Nevertheless, the instrument seeking to establish the union of the two countries was rejected in both Parliaments in 1607.

Another matter of pressing concern at the start of the reign was the need to bring an end to the ruinously expensive war with Spain. This was achieved with speed and efficiency – to a large extent, because Spain needed peace even more than England did – in a peace treaty signed in London on 18 August 1604.

THE GUNPOWDER PLOT

James's early reign was marked by rebellions against his rule. The first came in the very year of his accession, when Lord Cobham, Sir Walter Raleigh and other lords were arrested and found

Right: There was an outbreak of the plague at the time, but crowds still flocked to see the coronation of King James in 1603.

guilty of planning to depose James in favour of the king's cousin, Lady Arabella Stuart. On 10 December 1603 James spared Cobham at the very moment of execution, thus making a dramatic demonstration of his royal authority. The second and more serious plot aimed to depose the Protestant James

JAMES AND THE 'NEW WORLD'
THE SETTLEMENT OF AMERICA, 1603–1625

On 10 April 1606, James granted the Virginia companies in London and Bristol a royal charter to explore and settle land on part of the eastern seaboard of North America (roughly corresponding to the territory between northern Maine and Wilmington, North Carolina). Tudor adventurer Sir Walter Raleigh had founded the colony of Virginia, England's first in North America, but settlement there had foundered following the failure of the 'Lost Colony' of Roanoke.

THE JAMESTOWN SETTLEMENT

Three ships under the command of Captain Christopher Newport carrying 120 Virginia Company settlers set sail for North America in December 1606.

When they arrived in Virginia, in April 1607, they named the natural features of the area for the king and princes of the Stuart dynasty – the River James and Capes Henry and Charles – and honoured the king himself in the name of their settlement, Jamestown, which they established on 14 May 1607.

Under the terms of the charter, the land they claimed belonged to the king, with the settlers as sub-tenants of the Charter company. Jamestown had

the distinction of becoming the first permanent English settlement in North America. Government was undertaken by a royal council that was appointed by the king in London.

THE PRINCESS POCAHONTAS

Jamestown came under regular attack by local Native American Algonquians. One of the settlement leaders, Captain John Smith, was kidnapped and held by the Algonquian chief Wahunsonacock, or Powhatan, for four weeks, during which he survived a form of life or death trial in which, the story goes, his life was saved by Powhatan's 11-year-daughter, Pocahontas. Smith was released, became president of the Jamestown council and then was injured by a gunpowder burn and returned to England.

Pocahontas became a regular visitor to the Jamestown settlers, even bringing them gifts of food to help them survive. However, in 1613 one settler, Captain Samuel Argall, repaid her generosity by kidnapping her and holding her to ransom. He demanded the return of English prisoners and stolen firearms plus 'payment' of corn.

Pocahontas's father, Powhatan, paid a part of the ransom, but while Pocahontas was in captivity she was baptized a Christian as 'Lady Rebecca'

Above: This 1609 advertisement promises 'most Excellent fruites', but the first settlers of Virginia endured very lean times.

and fell in love with a European tobacco planter named John Rolfe. Pocahontas and John Rolfe were subsequently married and in 1616 sailed to England for a visit.

The Native American princess and convert was a great attraction in London society. Pocahontas was presented to King James I at court, and she sat with the king watching a masque written by the leading playwright Ben Jonson.

James was captivated by the young woman, and spoke of his plan to found a school in Virginia to educate young Native American children. Most unfortunately, before she and Rolfe could return to Virginia, Pocahontas contracted a fatal illness. She died in 1617 aged only 22.

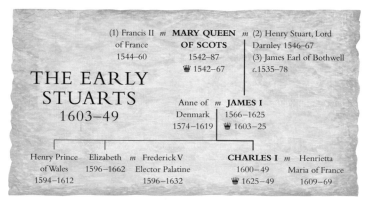

THE EARLY STUARTS 1603–49

(1) Francis II m	**MARY QUEEN**	m (2) Henry Stuart, Lord
of France	**OF SCOTS**	Darnley 1546–67
1544–60	1542–87	(3) James Earl of Bothwell
	♛ 1542–67	c.1535–78

	Anne of	m **JAMES I**
	Denmark	1566–1625
	1574–1619	♛ 1603–25

Henry Prince	Elizabeth	m Frederick V	**CHARLES I**	m Henrietta
of Wales	1596–1662	Elector Palatine	1600–49	Maria of France
1594–1612		1596–1632	♛ 1625–49	1609–69

THE KING'S ROYAL COLONY

A new royal charter of 1609 offered financial interests in the city of London the chance to invest in the Virginia colony. Government was in the hands of the Virginia company treasurer and his council in London, as well as that of a governor and advisory council in Jamestown. Profits were poor, because conditions were difficult and many ships were lost in the Atlantic.

Another royal charter, in 1612, widened the colony boundaries to include the Bermuda Islands and introduced a democratic assembly in Jamestown in 1619.

Conditions remained poor in the colony. James ordered an investigation: the result was that in 1624 he dissolved the London company and Virginia became the King's Royal Colony.

JAMES AND THE MAYFLOWER

On 16 September 1620 one of the most celebrated transatlantic voyages in history began under licence from King

Below: A map of Virginia, with scenes of its early settlement. The engraving was made and published by Thedore de Bry in the first part (1590) of a book on America.

James. Some 101 Puritans departed from Plymouth on board the *Mayflower* seeking a new life free from the religious persecution they suffered at home.

James and the Church of England authorities had been a major source of persecution for those – like many of the *Mayflower* pilgrims – who refused to accept the religious authority of king and church establishment. The king famously declared, 'I shall make them conform or I will harry them out of the land or else do worse'.

One group on board the *Mayflower* joined other travellers from the Netherlands: they were a congregation of English 'Separatists'. The 'Separatists' had been living in exile from James's persecution in the Low Countries for 12 years, since 1608. It was their declared belief that only Christ had authority over the Church.

Despite the fact that the *Mayflower* travellers had had major difficulties with the king, they sought and received royal backing for their venture before they departed. They won both the support of the Virginia Company and a licence from James after an interview in which the king was reportedly impressed by the adventurers' declaration that

Above: Pocahontas. This portrait is based on an engraving made during her 1616 visit to King James's court in London.

they would live by fishing. 'It is certainly an honest trade,' James responded, 'and was indeed the calling of the apostles themselves.'

Storms and high seas prevented the *Mayflower* from landing as intended in Virginia. The ship instead put in at Cape Cod (at the site of modern Provincetown, Massachusetts) on 21 November 1620 before unloading fully on 26 December at a nearby site that the new arrivals christened 'New Plymouth', 37 miles (60 km) south-east of Boston. William Brewster, leader of the Dutch 'Separatists', also became leader of the colony of New Plymouth. In 1621 the settlers in Plymouth gave thanks to God for the first good harvest of the colony with a three-day celebration to which they invited local Native Americans. This is celebrated in the modern 'Thanksgiving' holiday in the United States.

AT THE COURT OF KING JAMES
PLAYERS AND FAVOURITES, 1603–1625

The extraordinary 'English renaissance' of cultural life that began in the London of Queen Elizabeth continued in the reign of King James. In the first year of his reign James honoured William Shakespeare's theatrical company by making them the 'King's Men', and many of Shakespeare's greatest plays were performed at the royal court.

The tragedy *Hamlet*, first performed in 1601, just predated the new reign, but 1603 saw the first performance of *Othello* and the play is known to have been performed at James's court in November 1604. *All's Well that Ends Well* and *Measure for Measure* were first performed in 1604, *King Lear* in 1605, *Macbeth* in 1606 and *Antony and Cleopatra* and *Coriolanus* in 1607. The year 1611 was notable for the first productions of *Cymbeline*, *The Winter's*

Below: A scene from Ben Jonson's Masque of Queens *in the romantic style by Henry Fuseli (1741–1825).*

Tale and *The Tempest*. These later years also saw the publication of Shakespeare's extraordinary *Sonnets*, a collection of 154 poems printed in 1609 by the publisher Thomas Thorpe. The sonnets are mostly in praise of a young nobleman of great beauty, and the published edition was dedicated to 'Mr WH, the onlie begetter of these insuing sonnets'. Rival theories identify WH as William, Lord Herbert, or Henry Wriothesley, Earl of Southampton.

BEN JONSON AND THE MASQUE

In the years after 1605, King James, Queen Anne and their family and courtiers developed a great fondness for 'masques': theatrical performances with ornate costumes, choreographed dances and songs, often on classical themes. Rising playwright Ben Jonson forged a reputation as a creator of these entertainments. A clergyman's son and former bricklayer and soldier, Jonson had already made his mark in the late Elizabethan theatre world. His play

Above: 'Steenie'. This portrait of King James's great favourite George Villiers is by Flemish artist Paul van Somer (d. 1621).

Every Man in His Humour was performed at the Curtain Theatre in 1598 with Shakespeare himself in the cast.

Under King James, Jonson became a popular and well-rewarded figure at court. His first masque was created to give James's queen, Anne, the chance to make up and play a black woman: *The Masque of Blackness* was first put on to celebrate Twelfth Night in 1605. On the same day in 1610, Jonson's masque *Miles a Deo* ('Soldier of God') starred James's eldest son Henry in a performance to celebrate both the Christmas season and Henry's investiture that day as Prince of Wales. In these years Jonson also produced major plays, including *Volpone* (1605), *The Alchemist* (1610) and *Bartholomew Fair* (1614). In 1616 James granted Jonson a life pension: some scholars regard his court position as a forerunner of the 'poet laureate'.

In the first 12 years of the reign the poet John Donne (who was suffering from poverty after a secret 1601 marriage led to imprisonment and ruined his political prospects) made several

attempts to gain employment at court. He was repeatedly rebuffed by King James, who disliked his poetry and once declared, 'Dr. Donne's verses are like the peace of God; they pass all understanding'. James urged Donne to become an Anglican priest. When Donne finally agreed to enter the Church in 1615, James made him a royal chaplain and ordered Cambridge University to make the poet a Doctor of Divinity. Subsequently Donne won the favour of the new court favourite, George Villiers, Marquis of Buckingham, and with his support was made Dean of St Paul's, London. In addition to being a great poet, Donne was one of the greatest preachers of his day.

Also active at James's court was the architect and artist Inigo Jones, remembered as the founder of the English 'classical tradition' in architecture. Beginning in 1605, Jones made his name in London under the patronage of Queen Anne, designing the scenery and costumes for the court masques

Below: Shakespeare and friends. The great cultural figures of King James's London are portrayed by Victorian artist John Faed.

written by Ben Jonson. Then in 1615 he was appointed James's surveyor of building works. His first major work was the Queen's Palace at Greenwich, which he began in 1616 fresh from a 1613–14 tour of Italy in the company of Thomas Howard, second Earl of Arundel, during which Jones studied classical ruins and the work of modern Italian classical architect Andrea Palladio. Jones next rebuilt the Banqueting House in Whitehall in 1619–22.

COURT SCANDALS

King James's homosexual interest in and preferential treatment of handsome young men added spice to life at court. Early in the reign, the favourite was the 17-year-old Robert Carr (or Ker), the son of Scottish nobleman Sir Thomas Ker of Ferniehurst, who enjoyed a meteoric rise. The young man fell just as swiftly from favour, however, when he was found guilty of murder in 1616.

Around this time, James became enamoured of a new favourite, George Villiers, son of a Leicestershire squire. First introduced to the king at the age of 22 in August 1614, Villiers was made a gentleman of the bedchamber

Above: Shakespeare's fellow actors John Heming and Henry Condell prepared this first collected edition of his works (1623), known to scholars as the 'First Folio'.

in April 1615, Master of the Horse in January 1616, a Knight of the Garter in April 1616, Viscount Villiers and Baron Whaddon in August 1616, Earl of Buckingham in 1617, Marquis of Buckingham on 1 January 1618 and Duke of Buckingham in 1623. Villiers was tall and beautifully built with blue eyes and chestnut hair; courtiers reported that the king could scarcely keep his hands off the young man he called 'my Steenie', due to a supposed resemblance to St Stephen, who had 'the face of an angel'.

Buckingham made many enemies at court and among the aristocracy when he exploited his influence to raise his relatives to positions of power. He also succeeded in befriending the heir to the throne, Prince Charles, and travelled with Charles – in disguise – to Madrid on an unsuccessful attempt to negotiate a marriage with the Infanta, daughter of King Philip of Spain. Buckingham's almost entirely negative influence in government and at court lasted beyond the death of King James in 1625.

THE WISEST FOOL IN CHRISTENDOM
KING JAMES'S LEGACY, 1603–1625

James was dubbed 'the wisest fool in Christendom' by King Henry IV of France and he was certainly a king of contradictions: an intellectual who was a bawdy drunkard, a man who claimed regal dignity while behaving with none, a king who declared his divinely sanctioned authority but then allowed himself and his government to be dominated by incompetent 'favourites'. His reign was marked by repeated clashes with an increasingly troublesome and self-willed Parliament.

STRUGGLE WITH PARLIAMENT

As early as 1604 there were disagreements over the extent of the king's self-proclaimed royal prerogatives, and James's extravagance at court led to several angry encounters with Parliament over finance. When MPs refused to place a new series of import duties on merchants, James had the duties declared law by the courts in 1608 as he again

Below: King James left a difficult legacy for Charles I, particularly in the troubled relationship he had with MPs.

Plantation and Settlement of English and Scottish 1556–1620

sought to undermine Parliament's role as supreme legislative body. This led Robert Cecil, Lord Salisbury, to propose a 'Great Contract' under which the king would abandon his royal prerogative to raise money in this way in return for a guaranteed annual grant of taxation. The contract could not be agreed, however, and in February 1611 James dissolved Parliament, angry at its failure to help him solve his financial problems.

The next Parliament of his reign was an unmitigated disaster. James called the Parliament in April 1614 on the advice of Sir Francis Bacon, the attorney general. James wanted the House to vote him money, but MPs were opposed to the king's foreign policy and refused to

Above: The 'Plantation' of Protestants in 17th-century Ireland occurred mainly in the north, but also in pockets elsewhere.

cooperate. The Parliament lasted only two months and did not pass a single piece of legislation.

James's third Parliament, in 1621, brought about a total breakdown of relations between king and MPs. This dramatic clash was largely fuelled by MPs' distaste for James's plan to forge an alliance with Catholic Spain and to negotiate a diplomatic marriage for his son Charles (the future Charles I) with the Infanta, daughter of the Spanish king. When Parliament demanded that Prince Charles seek a Protestant bride,

Above: England and Scotland. The Tudor arms were quartered with the lion rampant of Scotland in the king's great seal.

determined that the marriage should go through) made secret commitments to the French on improved conditions for Catholics in England.

A KING OF CONTRADICTIONS
By this time King James was unwell, severely troubled by arthritis and swiftly ageing. Government was almost entirely in the hands of his favourite, the Duke of Buckingham. James died on 27 March 1625 at his favourite residence, the country mansion of Theobalds in Hertfordshire, after suffering a stroke. He had been a king for all but one of his 59 years and, given the circumstances of his accession to the throne of Scotland in 1567, it was remarkable that he survived his youth to achieve such a long and largely peaceful reign.

A BLOODY INHERITANCE
James left a tragic legacy in Ireland. He backed the 'Plantation' or settlement of Catholic Ulster by Protestant Scots and Englishmen, which began in 1611. Ulster was one of the most strongly Catholic parts of Ireland and was actively rebellious against English government. Under the scheme, Catholic landowners' estates were confiscated and six new counties of Tyrone, Donegal, Armagh, Fermanagh, Derry and Cavan were created. The land was given to Protestant settlers. The 'Plantation', under plans enthusiastically approved by King James in 1608, added further fuel to flames of religious conflict in the region.

that James declare war on Spain and that existing anti-Catholic laws should be imposed with greater force, the king was furious, telling MPs that they had no right to meddle. When MPs then made a protestation of their ancient privileges and declared that every member should enjoy freedom of speech, James dissolved Parliament once more on 30 December 1621. He ripped from the House of Commons journal the pages on which the 'protestation' had been written.

A fourth Parliament, in March 1624, again urged war against Spain and an end to marriage negotiations with the Infanta. Later that year the proposed Spanish marriage – which had been very unlikely since the failure of a diplomatic trip to Spain by Charles and the Duke of Buckingham in 1623 – was replaced with a French match: in November 1624 Charles was betrothed to Henrietta Maria, the 15-year-old sister of King Louis XIII of France. During negotiations James (under pressure from Buckingham, who was

Right: James enjoyed hearing sermons. He patronized John Donne, whom he appointed Dean of St Paul's Cathedral in London.

CHARLES I
1625–1649

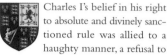

Charles I's belief in his right to absolute and divinely sanctioned rule was allied to a haughty manner, a refusal to change his mind and a damaging willingness to do anything to have his way. These characteristics made him profoundly ill-suited for the task history set him, of handling a troublesome Parliament and maintaining peace between religious factions. His failure led to civil war, his own execution, the abolition of the monarchy and Britain's reinvention as a 'commonwealth'.

Born in Dunfermline Palace in 1600, Charles was six years the junior of Prince Henry, heir to the throne. Charles was a sickly child, so feeble that he did not walk until he turned seven in 1607, and at first he was left behind in Scotland when James progressed southwards to claim the throne of England. However, in 1612 he became heir to the throne, when Henry died of typhoid, and thereafter he grew in confidence. He had a lonely childhood, missing Henry and his sister Elizabeth, who left England in 1613 when she married Frederick, the Elector Palatine of the Rhine. As an adult Charles remained short – he grew no taller than 5ft 4in (1.6m) – and was frail and shy, with a minor speech defect that he never conquered.

INFLUENCE OF BUCKINGHAM

Life at Charles's court was rather more civilized than it had been under the often boorish King James I. Charles was a believer in the importance of manners, ritual and appearances, and he was a keen patron of the arts with a very fine eye for painting. However, in one important sense, government and court life were unchanged: George Villiers, the Duke of Buckingham was

Left: This medal was struck in 1633 to mark the king's return to London following his Scottish coronation in Edinburgh.

Above: Charles I was 24 when he became king. He remained under the disastrous influence of the Duke of Buckingham.

a favourite of Charles, just as he had been of James, and he continued to exert a largely disastrous influence.

MPs were strongly critical of the Duke of Buckingham's disastrous diplomacy and military leadership. The duke's poorly resourced and incompetently led attack on Cadiz was driven back by Spain with humiliating ease in early summer 1626; in June 1626 Charles dissolved the second Parliament

Left: A contemporary woodcut depicts Charles's visit to Spain, before he became king, to negotiate a planned marriage.

Buckingham's death at the hands of a knife-wielding assassin in 1628. The killer, who stabbed Buckingham at the *Greyhound Inn* in Portsmouth, as the duke prepared for yet another raid on La Rochelle, was found to be John Felton, a disgruntled veteran of the previous La Rochelle campaign. He made himself many new friends by despatching the enemy of the House of Commons.

RELIGIOUS TENSIONS HEAT UP

One of Charles's first acts as king was to welcome his new bride to England. In May 1625, Charles and the princess Henrietta Maria, daughter of France's King Henry IV and Queen Marie

Above: Charles married Henrietta Maria in 1625. Their first son, Charles James, was born and died on 13 May 1629.

of his reign after MPs called for the Duke of Buckingham's impeachment. Buckingham, in 1627, led one of two failed attacks to help the Huguenots who were besieged in the French port of La Rochelle; in June 1628 MPs called again for Buckingham to be dismissed from court and government. The sorry saga finally ended with

de'Medici, were married by proxy, and the following month Henrietta Maria landed at Dover from her homeland. Although the Catholic princess was not the Protestant bride that the English Commons and people had hoped for, she was generally preferred to James and Charles's original choice – the Catholic Infanta, daughter of the Spanish king.

Unfortunately, religious tension interfered with Charles's coronation in February 1626: Henrietta Maria refused to attend because the ceremony was performed by a Protestant bishop. She also grew angry over Charles's failure to honour promises made by his father James in the marriage agreement that conditions for English Catholics would be improved.

Religious differences also led to the dissolution of Charles's first Parliament, in August 1625: Charles took offence at MPs' repeated attacks on a clerical group known as the Arminians, who argued – with Charles's sympathy – for a revival of early Church doctrine. They were viewed by members of the 'reformed religion' as Catholics.

CHARLES I, KING OF ENGLAND, SCOTLAND AND IRELAND, 1625–1649	
Birth: 19 Nov 1600, Dunfermline Palace	**12 May 1641:** Execution of Sir Thomas Wentworth, Earl of Strafford
Father: James VI of Scots (later James I of 'Great Britain')	**22 Nov 1641:** Parliament passes Grand Remonstrance against the king
Mother: Anne of Denmark	**3 Jan 1642:** Charles fails to arrest leaders of parliamentary opposition
Accession: 27 March 1625	
Coronation: 2 Feb 1626, Westminster Abbey; 18 June 1633, Holyrood Palace, Edinburgh	**13 Sept 1642:** Civil war: Charles raises royal standard
Queen: Henrietta Maria (m. 13 June 1625; d. 21/31 August 1669)	**23 Oct 1642:** First skirmish, Battle of Edghill
Succeeded by: His son Charles II in Scotland; after Charles I was executed in 1649, the monarchy was abolished and England declared a commonwealth	**25 Sept 1643:** Solemn League and Covenant allies English Puritans and Scots Presbyterians
	2 July 1644: Major royalist defeat at Battle of Marston Moor
Greatest achievement: Dignity with which he faced trial and execution	**14 June 1645:** Decisive Parliamentary victory in Battle of Naseby
23 Aug 1628: Buckingham assassinated	**Jan 1647:** After fleeing to Scotland, Charles is handed into the care of Parliament
10 March 1629: Dissolves Parliament and declares he will rule alone	
April 1630: John Winthrop leads Puritans into exile in Massachussetts	**20–27 Jan 1649:** On trial before High Court in London
1638–9: Defeated in the First Bishops' War in Scotland	**Death:** 30 Jan 1649, executed in Whitehall, buried in St George's Chapel, Windsor
1640: Defeated in the Second Bishops' War in Scotland	

COUNTDOWN TO CIVIL WAR
CHARLES I AND PARLIAMENT, 1625–1641

In the late 1620s Charles continued to be in direct conflict with Parliament over two main issues – revenue and religion.

Following great unrest provoked by his imposition of a 'forced loan' collected under threat of imprisonment, in 1628 Charles was forced to approve a 'petition of right' that guaranteed his subjects freedom from, among other things, arbitrary taxation. Henceforth, no man might be 'Compelled to make or yield any gift, loan, benevolence, tax or such like charge, without common consent by Act of Parliament'.

The same year William Laud, a supporter of the controversial Arminian doctrine became Bishop of London.

In a dramatic development on 2 March 1629, MPs outmanoeuvred the king to pass laws condemning attempts to raise taxes without parliamentary backing and attacking efforts to impose Arminianism. Charles had instructed the Speaker of the House, Sir John Finch, to rise when MPs began to debate and so prevent any laws being passed, but two MPs – Denzil Holles and Benjamin Valentine – forcibly held the Speaker in the chair, while others locked the door against the king's messenger, Black Rod, who had been sent to dissolve Parliament. In this way they were able to pass the laws that Charles opposed.

As a result on 10 March 1629 Charles dissolved Parliament, announcing that he would rule without its backing.

Above: Charles I. Anthony van Dyck, court painter from 1632, is celebrated for his sensitivity to the character of his subjects.

Speaking of the Commons, he declared, 'I know there are many there as dutiful subjects as any in the world; it being but some few Vipers amongst them that did cast this Mist of Undutifulness over most of their Eyes'.

DEFICIT IN ROYAL FINANCES
Thereafter, unable to levy taxation with parliamentary backing, Charles had to come up with ingenious schemes of doubtful legality to raise money in order to cover a deficit in the royal finances that was running at £20,000 a year by the mid-1630s. The 'ship tax' was levied on coastal areas – officially to fund the Royal Navy – and afterwards extended to inland areas also. Charles also raised customs duties and revived venerable 'forest laws'. These allowed fines to be imposed on those who encroached on ancient royal forests and were now applied to areas such as Essex, which had been forest in the past but had since been cleared. Having bypassed Parliament, the king was acting with no apparent restraint – a landowner named

RELIGIOUS EXILES

In 1630 John Winthrop led a mass exodus of Puritans to the New World, in flight from what they saw as excessive Catholic influence at court. In 1629 they obtained a charter from King Charles to establish the Massachussetts Bay Company. The king understood it to be a commercial venture, but Winthrop and friends were determined to found a Puritan colony. Winthrop was elected governor of the new colony before departure. He set sail aboard the *Arbella* at the head of a fleet of 11 ships containing 700 people in April 1630. In America, he was re-elected a number of times as governor of the fledgling colony. He wrote a celebrated sermon, 'The City on a Hill', which cast Puritan exiles as parties to a special agreement with God to found a sacred society. Another quite different religious exile founded

Maryland, named in honour of Charles's queen, Henrietta Maria. Cecilius Calvert, second Baron Baltimore, was a Roman Catholic who received a grant of territory from Charles to establish Maryland in 1632. Baltimore founded the colony both as a commercial enterprise and as a place of refuge where Catholics could live and worship in freedom.

Right: George, father of Cecilius Calvert. The colony of Maryland was his idea, but he died before it was realized.

John Bankes challenged the legality of the extension of the ship money but lost his case in court, in June 1638, in a decision that served to increase bad feeling against the king.

The fear of Catholic influence at home was heightened by Charles's reissue in 1633 of King James's *Book of Sports*. This specified the sports that were permissible on the Sabbath – and offended Puritans who argued that the Sabbath should be kept free of all sports and recreations, including music. Worse still in Puritan eyes was the 1634 visit to Queen Henrietta Maria of papal legate Gregorio Panzani and the public knowledge that the Catholic Mass was celebrated every day for the queen in the palace in Whitehall.

LAVISH ARTS SPENDING

Meanwhile at court, despite financial troubles and increasing public ill-feeling at Charles's unusual means of raising money from his people, the king spent lavishly on the arts. He hired the finest artists and put together a collection of Europe's greatest paintings. Charles commissioned works by leading artists such as Peter Paul Rubens and Anthony van Dyck and in 1632 made van Dyck court painter. He hired Rubens to paint scenes of King James I's apotheosis on the ceiling of the Inigo Jones's Banqueting House in Whitehall.

In 1634 van Dyck painted a celebrated equestrian portrait of King Charles and in 1637 the well-known *Charles I in Three Positions*.

The king bought works by Titian, Raphael and Mantegna for the royal art collection. He viewed the collection as an expression of his regal authority and dignity and wanted it to be the equal to that of any European royal house. To this end, he put the collection under the control of Dutch art expert Abraham van der Doort.

Left: John Winthrop, first governor of Massachussetts, believed that God had chosen him for sainthood in his lifetime.

Above: Van Dyck painted several imposing portraits of Charles, seeking to express the king's belief in his divine right to rule.

As in his father James's reign, masques were a popular form of entertainment at court, with many designed by the great Inigo Jones. Doubtless Charles enjoyed escaping from the troubling political and religious struggles of his day into a well-ordered world that honoured ruler and courtiers. Inigo Jones and Ben Jonson collaborated on more than 30 masques, but had a disagreement in 1631 after which other playwrights and poets including James Shirley and Thomas Carew authored the masques.

THE ENGLISH CIVIL WAR
1642–1649

 The beginning of the long struggle that became the English Civil War can be traced to Charles's 1637 decision to impose on the Scots a Book of Common Prayer almost exactly the same as the one used in England. This provoked strong opposition among Scottish Presbyterians, who saw the move as an Anglo-Catholic assault on the purity of their religion: in 1638 they signed a National Covenant to uphold their faith. Charles first attempted negotiation, at a general assembly of the Church of Scotland, in Glasgow, in November 1638, and when that failed, he found himself faced by a Scottish Covenanter army. He raised a royalist force and marched north, but in the First Bishops' War could not defeat the Covenanters and was forced to agree peace in June 1639.

Above: Key figures of the Civil War, including the Earl of Essex (top left) and Cromwell (bottom, second from left).

THE LONG PARLIAMENT

In April 1640, Charles called his first Parliament for 11 years to try to raise money for further military action in Scotland. He encountered concerted opposition in the Commons and so dismissed the Short Parliament after just three weeks. He then went ahead with the planned campaign in Scotland, but the Second Bishops' War ended in another defeat and Charles was forced into both a humiliating peace at Ripon and into recalling Parliament.

This Parliament would sit until 1660 and is known as the Long Parliament. The king's opponents in the Commons had Charles's most able minister, Thomas Wentworth, Earl of Strafford, impeached and then executed under a bill of attainder in May 1641. Charles was forced to concede that 'ship money' and his other financial levies were illegal and that Parliament could not be dissolved without its own agreement. On 22 November 1641 the Commons then passed a 'Grand Remonstrance' listing Charles's many failings since his accession. It called for royal ministers to be approved by Parliament and for the appointment of a Parliament-nominated assembly to oversee church reform.

A Catholic uprising in Ireland led Charles to raise another army, and MPs, fearful that he would use it against them, demanded that he relinquish control of the troops. He angrily refused and, in January 1642, took the bold step

Left: Captive king. This woodcut shows Charles under house arrest at Carisbrooke Castle, Isle of Wight, in late 1647.

of entering the Commons with an armed guard to arrest ringleader MPs for treason. He came too late. The MPs in question had been tipped off and escaped into hiding on a river barge.

Charles now fled London, heading for northern England. Queen Henrietta Maria and Princess Mary left the country to raise financial support for the king in Continental Europe, and England prepared for civil war.

FIRST SKIRMISHES

Charles raised the royal standard at Nottingham on 13 September 1642 and began to move on London as the Parliamentarians gathered an untrained army under the Earl of Essex. The first major clash, at Edghill near Banbury on 23 October 1642, was a victory for the king, although the Parliamentarian army retreated in good order. A second clash at Brentford, west of London, on 11 November was also a royalist victory, but a third, at nearby Turnham Green two days later, saw the 12,000-odd royalist troops defeated by a 25,000-strong Parliamentarian force.

The royalist advance on London was thus turned back, ending Charles's chances of securing a quick victory.

HONOURS EVEN

In 1643 fortunes swung to and fro, with royalist victories in Yorkshire and the south-west followed by a Parliamentarian fight-back that again blocked the king's approach to London. A key event was the signing of the 'Solemn League and Covenant', which pledged alliance between English Puritans and Scottish Presbyterians and provided a Scottish army to support the Parliamentary cause.

The Scottish Covenanters provided crucial support to the Parliamentarian army at the Battle of Marston Moor on 2 July 1644, when the royalists were swept away by a crack cavalry force led by Oliver Cromwell. However, later in the year Charles defeated the Earl of Essex at Lostwithiel, in Cornwall.

THE TIDE TURNS

1645 was the decisive year. Although royalist troops in Scotland under Montrose won a famous victory over Covenanters at Inverlochy in February, in England the Parliamentarians established the highly disciplined 'New Model Army' under the command of Fairfax and Cromwell and won a series of important victories; not least the overwhelming defeat of Charles's army at Naseby, Northants, on 14 June. In November Charles retreated to Oxford.

In spring 1646, as the Parliamentarians prepared to besiege Oxford, the king fled in disguise. He escaped to Scotland, but was handed back to the care of the English Parliament in January 1647. Kept at first under house arrest in Northants, Charles was taken into army custody in June 1647 as a new civil conflict developed between the New

Above: Major battles of the English Civil Wars. Parliamentarians won key victories at Marston Moor and Naseby in 1644–5.

Model Army and Parliament. After a final victory over Scottish royalists at Preston in August 1648, the army took control.

On 20 November, General Henry Ireton presented Parliament with the 'Remonstrance of the Army', which demanded that Charles be put on trial for treason. Parliament still hoped to reach a compromise with the king and rejected the document.

On 6 December Colonel Thomas Pride reduced the Commons to a 'rump' that would be obedient to the will of the military. At Christmas 1648 Charles was brought to Windsor Castle. The army hierarchy was determined to achieve its aims: the trial and execution of the king and the abolition of the monarchy.

THE EXECUTION OF CHARLES I
1649

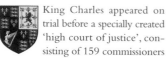

King Charles appeared on trial before a specially created 'high court of justice', consisting of 159 commissioners appointed by the 'Rump' Parliament, in the Painted Chamber at the Palace of Westminster on 20 January 1649. Security was tight: soldiers watched the movements of the crowd, guards perched on the palace roof and the high court president, John Bradshaw, wore a steel-lined hat to protect him from assassins' bullets.

CHARGED WITH TREASON

The king was charged with having governed according to his will and not by law, with having waged war 'against the present Parliament and the people there represented' and with having committed treason against his own people – a neat reversal of the usual definition of treason. Charles refused to defend himself, or enter a plea in response to the

Below: Charles tried to project an aura of authority despite losing control of his destiny. This portrait by Edward Bower (fl 1635–67) shows the king at trial.

charge, as he denied that the court had any authority over him. He declared, 'I would know by what power I am called hither…by what authority' and warned the court, 'Remember I am your king, your lawful king', adding, 'I have a trust committed to me by God, by old and lawful descent, [and] I will not betray it, to answer a new unlawful authority'.

'TYRANT AND PUBLIC ENEMY'

The trial lasted eight days. Witnesses described the king's physical involvement in the battles of the civil war, while alleging that he approved atrocities against the people and that he tried his utmost while in captivity to stir up and prolong the wars.

Sentence was passed on 27 January. The high court found the king guilty as a 'Tyrant, traitor, murderer and public enemy to the Commonwealth of England' and sentenced him to be 'Put to death by the severing of his head from his body'.

John Bradshaw, president of the court, addressed Charles for 40 minutes, declaring that when a king entered battle against his own people he lost his claim to their allegiance, and arguing that even a monarch was subject to the law as it issued from Parliament. Charles was shocked and upset to discover that

Above: Signatories of Charles's death warrant included army men Oliver Cromwell and Henry Ireton but not Sir Thomas Fairfax, army commander.

he was not allowed to reply. Instead, with the death sentence ringing in his ears, he was taken to St James's Palace to await his end. Just 59 commissioners of the 159 appointed signed the king's death warrant.

Below: The king faces his accusers in the High Court of Justice on 27 January.

'MARTYR OF THE PEOPLE'

The execution was planned for early in the morning of the following day, 30 January 1649. It was a bitterly cold day: Charles wore two shirts from fear that he would be cold and shiver, giving onlookers the impression that he was trembling with fear. He gave instructions for sharing out his intimate possessions among his children, including his gold watch and his Bible, and he received Holy Communion.

However, the execution was delayed because Cromwell was told that under current law a king's successor must be declared at the moment of a royal death. The king was forced to wait while Parliament drafted and hurried through three readings of a bill declaring it illegal to make a proclamation of succession. It was not until 2 p.m. that Charles came out from the Banqueting House in Whitehall on to the platform specially raised against its side, where a large crowd had gathered.

Charles walked forth confident and fearless and made a final statement, declaring his loyalty to the Church of England and arguing that the people should have no part in government, saying, 'A subject and a sovereign are clean

different things'. He then proclaimed, 'I am the martyr of the people' and forgave those who were responsible for his death. His last words were, 'I go from a corruptible to an incorruptible crown, where no disturbance can be'.

Because the executioner's block was very low, Charles had to lie down rather than kneel. When he was ready he made a pre-arranged signal with his hands and his head was cut off with one blow. The assistant to the executioner held

THE CULT OF THE KING

Mindful that Charles could indeed become a martyr in death, the authorities arranged for his burial in St George's Chapel, Windsor Castle, well away from the London crowds, rather than in Westminster Abbey. His embalmed body – with the head sewn back in place – was moved to Windsor by water and he was buried in the castle on 8 February 1649. The authorities outlawed public mourning and declared that there would be no state funeral for the king.

But they were unable to stop the tide of emotion that made a bestseller of a book of the king's supposed meditations

and prayers in his final days. The book – Eikon Basilike, The Pourtraicture of His Sacred Majestie in his Solitude and Sufferings, ghostwritten by John Gauden, chaplain to the earl of Warwick – went through 40 English-language editions in 1649 alone, and was translated into many languages including French, Latin, Dutch and Danish.

Subsequently, with the Restoration of the monarchy, the 'cult' of King Charles I was encouraged and in 1660 Parliament declared the king to be a martyr and made him a saint of the Anglican Church.

the decapitated head aloft and a moan – perhaps of grief, perhaps of horror at the killing of a king – was heard from the watching crowd.

Pandemonium broke out among the crowd as hundreds of people struggled to dip scraps of cloth in the royal blood.

Below: Charles was defiant unto death. Dutch artist Weesop painted this 'Eyewitness Representation of the Execution of King Charles I'.

COMMONWEALTH AND PROTECTORATE

1649–1660

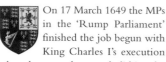

On 17 March 1649 the MPs in the 'Rump Parliament' finished the job begun with King Charles I's execution when they passed an act abolishing the monarchy and making England a 'Commonwealth and free state'. The act also abolished the House of Lords and proclaimed Parliament 'supreme authority of this nation'.

There was still powerful opposition to be faced, however. In September 1649, Cromwell was despatched to Ireland to put down a royalist uprising among Irish royalists. He won devastating victories at Wexford and Drogheda. Then in June 1650, having been made Commander-in-Chief of the Commonwealth forces, Cromwell marched north to Scotland, where the Covenanters were promoting the cause of Charles I's son, Charles.

Cromwell won a resounding victory over a Covenanter army at Dunbar on 3 September 1650, but royalist opposition

Below: Army commander, England's Protector. True to his convictions, Cromwell twice turned down the offer of the throne.

Above: Cromwell's crown. This gold five-shilling coin was minted in London in 1658.

persisted, and on 1 January 1651 Charles Stuart was crowned King Charles II of England, Scotland, Ireland and France (the last title traditional), at Scone in Scotland.

In August that year Charles led an army of Scots and royalist sympathisers across the border and marched on London. However, Cromwell inflicted a devastating defeat on him at Worcester on 3 September, forcing him to flee in disguise and go into hiding.

GOVERNING WITHOUT A KING

Although Oliver Cromwell had made the Commonwealth safe, the execution of the king had created a power vacuum and the search for a stable form of government proved a difficult one. As Commander-in-Chief of the army, Cromwell was the dominant figure. He eventually became frustrated at delays in the Rump Parliament, which was supposed to be planning for the election of a new assembly.

On 20 April 1653 Cromwell declared the Rump Parliament dissolved, angrily telling the House, 'You have sat here too long for the good you do. In the name of God, go!' He did not act in order to bolster his own position, but his behaviour was painfully reminiscent of

A SUCCESSION OF PARLIAMENTS

13 April–6 May 1640: 'Short Parliament' dissolved by King Charles I after three weeks

3 Nov 1640: Charles I calls 'Long Parliament'; not formally dissolved until 16 March 1660

7 Dec 1648: Col Thomas Pride 'purges' the Long Parliament to create the compliant 'Rump Parliament'

20 April 1653: Cromwell dissolves the Rump Parliament;

4 July 1653: New 'Barebones Parliament' assembles

12 Dec 1653: Barebones Parliament dissolved; Cromwell becomes Lord Protector

16 May 1659: Army leaders recall the Rump Parliament

Feb 1660: Members excluded in Pride's Purge are recalled to reconstitute the Long Parliament

16 March 1660: The Long Parliament votes to dissolve ahead of new elections

25 April 1660: The Pro-Royalist 'Convention Parliament' meets

the acts of Stuart 'tyranny' that had provoked the Civil War and led to the execution of a king.

KING OR LORD PROTECTOR?

A new Parliament was appointed, made up of 140 officially approved Puritans. The first parliament to represent the whole of the British Isles, it was nicknamed the 'Barebones Parliament' from the name of one of its members, the Anabaptist Praisegod Barebones. It was short lived, for in December 1653 it voted itself out of existence and put power into the hands of Cromwell. He thus became the first man to rule a unitary state of Great Britain and Ireland.

Above: 'In the name of God, go!' Like the Stuart kings before him, Cromwell dismissed troublesome MPs – including members of the Rump Parliament in 1653.

Major-General John Lambert was behind this development – essentially a coup – and he tried to persuade Cromwell to become king. Cromwell refused, however, providing proof of his religious sincerity and rectitude of character: he was convinced that it had been God's will for the monarchy to be abolished and he would not countenance its reintroduction. Instead he agreed to become 'Lord Protector'.

This change was introduced under England's first written constitution, the 'Instrument of Government', which made the country a Protectorate. Government was to be by the Lord Protector through a council of state and the House of Commons. Religious toleration was to be guaranteed for all, except Catholics.

When the new Parliament met in 1654 its attempts to alter the constitution and notably to restrict religious toleration led Cromwell to dissolve it once more. In July 1655 he introduced a new system of government under which 12 major-generals were appointed, with each ruling one of 12 English regions.

However, this system also proved unpopular and ineffective. Another House of Commons was elected in 1656.

In April-May 1657, the Commons again urged Cromwell to take the crown and become King Oliver, but after agonizing over the decision and, according to some accounts coming very close to accepting, Cromwell refused again. He declared, 'I would not seek to set up that that providence hath destroyed and laid in the dust'.

On 3 September 1658, Cromwell died aged 59. The extent to which he had become king in all but name, and in contradiction of his dearly held beliefs, was marked by the fact that he named his son, Richard, to be Lord Protector in his stead.

THE RETURN TO MONARCHY

Richard Cromwell's rule lasted only eight months. He resigned as Lord Protector when army leaders recalled the 'Rump Parliament' of 1648. The Rump Parliament could not impose its authority, however, and MPs and army still fought for supremacy.

In early 1660 General Monck, commander of the army in Scotland, marched to London and won the agreement of the Rump assembly to dissolve itself and recall the Long Parliament originally formed in 1640. This opened the way for a new election and another new Parliament and the prospect of a return of the monarchy.

A KING ON THE RUN

After the destruction of his hopes of regaining the crown at the Battle of Worcester on 3 September 1651, Charles II fled the battlefield in a charge of cavalry down Worcester High Street. He was on the run.

Changing into some old clothes and applying blacking to his face as disguise, he cut across country towards the sea. He attempted to take the ferry over the river Severn but, finding it guarded, he turned back to seek cover in woodland. By good fortune he met a Catholic royalist, William Carlis, who warned him that Cromwell's men were searching the woods. The pair decided to hide in the branches of a lone oak tree in an open field, reasoning that it was so prominent a spot that it would not be searched. Later Charles travelled in disguise as the servant of Miss Jane Lane, sister of a royalist colonel, and finally – some six weeks after Worcester – made it to Shoreham, west Sussex, from where he fled to safety in France aboard a coal brig, the *Surprise*.

Below: Before his failed invasion of England, Charles II was crowned at Scone in 1651.

CHAPTER EIGHT

THE RESTORATION
OF THE STUARTS

1660–1714

The execution of King Charles I on 30 January 1649 appeared to be
the end for the royal house of Stuart. Indeed, when Parliament
abolished the monarchy on 17 March 1649, it seemed to mark the
point of no return for all of England's royal rulers. However, after
the death of Oliver Cromwell in 1658 and the apparent failure of the
Commonwealth and Protectorate, Charles I's son Charles Stuart was
recalled from exile in the Low Countries. He returned to London amid
public rejoicing on 29 May 1660. Diarist John Evelyn recorded, 'This
day came in his Majesty Charles the 2nd to London after a sad and long
exile ... with a triumph of above 20,000 horse and foot, brandishing
their swords and shouting with unexpressable joy: the ways strewn with
flowers, the bells ringing, the streets hung with tapestry ... the windows
and balconies all set with ladys, trumpets, music, and ... people flocking
the streets.' Charles II was crowned on 23 April 1661.

Stuart monarchs reigned for a further 54 years. Even when
Charles II's Catholic brother, James II, was overthrown and replaced
according to the will of Parliament by the Protestant William III,
Stuarts remained on the throne, for William was Charles II's nephew
and William's wife and joint sovereign, Mary II, was James II's daughter.
The Stuart line is said to have ended with the death of Mary's sister,
Queen Anne, and the accession under the Act of Settlement of King
George, first ruler of the House of Hanover. However, even George
had a blood connection to the Stuarts, for he was the son of Sophia,
Electress of Hanover, who was King James I's granddaughter.

*Left: Monarchy restored, in an imposing figure. Charles II was powerfully built, standing
6ft 2in (1.88m) tall. He had black hair, an olive complexion and dark brown eyes.*

CHARLES II
1660–1685

Charles Stuart, son of the executed King Charles I, arrived in London to claim the English throne on 29 May 1660, his 30th birthday. Cheering crowds lined the streets, flowers were cast in the roadway and the bells rang out in the City of London to acclaim the restoration of the English monarchy following the harsh years of the English Commonwealth and Protectorate.

Some three and a half months earlier, on 16 March, the reconstituted Long Parliament of 1640 had voted to dissolve ahead of elections. The newly elected Convention Parliament that assembled on 25 April was strongly pro-royalist and on 1 May declared that the government should be by a restored king, House of Lords and House of Commons. MPs approved Charles's restoration on the basis of the king's Declaration of Breda, in the Low Countries, which he issued on 4 April. He promised a general pardon; liberty of conscience in religion; to pay the army and take soldiers into his own service on the same conditions they presently enjoyed; and to entrust Parliament with settling disputes over land ownership arising from the troubles of the previous 20 years. On this basis, the Lords and Commons proclaimed Charles king on 8 May.

CHARLES II, KING OF ENGLAND, SCOTLAND AND IRELAND, 1660–1685

Birth: 29 May 1630, St James's Palace, London

Father: Charles I

Mother: Henrietta Maria

Accession: 30 Jan 1649

Coronation: 1 Jan 1651, Scone (Scotland); 23 April 1661 (Westminster Abbey)

Queen: Catherine of Braganza (m. 21 May 1662; d. 1705)

Succeeded by: His brother, James II

Greatest achievement: Regaining and retaining the crown

4 April 1660: Charles Stuart issues Declaration of Breda

8 May 1660: Parliament proclaims him King Charles II

29 May 1660: Charles enters London

24 March 1663: Grants North American lands of 'Carolina' to eight wealthy noblemen

8 July 1663: Grants royal charter to Rhode Island colony

2–6 Sept 1666: Great Fire of London

1678: Former priest Titus Oates alleges Catholic plot to kill Charles

1681: Grants lands of Pennsylvania to Quaker William Penn

1683: Rye House Plot foiled

Death: 6 Feb 1685. Buried in King Henry VIII Chapel, Westminster Abbey

---

A FINE CORONATION

Colour, spectacle and glamour were emphasized in Charles's coronation on 23 April 1661. Wearing robes of crimson velvet and cloth of gold, riding a horse fitted with a gold- and pearl-encrusted saddle, he rode through the city in a magnificent procession past splendid theatrical tableaux, from Tower Hill to Westminster Abbey.

London diarist Samuel Pepys attended the Coronation ceremony in the Abbey. It was so crowded, he reported, that he had to take his place some seven hours before the service began. He saw, 'The king in his robes, bare headed, which was very fine … in the Quire at the high altar he passed all the ceremonies of the Coronacion … the crowne being put upon his head, a great shout begun … and three times the King-at-arms … proclaimed that if any one could show any reason why Ch.Steward should not be King of

Below: King Charles II's coronation procession. New crowns and regalia were made at a cost of £12,000.

Above: On the night of the Great Fire of London, flames illuminate Ludgate and old St Paul's. This anonymous oil painting of the disaster was made c.1670.

sacredness of absolute monarchy, Charles was not a pious or particularly serious man. He was charismatic and charming and a passionate collector of mistresses, even after his 1662 wedding to the Portuguese Infanta, Catherine of Braganza. He once declared that he did not believe God would 'Make a man miserable only for taking a little pleasure out of the way'.

PLAGUE AND FIRE

There were many among the new king's population who looked with horror at his court's devotion to pleasure. When two disasters struck England within years of the Restoration, Puritan critics could claim that the events were evidence of God's displeasure at the hasty abandonment of England's great republican experiment.

Bubonic plague was a regular threat to London's crowded streets from the start of the 17th century onwards, but it hit with particular virulence following a heat wave in June 1665. Charles, his court and Parliament fled to Oxford, while the exchequer was moved to Surrey. In London, fires burned in the streets in an attempt to cleanse the air. As many as 70,000 people died.

Then on 2–6 September 1666 the Great Fire of London ravaged the capital. Beginning in the early hours of 2 September at the king's bakery in

Above: The plague was a recurrent threat. Charles was happy to revive the traditional practice of royal cure by laying on hands.

Pudding Lane, close to London Bridge, the fire was whipped by a strong east wind and spread quickly through London's narrow streets of tightly packed wooden houses. Pepys wrote, 'We saw the fire as only one entire arch of fire…it made me weep to see it. The churches, houses, and all on fire and flaming at once, and horrid noise the flames made, and the cracking of houses at their ruin'.

The Great Fire made 100,000 people homeless and destroyed 13,000 houses and 87 parish churches as well as St Paul's Cathedral. On 4 September King Charles did his reputation no harm by turning out to fight the fire with his people in the streets. He could be seen, clothes sodden and face blackened with smoke, working side by side with the desperate Londoners. He also sent food to the poverty-stricken and money to boost fire control efforts. Afterwards he promised the devastated people of London that he would build a splendid new city of stone and brick.

England, that he should come and speak'. Afterwards silver medals were thrown into the congregation, but Pepys was unable to get hold of one. A splendid coronation feast followed, then as the day ended a great thunderstorm burst over Whitehall – which Pepys interpreted as a good omen for the new king's reign.

A LOVER OF PLEASURE

While he was astute in his handling of parliamentary, military and religious factions, and a convinced believer in the

OAK APPLE DAY

After Charles's triumphant entry into London on 29 May 1660, Parliament voted that this day should be kept as a national holiday; in the words of diarist Samuel Pepys, 'As a day of thanksgiving for our redemption from tyranny and the king's return to his Government'. It was named Oak Apple Day, a reference to Charles's escape from the troops of the Parliamentary army when he hid in an oak tree near Boscobel House, Shropshire, following the Battle of Worcester, in 1651.

Above: Protective species that sheltered a king, the oak tree is celebrated as a symbol of endurance and of Englishness.

THE MERRY MONARCH
RESTORATION LIFE

 On 21 May 1662 Charles II married the pious Catholic princess Catherine of Braganza, daughter of the King of Portugal. Under the marriage treaty, which cemented an English-Portuguese-French alliance against Spain, Catherine would maintain her allegiance to the Catholic Church while agreeing that any children of the marriage should be raised as Protestants. On the wedding day, the royal couple went through two ceremonies. The first, conducted in private, was a Catholic one. The second, conducted in public, was the official Church of England rite.

MANY MISTRESSES

Queen Catherine brought a vast dowry to the marriage, which included £360,000 and the Portuguese overseas possessions of Bombay and Tangier. Charles, for his part, promised that he intended to be a good husband. However, marriage vows did not prevent the promiscuous king from continuing to pursue his favourite sport of collecting mistresses. One of these, Lady Castlemaine, was a long-standing lover whom Charles had met before the Restoration, at Breda. At his wedding she was appointed among Queen Catherine's ladies of the bedchamber,

despite the fact that she had borne Charles a son the previous year. Subsequently, Charles recognized several children of this liaison as his own, and according to royal convention gave them the name 'Fitzroy'.

Another mistress of the early years was Lucy Walter, the daughter of a prominent Welsh family and 'Brown, beautiful and bold' according to diarist John Evelyn. She was intimate with the king in 1648–51, and her son of 1649, initially known as 'James Fitzroy', later became James Scott, Duke of Monmouth, who was championed as a possible Protestant successor to King Charles in his latter years.

Another mistress was Italian duchess Hortense Mancini, to whom Charles gave rooms in St James's Palace, where he visited her nightly. According to court gossips, he was drawn as much by her expertise in the arts of love as by her alluring dark beauty.

Among Charles's most celebrated lovers was actress Nell Gwynn, who became the king's mistress in 1670. She reportedly called him Charles the Third on the grounds that he was 'The third Charley' she had accepted into her bed. The following year the king also took up with a French Catholic noble-woman, Louise de Kéroualle. When

Above: Restoration gallant. The king's roguish love of pleasure is suggested in this portrait by Peter Lely (1618–80).

the outspoken Nell Gwynn had her carriage jostled by a crowd who had mistaken her for her unpopular Catholic rival, she exclaimed, 'Pray good people be civil, I am the Protestant whore'.

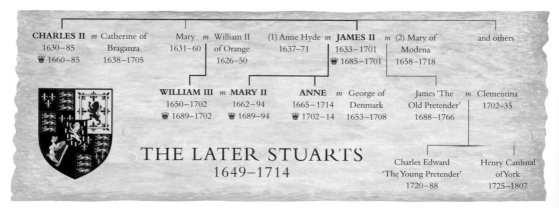

CHARLES II	*m*	Catherine of	Mary	*m*	William II	(1) Anne Hyde	*m*	JAMES II	*m*	(2) Mary of	and others
1630–85		Braganza	1631–60		of Orange	1637–71		1633–1701		Modena	
♕ 1660–85		1638–1705			1626–50			♕ 1685–1701		1658–1718	

		WILLIAM III	*m*	MARY II	ANNE	*m*	George of	James 'The	*m*	Clementina
		1650–1702		1662–94	1665–1714		Denmark	Old Pretender'		1702–35
		♕ 1689–1702		♕ 1689–94	♕ 1702–14		1653–1708	1688–1766		

THE LATER STUARTS
1649–1714

Charles Edward	Henry Cardinal
'The Young Pretender'	of York
1720–88	1725–1807

Above: Barbara Villiers, Lady Castlemaine. Charles II reputedly spent his first night as king in her company. Samuel Pepys reported her exceptional beauty.

Above: 'Pretty, witty Nell'. Nell Gwynn was the only one of Charles's mistresses to be popular with the public. She was widely liked for her impudence and indiscretions.

racing establishment, the Palace House Stables. His love of entertainment, coupled with his easy-going manner and enjoyment of pleasure, won him the nickname the 'Merry Monarch'.

RESTORATION THEATRE

Charles II was a keen and appreciative patron of the arts and sciences. London's theatres had been closed by the Puritan establishment in the years of the Commonwealth and the Protectorate. In 1662, Charles granted patents to Thomas Killigrew and Sir William Davenant to open theatres. Thomas Killigrew inaugurated the *Theatre Royal* in Covent Garden on 7 May 1663 with a performance of *The Humorous Lieutenant* by John Fletcher and Francis Beaumont.

After the years of repression, London's theatres burst forth once more in the vibrant stage scene of 'Restoration theatre'. The works of playwrights John Dryden (appointed Poet Laureate in 1668), Beaumont and Fletcher, and William Wycherley were widely performed and praised to the skies. Henry Purcell was appointed court composer in 1677.

Below: Londoners rejoiced at the reopening of the city's theatres at the Restoration. This engraving shows the Duke's Theatre, Lincoln's Inn Fields, in Charles II's time.

SPORT AND GAMES

Charles was also a lover of sports. Before the English Restoration, when he was crowned King by the Scots at Scone in 1651, he rounded off the celebrations that followed a vast banquet by playing a round of golf. He also pioneered yachting in England. His first taste of the sport came when he received a small racing yacht, the *Mary*, from the City of Amsterdam as a present to mark the Restoration. He himself then designed a larger version that was christened the *Jamie*. On 1 October 1661 he raced the *Jamie* against his brother, the Duke of York, sailing a Dutch yacht called the *Bezan* from Greenwich to Gravesend and back again. Charles's *Jamie* won by a distance of 3 miles (5km).

At Newmarket in Suffolk the king was a frequent visitor to the racecourse, and rode his own stallion, 'Old Rowley', in races on the heath. On 14 October 1671 the king won a race over 4 miles (6.5km) on the Newmarket course. He built a summer house, afterwards called 'the King's Chair', from which he could watch the races – and began his own

A ROYAL SOCIETY OF SCIENTISTS

The reign of Charles saw a powerful surge of scientific achievement. Robert Boyle, Robert Hooke, Isaac Newton, Edmond Halley and John Flamsteed were all at work during this period. This achievement was encouraged by the king, who granted a charter to a group of scientists to found the Royal Society on 22 April 1662.

In 1675 Charles appointed Flamsteed the first 'Astronomer Royal' and in 1675–76 built the Greenwich Royal Observatory. Boyle published his *The Sceptical Chemist* in 1661; Newton demonstrated his theories on the laws of gravity at the Royal Society in 1683–4, and in 1687 he published his masterwork, the *Philosophiae Naturalis Principia Mathematica* ('Mathematical Principles of Natural Philosophy' – generally known as the Principia).

Hooke experimented with early reflecting microscopes and published his *Micrographia* ('Small Drawings') in 1665. He was one of the earliest pioneers of the theory of evolution.

CHARLES II AND THE 'NEW WORLD'
THE GROWTH OF NORTH AMERICA

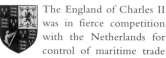

The England of Charles II was in fierce competition with the Netherlands for control of maritime trade around the globe and in particular the sea transport of West African slaves to North America.

'NEW AMSTERDAM'

In 1664 an English privateering fleet took possession of the Dutch fur-trading post at 'New Amsterdam' on the Hudson River in North America. This settlement, at the foot of Manhattan Island, had been established for almost 40 years, since 1625. In 1664 its Dutch director-general, Peter Stuyvesant, offered no resistance to the English occupiers.

However, the following year, in the wake of this attack and English raids on Dutch slave-trading posts in West Africa, the Dutch declared war on England.

Below: James, Duke of York, ruled the territory of 'New York' with absolute authority under the 'duke's laws'.

Above: A European treaty with major consequences for America. The Dutch ceded the future 'New York' to England under the Treaty of Breda, 31 July 1667.

The war lasted just two years. It began with a great English victory, as James, the Duke of York, sunk 16 Dutch vessels and captured nine more in the Battle of Lowestoft. However, in June and August 1666 ferocious sea battles caused vast losses of men and ships on both sides. England's position was further weakened by the effects of the 1665 Great Plague and the 1666 Great Fire of London. Then in 1667, with the English navy staying in port to conserve resources, the Dutch struck a humiliating blow: sailing brazenly up the Thames estuary, they burst into Chatham harbour, sunk four warships and left with no less a prize than the *Royal Charles*, the Duke of York's flagship. Both England and the Netherlands were by now keen to broker peace, and the Treaty of Breda ending the war was signed on 31 July 1667.

Under the treaty, the Dutch gave England 'New Amsterdam' and the surrounding area, while in return they gained possession of Surinam in South America. The English renamed the Manhattan Island settlement 'New York' in honour of the king's brother James, the Duke of York. The two principal boroughs were King's (for King Charles) and Queen's (for Queen Catherine); the first is now called Brooklyn but the second has retained its original name.

The wider surrounding area was the former Dutch colony of New Netherland, established by the Dutch West India Company in 1624 at Fort Orange (modern Albany, New York state) to provide access to the lucrative trade in furs from the Great Lakes. Charles gave this land to the Duke of York in return for an annual 'rent' of 40 beaver skins.

The Duke of York granted control of land between the Hudson and Delaware rivers to John, Lord Berkeley and Sir George Carteret. They named the land 'New Jersey' after the island of Jersey in the English Channel where Carteret was born and where he had served as Lieutenant Governor. The territory later passed into the hands of Quaker entrepreneurs, one of whom was William Penn, founder of Pennsylvania.

THE COLONY OF CAROLINA

Shortly after the Restoration, on 24 March 1663, Charles granted a wide tract of North America to a group of eight nobles, including Lord Ashley, the Duke of Albemarle, the Earl of Clarendon and the New Jersey founders Lord Berkeley and Sir George Carteret. These men founded the colony of Carolina (from the Latin form of their monarch's name). Lord Ashley's secretary, the philosopher John Locke, wrote the constitution for the new colony.

Two years later, the area of the colony, which already ran from the Atlantic to the Pacific, was further extended. In this form the vast land-holding included all the following US states: North and South Carolina, Alabama, Arkansas, Arizona, Georgia, Louisiana, Mississippi, New Mexico, Oklahoma and Tennessee, as well as parts of southern California, Nevada, Florida, Missouri and of Mexico.

A RELIGIOUS HAVEN

In 1663 Charles granted a royal charter to Baptist clergyman John Clarke for the colony of Rhode Island. The colony had been founded in 1636, by Roger Williams, a religious émigré. Charles's

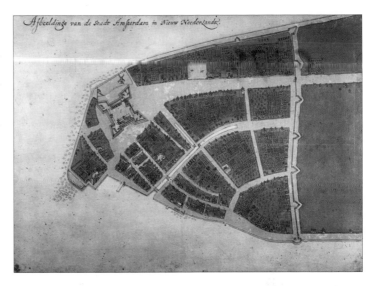

charter guaranteed the Rhode Island colonists freedom of religious conscience: 'No person within the said colony, at any time hereafter shall be any wise molested, punished, disquieted, or called in question, for any differences in opinion in matters of religion'.

In 1679 Charles declared the land of New Hampshire a separate royal province. The colony had been founded under King Charles I in the 1620s, and

Above: Manhattan as it was. This view of New Amsterdam is from 1660, before the settlement passed into English hands.

named New Hampshire in 1629. For almost 40 years prior to the 1679 declaration, New Hampshire was governed as part of Massachussetts Bay Colony. English colonization of North America was therefore well advanced by the end of Charles II's reign.

A CHRISTIAN COMMONWEALTH: PENNSYLVANIA

In 1681 King Charles made a large grant of land west of the Delaware river to his friend William Penn, a leading Quaker. The grant was by way of cancelling a large debt Charles owed to Penn's father, Admiral Sir William Penn.

On the land so given, William Penn founded the American Commonwealth of Pennsylvania (named in honour of his father). It was intended to be a refuge for Quakers and other religious groups exiled by European persecution, and an explicit attempt to create a perfect Christian commonwealth.

In the same year, Penn also received the 'lower counties' (the lands that became the modern US state of Delaware) as a

grant from the Duke of York. The city of Philadelphia was laid out on a grid pattern according to Penn's instructions.

Above: At court in London, a soberly dressed William Penn (right) receives the charter for Pennsylvania from the king.

THE REBUILDING OF LONDON
AFTER THE GREAT FIRE OF 1666

 The Great Fire of London broke out in a baker's shop in Pudding Lane on the night of 2 September 1666 and destroyed most of the City.

A NEW CITY

Just days after the fire, Charles II was presented with three separate plans for reconstruction. One was drawn up by chemist and architect Robert Hooke, one by diarist and courtier John Evelyn, who had already served on pre-fire commissions for improving London's streets (1662), and one by Christopher Wren, Savilian Professor of Astronomy at Oxford University (from 1661), who had already designed the Sheldonian Theatre in Oxford (1662).

All three plans recommended regularizing the street layout, but in the event none was adopted, principally because London's landlords were unwilling to countenance changes that would lead to drops in rent, and there

was a shortage of money to offer them compensation. In 1667 a Rebuilding Act provided for certain streets to be made wider, set improved standards for house-building and imposed a tax on coal imports to raise funds for rebuilding. This tax was increased in another act of 1670. Charles also gave a boost to redevelopment by repealing the tax on hearthstones. Hooke and Wren both played central roles in the reconstruction of the city. Hooke was appointed city surveyor for the building of houses, while Wren was made surveyor-general of the king's works in 1669.

In this capacity Wren supervised the rebuilding of St Paul's Cathedral and of London's parish churches. Although 87 churches had been destroyed, only 52 were rebuilt because smaller parishes were amalgamated. Wren personally designed or approved each one.

Above: Sir Christopher Wren, with St Paul's behind. Wren was a Mason, and full Masonic rites attended the laying of the St Paul's foundation stone in June 1675.

'RESURGAM'

Wren's new St Paul's Cathedral was built to the third design he produced: his second and favourite design was approved by King Charles but had to be dropped because of opposition to it among the canons of St Paul's. Building began in 1675 following the issue of a royal warrant that gave Wren liberty 'To make some variations rather ornamental than essential, as from time to time he should see proper'. For the foundation stone, Wren asked a workman to find a flat piece from the remains of the first cathedral. The stone, which Wren laid himself, was a fragment of a grave headstone bearing the Latin inscription

Below: Wren's masterpiece. The section, elevation and half-plan of the architect's third and final design for St Paul's.

Resurgam ('I will rise again'). St Paul's Cathedral was not finished until 1710 – although the structure was complete enough for the first service to be held there in 1697. Its magnificent dome became a London landmark.

THE SUCCESSION QUESTION

In the 1670s, after Queen Catherine had had several miscarriages, Charles's subjects began to suspect that he would not produce a legitimate heir, despite the fact that he had maintained a regular and generous output of illegitimate offspring with his many mistresses. The likelihood that the throne would pass to Charles's brother James, Duke of York, began to seem a potential calamity after James married the Catholic Mary of Modena in 1673 and word spread that the duke had himself secretly converted to Catholicism.

The staunchly Protestant Whig party in the Commons repeatedly sought to bar the Duke of York from the accession, but although bills were voted through in the Commons, Charles outmanoeuvred the Whigs to prevent them becoming law. However, the king was unable to prevent the passing of severe laws that barred Catholics from

Parliament and even from residing in London, and the Catholic Duke of York was sent into exile in 1679–80.

An assassination plan was uncovered in 1683. The Rye House Plot took its name from a house used by Charles and the Duke of York when they travelled from London to Newmarket in Suffolk to attend horse-racing meetings. The plan was to seize the royal pair and place Charles's illegitimate son, the Protestant Duke of Monmouth, on the throne. When the plot was uncovered, Monmouth, Charles's son by his mistress Lucy Walter, fled into exile.

Above: Whitehall Palace and St James's Park in the 17th century. In 1678, Titus Oates claimed that 'Popish plotters' intended to kidnap the king in the park.

Meanwhile in 1670, 1678 and 1681 Charles made secret deals allying himself with the French king Louis XIV in return for substantial payments. The first agreement contained an explosive clause in which Charles promised to announce his conversion to Catholicism and to accept military and financial aid from the French if – as it surely would – this provoked unrest among his subjects. Historians are divided over whether Charles was committed to these agreements or whether he played Louis along for the financial benefit, which was significant enough to make him independent of Parliament for the last four years of his reign, 1681–5.

'A PRETTY, WITTY KING'

Charles was remembered indulgently by his subjects as the 'Merry Monarch', celebrated in the Earl of Rochester's lines, 'We have a pretty witty king, Whose word no man relies on; Who never said a foolish thing, nor ever did a wise one.' Although he has been criticised for lacking seriousness of mind and application to the affairs of government, he did succeed in stabilizing the monarchy after the troubled years of the Commonwealth and Protectorate.

A CATHOLIC AT THE LAST

King Charles II died on 6 February 1685. On his deathbed he secretly converted to the Catholicism espoused by his wife and feared by his subjects. He was severely unwell for four days after suffering a stroke, but maintained his good humour and before he died made his peace with his queen and many illegitimate offspring. Queen Catherine, who had loved him powerfully throughout his years of philandering, sat patiently with him during the illness, but was absent at the end because she grieved so fiercely. When she sent an apology for not being present, the king exclaimed, 'Alas, poor woman. She beg my pardon? I beg hers with all my heart!'

Above: In his final hours, Charles found peace and listened to his conscience.

JAMES II AND VII

1685–1688

The Catholic succession to King Charles II's throne that had been so feared and agitated against by the Whigs in Parliament became reality on 6 February 1685. The king's avowedly Catholic brother, James, was crowned in Westminster Abbey on 23 April and almost at once had to deal with a Protestant challenge to his authority.

PROTESTANT REBELLION

Charles's illegitimate son, the Duke of Monmouth, landed at Lyme Regis on 11 June with a mere 82 supporters to stake his claim as the Protestant heir to the throne. Although he managed to gather a force of 4,000-odd soldiers, his army was routed by royalists at the Battle of Sedgemoor on 6 July.

Meanwhile the Presbyterian Earl of Argyll returned from exile in the Low Countries to try to provoke a Scottish uprising. He did raise an army of around 1,500 – largely from his own Clan Campbell – but, faced with royalist troops, Argyll was captured and the rebellion melted away.

Above: James II's three years on the throne were a brief interlude between life as a prince, before, and a long exile, afterwards.

King James was triumphant – and secure. Argyll was beheaded in Edinburgh on 30 June. Monmouth begged for his life but was despatched in a horribly bungled execution on 15 July in which six strokes of the axe were required to kill the duke.

In the wake of these revolts James greatly expanded the army and granted command of new regiments to Catholic officers, especially in Ireland. This latter issue provoked a row with Parliament, which the king prorogued in November 1685. It did not meet again during his brief reign.

JAMES II AND VII, KING OF ENGLAND, SCOTLAND AND IRELAND, 1685–1688

Birth: 14 Oct 1633
Father: Charles I
Mother: Henrietta Maria
Accession: 6 Feb 1685
Coronation: 23 April 1685, Westminster Abbey
Wives: (1) before accession married to Anne Hyde (m. 3 Sept 1660; d. 31 March 1671); (2) Mary of Modena (m. 30 Sept 1673; d. 7 May 1718)
Succeeded by: His daughter Mary II and his son-in-law Prince William of Orange
Greatest achievement: Putting down anti-Catholic revolts in 1685

6 July 1685: Battle of Sedgemoor: defeat of Duke of Monmouth
15 July 1685: Monmouth executed
4 April 1687: James issues Declaration of Indulgence
10 June 1688: Birth of King James's son, Prince James Francis Edward
30 June 1688: Nobles call on William of Orange to invade
5 Nov 1688: William of Orange lands at Torbay
23 Dec 1688: Formally deposed as king by Parliament
Death: 6 Sept 1701, in exile at St Germain, France

PRINCE OR FOUNDLING?

Protestant opponents of the Catholic King James II drew comfort from the fact that his only feasible heirs were Protestant. None of the 10 children of James and his queen Mary of Modena survived infancy, and his two surviving daughters from his previous marriage to Anne Hyde, Mary and Anne, had both made marriages to important Protestant royals; Mary to Prince William of Orange and Anne to Prince George of Denmark.

On 10 June 1688 all that changed as Queen Mary gave birth to a healthy boy, later given a Catholic christening as James Francis Edward and a powerful godfather in Pope Innocent XI. A Catholic succession was again a possibility. Some Protestants refused to accept this unwelcome development: they argued that the infant was not Mary's own, but was a foundling child who had been smuggled into the palace in a warming pan. Mary and Anne's representatives were absent from the birth and so they could not vouch for the child.

RELIGIOUS TOLERATION

James then tried to take on the Anglican establishment. On 4 April 1687 he issued a Declaration of Indulgence that suspended all laws punishing Catholic or Protestant dissenters against the Church of England. He began to promote Catholics to positions of authority in the Privy Council, courts and universities. Some of his public statements suggested that he acted out a desire for religious toleration, others that he was truly – as his opponents feared – seeking to re-establish Catholicism as the English state religion.

Matters came to a head in 1688 when Queen Mary gave birth to a healthy son after a long succession of miscarriages and infant deaths, suddenly and unexpectedly raising the prospect of a Catholic succession to the throne.

Above: The Duke of Monmouth begs for his life before the king. Victorian artist John Pettie painted this dramatic canvas.

Earlier James had ordered his Declaration of Indulgence to be reissued and read in churches, and when the Archbishop of Canterbury and six bishops wrote a petition asking him to withdraw the order, he had them cast into the Tower of London and prosecuted for seditious libel.

On 30 June all seven churchmen were acquitted of the charge. It became clear that public opinion had swung decisively against the king, for crowds on the London streets cheered the release of the bishops and bonfires were lit to celebrate their freedom. On the very same day, seven leading Protestant noblemen wrote to Prince William of Orange – husband of Princess Mary, the king's eldest daughter by his first marriage to Anne Hyde – asking him to invade and so secure Protestantism against the Catholic threat.

Prince William landed at Torbay with 15,000 troops on 5 November. The men of the West Country rose in support. A royalist army marched as far as Salisbury but was decimated by senior desertions. James fled back to London.

On 11 December, after William had marched into the capital and begun negotiations, James took flight again. As he crossed the Thames at Vauxhall, he let the Great Seal fall into the water. He got as far as Faversham and took ship for France, but was arrested and returned to London. Finally, William ordered him to leave and he escaped to France on 23 December 1688.

Below: In 1688 the Archbishop of Canterbury and six bishops were sent to the Tower of London on charges of seditious libel.

De Seven Bisschoppen, worden gevangen na den Tour gebragt

De Bisschoppen, weder uyt den Tour gehaelt, en vry verklaert

THE 'GLORIOUS REVOLUTION'

1688

When William of Orange and Princess Mary, daughter of King James II, jointly acceded to the throne on 13 February 1689, it marked the first time in English history that a royal succession had been settled not by hereditary right, military might or possession of the crown and treasury, but by the will of the two Houses of Parliament.

CONSORT OR KING?

On 23 December 1688 – the day that King James II succeeded in escaping to France – the peers and bishops of the House of Lords asked William to assume the duties of government. William summoned all the surviving MPs from the reign of Charles II to sit in the Commons. William turned down a suggestion that he should claim the throne himself by right of conquest.

On 28 January 1689 the Commons declared that James II's flight to France was an abdication of the government and that the throne was therefore vacant. The Protestant Whigs in the

Below: An allegory of the 'Glorious Revolution'. The pope (right) is offended, but Magna Carta and Liberty approve.

House of Commons were largely in favour of the throne passing to William and Mary, but in the Lords the Tory supporters of absolute monarchy were concerned to safeguard the principle of hereditary succession. Tory suggestions that Mary should rule alone (having inherited the throne as King James II's daughter), or that William and Mary should govern as regents until James II died, came to nothing. On 3 February 1689 William declared that he would not agree to rule as regent or as Mary's consort. He demanded the full power and sovereignty of a monarch, jointly held with his wife.

CONSTITUTIONAL MONARCHY

On 12 February 1689 Princess Mary arrived in London after travelling from the Netherlands, and both houses of Parliament agreed a 'Declaration of Rights'. When on the following day William and Mary accepted the terms of this declaration and were elevated to the throne as joint rulers, a new kind of royal government was brought into being: constitutional monarchy.

The Declaration of Rights, which was made formal in a Bill of Rights passed on 16 December 1689, made a

Above: A detail from James Thornhill's Painted Hall at Greenwich shows William and Mary enthroned in regal splendour.

number of ground-breaking changes to the relationship between monarch and Parliament. The monarch was barred from keeping a standing army, and Parliament had final authority in declaring war, raising taxes and passing laws. Free elections to Parliament would be held every three years, and MPs would be guaranteed freedom of speech. Subjects also had the right to petition the monarch on matters of concern. All Protestants had the right to carry arms for self-defence, to enjoy freedom from cruel and unusual punishments and excessive bail, and to live free from fines imposed without trial.

The new settlement also safeguarded the Protestant faith and made explicit a connection between Protestantism and the liberty of Englishmen. The Bill of Rights declared that, 'It hath pleased

THE CIVIL LIST

Under the Civil List Act 1697 Parliament granted William III annual funds of £700,000 for the rest of his life. These were to cover the king's royal and civil expenses.

The Civil List grant replaced an earlier parliamentary voting of funds, made on William's accession with Mary in 1689, of £600,000 annually. The custom of the Civil List was new: previous monarchs were expected to find money for these expenses from hereditary revenues and taxes. However, many earlier kings and queens had had far greater freedom to raise tax income without needing parliamentary approval.

Almighty God to make [William] the glorious instrument of delivering this kingdom from popery and arbitrary power'. Under the bill, all Catholics – including James II and his offspring – and all those married to Catholics were barred from the succession. The document declared, 'It hath been found be experience that it is inconsistent with the safety and welfare of this Protestant Kingdom to be governed by a popish prince'. When William and Mary were

Below: Queen and king. A beadwork bag made by Mary for William celebrates their loving relationship and their joint rule.

Above: A new relationship between monarch and subjects. The Bill of Rights is presented to William and Mary.

crowned on 11 April in Westminster Abbey, they swore new oaths that required them to uphold 'The Protestant reformed religion established by law' and to govern in accordance with the 'Statutes of Parliament'.

The Bill also specified the future Protestant succession: first, through the heirs of Queen Mary II, then through Mary's sister Princess Anne and her heirs and then through any heirs of William III by a later marriage.

SCOTTISH RIGHTS

In Scotland a Convention of Scottish Estates drew up a similar document to the declaration, called a Claim of Right, and passed it on 11 April 1689.

The document declared that James had 'Forfeited the right to the crown' since as a 'Professed papist' he had 'Assumed regal power without ever taking the oath required by law'; that is, 'To swear to maintain the Protestant religion'. He had also, the Claim declared, 'Invaded the fundamental constitution of the Kingdom, and altered it from a legal limited monarchy to an arbitrary despotic power'. Therefore, the Estates said, the throne was vacant.

The Claim, like its English counterpart, barred Catholics from the throne; it also declared the printing of 'popish books' to be illegal and outlawed the practice of sending children abroad for a Catholic education.

William and Mary accepted the Scottish crown on 11 May 1689 in Whitehall. However, they faced considerable opposition to their rule there, particularly in the Highlands, where allegiance to Catholicism and the House of Stuart was strong.

WILLIAM III AND MARY II
1689–1694

On 13 February 1689 William and Mary were jointly offered the throne under a Bill of Rights agreed in both Lords and Commons that made the monarchy subject to Parliament. On 11 April 1689 they were crowned England's joint rulers King William III and Queen Mary II. Almost at once they faced opposition in Scotland from those loyal to King James II. These opponents were called 'Jacobites' from the Latin form, *Jacobus*, of 'James'.

BONNIE DUNDEE
James II was in exile at the Versailles court of the French king, Louis XIV. He gave his backing to Scots nobleman John Graham, Viscount Dundee, to be his military commander in Scotland. Just two days after William and Mary's coronation, Dundee raised the Jacobite standard in Scotland. Rebels loyal to the ousted king began to muster under the command of this charismatic figure known as 'Bonnie Dundee', a veteran of 1679 struggles

against Presbyterians in the cause of Charles II. On 27 July 1689 Dundee led a force of highlanders in a famous victory over a royalist army commanded by General Hugh Mackay at Killiecrankie. This could have proved a turning point, but after the battle Dundee died from a

Above: Protestants ride to triumph. American artist Benjamin West painted this view of William's victory at the Boyne.

musket shot he received in conflict, and without his leadership the Jacobite cause foundered. The royalist forces regrouped and on 21 August at Dunkeld inflicted a major defeat on the Jacobites that was decisive in the short term.

William demanded oaths of loyalty from the leaders of the Highland clans. When the MacDonald clan chief Alastair MacIain failed to make the oath by the required deadline, troops of the Argyll regiment inflicted a terrible massacre on the MacDonalds at Glencoe on 13 February 1692. Public outrage at this incident combined with the fact that William did not try to punish those responsible for the massacre, undermined his popularity.

IRISH WAR
In Ireland the struggle to secure the Protestant succession provoked a two-year war. James II landed at Kinsale, County Cork, on 12 March 1689 to reclaim his throne. His 20,000-strong

---

WILLIAM III, KING OF ENGLAND, SCOTLAND AND IRELAND AND PRINCE OF ORANGE, 1689–1702

Birth: 4 Nov 1650, Binnenhof Palace, The Hague

Father: William II, Prince of Orange

Mother: Princess Mary, daughter of Charles I

Accession: 13 Feb 1689

Coronation: 11 April 1689, Westminster Abbey

Queen: Mary (m. 4 Nov 1677; d. 28 Dec 1694)

Succeeded by: His sister-in-law Anne

Greatest achievement: Battle of the Boyne

27 July 1689: Jacobites clash with royalists at Killiecrankie

21 Aug 1689: Royalists victorious at the Battle of Dunkeld

1689–90: Bloody siege of Londonderry

1 July 1690: Defeats James II at the Battle of the Boyne

3 Oct 1691: Irish 'Williamite War' ends with Treaty of Limerick

13 Feb 1692: Glencoe Massacre of MacDonald clansmen

31 Dec 1694: A griefstricken King William breaks down before Parliament

Feb 1695: William acknowledges Princess Anne as his heir

30 July 1700: Anne's only son, William Duke of Gloucester, dies aged 11

6 Sept 1701: Death of exiled King James II at St Germain

Death: 8 March 1702. Buried in Westminster Abbey

---

summoning John Churchill, the Duke of Marlborough, to command royalist forces in Ireland. The war continued for a further 15 months until the Peace of Limerick was signed on 3 October 1691.

A UNITED COUPLE

Although he was celebrated as the upholder of England's Protestant destiny, William was never really popular with his people. He was doubtless distrusted as a foreigner and, in sharp contrast to the flamboyant Charles II, he had an unattractive appearance and manner – short and stooped with severe asthma and a withdrawn character. Queen Mary, by contrast, had an elegant figure and charming manners and at 5ft 11in (1.8m) was a full 5in (12cm) taller than her husband. She was widely acclaimed and proved a dutiful wife. In the normal run of affairs, she left affairs of state and

Above: After defeat at the Battle of the Boyne, the former James II escapes from Ireland by boat, bound for France.

government to William, but when he was abroad at war she demonstrated fine judgement. Mary died aged just 32 from smallpox in 1694. Her devastated husband was left to rule alone.

French army was boosted by vast numbers of Irish Catholics loyal to his rule. On 4 May 1689 the Irish parliament in Dublin declared the country to be behind James. At first James swept Protestant opposition aside, but at Londonderry (Derry), Ulster, he found the gates closed against him. In December he embarked on a siege of around 105 days. Thousands of lives were lost and the enduring Irish Protestant slogan of 'No Surrender' was born as the city endured the siege until it was lifted by a relief ship.

William landed at Carrickfergus on 24 June 1690. On 1 July, at the head of a vast army of 36,000 soldiers that included Dutch, Germans, French Huguenots and Ulster Protestants as well as Englishmen, he inflicted a decisive defeat on James's army at the Battle of the Boyne, near Drogheda. James fled to France; William returned to England,

Right: Major battles of the 'Williamite war'. After victory at the Boyne, William's army swept across southern Ireland.

WILLIAM III RULES ALONE

1694–1702

 William was so devastated by the death of Queen Mary in 1694 that he was overcome by his emotions in Parliament and could not make a reply when offered the condolences of MPs.

He apparently saw the queen's untimely death as God's judgment on him for his sins. He withdrew from his long-standing affair with Elizabeth Villiers, the eldest daughter of Richmond gentleman Sir Edward Villiers. It seems that it was as a parting gift that he made over to Elizabeth Villiers all King James II's landholdings in Ireland in January 1695.

To escape his grief, William threw himself into the Continental war that had been running since the creation of a Protestant 'Grand Coalition' in 1689, and in September 1695 he led the army to victory over the French at Namur. In the absence of the heirs he had hoped to produce with Queen Mary, he also formally recognized his sister-in-law, the increasingly overweight 30-year-old Princess Anne, as his successor.

JACOBITE PLOTS

In 1696 a failed Jacobite assassination plot had the effect of rallying public opinion in William's favour. The

Above: Sir Godfrey Kneller's portrait masks William's physical failings. In reality the king had a short, stooping figure.

plan, developed at the French court, was for Sir George Barclay – a former associate of 'Bonnie Dundee' – to kidnap and kill the king at Turnham Green as he returned to London from Richmond. However, the details were leaked to the royal party and the attempt was never made; Barclay escaped back to France. Afterwards Parliament passed the Act of Association, laying a requirement on all holders of public office to swear that William was 'rightful and lawful king'; and, because Jacobites made trips to the court of the French king, Louis XIV, to hatch their plans, it was declared high treason to travel from France to England without official authority

Left: Namur. Despite troublesome swelling of his legs, William himself commanded the English army in France in 1695.

The Continental war came to an end in 1697 with the Treaty of Ryswick (on the outskirts of the Hague), signed on 20 September between William III, Louis XIV of France and Spain's Charles II. For the first time Louis – who had previously viewed James II as the rightful English king – accepted William as king of England. Other terms of the treaty saw Louis restore most of the conquests he had made since the start of the war in 1689 and recognize the independence of Savoy.

Following the death of James II on 6 September 1701 at St Germain, Louis recognized James's 13-year-old son, James Francis Edward, as the rightful king of England – in direct contravention of the treaty. In England opinion swelled in favour of war with the French. The Commons had voted in April to back the Dutch against the French and in June to ally with Austria and the United Provinces – and on 7 September in the Hague William agreed to ally Britain with the Netherlands and the Holy Roman Empire.

A NEW SUCCESSION CRISIS

At home, the death of the 11-year-old Duke William of Gloucester, only son of William's recognized successor, Princess Anne, put the Protestant succession in jeopardy. On 12 June 1701 Parliament passed the Act of Settlement, which nominated a new and unexpected Protestant heir to follow Anne. The heir was to be Sophia, Electress of Hanover, the daughter of Charles I's sister Elizabeth and her husband Frederick V the Elector Palatinate. The act made it abundantly clear where final authority now resided: in Parliament, which had the gift of the crown among its powers.

Parliament's decision was that it was better to pass the crown to a foreign royal family than to risk it falling into Catholic hands. The Act of Settlement excluded from succession any Catholics who married princesses of the Stuart line. It also tried to limit potential problems arising from giving royal power to

the Hanoverian royal line by stating that future monarchs would not be permitted to launch a war 'for the defence of dominions or territories which do not belong to the Crown of England, without the consent of Parliament'. It also stated that future monarchs would not be permitted to depart Britain without parliamentary consent. Additionally, monarchs would be prevented from appointing foreign courtiers to high position under a clause that declared that those born outside Britain might not serve on the privy council.

King William did not live to see the war with France towards which he was manoeuvring the country. On 21 February 1702 he fell from his horse and broke his collarbone after the animal stumbled over a molehill in Richmond Park. The fall plunged him into a terminal decline; he developed

Right: A king in waiting? This French portrait depicts James II's son, James Edward Stuart, in his early teens.

Above: William dies amidst courtiers in the royal bedroom. The crying figure (right) is probably the future Queen Anne.

pulmonary fever and died on 8 March. In France, gleeful Jacobites toasted the mole assassin, 'the little gentleman in his black velvet jacket'.

ANNE
1702–1714

Princess Anne, aged 37, plain of face and prematurely troubled by rheumatism and gout, did not make an inspiring queen when she was crowned in Westminster Abbey on 23 April 1702. She could not offer an heir: the veteran of six miscarriages and eleven stillbirths or infant mortalities, she was childless following the death of her only healthy child, Duke William of Gloucester, in 1700. Moreover, she was inexperienced in government and in affairs of state.

Nevertheless, she presided over a great period for her country, in which English armies won stunning victories over the French and re-established England as a significant European force with growing imperial possessions. The kingdoms of England and Scotland were formally joined in the Kingdom of Great Britain, and in decorative arts Britain reached a new height of elegance with the development of the Queen Anne style.

THE ACT OF UNION

The 1701 Act of Settlement that named the Protestant Hanoverian royal family as Anne's successors had provoked anger in Scotland. The Act of Security of the Kingdom, passed by the Scottish

Right: Queen Anne. The suddenness of her death seems to have caught pro-Jacobite Tories unprepared and so helped to secure the Protestant succession to the crown.

Parliament, in Edinburgh, in August 1703, declared the Scots' willingness to bar the Hanoverian accession and raised the possibility that a Stuart king could be installed in Scotland and join forces with France against England as in the days of the 'Auld Alliance'.

To rectify this situation, negotiations for the legal union of England and Scotland formally began in 1706 and on 22 July of that year a draft treaty was agreed by the 62 appointed commissioners, providing for a united kingdom with a single Parliament in Westminster, a single currency, a common union flag and, crucially, a guaranteed Protestant succession to the Hanoverian royal line. In addition, the treaty provided for the Scottish church, education and legal systems to be independent of those in England. With a few minor amendments, and thanks to the sweetening effect of a £400,000 one-off English payment to Scotland and numerous behind-the-scenes bribes – and despite Scottish public opposition strong enough to fuel riots in Edinburgh and

Glasgow – the Act of Union was passed by the Scottish Parliament on 16 January 1707. The Act received royal assent in Westminster on 6 March 1707. At a special service of thanksgiving in Sir Christopher Wren's recently completed St Paul's Cathedral on 1 May 1707,

Below: Queen of Great Britain. The articles of Anglo-Scottish union are presented to Anne in 1706.

ANNE, QUEEN OF GREAT BRITAIN AND IRELAND, 1702–1714	
Birth: 6 February 1665, St James's Palace	**Greatest achievement:** Her government's creation of the Kingdom of Great Britain
Father: James, Duke of York (afterwards James II)	**1702:** England at war with France
Mother: Anne Hyde	**August 1704:** The Battle of Blenheim
Accession: 8 March 1702	**16 January 1707:** Scottish Parliament approves Act of Union
Coronation: 23 April 1702, Westminster Abbey	**6 March 1707:** Royal assent to Act of Union
Husband: Prince George of Denmark (m. 28 July 1683; d. 28 Oct 1708)	**Death:** 1 August 1714, Kensington Palace. Buried at Westminster Abbey on 24 August
Succeeded by: Her second cousin George I	

Right: John Churchill, Duke of Marlborough, signs the despatch at the Battle of Blenheim in August 1704.

Queen Anne wore the insignia of the combined Order of the Garter and Order of the Thistle.

WAR WITH FRANCE

Queen Anne proved a more able and astute ruler than anyone had imagined. Her three principal ministers were all exceptionally able: John Churchill, Duke of Marlborough, who was commander-in-chief and in charge of diplomatic and military affairs; Sidney, Baron Godolphin, Lord Treasurer; and Sir Robert Harley, Secretary of State. The Continental war that was suspended following the 1697 Treaty of Ryswick reignited in 1702, largely in response to Louis XIV's backing of James' II's exiled son, James Francis Edward Stuart, in his claim for the English throne. In this conflict the English army and navy won a series of battles, most famously over Louis's army at the Battle of Blenheim (a village in south-central Germany) in August 1704, which was hailed by contemporaries as a new Agincourt or Crécy. For this great victory Churchill was rewarded with a victory parade in London on 3 January 1705 and the gift of the formerly royal manor of Woodstock, Oxfordshire, later that year. The war continued until 1713 – and one of its enduring consequences was British possession of Gibraltar in southern Spain.

QUEEN ANNE'S FAVOURITES

Before her accession Anne was very close to Sarah, wife of John Churchill, who was made Duke of Marlborough in 1702 and went on to military glory. However, after 1703, Anne's relationship with Sarah became increasingly troubled. The queen appeared to have a new favourite, Abigail Hill. Ironically she was Sarah's relation and had first gained employment as lady of the queen's bedchamber thanks to Sarah's influence. The dispute became very bitter: in 1708 Sarah even accused Anne of being a lesbian, declaring that she had 'no liking for anyone but only her own sex' and quoting a ribald poem that suggested that Abigail and Anne were involved in 'dark Deeds at night'. Anne's friendship with Sarah was cut off finally in 1710. Abigail Masham, as she became on her marriage in 1707, remained close to the queen and was created Lady Masham in 1711.

Right: This portrait of Sarah was made by Robert White (d. 1703) during the period in which she dominated Anne.

THE AILING MONARCH

Even at her accession, Queen Anne was visibly unwell, so troubled by rheumatism, weight and gout that she could walk for only a short way with the support of a stick. From at least 1707, she was virtually incapacitated by her poor health, although she continued to play her role in affairs of state. The loss of her devoted husband, Prince George of Denmark, who died in 1708, was a great blow to her. He was a dull but sensible man and she had relied greatly on his advice and support. She had a serious fever in 1713 and the following summer died on 1 August 1714, after falling into a coma. The Stuart line was ended. After some debate in cabinet, the government – in line with the Succession Act – invited Elector George of Hanover to take the throne.

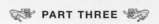

PART THREE

A UNITED KINGDOM

By the 18th century the power to govern was passing from the monarch to Parliament. From the 1714 accession of George I, kings and queens gradually lost their grip on the reigns of power while maintaining their prestige and status – particularly in the 100–odd years after 1850, when Britain's monarchs were symbolic rulers of the greatest empire known to history. Thereafter Queen Elizabeth II found stability for the monarchy in an era of intensive media scrutiny and rapid cultural and political change.

Left: Queen Elizabeth II met a warm welcome from flag-waving crowds during walkabouts marking the celebrations for the Golden Jubilee year of her reign in 2002.

CHAPTER NINE

THE HOUSE OF HANOVER

1714–1760

The 1701 Act of Settlement appeared to establish beyond doubt that on the death of Queen Anne the crown would pass to the Protestant Sophia, Electress of Hanover. However, in the summer of 1714 as Queen Anne was nearing death, the succession remained in the balance, with senior government figures, including Henry St John, Viscount Bolingbroke, supporting the accession of Anne's Stuart half-brother, James Francis Edward, Catholic son of James II. On the very day of Anne's death, 1 August 1714, Viscount Bolingbroke and senior Tories considered declaring James Stuart as King James III. In the end, however, they realized that James's refusal to abandon his Catholicism would make him an unworkable choice, and they acquiesced in the decision of their Whig parliamentary opponents to follow the Act of Settlement. Because the 84-year-old Electress Sophia had died two months earlier, the crown passed to her son, Prince George Louis of Brunswick-Lüneburg, who was declared 'George, by the Grace of God King of Great Britain, France and Ireland'. So the royal House of Stuart, founded in 1371 by Robert II of Scots and ruling in England since the accession of James VI of Scots as James I of England in 1603, came to its end. Its successor was the royal House of Hanover, which was destined to survive a series of attacks by 'Jacobite' supporters of the deposed Stuarts and to endure – through a change of family name to 'Windsor' in the reign of King George V in 1917 – right through to the 21st century.

Left: Hanoverian majesty. Sir Godfrey Kneller, an established Stuart court painter, added lustre to the newly established royal house when he painted this portrait of King George I.

GEORGE I
1714–1727

Prince George Louis, Elector of Brunswick-Lüneburg, was declared King George I outside St James's Palace, London on 1 August 1714, less than nine hours after Queen Anne had died in bed in Kensington. At the age of 54, he set a record as the oldest monarch on accession in British history.

George was in Hanover when he became king. As a monarch, he remained strongly attached to his German roots and throughout his reign as king of Britain was fonder of his birth country than he was of his new domains. He spent as much time as his duties permitted in Hanover and never learned

GEORGE I, KING OF GREAT BRITAIN AND IRELAND AND ELECTOR OF HANOVER, 1714–1727	
Birth: 28 May 1660, Hanover	**1715:** Jacobite rebellion led by Earl of Mar
Father: Ernst August of Brunswick-Lüneburg	**1717:** Handel's *Water Music* performed
Mother: Sophia, Electress of Hanover	**1719:** Jacobites defeated at Glenshiel, near Inverness
Accession: 1 Aug 1714	**1720:** South Sea Bubble scandal
Coronation: 20 Oct 1714, Westminster Abbey	**1722:** Jacobite 'Atterbury Plot' foiled
Married: Princess Sophia Dorothea of Celle (m. 22 Nov 1682; divorced Dec 1694; d. 13 Nov 1726)	**1726:** King George's divorced wife, Sophia Dorothea, dies
Succeeded by: His son George II	**May 1727:** George I becomes patron of the Royal Society
Greatest achievement: Establishing Hanoverian royal rule in Britain	**Death:** 11 June 1727, Osnabrück. Buried in the Leineschloss Church, Hanover

to speak English more than haltingly. He did not gain the affection of his British subjects. From the start he was distrusted as a foreigner, and he took little interest in British customs. He was short, overweight, bad-tempered and lacking in both manners and charm. He was dismissed as 'An honest blockhead' by Lady Mary Wortley Montagu and as 'An honest, dull German gentleman, as unfit as unwilling to act the part of a king' by Lord Chesterfield.

George's claim to the throne lay chiefly as a Protestant with a viable – if distant – blood relationship to the English ruling line. He acceded under the 1701 Act of Settlement, which in order to secure a Protestant succession, had raised George's mother Sophia, Electress of Hanover, above more than 50 Stuart relations with better claims. George's own relationship to the Stuart line was through his maternal grandmother, Princess Elizabeth, the daughter of James I, who had married Frederick, Elector Palatine of the Rhine in 1620.

Left: A detail from James Thornhill's epic decoration in the Painted Hall at Greenwich presents a regal George I.

THE OLD PRETENDER

George's potentially troublesome accession initially passed off peacefully. On 6 August, Parliament proclaimed George was to be crowned at Westminster Abbey on 20 October and, although there were demonstrations in favour of the Jacobite claim of James Stuart, the 'Old Pretender', the occasion went well.

In 1715 the new king faced a large-scale rebellion of Highlanders and northern English Jacobites in support of the 'Old Pretender'. The Stuart standard was raised at Braemar on 6 September by the Earl of Mar, a Tory landowner snubbed by King George, who gave open expression to his support for the staunchly Protestant Whig party at Westminster. Mar attracted some support. A minority of Scots favoured the Jacobite cause for several reasons: one

Above: At St Germain-en-Laye, France's King Louis XIV threw a party in honour of James Stuart, whom the French court recognized as the rightful king of England.

pressing factor was resentment at the Act of Union; another was affection for the House of Stuart, originally a Scottish royal family; a third was loyalty to the Catholic cause, which remained strong among the Highland clans although it had little appeal to most Presbyterian Lowland Scots.

However, Mar was not a great general and was unable to turn numerical superiority over the Hanoverian army into victory. The Battle of Sheriffmuir, near Stirling, on 13 November ended inconclusively and the English Jacobites were crushingly defeated the next day at Preston. The Old Pretender landed at Peterhead just before Christmas, but the uprising dwindled to nothing and on 4 February 1716 he returned to France, having achieved nothing.

Left: Before he became king of Britain and Ireland, George I became Elector of Brunswick-Lüneburg in January 1698.

Hanover at time of accession of George I

DENMARK

North Sea

GREAT BRITAIN

NETHERLANDS

AUSTRIAN NETHERLANDS

FRANCE

HOLSTEIN
LÜBECK
HAMBURG
BREMEN
KLOSTERZEVENO
MECKLENBURG
VERDEN
BREMEN
CELLE
HOYA
CELLE
BRANDENBURG
HERRENHAUSEN
HANOVER
BRUNSWICK
WOLFENBÜTTEL
CALENBERG
GÖTTINGEN

HOLY ROMAN EMPIRE

A GERMAN KING
THE FIRST JACOBITES AND OTHER TROUBLES, 1714–1727

The suspicion with which many Englishmen viewed their stout Hanoverian monarch was certainly not eased by the king's prolonged and spiteful falling out with his son, George, the Prince of Wales. This had its roots in King George's treatment of his divorced wife – and Prince George's mother – Sophia Dorothea. George punished her for a love affair by keeping her imprisoned in Germany and barring her from seeing her son or his sister (another Sophia Dorothea, who subsequently became Queen of Prussia as wife of Frederick William I) until her death.

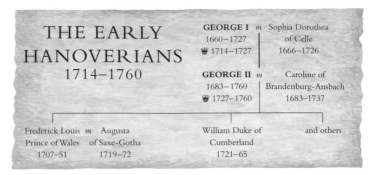

THE EARLY HANOVERIANS 1714–1760		
	GEORGE I *m* 1660–1727 ♛ 1714–1727	Sophia Dorothea of Celle 1666–1726
	GEORGE II *m* 1683–1760 ♛ 1727–1760	Caroline of Brandenburg-Ansbach 1683–1737
Frederick Louis *m* Prince of Wales 1707–51	Augusta of Saxe-Gotha 1719–72	William Duke of Cumberland 1721–65	and others

Below: 'German George'. The first Hanoverian king did not manage to win the affection of his British subjects.

Early in King George's reign, the Prince of Wales's growing popularity in London contrasted sharply with king's own public profile, exacerbating the difficulties. Tension erupted in an open quarrel in 1717 when, following the birth of the Prince of Wales's second son, George William, King George imperiously insisted on making the Duke of Newcastle the child's godfather. The Prince of Wales was angry and argued with Newcastle, who misunderstood what had happened and believed that the prince had challenged him to a duel. When the king discovered these events, he briefly imprisoned the Prince of Wales, then barred prince and princess from the royal palace. To further demonstrate his disapproval, he kept the Prince's children in his own care, took charge of their education and refused to allow the parents to see their offspring more than once a week.

JACOBITE TROUBLES
The collapse of the Jacobite uprising in Scotland in 1715 was by no means the end of efforts by supporters of James II's son, James Stuart, to undo the Hanoverian succession and put a Catholic Stuart monarch on the English throne. James – the self-declared King James III of England and King James VIII of Scots – could count on the intermittent backing of France and

Spain, for both countries wanted to destabilize an increasingly powerful Great Britain and also in principle supported the idea of a Catholic monarchy in London. In 1719 a planned Spanish invasion of Scotland went awry when the main fleet was forced back by storms and a tiny Spanish force of no more than 300 soldiers, supplemented by a small group of Jacobite Highlanders, was defeated by Hanoverians in a skirmish at Glenshiel.

Then in 1722 a Jacobite plot to take control in London was uncovered. The plan was for armed supporters of James Stuart to seize the Tower of London and St James's Palace while King George was visiting Hanover. The unlikely leader was Francis Atterbury, Bishop of Rochester, a secret supporter of the Jacobite cause. However, details of the 'Atterbury plot' were leaked to the King's mistress, Melusine von Schulenberg, and the uprising did not occur. Atterbury was exiled and only one plotter – a London barrister named Christopher Layer – was convicted of treason and executed.

THE SOUTH SEA BUBBLE

The sudden collapse of stock in the South Sea Company in September 1720 came closer than the Jacobites ever did to destroying the House of Hanover. The bursting of the 'South Sea Bubble' following a period of frenzied

Above: Sir Robert Walpole is generally remembered as Britain's first prime minister. His capable response to the Atterbury plot consolidated his position.

financial speculation left a huge hole in the monarch's finances, while the king and royal family's role in the affair left them looking very stupid if not corrupt.

The South Sea Company was formed in 1711 to trade with South America, primarily in slaves. When George became a governor of the company, stock sold very fast and was paying 100 per cent interest. There was a tremendous boom in shares and the king invested £60,000 of civil list funds. When the collapse came, it was very painful for all but a few canny investors. The royal court came under severe attack but survived thanks to Robert Walpole, appointed Chancellor of the Exchequer after the bubble burst. Walpole succeeded in stabilizing the situation and diverting blame from the king and the directors of the company.

Left: 'The Bubblers bubbl'd or The Devil take the hindmost'. James Cole's 1720 engraving satirizes the South Sea Bubble.

Above: James II's son, James Edward Stuart, in 1716. He was the focus of the Jacobite uprising of 1715 and became known as the Old Pretender or Chevalier de St George.

GEORGE'S FAILING HEALTH

From around 1724, King George, by now severely obese, was in failing health. He was regularly struck down by gout and often lost consciousness in fits of fainting. The king increasingly withdrew from public life, leaving control of government in the hands of the immensely capable Sir Robert Walpole, and went to Hanover whenever he could.

It was in Hanover that George I died, on 11 June 1727, in bed. While travelling to Hanover via the Netherlands from Greenwich, he had been struck down with severe diarrhoea, after consuming a very large quantity of fruit for dinner, and fainted more than once. The final fit was permanent: his courtiers could not revive him. He died aged 67 after a reign of 12 years. George was buried in the Leineschloss Church, Hanover. His son George Augustus, with whom he had had many disagreements, succeeded him as King George II.

GEORGE I, PATRON OF THE ARTS
MUSIC, ART AND ARCHITECTURE, 1714–1727

On 17 July 1717, King George, his mistress Sophia Charlotte von Kielmannsegge and an elite gathering of the nobility enjoyed a musical entertainment on the river Thames. In the early evening the party boarded barges at Whitehall and then sailed upriver as far as Chelsea, where they disembarked and took supper in a secluded garden. After the meal, which did not finish until 3 a.m, they climbed back into the barges and returned to Whitehall, where they arrived at St James's Palace at 4.30 a.m.

On both journeys the royal party was entertained by a group of 50 musicians sailing alongside them in their own barge playing a suite – later known as the *Water Music* – by the German-born composer George Frideric Handel. King George enjoyed the music – played on strings, trumpets, flutes, recorders, horns, oboes and bassoons – so much that he had the musicians play the one-hour suite three times over.

Above: Working life of a great composer. Handel's setting of the Coronation Anthem Zadok the Priest, first used in 1727, is stained with the mark of a coffee cup.

The triumphantly successful evening was arranged and paid for by Sophia Charlotte and her husband Baron von Kielmannsegge.

HANDEL'S PATRON
George had become a patron of the composer Handel before acceding to the throne: he appointed him Kapellmeister to the Hanover court in 1710. That same year Handel had made his first impact in England and over the next four years so pleased Queen Anne – with an *Ode for the Queen's Birthday* and a *Te Deum* to celebrate the Peace of Utrecht (both 1713) – that she awarded him a pension of £200 a year for life. As king, George appointed Handel music teacher to his granddaughters, regularly attended performances of Handel's operas – such as *Rinaldo* and *Amadigi* – and granted the composer a

Left: Sir Godfrey Kneller, who painted this portrait of King George, was the first painter to be made a baronet, in 1715.

Above: Handel's career as a royal musician extended from the success of his Water Music *in 1717 to his* Music for the Royal Fireworks *in 1749.*

further £200 annual pension. In 1726 Handel became a British subject and was appointed composer of the Chapel Royal. George also demonstrated his love of music by signing up for a £1,000 subscription to help establish the Royal Academy of Music.

George I was also a patron of the visual arts, a supporter of British-born artist James Thornhill, who painted allegories of the Protestant succession in the Painted Hall, Greenwich (1708–27) and eight scenes on the inner dome of St Paul's Cathedral (1715–19). George appointed Thornhill royal history painter in 1718 and knighted him in 1720.

GEORGIAN ARCHITECTURE
Many fine churches and residential buildings were raised or completed in George's reign. Hanover Square in London's West End (just to the south of modern Oxford Street) was named in honour of the new royal house when it was laid out in 1717–19. More tributes

Right: Vanbrugh had a theatrical triumph with The Provok'd Wife *in 1697. With Castle Howard (1702) and his work on Blenheim, he had also established himself as a leading architect by George I's reign.*

included the naming of its church (St George's) and of its southerly approach (George Street). At the end of Queen Anne's reign, architect Nicholas Hawksmoor, who had worked with his professional patron Sir Christopher Wren on St Paul's Cathedral, was appointed one of two surveyors to commission or design 50 new churches. Four of his celebrated designs were built largely within King George's reign, mainly in London's East End: St Anne, Limehouse, St Mary, Woolnoth, St George in the east, Wapping and Christ Church, Spitalfields.

In the year of his accession King George appointed leading architect John Vanbrugh comptroller of royal works. Vanbrugh's Blenheim Palace, in Oxfordshire, originally commissioned by Queen Anne in 1705 and designed and built with the help of Hawksmoor, was completed in 1719 for the Duke of Marlborough, hero of the Battle of Blenheim, after which the magnificent

Below: Blenheim Palace. Architects Vanbrugh and Hawksmoor, carver Grinling Gibbons and painters Thornhill and Laguerre all contributed to its grandeur.

country house was named. Vanbrugh was the first man to be knighted by the King George in 1714. He worked for the king on Kensington Palace, where three state rooms and a series of court-yards were added. Vanbrugh also won acclaim as a playwright, celebrated for plays such as *The Provok'd Wife* and *The Relapse or Virtue in Danger*.

King George was far less interested in the world of literature and theatre than in that of music and opera. French philosopher and poet François Voltaire, exiled in London from 1726 to 1729, dedicated his epic poem *La Henriade* (1723–28) to King George, but scholars believe that the king's support for the Frenchman – whom he received and gave £200 in January 1727 – was probably politically motivated, in the interest of promoting an Anglo-French alliance.

Many leading writers made or con-solidated reputations during George's reign. These included Alexander Pope, Jonathan Swift (whose *Gulliver's Travels* was published in 1726) and Daniel Defoe, who published *Robinson Crusoe* (1719) and *Moll Flanders* (1722). However, the king's very poor grasp of English inevitably limited his contact with writing in that language.

THE ROYAL SOCIETY

Like his predecessor Charles II, George showed a keen interest in scientific developments. He received a number of prominent scientists at court, including the Italian mathematician Schinella-Conti, although language difficulties caused problems. He became patron of the Royal Society – the scientific body founded in 1660 – in May 1727.

Below: St George's, Hanover Square. The king and ruling house were both honoured, but the plan to place a statue of George on the pediment was not carried through.

GEORGE II
1727–1760

George Augustus, Prince of Wales, was proclaimed King George II – the second ruler of the House of Hanover – on 15 June 1727. This was just four days after his father's George I's death in Osnabrück, Hanover.

On 27 June George II opened the first Parliament of his reign, and in its very first sitting it voted a generous rise in the king's civil list financial settlement. George was granted £800,000 a year – an increase of £100,000 on his father's entitlement – plus a further £100,000 entitlement for the king's popular consort, Queen Caroline.

WALPOLE RETAINED

The vote was a triumph for Sir Robert Walpole, who thereby consolidated his position as chief government minister. King George had intended to replace Walpole, so powerful in George I's reign, with Sir Spencer Compton. However, Walpole's generosity with the civil list settlement, combined with the influence of Queen Caroline, who was a close friend of Sir Robert, convinced the king to keep the minister on.

Below: House of a royal mistress. Henrietta Howard built the splendid Palladian villa of Marble Hill House in Twickenham.

GEORGE II, KING OF GREAT BRITAIN AND IRELAND AND ELECTOR OF HANOVER, 1727–1760

Birth: 30 Oct 1683, Hanover
Father: Prince George Louis, Elector of Brunswick-Lüneburg – later King George I
Mother: Princess Sophia Dorothea of Celle
Accession: 11 June 1727
Coronation: 11 Oct 1727, Westminster Abbey
Married: Caroline of Brandenburg-Ansbach (m. 22 Aug 1705; d. 20 Nov 1737)
Succeeded by: His grandson George III
Greatest achievement: Last British king personally to lead his troops in battle
1732: King signs royal charter for North American colony of 'Georgia'
1737: Queen Caroline dies
1742: Resignation of Sir Robert Walpole

27 June 1743: Leads troops to victory in Battle of Dettingen
21 Sept 1745: 'Bonnie Prince Charlie', the 'Young Pretender', defeats royal army at the Battle of Prestonpans
16 April 1746: Jacobites defeated at Battle of Culloden
20 March 1751: Frederick, Prince of Wales, dies
2 Jan 1757: Robert Clive retakes Calcutta from viceroy of Bengal, India
23 June 1757: Clive's victory at the Battle of Plassey
1 Aug 1759: British victory at Battle of Minden, Germany
18 Sept 1759: British troops capture Quebec
8 Sept 1760: British troops capture Montreal and have total control in Canada
Death: 25 Oct 1760, Kensington Palace. Buried at Westminster Abbey

---

The following month, July 1727, brought more good news for King George when Sir Robert Walpole's brother, Horatio Walpole, who was the English ambassador to Paris, arrived in London with the news that Louis XV of France was to back George II as England's king rather than support the claim of the Catholic claimant James Stuart.

A STATELY CORONATION

King George and Queen Caroline were crowned with great ceremony in Westminster Abbey on 11 October 1727. They approached the Abbey from Westminster Hall along a blue carpet strewn with herbs. The moment at which King George took the coronation oath was marked by the firing of guns at the Tower of London and in Hyde Park. Handel wrote four new anthems for the service, including the majestic *Zadok the Priest*, which so impressed king and court that it became standard fare for coronation services, and has been used at every British crowning from 1727 to the present day. Another of the Handel anthems, the beautiful *My Heart is Inditing*, was composed especially for the moment at which Queen Caroline was crowned. Other musical splendours of the service included *O Lord, Grant the King a Long Life* by William Child and a magnificent *Te Deum* by Orlando Gibbons.

ROYAL LIFESTYLE

King George settled into court life at St James's Palace, where he openly kept two mistresses: Henrietta Howard, the Countess of Suffolk and Mary Scott, the Countess of Deloraine. In company

Above: George II made Irish artist Charles Jervas, who painted this portrait, his principal court painter in 1723.

Above: Queen Caroline. She put up with George's long-term infidelities; he had a deep and lasting reliance on her.

was quick-witted and interested in ideas. She read widely, enjoyed theological and philosophical discussions and was a friend of Sir Robert Walpole. It was common knowledge at court that the way to promote a project was via Walpole and the queen. If a person convinced Walpole, Walpole would secretly convince Queen Caroline, who would convince King George and the king would ask Walpole to look into the matter. Writing of the queen's influence on the king, Walpole noted, 'She can make him propose the thing which one week earlier he had rejected'.

King George was a keen hunter and rode frequently in pursuit of stags in Windsor Great Park. However, in line with Hanoverian opinion, he was dismissive of British fox hunting. In an exchange with the Duke of Grafton, George declared that the fox, 'Was generally a much better beast than any of those that pursued him'.

he could be ill-mannered and, like his father, he was short-tempered. He spoke English with a heavy German accent and, according to contemporary accounts, was obsessively attentive to court etiquette. His main interest was in military uniforms and he had little time for painting or poetry, although he did enjoy music. In general, as in this particular, he considered things Hanoverian superior to things British.

Each night George would visit his mistress the Countess of Suffolk in her court apartments at 7 p.m. He would never go early: he could be seen pacing up and down looking at his watch for a full quarter of an hour before the time came. He was rude both about his mistresses and about the queen, but it was plain to all that behind the façade he was devoted to Queen Caroline, who had great influence over him. The queen, by contrast with King George,

Right: Sir Robert Walpole. He has been called 'the queen's minister' because he owed his influence to her hidden support.

THE UNPOPULARITY OF GEORGE II

THE ROYAL COURT, 1727–1743

King George and Queen Caroline shared a very low opinion of their first-born son, Frederick Lewis. Caroline appears unaccountably to have taken against the baby almost as soon as he was born, in 1707. George dismissed him as 'The greatest ass…in the whole world'. Some people unkindly suggested he was not the royal couple's offspring at all, but a foundling. In December 1728, Frederick, as heir to the British throne, now honoured as Prince of Wales, arrived in London for the first time from Hanover at the aged of 20.

King George made every effort to ostracize his son from society, limiting him to an annual income of £24,000 – significantly less than the £100,000 a year his own father had allowed him. Nonetheless, he became increasingly popular in London, effectively keeping a rival court, which became the focus of political opposition to George's favoured minister, Sir Robert Walpole.

ROYAL FAMILY SQUABBLES

On 25 April 1736 Prince Frederick married a 17-year-old German princess, Augusta of Saxe-Gotha, in London. In August the following year, when Princess Augusta was at the point of giving birth at King George's Hampton Court, Prince Frederick swept her off in a carriage to give birth away from his parents in St James's Palace. Enraged by this slight, the king split publicly with the prince in September 1737, declaring that any who attended the prince's rival establishment at Kew would not be welcome at Hampton Court.

The prince was kept away even when his mother, Queen Caroline, fell seriously ill in November 1737; indeed, as she approached death the queen declared that she was at least consoled by the thought that she would never

Above: Royal warrior George II in the saddle at the Battle of Dettingen on 27 June 1743. George was the last British king to lead soldiers into conflict.

again have to see 'that monster' her son. She died on 20 November 1737. The following year, on 4 June 1738, Princess Augusta gave birth to a second child, a boy named George William Frederick. He was a sickly infant and many expected him to die in infancy; he was christened on the day of his birth in case the worst happened. However, he proved the doubters wrong and grew into a healthy boy.

A KING MOCKED AND ABUSED

In the mid-1730s King George's popularity in Britain was at a very low ebb. His frequent absences in Hanover, where he had taken up with a new mistress named Amelia Sophia von Walmoden, were resented and mocked. One critic made a public display of his

Left: Frederick, Prince of Wales. This portrait, by Charles Phillips (d. 1747), shows the prince in 1732 aged 25.

THE BIRTH OF 'GEORGIA'

On 9 June 1732, King George granted a royal charter for the formation of a new English colony in North America, to be called 'Georgia' in his honour. The holder of the charter, James Oglethorpe, planned to allow imprisoned debtors and other people in severe poverty to make a new life in the colony. A group of 114 colonists departed from Gravesend on a frigate named the *Anne* and commanded by Captain John Thomas. After transferring to a group of small boats in South Carolina, some of these settlers landed at Yamacraw Bluff on the Savannah river on 12 February 1733 and founded the settlement of Savannah. Local Yamacraw Indians helped the first Georgians, and after a difficult beginning the colony soon began to thrive and prosper.

Above: James Oglethorpe (d. 1785) meets Yamacraw Indians after landing in the future colony of Georgia in 1733.

THE AUSTRIAN SUCCESSION

Following Walpole's resignation from government in February 1742, Britain plunged into the Continental 'War of the Austrian Succession' in 1743. This conflict arose from the inheritance and succession disputes that followed the death of Holy Roman Emperor Charles VI in 1740.

On 27 June 1743, King George II led British troops to victory over a French army commanded by Marshal Noailles at Dettingen, in Germany, boldly declaring, 'Now boys, fight for England's honour – shoot and be brave and the French will not stand their ground!' In fact the victory brought few if any benefits because the king did not press home his advantage. Yet, when he returned to London in November, he was greeted like the victor of Agincourt by rapturous crowds, the pealing of church bells and the burning of huge victory bonfires.

contempt by setting an old nag loose on the streets of London with the following words pinned to a broken saddle: 'Do not stop me, for I am the King of Hanover's horse galloping to fetch his majesty and his whore to London'. In December 1736 news circulated in London that the king had been drowned in a Channel storm as he tried to return from Hanover to London. This news provoked brief celebration – and the arrival of the Prince of Wales's supporters at his palace to hail a new king – until it emerged that King George II was safe and well.

GEORGE'S MILITARY TRIUMPH

The Prince of Wales's supporters opposed Walpole's efforts to keep Britain out of Continental wars and pressed for England to assert its military might, particularly against France. Walpole dismissed them as the 'Patriot Boys'. However, the king was also inclined to favour war, since he was fascinated by military matters and was himself a soldier of proven ability

who had covered himself in glory when fighting under John Churchill, the Duke of Marlborough, at the Battle of Oudenarde in 1708.

Below: Musicians in the bandstand (right) entertain Georgian society. This 1751 engraving shows the tree-lined Grand Walk in Vauxhall pleasure gardens.

CHARLES EDWARD STUART
BONNIE PRINCE CHARLIE AND THE 1745 RISING

In 1745 Prince Charles Edward Stuart, grandson of the ousted King James II of England, launched the last attempt by Jacobite supporters of the Stuart claim to regain the British crown. The charismatic 24-year-old was the elder son of James Stuart, the man derided as the 'Old Pretender', who had been the figurehead of failed Jacobite revolts in 1708, 1715 and 1722. Charles sailed from France to Scotland to claim the throne for his father.

On 23 July 1745, Charles Stuart landed in the Outer Hebrides and declared, 'I am come home'. He was supported by just 12 men and had lost a large part of his military supplies when the Royal Navy drove back a French support ship. However, after travelling on to the mainland he was able to raise the support of the largely pro-Stuart and virulently anti-English Highland clans. On 17 September 1745 he entered Edinburgh at the head of a force of 2,400 men. His Scots supporters acclaimed him as 'Bonnie Prince Charlie' while the Hanoverians mocked him as the 'Young Pretender'. In Edinburgh he proclaimed his father King James VIII of Scots.

BATTLE OF PRESTONPANS

On 21 September the Jacobites surprised and defeated a government force of around 2,500 at Prestonpans, 10 miles (16km) to the east of Edinburgh. The government commander in Scotland, Sir John Cope, had encamped beside a marsh at Prestonpans, thinking that the Jacobites would not be able to cross it without giving themselves away. However, a local guide led the Jacobite troops safely through by night and at first light they overwhelmed the unprepared

Above: 17 September 1745. On entering Edinburgh in triumph, the 'Bonnie Prince' proclaimed his father King James VIII.

government troops. Three hundred Hanoverian soldiers were killed and the rest of Cope's army fled.

'GOD SAVE THE KING'

In London King George and the Hanoverian establishment began to fear that, after so many failed attempts, the Jacobites might finally succeed. A popular song began to do the rounds, lauding King George and begging God for help. It was first played in public after a performance of Ben Jonson's play *The Alchemist* at the Theatre Royal, Drury Lane, on 28 September – just one week after the Jacobite victory at Prestonpans. Three days later, the words were printed in *The Gentleman's Magazine*.

At this stage, the song consisted of the first three verses, but a fourth, virulently anti-Jacobite verse was later added. The words were by an unknown author while the tune may have been

Left: The Jacobites' hopes of a Stuart restoration were undone at Culloden.

based on a Tudor galliard or a tune by French composer Jean-Baptiste Lully. By 1819 it was established as the national anthem.

MARCH ON LONDON

Buoyed by his success at Prestonpans, Charles wanted to march on London. His Jacobite generals advised him to consolidate in Scotland and wait – for French support or perhaps a rising against the Hanoverians in England. However, Charles was both impatient and impetuous. He held a ballot of his advisors and won a majority of just one in favour of pressing on. He marched into England, capturing Carlisle in passing on 15 November. The 5,000-strong Jacobite army got as far as Derby, where on 5 December it was faced by a government force six times its size.

Charles wanted to make a dash for London, since he thought resistance would collapse if he took the capital quickly, but he was persuaded by his council and generals to retreat.

Under the skilful command of Lord George Murray, his army extricated itself from a difficult situation and

Above: Flora MacDonald became a heroine to Scottish Jacobites for her role in facilitating Bonnie Prince Charlie's escape.

retreated safely to Scotland. On 17 January, after gathering reinforcements from Glasgow, the Jacobite army defeated a government force commanded by General Hawley at Falkirk before retreating to Inverness to regroup and reconsider its position

Above: The tall prince was unconvincing as a woman. An onlooker called him 'a very odd, muckle, ill-shapen up wife'.

SLAUGHTER AT CULLODEN

The Jacobites were pursued northwards by the Duke of Cumberland at the head of a large Hanoverian army. Charles insisted on facing the pursuing Hanoverians in a pitched battle, despite the urging of Lord Murray to hold back and fight a guerrilla war in the difficult northern country. Moreover, Charles's supplies began to dwindle, so his 5,000-strong force was ill equipped when on the morning of 16 April 1746 they went into battle against the 9,000-odd troops of Cumberland's army on Culloden Moor, near Nairn.

Cumberland's army overwhelmed Charles's bedraggled force and brutally slaughtered the wounded and prisoners. Few escaped the massacre, but Prince Charles was one of them. He eluded his pursuers – despite the offer of a £30,000 reward for his capture and many near misses – for five months. The most dramatic moment was, without doubt, when he escaped from South Uist in female disguise as the Irish maid of local woman Flora MacDonald. On 20 September 1746 at Loch na Uamh he boarded a French frigate, *L'Heureux*, and escaped into exile forever.

GOD SAVE THE KING

This patriotic song of 1745 became Britain's national anthem in 1790 – without the final verse about Wade.

God save great George our king,
Long live our noble king,
God save the king.
Send him victorious,
Happy and glorious,
Long to reign over us,
God save the king!

O Lord our God arise,
Scatter his enemies,
And make them fall;
Confound their politics,
Frustrate their knavish tricks,
On him our hopes we fix;
God save us all!

Thy choicest gifts in store,
On George be pleased to pour,
Long may he reign;
May he defend our laws,
And ever give us cause
With heart and voice to sing
God save the king!

God grant that Marshal Wade
May by Thy mighty aid
Victory bring!
May he sedition hush
And like a torrent rush
Rebellious Scots to crush
God save the king!

Some accounts suggest the words, including the final verse about the royalist Wade, were written in 1740 by Henry Carey.

GEORGIAN BRITAIN
A VIBRANT COUNTRY, 1745–1760

In the latter years of King George II's reign, a vibrant Britain greatly expanded its colonial holdings. This took place in the course of the French and Indian War (1754–63), which was the North American phase of the Seven Years War fought with France in Europe (usually dated 1756–63). The military triumphs of James Wolfe in North America settled Anglo-French colonial rivalry in Britain's favour and further established the foundations of Britain's overseas empire.

IMPERIAL TRIUMPHS

In North America, British and American colonial forces came into conflict with the better-equipped armies of New France, the French colonial holding in the region. Fighting began in 1754 in the upper valley of the Ohio River and for four years resulted in uninterrupted French victories.

Below: The king in ripe old age. This portrait shows him at the age of 76 in 1759, the year before his death.

However, in 1758–9, thanks to a British naval blockade that prevented French supplies getting through, the British won a series of astonishing victories. These culminated in the Battle of Quebec on 13 September 1759, which forced the surrender of Quebec. In October 1760, the month of King George II's death, the British also captured the city of Montreal.

These triumphs reflected well on King George II, who was a strong supporter of the hero of the North American campaign, General James Wolfe, (unfortunately killed in the Battle of Quebec). Other victories came in India, where Robert Clive defended British interests and chipped away at French holdings and on Continental Europe, where British troops crushed a French army under Marshal de Contades at the Battle of Minden on 1 August 1759. Horace Walpole commented that in 1759, 'The church bells are worn threadbare with the ringing-in of victories', while Lord Temple,

Above: Italian artist Antonio Canaletto lived in London 1746–56 and painted several masterful views of the city. This is of the Thames on Lord Mayor's Day 1747.

commented with satisfaction that, 'The closing years of the king's reign are distinguished by lustre of every kind'.

A RICH CULTURE

Meanwhile, at home, a king who declared his lack of interest in books and learning presided over and made a major contribution to the foundation of the British Museum, as well as a culture of glittering musical, artistic and literary achievement.

The British Museum was established by an Act of Parliament on 7 June 1753. Its principal collection consisted of 71,000 objects and 50,000 books left to King George for the nation in a will that year by physicist Sir Hans Sloane. In 1757 King George then donated the 'Old Royal Library' belonging to the monarchs of England, a rich and venerable collection of 10,000 books and 1800 manuscripts. The new collection was housed in Montagu House in Bloomsbury and opened to the public on 15 January 1759.

At this time London had a thriving literary culture: Dr Samuel Johnson's *Dictionary of the English Language* was published in 1755, while the novels *Clarissa* by Samuel Richardson and *Tom Jones* by Henry Fielding had recently been published. In the visual arts William Hogarth was at the height of his powers. He was named painter to the court of King George in June 1757.

In music, George Frideric Handel remained an active composer for his royal patrons throughout the reign, producing the *Funeral Anthem for Queen Caroline* (1737), the *Dettingen Te Deum* (1743) to celebrate the king's triumph at the Battle of Dettingen and the *Music for the Royal Fireworks* in 1749 for a celebration planned to mark the Peace of Aix-la-Chapelle that ended the War of the Austrian Succession. German-born, but a British citizen since 1726, by the time of his death on

Above: Triumph in North America. A Victorian engraving celebrates General James Wolfe's victory in Quebec in 1759.

14 April 1759, Handel was established as a British institution. He was buried in Poets' Corner, Westminster Abbey.

DEATH OF THE KING

King George II died an undignified death at Kensington Palace on 25 October 1760 shortly before his 77th birthday. He suffered a fatal heart attack while seated on the lavatory. His 33-year reign had seen a consolidation of the arrangements of constitutional monarchy, under which the king reigned but scarcely ruled. In his latter years, he was involved less and less in government as power became concentrated in the hands of ministers such as William Pitt.

The threat presented by the Jacobites in 1745 and the string of military victories in the late 1750s had repaired the king's formerly antagonistic relationship with his people. He may have preferred Hanover to Britain, but on his death he left an increasingly secure and successful nation, with British naval and military might bringing rapid expansion

in overseas possessions. He would be remembered as the last British monarch to lead his army into battle. Following the death of his hated son Frederick in 1751, George's heir was his grandson George William Frederick, who succeeded as King George III.

Below: William Hogarth's engraving Gin Lane. *Hogarth won a wide reputation for what he called 'modern moral subjects'.*

Below: Handel. Although he was German-born, his music was seen as an embodiment of England's national character.

CHAPTER TEN

BRITISH
HANOVERIANS
1760–1837

George III, third king of the Hanoverian line, acceded to the throne, aged 22, on 25 October 1760. He was the first of the Hanoverian kings to have been born in England and to speak English without a German accent. At his coronation in Westminster Abbey on 22 September 1761, he declared, 'I glory in the name of Briton'.

King George III saw it as his duty to maintain the authority and power of the British monarchy, but failed in his struggle to do so. The king, remembered as the ruler who lost Britain's North American colonies, who saw the rise to independence of the United States of America, was increasingly sidelined at home, as powers of government passed to ministers in Parliament. The monarch became a figurehead, who reigned more than he ruled. In his final years, Parliament appointed the Prince of Wales to serve as Regent during his father's mental illness. The Prince Regent oversaw a great flowering of architecture and the arts in Britain. The architect John Nash reshaped the face of London with developments in and around Regent's Park and Buckingham Palace and extravagantly transformed the Royal Pavilion in Brighton. George III (1760–1820) and his successors George IV (1820–30) and William IV (1830–7) occupied the throne at a time in which Britain defied Napoleon Bonaparte and restored its reputation as a great military power. It won feted victories such as those under Nelson at Trafalgar in 1805 and under Wellington at Waterloo in 1815. In this period, Britain gained widespread overseas territories that formed the basis for the great worldwide empire of the Victorian era.

Left: His Majesty enthroned. On 19 July 1821, in Westminster Abbey, the former Prince Regent was finally crowned King George IV, at the age of 58.

GEORGE III
1760–1820

George III was proclaimed King of Great Britain and Ireland on 25 October 1760. He was told of his elevation as he rode across Kew Bridge and asked for the announcement to be delayed until he could inform his mentor John Stuart, Earl of Bute, whom he called his 'dearest friend'.

Aware of the need to produce an heir to the throne, King George almost at once set about the task of finding a suitable bride. He was reliant in this, as in all matters at this time, on the advice and help of Bute. Within a year, even before the coronation took place, George married Princess Charlotte of Mecklenburg-Strelitz on 8 September

Above: George III was admired for his upright character and humility. At the coronation, he removed his crown when receiving Holy Communion.

1761 in St James's Palace, London. The couple's first child, a boy, was born on 12 August 1762 and christened George Augustus Frederick.

THE KING'S CHARACTER
George III was moral, devout and hardworking, usually kind-hearted although sometimes uncharitable, viewing others' failings with a certain censorious superiority. Before he established such a close relationship with the Earl of Bute, he had been through a number of tutors, many of whom complained of his 'indolence' and 'inattention', and highlighted a certain melancholy in his character that could cause him to become withdrawn, 'sullen and silent'.

Under Bute's tutelage George gradually overcame his shyness and self-doubt, although early in his reign he

---

GEORGE III, KING OF GREAT BRITAIN AND IRELAND AND ELECTOR OF HANOVER, 1760–1820

Birth: 24 May 1738, Duke of Norfolk's house, St James's Square, London
Father: Frederick Lewis, Prince of Wales
Mother: Princess Augusta of Saxe-Gotha
Accession: 25 Oct 1760
Coronation: 22 Sept 1761, Westminster Abbey
Queen: Princess Charlotte of Mecklenburg-Strelitz (m. 8 Sept 1761; d. 17 Nov 1818)
Succeeded by: His son George Augustus Frederick, who rules as Prince Regent 1811–20 and as George IV 1820–30
Greatest achievement: Despite loss of North American colonies, his reign saw the gain of overseas territories that formed the basis of Britain's 19th-century empire
1762: George suffers from mystery illness
1768: George founds Royal Academy of Arts
16 Dec 1773: Boston Tea Party
1775: Parliament gives Buckingham House to Queen Charlotte
19 April 1775: War of the American Revolution begins with the Battle of Lexington and Concord, Massachusetts
4 July 1776: Americans denounce George as a tyrant in the Declaration of Independence
June 1780: Anti-Catholic 'Gordon riots' kill 850 in London

19 Oct 1781: American war effectively ends with surrender of British General Cornwallis to American troops at Yorktown
3 Sept 1783: Treaty of Versailles recognizes an independent United States of America
1788–9: Madness strikes the king as illness recurs
1793–1802: Britain at war with France
1 Aug 1798: Horatio Nelson destroys a French fleet in the Battle of the Nile
1 Jan 1801: Act of Union creates the United Kingdom of Great Britain and Ireland
1803: Britain is at war with France (until 1815)
1801, 1804: The king's madness recurs
21 Oct 1805: Nelson victorious over French and Spanish in Battle of Trafalgar
25 Oct 1810: King George's Golden Jubilee is celebrated
2 Nov 1810: George devastated by the death of Princess Amelia
3 Nov 1810: George confined in a straitjacket
6 Feb 1811: King George declared unfit to rule; Prince of Wales becomes regent
18 June 1815: Generals Wellington and Blucher defeat Napoleon Bonaparte at the Battle of Waterloo
Death: 29 Jan 1820 dies at Windsor Castle. Buried in St George's Chapel, Windsor, on 15 Feb 1820

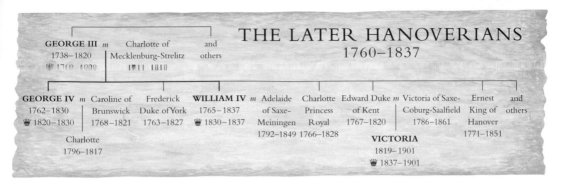

THE LATER HANOVERIANS
1760–1837

GEORGE III *m*	Charlotte of	and
1738–1820	Mecklenburg-Strelitz	others
♔ 1760–1820	*m* 1761 1818	

GEORGE IV *m* Caroline of	Frederick	WILLIAM IV *m* Adelaide	Charlotte	Edward Duke *m* Victoria of Saxe-	Ernest and
1762–1830 Brunswick	Duke of York	1765–1837 of Saxe-	Princess	of Kent Coburg-Saalfield	King of others
♔ 1820–1830 1768–1821	1763–1827	♔ 1830–1837 Meiningen	Royal	1767–1820 1786–1861	Hanover
		1792–1849	1766–1828		1771–1851
Charlotte				VICTORIA	
1796–1817				1819–1901	
				♔ 1837–1901	

found making speeches and granting audiences something of an ordeal. In 1766 the young king began a letter to his son, then only five years old, in which he offered a statement of his own character and aims. 'I do not pretend to any superior abilities, but will give place to no-one in meaning to preserve the freedom, happiness and glory of my dominions, and all their inhabitants, and to fulfil the duty to my God and my neighbours in the most extended sense.'

His mind and character, however, would be quite unbalanced by repeated attacks from the late 1780s onwards of a mysterious illness that made him unfit to govern by 1811, when the 48-year-old Prince of Wales became 'Prince Regent'.

Left: The king's brother Henry, Duke of Cumberland, secretly wed commoner Ann Horton. George was furious.

VICE AND ROYAL EXAMPLE

George's moral nature, together with a strongly developed sense of the dignity of the monarchy, found expression in his attempts to place limits on the amorous exploits of members of the royal family. His own marriage was happy and he was the first king since Charles I not to keep a royal mistress. However, the behaviour of many of his close relatives fell far below his own standards.

In 1770 an affair between his brother Henry, the Duke of Cumberland, and Lady Grosvenor led to a divorce case in which costs and damages of £13,000 were awarded against the duke. George himself had to cover the bill.

Two years later the king broke off relations with Henry after learning that the duke had secretly married a commoner named Ann Horton. Then, in 1772, George discovered that another brother – William Henry, Duke of Gloucester – had secretly wed Maria, Lady Waldegrave, and kept the marriage secret for no less than six years.

Although George was gratified by the passing, on 24 March 1772, of the Royal Marriages Act – which provided that, almost without exception, royal marriages required the king's permission before they could go ahead – he remained concerned that the royal family set a poor example to their subjects at a time of increasing vice. In 1780 he had to pay

off an actress who had demanded a bribe in order to return compromising letters that she had received from the Prince of Wales. He wrote to his son, exhorting him to remember his position:'In the exalted station you are placed in, every step is of consequence'.

On 1 June 1787 came the embarrassment of the revelation of the Prince of Wales's secret 1785 marriage to a Catholic widow named Maria Fitzherbert. In response, King George issued a royal proclamation against immorality and vice that was sent to mayors and sheriffs across the country.

Below: Princess Charlotte of Mecklenburg-Strelitz became Queen Charlotte on 8 September 1761 at the age of 17.

WAR WITH AMERICA
REVOLUTION, 1773–1783

King George III's reign saw Britain at war with its American colonies and the issue – in Philadelphia on 4 July 1776 – of the American Declaration of Independence. This document declared George 'Unfit to be the Ruler of a free People' and stated that 'The History of the present King of Great-Britain is a History of repeated Injuries and Usurpations, all having in direct Object the Establishment of an absolute Tyranny over these States'.

ROAD TO INDEPENDENCE

Conflict began around a decade earlier over the Stamp Act, imposed in March 1765 on legal documents, newspapers, pamphlets and many other paper items, including playing cards, as a way of raising revenue to help cover the costs of the Seven Years War (1756–63). Americans resisted, declaring that Parliament in London could not impose an internal tax in this way in distant colonies; the Stamp Act was repealed in 1766. However, further taxes on tea, glass, lead, paper and paint were introduced under the 1767 Townshend Act (named after the Chancellor of the Exchequer, Charles Townshend). In Boston, Massachusetts, they provoked

a boycott of British goods and rioting. British regiments were called in to try to uphold the law and impose a peace, resulting in the 'Boston Massacre' of 5 March 1770, when British soldiers fired on a group of Americans at the custom house, killing five people. In the same month in Westminster all the taxes were repealed, save that on tea.

Then, in October 1773, Parliament passed the Tea Act, which attempted to establish for the East India Company a monopoly on importing tea to North America. This provoked further unrest in Boston, including the 'Boston Tea Party' of 16 December 1773, when American colonists armed with axes and dressed as Native Americans attacked and boarded three British ships in the harbour, casting overboard hundreds of tea chests containing 90,000lb (41,000kg) of tea.

The disagreement escalated. In 1774 Parliament passed the Coercive Acts, containing punitive measures against the colonists and, in February 1775, Massachusetts was declared to be in a state of rebellion.

Below: Tea overboard. Americans angry at the duties imposed by the Tea Act hurl a precious cargo into Boston Harbour.

Above: American triumph. Britain's Charles Cornwallis surrenders to George Washington at Yorktown in October 1781.

CONFLICT BREAKS OUT

The American War of Independence began on 19 April 1775. In clashes between British troops and colonial soldiers at Lexington and Concord, Massachusetts, the British were foiled in their efforts to destroy arms and supplies.

The next principal event was the besieging of Boston by 15,000-odd colonial troops gathered from Rhode Island, New Hampshire, Connecticut and Massachusetts. The Battle of Bunker Hill, fought nearby on 17 June 1775, was boosted American confidence and self-belief because British casualties were so high: around 1,000 troops were killed or injured, between one quarter and one fifth of the total force. The colonial army, under General George Washington, drove the British out of Boston on 17 March 1776.

King George was not greatly interested in the American colonies until the revolts there called for an official response. Then it became apparent that he was in favour of strong action, to defend the dignity and authority of both monarch and Parliament.

In November 1774 he wrote, 'The New England governments are in a state of rebellion. Blows must decide whether they are to be subject to this country or be independent'.

Above: The American Declaration of Independence of 4 July 1776 was a ringing statement of human equality.

Above: In 1776, after a public reading of the Declaration of Independence, New Yorkers tore down a statue of the king.

The conflict in North America was prolonged and expensive. Britain found itself in the hugely expensive and strategically difficult position of being at war with France, Spain and the Netherlands as well as General George Washington's colonial armies. British troops won a few major victories, but could not build on them, not least because their supply lines were being almost constantly attacked by American guerrilla forces.

After Britain lost control of the seas to the French in the five-day Battle of the Capes, 5–9 September 1781, final defeat in America was only a matter of time. General Cornwallis surrendered to American forces at Yorktown on 19 October 1781.

INDEPENDENCE RECOGNIZED

Back in London, King George refused to accept that the conflict was over. However, the House of Commons voted against continuing the struggle and the Prime Minister, Lord North, who had wanted to scale down rather than conclude the conflict, resigned on 20 March 1782. King George contemplated abdication and drafted a message explaining his decision, but stayed on and accepted a Whig ministry led by the Marquis of Rockingham.

British naval victories in 1782 – notably Admiral Rodney's defeat of the French in the Battle of the Saints, off Dominica, on 12 April – meant that the peace agreed in the Treaty of Versailles, on 3 September 1783, was far more favourable to Britain that it might have otherwise have been.

The United States of America gained its independence; France took Tobago and Senegal; Spain had Minorca and Florida; Britain retained possession of Gibraltar, India, Canada and the West Indies. King George had by this time reconciled himself with some sadness to the loss of Britain's American colonies.

AMERICANS DENOUNCE GEORGE'S RULE

The Declaration of Independence contained a list of George's despotic acts, including the following.

• He has refused his Assent to Laws, the most wholesome and necessary for the public good.

• He has dissolved Representative Houses repeatedly, for opposing with manly firmness his invasions on the rights of the people.

• He has erected a multitude of New Offices, and sent hither swarms of Officers to harass our people and eat out their substance.

• For cutting off our Trade with all parts of the world:

• For imposing Taxes on us without our Consent:

• He has kept among us, in times of peace, Standing Armies, without the Consent of our legislature.

• He has combined with others to subject us to a jurisdiction foreign to our constitution, and unacknowledged by our laws; giving his Assent to their Acts of pretended Legislation:

• For depriving us in many cases, of the benefit of Trial by Jury:

• For transporting us beyond Seas to be tried for pretended offences.

• He has abdicated Government here, by declaring us out of his Protection and waging War against us.

• He has plundered our seas, ravaged our Coasts, burnt our Towns, and destroyed the Lives of our People.

THE GOVERNMENT OF GEORGE III
CONFLICT AT HOME, 1760–1780

King George III's attempts to maintain the power of the monarchy both at home and in the American colonies were attacked as tyranny or attempts at absolutism. However, George did not want to turn the clock back to the Stuart era of absolute royal rule. Devout and conscientious, he saw it as his God-given duty to rule with authority and expected the willing consent of Parliament. Right from the start of the reign he struggled to maintain this authority in the face of an ever-stronger and more independent Parliament and public criticism of his actions.

GEORGE III IN GOVERNMENT
The first ten years of the reign, 1760–70, saw a succession of ministries come and go. George had expected to enjoy a lengthy rule alongside his for-mer tutor the Earl of Bute when he appointed him Prime Minister in May 1762, but Bute resigned in April 1763 after a short and extremely ineffective

spell in government. His successor, George Grenville, lasted only until 16 July 1765, when he was replaced by the Marquis of Rockingham. He in turn was replaced on 4 August 1766 by William Pitt, Earl of Chatham, who resigned due to ill health on 19 October 1768 and was replaced by the Duke of Grafton. Only with the government of Lord North, Prime Minister from 28 January 1770, was some measure of stability achieved. Nonetheless, North's 12-year tenure saw the escalation of troubles in North America and the loss of the American colonies.

'THAT DEVIL WILKES'
The reign's first decade was also marred for King George by the activities of politician and journalist John Wilkes. MP for Aylesbury from 1757, Wilkes was also editor of the *North Briton* newspaper, in which he made raucous attacks on King George and the Earl of Bute's government.

The man dismissed by the king as 'that devil Wilkes' was initially thrown in the Tower of London, provoking a

Above: Hogarth's engraving shows John Wilkes in 1763, the year in which the radical published issue 45 of the North Briton, *which attacked the king.*

public outcry under the slogan 'Wilkes and Liberty!' He was released after less than a week on the grounds that his detention violated parliamentary privi-lege. However, following the discovery of an obscene poem at his printing press he was expelled from the Commons and found guilty of seditious libel and

END OF AN ERA
James Stuart, son of King James II and figurehead for the Jacobite revolts of 1715, 1719 and 1745, died in Rome on 1 January 1766 at the age of 77. He was buried in St Peter's after a truly splendid memorial ceremony – in which his body, dressed in robes of crimson velvet and wearing a crown, was laid beneath a banner proclaiming him *Jacobus Tertius Magnae Britannia Rex* ('King James III of Great Britain'). His son, 'Bonnie Prince Charlie', survived him. But he, too, died on 30 January 1788 in Rome. The deaths of the men known as the 'Old Pretender' and the 'Young Pretender' marked the end of the Stuart era in European royal life.

Below: This Protestant demonstration against the 1778 Catholic Repeal Act sparked the week-long Gordon Riots.

Above: The future Buckingham Palace was built to William Talman's designs in 1702. It belonged to the Duke of Buckingham before becoming a royal possession in 1762.

obscenity on 21 February 1764. He was by now in French exile, having travelled to Paris at Christmas 1763.

In a general election of March 1768 he was elected MP for Middlesex and the following month returned to London, where he gave himself up for imprisonment. He remained in jail until April 1770, despite being re-elected MP and expelled from the Commons no fewer than three times in the period. He was a persistent problem for king and government. Always popular with Londoners, in October–November 1774 he was elected Mayor of London and returned again as MP for Middlesex.

THE KING DENOUNCED

Criticism of the king and his role in government remained strong. In April 1780, MPs in the House of Commons voted by 233 to 215 to pass the motion that, 'The influence of the crown has increased, is increasing and ought to be diminished'. As the war in North America ran down to a humiliating defeat, the king and Lord North's government were cast as incompetent.

In Parliament, Charles James Fox, the MP for Westminster, was a committed opponent of George and of royal power. He declared that, 'The influence of the

crown', which he called 'one grand evil', was the primary cause of Britain's troubles at home and abroad.

The year 1780 saw violent London riots, sparked by an atmosphere of anti-Catholic hysteria that had developed in the wake of the passing of the 1778 Catholic Relief Act, which lifted some anti-Catholic laws. This troubling atmosphere exploded in June 1780, when Wiltshire MP Lord George

Gordon incited a five-day London riot in which Catholic churches and houses were burned and around 850 people were killed. In the face of this unrest King George acted with calm authority. Indeed, although he endured criticism in Parliament and from radicals such as Wilkes and Fox, among the people George III maintained a significant level of popularity – even after the loss of the American colonies.

KING GEORGE AND THE ARTS

George III was a keen musician and an able performer on harpsichord and flute. He liked chess, was an amateur painter and also enjoyed collecting books. He took an interest in mechanics and science, investigating the workings of clocks as well as studying astronomy.

George was also a significant patron of the arts. In 1768 he founded the Royal Academy, 'For the purpose of cultivating the arts of painting, sculpture and architecture'. Its first president was portrait painter Sir Joshua Reynolds.

King George and Queen Charlotte received the eight-year-old boy genius Wolfgang Amadeus Mozart in 1764. Later in the reign the Austrian composer Joseph Haydn became a favourite.

George also bought Buckingham House, the future Buckingham Palace, in 1762 and had Dr Johnson create a library there in 1767. Robert Adam was appointed to the post of royal architect 1761–9 and Josiah Wedgwood served as the Queen's potter from 1765.

Right: Wolfgang Amadeus Mozart performed twice for the king and Queen Charlotte during his 1764 visit.

THE MADNESS OF GEORGE III
INSANITY AND THE KING, 1810–1820

On 3 November 1810 King George was confined in a straitjacket. The death on the previous day of his beloved youngest child, Princess Amelia, at the age of 27, brought on a recurrence of the mysterious illness that robbed him of his mental faculties. He had recovered from previous attacks but this time, despite initial intervals of mental clarity, he descended beyond the reach of his doctors into a decade-long darkness that lasted until his death in January 1820.

A MYSTERY ILLNESS

The king was struck down with serious illness very early in the reign. In 1762 and 1765 he suffered attacks of serious chest pains, hoarseness, a racing pulse and violent coughing. Following an official visit during the second bout, the Prime Minister George Grenville reported that George's '...countenance and manner were a good deal estranged'. George himself was brought to an awareness of his own mortality and was sufficiently alarmed to propose that plans should be made to establish a regency should he die suddenly.

The first attack of madness came in the autumn of 1788. The illness affected the king's eyesight – he complained of a mist clouding his vision and his eyes appeared bloodshot – and also made him talk in a rambling, incoherent and sometimes lewd manner. He also

Above: Princesses Mary, Sophia and Amelia. The death of George's beloved Amelia precipitated his final madness.

behaved violently on occasion. During a walk in Windsor Great Park at this time he was discovered talking to an oak tree, which he had apparently mistaken for the king of Prussia. At another point during this bout he attacked his son, the Prince of Wales.

King George's doctors were at a loss. In 1788, Queen Charlotte lost faith in them and entrusted her husband to the care of the Reverend Francis Willis, owner of an asylum for the mentally unbalanced in Wiltshire but not a qualified doctor. Willis promised a cure. The first attack ended after three months in the spring of 1789, and the recovery was celebrated in a service of thanksgiving in St Paul's Cathedral on 23 April 1789. Afterwards he and Queen Charlotte spent the summer of 1789 recuperating at a house belonging to the Duke of Gloucester in Weymouth, Dorset.

A second attack, with identical symptoms to the first, including the profound mental confusion so alarming to the

BRITAIN ABROAD

In King George III's long reign the foundations were laid for Britain's great global empire of the 19th and early 20th centuries. At the close of the Seven Years War, the 1763 Treaty of Paris brought Britain widespread territories. Many of these were retained, following the loss of the North American colonies, in the 1783 Treaty of Versailles, when Britain remained in control of the West Indies, India, Canada and Gibraltar. Captain James Cook also claimed Australia and New Zealand for Britain in the early 1770s; the penal colony of Botany Bay was established near the 'new town' of Sydney in January 1788. The 1801 Act of Union eased British anxieties that following the creation of the USA and the French Revolution of 1789, Ireland would achieve independence.

Below: By George III's reign, Britain's overseas empire took in parts of Africa and India as well as North America.

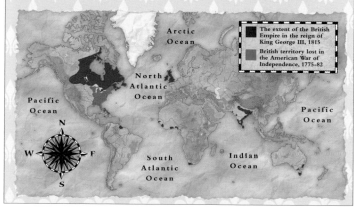

WHAT WAS THE KING'S ILLNESS?

Historians once thought that the king's sickness was largely psychosomatic, brought on by the enormous stresses of political upheaval, the loss of Britain's North American colonies, and family tragedy, including the death in 1810 of his youngest and favourite daughter Amelia.

However, we now know that George III probably suffered from acute intermittent porphyria, a hereditary condition in which, from time to time, the body cannot manufacture the blood pigment haemoglobin and as a result porphyrins (substances normally used to make haemoglobin) accumulate in the

blood stream and damage the nervous system. Attacks normally come and go because the body's failure to make haemoglobin is triggered by other illness or profound emotional stress.

Right: In his pathetic final years, George often wore nothing more formal than a dressing gown and was bullied by doctors.

government, struck on 13 February 1801 and lasted around four weeks. George's recovery was, however, assured on 11 March 1801.

Another attack in February 1804 led to the appointment of Dr Simons, from St Luke's Hospital for Lunatics, a great believer in the use of the straitjacket to confine disturbed individuals. George had fully recovered by the summer when he visited Weymouth once more to recuperate.

KING GEORGE'S LAST YEARS

After 1811 the king was a truly pathetic figure, completely blind and increasingly deaf, with long straggling white hair and beard. He did not recognize Queen Charlotte when she visited him and he could not sleep, even after taking laudanum. He took comfort in a harpsichord that had once belonged to Handel, but could not play it as he once had because of his deteriorating hearing. He was detached from his former self and the glorious life he had once lived. He reportedly told a courtier that the harpsichord in question had once been a favourite of the late King

George, when that monarch was alive. He conducted conversations with Lord North, who had been dead since 1792, and inspected invisible military parades.

THE KING'S REPUTATION

History has not been kind to King George III. He is remembered as a pathetic figure in his madness. As a sane man, he is generally remembered as something of a fool; an incompetent king who rode roughshod over

American sensibilities, provoking a war that brought about the loss of the North American colonies – a catastrophic event for Britain if a proud one for the nascent United States of America. He is made the source of foolish quotes: his diary entry for 4 July 1776, the day of the American Declaration of Independence, read, 'Nothing of importance happened today'; but of course events in America were not known in Europe for weeks.

King George is viewed as a family ridiculous figure in his guise as 'Farmer George'. The epithet refers to the interest he took in modern agricultural methods, which he applied with some success in farms at Windsor and Richmond. In the years before madness carried him off, George was a devout and highly conscientious ruler, with a developed sense of his destiny that was somewhat at odds with his achievements. He endeavoured to follow his appointed duty.

As he said to the US ambassador John Adam at their first meeting, in reference to the American War of Independence, 'I have done nothing in the late contest, but what I thought myself indispensably bound to do by the Duty which I owed to my people.'

Below: A cartoon by William Charles shows Charles James Fox, a persistent enemy of George III, with fellow radicals.

THE PRINCE REGENT

1811–1821

 Parliament passed the Regency Act on 5 February 1811, under which the Prince of Wales, 'by reason of the severe Indisposition with which it hath pleased God to afflict the King's Most Excellent Majesty', took 'Full power and authority, in the name and on behalf of His Majesty, and under the stile and title of Regent of the United Kingdom of Great Britain and Ireland, to exercise and administer the royal power'. The 'Prince Regent' swore oaths of office on 6 February 1811.

Initially both the prince and the government hoped that the Regency would be short-lived, for the king had previously recovered from his bouts of illness after a few weeks or months and the regency provision were set to expire after a year. However, by February 1812 it was becoming increasingly apparent

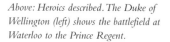
Above: Heroics described. The Duke of Wellington (left) shows the battlefield at Waterloo to the Prince Regent.

that the king would not recover and accordingly the Prince of Wales's regency was made permanent.

HANOVERIAN CENTENARY

On 1 August 1814 the Prince Regent hosted lavish celebrations in the parks of central London to mark the 100th anniversary of the Hanoverian accession. The celebrations included the erection of a spectacular seven-storey Chinese pagoda in St James's Park and of arcades and roundabouts in Hyde Park; meanwhile, a 'sea battle' was enacted on the waters of the Serpentine. After dark, fireworks lit the sky above Green Park, where a gothic castle had been temporarily built.

Earlier that summer, Prince George had helped King Louis XVIII celebrate the restoration to the French throne of the House of Bourbon. This followed the abdication of the French emperor, Napoleon, on 6 April and his subsequent exile to the island of Elba. The prince processed through central London in a state carriage with the restored king and, after a short London

Left: Prince regal. This imposing portrait by royal painter Sir Thomas Lawrence shows George in his Garter robes in 1816.

stay, Louis was escorted by the Royal Navy on his return to France. Prince George also threw a gala at Carlton House to celebrate the military triumphs of the Duke of Wellington.

THE DEPARTURE OF CAROLINE

On 8 August 1814 Caroline, Princess of Wales, left the Prince Regent and returned to her native Duchy of Brunswick (northern Germany). This followed many years of open marital difficulties exacerbated by the fact that the Princess was far more popular than the dissolute Prince with the British public. The Prince of Wales was not only openly unfaithful with a string of mistresses but also tried to exclude the princess from public life.

VICTORY AT WATERLOO

The Duke of Wellington's defeat of the French emperor Napoleon at the Battle of Waterloo on 18 June 1815 was one of the great events of the prince's regency. The prince learned the news on the very evening of the battle, when the society party he was attending was interrupted by the arrival of Major Henry Percy, who had ridden directly from the battlefield in Belgium. Major Percy, dirty and bloodspattered, dropped to one knee as he laid the captured

battle insignia of the French army on the floor at the Prince Regent's feet and Lord Liverpool read aloud the battle despatch from Wellington. On the spot the Prince Regent promoted Major Percy to Colonel. A little later, Prince George commented, 'It is a glorious victory and we must rejoice at it. But the loss of life has been fearful.'

A NEW SUCCESSION CRISIS

The Prince Regent's only child, Princess Charlotte, died on 6 November 1817 after a stillbirth. The succession was

Left: The prince's only child, Princess Charlotte. Her death sparked a royal scramble to produce a suitable heir.

Above: James Gillray's cartoon shows the voluptuary Prince Regent hard at work digesting his latest epic dinner.

suddenly plunged into doubt and later in the month Parliament recommended that all unmarried royals of suitable age should be wed. On 24 May 1819 the Duke of Kent's wife, Princess Victoria of Saxe-Coburg, who had travelled all the way from Germany to England in a coach to ensure that her child was born in England, gave birth to the future Queen Victoria.

With the death of the 82-year-old King George III on 29 January 1820, the Prince Regent acceded to the throne as King George IV.

REGENCY ARTS AND ARCHITECTURE
A CLASSICAL REVIVAL, 1811–1821

First as Prince of Wales, then Prince Regent and finally King George IV, George Augustus Frederick was forcibly criticized for self-indulgence and extravagance. However, in one important area his free spending left an enduring and positive legacy, for he was an enthusiastic and discerning patron of the arts, particularly in the field of architecture. He indisputably enriched his realm through his association with architect John Nash, designer of Regent's Park and Regent Street in London and extravagant remodeller of the Royal Pavilion in Brighton.

NASH'S GREAT PROJECTS

After an unsuccessful period in 1780s London, Nash made his name as an architect of country houses in Wales before returning to London and entering the employment of the Prince of Wales in 1798. In 1806, as Prince Regent, George engineered Nash's appointment as Architect in the Office

Below: East meets West. John Nash's 'Hindu-Gothic' designs transformed George's Marine Pavilion in Brighton.

Above: The Prince's lavish London home, Carlton House. Novelist Jane Austen visited, at George's invitation, in 1815.

of Woods and Forests, which allowed Nash to make his mark in the design of the 'New Street' proposed to link the Regent's palace, Carlton House, to planned new developments in Marylebone Park (now Regent's Park). The twin projects came under the aegis of this office because they involved building on Marylebone Park, where large areas were due to revert to the crown on the expiry of leases in 1811. In the event, Nash was architect both of the 'New Street' and of the Marylebone Park developments.

Work began on the street under the New Street Act of 1813 and was completed around 1825. Nash's design included the development of partly residential Lower Regent Street, Piccadilly Circus, a curved shopping section (the Quadrant) between Piccadilly Circus and Oxford Circus, and north of Oxford Circus an upper residential stretch running as far as Portland Place. The grandest section was the Quadrant, laid out with rows of cast-iron colonnades, creating covered walkways that allowed shoppers to carry on their business despite London rain. Nash's original and highly stylish plans for the park, which created an elegant layout with grand terraces, scattered villas, a

Surprise (Number 94), *The Drumroll* (Number 103) and the *London Symphonies* (Numbers 99–104).

In 1820 George was a founding member of the Royal Society of Literature. He was a friend of Sir Walter Scott and reportedly a keen reader of the novels of Jane Austen.

George invited Austen to Carlton House in 1815 and she is known to have attended, although it does not appear that she actually met the prince, rather spending her time with George's librarian, a Mr Clarke. She was informed that George kept a set of her novels in each of his houses. She returned the compliment by putting this dedication at the start of her next novel, *Emma* (1816): 'To His Royal Highness, The Prince Regent, this work is, by his Royal Highness's permission, most respectfully dedicated, by His Royal Highness's dutiful and obedient humble servant, the Author'.

Below: John Nash set about adding regal grandeur to Buckingham Palace. This view of the imposing Saloon appeared in WH Pyne's Royal Residences *(1818).*

lake and a wooded area, attracted considerable criticism, but the Prince Regent strenuously defended them and ensured they came to fruition. Building work began in 1817 and was largely complete by 1828.

In the years 1815–23 Nash remodelled George's Royal Pavilion in Brighton in an extravagant 'Hindu-Gothic' style that combined classical architecture with elements derived from Indian temples and palaces. Originally a farmhouse, the building had been rebuilt for George as a 'Marine Pavilion' by architect Henry Holland in 1787.

Other Nash projects included the redesign of St James's Park (1827–29) and the redevelopment of Buckingham House as a palace. On the death of King George IV in 1830, however, Nash was removed from the Buckingham Palace job because of escalating costs and doubts about the building's structural soundness.

ART, MUSIC AND LITERATURE

In the field of the visual arts, George commissioned works from John Constable, George Stubbs, Thomas Gainsborough, Thomas Lawrence and Joshua Reynolds, while also buying art by masters such as Rubens and Rembrandt for his Carlton House collection. He showed his appreciation of Italian neoclassical sculptor Antonio

Canova by welcoming him on his visit to London in 1815 and commissioning the life-size group sculpture 'Venus and Mars'. He opened his collection to the public, and he played an important role in the 1824 establishment of the National Gallery.

In music George was a keen patron of the Austrian composer Joseph Haydn, whom he first met in the course of the composer's 1791–2 visit to London. On this and a second visit to London in 1794, Haydn wrote 12 symphonies, which were ecstatically received by the royal family and the London public. They included *The*

GEORGE IV

1820–1830

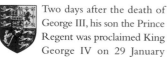 Two days after the death of George III, his son the Prince Regent was proclaimed King George IV on 29 January 1820. The portly, self-indulgent prince had pursued a hard-drinking, womanizing lifestyle since at least 1779 when, at the age of 17, he began a love affair with a married actress. His behaviour made him unpopular, and this was exacerbated by his refusal to mend his ways following his marriage to Princess Caroline of Brunswick-Wolfenbüttel in 1795. The royal couple lived together for only one out of the 19 years from that date until 1814, when the princess abandoned her husband and returned to Brunswick.

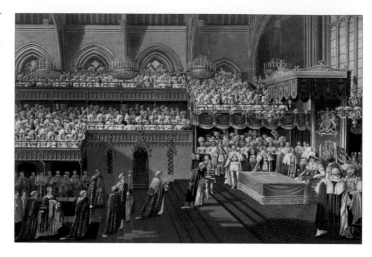

THE INJURED QUEEN

Within six months of George's accession, the former Princess of Wales returned from the Continent in June 1820 to claim her rightful position as Queen of England. A bill was introduced in the House of Lords to dissolve the marriage on the grounds of the queen's alleged adultery and so exclude her from the

Above: In his coronation sermon the Archbishop of York urged the king to deliver Britain from the 'contagion of vice'.

monarchy. Public feeling was aroused by the king's ill-treatment of his wife and, when the bill failed to pass in November 1820, the news sparked wholly remarkable scenes of public rejoicing: bonfires were lit, processions and dances were laid on and Londoners celebrated in the streets.

The following year, when King George IV was crowned in the utmost splendour at Westminster Abbey, his queen tried several times without success to gain admission to the abbey.

George's coronation was as extravagant as the rest of his life: he wore a crimson velvet train some 27ft (8.2m) long and processed from Westminster Hall to the abbey beneath a canopy of cloth of gold. The celebrations, which included a five-hour service, a vast banquet and fireworks in Hyde Park, cost around £240,000.

Queen Caroline did not live long to trouble her royal husband. She was taken ill on the very night of the coronation, and died from an inflammation

---

GEORGE IV, KING OF THE UNITED KINGDOM OF GREAT BRITAIN AND IRELAND AND ELECTOR OF HANOVER, 1820–1830

Birth: 12 Aug 1762, St James's Palace, London

Father: George III

Mother: Charlotte of Mecklenburg-Strelitz

Accession: As Prince Regent, 6 Feb 1811; as King: 29 Jan 1820

Coronation: 19 July 1821

Queen: Princess Caroline of Brunswick-Wolfenbüttel (m. 8 April 1795; d. 7 Aug 1821)

Succeeded by: His brother William IV

Greatest achievement: Artistic patronage, especially the creation of Regent's Park and Regent Street

6 Feb 1811: Becomes Prince Regent due to King George III's illness

8 Aug 1814: Princess of Wales abandons George and returns to Brunswick

6 Nov 1817: George's only daughter, Princess Charlotte, dies

29 Jan 1820: Accedes to throne on death of King George III

23 Feb 1820: 'Conspirators of Cato Street', plotting murder of the cabinet, are arrested

29 Nov 1820: Inquiry clears Queen Caroline of adultery

7 Aug 1821: Queen Caroline dies

Aug–Sept 1821: George makes triumphant visit to Ireland

Aug 1822: George visits Edinburgh and dons a kilt

16 April 1829: Catholic Emancipation Act lifts restrictions on Catholics holding public office

Death: 26 June 1830 at Windsor. Buried in St George's Chapel, Windsor

---

Above: Queen Caroline appears to loom out of George's mirror in an anonymous cartoon published on his accession.

or blockage of the bowels on 7 August 1821 in Hammersmith, west of London. One of her final requests was that she be interred not in England but in Brunswick. Her coffin was carried on a funeral procession to Harwich, where those sympathetic to her memory placed on it the inscription 'Caroline, the injured Queen of England'.

THE KING KILTED

King George IV made a royal visit to Edinburgh in August 1822, as part of a post-coronation 'royal progress' through his kingdom. Arrangements were placed in the hands of the king's friend, the novelist Sir Walter Scott, who had been a guest at the coronation the previous year. Keen to stress the independence and richness of Scots culture, Scott arranged for Highland clan chiefs, bagpipes and kilts to play a prominent part in the proceedings.

George sailed to Scotland on board his yacht, the *Royal George*, and disembarked at the port of Leith. As he processed through the streets of Edinburgh he was greeted by banners emphasizing Scottish links to the royal line. One read, 'Descendant of the immortal Bruce, thrice welcome', another, 'Welcome to the land of your ancestors.' He attended a levée at Holyrood Palace dressed in a kilt, much to the delight of his hosts, and processed alongside MacGregor, Drummond and MacDonnell clansmen from Holyrood to Edinburgh Castle. From the castle, he looked down on the city and exclaimed, 'What a fine sight...the people are as beautiful and extraordinary as the scene.' He also attended several balls and a dramatization at the Theatre Royal of Scott's novel *Rob Roy*. The popularity of Scott's novels and also of King George's visit to Scotland was to spark a revival of interest in the history and traditions of the Highland clans – not least in the wearing of clan tartan in the late Victorian period.

THE KING'S ILLNESS

From 1823 George increasingly kept away from London, living in his extravagant Brighton Pavilion and at Windsor Castle with his latest mistress, Marchioness Conyngham. Years of debauchery had ruined his physique, which was severely bloated by dropsy

Below: Caroline. She accepted a payment of £50,000 per annum to go abroad, but died within a fortnight of the coronation.

and wracked with pain from rheumatism. He continued in his bad habits, drinking very heavily, while also complaining of his afflictions. The Duke of Wellington, who visited him in Windsor, declared that there was nothing wrong with the king save the troubles caused by 'Strong liquors taken too frequently and in too large quantities', adding that George 'Drinks spirits morning, noon and night'.

The king also took laudanum – often as much as 250 drops per day – to counter bladder inflammation; he may also, like his father, have suffered from porphyria. He had attacks of severe breathlessness in which he would have to struggle so hard to draw breath that his fingertips tuned black. He died at Windsor on 26 June 1830. His last words, delivered to his doctor Sir Wathen Waller in a paroxysm of pain, were, 'My dear boy! This is death!'

There was little sadness at his passing. *The Times* declared that there had never been 'An individual less regretted by his fellow creatures than this deceased king'. George was succeeded by his brother William, Duke of Clarence, who reigned as King William IV.

Below: King of Scots. George's visit to Scotland in 1822 was the first by a ruling monarch since that of Charles II.

WILLIAM IV

1830–1837

William, Duke of Clarence, was woken at 6 a.m. on 26 June 1830 to be told that he was king because his older brother, George IV, had died in the small hours. William reportedly shook the messengers by the hand and retired to bed with the joke that it had long been his ambition to sleep with a queen. Later that morning he rode from his home, Bushy House, Teddington, to Windsor, cheerfully receiving the acclamations of the people he passed and exhibiting no signs of grief at his brother's death.

A VERY DIFFERENT BROTHER

The 64-year-old duke had been heir to the throne for only three years following the death in January 1827 of Frederick, Duke of York. He had a bluff, easy-going manner, perhaps explained by the fact that he joined the navy aged 13. He had risen to the rank of lieutenant and taken command of a frigate of 28 guns before he was recalled to civilian life by the Prince of Wales in 1788 at a time when their father was incapacitated by physical illness and mental confusion.

Below: The king's name is forever linked to the 1832 Reform Act, which moved Britain towards fuller democracy.

WILLIAM IV, KING OF THE UNITED KINGDOM OF GREAT BRITAIN AND IRELAND AND ELECTOR OF HANOVER, 1830–1837	
Birth: 21 Aug 1765 at Buckingham House, London	the passage of the first Reform Act, which marked Britain's progress towards full democracy
Father: George III	
Mother: Charlotte of Mecklenburg-Strelitz	**7 June 1832:** Reform Act passed
Accession: 26 June 1830	**Nov 1834:** Fire destroys the Houses of Parliament
Coronation: 8 Sept 1831, Westminster Abbey	**24 May 1837:** Princess Victoria, heir to the throne, celebrates her 18th birthday; she can now inherit the throne in her own right
Queen: Princess Adelaide of Saxe-Meiningen (m. 11 July 1818; d. 2 Dec 1849)	
Succeeded by: His niece, Victoria	**20 June 1837:** Dies at Windsor and is buried in St George's Chapel, Windsor
Greatest achievement: Intervening in	

William lived from 1791 to 1811 with the celebrated actress Mrs Dorothy Jordan, with whom he had ten illegitimate children (five daughters and five sons). In 1818, when the death of Princess Charlotte sparked a mini succession crisis, he married Princess Adelaide of Saxe-Meiningen in a double ceremony on 11 July with his brother Edward, Duke of Kent (who married Princess Victoria of Saxe-Coburg). However, all the children of William's marriage died, so on his accession he was unable to offer a succession through legitimate heirs.

A POPULAR KING

William was immediately popular with his people. In Windsor he opened the East Terrace and various parts of the Great Park to the public and threw an open-air banquet for 3,000 impoverished locals to mark his birthday on 21 August 1830. The king sat with his people to eat from a menu of veal, ham, beef and plum pudding.

He regularly walked the streets of Windsor, London and Brighton rather than ride in a carriage and had the facility of talking easily to strangers.

Acutely aware of the resentment that had been caused by the extravagance of his self-indulgent brother George IV, he took care to have a relatively frugal, low-key coronation in Westminster Abbey on 8 September 1831.

The ceremony cost around £30,000, one-eighth of the £240,000 lavished by George IV on his coronation. One wag called King William's event the 'half-crownation', a reference to the low-denomination half-crown coin.

Below: J.M.W. Turner's painting of Parliament ablaze. The king's household troops were unable to stop the 1834 fire.

'REFORM BILLY'

The king's actions in April 1831 earned
him the nickname 'Reform Billy'. The
Tory-dominated House of Lords was
attempting to block the Reform Bill
introduced by Prime Minister Lord
Grey and already passed by the Whig-
dominated House of Commons. The
Bill extended the franchise and made
much-needed changes in seat distribu-
tion. On 21 April 1831 King William
went personally to the Lords and used
his power to dissolve Parliament, thus
forcing an election in which the Whigs
won a greater majority.

The following year, after a prolonged
Parliamentary struggle and street riots
to protest against the Lords' continuing
efforts to block the bill, William created
sufficient Whig peers to pass the bill and
for the Act to become law.

PARLIAMENT DESTROYED

A terrible fire in November 1834
reduced the Palace of Westminster,
location of the House of Commons and
the House of Lords, to a ruin. The fire
began when two workmen overstocked
a stove in which they were burning
elm-wood tally-sticks that had been
discarded by the Exchequer. The stove,
situated beneath the chamber of the
House of Lords, overheated and began
a fire that took hold.

In the aftermath, King William
offered Buckingham Palace, which he
did not like because he associated it
with the over-indulgence of his
brother's reign, as a replacement home
for the two houses of Parliament. His
offer was declined.

VICTORIA COMES OF AGE

King William had a long-running feud
with his sister-in-law Victoria, Duchess
of Kent who, in the event of his death,
was set to become regent for her
daughter Victoria. He publicly declared
that he would live at least as long as
Victoria's 18th birthday – 24 May 1837
to thwart the Duchess of Kent.

In the event, William fell ill just
before that day, in April 1837: the death
of his daughter Sophia, Lady de L'Isle,
in childbirth appeared to deprive him
of much of the will to go on. He
nonetheless survived until 20 June 1837,
so that on his death aged 71 the 18-
year-old princess acceded to the throne
as Queen Victoria.

*Below: Like George III before him,
William fell into an irreversible decline
after hearing of a beloved daughter's death.*

CHAPTER ELEVEN

THE AGE OF VICTORIA

1837–1901

When the 18-year-old Princess Victoria came to the throne on 20 June 1837, the reputation of the monarchy had been considerably damaged by the excesses of the first four kings of the House of Hanover – from George I (1714–27) to George IV (1820–30) – and its reputation was only partially restored by the more restrained William IV (1830–37). However, by the time Queen Victoria died on 22 January 1901, after a reign of sixty-three-and-a-half years, the monarchy was a well-respected and essential British institution: the queen had become a proud symbol of the stability and power of Britain, a country that now possessed 20 per cent of global territory in the greatest empire known to history. The presence of representatives from across the British Empire at the celebrations that marked the Queen's Golden and Diamond Jubilees in 1887 and 1897, marked the establishment of Britain as a worldwide empire.

Largely as a result of this imperial expansion, Queen Victoria's reign saw a tremendous rise in the prestige of the British monarchy. After 1877, when she became Empress of India, the queen was proud to sign herself *Victoria Regina et Imperatrix* ('Victoria, Queen and Empress'). Yet the reign also saw a steady decline in the monarch's real power in government in a continuation of the transformation of the British monarch from ruler to figurehead that was set in motion by the 'Glorious Revolution' of 1689.

Left: The domestic calm of the royal family is presented in a group portrait of Queen Victoria and Prince Albert in 1847 with the eldest five of their offspring – Princess Victoria, Prince Edward, Princess Alice, Prince Alfred and Princess Helena. Victoria would eventually have nine children and 31 surviving grandchildren.

VICTORIA
1837–1901

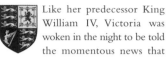

Like her predecessor King William IV, Victoria was woken in the night to be told the momentous news that the previous occupant of the throne had died. At around 6 a.m. on 20 June 1837 the Archbishop of Canterbury, William Howley, and the Lord Chamberlain, Marquis Conyngham, informed the 18-year-old princess that she was now queen. Within three hours the young queen held a meeting with the Prime Minister Lord Melbourne and informed him that she wanted him to remain in government.

DESTINED TO BE QUEEN?

Victoria came to the throne as the only legitimate child of Edward Augustus, Duke of Kent, the fourth son of King George III. In 1818, Edward married Princess Victoria of Saxe-Coburg-Saalfeld, and their daughter Alexandrina Victoria was born in Kensington Palace on 24 May 1819. The duke was

Below: Princess Victoria aged four. Her upbringing was lonely, in the hands of strict German governess Baroness Lehzen.

VICTORIA, QUEEN OF THE UNITED KINGDOM OF GREAT BRITAIN AND IRELAND AND EMPRESS OF INDIA, 1837–1901

Birth: 24 May 1819, Kensington Palace, London

Father: Edward Augustus, Duke of Kent

Mother: Victoria of Saxe-Coburg-Saalfeld

Accession: 20 June 1837

Coronation: 28 June 1838

Married: Albert Augustus Charles Emmanuel of Saxe-Coburg-Gotha (m. 10 Feb 1840; d. 14 Dec 1861)

Succeeded by: Her son, Edward VII

Greatest achievement: Figurehead as Empress of the British Empire

10 Feb 1840: Marries Prince Albert of Saxe-Coburg and Gotha

21 Nov 1840: Birth of Victoria's first child, Princess Victoria Adelaide

9 Nov 1841: Birth of Prince Albert Edward, future King Edward VII

1 May 1851: Victoria and Albert open the Great Exhibition

25 June 1857: Albert is 'Prince Consort'

10 March 1863: Prince of Wales marries Princess Alexandra of Denmark

14 Dec 1861: Prince Albert dies

8 April 1871: Queen Victoria opens the Royal Albert Hall as a memorial

1 Jan 1877: Queen Victoria becomes Empress of India

29 March 1883: Death of John Brown, Victoria's 'Highland servant'

20 June 1887: Victoria's Golden Jubilee

20 June 1897: Victoria's Diamond Jubilee

Death: 22 Jan 1901, Osborne House, Isle of Wight. Buried at Frogmore

---

extremely proud of his baby daughter, and would tell people she was destined to be queen. Unfortunately, within months of the princess's birth he died of pneumonia.

WILLING TO LEARN

Victoria grew up into a serious-minded young woman. On her accession she noted in her diary, 'Since it has pleased Providence to place me in this station, I shall do my utmost to fulfil my duty towards my country; I am very young, and perhaps in many, though not all things, inexperienced, but I am sure that very few have more real good will and more real desire to do what is fit and right than I have'. She was crowned in great splendour in Westminster Abbey on 28 June 1838.

The young queen was just 4ft 11in (1.5m) tall. Despite rather large blue eyes and a small mouth, she could not be described as beautiful, but she was engaging and charming and observers often described her as 'lovely'.

Left: Victoria had a thorough education. By the age of ten, she was having formal lessons five hours a day, six days a week.

Above: Royal newly weds and leaders of musical fashion. A piece of sheet music shows the queen dancing with Albert.

'LORD M'

The young queen was aware that she lacked experience in the ways of government and became devoted to her Prime Minister Lord Melbourne, whom she called 'Lord M'. Melbourne was a Whig and Victoria supported the Whigs over the Conservatives, in part because she believed her late father to have been a Whig himself.

However, having lost the support of the House of the Commons, Melbourne was forced to resign on 7 May 1839. Victoria was distressed and wrote in her diary, 'All my happiness gone!...dearest kind Lord Melbourne no more my minister!'

Victoria was obstructive to Melbourne's Conservative successor, Sir Robert Peel. When Peel sought to replace Whig-supporting ladies of the bedchamber with Conservative-supporting ladies, the queen refused to accept the new appointments. After a standoff, Peel declined to form a government and Melbourne returned. Some interpreted this crisis as an attempt by the queen to reassert the monarch's authority over ministers, while many others have seen it as an inappropriately emotional outburst.

PRINCE ALBERT

Victoria announced her engagement to Prince Albert of Saxe-Coburg-Gotha on 23 November 1839. Victoria's uncle King Leopold of the Belgians, had long envisaged Albert as a suitable match for his niece and had arranged a visit to Britain in May 1836 for Albert and his brother Ernest.

Victoria met Albert then and found him to have 'Every quality that could be desired' but subsequently, and even as late as June 1839, she was convinced that she would prefer to remain single for several years. However, on 10 October, when Albert arrived at Windsor at the start of a prearranged visit, Victoria fell swiftly in love. She afterwards recalled, 'It was with some emotion that I beheld Albert, who is *beautiful*'. Five days later she proposed to him declaring, as she later recalled, that, 'It would make me too happy if he would consent to what I wished (to marry me)'.

ROYAL WEDDING

Victoria and Albert were married at St James's Palace on 10 February 1840. After a magnificent wedding breakfast at Buckingham Palace, they travelled to Windsor for their honeymoon. Their first child, Victoria Adelaide, was born on 21 November 1840. When the doctor announced that the baby was a daughter, a princess, Victoria replied, 'Never mind, the next one will be a prince'. Sure enough, a boy – Albert Edward, the future King Edward VII – was born on 9 November 1841.

Below: Young queen with a great future. In her coronation robes in 1838 Victoria appears to look heavenwards for guidance.

THE CROWN UNDER THREAT
1840–1850

In the 1840s the youthful Queen Victoria survived a number of botched assassination attempts, at a time of growing republican sentiment among radical groups. The first attack came on 10 June 1840, when an 18-year-old named Edward Oxford fired pistols twice at Victoria and Prince Albert as they rode up Constitution Hill in London. The royal couple calmly continued their drive after the attack, as the assailant was captured by a bystander, Mr Millais, and his art student son.

Oxford was tried for high treason, but claimed insanity and was acquitted. Some contemporaries suggested that he was part of a conspiracy by 'Chartists' (working-class supporters of parliamentary reform, in particular of universal suffrage for all males over 21).

THE 'VICTORIA CROSS' AND THE CRIMEAN WAR

Victoria took great pride in the valorous achievements of the British Army in the Crimean War of 1854–6. On 29 January 1856 she introduced a new decoration for bravery called the Victoria Cross and inscribed 'for valour': it brought with it a pension of £10 a year.

Britain had declared war on Russia on 28 February 1854 to defend Turkey against Russian expansion in the regions of the Balkans and the Mediterranean. When Britain's French allies stormed Russian-held Sebastopol in September 1855, Victoria and Albert celebrated by dancing wildly around a bonfire on Craig Gowan near Balmoral. Albert reported it 'A veritable witches' dance supported by whisky'.

At other times Victoria played out her part in the conflict by knitting socks and mittens for the soldiers and writing letters of condolence to be sent to relatives of those killed in the fighting. When the troops returned she reviewed them with great pride at Aldershot on 30 July 1856.

Right: An 1856 engraving celebrates the new honour and various acts of bravery.

Above: On 18 May 1856 the queen presented the Victoria Cross to crippled Crimean war veteran Sir Thomas Troubridge.

Two more attacks followed in summer 1842. The first was made on 30 May, when John Francis attempted to shoot the queen from a distance of only five paces as she and Albert drove down the Mall; the man's pistol was unloaded and he was easily overpowered. The second was made on 3 July, when a youth named John William Bean succeeded in firing a pistol at the queen, but did not hurt her as the weapon was not correctly loaded. Francis was convicted of high treason, but the sentence was commuted to transportation; Bean was sentenced to 18 months' imprisonment.

The more lenient sentence came under a new act passed by Parliament under which hitting the queen or producing a weapon in her presence was no longer considered treason but was made subject to a seven-year prison term and a flogging; in this case, Bean

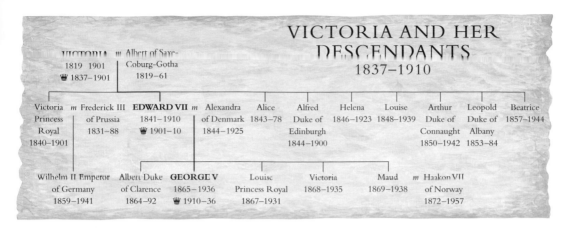

VICTORIA AND HER DESCENDANTS
1837–1910

VICTORIA
1819 1901
♛ 1837–1901
m Albert of Saxe-Coburg-Gotha
1819–61

| Victoria Princess Royal 1840–1901 | *m* Frederick III of Prussia 1831–88 | **EDWARD VII** 1841–1910 ♛ 1901–10 | *m* Alexandra of Denmark 1844–1925 | Alice 1843–78 | Alfred Duke of Edinburgh 1844–1900 | Helena 1846–1923 | Louise 1848–1939 | Arthur Duke of Connaught 1850–1942 | Leopold Duke of Albany 1853–84 | Beatrice 1857–1944 |

| Wilhelm II Emperor of Germany 1859–1941 | Albert Duke of Clarence 1864–92 | **GEORGE V** 1865–1936 ♛ 1910–36 | Louise Princess Royal 1867–1931 | Victoria 1868–1935 | Maud 1869–1938 | *m* Haakon VII of Norway 1872–1957 |

escaped the flogging. Prince Albert supported the introduction of the act. He felt that if attacks were treated as treason and subject to a death penalty they often ended with acquittal, whereas if a less draconian punishment were made available it would be more likely to be imposed – and so act as a deterrent.

FEAR OF REVOLUTION

The year 1848 saw an explosion of revolutionary activity in Europe. In February, King Louis Philippe of France was deposed and took refuge with Queen Victoria. This was followed a month later by revolutionary outbursts

Below: Assassination attempts continued throughout the reign. This one, by Roderick MacLean in Windsor, was in March 1882.

in Italy, Germany, Hungary and Austria. Marx and Engels' *Communist Manifesto* was also published in German and French. Given this climate, the British government, royal family and aristocracy were understandably nervous.

On 8 April 1848, two days ahead of a planned Chartist rally in London, Victoria, Albert and their six children left the capital for the safety of their house on the Isle of Wight. They left London in the hands of the Duke of Wellington, who was commanding yeoman regiments with guns arranged to defend the bridges across the Thames. In the event the feared uprising did not take place.

The queen's everyday movements around London nonetheless left her very vulnerable to attack and by the

start of the 1850s she had been attacked twice more on the streets of the capital.

On 19 May 1849 an Irishman named William Hamilton shot at her from almost point-blank range as she drove in her carriage down Constitution Hill towards Buckingham Palace following her official birthday celebrations. Once again, and most fortunately, the pistol had not been properly loaded.

On 27 July 1850 she was actually struck by a man named Robert Pate who attacked her with a stick as she travelled in an open carriage through Piccadilly. The queen was left with facial bruises and a very bad headache.

Below: Victoria and Albert had been married only four months when they were attacked by Edward Oxford in June 1840.

THE GREAT EXHIBITION

CRYSTAL PALACE, 1851

On 1 May 1851, Queen Victoria and Prince Albert rode in a fleet of nine state carriages from Buckingham Palace to Hyde Park to open an 'Exhibition of the Works of Industry of all Nations'. The 'Great Exhibition' had been organized principally by Prince Albert and civil servant Henry Cole to celebrate the achievements of modern industry, to 'Combine engineering, utility and beauty in one staggering whole'.

More than 100,000 items were put on display by 14,000 exhibitors from around the world: more than half were from Britain and the British empire. There were 560 exhibits from the United States, including a Colt pistol, Goodyear India rubber products and false teeth.

British exhibits included automated spinning machines, steam engines and pumps. Other magnificent display items included the world's largest pearl and the Koh-i-Noor ('Mountain of brightness') diamond, a Mughal Indian stone that had been acquired by Britain in the 1849 annexation of the Punjab and since placed among Victoria's crown jewels.

THE CRYSTAL PALACE

The exhibition was housed in the magnificent Crystal Palace, made of glass and cast-iron. It was designed by Joseph Paxton and based on the design of the conservatory of Chatsworth House, where he worked for the Duke of Devonshire as garden superintendant. The palace stood 1848ft (563m) long and 408ft (124m) across. It covered 18 acres (7 hectares) of parkland, while the exhibition floorspace was 23 acres (9 hectares). It contained almost 300,000 panes of glass and 4000 tons of iron. William Thackeray wrote of the palace, 'A blazing arch of lucid glass/Leaps like a Fountain from the grass'.

Above: This picture of the Italian Court was taken after the Palace and Exhibition were moved to Sydenham, south London.

At its tallest point, the Crystal Palace was 108ft (33m) tall; its roof rose above the tops of the ancient elms that stood in the part of Hyde Park chosen to erect the building. Initially the developers had problems with sparrows, which flew in and out of the vast building and spattered exhibits with their droppings, but the problem was solved by the Duke of Wellington, who had the idea of deterring the sparrows by introducing sparrowhawks to hunt them.

The sun shone brilliantly through the glass roof as Victoria, Albert and their eldest offspring, 'Vicky' and 'Bertie', took their place on a dais in the centre of the building. A 600-strong choir sang the National Anthem, before the Archbishop of Canterbury read a prayer and the choir performed Handel's 'Hallelujah' Chorus. The Marquis of Breadalbane declared, 'Her Majesty commands me to declare the Exhibition opened'. Victoria was overwhelmed by the triumph. As she afterwards reported, the occasion was 'The greatest day in our history...the triumph of my beloved

Left: On 1 May 1851, the royal party arrives at the Crystal Palace in Hyde Park to open the fêted Great Exhibition.

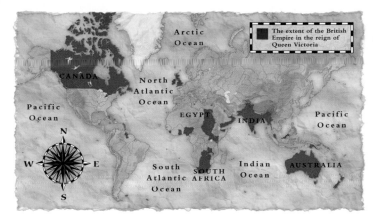

Above: The Exhibition celebrated the pride of queen and people in the achievements of industry and the spread of the empire.

Above: Victoria reported that the opening was 'The most beautiful and imposing and touching spectacle ever seen'.

Albert…It was the happiest, proudest day in my life, and I can think of nothing else, Albert's dearest name immortalized with this great conception…The triumph is immense.'

The project was closely associated with Prince Albert, who at a meeting of the Royal Society of Arts in 1849 had promoted an earlier suggestion by Henry Cole to put on such an exhibition. Albert chaired a Royal Commission, established in 1850 and containing many members of the great and the good, including Gladstone, Peel and the Duke of Devonshire, to raise funds and make practical preparations.

At a meeting at the Mansion House on 21 March 1850 to launch preparations for the exhibition, Albert declared that it would promote 'Achievements of modern invention' and be a 'Living picture of the point of development at which mankind has arrived, and a new starting point from which all nations will be able to direct their future exertions'. For three months after the

Right: A writer in The Times *likened the crowds gathered around Victoria at the opening to the heavenly host: 'Some were reminded of that day when all…should be gathered round the Throne of their maker'.*

opening, Victoria came as often as every other day to the exhibition: she even visited the Crystal Palace on her 32nd birthday, 24 May.

SYMBOL OF AN AGE

The Great Exhibition was open from 1 May to 15 October 1851. It attracted six million visitors from around the world and made a profit of £186,000, which was used to build the Natural History Museum, the Victoria and Albert Museum and the Science Museum in the second half of the 19th century; the area of South Kensington in which the museums were built was nicknamed 'Albertopolis' in the Victorian age. The Crystal Palace was dismantled and

rebuilt in Sydenham Hill, south London where, such was the quality of its construction, it survived intact until 1936, when it burnt down.

The Great Exhibition and the Crystal Palace are generally seen as symbols of the Victorian age. The exhibition contained many modern industrial items and exhibits. The world was changing: in the 1851 population census, for the first time in British history, town-dwellers outnumbered people living in the country. At the centre was the queen, a reassuring source of stability.

ALBERT AND THE ROYAL FAMILY
1840–1861

In the first years after Victoria's marriage to Prince Albert in 1840, the queen was determined that the responsibilities of government should not be shared by her husband, but she very quickly became dependent on his advice and – particularly during her pregnancies – he played an increasingly central role in affairs of state and meetings with ministers.

As early as 1845, Charles Greville commented, 'It is obvious that while she has the title, he is really discharging the functions of the Sovereign. He is the King to all intents and purposes.'

When Prince Albert died in 1861, Victoria reflected that she had 'Leant on him for all and everything – without whom I did nothing, moved not a finger, arranged not a print or photograph, didn't put on a gown or bonnet if he didn't approve it'.

A MODEL FOR DOMESTIC LIFE

Victoria and Albert's marriage, stable life and large family did much to restore the dignity and standing of the monarchy after the excesses and public disgraces of the early Hanoverian kings.

The royal couple had no fewer than nine children, all of whom survived to adulthood, which was highly unusual even among the wealthy at the time. In addition to Princess Victoria and Prince Edward, the queen gave birth to seven other children: Princess Alice (born 25 April 1843), Prince Alfred ('Affie', born 6 August 1844), Princess Helena (born 25 May 1846), Princess Louise (born

Above: Prince Consort. This celebrated portrait by Franz Winterhalter shows Prince Albert in 1859, at the age of 40.

18 March 1848), Prince Arthur (born 1 May 1850), Prince Leopold (born 7 April 1853) and Princess Beatrice (born 14 April 1857). In 1853 Victoria did much to popularize the use of anaesthesia during childbirth when she took chloroform while in labour prior to the birth of Prince Leopold. She later reported that it was 'Soothing, quieting and delightful beyond measure'.

Many of Victoria's children married into other European royal families, weaving a complex web of dynastic relationships that led her to become known as the 'matriarch of Europe'. When she died, she had 31 surviving grandchildren and 40 great-grandchildren. Her granddaughters included the queens of Sweden, Norway, Greece, Romania and Spain, and the Tsarina of Russia. One of her grandsons became Kaiser Wilhelm II of Germany.

In their life together at Windsor, Balmoral and the family home of Osborne House on the Isle of Wight, the royal family was held up to the nation as the perfect exemplar of

GATHERED AROUND THE CHRISTMAS TREE

Prince Albert is generally credited with introducing to Britain the German custom of decorating a tree as part of a family's Christmas celebrations. The custom became popular following its use by Victoria and Albert and particularly after

the publication in the December 1848 *Illustrated London News* of a picture of the royal family gathered around the Christmas tree. However, the true royal pioneer of the tradition in Britain was Queen Charlotte, wife of King George III. She first had a Christmas tree in 1800. Victoria, indeed, had been enchanted by the custom in her own childhood and reported enjoying Christmas trees in 1832, when she was 13. Prince Albert's first Christmas tree, in Windsor Castle, in December 1841, was hung with German glass ornaments, candles, gingerbread, sweets and fruit. That Christmas, Victoria and Albert had two infant children – Victoria and Edward – to entertain. Albert noted that his children were 'full of happy wonder' on Christmas Eve.

Left: This Illustrated London News *engraving, of royal children around the tree in 1848, popularized the custom.*

Above: At Osborne, 26 May 1857. Left to right: Alfred, Albert, Helena, Alice, Arthur, Victoria holding Beatrice, Vicky, Louise, Leopold and Albert Edward.

domestic life. However, the reality of family life, even for a king and queen, was somewhat different. Victoria had a fierce temper and would sometimes throw tantrums when her will was crossed. Albert became distant and withdrew in the face of sharp words, but usually managed to bring the queen around to a mood of repentance and deference. Victoria also feared childbirth, which she called the 'Shadow-side of marriage'. She wrote to Vicky, the Princess Royal in 1858, that giving birth made her feel 'Like a cow or a dog'. Our poor nature becomes so very animal and unecstatic'.

DEATH AND MOURNING

Prince Albert's death from typhoid fever aged just 42 was unexpected until a few days before he died at Windsor on 14 December 1861. He had been unwell for years – modern doctors believe he may have suffered from bowel or stomach cancer – and the fatal attack was initially seen by the queen as another in

a series of episodes. It was only in the last three days that she was aware that he was dying. At the last she knelt by his bedside and held his hand.

Albert's death came at the end of a truly terrible year for the queen, in which she lost her mother, the Duchess of Kent (d. 16 March 1861) and may herself have suffered from a mental

Below: The Albert Memorial (1872) in Kensington Gardens, London. The golden statue of the Prince was added in 1876.

breakdown. She also learned that the Prince of Wales had been conducting an affair with the Irish courtesan Nellie Clifden while official negotiations were being conducted for his marriage to Denmark's Princess Alexandra.

The loss of the man she described as 'The purest and best of human beings' devastated Victoria. 'He was my life', she wrote. She later recalled the deep desolation she felt, 'Those paroxysms of despair and yearning and longing and of daily, nightly longing to die...for the first three years never left me'. She withdrew to the Isle of Wight and was represented at her husband's funeral, in Windsor on 23 December 1861, by the Prince of Wales.

Victoria's withdrawal from public life was almost total and lasted at least ten years. She was effectively invisible as queen until the early 1870s. The public was initially respectful and sympathetic, but as time passed and the queen did not re-emerge to play her public role, the national mood became impatient. In 1871, however, Victoria was able to open a lasting memorial to her husband in the form of the magnificent Royal Albert Hall in Kensington, London, and that same year she began to re-emerge.

QUEEN VICTORIA'S SCOTLAND
1843–1901

In 1843 Queen Victoria and Prince Albert began a long love affair with Scotland when they visited Lord Breadalbane in Taymouth Castle. The royal couple were keen readers of the novels of Sir Walter Scott, with their taste for romances of the Highlands and for the traditional tartans worn by the clans. Prince Albert wrote, 'Scotland has made a most favourable impression on us both'. He praised the beautiful countryside, the many opportunities for sport and the 'Remarkably light and pure' air.

BALMORAL

The couple leased the manor house of Balmoral – which Victoria described as 'A pretty little castle in the old Scotch style' – in September 1848. In 1852 they bought the castle and its estate of 20,000 acres on the bank of the river Dee in Grampian for 300,000 guineas.

The 15th-century building stood on the site of an earlier hunting lodge belonging to King Robert II (1371–90). It was demolished and a significantly larger castle was built

Below: The romance of Scotland. This image of Balmoral is from sheet music entitled 'The Highland Home'.

Above: Balmoral Castle. Albert's design made the Scottish baronial style popular.

following Prince Albert's own designs in the 'Scottish baronial style', using grey granite from the nearby quarries of Glen Gelder. It was finished in 1855.

The queen was enchanted by the finished building, and the royal couple made repeated visits. She wrote in her journal, 'Every year my heart becomes more fixed in this dear paradise and so much more so now that all has become my dearest Albert's own creation'.

The queen was particularly appreciative of the service of John Brown, Prince Albert's hunting guide or *ghillie* and later her own personal attendant, whom she praised as 'Really the perfection of a servant.'

Victoria continued to visit Balmoral after Albert's death in 1861, often staying in its secluded surroundings for as much as four months at a time while she pined for her late husband. She ordered a large statue of Albert to be raised on the estate. She was greatly helped in her mourning by the loyalty and devotion of John Brown. In 1868 she published a book, based on her journal, detailing her stays there with

Albert and family. *Leaves from the Journal of Our Life in the Highlands 1848–61* was an instant bestseller. Such was its success that Victoria produced a follow-up, *More Leaves*, in 1883, based on journal entries for the years 1862–63, immediately after Albert's death. The queen's books and interest in Balmoral helped restore the link between the monarchy and Scotland, which had been lacking since the Act of Union.

Below: After Albert's death, Victoria was so close to former Balmoral guide John Brown that she was nicknamed 'Mrs Brown'.

VICTORIAN PALACES
1844–1901

Victoria and Albert found a pleasant retreat from the formal surroundings of Buckingham Palace on the Isle of Wight, where they bought Osborne House and around 1,000 acres (400 hectares) in 1844.

OSBORNE HOUSE

The house was demolished and a new villa in the Italian renaissance style built to the designs of Prince Albert and architect Thomas Cubitt. The very large villa contained a 'pavilion wing' for the royal family and another, less grand, wing for the household servants. A grand corridor between the two wings was used to display classical statues.

The royal family moved in in September 1846. Osborne House was subsequently the setting for many family holidays. It was at Osborne House on 26 May 1857 that the queen's family posed for the first official royal group photograph in British history.

BUCKINGHAM PALACE

At the start of Victoria's reign Buckingham Palace was made the monarch's official state residence in London, and the period of her rule saw significant work on the palace. Earlier, in the reign of George IV (1820–30),

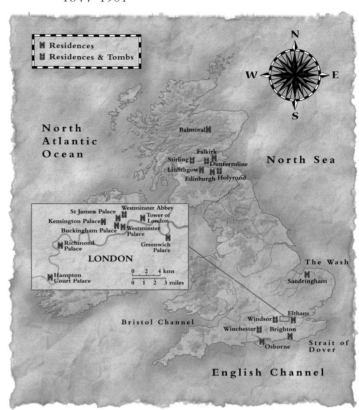

Above: Royal palaces, residences and tombs range from Anglo-Saxon Winchester to Victorian Balmoral and Sandringham.

John Nash had raised a large three-sided courtyard that gave on to the Mall through a grandiose arch. In 1847 Edmund Blore completed a fourth wing that enclosed the courtyard: this is the side of the palace currently visible from the Mall. In 1851, Nash's archway was moved to the former Tyburn execution ground at the northeast corner of Hyde Park – the spot now known as 'Marble Arch'. In 1851–5, James Pennethorne built a ballroom and supper-room in Buckingham Palace.

Left: The Victoria Memorial (1911) stands in front of Buckingham Palace today.

Right: The Italianate terrace at Osborne House gives onto an ornate courtyard.

EDWARD, PRINCE OF WALES

1841–1901

 Queen Victoria and Prince Albert tried hard to raise their offspring with a highly developed sense of duty, an industrious attitude and respect for others. Right from the start the royal parents took a close, controlling interest in their children's education and most particularly in that of their eldest son, 'Bertie', the Prince of Wales and heir to the throne. However, from an early age he disappointed his mother and father by exhibiting a wilful attitude and a lack of commitment to his studies.

BERTIE'S 'FALL'

In 1861 the Prince of Wales caused great distress to his parents by losing his virginity in an all-too-public affair with a Dublin courtesan named Nellie Clifden. Prince Albert was horrified by the potential impact of this unwelcome news upon the hard-won moral image of the royal family and within months succumbed to an attack of typhoid fever. Victoria afterwards blamed Bertie

Below: By 1863, when Bertie married Princess Alexandra, Queen Victoria was 44 and in the 26th year of her reign.

Above: In the company of Lt.-Col. Baker, the Prince of Wales reviews the 10th Hussars at Aldershot on 8 September 1871.

for causing his father's death. She refused to grant her son a public role and found his mere presence a provocation. 'It quite irritates me to see him in the room', she told Lord Clarendon, while she wrote to her eldest daughter, Vicky, 'Much as I pity him, I never can or shall look at him without a shudder'.

A FAMILY LIFE?

On 10 March 1863, with his mother's full blessing, Prince Bertie married Princess Alexandra of Denmark. The royal couple made their London home in Marlborough House, in Pall Mall, while their country residence was Sandringham. On 8 January 1864 Bertie became a father when Princess Alexandra gave birth to a son two months prematurely. He was christened Albert Victor. A second son, George Frederick, (the future George V) was born on 3 June 1865.

The queen remained determined to exclude the Prince of Wales from an active life as a royal. Although he took a seat in the House of Lords, where he occasionally made speeches, and served

Below: The 'Jersey Lily'. Lillie Langtry, Bertie's mistress after 1877, was the first society lady to work as an actress.

in positions such as President of the Society of Arts, he gave most of his energy to a wild social life, gambling at whist, attending music halls, visiting pleasure gardens, enjoying himself on the Riviera and in Paris, attending meetings of horse racing at Goodwood and yachting at Cowes; and hosting lavish house parties at Sandringham.

THE PRINCE AS WITNESS

In 1869–70 the prince became embroiled in a scandalous divorce case involving Lady Harriet Mordaunt, the mentally unhinged wife of Sir Charles Mordaunt, Conservative MP for South Warwickshire. Sir Charles brought a divorce case against Lady Mordaunt on the grounds of adultery with two of the prince's friends; there was press and public outcry after it emerged that Lady Mordaunt had also named the prince as her lover. On 21 February 1870 the prince appeared in court as a witness and was openly asked whether he had been drawn into 'improper familiarity' with Lady Harriet; his simple negative reply was not enough to calm the storm of public feeling, and he was hissed when out and about in London.

Below: Prince 'Bertie' married the beautiful Princess Alexandra of Denmark in St George's Chapel, Windsor, in March 1863.

Then in 1871 two of the Prince of Wales's indiscretions came back to haunt him. A former mistress, Lady Susan Vane Tempest, was left badly off on the death of her husband and repeatedly pressed the prince for money, which he was forced to provide. In addition, the prince was blackmailed over indiscreet letters he had written to Giulia Baruci, a renowned Italian prostitute. In the end he had to pay £240 to retrieve the letters from Giulia's brother, Pirro Benini.

These problems could not have come at a worse time. In 1870, France proclaimed a republic, and republican feeling was running high in Britain too, where Liberal MP Sir Charles Dilke was a figurehead for a movement calling for an English republic. Dilke declared that the monarchy was politically corrupt and accused the mourning queen of 'dereliction of duty'.

Above: Four princes. Bertie and his brothers Alfred Duke of Edinburgh, Arthur Duke of Connaught and Leopold Duke of Albany.

However, potential disaster was averted. In December 1871 the Prince of Wales fell very seriously ill with typhoid and it was feared he would die. The public mood swung immediately and firmly behind the royal family. On 27 February 1872, when a Service of Thanksgiving for the prince's recovery was held in St Paul's Cathedral, crowds lined the streets to cheer Victoria and the Prince of Wales.

This was far from the end of the Prince of Wales's scandals and indiscretions, but the republican crisis of 1870–2 was over and, as Queen Victoria emerged from her period of mourning for Prince Albert, the popularity of the monarchy reached new heights.

VICTORIA, QUEEN AND EMPRESS
YEARS OF JUBILEE, 1877–1901

 On 22 June 1897 Queen Victoria paraded for 6 miles (10km) through London past vast, cheering crowds to celebrate her Diamond Jubilee – the 60th anniversary of her accession to the throne. The Jubilee procession included representatives from far and wide across the vast British empire – from Australia, Borneo, India, Canada and British parts of Africa.

In a landau carriage pulled by a splendidly attired team of eight horses, she paraded to St Paul's Cathedral, where a service of thanksgiving was held, then on across London Bridge and through the poorer parts of London south of the river Thames. Everywhere she went, she was cheered to the skies and was several times reduced to tears. She wrote in her diary, 'A never to be forgotten day. No one ever, I believe, has

Right: This combination of family portraits and views of royal residences was published in Victoria's Golden Jubilee Book.

Below: This rare picture of Victoria smiling was taken on the occasion of her Golden Jubilee celebrations in June 1887.

met with such an ovation as was given me…The crowds were quite indescribable…The cheering was quite deafening, and every face seemed to be filled with real joy.'

THE VICTORIAN EMPIRE

Since 1877, Queen Victoria had been Empress of India – *Victoria Regina et Imperatrix* ('Victoria, Queen and Empress'). She was ruler of history's greatest empire and revered in many far-flung parts of the world. No fewer than eleven colonial prime ministers travelled to London for the Diamond Jubilee and afterwards held an imperial conference. From Buckingham Palace Victoria sent greetings to the empire: 'From my heart, I thank my beloved people. May God bless them!'

On 23 September 1896 Victoria had become the longest-reigning monarch in British history, when she passed the previous record, set by George III, of 59

Above: The privileged few received this invitation to Queen Victoria's Diamond Jubilee Reception and Ball in 1897.

Right: On 'A never to be forgotten day', crowds lined the streets to watch the queen's Diamond Jubilee procession.

years and 96 days. George III, of course, was a forgotten man for the final ten years of his reign, reduced by the madness that accompanied his undiagnosed porphyria to a shadow of his former self. However, Victoria remained active and had never been more popular.

THE GOLDEN JUBILEE

At the close of the previous decade, equally lavish ceremonies had been held in July 1887 to mark the Golden Jubilee – the 50th anniversary of Victoria's accession. In 1887, London's streets were packed by thousands of well-wishers, who cheered Victoria as she rode in

procession to Westminster Abbey. At a party in Hyde Park 30,000 children were treated to buns and milk in special Jubilee mugs. She received telegrams of congratulation from across the empire including one from India which read, 'Empress of Hindoostan, Head of all Kings and Rulers, and King of all Kings, who is one in a hundred, is Her Majesty Queen Victoria'.

THE LAST MONTHS

In 1900 Victoria's health began to give way. In the year that she turned 81, she was plagued by indigestion, loss of appetite, insomnia and exhaustion.

She was badly shaken by reverses for British troops fighting Boer irregulars in Cape Colony (southern Africa) and by the death in July 1900 of her third child and second son, Prince Alfred, of cancer of the throat, aged 55.

Queen Victoria slipped into a terminal decline. She spent her final weeks at Osborne House on the Isle of Wight. She suffered a stroke on 17 January and died on 22 January 1901 at 6.30 p.m. in the company of her children and grandchildren. At the last she was reconciled with her eldest son and heir to the throne, with whom she had had so many difficulties and endured so many estrangements: her final act was to breathe his name 'Bertie!' and stretch out her arms to him.

Victoria's death was truly the end of an era. From the 1850s, the adjective 'Victorian' had been given to the reign and the historical age in Britain, in the United States and across Europe. When she died, none of her subjects below the age of 64 years knew what it was like to live under any other monarch.

The 63 years of her reign saw sweeping changes, with widespread industrialization and the advent of trains, photography and moving pictures, the telephone, electric lighting and the motor car. However, on 22 January 1901 the 'Victorian age' ended.

VICTORIA'S EMPIRE

By 1900 Britain's empire included the dominions of Canada and Australia and colonies in the Honduras, the Bahamas, the West Indies, Guyana, southern, western and eastern Africa, Kuwait, India and Burma, Hong Kong, Malaya, North Borneo and the South Solomon islands. The empire contained 20 per cent of the world's territory and 23 per cent of the global population.

Right: Queen Victoria was hailed as the 'mother of the Empire'. Her reign saw the consolidation of a vast trading empire.

CHAPTER TWELVE

THE HOUSE OF WINDSOR

1901–

Victoria reigned for over 60 years and celebrated her Diamond Jubilee in 1897. Her death on 22 January 1901 marked the end of British rule by the House of Hanover, which had reigned since the accession of George I in 1714. Victoria's son, Edward VII, was the first king of the House of Saxe-Coburg and Gotha: its name came from that of Victoria's husband, Prince Albert of Saxe-Coburg and Gotha. Edward VII and his son George V ruled as kings of the House of Saxe-Coburg and Gotha. However, on 17 July 1917, in the midst of the First World War against Germany, George V decreed that henceforth he and his descendants would be known as 'Windsor'. The name was that of one of his principal palaces, Windsor Castle, and was thought to have a reassuringly British resonance.

George V's descendants have ruled under this name to the present day. The children of Elizabeth II would normally be expected to take the surname Mountbatten, that of Elizabeth's husband Prince Philip (and an Anglicized form of the German 'Battenberg'). However, in the first year of her reign, 1952, Elizabeth II declared that her descendants would be called Windsor. Thus her successor – for instance, her son, ruling as King Charles III, or his son, ruling as King William V – will maintain the rule of the House of Windsor. The enthusiasm with which the British people celebrated the marriage of Prince William and Kate Middleton in 2011 and international involvement in plans for the Queen's Diamond Jubilee in June 2012 show the long-lasting appeal of the British monarchy at the start of the 21st century.

Left: For sixty years, Queen Elizabeth II has attended the State Opening of Parliament. In 2004 she was accompanied by Prince Philip and her Ladies in Waiting.

EDWARD VII
1901–1910

Edward VII lived a large part of his life as Prince of Wales, prevented by his mother Queen Victoria from taking a role in government affairs. On his accession in 1901, he was 59 years old and keen to make his mark.

FROM PRINCE TO KING

The new king, who had been christened Edward Albert, made clear his desire to put some distance between his rule and that of his mother when he declared that he would be known as Edward VII and not – as Victoria had wanted in honour of his father – as Albert I. He was proclaimed King Edward VII on 23 January 1901.

In his long period as Prince of Wales, Edward had become associated with a riotous social life in which he indulged his taste for 'fast' living, with gambling, and horse racing. However, he had also proved, during trips to Canada and the United States in 1860 and to India in 1876, that he made a very effective overseas ambassador for his country. Both his personality and his achievements as ambassador would play a notable part during his reign as king.

Above: Regal grandeur. Edward combined the dignity proper to his position with a modern outlook and charming manner.

EDWARD VII, KING OF THE UNITED KINGDOM OF GREAT BRITAIN AND IRELAND AND EMPEROR OF INDIA, 1901–1910

Birth: 9 Nov 1841, Buckingham Palace
Father: Prince Albert
Mother: Victoria
Accession: 22 Jan 1901
Coronation: 9 Aug 1902
Queen: Princess Alexandra of Denmark (m. 10 March 1863; d. 20 Nov 1925)
Succeeded by: His son George V
Greatest achievement: The Entente Cordiale with France
1 Jan 1901: Australia becomes a British dominion

1 Jan 1903: Edward VII created Emperor of India
29 April 1903: Edward visits Rome and has audience with Pope Leo XIII
8 April 1904: Entente Cordiale signed with France
1907: New Zealand becomes a British dominion
9 June 1908: Edward makes state visit to Tsar Nicholas II in Russia
Death: 6 May 1910, dies at Buckingham Palace. Buried in the vault beneath St George's Chapel, Windsor

A NEW AGE

Edward VII's relatively brief nine-year reign matched his mother's 63-year rule by giving a name to an age and culture: 'the Edwardian era'. Edward embodied this new culture in the way he modernized the monarchy and brought new life and a sense of fun to a royal court that had become staid and rather gloomy over the long years of Queen Victoria's reign. He lived principally in London, redecorating Buckingham Palace, where he held balls and sessions

Above: Before he was king. A family shot shows 'Bertie' with wife Alexandra and offspring Albert, George and Louise.

of court. He enthusiastically took to the motor car, which his mother had hated, and owned both a Renault and a Mercedes-Benz.

THE 'ENTENTE CORDIALE'

Edward fell in love with France as a teenager in 1854. He spoke perfect French and made visits to Paris and the southern resorts of Biarritz and Cannes throughout his years as Prince of Wales. He came up with the phrase 'Entente Cordiale ('Friendly Understanding') as

THE SPORT OF KINGS

Both as Prince of Wales and as king, Edward had a passionate interest in horse racing. He achieved great successes as a horse owner in the last years of Victoria's reign. In 1896 his horse Persimmon won the Derby, while in 1900 he was the most successful horse owner in the country. His horse Diamond Jubilee won no fewer than five major races (including the Derby, the St Leger and the '2000 Guineas') and another horse, Ambush II, won the Grand National steeplechase. He won a third victory at the Derby in 1909 with his horse Minoru. As he was dying from bronchitis in 1910, Edward was cheered in his last moments by the news that another of his horses, Witch of

Air, had won a race at Kempton Park. In fact his last words were a reference to this fact. 'Yes I have heard of it', he replied to a question. 'I am very glad.'

Right: This image of Edward in the grandstand at Epsom was published in the Illustrated London News *(1902).*

early as 1870, but the impetus for the signing of the agreement known by that name came from his visit as king in 1903, when he proved a skilled diplomat. The Entente of 8 April 1904 established a mutual agreement that Britain could pursue its interest in Egypt, and France could do likewise in Morocco, and settled various colonial

disagreements in Africa and Asia. In June 1908 Edward also made a state visit to his nephew-in-law Tsar Nicholas II of Russia, cementing an alliance established in a diplomatic agreement the previous year. The king's active diplomacy helped his country to establish itself in a new alignment of European countries: Britain would have the backing of France and Russia in any conflict with Germany, Austria or Italy.

BRONCHITIS AND DEATH

King Edward VII suffered from bronchitis for many years, but in 1910, after catching a chill, he had a very serious attack and died on 6 May. At the last, Queen Alexandra behaved with the greatest dignity in allowing her husband's long-term mistress, Mrs Keppel, to visit him as he prepared for death. He was succeeded by his son, the Prince of Wales, who became King George V.

Left: Royal hospitality. Edward VII receives maharajahs and other dignitaries from around the empire before his Coronation.

GEORGE V
1910–1936

George V was not raised to be king. He was recalled from naval duty in January 1892, when the death from pneumonia of his older brother Albert, Duke of Clarence, made George heir to his father, then still Prince of Wales.

On 6 July 1893, George married his late brother's fiancé, Princess Mary of Teck. A genuinely devoted family man, he produced six children with Princess Mary, including the future King Edward VIII and the future King George VI.

MYSTIQUE OF MONARCHY

As king, George V maintained the mystique of the monarchy, projecting a regal grandeur through elaborate ceremonial. He led the mourning for his father in a very grand funeral attended by leading members of all the European royal houses on 20 May 1910. His coronation in Westminster Abbey in 1911 was attended by rulers and government

Above: The man who did not expect to become king enjoyed a sumptuous coronation ceremony in June 1911.

figures from across the empire. Later that year, on 12 December in Delhi, George was hailed as Emperor of India in a lavish enthronement ceremony in which he wore a new crown worth £60,000.

FROM CRISIS TO CRISIS

George V's reign saw the years of the First World War, which erupted in 1914. The royal family came out of the war with great credit, largely because George displayed good sense in acting as a national figurehead while leaving the politicians to manage the war. Another difficult development in a period of rapid and profound change was the break-up of the British empire. An Imperial Conference of October–November 1926 agreed the autonomy

---

GEORGE V, KING OF THE UNITED KINGDOM OF GREAT BRITAIN AND IRELAND AND EMPEROR OF INDIA, 1910–1936

Birth: 3 June 1865, Marlborough House, London

Father: Edward Albert, Prince of Wales (later Edward VII)

Mother: Princess Alexandra of Denmark

Accession: 6 May 1910

Coronation: 22 June 1911

Queen: Princess Mary of Teck (m. 6 July 1893; d. 24 March 1953)

Succeeded by: His son Edward VIII

Greatest achievement: Preserving the monarchy in a time of great change

Dec 1911: George enthroned as Emperor of India in Delhi

4 Aug 1914: Start of World War I – Britain declares war on Germany

26 May 1917: George decrees that Britain's ruling royal house will be

known as 'Windsor' rather than 'Saxe-Coburg-Gotha'

15 Nov 1918: George parades through London on 'Victory Day', celebrating end of World War I

Jan 1919: George's youngest son, John, dies at Sandringham aged 13

23 April 1924: George opens British Empire Exhibition at Wembley

Oct 1931: George receives Gandhi at Buckingham Palace

11 Dec 1931: Statute of Westminster establishes the British Commonwealth of Nations

6 May 1935: King and people celebrate the Silver Jubilee of his reign

Death: 20 Jan 1936 at Sandringham. Buried in St George's Chapel, Windsor

Above: George V saw himself as a family man and took seriously the responsibility of training his children to take up royal duties.

British Commonwealth of Nations. In India, Mohandas Gandhi led a peaceful campaign for independence. In October 1931, while in London for an India Round Table Conference, Gandhi was received at Buckingham Palace. India finally achieved independence in August 1947, in the reign of George VI.

At home, George faced the formation of the first Labour government in 1924, the General Strike of 1926 and the economic crisis of 1930–31. He was a force for common sense and decency, urging moderation and national unity.

SILVER JUBILEE

King George celebrated the Silver Jubilee of his reign in May 1935, riding through cheering crowds of Londoners to a service of celebration in St Paul's Cathedral, while, across the country, hill-top beacons were lit and church bells rang out. The king was serenaded at Buckingham Palace by a crowd singing 'For He's a Jolly Good Fellow'. King George V died aged 70 at Sandringham

Above: In 1915, during a visit to the front line, George accompanied French dignitaries to inspect troops at Blincourt.

from chest and heart problems probably brought on by his long-term cigarette-smoking habit. His eldest son, Edward, succeeded at the age of 41 as King Edward VIII.

in domestic and foreign policy of the British 'dominions over the seas' (Australia, Canada, New Zealand and South Africa). The Statute of Westminster of 11 December 1931 established the

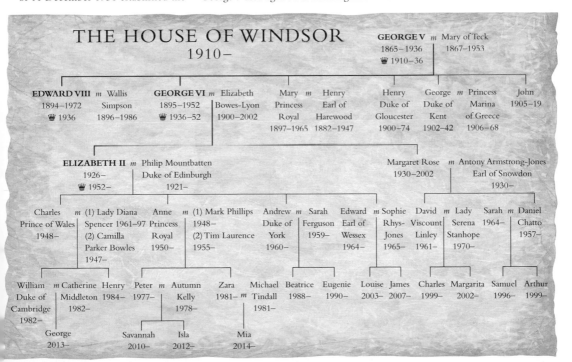

THE HOUSE OF WINDSOR
1910–

GEORGE V _m_ Mary of Teck
1865–1936 | 1867–1953
♛ 1910–36

EDWARD VIII _m_ Wallis
1894–1972 Simpson
♛ 1936 1896–1986

GEORGE VI _m_ Elizabeth
1895–1952 Bowes-Lyon
♛ 1936–52 1900–2002

Mary _m_ Henry
Princess Earl of
Royal Harewood
1897–1965 1882–1947

Henry
Duke of
Gloucester
1900–74

George _m_ Princess
Duke of Marina
Kent of Greece
1902–42 1906–68

John
1905–19

ELIZABETH II _m_ Philip Mountbatten
1926– Duke of Edinburgh
♛ 1952– 1921–

Margaret Rose _m_ Antony Armstrong-Jones
1930–2002 Earl of Snowdon
1930–

Charles _m_ (1) Lady Diana
Prince of Wales Spencer 1961–97
1948– (2) Camilla
Parker Bowles
1947–

Anne _m_ (1) Mark Phillips
Princess 1948–
Royal (2) Tim Laurence
1950– 1955–

Andrew _m_ Sarah
Duke of Ferguson
York 1959–
1960–

Edward _m_ Sophie
Earl of Rhys-
Wessex Jones
1964– 1965–

David _m_ Lady
Viscount Serena
Linley Stanhope
1961– 1970–

Sarah _m_ Daniel
1964– Chatto
1957–

William _m_ Catherine
Duke of Middleton
Cambridge 1982–
1982–

Henry Peter _m_ Autumn
1984– 1977– Kelly
1978–

Zara
1981– _m_ Tindall
1981–

Michael

Beatrice
1988–

Eugenie
1990–

Louise
2003–

James
2007–

Charles
1999–

Margarita
2002–

Samuel
1996–

Arthur
1999–

George
2013–

Savannah
2010–

Isla
2012–

Mia
2014–

EDWARD VIII

1936

 The reign of King Edward VIII lasted less than 11 months. After acceding to the throne on the death of his father King George V on 20 January 1936, he abdicated in a storm of controversy on 10 December the same year in order to marry American divorcée Wallis Simpson. Edward is generally remembered without fondness as the king who put private pleasure before public duty.

UNFIT TO BE KING?

The memory of Edward VIII is further tarnished by evidence that he was sympathetic to the Nazi regime in Germany. He made a visit to Germany with Wallis Simpson in October 1937 and was photographed smiling broadly as he was introduced to Nazi *führer*

Adolf Hitler at Berchtesgaden. On this occasion he made a modified Nazi salute and on two other occasions was seen making full forms of the salute.

There is, furthermore, evidence in the form of official German papers discovered after the Second World War that the Germans intended to restore Edward to the throne at the head of a British fascist state allied to Germany. Many historians argue that it was a blessing for the British monarchy and the House of Windsor that Edward's reign was truncated.

As Prince of Wales, Edward won admirers in the army during the First World War, on trips to working-class areas of Britain in 1919 and on tours of Canada, the United States and Australia in 1919–20. However, long before his accession, he was exhibiting troubling

Above: On 13 July 1911, aged 17, Edward was invested at Caernarfon as Prince of Wales.

signs of boredom with official duties. He evidently did not have his father's strong character and sense of duty. The

Below: Edward inspects troops in 1921. He won the Military Cross for army service in France in the First World War.

EDWARD VIII, KING OF THE UNITED KINGDOM OF GREAT BRITAIN AND IRELAND AND EMPEROR OF INDIA, 1936

Birth: 23 June 1894, White Lodge, Richmond Park
Father: George, Duke of York (later King George V)
Mother: Mary, Duchess of York (later Queen Mary)
Accession: 21 Jan 1936
Abdication: 10 Dec 1936; becomes the Duke of Windsor
Married: Mrs Wallis Simpson (m. 3 June 1937; d. 24 April 1986)
Succeeded by: His brother, George VI
Greatest achievement: Tours as Prince of Wales
21 Jan 1936: Edward takes oath of accession
22 Jan 1936: Edward is proclaimed King Edward VIII
28 Jan 1936: Edward leads national mourning at Windsor funeral of King George V

14 Sept 1936: Edward returns from a summer holiday with Mrs Simpson, that is widely covered in the international press
27 Oct 1936: Mrs Simpson wins *decree nisi* from her second husband, Ernest
16 Nov 1936: Edward informs Prime Minister Stanley Baldwin that he is determined to marry Wallis Simpson, even if it results in his abdication
2 Dec 1936: First British press reports of abdication crisis
10 Dec 1936: Edward signs instrument of abdication
11 Dec 1936: Edward makes abdication broadcast on radio from Windsor
3 June 1937: Edward, now Duke of Windsor, marries Wallis Simpson in France
Death: 28 May 1972, Edward dies in Paris and is buried at Frogmore

likelihood is that he would have made a disastrous king in the long term. George V certainly feared the worst, saying with remarkable prescience of his eldest son, 'After I am dead, the boy will ruin himself in 12 months'.

AN ADVISABLE SUCCESSION

Edward suggested, in a book he published in 1951 entitled *A King's Story*, that he was constitutionally ill-equipped to rule. 'The fault', he wrote, 'lay not in my stars but in my genes'.

Some writers propose that Edward was happy to escape the life of a king and that he used the circumstance of his romance with the divorcée Wallis Simpson as a way out of an intolerable situation. Others argue that, while Edward wished to remain king, his obvious unsuitability meant that leading religious and political figures in the drama – such as Cosmo Gordon Lang, the Archbishop of Canterbury, and Prime Minister Stanley Baldwin – were happy to see him depart. It is argued that they preferred to see the throne pass to his brother Prince Albert (subsequently George VI) and

Below: A nation's hopes. This poster for Edward VIII's accession offers prayers for a bright future under the new king.

Above: The common touch? At a time of great economic hardship, Edward made successful visits to British mining towns.

later to George VI's daughter Elizabeth (the future Elizabeth II) who, it was already clear, were better equipped to reign.

Such, indeed, was the will of the late King George V, who had declared, 'I pray to God that my eldest son Edward will never marry and have children and that nothing will come between Bertie and Lilibet and the throne'. ('Lilibet' was the family name for Princess Elizabeth.)

Yet while Edward's departure may have been convenient, the act of abdication set a troubling precedent and undermined the constitutional monarchy. Under generally accepted rules, monarch and subject were bound by duty: the one to rule, the other to serve with loyalty. If a king could set aside duty and choose not to rule when it pleased him, surely subjects could set aside loyalty and unseat an unpopular king or queen?

As part of his abdication negotiations, Edward thrashed out a settlement covering his finances and royal status with his younger brother and successor, George VI. Under this agreement, Edward would receive £25,000 a year and the title His Royal Highness the Duke of Windsor. The title HRH was denied to Wallis, who was to be known simply as the Duchess of Windsor.

Edward reportedly was unable to forgive George for this rebuff. Some sources suggest that King George did not expect the marriage to last and therefore did not want to confer a title that is traditionally permanent.

'SOMETHING MUST BE DONE'

Edward more than once suggested that he had sympathy with the plight of the working man.

On 19 November 1936 Edward made a well-publicized visit to economically devastated areas of South Wales. At the Bessemer Steel Works, at Dowlais, a group of unemployed and largely destitute men serenaded him with an ancient Welsh hymn. He declared 'Something must be done to find them work'.

He established a connection with servicemen during the First World War and in 1919 was well received when touring mining areas of South Wales. Later, as Governor of Bahamas, he achieved a number of improvements for unemployed black workers there.

THE ABDICATION
YEAR OF CRISIS, 1936

 Edward VIII first met Wallis Simpson, the American woman for whom he gave up the British throne, on 10 January 1931, when he was still Prince of Wales. The prince's close friend and then lover, Thelma, Lady Furness, introduced him to Pennsylvania-born Wallis and her Anglo-American husband Ernest Simpson in Lady Furness's house at Melton Mowbray. Edward soon became a close associate of the Simpsons, with whom he frequently dined in London.

THE AMERICAN BELLE

Wallis was born Bessie Wallis Warfield in Blue Ridge Summit, Pennsylvania, on 19 June 1896, the only child of American businessman Teackle Wallis Warfield and Alice Montague. After her father's death when she was five months old and throughout her childhood, 'Bessie Wallis' and her mother were extremely poor.

In 1916, aged 19, she married Earl Winfield Spencer, but divorced him in 1927. On 2 July 1928 she married her second husband, Ernest Simpson. They came to London, where Ernest managed an office of his father's shipping

Above: Edward broadcasts. After breaking the news of his abdication and his brother's accession he declared, 'God save the king'.

Below: After abdication, Edward and Wallis visited Nazi Germany and had a friendly meeting with Adolf Hitler.

company. By mid-1934 the prince had cut contacts with Lady Furness and his other long-term female intimate, Freda Dudley Ward, and concentrated all his attentions on Wallis – although to the end of his life he denied that they had become lovers before they were married in 1937.

Edward appears to have convinced himself that he could not live without Wallis and must marry her at all costs. Many writers comment on the bullying and aggressive nature of her interaction with the prince and speculate that the relationship may have had a sado-masochistic element.

Prince Edward's intimacy with Wallis was a matter of increasing public comment and scandal on the international scene. In Britain the press kept silent, but American and European newspapers followed the developing drama in lurid detail. In 1934–5 Wallis spent three holidays with the prince, first in the Mediterranean, then skiing in Austria and third, cruising the Mediterranean and visiting Budapest and Vienna. Meanwhile, her husband stayed home.

Edward's accession to the throne only strengthened his desire to make Wallis Simpson his wife. In summer 1936 they holidayed as a couple more openly than ever before on a chartered yacht, the *Nahlin*, in the eastern Mediterranean. International pressmen followed their every move and a crowd was heard to shout, '*Vive l'amour!*' ('The wonders of love!') when the couple came ashore.

On 27 October 1936 Wallis won a *decree nisi* divorce from Ernest at a court in Ipswich, adding further weight to international speculation that Edward planned to marry her. Prime Minister Stanley Baldwin asked Edward his intentions. The prince confirmed, on 16 November 1936, that he was determined to marry the woman he loved.

POSSIBLE SOLUTIONS

Edward's abdication was by no means inevitable. The difficulty was that Wallis had been married twice and was in the throes of gaining her second divorce. As Supreme Governor of the Church of England, which did not allow church marriage for divorced people, Edward would undermine his coronation oath to uphold the Church if he married her and made her his queen. A possible

Above: In the summer of 1936, the king and Wallis Simpson were clearly travelling as a romantic couple on holiday in Yugoslavia.

solution was a 'morganatic marriage', in which Edward would marry Mrs Simpson but she would not become queen and their children would not inherit the throne. Edward apparently backed this option, but Baldwin opposed it. Such a development would have required an Act of Parliament, and

Baldwin did not believe that he could win a debate on the issue. As the crisis came to breaking point, events developed quickly.

On 3 December Mrs Simpson fled London for Paris. Four days later she issued a statement declaring her willingness to withdraw from the relationship. However, Edward would not give up. On 10 December he signed an instrument of abdication. 'I Edward the Eighth, of Great Britain, Ireland, and the British Dominions beyond the Seas, King, Emperor of India, do hereby declare my irrevocable determination to renounce the throne for Myself and for My descendants, and My desire that effect should be given to this Instrument of Abdication immediately'.

On 11 December he made an abdication broadcast from Windsor Castle declaring, 'I have for 25 years tried to serve...But you must believe me when I tell you that I have found it impossible to carry the heavy burden of responsibility and to discharge my duties as king as I would wish to do without the help and support of the woman I love...And now we have a new King. I wish him, and you, his people, happiness and prosperity with all my heart.'

LIFE AFTER ABDICATION

The former King Edward VIII departed Portsmouth on board HMS *Fury* on 12 December 1936, headed for Paris, where he set up home with Wallis. The couple were married at the Château de Condé, near Tours, on 3 June 1937. An Anglican clergyman married them using the Church of England service despite official opposition to church marriage of divorced people. No members of the royal family attended, and thereafter the Duke and Duchess of Windsor were effectively excluded from royal life.

In the Second World War, Edward initially served as a member of the British military mission to France. With the fall of France in June 1940, he and Wallis fled

to Madrid and then Lisbon. They left Lisbon to enable Edward take up the governorship of the Bahamas, safely out of the war.

After the war they returned to Paris, where they largely lived for the rest of their lives. Edward died from throat cancer aged 77 in his Paris home on 28 May 1972. His body was flown back to Windsor, where 60,000 mourners viewed it as it lay in state in St George's Chapel. He was buried in the Frogmore Mausoleum following his funeral on 5 June. Wallis died on 24 April 1986 and was buried beside Edward.

Right: Edward and Wallis at a film premiere in 1967. In Parisian exile, the former king and his wife lived in style.

GEORGE VI

1936–1952

 George VI was crowned in Westminster Abbey on 12 May 1937, the day originally set for the coronation of his older brother, Edward VIII. The new king's elevation to the throne had been swift and unexpected.

Albert Frederick Arthur George, Duke of York, learned that he was to be king on 8 December 1936, two days before Edward VIII's abdication. As a shy man with a stammer that made public speaking a trial and who had had an undistinguished naval education, he would not have wished for the role of king – he told Lord Louis Mountbatten, 'I'm quite unprepared for it…I've never even seen a state paper. I'm only a Naval Officer, it's the only thing I know'.

A DUTIFUL MAN

The new king had a strong sense of duty and set out to restore the good name and dignity of the royal family,

Above: 'Long to reign over us'? After the abdication crisis, George's subjects looked for stability and propriety in the new king.

which he felt had been blemished by the abdication crisis. To this end, the man known before his accession as

Prince Albert – and in the royal family as 'Bertie' – chose the name George VI to reassert the qualities of decency and dutiful service embodied by his father.

In his unlooked-for role as king, George VI was greatly supported by his elegant and charming wife Elizabeth,

---

GEORGE VI, KING OF THE UNITED KINGDOM OF GREAT BRITAIN AND NORTHERN IRELAND AND EMPEROR OF INDIA, 1936–1952

Birth: 14 Dec 1895, York Cottage, Sandringham
Father: George, Duke of York (later George V)
Mother: Mary, Duchess of York (later Queen Mary)
Accession: 11 Dec 1936
Coronation: 12 May 1937
Married: Lady Elizabeth Bowes-Lyon (m. 26 April 1923; d. 30 March 2002)
Succeeded by: His daughter Elizabeth II
Greatest achievement: Restoring dignity to the monarchy after the abdication crisis
July 1938: George and Queen Elizabeth make triumphant state visit to Paris
May–June 1939: George and Queen Elizabeth tour Canada and the US

Dec 1939: George visits British troops in France
9 Sept 1940: Buckingham Palace hit by German bombs
June 1943: George inspects British troops in Africa
8 May 1945: Royal family lead London celebrations of the end of the war in Europe
15 Aug 1947: Under the India Independence Act, the British monarch loses his title of Imperator (Emperor) of India
30 April 1948: George and Queen Elizabeth celebrate their silver wedding anniversary
Death: 6 Feb 1952 at Sandringham. Buried in St George's Chapel, Windsor

Below: Royal wed commoner when the future George VI (then Albert, Duke of York) married Elizabeth Bowes-Lyon.

Left: On Coronation Day, George and the royal family greet adoring crowds from the balcony at Buckingham Palace.

of Canada and the USA. The visit, the first by a reigning British king and queen to North America, had the added purpose of countering 'isolationism' in the USA and reasserting links with the Dominion of Canada, in the hope that both countries would give Britain much-needed backing in the war against Germany. The trip was a triumph. A total of 15 million people flocked to see the couple during their 10,000-mile (16,000-km) journey.

and by the tranquil home life he enjoyed with her and their two daughters Elizabeth (the future Elizabeth II) and Margaret Rose. The happiness and intimacy of his immediate 'royal family' was a genuine help to the king, but it was also publicly promoted as a means of establishing common ground with George's subjects. The image of domestic calm also helped to distance the new king and his heir Elizabeth from the raffish 'bachelor' lifestyle adopted by Edward VIII as Prince of Wales and, briefly, as king.

The public emphasis on King George's sense of duty was another key part of the monarchy's attempt to repair the damage done by Edward VIII's abdication. Edward's decision to stand down seemed to imply that the obligations of kingship could be taken up or set aside at will, but George's dutiful acceptance of a role he did not apparently desire restored gravity to the monarchy.

DUTY'S REWARD

Within three years of George's accession, Britain was plunged into the Second World War. In summer 1939, as war loomed over Europe, George and Queen Elizabeth made a six-week tour

Right: George VI and Elizabeth provided a calm domestic setting for the childhood of Princesses Margaret and Elizabeth.

GEORGE AND ELIZABETH
A ROYAL PARTNERSHIP, 1939–1952

After the beginning of the Second World War on 3 September 1939, George and the royal family played a major role in rallying the spirits of British servicemen and public. They visited bombed-out areas of the East End of London as well as other cities, including Coventry, Bristol and Southampton. On 9 September 1940 Buckingham Palace itself was hit by two bombs, prompting Queen Elizabeth to observe, 'I'm glad we have been bombed. We can now look the East End in the face'.

The royals set out to share in the hardships of the British people, enduring food and clothes rationing, and turning off the central heating in

VICTORY IN EUROPE

On 8 May 1945 Buckingham Palace was a focus for victory celebrations. At one point the princesses left the palace and mingled *incognito* with the crowd.

Above: King George and Queen Elizabeth appeared on the palace balcony eight times. George declared, 'We give thanks for a great deliverance'.

Left: In 1940, as Britain endured the German bombing of the Blitz, George VI and Queen Elizabeth inspected air-raid damage at Buckingham Palace.

Below: An informal portrait of the royal family in 1936 shows the king and queen relaxing with their daughters Elizabeth and Margaret Rose.

by previous monarchs for jubilees of their rule. In a thanksgiving service in St Paul's Cathedral, the Archbishop of Canterbury gave thanks to God 'That He has set such a family at the seat of our royalty'. Later both king and queen made radio broadcasts to mark the occasion.

LAST MONTHS

King George developed lung cancer and in autumn 1951 had an operation to remove his right lung. He died from a heart attack during his convalescence at Sandringham on 6 February 1952, aged 56, and was buried in St George's Chapel, Windsor.

His memory was honoured: the man who had not expected or wanted to be king rose to the daunting challenge presented by Edward VIII's abdication. He re-established the public standing of the monarchy, led the country with dignity through the traumas of the Blitz and the Second World War, and produced an heir, Princess Elizabeth, who was herself devoted to preserving the standing of the monarchy in rapidly changing times.

Buckingham Palace. To help counter food shortages, the king authorized the ploughing of 1,500 acres (600 hectares) of Windsor Great Park to plant cereal crops. Towards the end of the war, in March 1945, Princess Elizabeth joined the ATS (Auxiliary Transport Service).

A ROYAL WEDDING

The post-war years brought marriage celebrations, as well as declining health for King George. On 10 July 1947 the king announced the engagement of Princess Elizabeth, heir to the throne, and Lt Philip Mountbatten of the Royal Navy. Prince Philip was the son of Prince Andrew of Greece and Denmark. Before his engagement, he renounced his Greek nationality and became a British citizen, adopting the surname Mountbatten.

The couple were married in Westminster Abbey, amid post-war austerity, on 20 November 1947. The king gave Elizabeth's husband the title of Prince Philip, Duke of Edinburgh.

On 14 November 1948, Elizabeth gave birth at Buckingham Palace to a boy, later christened Charles Philip Arthur George, and on 15 August 1950 at Clarence House she produced a daughter, Anne Elizabeth Alice Louise. The domestic tranquillity of the royal family was again celebrated on 30 April 1948, when King George and Queen Elizabeth marked their silver wedding anniversary with much of the pomp used

Right: Three queens in black. Elizabeth II, Mary and Elizabeth the Queen Mother attend George VI's funeral.

ELIZABETH II

FROM 1952

Princess Elizabeth learned of her father's death and her elevation to the British throne on 6 February 1952 while on safari in Kenya. A local newspaperman brought the news that King George had died to the lodge where Elizabeth and Philip were staying. It was Prince Philip who broke the news to Elizabeth, who reportedly received it 'Bravely, like a queen'. Her accession as Queen Elizabeth II was proclaimed on 8 February 1952. At the age of 25, she was the youngest British monarch on accession since Queen Victoria came to the throne at 18 in 1837.

The young queen stood just 5ft 4in (1.62m) tall. While she did not possess the large-eyed beauty of her sister Margaret, she cut an elegant and attractive figure and was flattered by the styles of the 1950s. Moreover, from the start of her reign Elizabeth impressed all with the calm and dignity she displayed in taking on large responsibilities at a young age. Not least among her difficulties was that of coming to terms with a new level of press and television scrutiny of her doings and those of her family.

Above: A formal portrait of the Queen in robes of the Order of the Thistle, 1956, one of Sir William Hutchison's finest works.

Below: Elizabeth's coronation, on 2 June 1953, was the first to be shown live on TV.

ELIZABETH II, QUEEN OF THE UNITED KINGDOM OF GREAT BRITAIN AND NORTHERN IRELAND, 1952–

Birth: 21 April 1926, 17 Bruton St, London
Father: Prince Albert, Duke of York (later George VI)
Mother: Elizabeth, Duchess of York (later Queen Elizabeth and Queen Elizabeth, the Queen Mother)
Accession: 6 Feb 1952
Coronation: 2 June 1953
Married: Philip Mountbatten (Prince Philip, Duke of Edinburgh; m. 20 Nov 1947)
Greatest achievement: Figurehead for the Commonwealth

Dec 1953–April 1954: First visit by monarch to Australia and New Zealand
18 Oct 1957: Welcomed by President Eisenhower at the White House
25 Dec 1957: Elizabeth makes first televised Christmas broadcast
1 July 1969: Prince Charles invested as Prince of Wales
7 June 1977: National holiday celebrates Elizabeth II's Silver Jubilee
1–4 June 2002: Elizabeth II's Golden Jubilee
2–5 June 2012: Diamond Jubilee Weekend celebrating 60 years

Above: Elizabeth has had a good relationship with several US Presidents. John and Jackie Kennedy visited the UK in 1961 and met the Queen and Prince Philip.

THE COMMONWEALTH

In the early years of her reign Elizabeth made several tours to visit her subjects, the peoples of the Commonwealth and the USA. In 1953 she made an extensive coronation tour to various parts of the United Kingdom, including Scotland and Northern Ireland. In 1953–4, she became the first ruling monarch to visit Australia and New Zealand, in a three-month tour during which she made the first Christmas broadcast ever given from outside Britain. In this broadcast, made from New Zealand, she declared, 'The Crown is not merely an abstract symbol of our unity, but a personal and living bond between you and me'.

Africa was next on the agenda. In January–February 1956 Elizabeth and Philip received a wildly enthusiastic welcome on a visit to Nigeria, which at that stage was still a British colony. During the tour, the royal couple made a visit to a leper colony situated on the river Oji and agreed to sponsor a leper child. Their visit was praised by the colony manager for its positive effect in diluting public fear of and hostility towards lepers.

The following year Elizabeth and Philip toured North America. In Canada, Elizabeth became the first ruling monarch to open the Canadian parliament, in Ottawa.

Later Elizabeth travelled south to the USA, where she visited Jamestown, Virginia, to mark the 350th anniversary of the establishment of England's first

Above: On 1 July 1969, Elizabeth's eldest son, Charles, became the 21st Prince of Wales on his inauguration at Caernarfon.

permanent overseas colony, before being received at the White House by President and Mrs Eisenhower. Elizabeth also gave an address to the United Nations general assembly in New York City.

THE COMMONWEALTH AND ELIZABETH II

The Commonwealth grew out of the British empire. It began as a collection of former British colonies that had been transformed into self-governing 'dominions' and which maintained ties with Britain to promote cooperation and friendship. A 1931 British parliamentary act, the Statute of Westminster, referred to a number of dominions – principally Australia, Canada, the Irish Free State, New Zealand and South Africa – as the 'British Commonwealth of Nations'. The word British was dropped in 1946.

The monarch has an important symbolic role as head of the Commonwealth, and Elizabeth II has always taken this very seriously. On 21 April 1947, when she was still Princess Elizabeth and a subject of King George VI, she turned 21 in South Africa. In a radio broadcast, she declared: 'my whole life, whether it be short or long, shall be devoted to your service, and the service of our great Imperial Commonwealth to which we all belong'. In the early 21st century the Commonwealth consists of 53 countries, and has a total population of 1.8 billion.

Map labels: Arctic Ocean; CANADA; North Atlantic Ocean; Pacific Ocean; Pacific Ocean; INDIA; South Atlantic Ocean; SOUTH AFRICA; Indian Ocean; AUSTRALIA; N, E, W, S (compass)

The extent of the Commonwealth, 2000

CROWN AND COMMONWEALTH
THE NEW ELIZABETHANS, 1952–1977

In 1977, Queen Elizabeth II, her British subjects and millions of people around the world celebrated the 25th anniversary of her reign. 'Jubilee Day', 7 June 1977, was a national holiday at Elizabeth's decree.

A YEAR-LONG CELEBRATION

Across the country people threw street parties in an explosion of communal goodwill and royalist fervour. A string of beacons on hilltops from the Shetlands to Land's End included one at Windsor lit by the Queen herself.

In London, Elizabeth processed with Prince Philip in the golden state coach from Buckingham Palace to St Paul's Cathedral for a service of thanksgiving. Afterwards she attended lunch at the Guildhall and then, watched by around 500 million people worldwide on television, she processed down the Mall to Buckingham Palace, where a crowd of a million people had gathered to acclaim her appearance on the balcony.

The year-long celebration began on 6 February, the 25th anniversary of Elizabeth's accession in 1952. The Queen,

Above: Elizabeth 'at home' in 1969. This was the year of the first TV documentary to show scenes of the royals' private lives.

CHARLIE'S ANGELS

In 1977 Prince Charles was 29 and touted in the press as the world's most eligible bachelor. He was linked to a string of beautiful women, dubbed 'Charlie's Angels' after the popular 1970s TV show.

The prince's close friends included Lady Sarah Spencer (elder sister of his eventual first wife, Lady Diana Spencer), Lady Jane Wellesley, Sabrina Guinness, Lucia Santa Cruz, Davina Sheffield and Princess Marie Astrid. Earlier, in 1970–1, he had been very close to Camilla Shand (subsequently Camilla Parker Bowles and now his second wife).

Above: Charles and Camilla at a polo match in Cirencester Park in 1975. Their paths continued to cross after their initial romance foundered.

who had declared that she wanted to mark the Jubilee by meeting as many of her people as possible, made official visits with Prince Philip to Western Samoa, Australia, New Zealand, Tonga, Fiji, Tasmania, Papua New Guinea, Canada and the West Indies in a series of globetrotting tours that totalled 56,000 miles (90,000km) in the year. At home she made six Jubilee tours in the UK and Northern Ireland. Again with Prince Philip, she visited no fewer than 36 counties, beginning in Glasgow on 17 May.

Above: In 1979 the Queen's cousin, Earl Mountbatten of Burma, congratulates Prince Charles after a polo success.

THE ROYAL FAMILY'S IMAGE

In the first 25 years of her reign Elizabeth II presided over an expanding family, with the births of Prince Andrew (1960) and Prince Edward (1964) and the growth to adulthood of her two older children, Charles and Anne. Charles passed through private school and attended Cambridge University, where he enjoyed taking part in student theatrical revues. Anne began official duties, married Captain Mark Phillips on 14 November 1973, survived a bungled kidnap attempt on 20 March 1974 outside Buckingham Palace and rose to become a prominent horsewoman.

Elizabeth steered the monarchy through the choppy waters of increasingly egalitarian times. She came face to face with symbols of change rather than avoiding them. In June 1965 she met

Right: Queen Elizabeth pioneered the 'royal walkabout', a new and informal way of meeting her subjects, in the 1970s.

the Beatles and awarded them the MBE. In 1976 she accepted that her sister's marriage to Lord Snowdon (Antony Armstrong Jones) was over and that the couple were to separate.

She also coped with many television-led 'modernizations' in the image and role of the royal family. These included the first televised Christmas broadcast (1957), the first TV documentary showing scenes of the private apartments in royal palaces (1966) and the first TV documentary showing scenes of the royal family's private life (1969). In the course of her reign, the monarch and the royal family had to accept more intrusive scrutiny than ever before.

THE END OF EMPIRE

Meanwhile the remaining British empire had been almost entirely broken up, with the grant of independence to former British colonies in Africa and south-east Asia. However, Elizabeth worked hard to maintain the importance of the Commonwealth. After 1949 it was no longer a requirement for Commonwealth countries to pledge 'an allegiance to the crown' (in the words of the 1926 Balfour report), which opened the way for republics such as India to join, but the British monarch still held an important role as symbolic

Above: The Queen addresses a Silver Jubilee reception in Canberra, Australia, during a 'world tour' of official visits in early 1977.

figurehead. Ghana, which Elizabeth visited in 1961, was one of many former African and Caribbean colonies to join the Commonwealth, which increasingly gained the multiracial character that it has in the early 21st century.

CHARLES AND DIANA

A MODERN FAIRY TALE?, 1977–1992

Prince Charles met his first wife, Lady Diana Frances Spencer, in November 1977 when he visited the country estate of Althorp, Northamptonshire, which belonged to her father John, 8th Earl Spencer. That year the prince had been romantically connected to Lady Diana's older sister, Lady Sarah Spencer, and Lady Diana was still a schoolgirl, at West Heath school, Sevenoaks, Kent.

BACKGROUND TO ROMANCE

The Spencer family were from the 'top drawer' of the British aristocracy and could trace their lineage back to Henry VII. Lady Diana did not excel academically at school, but she had the attributes expected of a young lady of her class, not least beauty and charm.

At the close of 1977 Lady Diana moved on to finishing school in Switzerland, before settling in London. She lived in Kensington on an inheritance from her great-grandmother, Lady Fermoy, and took a string of part-time jobs as a nanny. She met the Prince again in July 1980, at a party in Sussex. He proposed to her on 6 February 1981, and their engagement was made public on 24 February 1981.

Below: After their wedding, Charles and Diana greeted the crowds from the balcony of Buckingham Palace.

Above: Lady Diana wore a £28,500 diamond and sapphire engagement ring as her engagement was announced.

A ROYAL ENGAGEMENT

The prince was 31, Diana 19. At the engagement press conference, he made light of the age difference, declaring, 'I just feel you're as young as you think you are. Diana will certainly help to keep me young'. It appeared to be a fairy-tale match: Diana was said to have harboured a crush on the prince, like so many of her female contemporaries.

Asked if they were in love, she replied instantaneously, 'Of course'. Ominously, the prince gave a less enthusiastic reply, saying, 'Whatever "in love" means'.

To protect Diana from the attentions of the international press pack she was moved first into Clarence House and then into Buckingham Palace. At this time before the wedding, she was isolated from her family and friends. Diana reportedly learned of Charles's former relationship with Camilla Shand (Parker Bowles). She lost weight and may have begun to be troubled by the eating disorders of anorexia and bulimia that later plagued her.

THE WEDDING DAY

Prince Charles married Lady Diana Spencer in St Paul's Cathedral on 29 July 1981. The Archbishop of Canterbury, Robert Runcie, declared, 'This is the stuff of which fairy tales are made'. Diana's ivory silk crinoline wedding dress had a 'train' 25ft (7.5m) in length. The wedding was televised live in 74 countries, producing a global TV audience of 750 million people.

The newlyweds spent their honeymoon on the royal yacht *Britannia* and then visited Balmoral. Almost at once the press began to suggest that all was not as it should be in the marriage. Diana appears to have been less than stimulated by the country pursuits favoured by the royal family and by the Prince's established group of friends. She quickly became pregnant, however, and their first child, a boy, was born on 21 June 1982 at St Mary's Hospital, Paddington. He weighed 7lb 10oz (3.5kg) and had the blond hair of his mother. The baby prince, later christened William Arthur Philip Louis and known as Prince William, was third in line to the throne. A second son, Henry Charles Albert David, was born in the same hospital on 15 September 1984.

THE QUEEN'S 'ANNUS HORRIBILIS'

On 24 November 1992, in a speech at London's Guildhall to mark the 40th anniversary of her accession, the Queen declared, '1992 is not a year on which I shall look back with undiluted pleasure. In the words of one of my more sympathetic correspondents, it has turned out to be an *annus horribilis*'.

The Latin words ('horrid year') were a joking reference to the often-used phrase *annus mirabilis* ('wonderful year'), and were apt because in 1992 the Queen had endured the separation of Prince Andrew, Duke of York, from his wife, Sarah (in March); the divorce of Princess Anne and Captain Mark Phillips (April); and the final and very public death throes of the Prince and Princess of Wales's marriage, which resulted in their formal separation in late 1992.

Right: 1992 proved to be one of the most testing years of Elizabeth's reign.

In addition to all this, a serious fire struck Windsor Castle and there was public outrage when it was proposed that the government would pay the £40 million repair costs. The Queen repeated her description of 1992 as an *'annus horribilis'* in her Christmas broadcast.

MARRIAGE AND THE MEDIA

As early as December 1981 the Queen appealed to British newspaper editors to give the Prince and Princess more privacy, but her efforts had little effect: the Waleses were a fatally fascinating couple for the media. Most early press coverage was supportive of Diana and far more critical of her husband, but rumours that she suffered from the eating disorder anorexia nervosa could not be silenced and were fuelled by fainting fits in 1986 – including one while on royal duty in Vancouver in May 1986.

The Princess of Wales appears to have entered her marriage believing in the fairy-tale imagery of her romance and wedding, which had been so heavily publicized in the press. The royal marriage was conducted in the full glare of global press and television attention. By 1986–7, the marriage was in serious trouble. Both, by now, had probably taken lovers. Some reports suggest Charles had already returned to his old flame, Camilla Parker Bowles, while Diana may have been seeing James Hewitt, a captain in the Life Guards and polo player. Diana first met Hewitt in 1986 and most accounts suggest that they were lovers in 1987–9 and 1990–1.

SCANDAL UPON SCANDAL

By the early 1990s the Waleses were in open conflict. Information was leaked to the press about the prince's extramarital affair with Camilla Parker Bowles, with the suggestion that Charles was an old-fashioned and distant father to his sons. From the Prince's camp came indications that Diana was mentally unhinged, and driven by jealousy.

Revelations came thick and fast. Diana cooperated with the journalist Andrew Morton on his book *Diana: Her True Story*, which was published in June 1992. Morton presented the princess as a loving mother and wife who had been ignored and mistreated by her husband and his emotionally frigid family.

In August that year a transcript of two-year old tapes of an intimate phone conversation between the Princess of Wales and her then lover James Gilbey (a motor-car salesman) were published in *The Sun* newspaper.

The Prince of Wales asked for a formal separation on 25 November 1992, and this was made public in a House of Commons announcement on 9 December 1992.

Below: Despite the best efforts of 200 firefighters, Windsor Castle was badly damaged by fire on 20 November 1992.

ROYAL CRISIS
THE FAMILY FIRM, 1992–1996

Charles and Diana's public agony at the hands of the media continued after their formal separation in 1992. A transcript of a taped conversation between the prince and Camilla Parker Bowles, recorded in 1989, was published in January 1993 and proved publicly once and for all that Charles had been unfaithful to Diana. In 1994 Anna Pasternak's book *Princess in Love* revealed details of Diana's long love affair with Captain James Hewitt.

'QUEEN OF PEOPLE'S HEARTS'
In 1995 Diana gave an interview to the BBC news programme *Panorama*, watched by over 23 million people, in which she produced the enduring phrase that she wanted to be 'Queen of people's hearts'. Diana admitted her affair with Hewitt and declared the prince's love for Camilla Parker Bowles had made the marriage very difficult. She suggested Charles was unfit to be king and said she would not be silenced by the royal family – 'I'll fight to the end, because I believe that I have a role to fulfil and I've got two children to bring up'.

Below: Prince Andrew's marriage to Sarah Ferguson, which began with high hopes in 1986, lasted only until March 1992.

A ROYAL DIVORCE
The Queen saw that matters had to be brought to a head and proposed a swift divorce. Charles and Diana received their *decree nisi* on 15 July 1996 and their *decree absolute* on 28 August 1996. In the negotiated settlement Diana was given around £17 million but was denied the title 'Her Royal Highness'; she would be called Diana, Princess of Wales.

Following her divorce, Diana remained in the public eye with her high-profile charitable work and support of an International Red Cross campaign against landmines. Her jet-setting holidays remained a draw for the press. On a Mediterranean cruise in July 1997, she met Dodi Al Fayed, eldest son of the hugely wealthy Egyptian businessman Mohamed Al Fayed, and spent much time with him over the summer.

On the night of Saturday 30 August 1997 Diana dined with Dodi at the Ritz Hotel in Paris. They left in her armoured Mercedes car, driven by bodyguard Henri Paul, chased by a waiting pack of photographers. The ensuing car chase ended in tragedy at 12.24 a.m. when Diana's Mercedes crashed in an underpass beneath the

Above: Fairy tale soured. By 1991, when this picture was taken in Toronto, the Waleses' marriage was beyond salvage.

Pont d'Alma. The driver and Dodi were killed instantaneously. Diana was taken to La Pitié-Salpêtrière Hospital where she was declared dead at 4 a.m. on Sunday 31 August. Accompanied by Prince Charles and her sisters, her body was flown back to England.

Below: Diana's affair in the late 1980s with Life Guards captain and polo player James Hewitt was made public in 1994.

Right: Prince Charles, Diana's brother Earl Spencer and Princes William and Harry were united in grief at the funeral.

THE PEOPLE'S PRINCESS

Diana's death provoked an extraordinary outpouring of public emotion in Britain. Crowds flocked to her London home, Kensington Palace, creating an ocean of around one million bouquets. At St James's Palace, mourners queued for up to 12 hours to sign books of condolence. Prime Minister Tony Blair declared her, 'The people's princess'. On Friday 5 September, the eve of the Princess's funeral, Queen Elizabeth made a television broadcast in which she paid glowing tribute to her former daughter-in-law as 'an exceptional and gifted human being'.

On Saturday, 6 September 1997 the princess's coffin was transported from Kensington Palace to Westminster Abbey. The carriage was followed on foot for the final mile by the Prince of Wales and Diana's sons, Princes William and Harry, as well as by Diana's brother Earl Spencer and Prince Philip. Three million people lined the route.

The funeral was televised live in 187 countries around the world. At the close of the funeral, the nation observed a minute's silence. Afterwards Diana's coffin was driven to the Spencer family estate of Althorp, where she was buried on an island in a lake.

Below: Diana's sons were inspired by their mother's charitable work. William visited a New Zealand children's hospital in 2005.

A CITIZEN OF THE WORLD

In November 1997, just two months after her death, South African President Nelson Mandela praised her work with the poor and sick, and hailed her as, 'One who became a citizen of the world through her care for people everywhere'. At the time of her death, US President Bill Clinton declared, 'Hillary and I knew Princess Diana and were very fond of her…We admired her work for children, for people with AIDS, for the cause of ending the scourge of landmines in the world and for her love for her children, William and Harry'.

Diana's charitable work was an important part of her legacy. From the mid-1980s until her death, she represented a wide range of charities, including those supporting victims of AIDS and leprosy, the Red Cross, hospices, the marriage guidance body RELATE and refuges for abused women. In 1987 she visited the first British ward for AIDS victims. In 1997, Diana served as an International Red Cross VIP volunteer in the organization's campaign against landmines, helping lead the way for the signing of the Ottawa Treaty in December 1997.

DIANA MEMORIALS

The Diana, Princess of Wales Memorial Fountain in Hyde Park, London, a £3.6 million water feature, was opened by Queen Elizabeth on 6 July 2004 with Princes Philip, Charles, William and Harry in attendance. The £1.7 million Diana, Princess of Wales Memorial Playground for children, close to her former home in Kensington Palace, London, opened in June 2000. In Northampton,

Right: The Diana, Princess of Wales Memorial Fountain was designed by American architect Kathyrn Gustafson.

close to Diana's burial place at Althorp, a bronze plaque to her memory was unveiled by her brother Earl Spencer.

THE GOLDEN JUBILEE OF ELIZABETH II
YEAR OF TRIBUTE, 2002

 In the months leading up to the celebrations planned for Elizabeth II's Golden Jubilee in 2002, the Queen lost both her mother, who died at the age of 101, and her sister Margaret. Criticism of the royal family's response to Diana's death had led to some anxiety in royal circles about public response to the Jubilee. In the event, the Queen's enduring popularity was triumphantly demonstrated in the nationwide celebrations of the 50th anniversary of her acccession.

JUBILEE WEEKEND
The celebrations climaxed in a four-day 'Jubilee Weekend' of festivities in London, beginning on Saturday 1 June, with a classical music concert at Buckingham Palace by the BBC Symphony Orchestra and Chorus and star vocalists including Kiri Te Kanawa and Thomas Allen. The event, known as the 'Prom at the Palace', was attended by 12,000 people from across the UK

Below: Prince Charles declared the Queen Mother to be, 'the most magical grandmother you could possibly have'.

who had been chosen by a ballot the previous March. On 2 June, a Sunday, the Queen and Prince Philip attended a service of thanksgiving at St George's Chapel, Windsor, while other members of the royal family attended Jubilee church services across the country.

On 3 June, another Buckingham Palace concert, this time of pop music and known as the 'Party at the Palace', was held. The Queen and all the members

Above: Walkabout 2002 style. The Queen was greeted by crowds wherever she went during the Golden Jubilee celebrations.

of her immediate family attended the concert, which included performances by Paul McCartney, Tom Jones, Brian Wilson, Cliff Richard, Shirley Bassey and Tony Bennett. A crowd of 12,000 people within the grounds – again chosen by ballot – was supplemented by more than a million more gathered outside in the Mall, and the event was broadcast live on TV. On this day street parties were held in honour of the Jubilee, though in reduced numbers

Below: The Queen Mother died in March 2002. Her son-in-law and grandchildren followed her coffin. Left to right – Andrew, Charles, Philip, Anne and Edward.

Above: On 4 June, the supersonic airliner Concorde led the Red Arrows display team in a celebratory Jubilee fly-past over the Mall and Buckingham Palace.

compared to the 1977 celebrations of the reign's Silver Jubilee. In the evening of 3 June, Queen Elizabeth lit a beacon at the Queen Victoria Memorial in front of Buckingham Palace, the last in a worldwide line of beacons in an echo of the previous royal Golden Jubilee celebrated by Queen Victoria in 1887. A *son et lumière* firework display

AMERICAN TRIBUTE
New York City joined in the Queen's 50th anniversary celebrations when, on the evening of 4 June 2002, the Empire State Building was illuminated in her Golden Jubilee colours of purple and gold for several hours. It was the first time the building had been illuminated in tribute to a non-American since the visit of Nelson Mandela shortly after his release from prison in 1990. The tribute was in part a gesture of thanks to Queen Elizabeth for having ordered the playing of the American national anthem at Buckingham Palace two days after the terrorist attacks of 11 September 2001.

followed, in which, for the first time ever, fireworks were fired from the roof of Buckingham Palace.

PRIDE AND GRATITUDE
On 4 June the Queen processed with the Duke of Edinburgh in the golden state coach from Buckingham Palace via Temple Bar to a service of thanksgiving in St Paul's Cathedral and then, as in 1977, attended lunch at the Guildhall.

She declared herself 'Deeply moved' by the public acclamation of her reign, adding, 'Gratitude, respect and pride, these words sum up how I feel about the people of this country and the Commonwealth and what this Golden Jubilee means to me'. She also said, 'I think we can all look back with measured pride on the achievements of the last 50 years'.

A Jubilee festival procession in the Mall was designed to celebrate the many changes in British life during the 50 years of Elizabeth II's reign. It also celebrated the great diversity of life and peoples in the Commonwealth.

At its climax, 4,000 people from 54 countries of the Commonwealth paraded in national costume. The Anglo-French supersonic airliner, Concorde, led a celebratory fly-past, accompanied by the Red Arrows aerobatic display team.

Above: The Queen and Prince Philip celebrated their Diamond Anniversary in 2007. Here they enjoy a private joke during the Golden Jubilee celebrations of 2002.

Throughout the year the Queen made a series of celebratory trips throughout the Commonweath. These included visits to Jamaica, New Zealand, Australia and Canada. The royal couple also visited every region of the UK.

Below: Elizabeth said on 4 June 2002, 'I think we can all look back with...pride on the achievements of the last 50 years'.

THE ROYAL FAMILY TODAY
2002–TODAY

In the years since the Golden Jubilee, many marriages have occurred among the younger royals. The Queen is now a great-grandmother, a status achieved by few reigning monarchs. Meanwhile, her eldest son, Charles, has served as Prince of Wales for over 40 years since his investiture in 1969.

On 10 February 2005, Prince Charles announced that he was to marry his long-term lover, Camilla Parker Bowles. The royal wedding was held in Windsor Guildhall on 9 April 2005. The witnesses were Prince William and Camilla's son (and Charles's godson) Tom Parker Bowles. The civil marriage was followed by a service of prayer and blessing in St George's Chapel, led by the Archbishop of Canterbury, Rowan Williams, and attended by the Queen and Prince Philip, leading royals and 750 guests. After a buffet in Windsor Castle, the new Duchess of Cornwall and her husband departed for their honeymoon at Birkhall, a lodge on the Balmoral estate.

Below: Harry and William clash in a polo match played to raise money for those affected by the 2004 tsunami in Asia.

AN ACTIVE MONARCHY

In the early 21st century, at a time when traditional forms of deference and respect for rank have all but disappeared, the future popularity of the monarchy may well depend on the extent to which its leading members appear to be responsive to pressing environmental, social and political problems.

Diana, Princess of Wales, won many admirers for her charitable and campaigning work, and Princes William and Harry have been keen to follow their mother's lead. In summer 2000, during his 'gap year' between Eton College and St Andrew's University, William volunteered in Chile with Raleigh International, a body that carries out environmental and community projects around the world. In 2004, Prince Harry built on his mother's work for AIDS sufferers when he visited African children orphaned by the disease in Lesotho. In a 2004 interview, Prince William declared that he shared his

Above: Charles, Harry and William on a skiing holiday in Switzerland in 2005.

Below: Princess Anne, the only member of the British Royal Family to have competed in the Olympic Games, helped secure the 2012 Olympics for London.

Above: Throughout her 60-year reign, the Queen has been renowned for the grace and good humour she brings to her public duties.

younger brother's desire to help combat AIDS in Africa and that he also wanted to help the homeless in Britain. He said, 'My mother introduced that sort of area to me...it was a real eye-opener and I'm very glad she did'.

ANNE AND THE OLYMPICS

The princes' aunt Anne, the Princess Royal, carries out more engagements than any other member of the Royal Family and is involved with over 200 charities. After competing for the British equestrian team in the 1976 Olympics, she became a British representative in the International Olympic Committee and helped present London's successful campaign to host the 2012 Olympic games.

THE PRINCE OF WALES

Prince Charles has attempted to use his status and wealth to develop solutions for social and environmental problems.

Right: Graduation day, June 2005. Kate Middleton and Prince William became friends at St Andrews University, Scotland.

In 1976 he founded the Prince's Trust to help disadvantaged young people in the UK through practical support and training. Charles began to convert his Highgrove estate and Duchy Home Farm, in Gloucestershire, to organic methods in 1986. His Duchy Originals brand of organic foods was launched with an oat biscuit in 1992.

Charles has also made several public statements of his concern about environmental issues. On his first joint overseas engagement with Camilla, Duchess of Cornwall, at a lunch hosted by President Bush in Washington, DC, the prince said, 'So many people throughout the world look to the United States for a lead on the most crucial issues that face our planet and indeed the lives of our grandchildren'.

COMMEMORATION AND CRISIS

Following terrorist bomb attacks on London on 7 July 2005, Queen Elizabeth rallied the spirits of survivors when she visited victims in hospital. Then, on 9 July 2005, she unveiled a memorial to the women of World War II, in Whitehall, as part of ceremonies to commemorate the 60th anniversary of the end of the Second World War.

Above: On 9 April 2005, Charles and Camilla posed for their official wedding photograph in Windsor Castle.

The combination of formal ceremony and informal symbolic leadership typified the way in which the Queen and the royal family continue at the start of the 21st century to play a widely valued role as figureheads for the nation.

CELEBRATING THE MONARCHY
PRINCE WILLIAM'S WEDDING AND THE DIAMOND JUBILEE

Elizabeth II celebrated the Diamond Jubilee of her reign in 2012, becoming only the second British monarch – after Queen Victoria – to mark 60 years on the throne. In January 2010 the Government announced elaborate plans to mark the Jubilee: a Diamond Jubilee Pageant at Windsor Castle in May, followed by a long weekend of events on 2–5 June, including a special concert at Buckingham Palace, a Service of Thanksgiving at St Paul's Cathedral and the lighting of 2012 beacons up and down the UK. Sunday 3 June featured the Thames Diamond Jubilee Pageant with around 1,000 boats on the river Thames in London, and the Big Lunch, a series of locally organized street parties.

ROYAL PAGEANTRY

London was also the setting for royal pageantry and celebrations in 2011 when the Queen's grandson Prince William,

Below: The Queen in Australia in 2011. She attended the Commonwealth Heads of Government Meeting, where changes to the laws of royal succession were announced.

Above: Prince William and Kate exchange a kiss on the balcony at Buckingham Palace, after their wedding in April 2011.

the new Duke of Cambridge, married Catherine (Kate) Middleton on Friday 29 April at Westminster Abbey. William – second in line of succession to the throne after his father Charles – met Kate in 2001 when both were students at St Andrew's University, Scotland; they

announced their engagement on 16 November 2010, when William presented Kate with the sapphire and diamond engagement ring given to his late mother Diana, Princess of Wales in 1981. After the service the royal couple rode in the 1902 state Landau carriage to

Below: As the newest member of the Royal Family, Prince William's wife Kate charmed press and public alike.

Above: Prince Harry saw active service with the British Army in Helmand Province, southern Afghanistan, in 2008.

Buckingham Palace, where – in line with tradition – they kissed on the balcony before cheering crowds in the Mall.

Ten days after the wedding the royal couple departed on honeymoon to a private island in the Seychelles, then on 30 June–8 July they made their first royal tour together, visiting Canada.

EDINBURGH CEREMONY

On 29 July 2011 another of the Queen's grandchildren, Zara Phillips (daughter of Anne, the Princess Royal and Captain Mark Phillips), married Mike Tindall, at the time captain of the England rugby team, at Canongate Kirk, Edinburgh. The bride, 17th in line to the throne and a successful equestrian athlete, announced that she would keep her own name after the marriage.

SECRET SERVICE

News emerged on 28 February 2008 that for ten weeks Prince Harry had secretly been serving with his regiment of the Household Cavalry in Afghanistan. Harry, who entered Sandhurst in 2005 and was commissioned in the Blues and Royals regiment in 2006, was ear-marked for service in Iraq in May–June 2007 but his involvement then was can-celled amidst fears he would become a target. After his role in Afghanistan became public, he was withdrawn from active service there and subsequently trained to fly Apache attack helicopters.

OFFICIAL VISITS

Elizabeth II and Prince Philip, Duke of Edinburgh, made a tour of Canada on 28 June–6 July 2010, then visited New York City, where the Queen addressed the United Nations General Assembly on 6 July. This was her second speech to the UN, following an earlier address in 1957. In May 2011 they made a state visit to the Republic of Ireland, the first visit by a British monarch to Ireland since 1911.

Before the next trip, Prince Philip celebrated his 90th birthday on 10 June. He announced he would reduce his royal responsibilities and told an interviewer he was "winding down". In what was seen as a gesture of affection on his birthday the Queen announced he would be Lord High Admiral of the Navy, a title she had held herself since 1964. Philip was a naval officer before his marriage to the Queen in 1947.

The Queen and Prince Philip made an official tour of Australia in October 2011, her 16th since 1954. She attended the Commonwealth Heads of Government Meeting in Perth where changes to the laws of royal succession were announced. In Perth, the Queen said to the crowds, "We have been overwhelmed by your kindness and support … Once again we will return to the United Kingdom with fond memories of our time here."

PRINCES GIVE WAY TO THEIR OLDER SISTERS

The laws of succession to the throne were changed on 28 October 2011. Under existing laws, which dated back to the late 17th century, a male child outranked his older sisters in the line of succession, but under the new provisions, which will first be effective in the case of the children of Prince William and the Duchess of Cambridge, the first-born child – whether a girl or a boy – will be next in line to the throne. All 16 of the Commonwealth countries that recognize the Queen as head of state (including Australia, New Zealand and Canada) granted their assent when the change was agreed at the Commonwealth Heads of Government Meeting in Perth, Australia. Rule changes will also allow a monarch to marry a Roman Catholic, although the monarch cannot be a Catholic since as head of the Church of England the king or queen must be in communion with that church.

Below: Queen Elizabeth II and Prince Philip, Sovereign and Knight of the Order of the Garter at Windsor Castle, 2011, the weekend of Prince Philip's 90th birthday.

CASTLES, PALACES & STATELY HOUSES OF BRITAIN

From the medieval castles of Edward I at Beaumaris and Caernarvon
to the glories of Hampton Court Palace and Castle Howard, and
the splendours of Chatsworth and Holyroodhouse, Britain's glorious
architectural heritage is among the finest in the world. The international
importance of Britain's historic houses is demonstrated in these
descriptions of the lives and work of their great architects, builders
and garden designers, with colourful stories about the famous people
who lived in them. This comprehensive survey of the historic houses
and national treasures of the United Kingdom, with in-depth features
on over 120 buildings, an A–Z gazetteer, a glossary of building terms
and detailed location maps and timelines, will lead every reader to
appreciate anew Britain's unique architectural legacy.

Left: Castle Howard, masterpiece of architect Sir John Vanbrugh and one of Britain's finest country houses.
Below: Shields representing England, Wales, Scotland and Northern Ireland.

BRITAIN'S HISTORIC HOUSES

Castles summon a stirring vision of the past, including mounted knights and their ladies, jousting in the lists, fearless swordfighting and the heroic deprivations of siege warfare. When we visit castle sites in England and Wales, we find evocative ruins or romantic Victorian reconstructions to encourage these reveries of the 'age of chivalry'.

No English or Welsh castles survive in their original form from the Middle Ages because they were brought to ruin by natural decay, damaged in the fighting of the English Civil War or deliberately slighted (made indefensible) by the victorious Parliamentary army. In Scotland, however, castles survived for longer. Some played a part in the Jacobite conflicts of the 18th century, when an alliance of highlanders, English rebels and foreign supporters failed to restore the House of Stuart to the throne.

One cause of the enduring appeal of castles (and the key reason why some 19th-century landowners wanted to rebuild their great country houses with turrets and gatehouses) is that these fortresses are centuries-old symbols of social status and authority.

Below: The oldest-surviving part of the Tower of London, the White Tower of c. 1078, was once painted with whitewash.

Above: Harlech Castle in North Wales, built by Edward I c. 1283, has the double defensive walls of the 'concentric castle'.

THE FEUDAL SYSTEM

Castle-building was introduced to England by William the Conqueror and his Norman army in 1066. (A few English castles in Herefordshire and Essex did predate the Conquest, but they were built by Norman friends and associates of Edward the Confessor.) The invaders swept aside the Anglo-Saxon aristocracy, imposing a new Norman ruling class bound to King William I and his descendants by the ties of the feudal system. The castles they built were symbols of feudal authority. They were the fortified homes of knights and great lords, who held them as vassals of the king or a superior lord in return for military support and loyal service.

Castles were, of course, regal as well as lordly residences. Most medieval English kings were great castle-builders, from William I to Edward I and beyond. At the Tower of London and Windsor, William I founded great royal strongholds that have endured to this day as embodiments of royal tradition.

FROM TIMBER TO STONE

In the early years, most Norman castles were timber and earthwork fortifications. The typical early Norman castle was the 'motte and bailey'. The motte, or

mound, stood within its own defensive barrier, and often supported at its summit a tower containing the lord's living apartments. The bailey was the larger area around the motte, enclosed by a ditch and a bank topped with a palisade. The motte might be a natural hill or outcrop, or it might be a man-made mound; it was usually linked by a wooden bridge to the bailey, which contained essential buildings such as stables, kitchens, chapel and hall.

Gradually, timber and earthwork were replaced with stone – although in a few cases, for instance at Richmond in Yorkshire and Ludlow in Shropshire, castles were built partly or mostly in stone from the start. Castles were usually enlarged and improved in a piecemeal fashion, and often details of history or topography dictated the kind of solution found in a particular place to a particular need.

When the summit of the motte was encased in stone, the result was what historians call the 'shell keep', which often, as at Windsor and Restormel, enclosed timber or stone buildings for the lord's use in an inner courtyard. Elsewhere, the lord's stronghold was often in a great stone tower – the *magna turris* ('great tower') of contemporaries and the 'tower keep' of historians. Some tower keeps were built in the late 11th century, such as the Tower of London and Colchester. Throughout the following century, tower keeps, whether rectangular, cylindrical or polygonal, were regularly added to castles.

The tower or shell keep, like the palisaded motte in the early castles, formed an inner stronghold to which the lord and his bodyguard, could retreat. This stronghold within the castle was called the 'dungeon' (from the Latin *dominium* via French *donjon*, meaning lordship). The word acquired its modern meaning, of a dank and dark prison for the lord's enemies, only in later times.

TOWERS AND GATEHOUSES
Stout towers were an important feature of the defensive walls around the bailey. If they were projecting from the wall, they provided a strong position from which defenders could shoot at anyone trying to scale or undermine the wall. They also provided a raised shooting point from which defenders could attack people who had gained access to the top of the wall.

The entrance was a particularly vulnerable point, and towers built above it or to either side of it resulted in the development of the gatehouse. This became a major feature (and the most

secure part of the castle at Caerphilly and Beaumaris in Wales), containing some of its most prestigious apartments.

THE CONCENTRIC CASTLE
In the late 13th century, the concentric castle – regarded by historians as the climax and perfection of British castle design – was developed in Wales, most notably at Caerphilly, built *c.*1271–80 by Gilbert de Clare, Lord of Glamorgan, and at Beaumaris, begun in 1295 by Edward I. This design consisted of two rings of fortifications – an outer wall overlooked and protected by a taller and more heavily fortified inner wall. This idea was as old as ancient Egypt, but was new to Britain. Edward and others had seen its effectiveness on Crusade.

THE FORTIFIED MANOR HOUSE
In early medieval warfare, the possession of castles provided the key to victory. King Stephen's long struggle against the

Above: At Dover, the vast stone square keep built by Maurice the Engineer for Henry II after 1168 still dominates the castle.

Empress Matilda – through the '19 long winters' (1135–54) remembered by chroniclers – was conducted as a series of castle sieges. King John's battle against rebel lords in 1215 climaxed in a two-month siege of Rochester Castle. However, by the time of the Wars of the Roses in the 15th century, conflicts were decided on the battlefield.

Lords still wanted battlements and gatehouses on their property – partly because a fortified house was prestigious, and partly because lawlessness had by no means been entirely eliminated – and so applied for a royal 'licence to crenellate'. But, increasingly, they looked more for comfort than security. At Penshurst Place in Kent and Stokesay Castle in Shropshire, the level of fortification was sufficient only to deter passing marauders.

Left: The imposing gatehouse tower of Pembroke Castle, built in the 13th century by William Marshall, Earl of Pembroke.

> **USING THIS SECTION**
> Many of the houses described in the following pages changed over time as architects added new buildings to the original design or modernized old structures. Therefore, some great houses appear in several sections of the book.

The Tudor age brought about social changes in England and Wales as profound as those that followed the Norman Conquest of 1066. The accession of Henry Tudor as Henry VII in 1485 ended the long Wars of the Roses: as the heroic age of warrior lords and knights drew to a close, a new elite class of merchants and statesmen arose to take their place. Then, *c.*1536–41, as Supreme Head of the Church of England, Henry seized the lands and assets of the country's religious houses, including around a quarter of England's agricultural land, in the Dissolution of the Monasteries. To raise money, he sold much of it to the merchants and political operators of the new Tudor gentry, resulting in an unprecedentedly extensive and swift change of land ownership in England.

A NEW LEVEL OF COMFORT

Great new country houses were built by these men, houses constructed and decorated by the masons and craftsmen who had previously worked for the Church. Initially, many lords continued to raise battlements and gatehouses, but increasingly, also, they fitted their houses with large glass windows – a sign that they did not fear attack.

By 1540, Henry VII and Henry VIII had between them reigned for more than 50 years. Although there were continuing fears of foreign invasion, particularly since the establishment of the Church of

England had inspired a Franco-Spanish Roman Catholic alliance, the Tudors had resoundingly succeeded in delivering the domestic peace they promised the people following the Wars of the Roses.

The new Tudor country houses offered far greater comfort: the windows let in more light and the fitting of flues led to the introduction of coal-burning fireplaces and chimneys. The houses also began to provide more private living space for their owners. The Great Hall began to be neglected in favour of the warm 'solar' room and other private chambers on the first floor of the house.

TUDOR PALACES

The early Tudor decades were also a time of lavish palace building. Henry VII replaced his fire-ravaged palace at Sheen in Surrey with the vast and ornate

Above: The west front at Hampton Court was the entrance in Tudor times. Henry VIII's arms are carved above the gateway.

Richmond Palace, laid out over 10 acres (4ha) around wide courtyards and with a magnificent timber-roofed Great Hall 100ft (30m) in length. He also built a new palace at Greenwich, where Henry VIII was born in 1491, and developed Baynard's Castle from a Norman fortification in London.

Henry VIII created magnificent royal residences at Whitehall and Hampton Court out of houses seized from Cardinal Wolsey; he took possession of great episcopal palaces such as Hatfield House in Hertfordshire and Knole in Kent; he built many new houses, for example at Bridewell in London and Beaulieu in Essex; and he established the extravagantly splendid new palaces of St James's in London, Oatlands at Weybridge and Nonesuch near Ewell (both in Surrey). By his death in 1547, Henry possessed more than 40 palaces and houses – more than any other English monarch.

PRODIGY HOUSES

Edward VI, Mary and Elizabeth I added nothing to the collection of royal palaces, beyond minor additions and

Left: Fit for Queen Elizabeth I. Sir William Cecil's 'prodigy house' at Burghley, Lincolnshire, was 32 years in construction (1555–87).

Above: Holyroodhouse Palace, in Edinburgh, was founded as a priory in 1128. It is the Queen's official residence in Scotland.

necessary maintenance under Elizabeth. But although no new royal buildings were erected, the 45-year reign of Elizabeth saw the construction of a series of astonishingly grand country houses built in her honour. Burghley House in Linconshire, Longleat in Wiltshire, Holdenby in Northamptonshire, Wollaton Hall in Nottinghamshire and Loseley House in Surrey were all 'prodigy houses', built by leading courtiers competing to create a country estate worthy of the monarch revered as England's greatest treasure, and fit to receive her on one of her annual 'summer progresses' around England.

The desire to create a country house grand enough to receive a monarch also inspired lords in the reign of James I, when Robert Cecil, 1st Earl of Salisbury, built the majestic Hatfield House in Hertfordshire and Thomas Howard, 1st Earl of Suffolk, built Audley End, Essex. Like Knole in Kent, Hatfield was originally an ecclesiastical palace and then one of Henry VIII's many grand

residences, before it was transformed into the country seat of England's leading political family. Mary I and Elizabeth I spent much of their childhood at Hatfield, and Elizabeth received the news there that she was queen.

CLASSICAL ARCHITECTURE

The era of James I and Charles I saw the rise of Inigo Jones, one of the greatest English architects. With the creation of the Queen's House in Greenwich, the Banqueting House in Whitehall and Wilton House in Wiltshire, Jones became

the pioneer in England of 'classical' building inspired by both ancient Roman and Italian Renaissance architecture, and particularly by the writing and designs of Andrea Palladio. Jones's elegant buildings were a major influence on future generations of patrons and architects – especially on the members of the 18th-century Palladian movement, who drew their inspiration from the works of Palladio.

Below: The honey-coloured Montacute in Somerset, built in the 1590s, is one of the loveliest of Elizabethan country houses.

ROYAL BUILDERS

The first decades that followed the accession of the Hanoverian dynasty in 1714 represent the nadir of royal building in England. When in London, George I and George II made do with the modest Kensington Palace, created by William III, and the increasingly shabby redbrick St James's Palace, built by Henry VIII; they did not attempt to rebuild the previous royal residence in London, Whitehall Palace, which had been destroyed by fire in 1698. Neither king liked England much and their affections really lay with their preferred palace of Herrenhausen in Hanover.

For much of the 18th century, indeed, many Englishmen were rather uncomfortably aware that the monarchy lacked a grand palace in the capital. St James's was considered inadequate: the novelist and journalist Daniel Defoe dismissed it as 'really mean' in comparison to the glories of the royal court it housed. He also added that, while the English court was more magnificent than any other in Europe. 'this palace comes beneath those of the most petty princes'.

Below: The Prince Regent and John Nash used an Islamic-influenced 'Hindoo' style for the Brighton Pavilion, begun in 1815.

LATE GEORGIAN CHANGES

In his 60-year reign (1760–1820), George III did undertake improvements at Windsor Castle, previously left empty. He also bought Kew Palace and – as a family retreat from court life at St James's – Buckingham House, which in the 19th and 20th centuries was to become the kind of grand metropolitan palace that might have pleased Defoe. But it was only with George III's son, first as Prince of Wales, then as Prince Regent (1811–20) and finally as George IV (1820–30) – that royal building really began once more. With Jeffry Wyatville, George was largely responsible for transforming Windsor Castle into the picturesque 'Gothic' residence that wins the admiration of visitors from all over the world; with John Nash, Henry Holland, Thomas Hopper and James Wyatt, he created the extravagant Carlton House in central London (demolished in 1827); and, again with Nash, he built the exotic Royal Pavilion in Brighton and began the transformation of Buckingham House into a great palace.

VICTORIA'S CONTRIBUTION

In Queen Victoria's reign, Buckingham Palace was named the monarch's official London residence and given the east front that is now its celebrated 'public

Above: Robert Adam transformed the 16th-century Osterley House, Middlesex, by adding a 'neoclassical' facade in c.1763.

face', facing the courtyard and the Victoria Memorial and, beyond, the Mall. However, Victoria's principal contribution to royal building was the result of her carrying to new lengths the separation between the monarch's public and private lives that George III had begun when he bought Buckingham House as a family home. With her husband, Prince Albert, she built two substantial family retreats far removed from London: Osborne House on the Isle of Wight and Balmoral Castle in the Grampian region of Scotland. Balmoral Castle has remained popular with the royal family and together with Sandringham House in Norfolk – acquired by Edward VII in 1862 while still Prince of Wales – is Elizabeth II's principal retreat from royal life at Buckingham Palace, Windsor Castle and Holyroodhouse in Edinburgh.

BRITISH COUNTRY HOUSES

In the 18th century, when Britain's kings occupied the rundown St James's Palace and the uninspiring Kensington Palace, the country's powerful Whig aristocrats lived and entertained in extravagant style in country houses such as Castle Howard in Yorkshire, Stowe House in Buckinghamshire and Chatsworth in Derbyshire. With buildings designed by architects of genius, such as John Vanbrugh, William Kent, Nicholas Hawksmoor and Colen Campbell, standing in gardens and parklands designed by Charles Bridgeman, Kent

and 'Capability' Brown, 18th-century aristocrats may well have enjoyed the period of highest achievement in the history of the British country house.

In the 19th century, the wealth generated by Victorian Britain's empire and industry funded another great age of country house building. Architects such as Anthony Salvin and William Burges romantically renovated some great castles such as Alnwick, Muncaster, Cardiff and Castell Coch.

DECLINE AND FALL

In the 20th century, however, although fine new houses such as Castle Drogo and Manderston were built, the general picture for country houses was bleak. Following agricultural depression and swiftly moving social changes, partly resulting from wider democratization, and in the face of heavy taxation and punitive death duties of potentially 80 per cent of the estate, many owners of great houses struggled to survive. Houses fell into ruin, and were demolished or sold for institutional use, while treasured collections of paintings, sculpture and books were sold to overseas buyers.

Below: Robert Adam evoked the grandeur of ancient Rome in his lavish decoration of the Ante-room at Syon House, Middlesex.

SAVED FOR THE NATION

Some estate owners showed great ingenuity in making their houses pay: in the 1960s, Henry Thynne, 6th Marquess of Bath, introduced lions to his estate at Longleat in Wiltshire to help attract paying visitors in order to fund the house; at Loseley Park in Surrey, James More-Molyneux established a thriving dairy business. Many other houses were saved by the Country House scheme of 1937, under which owners unable to meet death duties could pass the property to the National Trust, an independent charity founded

Above: Belvoir Castle, Leicestershire, is one of many castles rebuilt in the 'Gothic Revival' style in the 19th century.

in 1895, and later government schemes under which restoration and maintenance grants were made and tax concessions granted in return for house owners opening their doors to the public for an agreed number of days each year.

House after house passed from private hands into those of the National Trust and English Heritage (a government organization charged with caring for England's historic environment) or to their equivalents in Scotland, Wales and Ireland. As they did so, they found a new status as cherished repositories of British achievements in art and architecture.

The country house was for many centuries a central point in local life: its owner was supported by and supportive of the locality, and had many responsibilities as a result. In the 19th and early 20th centuries, these houses briefly became little more than a locus of privilege, a treasured private possession. Since the end of World War II, however, they have become part of a shared and treasured national heritage – an embodiment, like the ruined castles that also dot the countryside, and the palaces and other royal residences, of the glories and storied achievements of Britain's past.

PART FOUR

ANCIENT CASTLES

TO 1485

In the years after 1066, the great Norman lords built castles wherever they settled. Castles were immensely effective as instruments of war, yet they were also the proud homes of the new Norman aristocracy. Fortifications became symbols of lordly authority, and so were added to country houses; later, fortified manor houses were built that combined comfort with security.

Left: The original Pembroke Castle was built by Roger, Norman Lord of Dyfed. William Marshall, Earl of Pembroke, added the cylindrical tower keep (centre) c.1200.

ENGLAND TIMELINE, TO 1485

Above: The Round Tower at Windsor Castle, Berkshire, was built in the 12th century.

Above: Middleham Castle, North Yorkhire, was the childhood home of Richard III.

Above: Bodiam Castle, East Sussex, is one of the finest examples of medieval building.

TO 1086

*c.*300BC At Maiden Castle in Dorset, Iron Age Britons begin building a vast hillfort. In AD43 the Roman army takes it from the Durotriges tribe.

*c.*AD75 Fishbourne Villa near Chichester, West Sussex, is a palace for King Cogidubnus of the Regnenses tribe.

*c.*AD250 At Porchester in Hampshire, the Romans build one of a series of 'Saxon shore forts'. Remains of other forts are at Richborough, Lympne and Pevensey.

*c.*AD850 Leede builds the original Leeds Castle in Kent.

1066 Duke William's army builds castles at Pevensey, Hastings, Dover, Canterbury, Wallingford, Berkhamsted and London.

1068 William the Conqueror founds castles at Warwick, Nottingham, York, Lincoln, Huntingdon and Cambridge.

*c.*1070 Alan Rufus, Earl of Yorkshire, builds Richmond Castle.

1072 William founds castles in Durham and at Bambrugh in Northumberland.

1075 William founds Windsor Castle.

*c.*1076 William orders the rebuilding in stone of the original earthwork castle in London. The White Tower at the Tower of London is complete by 1100.

*c.*1076 Norman monk Gundulf begins building Colchester Castle on the site of the Roman Temple of Claudius.

1085 Roger de Lacy builds Ludlow Castle in Shropshire.

1087–1299

1087–9 Rochester Castle, originally built of earth and stone, is rebuilt in stone by Bishop Gundulf of Rochester.

1097 King William Rufus begins building Westminster Hall on the site of King Edward the Confessor's palace.

*c.*1100 Roger de Bigod builds Framlingham Castle in Suffolk.

*c.*1140 Aubrey de Vere III, Earl of Oxford, builds Castle Hedingham in Essex.

1145 Reginald, an illegitimate son of Henry I, builds a castle on the site of an Iron Age Celtic fortress and Saxon fort at Tintagel in north Cornwall.

*c.*1150 Robert Fitz-Ranulph builds Middleham Castle in North Yorkshire.

1153 Robert Fitz-Harding, 1st Lord Berkeley, builds Berkeley Castle in Gloucestershire.

1165 Henry II builds the polygonal keep at Orford Castle in Suffolk.

1180 Hamelin de Plantagenet builds a cylindrical keep at Conisbrough Castle in South Yorkshire.

*c.*1250 Henry III makes lavish improvements to Westminster Palace, creating the superb King's Great Chamber.

1280 William de Valence, uncle of King Edward I, begins rebuilding Goodrich Castle in Hereford and Worcestershire.

1290 Wool merchant Lawrence of Ludlow fortifies his fine manor house of Stokesay Castle in Shropshire.

1300–1485

1300 Sir John de Broughton builds Broughton Castle near Banbury, Oxfordshire.

1302 A fire destroys much of the royal palace at Winchester, but the Great Hall survives.

*c.*1340 Sir John de Poulteney begins major rebuilding at Penshurst Place in Kent; Thomas, 3rd Lord Berkeley, builds the superb Great Hall at Berkeley Castle in Gloucestershire; Sir Thomas Cawne builds the Great Hall in the moated manor house of Ightham Mote, near Sevenoaks, Kent.

1370 The magnificent Banqueting Hall is built at Haddon Hall, Derbyshire.

*c.*1375 The Neville family builds Raby Castle in County Durham.

1385 Sir Edward Dakygrigge begins building Bodiam Castle in East Sussex.

1432 Sir John Falstaff begins building Caister Castle in Norfolk and Ralph, Lord Cromwell, builds his Great Tower at Tattershall Castle in Lincolnshire.

1441 Sir Roger de Fiennes begins building the fine fortified manor house of Herstmonceux Castle in East Sussex.

1477 King Edward IV begins building St George's Chapel at Windsor Castle.

*c.*1480 Edward IV builds a splendid Great Hall at Eltham Palace in Kent.

1482 Sir Edward Bedingfeld begins building the fortified manor house of Oxburgh Hall, near King's Lynn, Norfolk.

N

W **E**

S

SCOTLAND

Chesters
Roman Fort

Housesteads
Roman Fort

Raby
Castle

Richmond
Castle

Middleham
Castle

Norton
Conyers

North Sea

Irish Sea

Peveril
Castle

ENGLAND

Tattershall
Castle

The Wash

Haddon
Hall

Belvoir
Castle

Oxburgh
Hall

Caister
Castle

Stokesay
Castle

Warwick
Castle

Framlingham
Castle

Ludlow
Castle

Sudeley
Castle

Broughton
Castle

Orford Castle

WALES

Goodrich
Castle

Berkhamsted
Castle

Castle
Hedingham

Tower of
London

Layer Marney
Tower

Palace of Westminster
& Jewel Tower

Lullingstone
Roman
Villa

Colchester Castle

Berkeley
Castle

Windsor Castle

Hever
Castle

Ightham
Mote

Rochester Castle

Dover
Castle

Bristol Channel

The Vyne

Leeds
Castle

Winchester Castle
Great Hall

Penshurst Place

Great Dixter House

Bignor Roman Villa

Strait of Dover

Maiden Castle

Porchester Castle

Lewes
Castle

Camber
Castle

Tintagel
Castle

Launceston
Castle

Fishbourne
Roman Palace

Herstmonceux
Castle

Pevensey
Castle

Hastings
Castle

English Channel

SCOTLAND, WALES
AND NORTHERN IRELAND TIMELINES, TO 1485

Above: Edinburgh Castle houses the Scottish Crown Jewels and the Stone of Destiny.

SCOTLAND, TO 1485

1093 David I builds a chapel in Edinburgh Castle in memory of his mother Margaret. St Margaret's Chapel is the oldest surviving part of the castle.

1204 Alan, 2nd High Steward, begins work on Rothesay Castle, Isle of Bute.

1279 Unknown builders begin the unusual triangular castle of Caerlaverock in Dumfriesshire.

1296 William Wallace captures Dunnottar Castle, Aberdeenshire.

1300 King Edward I repairs Hermitage Castle, Borders, during the Scottish Wars of Independence.

1368-72 The future Robert II of Scots builds the 60ft(18m)-high David's Tower at Edinburgh Castle, the first known example in Scotland of the tower house.

1375 1st Earl of Douglas begins building Tantallon Castle, East Lothian, on a rocky promontory opposite the Bass Rock.

1424 King James I of Scots begins rebuilding Linlithgow Palace in West Lothian.

*c.*1435 King James I of Scots builds a Great Chamber at Edinburgh Castle.

*c.*1440 The main tower is added to Glamis Castle, Angus.

1460 Robert, 2nd Lord Maxwell, completes the building of Caerlaverock Castle, Dumfries & Galloway.

N
W   E
S

Broch of Gurness

North Sea

Moray Firth

Dunvegan Castle

Cawdor Castle

Huntly Castle

Braemar Castle

Dunnottar Castle

Blair Castle

Glamis Castle

SCOTLAND

Scone Palace

Castle Campbell

Doune Castle

Blackness Castle

Firth of Forth

Rothesay Castle

Linlithgow Castle

Tantallon Castle

Edinburgh Castle

Brodrick Castle

North Atlantic Ocean

Hermitage Castle

Caerlaverock Castle

Solway Firth

ENGLAND

Irish Sea

Above: Beaumaris Castle, Wales, is the most technically perfect medieval castle in Britain.

WALES, TO 1485

1067 Chepstow Castle built.
1090 Abergavenny Castle built.
1106 Kidwelly Castle begun.
*c.*1200 Pembroke Castle begun.
1271 Caerphilly Castle begun.
1277 Edward I begins building Flint and Rhuddlan Castles, Denbighshire.
1283 Edward I begins building Conway, Caernarvon and Harlech castles.
1295 Edward I begins Beaumaris Castle.
1430 Sir William ap Thomas builds the Yellow Tower at Raglan Castle.

Above: Carrickfergus Castle, Northern Ireland, is dominated by its great keep.

NORTHERN IRELAND, TO 1485

*c.*1177 John de Courcy builds Dundrum Castle on the site of a Celtic hillfort overlooking Dundrum Bay.
*c.*1180 De Courcy builds Carrickfergus Castle overlooking Belfast Lough.
*c.*1180 De Courcy builds Killyleagh Castle to protect the inhabitants from Viking invaders.
1200s Building of Dunluce Castle begins.
1300s Building of Ardglass Castle begins.

ENTRY TO THE TRAITORS GATE

CHAPTER THIRTEEN

FROM ROMAN VILLAS TO NORMAN CASTLES

TO 1154

Few buildings and fortifications remain of those that were constructed before the Norman followers of William the Conqueror invaded England in 1066. Wood and other biodegradable building materials have decayed, and what stone structures there were have generally been dismantled or incorporated into later buildings. With a few exceptions, we cannot visit pre-Norman buildings. However, there are extensive archaeological remains from which we can get an idea of the houses, palaces and fortresses built by native Britons, Romans and Anglo-Saxons.

Chronicle accounts of the dramatic events of 1066 repeatedly make plain the Normans' reliance upon the castle as both a military base and a means of overawing the people they came to conquer. Upon landing at Pevensey, Duke William of Normandy built a castle amid the remains of the Roman fort there, and at Hastings he raised another. At Dover, within days of the Battle of Hastings, he built a further castle, then at Canterbury yet another. Before the year was out, he had even erected a fortification at the south-east corner of the city wall of London itself. By 1100, the Normans had built 400 castles in England. Each of the major Saxon towns had its Norman castle, and the borders were securely guarded by fortresses. Most comprised earthwork fortifications and timbers, and they were gradually rebuilt in stone in the late 11th and 12th centuries. Indeed, before the end of William I's reign in 1087, the first castles made entirely of stone were being built.

Left: The imposing Norman White Tower at the Tower of London was begun in 1078, using stone specially imported from Willliam the Conqueror's homeland in France.

BEFORE THE NORMANS
ROMAN AND ANGLO-SAXON BUILDING

The ancient Romans' version of the country house or palace was the summer villa, an elegant building often lavishly decorated with murals and mosaics and equipped with the latest comforts, such as underfloor heating, and set in a well-tended estate. During the Roman occupation of Britain, villas were considered to be a status symbol both for the Romans and for the richest and most prominent of their subjects – as is still evident from the impressive remains of those buildings that have been excavated.

ROMAN VILLAS

At Fishbourne, near Chichester in West Sussex, are the remnants of a magnificent villa built *c.*AD75 for King Cogidubnus (or Togidubnus) of the Regnenses tribe. Archaeologists have determined that the villa had four wings arranged around a central courtyard, with a large reception chamber in the west wing. As many as 100 rooms at Fishbourne had mosaic floors, of which 20 survive, including a beautiful one representing the Roman love god Cupid riding a dolphin.

Below: The broch of Gurness, a fort on Orkney, is around 65ft (20m) across and was probably in use until around AD100.

Fishbourne was probably the grandest villa in the whole of Britain, and it was so large that it bears comparison with imperial villas in Italy. Other less magnificent but still remarkable Roman villas in Britain include Bignor near Arundel in West Sussex, Chedworth in Gloucestershire and also Lullingstone in Kent.

ANGLO-SAXON PALACES

There are also a few tantalizing remains of the palaces and grand houses built by Anglo-Saxon kings in the years after the

Above: The ancient British fort of Maiden Castle, Dorset, covers 45 acres (18ha). Vespasian's forces captured it in AD43.

Roman withdrawal from Britain. The kings of Northumbria, for example, built a palace complex on raised ground at Yeavering in Northumberland in the 7th–9th centuries AD. The most important building of the complex, the Great Hall, was built entirely of wood and had a great central hearth and entrances in the long sides of the building. Roof posts were erected in pairs down the length of the building, which had the effect of dividing the space into three separate aisles.

Archaeologists have uncovered what may be the remains of palaces kept by the great King Offa of Mercia at Sutton in Herefordshire and on the banks of the River Thames at Chelsea in London. Another great Anglo-Saxon hall that may have been a palace was found at Northampton; while at Cheddar in Somerset, a building once thought to be a palace is more likely to have been a less grand building, perhaps a hunting lodge.

FORTS AND FORTRESSES

The remains of more than 2,500 hilltop fortresses built by ancient Britons have been identified. Most are small, and offered protection to just a few peasants and their cattle, but the remnants of very extensive hilltop fortresses from the 1st millennium BC can be seen at Maiden Castle in Dorset, Hengistbury Head in Hampshire and Old Sarum in Wiltshire.

In northern Scotland and on Orkney and the Shetland Isles, locals seeking protection against raiders built fortified round towers, or brochs, at about this time. The Broch of Gurness on Orkney is 65ft (20m) across and once stood 32ft (10m) tall; Mousa Broch, on the isle of Mousa off Shetland, still stands 42ft (13m) tall and is 50ft (15m) in diameter.

When the Romans conquered Britain, they very rarely used the existing British fortifications as strongholds, preferring to build their own fortresses. Some of these Roman forts have been excavated, giving an indication of their size and importance. Caerleon in Monmouthshire was a 50-acre (20-ha) fort. Its wall had defensive turrets every 150ft (46m) and the fortress had an amphitheatre for both military manoeuvres and entertainment.

At the northern limit of their empire, the Romans built Hadrian's Wall, which ran for 73 miles (117km) from

Below: The Roman camp at Caerleon was one of three permanent legionary forts in Britain in the late 1st century AD.

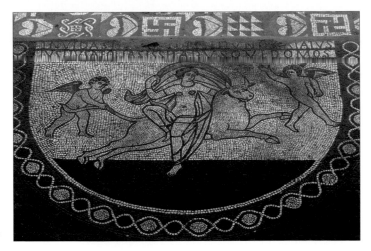

Newcastle to Carlisle. After every mile (1.6km), soldiers built a small 'Mile Castle' fortification, and after every 4 miles (6.5km), they erected a garrison fort, such as the one at Housesteads in Northumberland, which was built c.AD124 and has been fully excavated. It had room to garrison up to 1,000 men.

In south-east England are the remnants of Roman coastal fortifications, the Saxon shore forts, built to repel a possible sea-borne invasion. The most complete remains are at Portchester Castle in Hampshire. The 9-acre (3.6-ha) fort had walls 20ft (6m) high and 10ft (3m) thick, with D-shaped towers every 100–200ft (30–60m), from which defenders would have fired catapults. Large parts are still standing.

Anglo-Saxon kings needed to fortify their palace settlements against Viking raiders. King Alfred (r.871–99), for instance, garrisoned a series of forts for this purpose throughout his kingdom of Wessex, remains of which can be seen.

Many Roman and Anglo-Saxon forts later formed the basis of Norman stone castles: including the Roman fortresses at Pevensey, Porchester, Caerleon and Caerphilly. Excavations at Goltho, Lincolnshire, reveal how an Anglo-Saxon hall-palace complex was given ditch and bank defences in AD850–1000 and then was the site of a Norman motte-and-bailey castle in 1080–1150.

Above: This mosaic from the Roman villa at Lullingstone, Kent, shows the god Jupiter (in the form of a bull) carrying off Europa.

Below: King Alfred the Great – for whom this fine jewelled bookmark head was made – established around 30 fortified burghs (boroughs) to keep the Vikings at bay.

PEVENSEY AND HASTINGS
THE FIRST CASTLES

Along with Hastings, Dover and Canterbury, Pevensey Castle was among the first four Norman castles built in England. Duke William of Normandy began to build a castle at Pevensey within the west gate of the Roman fort there, on the very first day of the Conquest campaign, 28 September 1066. According to one chronicler, William's invasion force carried with it, packed in boxes, the materials needed for quickly raising a wooden tower and other defensive structures.

OCCUPATION OF ANDERIDA
The Roman fort of Anderida at Pevensey – later one of the Saxon shore line of fortresses – was sited on a peninsula overlooking the sea, for at the time of the Roman occupation, and indeed of the Norman Conquest, the waves came in as far as the castle walls,

although the sea has now fallen back to leave marshland. In 1066, the fort was the site of an Anglo-Saxon burgh, or fortified town, and the remains of a chapel excavated within the castle walls are probably those of this burgh. William and his Norman forces encountered no resistance when they took control and hastily erected their castle.

ROBERT, COUNT OF MORTAIN
In the autumn of 1066, Duke William did not linger at Pevensey, but moved his army swiftly on to Hastings. After the Conquest, he gave Pevensey Castle and its lordship to his half-brother Robert, Count of Mortain. Robert was also made Lord of Berkhamsted, Lambeth and Bermondsey, and in 1072 of Cornwall. He was England's second-largest lay landowner, although he spent little time in the country, preferring to live in Normandy.

Above: Pevensey Castle in Sussex survived sieges by the forces of King William Rufus (1088) and Simon de Montfort (1264).

PEVENSEY CASTLE
Robert strengthened the existing walls of the Roman fort at Pevensey to form the outer bailey wall of the castle. He repaired the eastern gateway and built a new entrance to replace the ancient one at the south-west. He then erected a second walled enclosure within and at the eastern end of the ancient fort.

The castle's stone tower-keep was probably built after Robert's death (1095), in the early 1100s, when many of the wooden Conquest castles were rebuilt in stone. It made use of part of the Roman wall and a Roman tower. On the other three sides of the inner bailey (or enclosure), the walls and D-shaped towers were probably erected in the mid-1200s by Peter of Savoy, Earl of Richmond and uncle of Henry III's wife, Queen Eleanor. Henry made Peter Lord of Pevensey in 1246. Peter built residential apartments set against the inside of the castle walls in a very grand style befitting his status.

As the sea retreated, uncovering Pevensey Marshes, the castle declined in importance. By the Tudor period, it had begun to fall into ruins. Nevertheless, it was partially refortified as a gun emplacement in the 1580s to defend

MOTTE-AND-BAILEY CASTLES
The early Norman castles combined a motte (a mound) surrounded by a ditch and a bailey (an enclosed, defended area). The bailey was enclosed by a wooden fence, and outside that by another ditch or a moat. Sometimes the motte was a hill; at other times it was an artificial mound built up using the earth that had been dug out when the ditch was made.

On the motte stood a keep (a look-out tower), in the early years also made of wood. It often contained accommodation for the castellan (keeper of the castle). Within the bailey were the buildings necessary to house and maintain the garrison – perhaps a Great Hall, kitchens, chapel, stables and other farm buildings.

In the late 11th–12th century, the wooden keep was often rebuilt in stone. The outer wall around the bailey was also remade in stone, with the addition of a strong 'gatehouse' and a drawbridge across the moat.

Right: At Launceston, Cornwall, a timber keep was built on a steep motte c.1067. The stone castle is late 12th century.

Above: The original timber motte-and-bailey castle of 1066 at Hastings, Sussex, was rebuilt in stone as early as 1070.

against a Spanish invasion. Almost 400 years later, it housed military billets and machine-gun posts during World War II.

HASTINGS CASTLE

An image in the Bayeux Tapestry shows William's men digging to create a ditch and raise a motte at Hastings. As he would later do at Dover, he built the motte of his castle within the outline of an Iron Age hill fortress and an Anglo-Saxon burgh, and close to a pre-existing church, which is now known as St-Mary-in-the-Castle. The castle occupied a commanding position on a coastal hilltop overlooking the beach and harbour. A tower was added in the 12th century; an eastern curtain wall (with a twin-

towered gatehouse) and the South Tower were built in the 13th century. Later the cliff was so severely eroded by the sea that parts of the castle fell into it.

After victory at Hastings, and building a castle at Dover, William marched in a circuitous route on London and

erected castles *en route* at Canterbury in Kent, Wallingford in Oxfordshire (where Archbishop Stigand of Canterbury submitted to him) and Berkhamsted in Hertfordshire. Earthworks and other castle remains can still be seen in all these towns.

Right: At Hastings, William, then Duke of Normandy, supervises his men digging out a ditch and using the earth to build a motte, in this scene from the Bayeux Tapestry.

DOVER CASTLE
THE STONE KEEP

In October 1066, within days of victory at the Battle of Hastings, and after building Pevensey and Hastings Castles, William the Conqueror began to build his castle at Dover. He set to work inside the boundaries of an Iron Age hillfort that had been adapted by the Romans and then become a fortified town. The pre-Norman church of St Mary-in-Castro, dating from the late 10th or early 11th century, survives within the castle precincts – alongside a Roman *pharos*, or lighthouse. The earth bank and ditch outside the castle's later 12th-century walls are probably the remains of the fortifications that were established on the site by its Iron Age colonizers.

According to the account of William of Poitiers, the first Norman castle at Dover was built in just eight days. Presumably, it was an earthwork and wooden motte-and-bailey fortification. This would have been quite a feat, as

Below: English stronghold. Constables of Dover Castle have included Henry V and Henry VIII (while princes), the Duke of Wellington and Sir Winston Churchill.

motte construction was very labour intensive, and the soldiers needed to be on constant guard. All that remains today is a stretch of the ditch and bank alongside the south transept of the church. King William made his half-brother Bishop Odo of Bayeux the first constable of the castle at Dover.

THE STONE KEEP

William's castle at Dover was greatly strengthened by Henry II (r.1154–89) and his architect Maurice the Engineer in 1168–88. Maurice built the vast square stone keep, or tower, which is the dominant building in the castle complex

Left: Henry II, who built the great keep at Dover, brought stability to England after the civil war of King Stephen's reign.

to this day. Measuring 96 x 96 x 98ft (29 x 29 x 30m), with walls 16–21ft (5–6.5m) thick, this massive rectangular stone keep was the largest in Europe. It contained four great rooms measuring 20 x 50ft (6 x 15m), and two chapels, in addition to a further 12 rooms, each roughly 10 x 15ft (3 x 4.5m), within the extremely thick walls.

THE CASTLE WALLS

Maurice also raised the inner bailey wall at Dover, complete with ten rectangular towers, and two twin-tower gateways with barbicans (outer fortifications defending a drawbridge or gateway) – one to the north (the King's Gate) and one to the south (the Palace Gate). Furthermore, Henry and Maurice began work on an outer curtain wall, in this way anticipating the principles of the concentric castle design, with its twin defensive walls, around 100 years ahead of the design's more general application in the reign of Edward I.

Above: The castle at Dover with (beyond, left) the Church of St Mary-in-Castro and the Roman lighthouse.

NORMAN RINGWORKS

In addition to motte-and-bailey castles, the Normans built fortifications known as 'ringworks' – defensive strongholds enclosed by earthworks but without a motte. These were sometimes quite small, less than 30m (100ft) across within the earthworks, but in other places they were of considerable size: a ringwork excavated at Huttons Ambo in Yorkshire measured 120 x 180ft (35 x 55m) within its bank and ditch defences.

Historians emphasize that the castle was a symbol of high status within the rigidly hierarchical feudal system, adding that ringworks may have been built for landowners who did not have sufficient feudal standing to justify a motte and a castle. Another explanation is that ringworks were preferred in places where a large garrison force was needed, since the castle and motte fortification could leave little room to house defenders.

The outer wall of the castle was completed by King John (r.1199–1216). At the close of John's reign, when the King was in open conflict with many of his barons, the castle was besieged by Prince Louis of France, who had been invited by the barons to invade. Despite the great expenditure on its walls by King Henry II, and a determined defence by constable Hubert de Burgh, the castle came close to being captured when Louis of France and his engineers succeeded in undermining the King's Gate, part of which collapsed. However, King John's death brought the conflict to an end before matters could get worse.

Henry III (r.1216–72) carried out extensive improvements at Dover Castle. Most notable was the erection of the Norfolk Towers in place of the former King's Gate and the addition of the Constable's Gate, containing residential quarters for the castellan or keeper of the castle, c.1227.

LATER YEARS

Dover Castle's position ensured that it remained an important element of England's maritime defences across the centuries. Many later alterations were made that, sadly, damaged the remains of the medieval castle. These included knocking down towers in the outer wall to establish gun emplacements during the Napoleonic War, when an extensive network of tunnels was first dug into the cliff beneath the castle. In World War II, Operation Dynamo (the May 1940 evacuation of 338,000 British soldiers from Dunkirk, northern France) was masterminded by 700 top-secret staff from the tunnels. Within the tunnels there was a hospital as well as a command centre that Churchill visited to see the plans that led to eventual victory.

Below: An early concentric castle in England? This reconstruction of Dover Castle in the mid-1300s shows inner and outer defences.

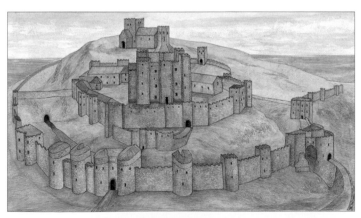

THE TOWER OF LONDON
AND WILLIAM I

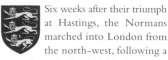

Six weeks after their triumph at Hastings, the Normans marched into London from the north-west, following a route from the battlefield via Dover, Canterbury, Winchester, Wallingford and Berkhamsted. The main aim of this long march was to make an impressive show of military force and to cow the population into submission. William sent an advance party into London to build a castle there, and, after his coronation on 25 December 1066, he retreated to Barking until it was finished.

The first London fortification was built in the south-east corner of the city's Roman walls. With the River Thames to the south and the city walls also to the south and to the east, the castle-builders built trenches and an

THE SQUARE KEEP

The rectangular tower of Colchester Castle and the White Tower of London are the earliest examples of the square keep in England. The former, at 107 x 151ft (32.5 x 46m), was larger even than the White Tower. These towers may have been based on the design of the ducal palace at Rouen of c.950. They were intended more as an expression of the might of the Norman invaders than as military strongholds.

Below: The vast Norman keep at Colchester was built over the vaults of the ruined Roman Temple of Claudius.

earthwork wall with a wooden palisade to the north and west. The trenches were 25ft (8m) wide and 11ft (3.5m) deep.

THE WHITE TOWER
Around a decade later, in 1078, William ordered the building of a great square stone keep, the White Tower, which was intended to strike fear into the hearts of any subversive Londoners. This vast and forbidding building, which survives to this day (see also page 102), was largely complete by c.1100. The tower, 90ft (27m) high with walls 11–15ft (3.5–4.5m) thick, measured 105 x 118ft (32 x 36m).

Above: The Tower of London was already being used as a prison by 1100, when Bishop Flambard of Durham escaped through a high window using a rope.

It contained a basement beneath two floors of residential apartments, both containing a hall, chamber and chapel. The top floor was set aside for the King himself. The tower's sole entrance was on the south side, some 15ft (4.5m) above ground and accessed by steps that could be removed. The White Tower was probably designed by Gundulf, a Norman monk who became Bishop of Rochester.

WESTMINSTER HALL
HEART OF THE PALACE

When William the Conqueror was satisfied with the fortifications he had built in the city of London, he moved his court into King Edward the Confessor's palace at Westminster. Edward had built this in 1060 on ground between the River Thames and the abbey church of Westminster (subsequently Westminster Abbey).

KING WILLIAM RUFUS

William the Conqueror's son, William Rufus, had grand plans to build a new palace on the site, and in 1097 he built the first stage: Westminster Hall. His structure is the only part of the 11th-century palace still standing today, since it survived the fire that devastated the ancient buildings in 1834.

William Rufus's hall was used for banquets. It measured a massive 240ft (73m) in length and was almost 40ft (12m) high, with walls 6ft 8in (2m) thick.

Below: King George IV's lavish Coronation Banquet was held in Westminster Hall, in 1821. The Earl of Denbigh wrote of the event that 'it exceeded all imagination'.

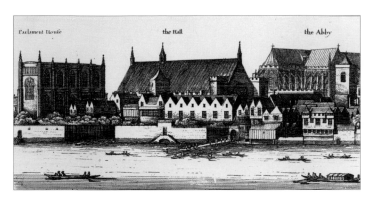

A raised gallery ran around the hall 20ft (6m) above the ground. The walls were plastered and painted, and contained round-headed windows. The roof was supported by great timber posts, which divided the vast room into a central nave and two side aisles. Although William was reputedly not very impressed with the new building – declaring it a 'mere bedchamber' – he held a great banquet in 1099 to celebrate its completion. The Royal Council of bishops, nobles and ministers, which later assembled there, was the forerunner of the present House of Lords.

Above: This engraving by Wenceslaus Holler shows Westminster Hall (centre) as it appeared in the English Civil War.

AFFAIRS OF STATE

The hall's appearance has significantly changed since King William Rufus's day. After it was damaged by fire in 1291, Edward II carried out restoration; in addition, Richard II made several major improvements in 1397–9, including installing a vast hammer-beam roof (see page 322). Later, the hall was the setting for the coronation feast of each new monarch, when, following tradition, the king or queen's champion would ride to the centre of the hall and challenge to single combat anyone who opposed the sovereign's right to rule. The last coronation feast held in the hall was for George IV in 1821, which was, like all his entertainments, incredibly lavish.

The hall has also been the setting for a number of important trials, including those of Sir Thomas More in 1535, the Gunpowder Plot conspirators in 1606 and King Charles I in 1649. Its main everyday function is as the vestibule of the House of Commons. Since the death of Queen Victoria, it has also been used for the lying-in-state of deceased royals, such as Edward VII (1910), George VI (1952) and Queen Elizabeth, the Queen Mother (2002).

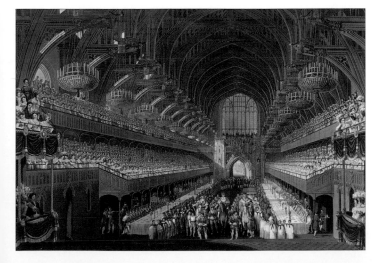

CHEPSTOW CASTLE
NORMAN BUILDING IN WALES

William FitzOsbern was the childhood friend of William the Conqueror and veteran of the Battle of Hastings. He began work on a stone castle at Chepstow in south-east Wales in 1067. Created Earl of Hereford, FitzOsbern established Chepstow as a base for Norman penetration into Wales. It was built in stone from the beginning.

The castle was built in a strategic position – a long, high cliff overlooking the River Wye and the place where the Roman road from western England into South Wales forded the river. Its principal building was a stone Great Hall, initially of two storeys; this was altered and raised in the 13th century, but its original walls are still standing, making it Britain's oldest surviving stone castle building. FitzOsbern and his masons used bands of red tiles thought to be from the nearby Roman fort of Caerwent; they also inserted Norman round-headed windows on the ground floor, which can still be seen today. There are also surviving sections of the 11th-century stone defensive walls to the east (now in the middle bailey) and west (now in the upper bailey).

FitzOsbern's castle was largely complete by 1071, when the Earl was killed in battle in Flanders. By then he had made good use of his base to stamp his authority on much of the Welsh

THE NORMANS IN WALES

Chepstow was the earliest of several castles erected on the borders of Wales (the Marches) by the Norman 'Marcher lords', who took an iron grip on the English-Welsh border. (The term 'Marcher' derives from the Frankish *marka*, meaning 'boundary'.) Just as William FitzOsbern was given the earldom of Hereford and built a castle at Chepstow, so Roger of Montgomery was created Earl of Shrewsbury and raised a castle at Pembroke, South Wales, and Hugh de Avranches was made Earl

of Chester and built a castle in that city. Many other Norman castles followed in Wales, including notable examples at Cardiff (built *c.*1091 by Robert Fitzhamon, Norman lord of Gloucester), Abergavenny (built *c.*1090 by Hamelin de Ballon), Kidwelly (built in the 12th century by Roger, Bishop of Salisbury) and Caerphilly (built from 1271 onward by Gilbert de Clare).

Below: Kidwelly Castle was rebuilt after c.1275 by Payn de Chaworth.

kingdom of Gwent. However, his son, Roger Fitzwilliam, lost possession of Chepstow when he joined the doomed uprising against the Conqueror in 1075. Roger was imprisoned, his castle and lands reverting to the Crown.

WILLIAM MARSHALL
In 1115, Henry I gave the castle to the powerful de Clare family, who seem to have made no notable alterations. Then, in 1189, the de Clare heiress, Isabel, daughter of Richard 'Strongbow' de Clare,

Left: Chepstow Castle's walls are 18ft (5.5m) thick in parts. They are notable for an early use of round and square towers.

Earl of Pembroke, married the great knight William Marshall, and the castle passed into his hands along with all her other estates. Marshall upgraded the defences at Chepstow significantly, rebuilding the eastern defensive wall and adding two projecting round towers with arrow slits through which archers could defend the land immediately outside the wall. (The curtain wall he raised was, in his day, the eastern boundary of the castle, but because of subsequent developments, it is now the dividing wall between the middle and lower baileys.)

In the years to 1245, William Marshall's sons continued to redevelop the castle, adding a further enclosure to the east (now the lower bailey) with a twin-towered gatehouse, and at the other, western, end of the castle building a barbican with a cylindrical tower. They also improved the Great Keep, adding large windows on the safer northern side overlooking the Wye.

ROGER BIGOD III

In 1270–1300 the castle was in the hands of another great landholder, Roger Bigod III, Earl of Norfolk. He built a new hall along the northern (cliff) side of the lower bailey, including a cellar, kitchen, service rooms and accommodation, as well as the public space of the hall. In addition, he erected what is now known as Marten's Tower, containing elegant accommodation for the lord of the castle and a richly decorated chapel, at the south-east angle of the lower bailey. Earl Roger also built a new three-storey gatehouse for the barbican, added an extra storey to William FitzOsbern's Great Keep and erected the town walls for the developing

Below: Interior of Marten's Tower, Chepstow. Henry Marten, who was jailed there, was a leader of the Levellers in the Civil War.

Above: River fortress. The Wye runs along the north edge of the escarpment on which the elongated castle stands at Chepstow.

settlement alongside the castle. The town of Chepstow grew in the 13th and 14th centuries and received a charter in 1524.

The castle was garrisoned for Charles I and came twice under siege during the Civil Wars of the 17th century. In forcing its surrender, parliamentary guns caused damage, but the castle was later repaired and garrisoned by both Cromwell and Charles II. Marten's Tower takes its name from Henry Marten, one of the judges who signed Charles I's death warrant and who, after the Restoration in 1660, was imprisoned with his wife (in some comfort) in the tower by Charles II. Marten died there in 1680.

ROCHESTER CASTLE
STRONGHOLD IN STONE

The original Rochester Castle was one of the earliest Norman fortifications, built shortly after the Conquest as a show of strength and to guard the point at which the Roman road from London to Dover crossed the River Medway in Kent. It was constructed of timber and earthworks in the south-west angle of the Roman city wall at the point where the medieval bridge spanned the river. In 1087–9, the first years of King William Rufus's reign, Bishop Gundulf – architect of the White Tower in London – rebuilt the castle walls in stone. Rochester was therefore one of the first Norman castles to be reworked in stone.

THE SQUARE KEEP

In 1127, King Henry I granted the castle to William de Corbeil, Archbishop of Canterbury, and his successors. The archbishop built a remarkable square keep, 70 x 70ft (21 x 21m), 113ft (34.5m) high to the parapet, with turrets at the corners soaring another 12ft (3.5m). The walls were 12ft (3.5m) thick at their base. The keep was forbidding

Below: A 19th-century painting of Rochester shows how close the cathedral stands to the castle, which guards the crossing of the River Medway.

Above: The square keep at Rochester Castle, showing the rounded south-east tower, rebuilt after damage in the siege of 1215.

without but luxurious within: the second floor housed a chapel, a Great Chamber and a Great Hall, with magnificent carving around the fireplaces, windows and doors, and a raised gallery to the hall. The keep also contained a defensive cross wall, behind which defenders could retreat if the tower was partially breached, and which came in

Above: The interior of the great keep of Rochester Castle is now little more than a shell, but the sheer size of the ruins gives a sense of its original luxury and grandeur.

useful for the castle defenders in 1215 (see below). A smaller tower, built against the north face of the keep, guarded the entrance, which was at first-floor level.

THE FIRST SIEGE

Archbishop de Corbeil's square keep at Rochester faced two major sieges in its history. The first came in 1215, when, with many of England's leading barons openly opposing King John, the Archbishop of Canterbury, Stephen Langton, refused to open the castle to the pro-Royalist Bishop of Winchester. King John and his army arrived, and laid siege for around two months, held at bay by a garrison of little more than 100 men. The King's men used five stone-throwing engines, which did great damage to the curtain wall but could make no significant impact on the tremendous fortifications of the keep itself, so instead they set out to undermine the south-east angle of the tower. They dug beneath the corner of the building and shored up the brickwork with wooden props, then set fire to the props, causing part of the tower to collapse. The defenders retreated behind the defensive cross wall and continued the fight, but the garrison was reduced to surrender by starvation.

After the siege of 1215, the damaged south-east corner of the keep was restored in the contemporary style as a cylindrical (circular) turret, in contrast to the square turrets at the other corners of the tower. Other repairs and improvements included reconstruction of the castle's outer gate and the building of a drawbridge in the southern curtain wall.

In 1264, Rochester Castle was besieged by Simon de Montfort and other rebels during the baronial uprising against King Henry III. The castle was badly damaged, but withstood the assault for a week, until de Montfort and his men withdrew at the news that the King's army was on its way to relieve the castle.

LATER YEARS

In later years, the castle fell into disrepair, but it was restored and rebuilt in the 14th century by Kings Edward III and Richard II. Then it suffered many more years of neglect before being passed from the Crown to private owners in the reign of James I.

MARCHER FORTRESS: LUDLOW CASTLE

Ludlow Castle in Shropshire was built in 1085 as a Norman stronghold to subdue the 'Marches' (the English–Welsh border). Its first lord, Roger de Lacy, was granted land in south Shropshire by William FitzOsbern, Earl of Hereford and builder of Chepstow Castle. At Ludlow, using locally quarried stone, de Lacy built one of the great stone keeps of the 12th century, on high land overlooking the River Terne. The de Lacy family lost the castle for some years, during which, *c.*1130, Sir Joyce de Dinan built a remarkable circular chapel in the Middle Ward, but the castle subsequently returned to its original owners. The town of Ludlow was laid out in the 12th century to the east of the fortress.

In later years, Ludlow Castle belonged to Roger Mortimer, the ruthless Earl of March; his descendants probably built the fortifications on the castle's northern front. The castle then passed to Edward IV. Many improvements were made to the castle in the Tudor period, when it was briefly the home of Prince Arthur (elder brother of the eventual King Henry VIII) and his bride, Catherine of Aragon. In the tower named after Prince Arthur, the sickly heir to the throne died in 1502 – an event with momentous consequences for England's royal family.

Below: In Ludlow's inner bailey stands the Chapel of St Mary Magdalene – the only round 'church' in an English castle.

CASTLE HEDINGHAM
THE GREAT TOWER

Castle Hedingham in Essex is celebrated as one of the most splendid 12th-century rectangular keeps in England. The vast stone tower, 110ft (33.5m) high, was built *c*.1140 by Aubrey de Vere III, probably to celebrate his elevation to the earldom of Oxford.

TOWER CASTLE
The keep has four floors above a basement: the first contains the entrance chamber and the second and third floors combine to make the great Banqueting Hall. Around the hall, built into the 12ft (3.5m) thick walls, runs an elevated minstrels' gallery. The hall and gallery make Hedingham comparable to the Great Keep at Rochester, built perhaps a decade earlier.

Above: The 28ft (8.5m) transverse arch in the Banqueting Hall at Hedingham is one of the largest Norman arches in England.

Castle Hedingham once had four corner turrets and a forebuilding on the west face containing the first-floor entrance to the tower, again as at Rochester. But two of Hedingham's turrets and most of the forebuilding have now been demolished. In other respects, however, it survives in remarkably good condition, with floors and roof intact.

The keep stood in the inner bailey, separated from the outer bailey to the east by a ditch (now crossed by a Tudor bridge). Remains of a Great Hall and a chapel have been found in the inner bailey. The inner and outer bailey were enclosed by earthwork and ditch defences.

The castle remarkably remained in the de Vere family until 1703, on the death of the 20th Earl of Oxford.

Left: Only two of the original four corner turrets survive on the four-floor rectangular tower at Castle Hedingham.

BERKELEY CASTLE
THE ROUND KEEP

The first documented castle at Berkeley in Gloucestershire was built by Roger de Berkeley, as recorded in the Domesday Survey of 1086. Earlier, the land had belonged to Earl Godwin of Wessex, father of Harold II, and after Harold's defeat at Hastings was granted by the Conqueror to the immensely powerful William FitzOsbern, Earl of Hereford, builder of Chepstow Castle and holder of large swathes of land in western and south-western England. There were fortifications on the site before Roger de Berkeley's castle.

THE KEEP

The oldest surviving building at Berkeley is the magnificent round keep, completed in 1153 by Robert Fitz-Harding, 1st Lord Berkeley. Lord Robert received the estate from King Henry II, who had taken the castle from its previous lord, another Roger de Berkeley, following the lawlessness of King Stephen's reign. The keep stands 62ft (19m) high and is 90ft (27m) in diameter. Its walls

Below: Berkeley Castle's inner bailey, 1822. In one of the apartments are the ebony bed and chairs used by Sir Francis Drake on his round-the-world voyage of 1577–80.

enclose the mound of the earlier motte-and-bailey Norman fortification, although rather than being placed on top of the motte, the tower here surrounds it. The entrance was by a staircase on the eastern side, enclosed in a forebuilding in the 14th century. The ascent was by 'trip steps', made deliberately in varying sizes so that attackers mounting in a hurry would be likely to lose their footing.

Above: Edward II was murdered at Berkeley in 1327. The Berkeley descendants of Robert Fitz-Harding still live at the castle.

The keep originally had four semi-circular turrets, all now gone. Two were incorporated into 14th-century buildings within the enclosure, one was replaced by a new gatehouse and the fourth by Thorpe Tower. The remodelling was carried out largely by Thomas, 3rd Lord Berkeley, in 1340–50, when he added the magnificent Great Hall in the castle's inner bailey (see page 320). This hall, 32ft tall and 62ft in length (10 x 19m), was raised on the site of the original hall. It is hung with fine tapestries and has beautiful stained glass windows.

LATER HISTORY

Berkeley Castle was besieged by a parliamentary army during the Civil War in 1645, when their guns made a breach measuring 35ft (11m) in the walls of the keep. This breach has never been repaired, remaining to this day as a reminder of the castle's past as a working fortress.

RICHMOND CASTLE
NORTHERN STRONGHOLDS

The Norman castle of Richmond in North Yorkshire dates to within a decade of the Conquest and occupies a commanding position on a spur overlooking the River Swale. It was built by Alan Rufus of Brittany, Earl of Yorkshire, who was given the vast lands of Edwin, the Saxon Earl of Mercia, as a reward for loyal service to William the Conqueror at Hastings. Richmond Castle was probably built after the Normans had decisively stamped their authority on northern England in the ruthless 'Harrying of the North' during the winter of 1069–70.

SCOLLAND'S HALL

The oldest surviving part of the castle is Scolland's Hall, a sizeable, very early stone two-storey keep built c.1071–5. The now-ruined building once contained a Great Hall on the first floor, as well as private apartments for the lord and a tower containing a garderobe, or area for dressing. Alan Rufus also

built a long curtain wall enclosing a large, roughly triangular bailey called the Great Court of around 2.5 acres (1ha), which takes its curious shape from that of the hilltop land it occupies. He fortified the south-west corner of the

Above: The two-storey building that survives in the corner of the triangular Great Court at Richmond is Scolland's Hall of c.1075.

enclosure with a rectangular defensive tower and added three more towers along the eastern stretch of the curtain wall. In the most northerly of these, Robin Hood's Tower, was a fine chapel dedicated to St Nicholas. This tower is also believed to have been the prison of King William 'the Lion' of Scots in 1174 after he was captured at Alnwick. Another chapel (now gone) appears from archaeological evidence to have stood in the western part of the Great Court. Beyond Scolland's Hall to the south was an outer defensive ward called the Cockpit.

A gatehouse originally stood at the north end of the Great Court, but this was incorporated into a new keep, begun c.1170 by Conan, 5th Lord of Richmond, and completed by King Henry II, who took possession of the castle after Conan's death in 1171. In the 14th century, John, Duke of Brittany, carried out some improvements, adding

---

THE CONQUEROR'S NORTHERN EXCURSIONS

King William travelled north in 1068 to deal with a threatened revolt. In the Anglo-Scandinavian city of York, he founded two motte-and-bailey castles, now known as Clifford's Tower and Baille Hill. On his way, he established castles at Warwick and Nottingham, and on the way back south built castles at Lincoln, Huntingdon and Cambridge. He returned to York in early 1069 to relieve the castles and again later the same year to unleash the celebrated 'Harrying of the North' in the face of Danish raids and English insurrection. He refortified both York castles and celebrated Christmas 1069, the third anniversary of his coronation day, in Clifford's Tower.

Above: Clifford's Tower, York. It takes its name from Roger de Clifford, hanged there in 1322 for disloyalty to Edward II.

NORMAN POWER

Other major Norman castles in northern England included the one at Bamburgh, ancient capital of the kings of Northumberland. Little today remains of the Norman fortifications, which may have been built by William the Conqueror in the 1070s; the castle underwent major restoration and rebuilding in the 18th and 19th centuries. The Conqueror also founded another once-significant castle at Lincoln. Begun in 1068, it was built in the south-west part of the walled city established by the Romans. The castle had stone walls from at least 1115, with gateways to east and west and two keep towers on the southern edge.

At Durham, the Normans built a magnificent motte-and-bailey castle to protect the Bishop of Durham, of which only the crypt chapel and part of the gatehouse survive. By the 1140s, Durham Castle consisted of a timber tower on the motte, with a stone curtain wall around the mound; in the bailey stood a chapel, a hall and a chamber block. The proud Norman Romanesque Cathedral, begun in 1093, already stood alongside the castle.

Above: Richmond's 12th-century keep has walls 11ft (3.4m) thick. The arch at its foot may be part of the original gatehouse.

a first-floor Great Chamber and chapel on the northern side of Scolland's Hall and raising the height of the curtain walls and some of the towers.

The castle is of great interest to archaeological historians because it was built with a keep-hall and a curtain wall but without any motte at a time when the Normans were building motte-and-bailey castles. At Richmond, the design was adapted to the location, which, due to its hilltop and riverside location, enjoyed excellent natural defences. Scolland's Hall is the second oldest surviving stone keep in England, after that at Chepstow Castle.

ROYAL RICHMOND

The earldom of Richmond has a famous history and many royal associations. Edward IV's brother, Richard of Gloucester, was Earl of Richmond and held on to the title after he became King Richard III. Henry VII took the title and then bestowed it upon his favourite palace of Sheen by the River Thames in Surrey, the palace he rebuilt following a calamitous fire of Christmas 1498. But the original Richmond Castle had a largely uneventful history. It was not attacked or besieged during either the Wars of the Roses or the English Civil War. Indeed, it was in a ruinous state as early as the mid-16th century.

Below: Richmond Castle's isolated position meant that it did not play a significant part in any national conflicts.

CHAPTER FOURTEEN

PLANTAGENET MIGHT

1154–1307

The formidable warrior-king Edward I (1239–1307) was the greatest royal castle-builder in English history. He was memorialized on his tombstone as *Scotorum Malleus* ('the Hammer of the Scots') for his battle exploits beyond England's northern border, but he is also remembered for the brutally efficient campaigns he fought in Wales and the network of great castles he erected to impose English rule there. Of the ten castles Edward built during his campaigns against the Welsh, those of Beaumaris, Caernarvon and Harlech are lauded as elegant and innovative examples of the art of castle-building.

Before his accession to the throne, Edward travelled to the Holy Land on Crusade in 1271–2. There, he saw and admired Crusader castles, learning much from their 'concentric' design. The castles had two concentric sets of walls: troops on the higher inner walls could defend the outer walls that they overlooked, but, if necessary, could withdraw within the inner stronghold. On his way back from the East, Edward stopped in Savoy (France), where he met an ambitious castle-builder who had established his reputation by building the widely admired stronghold of St Georges d'Espéranche for Edward I's uncle, Count Philip I of Savoy. Called Master James of St Georges in honour of Count Philip's castle, he became Edward's chief military architect. As Master of the King's Works in Wales, he was largely responsible for the magnificent ring of 'Edwardian' castles erected there.

Left: Symbol of an English king's power in Wales. The eight drum towers and high curtain wall of Conway Castle dominate the shore of the estuary.

ORFORD CASTLE
AND CYLINDRICAL KEEPS

Orford in Suffolk was once on the coast, but now the Orford Ness shingle bank intervenes between the village and the sea. The castle was built by King Henry II, both as a coastal defence against possible invasion and to strengthen the King's hand against the troublesome Earl of Norfolk, Hugh Bigod. Happily for the King, Orford Castle was finished in 1173, just in time to provide a royal stronghold in the face of a rebellion in Suffolk, supported by Bigod, in 1173–4. Following Henry's victory over the rebels, he destroyed Bigod's castles at Framlingham, Bungay, Thetford and Walton.

EXPERIMENTAL KEEPS

The keep, or tower, at Orford was polygonal (many-sided). Three rectangular turrets adjoined the keep, one of which had a forebuilding attached.

Below: The thick wall, round mural towers and outer gatehouse complement the vast circular keep at Pembroke Castle.

In the later 12th and early 13th centuries, castle-builders experimented with new forms for the keep, the main stronghold of the castle. As the techniques and weapons of siege warfare developed during the 12th century, the traditional rectangular keep proved unsatisfactory in two ways: it was vulnerable to attack (its corners could be undermined or destroyed, as at Rochester, making it unstable), while its rectangular shape restricted the defenders' field of fire.

At Orford, the keep's inner design was also experimental. Above the basement, with its own well, were two self-contained residential quarters on the first and second floors, each with kitchen, chambers, garderobe and spacious circular hall. The upper 'apartment' was very grand and evidently intended for the King himself. The forebuilding, on the southern side, contained the entrance way on the ground floor, and the chapel on an upper level between the first and second floors of the main tower. Today, only the keep survives at Orford, but originally it

Above: The turrets of the polygonal keep at Orford are 90ft (27m) tall. The keep is all that survives of a once substantial castle.

stood within a large bailey, or enclosure, surrounded by a defensive wall set with rectangular defensive towers.

The design of the keep at Orford is unusual among English castles. As builders moved on from the 'square' (rectangular) keep, they more often built 'cylindrical' (circular) rather than polygonal towers.

Above: Dundrum Castle is one of John de Courcy's finest castles, set high on a hill overlooking Dundrum Bay.

CONISBROUGH CASTLE

Henry II's illegitimate half-brother, Hamelin Plantagenet, built a splendid keep at Conisbrough, in Yorkshire, in the 1180s. The castle at Conisbrough had been established a little over a century earlier by William de Warenne, a close friend of William the Conqueror. It came into Hamelin's hands on his marriage to Isabel, Warenne's descendant and heiress, in 1164. Hamelin built a circular tower-keep surrounded by six turrets that rise above the main tower to provide elevated defensive positions. These buttress towers are therefore similar to the ones built around ten years earlier at Orford. Archaeological historians also see a fore-runner to the Conisbrough keep in Earl Hamelin's fortified cylindrical keep at Mortemer in Normandy.

At Conisbrough, the keep stood in the north-eastern part of an extensive bailey, surrounded by a thick curtain wall set with semicircular turrets. Within the tower was a basement with a well, a first-floor storage area and residential quarters on the second and third floors – a hall (second floor) beneath a chamber

Right: At Conisbrough Castle in Yorkshire, the cylindrical keep, with its six wedge-shaped buttresses, is 100ft (30m) in height.

(third floor), both luxuriously fitted with fireplace, garderobe and washbasin. Adjoining the chamber, in the easterly turret, was a splendid chapel.

PEMBROKE AND DUNDRUM

Other fine cylindrical keeps were built in the late 12th century at Pembroke in South Wales and at Dundrum (then Rath) in Co Down, on the east coast of Northern Ireland. Built in the years either side of 1200 by William Marshall, Earl of Pembroke, the castle at Pembroke was on the site of an 11th-century stronghold raised by Roger, Earl of Montgomery and Norman Lord of Dyfed. The keep is 75ft (23m) high, with a basement beneath three floors of residential apartments and a domed stone roof. It has a large gatehouse and barbican tower – part of an extensive curtain wall that encloses a sizeable bailey. Pembroke was South Wales's strongest castle. It also has a significant place in history as the birthplace of Henry Richmond, the future King Henry VII.

Dundrum Castle was built by John de Courcy, a Somerset knight who travelled to Ireland in 1171 as part of the Norman incursion and, pushing north on his own, conquered parts of Ulster.

Above: The impressive courtyard at Pembroke Castle is so big that the whole of Harlech Castle could fit within it.

De Courcy established the castle in a formidable position, on the site of a former Celtic fort atop a 200ft (60m) hill overlooking Dundrum Bay. His cylindrical keep was 52ft (16m) high and contained two storeys above a basement. The walls were 8ft (2.5m) thick and in places contained passageways and chambers. The castle's boundary was defined by an imposing curtain wall that ran around the edge of the flattened hilltop.

FRAMLINGHAM CASTLE
THE THIRTEEN TOWERS

The construction of the first castle at Framlingham is traditionally credited to the Norman knight Roger de Bigod, who fought in William the Conqueror's army at Hastings and was rewarded with extensive landholdings. Later, he received the Framlingham estate from Henry I in 1101. Following his death six years later, the castle and land passed first to his eldest son, William, and then, after William died in the '*White Ship*' disaster' in 1120, to Roger's second son, Hugh.

Hugh, the powerful and fiercely independent 1st Earl of Norfolk, provoked the wrath of King Henry II, as a result of which the castle of Framlingham was first confiscated by the Crown in 1157–65 and then partially destroyed in 1175, following the failure of a revolt (in which Hugh took part) in 1173–4.

THE CURRENT CASTLE

Hugh's son Roger, 2nd Earl of Norfolk, built Framlingham in its current form in 1190–1210. Earl Roger's design for Framlingham did away with the fortified keep altogether. Instead, probably in tribute to the Byzantine fortresses seen and admired by English knights on

Crusade, the castle's main fortification was a curtain wall containing 13 towers. This enclosed an extensive inner bailey and was complemented by earthwork defences surrounding an even larger outer bailey to the south, west and east. It appears that these were never rebuilt in stone. Additional defence was

Below: The rather inappropriate ornamental chimneys in the courtyard at Framlingham were added in the early 16th century by the castle's then owners, the dukes of Norfolk.

Above: Framlingham is a castle without a keep. Its strength lay in the 13 mural towers in the 44ft (13m)-high wall.

provided by an artificial lake, on the castle's western side, created by damming the nearby river. In the inner bailey, Earl Roger built a Great Hall, which in later years was partially demolished and used as a poorhouse.

ROYAL VISITS

King John was entertained at Framlingham Castle in 1213. Three years later, he besieged and captured the Bigod stronghold in the course of the civil war that ended his reign. The castle was returned to the ownership of the Bigods, who later served as Marshals of England, but after once more falling foul of the Crown, they were finally removed from office and relieved of all their landholdings by King Edward I (r.1272–1307).

In 1553, at a time when the castle had been forfeited by the dukes of Norfolk to the Crown, Mary Tudor was staying at Framlingham when she received the news that she had become Queen of England.

CARRICKFERGUS CASTLE
THE NORMANS IN IRELAND

Situated on a rocky outcrop overlooking Belfast Lough is Carrickfergus Castle, which is celebrated as the most complete surviving early medieval castle in the whole of Ireland. John de Courcy, Norman knight and builder of Dundrum Castle in Co Down, built the earliest part of the castle (later its inner ward) in the 1180s.

Above: Carrickfergus Castle commanded the waters of Belfast Lough and protected the walled town that grew up alongside it.

CASTLE CONSTRUCTION
De Courcy was defeated by Hugh de Lacy, Earl of Ulster, at Carrickfergus. He took possession of the castle, and began work on a massive four-storey rectangular keep some 90ft (27m) high, with a principal chamber measuring 40 x 38ft (12 x 11.5m). De Lacy doubled the size of the castle by enclosing the remainder of the peninsula and raised a substantial curtain wall with projecting towers, arranged to allow for covering arrow fire. Architectural historians compare the layout of the curtain wall and its towers to that at Framlingham. Like Framlingham, Carrickfergus was besieged and captured by King John and passed to the Crown.

Below: The entrance to the four-storey keep at Carrickfergus is on the second floor.

The distinctive gatehouse at Carrickfergus had flanking towers and a high arch that supported a wooden platform used by the defenders. It was added *c*.1250, when the curtain wall enclosing the outer ward was raised.

SCOTTISH BESIEGERS
In 1315, Carrickfergus was besieged by the army of Edward Bruce, brother of King Robert I of Scots. Edward led a Scots force into Ireland that year and was proclaimed High King in 1316; but despite the arrival of reinforcements commanded by his royal brother, he was defeated and killed by Ireland's English rulers in 1318. At Carrickfergus, the English garrison withstood the siege for a full year, apparently forced to eat the flesh of eight dead Scottish prisoners to fend off starvation. However, the castle finally fell to Robert Bruce himself.

Almost 400 years later, the castle played a role in the 'Williamite War', fought to decide the future of the English monarchy after the deposition of King James II and his replacement by Prince William of Orange as William III.

In 1690, the 'Williamite' army under General Schomberg besieged and captured the castle. The following year, William himself landed at Carrickfergus to lead the campaign that ended in his victory at the Battle of the Boyne.

Below: The massive walls of Carrickfergus Castle are over 3ft (1m) thick.

MIDDLEHAM CASTLE
HOME OF RICHARD III

In some places the square keep remained in favour. At Middleham in North Yorkshire, *c*.1150–70, Robert FitzRanulph built one of the largest square keeps in western Europe, measuring 110 x 80ft (33.5 x 24m), with walls 12ft (3.5m) thick. Even in its ruinous condition today, it rises to a height of 66ft (20m). Architectural historians use the term 'hall-keep castles' for fortified buildings such as Middleham, which are dominated by substantial keeps containing large halls.

At Middleham, the keep was built close to an earlier castle, an earthwork motte-and-bailey fortification constructed in the last decade or so of the 11th century by Alan Rufus, first Norman Lord of Richmond, or his brother Ribald. The remains of this fortification, now known as 'William's Hill', can be examined today around 500 yards (460m) to the south-west of the main castle.

Below: The remains of Robert FitzRanulph's great square keep (centre back) still dominate the ruined castle at Middleham.

A KING AT HOME IN MIDDLEHAM CASTLE

Richard III loved Middleham Castle. It was the home of his wife, Anne, daughter of Richard Neville ('Warwick the Kingmaker'), and they lived there with her mother, the Countess of Warwick, and Richard and Anne's son, Prince Edward, who was born in the castle's south-west tower (henceforth known as the Prince's Tower) in 1473. It was at Middleham, on 9 April 1484, that Edward died aged just ten, the year before his father was killed at Bosworth Field.

Right: Richard III (1452–85) is often assumed to have been responsible for the murder of the Princes in the Tower.

FAVOURED ROYAL CASTLE

Middleham Castle was a residence fit for a king. Indeed, it later became a favoured royal residence in the 15th century as the home of Richard III and his wife, Anne. Although its builder, Robert FitzRanulph, Ribald's grandson, had close family ties to the lordship of Richmond, he came from only a minor branch of the family, which makes the grandeur of Middleham Castle therefore somewhat surprising.

The keep's two storeys were constructed above a vaulted basement with two wells. The ground floor was occupied by a large kitchen and an extensive cellar-pantry; two circular stone pits are thought to have been used for keeping live fish prior to their preparation for the table. A circular stair in the south-east corner led up to the first floor, which contained a buttery, pantry, small chapel and the Great Hall in its eastern half; beyond a central wall in the western half was a Great Chamber and a privy or private chamber for the Lord of Middleham's personal use. The Great Hall was used both for feasting and as a law court.

DEFENDED STAIRWAY

The keep's main entrance was on the first floor, approached by a heavily fortified stone staircase (now destroyed) on the building's east face. Anyone approaching the keep had to gain access via a manned gateway at the foot of the

Above: The compact castle at Middleham is square. Although once luxuriously fitted as a palace, it was also a sturdy fortress.

stairs, then pass through another guarded gatehouse halfway up the stairs, and a third at the top of the stairs. All the way up, people climbing the stairs could be watched or, if need be, attacked from a defensive wall with a wall-walk along the top and also from the battlements on top of the keep.

LATER ALTERATIONS
From 1270 onward, the castle was in the hands of a branch of the Neville family, whose descendants later rose to great prominence in the north and, indeed, nationally. Under the Nevilles, a curtain wall was added around the keep in the late 13th century. A three-storey gate-house with battlements and a projecting 'gallery' from which defenders could throw missiles or pour boiling oil on attacking forces was built in the 15th century. The castle's four towers were built and gradually developed in stages from the 13th to 15th centuries.

In the 13th century, a substantial three-storey building was raised on the eastern side of the keep, linking it to the castle's eastern wall. It contained two floors of living quarters and a large chapel on the third floor to replace the rather small chapel originally provided within the main keep.

LUXURIOUS ACCOMMODATION
In the late 14th century, Ralph Neville, created Earl of Westmoreland by Richard II, constructed a series of residential chambers within the castle's thick curtain wall to supplement the accommodation provided in the keep. Ralph had a total of 23 children, including 14 by his second wife, Joan Beaufort, the illegitimate daughter of John of Gaunt. In his time, King Henry IV stayed at Middleham Castle and was reportedly impressed by the luxurious accommodation provided.

Ralph's descendant Richard Neville, Earl of Warwick, was the celebrated 'Warwick the Kingmaker', a power-broker during the Wars of the Roses. On his death at the Battle of Barnet on

Easter Sunday, 1471, Middleham Castle passed to Edward IV, who gave it to his brother Richard, Duke of Gloucester, subsequently King Richard III.

Below: Middleham's keep's original staircase has collapsed, but modern steps allow visitors to climb up for views of the town and surrounding Yorkshire countryside.

TINTAGEL CASTLE
KING ARTHUR'S BIRTHPLACE

The ruins of Tintagel Castle in north Cornwall, on a headland and adjacent outcrop, are among the most romantic military remains in Britain. Most of what is visible dates from the 13th century, but the castle's name is forever associated with the story of King Arthur of Camelot, the legendary king of Britain usually associated with a historical Celtic prince of the 5th–6th centuries AD.

THE ARTHURIAN LEGEND
It was in Tintagel Castle, according to the 12th-century Welsh chronicler Geoffrey of Monmouth, that Arthur was conceived. The magician Merlin transformed Uther Pendragon, King of Britain, into the likeness of Gorlois, Duke of Cornwall, so that he could lie with Gorlois's ravishing wife, Ygerna. The result was Arthur, who may also have been born at Tintagel. Later, he became – according to the legend – Britain's greatest king, Celtic defeater of the Saxons, embodiment of chivalric

Below: This watercolour of the remains of Tintagel Castle is by 19th-century American artist, William Trost Richards.

virtue, lord of Camelot and leader of the knights of the Round Table. Some versions of his legend suggest that he himself held court at Tintagel.

FROM MONASTERY TO RUIN
The headland at Tintagel may have been used as an Iron Age Celtic fortress or later as a Saxon fort, but no evidence remains of these fortifications. Tintagel was certainly the site of a monastic community established by the Celtic Christian missionary St Juliot in the

Above: Gateway to a romantic past? Tintagel's dramatic setting encourages visions of Merlin, Arthur and Ygerna.

early 6th century, and there are traces of a monastic cell (dwelling) and of an underfloor heating system thought to have been used by the monks.

In 1145, Reginald, an illegitimate son of Henry I, built a castle on the headland; the chapel and Great Hall are believed to survive from his time. His castle was extended by Richard, 1st Earl of Cornwall and Knight of the Holy Roman Empire. Most of the surviving castle buildings are from his stronghold.

The gate and upper ward of the castle were constructed on the headland, while a separate ward containing the Great Hall stood on the outcrop, which could be reached by a very narrow rock causeway. This has since been eroded by the sea, and access to the outcrop is now by steps cut into the rock.

Tintagel Castle fell into ruins after Earl Richard's time, and it was for many years a largely unregarded, if beautifully situated, ruin. However, the 19th-century revival of interest in Arthurian legend put the castle back on the map.

WINCHESTER GREAT HALL
AND THE ROUND TABLE

Winchester, in Hampshire, southern England, was the capital of the Anglo-Saxon kingdom of Wessex and the burial place of kings, including Alfred and Canute II. It remained England's principal city until the 12th century.

A Norman castle was built there soon after the Conquest, in the reign of King William I the Conqueror. King Henry III was born in the castle, on 1 October 1207, and in his time the Norman castle was rebuilt after having fallen into disrepair during King John's reign. Henry was a man of culture and refinement, whose reign saw the major rebuilding of Westminster Palace and Abbey, Windsor Castle and the construction of magnificent English cathedrals at Lincoln, Wells, Salisbury and St Alban's. At Winchester, the Great Hall is all that survives of his work.

> ### ARTHUR'S ROUND TABLE
> A magnificent round table that hangs on the wall of the Winchester Great Hall was for many years identified as the Round Table of King Arthur of Camelot. The table, 18ft (5.5m) in diameter and 2,640lb (1,200kg) in weight, is decorated with the names of the 24 knights of Arthur's company and a portrait of the King himself. According to the *Roman de Brut* (1155), one of the early medieval romances that developed the Arthurian legend, Arthur introduced a round table so that none of the knights could claim precedence over any other. Historians have established that the table in question was not made until the 14th century and was decorated in the reign of Henry VIII, who had a keen interest in knightly exploits, the Arthurian story and the chivalric tradition.

THE KING'S HALL
The Winchester Great Hall was an early example of a new development in such buildings, a movement away from the dark and shadowy halls of the 12th century to a lighter, more elegant design. Henry's hall contained columns of Purbeck stone, fashionable plate tracery windows and pointed arches. Its walls were plastered and decorated in brilliant colours. When he was in Winchester, Henry used the hall for dining, sitting in council with leading barons and

Above: The legend of King Arthur's round table inspired this vast 14th-century tribute, now hung in the Great Hall at Winchester.

clergy and as a courtroom. It is a fine example of the early English Gothic style of architecture.

In the reign of Henry's successor, Edward I, a major fire destroyed most of the royal apartments at Winchester in 1302. Edward and Queen Margaret, his second wife, were in residence at the time and were almost burned alive.

CAERPHILLY CASTLE
CONCENTRIC DEFENCES

The forbidding Caerphilly Castle in Glamorgan, South Wales, was built in 1271–*c.*1280 by Gilbert de Clare (1243–95), Lord of Glamorgan and one of the most powerful men in the realm. It covers 30 acres (12ha), and is the largest castle in Wales, as well as the second largest British castle, after Windsor. Both in size and in the splendour of its residential quarters, Caerphilly Castle rivalled the great Welsh strongholds, such as Beaumaris and Harlech, built shortly after by King Edward. It is rightly regarded by historians and architects as one of the most splendid castles in all Europe and as one of the finest medieval buildings erected in the British Isles.

As a 'Marcher Lord' (a descendant of the Norman lords created by William the Conqueror to subdue the natives in the Welsh Marches), de Clare had the right to build castles without royal licence and to wage war on his own behalf. He had become a man of great wealth when he inherited the earldom of Gloucester in 1262 and had driven Welsh prince Gruffudd ap Rhys out of upland Glamorgan in 1266.

LLYWELYN'S THREAT
De Clare's vast castle at Caerphilly, begun at the very end of Henry III's reign when the future Edward I was abroad on Crusade, must by its overwhelming size have provoked some misgivings at the royal court. However, de Clare's principal concern was to counter the threat of Welsh prince Llywelyn ap Gruffudd, who had control of much of northern and middle Wales and was aiming to move southwards and capture

Above: Gilbert Clare, Lord of Glamorgan. This Victorian image is based on a near-contemporary stained glass window (c. 1340) at Tewkesbury Abbey Church.

Glamorgan. With his powerful siege engines, Llywelyn had in 1270 overrun and destroyed an earlier castle that de Clare had begun to build at Caerphilly.

WALLS OF DEFENCE
The surviving stronghold at Caerphilly is notable as Britain's first truly concentric castle, one with twin defensive walls. The low outer wall has two gatehouses, each with two towers, as well as a water gate in the south front. The inner wall is rectangular, fortified with one gatehouse facing east and one facing west, a great kitchen tower and a tower at each of the corners of the rectangle.

THE CONCENTRIC CASTLE
A stronghold with two defensive boundaries (an outer wall overlooked and protected by a taller and stronger inner round of fortifications) is known as a concentric castle. The design was used by the Romans and put to very effective use in Crusader castles, such as Krak des Chevaliers in Syria. Shortly after the construction of Caerphilly, Edward I and his chief architect, Master James of St Georges, used the concentric design in the castle of Beaumaris, Anglesey, in 1295.

Below: This aerial view of Caerphilly shows impressive double walls – with higher inner fortifications – and extensive water defences.

Above: As part of a programme of modern repairs to Caerphilly Castle begun c.1870 by John Crichton Stuart, the 3rd Marquess of Bute, the water defences were restored by reflooding the lake.

Along the south side of the inner rectangle were the Great Hall and luxuriously appointed state apartments. The Great Hall was remodelled in 1322–6, when the castle was in the possession of Hugh le Despenser the Younger, favourite of Edward II.

The castle's main stronghold was the eastern gatehouse of the inner wall, intended as the residence of the castle constable. Its entrance passage could be closed with door and portcullis towards both the outer ward (the area within the outer wall, but outside the inner wall) and the inner ward (the area enclosed by the inner wall), and so could be defended from both directions. If the castle were overrun, its remaining defenders could retreat to this gatehouse.

The castle's forbidding stone defences were supplemented by a vast encircling moat that was probably inspired by the siege of Kenilworth Castle in 1266, in which its water defences greatly prolonged the encounter, which de Clare witnessed.

CAERPHILLY'S LEANING TOWER

Caerphilly's south-eastern tower leans dramatically 9ft (2.75m) from the perpendicular. The most likely explanation for this is that it was partially demolished during the English Civil War by parliamentarian forces determined to spoil the castle defences.

A more romantic tale maintains that when Edward II, at the close of his reign, took refuge in Caerphilly Castle, then held by his favourite Hugh le Despenser, his estranged wife, Queen Isabella, pursued him with armed force. Edward moved on, but Isabella besieged the castle and captured the tower, later setting off a vast explosion that almost brought it down.

RESTORATION

In the early part of the 15th century, Owain Glyndwr held Caerphilly Castle in the course of his failed revolt against Henry IV. By 1536, the castle had become derelict, except for one part, which remained in use as a prison. The stronghold was restored c.1870 by the 3rd Marquess of Bute, the builder-restorer of Cardiff Castle and Castell Coch, and then by his son, the 4th Marquess, in the early 20th century. The 5th Marquess placed Caerphilly Castle in state care in 1950.

Below: Beyond the Lower Eastern Gatehouse at Caerphilly is the Inner East Gate, with the celebrated leaning tower to the left.

CAERNARVON CASTLE
CONSTANTINOPLE'S INFLUENCE

In 1283, Edward I began building an impressive castle and walled town at Caernarvon in North Wales, as a symbol of his conquest of the Welsh. The King was fresh from triumph in the Second Welsh War (1282–3), in which he had slain Welsh prince Llywelyn ap Gruffudd and captured his brother Dafydd, Prince of Gwynedd.

STRATEGIC POSITION

As he prepared to establish English government in Wales, Edward wanted to make a triumphalist expression of his imperial ambitions at Caernarvon. He chose the town because it was an ancient stronghold for the princes of Gwynedd and because of its strategic position overlooking the Menai Straits, where the River Seoint reaches the sea, and controlling access to Snowdonia – but principally because it was the site of Roman Segontium, which had defended the north-west frontier of the empire.

Below: With his magnificent fortress at Caernarvon, Edward wanted to impress his regal power on his new Welsh subjects.

AN EMPEROR'S DREAM CASTLE

In appearance and design, Caernarvon is quite different to the other great castles Edward raised in Wales, at Harlech, Conway and Beaumaris. Caernarvon has polygonal rather than circular drum towers, and cross-banded masonry (alternate strips of light and dark stone) in the defensive walls.

Edward built Caernarvon as the fulfilment of a dream traditionally said to have come to Roman Emperor Magnus Maximus, son of Constantine I, in which he travelled to a land of mountains and found there a marvellous fortress with walls of varied hues, containing an ivory throne capped with golden eagles. The polygonal towers and cross-banded walls were apparently a homage to the Theodosian Wall at Constantinople, which Edward and his chief architect, Master James of St Georges, had seen while on Crusade.

King Edward and Master James incorporated into the castle an 11th-century Norman motte-and-bailey fortification built at Caernarvon by Hugh, Earl of Chester. In this way, Edward made the symbolic statement

Above: The towers of Caernarvon have stood proud for centuries. This watercolour shows the Eagle Tower c. 1850.

HISTORY TIMELINE

1294 The castle is besieged by land forces in the Welsh uprising led by Madog ap Llewelyn; the benefit of its maritime location is proven as the garrison takes in supplies by sea and survives until a relieving army arrives in the spring of 1295.

1323 The castle assumes roughly its modern form, after 40 years' building.

1399 Richard II visits. Furnishings and decorations must be unfinished, for he has to sleep on straw.

1401-3 Owen Glendower tries unsuccessfully three times to take the castle. The third time, he uses heavy siege machinery, but is still repulsed by a garrison of only 28 men.

1646 During the English Civil War, the castle, garrisoned by Royalists, is captured by Major-General Mytton for the Parliamentarians.

c.1890 After centuries of neglect, the castle is repaired.

that his claim to Wales was merely the renewal of an ancient right established by the Normans. A walled borough, or town, was built alongside the castle, the two making a heavily fortified seat for English royal government in Wales. Defences were strengthened further by the tidal waters that the castle overlooks: originally the castle and town stood on a peninsula that was almost completely surrounded by water. The castle has an irregular oblong design because it was built in the shape of the rock it occupies.

At the western end of the castle stands the majestic Eagle Tower, at 124ft (38m) high one of the tallest single towers erected in the Middle Ages. When first built, it had a stone eagle on each of its three turrets. The tower contained the splendid residence of the castle's keeper, the Justiciar (or regent) of North Wales.

BUILT FOR DEFENCE

At Caernarvon, Master James designed a forbidding fortress. Defenders in the 13 polygonal towers could cover the entire circumference of the castle. In the south front, soldiers and archers could rain weapons on attackers from two 'firing galleries' that ran, one above the other, right along the wall. There were two main gateways: at the east end, the Queen's Gate gave into the inner bailey

ENGLISH PRINCE OF WALES

On 25 April 1284, Edward I's wife, Queen Eleanor, gave birth to their first-born son at Caernarvon. According to tradition, he then presented the infant to his Welsh subjects as their next ruler, pointing out that the baby was currently without blame, had been born in Wales and spoke not a single word of English. Seven years later, again at Caernarvon, the boy was invested as Prince of Wales. In 1911, in a romanticized 'medieval' ceremony, Edward, eldest son of George V, was invested as Prince of Wales in the castle. The ceremony was devised for Prince Edward and his father by David

Lloyd George, MP for Caernarvon. Some 58 years later, Queen Elizabeth II's eldest son, Charles, was invested as Prince of Wales at Caernarvon on 1 July 1969.

Right: Famous for his castle-building and battlefield exploits, Edward I also recodified English common law.

by way of a drawbridge; on the north front, the King's Gate gave access to the castle from the walled town. The latter had impressive defences, for it contained six portcullises and five doors.

Master James' plan was for the enclosure within the castle walls to be divided across the middle by the gate-house, but the interior of the castle was never completed, as was a tower on the

mound of the Norman castle within the walls. Building work on the castle went on until 1330, yet much of it was left unfinished. In its surviving form, it is the shell of a magnificent fortress.

Below: Coastal stronghold of Caernarvon. Edward built his major Welsh fortresses on the coast because the Welsh intercepted land supplies and he needed access to the sea.

CONWAY CASTLE
DRUM TOWERS

The castle and walled town of Conway in North Wales were built by King Edward I in just five years (1283–8). Again designed by Edward's great architect, Master James of St Georges, the castle comprises eight massive drum towers linked by a high curtain wall that is 15ft (4.5m) thick in parts. The sturdy walls of the adjacent town contain three gates and 21 strong towers; on average 24ft (7.5m) in thickness, they run for over ¾ mile (0.5km). They survive in good condition over seven centuries later.

RING OF STONE

Conway was part of the ring of Welsh castles planned by King Edward I to impose English rule, enforced by English-garrisoned strongholds, on the Welsh. At Conway, however, in contrast to Beaumaris, Caernarvon and Harlech, Master James elected not to raise strongly fortified gatehouses with twin

Above: Stephenson's rail and Telford's road bridge run past Edward I's castle at Conway.

MASTER JAMES OF ST GEORGES

Edward's chief architect, the builder of the 'Edwardian' castles of North Wales, was Master James of St Georges (c.1230–c.1308). A native of Savoy, Master James took his full title from the magnificent castle of St Georges d'Espéranche, which he built for Edward I's friend and relative, Count Philip of Savoy. Like the castle at Caernarvon, St Georges d'Espéranche had polygonal towers. Master James built eight Welsh castles for Edward I: Aberystwyth, Beaumaris, Builth, Caernarvon, Conway, Flint, Harlech and Rhuddlan. Master James won a position of great eminence, was styled Master of the King's Works in Wales, and earned the then vast amount of three shillings a day.

---

towers. The drum towers in the castle walls defended both western and eastern entrances to the castle and made extra fortifications on the gate unnecessary.

INNER AND OUTER WARDS

Like Caernarvon, the castle at Conway has a narrow, elongated shape because it was designed to fit the rock on which it stands: a high promontory in a commanding position alongside the tidal waters of the river estuary. Within the high defensive walls, the castle was divided by a gateway into the outer and inner wards on an east–west axis. Access from the town was via a drawbridge across the moat at the north-western end of the rock. A steep flight of steps led into the west barbican (outer defence), which was defended by the western-most two of the castle's eight great towers. From there a gateway led into the outer ward, which contained the kitchen, stables and Great Hall. The constable had his quarters in the great towers overlooking the west barbican.

Right: Conway Castle's intimidating towers and vast curtain wall appear to grow naturally from the rocky outcrop on which they stand.

The smaller inner ward was the heart of the castle, containing the royal quarters: the King's Hall, Privy Chamber and Presence Chamber. The castle's south-east tower housed the king's sleeping rooms, while the north-east tower contained a well-appointed chapel. Beyond was the east barbican and stairs leading down to a water gate.

'BASTIDE' FORTIFIED TOWN

Conway Castle and town were, like Caernarvon and Flint, planned as a single defensive and trading unit.

Edward I had seen the success of building planned towns beside garrisoned castles in English-held Gascony (south-west France), and applied the idea in North Wales. The Welsh towns were planned as centres for the English administration of an occupied country. They were settled with English people, and the Welsh locals were often forbidden to enter the town or to trade with its people, and could risk hanging if found within the walls after sunset.

In 1401, according to tradition, a local carpenter won control of Conway Castle from Henry IV's garrison. Gaining access to the stronghold on Good Friday, when the majority of the defending garrison were at church, he then opened the gates to Welsh rebels, who declared for Owen Glendower, self-styled native Prince of Wales. The occupation itself did not

Below: Looking down to the west from the King's Tower on Conway's outer ward, the remains of the Great Hall lie on the left.

last long, however; Glendower's revolt against Henry IV failed, although subsequently, it is said, most of the rebels were granted pardons.

DECLINE AND RUIN

Over the next two centuries, the castle fell into disrepair. According to a state paper of 1609, it was already 'utterlie decayed', and in this condition was sold for £100 to Viscount Conway. The castle was repaired for use in the Civil War by John Williams, a Conway man

Above: Four of Conway's eight towers guard the castle's outer ward, while the other four protect the inner ward.

who had risen to be Archbishop of York. In the war, Conway was besieged and captured by Parliamentarians commanded by Major-General Mytton and afterwards was slighted. In 1665, the 3rd Earl of Conway reduced the castle to little more than a ruin by removing all the ironwork, lead and timbers. It was restored in the 19th and 20th centuries.

RHUDDLAN, FLINT AND GOODRICH
CASTLES BY THE WATER

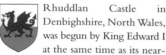

Rhuddlan Castle in Denbighshire, North Wales, was begun by King Edward I at the same time as its near-neighbour at Flint, in 1277. Rhuddlan and Flint, the first of the ten castles built by Edward I in Wales, were both raised alongside new towns set within earthwork fortifications. At Rhuddlan, the River Clwyd was diverted and canalized for 2–3 miles (3–5km) to allow seagoing vessels to approach the newly constructed landing stages, which were built separately for castle and town.

Rhuddlan was a long-established military and royal base. It was originally the setting for a fort built in AD971 by Edward the Elder, son of Alfred the Great, and was afterwards the kingly seat

Below: Loading bay. At Rhuddlan, the smooth waters of a canalized stretch of the Clwyd approach the castle's landing stage.

of Welsh ruler, Gruffydd ap Llywelyn. Gruffydd's stronghold was destroyed by Harold Godwinson in 1063. After the Norman Conquest, a motte-and-bailey castle was built there in 1073 by leading nobleman, Robert of Rhuddlan. In 1276–7, Edward I marched into the region to stamp out the threat posed by Welsh ruler, Llywelyn ap Gruffydd, self-styled 'Prince of Wales'. In the course of this campaign, Edward began the castles at Flint and Rhuddlan, and received the submission of Llywelyn at Rhuddlan in November 1277.

Edward's castle at Rhuddlan, raised around 650–1,000ft (200–300m) north-west of the Norman fortifications, was begun by Master Bertram de Saltu, a Gascon engineer, but finished by Master James of St Georges, to whom the castle is usually attributed. Rhuddlan Castle was built swiftly, and was largely complete by 1280.

Above: The remains of the south tower overlook the inner ward at Rhuddlan.

INNER WARD AND MOAT
The design was for a concentric castle, with a relatively low outer wall that was overlooked by the much more formidable fortifications of the inner ward. Beyond the outer wall was an artificial moat, itself protected by a further outer wall on three sides of the castle.

GOODRICH CASTLE: BUILT IN RED SANDSTONE

Goodrich Castle in Hereford and Worcester was largely rebuilt by Edward I's uncle, William de Valence, and William's son, Aymer, in the years after 1280. The Valences' castle, which overlooks the River Wye and defends an ancient river ford, incorporates an earlier tower-keep (of the mid-1100s). The Valences rebuilt the curtain wall and added impressive angle towers together with ditches on the east and south sides, and an outer defensive wall to the west and north, with a barbican to the north-east. The barbican, in a half-moon shape, seems to be derived from the similar Lions' Tower raised by Edward I at the Tower of London.

Right: The south-east tower largely hides the square keep (centre left). A modern rail lines the approach to the gatehouse (right).

To the south, however, giving on to the river, a short section was filled with water and used as a dock. In fact, the other three sections of the moat appear to have been kept dry to serve as a defensive ditch.

The symmetrical inner ward took the shape of a diamond. Matching towers rose at the north and south corners of the diamond, and double-towered gate-houses stood at the east and west corners. Within, a Great Hall, chapel, private rooms and kitchens once stood against the curtain wall. The inner fortifications were forbidding, with four-storey towers and walls 9ft (3m) thick, with a plentiful supply of arrow slits for the defenders.

BEYOND THE CASTLE

Four gates led out from the castle's outer ward: the main one leading north-wards to the newly built town, another gate giving on to the river, a third gate on to the dock, defended by a rectan-gular defensive tower, and a fourth, the Friary Gate (later blocked), opening to the south-east.

THE DONJON TOWER AT FLINT

The main strength of Flint Castle, completed with its adjacent town in nine years (1277–86), is its circular great tower at the south-east corner of the rectangular inner ward, which is set apart, surrounded by a moat. Castle historians liken the tower to the celebrated Tour Constance at the French port of Aigues-Mortes, from which Edward set sail with his troops for North Africa, while on Crusade in 1270.

The tower is the donjon, the lord's residence within the castle and the heavily fortified position to which the defenders would fall back as a last resort. It is supplemented by three more towers, one at each angle of the rectangular inner wall. (The French word *donjon* later became the English 'dungeon'; but in its earliest use in England, it signified the lord's dwelling rather than a gloomy jail-room.)

Another notable feature at Flint was the internal arrangement of rooms within the great tower. Above a large circular storage basement, the residential rooms and chapel on the first storey are arranged around a large, central, octagonal shaft, designed to bring light and air to residents. (Originally the building contained a basement and two storeys, although only the first storey now remains.) This arrangement is supposedly unique.

Below: The ruined north-east tower at Flint. The great tower at the south-east corner was complemented by three smaller towers at the other angles of the rectangular inner ward.

HARLECH CASTLE
IMPREGNABLE FORTRESS

At Harlech, Edward I and Master James of St Georges raised a concentric castle with a great twin-towered gatehouse on top of an imposing, steep-sided 200ft (60m) rock. When Edward and Master James built the castle in the late 13th century, the rock directly overlooked the sea and the tidal estuary of the River Dwyryd. Indeed, there was a landing stage for receiving seaborne supplies, accessed from the castle by a heavily fortified stairway, the 'Way from the Sea'. Today, however, the tidal creek is dry and the sea has retreated more than ½ mile (0.8km). Yet, because an approach up the cliff-like sides of the castle rock would be almost impossible, Harlech Castle retains an almost impregnable aspect – with land attack feasible only from the east. The castle was, in fact, taken four times: in 1404, 1408, 1468 and 1647.

The castle, begun in the summer of 1283 during King Edward I's second military campaign in North Wales, was built at a cost of £9,500 over the seven years to December 1290. At one point, in 1286, Master James had an army of 950 labourers at his disposal.

Above: Harlech Castle's position on a hilltop meant that space was tight. The outer ward is narrow and the inner ward small.

Below: Safe within the castle walls, the inner face of the gatehouse at Harlech can risk windows and a gentle staircase.

THE INNER WARD

The castle's outer defences are largely ruined, and the outer ward is very narrow, due to lack of space. However, the inner ward boasts four drum towers and the massively fortified gatehouse facing east. The gatehouse consists of two projecting semi-cylindrical towers flanking a narrow entranceway defended by three portcullises and gates, and seven 'murder holes' from which defenders could launch missiles or scalding water at the attackers.

The gatehouse contained guard-houses on the ground level at either side of the entrance, and on the first floor were the well-appointed quarters of the castle constable. On the second floor were even more luxurious rooms for the use of important visitors, doubtless including King Edward I. Both sets of rooms included a hall, a chamber, a bed-chamber and a private chapel. Although the outer face of the gatehouse presents a stern aspect, its inner walls contain large windows, and there is a fine external

KIDWELLY CASTLE

Where Harlech Castle failed to repulse Owain Glyndŵr, Kidwelly Castle in Dyfed succeeded, twice withstanding siege attacks by the 'Prince of Wales' in 1403–05. Kidwelly Castle was originally Norman, built by Roger, Bishop of Salisbury and Justiciar of England under Henry I, and dominating and commanding the upper tidal reaches of the River Gwendraeth. After being captured more than once by the Welsh and partially rebuilt by Lord Rhys in 1190, it passed to Edward I's nephew, Henry, Earl of Lancaster, in 1298. Around the inner castle with four drum towers, Henry built a heavily fortified outer defensive wall in imitation of the concentric castles of his uncle and Master James of St Georges. The impressive outer wall had four towers (one of which contained a chapel) and two gatehouses.

Left: The Great Gatehouse at Kidwelly Castle. On the first floor, directly above the gate, was a large and well-appointed hall.

staircase giving access to the constable's apartments, in which Master James, who was made the castle constable in July 1290, lived for the next three years.

There were further, less grand, residential rooms in the towers at the angles of the rectangular inner ward. Functional rooms, such as the Great Hall, buttery, granary, bake house and kitchens, were situated within the walls of the inner ward quadrangle.

HARLECH SIEGES

The castle may have been almost impregnable in the face of violent attack, but it could be vulnerable to being cut off from reinforcements and supplies. If the garrison maintained access to the sea, then all was well: when besieged by the troops of Madog ap Llywelyn in the 1294–5 uprising, the castle defenders received supplies by sea from Ireland. However, when the Welsh rebel and self-styled 'Prince of Wales', Owain Glyndwr, took the castle in 1401, he was able to block all supplies, since a fleet of his French allies was active in the waters beneath the rock while his own troops blocked land access.

During the Wars of the Roses in the 15th century, the castle was garrisoned by men loyal to the Lancastrian cause under Dafydd ap Iuean, and was besieged by a Yorkist army commanded by Lord Herbert, Earl of Pembroke. The garrison withstood immense hardship before surrendering in 1468 – a feat that inspired the marching song *Men of Harlech*. A royalist garrison defended Harlech Castle during the Civil War in the 17th century. Surrendered as late as March 1647, it was the last castle to fall to the Parliamentarian army.

Below: Harlech's rocky heights. The land falls steeply away on all sides save the east, and the position commands superb views.

BEAUMARIS CASTLE
MASTER JAMES'S MASTERPIECE

Beaumaris Castle on Anglesey was the last of the great castles built in Wales for Edward I by his chief builder, Master James of St Georges. Although it remained unfinished, it is celebrated today as a triumphant culmination of Edward's two decades of Welsh castle-building. Its plan, an octagon enclosing a rectangle, is lauded as the perfection of the concentric castle design. Set amid meadows rich in bulrushes, with distant views across into Snowdonia, it is also known for the great beauty of its location.

WELSH UPRISING
Beaumaris was begun in the spring of 1295. The previous year, during an uprising led by Llywelyn ap Gruffud's kinsman, Madog ap Llywelyn, Welsh rebels had overrun Anglesey and killed the royal sheriff, Roger de Pulesdon. Edward launched fierce reprisals over the winter of 1294–5 and was still in the area when the building of Beaumaris Castle began.

Below: The northern gate, or Llanfaes Gate, Beaumaris, viewed from the inner ward. A further storey was planned but never built.

THREE LAYERS OF DEFENCE
Built on flat marshy land, the castle had no natural defences, save the sea to the south, and needed to be heavily fortified. The design called for three concentric layers of defence: a moat, 18ft (5.5m) wide and filled with tidal water, and two sets of defensive walls. The octagonal outer wall contained 12 towers and two gatehouses. The rectangular inner wall, in places 15ft (4.5m) thick, contained four round towers (one at each corner), two gatehouses and two D-shaped towers.

Above: Beaumaris dwarfed by Snowdonia. In this view from the north, the waters of the Menai Strait are visible beyond the castle.

The main entrance in the outer wall to the south gave on to the sea at high tide. Known as the Gate-next-the-Sea, it overlooked a small dock area where ships could land supplies at high tide. The second gateway, called the Llanfaes Gate from the name of the Welsh town nearby, opened landwards to the north. The outer wall was lower and less thick than the forbidding inner fortification. The gates in the outer wall were set at an angle to those in the inner one, so that any attacker who succeeded in breaching the outer defences would have to make an awkward turn to the right under fire from the defenders of the inner stronghold. The outer ward, the area between the outer and inner walls, was just a narrow strip of land.

The two imposing inner gatehouses stood in the north and south stretches of the rectangular inner wall. The west and east walls, without gatehouses, contained formidable D-shaped towers, planned as three-storey buildings but never completed beyond the second floor. In addition, a circular tower rose

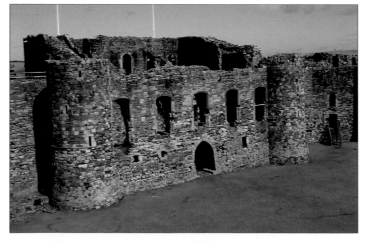

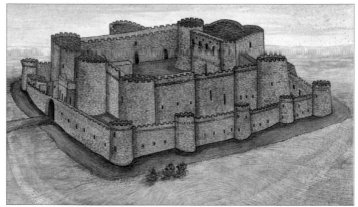

Above: Stones piled high – the bulk of the castle at Beaumaris and its superb design made up for its lack of natural defences.

A WHITE ELEPHANT

Edward I poured lavish resources into the work: Master James employed no fewer than 200 quarrymen, 30 smiths and carpenters, 400 masons and 2,000 general labourers. He had spent £6,000 by the autumn of 1295. The bulk of the building was carried out in the three years after 1295; by 1298, royal funds for building were running low, and the King was increasingly focused on events and building works in Scotland and Gascony.

Further building was carried out at Beaumaris beginning in 1306 and continuing intermittently after Edward's death in 1307 until 1330, without ever reaching completion. The castle remains

Above: Never finished, but formidable nonetheless – Beaumaris Castle in the 14th century has a moat and double walls.

an example of 'what might have been': a magnificent plan that was never brought to fulfilment.

Moreover, its formidable defences were never needed. Beaumaris, for all its might, saw little military action – for even by the time the castle was begun, Welsh resistance had been almost entirely crushed. Some 200 years later, it was garrisoned by Royalists in the Civil War, but was taken without a struggle by the Parliamentarian scourge of Edward's Welsh castles, Major-General Mytton, on 14 June 1646.

in each corner of the rectangle. The plans called for lavishly appointed chambers and halls, mainly in the first and second floors of the gatehouses. These were never fully built, but the castle's main room, the Great Hall on the first floor of the north gatehouse, gives an idea of the splendour awaiting the Prince of Wales or the king. The Chapel Tower, also part of the inner walls, contains a magnificently appointed chapel with vaulted ceiling and point windows. Within these formidable walls, the inner ward is surprisingly large, covering ¾ acre (0.3ha).

CAERLAVEROCK CASTLE, DUMFRIES

The builders of Caerlaverock were clearly influenced by Beaumaris and Master James's other great concentric castles. Caerlaverock combines a twin-towered gatehouse with two drum towers, the whole laid out to a triangular design within a defensive moat and an earthen rampart. The main defence and final refuge is the gatehouse, which – as at Beaumaris – contained the residential quarters of the castle constable.

Right: Within the castle lie the remains of 18th-century courtyard residences.

CHAPTER FIFTEEN

THE RISE OF THE FORTIFIED HOUSE

1307–1400

In 1290, wealthy wool merchant Lawrence of Ludlow obtained a royal licence to crenellate his manor at Stokesay in Shropshire. He declared that he needed to fortify the house because of the potential threat of the unruly Welsh just 20 miles (32km) away across the border. In fact, Edward I's forceful campaigns of the 1280s in Wales had effectively stamped out resistance there.

Lawrence's home, Stokesay Castle, was not a castle proper but an early example of a type of building that would become popular with wealthy householders in the 14th and 15th centuries: the fortified manor house. Other splendid examples include Penshurst Place, Hever Castle and Ightham Mote, all in Kent; Broughton Castle in Oxfordshire; and Raby Castle in Co Durham. Many of these buildings were fortified towards the end of the 14th century, when England had seemingly lost control of the English Channel and there were fears that France might invade. At this time (under Richard II) and again in the 15th century (under Henry VI), central authority was weak, so landowners needed to project at least an appearance of strength.

Yet, while fortified manor houses had a degree of defensive strength, none of them was a fortress. The houses may have been well enough defended to deter passing marauders, but they generally could not have withstood an attack by an organized army; they certainly could not have repelled a siege in the way that Rochester Castle almost did, and Kidwelly Castle in Dyfed twice succeeded in doing. The men who built the fortified manor houses put comfort before the needs of defence.

Left: The charming manor house of Ightham Mote, in Kent, combines a crenellated gatehouse and defensive moat with windows and a half-timbered upper storey.

STOKESAY CASTLE
AN ENGLISH STONE HOUSE

Stokesay Castle's name comes from that of a family – Say – who had their dairy farm ('stoke') here from around 1115. Wool merchant Lawrence of Ludlow fortified the house in the early 1290s.

Lawrence's father, John, had purchased the manor in 1281. Earlier, in 1240, the Says had built a tower at the north end of the house's west front. Lawrence added a new upper storey with projecting timberwork, which remarkably survives to this day. He also built a new Great Hall, 34ft (10.3m) high and measuring 52 x 31ft (16 x 9.5m), with partly shuttered, partly glazed windows – proof of his substantial wealth, for at this time glass cost so much that wealthy families with more than one house carried their window panes with them as they moved about. Much of the timberwork survives from the 13th century. The rafters are blackened by the smoke that rose from the chimney-less central hearth to find its way out via the louvres in the roof.

Below: Stokesay Castle's spacious hall is flanked by the north tower (left) and the solar with the turreted south tower (right).

A ROOM FOR RETIRING TO

Attached to the hall on the south side, Lawrence erected the 'solar block', containing a chamber to which the family withdrew from the more public space of the Great Hall. The private chamber, known as a 'solar' because the room was designed with large windows to allow in as much sunlight as possible, was on the upper floor, and reached by an external staircase, while the ground-level space beneath was used for storage.

Above: The magnificent beams of the Great Hall's roof were made from whole trees.

DEFENSIVE ADDITIONS

At the Great Hall's south end, Lawrence built the impressive, three-storey South Tower, complete with battlements. The only access to this stout construction – whose walls are 5ft (1.5m) thick – was via a drawbridge from outside the entrance to the 'solar' room. He also added a defensive curtain wall, topped with battlements, a stone gatehouse,

was let on a long lease to Charles Baldwyn, MP for Ludlow, who replaced the original stone gatehouse with a charming half-timbered building, which still survives. In the Civil War, Stokesay's then owner, Lord Craven, declared for the King, but surrendered to a parliamentary army in 1645 before any damage was done to the 'castle'. In line with their normal policy of slighting fortified defences, the Parliamentarians reduced the height of the curtain wall.

UNUSUAL ATTRIBUTES

Stokesay Castle is notable as one of the earliest English stone houses. It was built of local Silurian limestone, quarried just across the valley. Unless good-quality building stone was available locally, as here or in the Cotswolds, building in stone in this period was prohibitively expensive for all but the wealthiest landowners because it involved not only quarrying but also transporting the very heavy material over great distances. Generally, it was only the king, his leading barons and churchmen who could meet the necessary cost.

Stokesay Castle is also highly unusual in that its central buildings survive largely unaltered from the time of Lawrence of

Above: The gabled windows in the Great Hall were part-glazed: the upper part and the circular 'eye' above were glazed; the lower part was closed with shutters in the cold.

a drawbridge and an encircling rock-cut moat supplied with water from a large pond just to the south-west. The wall originally stood 34ft (10.3m) high from the bottom of the moat. Yet, although Stokesay Castle had some defensive capability, it was not designed to withstand a serious attack. The Great Hall, for example, was built with large windows facing Wales, the direction from which Lawrence said he feared attack. As in other fortified manor houses, comfort was deemed more important than defence. However, although far from impregnable, Lawrence's fortified manor was certainly sufficiently grand for him to entertain the Bishop of Hereford and his retinue for ten days.

LATER DEVELOPMENTS

Lawrence did not live to enjoy his castle for long, as he drowned in a shipwreck in 1294. Nevertheless, his descendants remained in possession of Stokesay for more than three centuries, and in the 14th and 15th centuries often served as sheriffs of Shropshire. The castle and lands were sold to pay off debts in 1598. In the 1630s, Stokesay

Ludlow in the 13th century. The buildings were unoccupied after 1706, and so were not altered in line with prevailing fashions. After 150 years, during which Stokesay fell gradually into picturesque ruins, and was used by a nearby farm, the 'castle' was bought and restored by Victorian philanthropist and glove-manufacturer J.D. Allcroft. It was further repaired in the 1980s and has been held by English Heritage since 1992.

Below: The solar chamber in the South Tower was warmed by sunlight through the large windows and the fire of its chimneypiece.

PENSHURST PLACE
HOME OF SIR PHILIP SIDNEY

Penshurst Place in Kent is one of England's earliest and finest fortified manor houses.

Celebrated above all for its later association with Renaissance poet and soldier, Sir Philip Sidney, and the Sidney family, Penshurst began life as a 13th-century house owned by Sir Stephen de Penchester (d.1299). In *c*.1340, Sir John de Poulteney, four times Lord Mayor of London, transformed the house into a country mansion where, within a day's ride of the capital, he could entertain and hunt.

HALL AND 'SOLAR'

The magnificent Barons' Hall, with a 60ft (18m) high roof made of chestnut wood and large octagonal central hearth, was completed in 1341. In this cavernous, smoky chamber, Sir John's servants ate and slept. Vast trestle-mounted wooden tables were used: the two wooden tables at Penshurst are 13th-century originals,

the only surviving examples of their kind in England. As at Stokesay and in other medieval halls, the smoke rose to the ceiling to escape through smoke louvers or slatted openings.

Three Gothic screens disguise the passage to the kitchen and offices. A stone staircase leads up to the house's state apartments. The first was originally a 'solar room'. It subsequently became an ante-room (reception area) in the Elizabethan era and, later still, the State Dining Room. (In 1430, Henry V's brother, John, Duke of Bedford, built a second hall to the south-west of the solar block adjoining the original Barons' Hall. The new hall, now called the Buckingham Building, had mullioned windows added in the 16th century.)

A FORTIFIED MANOR

In *c*.1390, amid fears of a French invasion, the owner of Penshurst Place was granted a licence to crenellate, and fortified the

Above: Sir Philip Sidney served Elizabeth I and knew many other great figures of the age, including Sir Walter Raleigh.

Below: From the ornate fountain in the Italian Garden at Penshurst Place there is a splendid view of the south front of the house.

mansion with a curtain wall containing eight defensive towers. As at Stokesay, the house was sufficiently well fortified to repel a minor assault, but a well-armed army would have had little difficulty in gaining entry. Today, the bulk of these fortifications have gone. Some were dismantled and others used as part of later extensions, but one tower remains, standing alongside a stretch of wall in the gardens to the south of the main house.

CROWN PROPERTY

In the late 15th and early 16th century, three dukes of Buckingham owned Penshurst, and all were beheaded. The third was Edward Stafford, who was executed on 17 May 1521, having been found guilty of high treason, supposedly for plotting the King's death and his own elevation to the throne.

As the property of a traitor, the estate was forfeit to the Crown. Penshurst Place came into royal hands, and Henry VIII stayed there when paying court to Anne Boleyn at Hever Castle nearby.

THE SIDNEY FAMILY

Edward VI granted the house and estate to the Sidney family in 1552. Sir Henry Sidney (1529–86) erected a new range and gatehouse to the north of the Barons' Hall. This included an arcade with Tuscan columns, completed in 1579 and perhaps England's earliest classical loggia.

This new building incorporated one of the 14th-century defensive towers; the arcade was later glazed. Sir Henry also created magnificent gardens around the house.

Sir Henry Sidney, whose father was tutor to the future Edward VI, was a childhood friend of the King and grew up at court. He became a trusted servant of the Crown, serving both Mary I and Elizabeth I with distinction, and naming his own son, the celebrated Sir Philip Sidney, after Mary's husband, Philip II of Spain, who was the boy's godfather. Sir Henry's wife, Mary Dudley, was the sister of Queen Elizabeth I's favourite, Robert Dudley, Earl of Leicester. Elizabeth often visited Sir Henry's

home, and the Queen Elizabeth Room, in which she held court when in residence there, is named in her honour.

Sir Philip Sidney, poet, soldier and courtier, author of *Arcadia* and *Defence of Poetry*, was born at Penshurst Place on 30 November 1554. After his death in a military encounter in the Netherlands at the early age of 31, he was given a state funeral in St Paul's Cathedral, becoming the first commoner to be accorded this honour (Nelson was next, in 1805). Sir Philip's brother, Sir Robert, inherited the house and built the Long Gallery, completed in 1601, as an extension to the staterooms. Lit by mullioned windows on both sides, it has elegant oak wainscoting and houses today, as in the early 17th century, many portraits of Sidney family members.

The house still remains in the hands of the Sidney family. Later owners have continued to modify the house, in particular remodelling the staterooms. In the second half of the 20th century, William Sidney, 1st Viscount De l'Isle, lovingly restored the house and estate.

Below: Penshurst's lavish Queen Elizabeth room. The Queen's great favourite, Leicester, was Sir Philip Sidney's uncle.

LEEDS CASTLE
A GIFT FOR QUEEN MARGARET

The full defensive potential of Leeds Castle in Kent was realized only in the late 13th century, when the River Len was dammed to form an artificial lake. By then, Leeds, a royal castle, had been standing on the site for about 200 years.

Before it was dammed, the Len naturally widened at this spot around two small islands. This caught the eye of a minister at the court of King Ethelbert IV of Kent, named Leede. After the Norman Conquest, William I granted the lands to Hamon de Crèvecoeur, whose son Robert built the first stone castle, which took the form of a keep and a gatehouse. Part of a cellar and some of the Gloriette Tower on the smaller northern island survive from this time.

Leeds Castle remained in the hands of the Crèvecoeur family until 1265, when the castle-builder's great-grandson was dispossessed after siding with the rebel baron, Simon de Montfort. Henry III then made a gift of the castle to Roger de Leyburn, whose son William sold it back to the Crown in 1298 to clear debts.

Below: Leeds Castle was much altered in the Tudor era, but some parts date back to the time of the Norman Robert de Crèvecoeur.

A CASTLE FOR QUEENS

Edward I and his first queen, Eleanor, loved the castle and often stayed there. He built a new curtain wall around the larger island, rebuilt the gatehouse on the northern island and added a chapel in the Gloriette Tower.

When Edward I remarried in 1299, he spent his honeymoon at Leeds Castle and then gave the beautifully situated fortress-palace to his new wife, Margaret of France. Their son, Edward II, by

Above: Busts of Henry VIII and his three children, Mary I, Elizabeth I and Edward VI, are on display in the Queen's Gallery.

contrast, gave the castle to a leading courtier – Bartholomew de Badlesmere – who, in 1321, earned the King's wrath when his wife refused to allow Queen Isabella access to the castle. Edward besieged and took the castle, threw Lady Badlesmere in jail and subsequently beheaded Bartholomew.

Edward III also admired the castle, and between 1359 and 1377 was engaged in redecorating the royal apartments in the Gloriette Tower. His son and successor, Richard II, hired master mason Henry Yevele, builder of the nave at Canterbury Cathedral and designer of improvements at Westminster Hall, to carry out buiding work at Leeds Castle. Richard followed the royal tradition by giving the castle to his queen, Anne of Bohemia. He must also have liked the place himself because after her death in 1394 he spent a good deal of time there. In 1395, Richard received the French chronicler Jean Froissart at the castle.

Henry Bolingbroke, who deposed Richard II in 1399 and ascended the throne as Henry IV, gave Leeds Castle to his queen and second wife, Joan of Navarre. The couple stayed at the castle in 1403 to escape the plague in London.

IN THE HANDS OF THE TUDORS

Following Henry IV's death, Queen Joan was declared forfeit on charges of sorcery. She was confined in Pevensey Castle, and her stepson, Henry V, was

Above: Black swans live on the lake. They were a gift to British leader Sir Winston Churchill, who gave them to the castle.

free to give Leeds Castle to his beautiful French wife, Catherine of Valois. At Leeds Castle, after Henry V's death, Catherine fell in love with and secretly married Owen Tudor, a Welsh squire. After the secret of their marriage was revealed, Queen Catherine retired to a nunnery at Bermondsey, where she died

in 1437, but the union with Tudor had far-reaching consequences, for her grandson by Owen, Henry Tudor, would win the crown in the Battle at Bosworth Field in 1485 and occupy the throne as King Henry VII.

The next royal to be associated with Leeds was Henry VIII, who spent lavishly on the place. He retained the fortifications, but his alterations to the royal apartments made Leeds more palace than fortress (see page 353).

CHAPEL ROYAL

When Edward I's beloved Queen Eleanor died in 1290, a grief-stricken Edward provided for mass to be said daily for her soul in the chapel he had added to the Gloriette Tower on the smaller northern island.

This benefaction – known as a chantry – was extended by Edward II, Richard II, Henry VI and Henry VII. The chapel itself was reconsecrated and made a Chapel Royal by the Archbishop of Canterbury, Donald Coggan, in 1978.

Above: The chapel has a serene atmosphere.

RABY CASTLE
STRONGHOLD OF THE NEVILLES

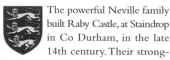

The powerful Neville family built Raby Castle, at Staindrop in Co Durham, in the late 14th century. Their stronghold stands on a place with venerable royal associations, reputedly the site of a palace belonging to Canute (r.1016–35).

The Nevilles were a significant Norman family who fought alongside William the Conqueror at Hastings and were rewarded with lands in the north of England. They acquired the manor of Raby through marriage in the 13th century, when Isabel Neville married the Lord of Raby, Robert FitzMaldred.

Among prominent early Nevilles was Robert Neville, who was killed at the 1319 Battle of Berwick. From 1334, another Neville, Ralph, served the English Crown as Warden of the Scottish Marches – a key position he shared with Henry Percy, 2nd Baron of Alnwick. The Neville and Percy families became fierce competitors for prominence and royal favour.

Below: In the 18th century, when this view of Raby was painted, the Vane family reworked the west wing and entrance hall.

Above: Fortified mansion. Grandeur and comfort outweighed defensive effectiveness in the considerations of the builders at Raby.

NEW DEFENCES

Ralph's son, Sir John Neville, was granted a licence to crenellate and embattle all the towers, houses and walls at Raby by the Bishop of Durham in 1378. By this date the castle was well established, and doubtless fortified, but Sir John added new defences to his family stronghold, so that the castle had the key elements of a defensible fortress, with a moat, drawbridge, gatehouse and curtain wall 30ft (9m) high. But within the inner enclosure, the arrangement of towers and other fortifications was planned not to maximize defensive capabilities, but rather to emphasize both the power and the grandeur of the Neville family.

THE NEVILLE GATEWAY

In the late 14th century, Sir John built the Neville Gateway in the western part of the castle, where the majority of the surviving medieval work is found and some of the walls are 20ft (6m) thick. The gateway is a celebration in stone of the family's ascent to power and pre-eminence: it bears the symbols of the Cross of St George (in reference to Sir John's acceptance as a Knight of the Garter in 1369) alongside the Nevilles' own saltire (St Andrew's cross) and a Latimer cross (because Sir John's second wife, named Elizabeth, was the heiress of the prominent Latimer family of Corby).

The gateway was the sole point of access to the inner court, and was originally fitted with a gate and drawbridge across the moat. From the gateway,

a tunnel 70ft (21m) long leads to the inner court. Other elements surviving from the 14th century are the Chapel Tower (although this has an 18th century doorway), the Servants' Hall and the splendid Kitchen Tower, which is almost entirely unchanged since its construction *c.*1360. The Great Hall may have been begun as early as 1320. Records show that in the mid-14th century, master mason John Lewyn was active at Raby, as he was at nearby Durham Cathedral.

IMPRESSIVE TOWERS

Sir John's son, another Ralph, was an active builder at Raby and at another Neville property, Middleham Castle. In all, at Raby there were two gatehouses (an outer one, in the north, in addition to the inner Neville Gateway) and nine towers. Eight of the towers survive, including the majestic Clifford's Tower, 80ft (24m) in height. However, one in the southerly part of the castle was replaced by a dining room in the 1840s, when the south range was entirely rebuilt. At the south-east corner of the castle is the 11th-century Bulmer's

Above: In the Barons' Hall at Raby, 700 knights gathered in 1569 to plot the ill-fated Rising of the North against Elizabeth I.

Tower, a uniquely unusual five-sided 11th-century building, named after the Norman knight Bertram de Bulmer. The only other tower of this shape is found in Denmark.

LATER ALTERATIONS

The Nevilles fell dramatically from power and influence in 1569, and in the late 16th century, Raby Castle was forfeit to the Crown. In 1626, the castle and estate were bought by Sir Henry Vane, who built an arcade on the court-yard's eastern edge and added a five-bay façade on the central block. In the 18th century, his descendant Gilbert Vane employed the architect James Paine to produce the Hunter's Gallery and remodel the interiors of much of the west wing. In the 1780s, Sir Gilbert's son employed architect John Carr of

York in the extraordinary project of refashioning the entrance hall so that a coach and horses could pass through it.

The 19th-century alterations by William Burn, a fashionable designer and remodeller of country houses, were unfortunately of the 'improving' early Victorian kind that swept away much that would have been of interest to later generations. In particular, Burn removed medieval vaulting from the Clifford and Bulmer Towers. Yet Raby Castle still makes an undeniably impressive impact, not least because of its size, but also because it retains a large number of authentic architectural elements surviving from the 14th century.

BODIAM CASTLE
CASTLE ON AN ISLAND

Of all the fortified great houses of the 14th century, Bodiam Castle in East Sussex probably has the best claim to being a truly defensible stronghold. It was clearly a comfortable and splendid dwelling, with elegant and well-designed residential quarters, but it also boasted four strong corner towers, a twin-towered gatehouse and wide water defences with a complex approach designed with defence much in mind.

The castle was built under a licence to crenellate ('for the defences of the adjacent county and the resistance against our enemies') granted to Sir Edward Dakygrigge by Richard II in 1385, at a time when the French had the upper hand in the English Channel, and at the height of English fears of an invasion. Sir Edward's manor of Bodiam stood in the valley of the River Rother, which at that time was large enough to be navigable by sizeable ships as far as Bodiam itself.

FRENCH DESIGN

Sir Edward built his fortified manor house at Bodiam from scratch, having abandoned the existing manor house nearby, which he had acquired through marriage, to create a compact castle. He based the design on continental fortifications he had seen first-hand when fighting in France under the command of Sir Robert Knollys during the reign of Richard II's predecessor and grandfather, King Edward III. The castle was rectangular. Four corner towers 60ft (18m) tall were linked by a defensive wall two storeys high, which included a square tower in the west and east walls, a vast gatehouse facing north and an additional postern tower situated in the south face.

BODIAM'S DEFENCES

The castle is, today, approached along a straight causeway from the north across the moat via a small octagonal island, but originally visitors – or, perhaps more

Above: The view of Bodiam across the moat from the south-east shows the postern tower (left, centre) in the two-storey south wall.

relevantly, attackers – had to approach from the west side of the moat and make a right-angled turn on the small island, all the while leaving themselves vulnerable to attack from the castle. Once on the octagonal island, the approach involved passing across a drawbridge to a barbican tower, then across another drawbridge to the castle's main gatehouse. The gatehouse itself was

BERKELEY CASTLE'S GREAT HALL

A majestic Great Hall was added to the 12th-century castle at Berkeley in Gloucestershire c.1340 by Thomas, 3rd Lord Berkeley. With large windows and a cavernous timbered roof, it stands 62ft (19m) long and 32ft (10m) high. Only 13 years earlier, the castle had been the scene of one of the most infamous events in English royal history: the murder in captivity of King Edward II, on 21 September 1327. Lord Thomas was cleared of responsibility for the deed and is remembered in both the Berkeley family and wider tradition as a man of compassion. However, closer investigation suggests that he must have known of the dark deeds and indeed sent news of the King's death to Queen Isabella and her lover, Roger Mortimer, Earl of March.

Above: Terraced gardens surround Berkeley Castle. From the gardens there are fine views of the country and the River Severn.

Above: A succession of monarchs, from Henry VII and Elizabeeth I to George IV, has been entertained in the Great Hall.

fitted with three portcullises and three gates, as well as gun-holes, and 'murder holes' through which materials could be thrown at or poured down on anyone trying to attack the castle.

The castle came under attack twice. The first occasion was in 1483, when Bodiam's then owner, Sir Thomas Lewknor, had provoked the anger of Richard III. The King sent the Earl of Surrey to seek revenge, and Sir Thomas surrendered his castle without a struggle. Then, in 1643, during the English Civil War, Parliamentarian forces took the castle, again without a fight. The Roundheads left the outer castle intact, but caused severe damage within.

LUXURY WITHIN

Today, the castle's inner buildings remain in ruins, but it is possible to recreate a picture of the luxurious accommodation provided for Sir Edward Dalyngrigge in the 14th century. The public buildings included a large chapel, a Great Hall and a large Public Chamber. Sir Edward's

elegant private chambers were in the east range's first floor and included a hall – complete with crenellated fireplace – giving access to two sleeping chambers, each with a garderobe, situated in the square tower on the castle's east wall. Sir Edward's private hall also gave access to a reserved side-chapel at first-floor level overlooking the altar in the main castle chapel. Thus, Sir Edward and his family could maintain their privacy while joining garrison soldiers at worship in the main chapel below.

RESTORATION DISCOVERIES

The castle at Bodiam was purchased and meticulously restored in the early 20th century by Lord Curzon, one-time Viceroy of India. Another indication of the level of luxury provided in this elegant fortified manor house was that, during restoration, Curzon found evidence of 33 fireplaces and no fewer than 28 lavatories, which were constructed in the curtain wall and gave directly into the moat.

Above: Easy access. On Bodiam's north face, a railed walkway now leads across the moat to the barbican and the gatehouse.

Below: The 60ft (18m) cylindrical corner towers of the four-sided castle at Bodiam each contain four storeys.

WESTMINSTER PALACE
HENRY III'S RESIDENCE

King Henry III (r.1216–72) was one of the greatest of England's royal builders. He spent £10,000 improving Westminster Palace, the royal residence first built alongside the Thames to the east of Westminster Abbey by Edward the Confessor (r.1042–66). Westminster was Edward's favourite palace and, in his time, as a result of his improvements, the finest in Europe (see page 279).

Henry's reign saw the building of the reputedly magnificent King's Great Chamber, or Painted Chamber, which measured 80 x 26ft (24 x 8m) and 31ft (9m) high, with a beautiful timbered ceiling and patterned floor tiles. Its walls were covered with superb murals by Masters William of Westminster and Walter of Durham, showing scenes from the Old Testament and the life of St Edward the Confessor. Nearby, Henry built new apartments for his queen, Eleanor, but these and the Painted Chamber were both destroyed in the fire that devastated the palace in 1834 – only the crypt of St Stephen's Chapel, the Jewel Tower and Westminster Hall, with its magnificent hammerbeam roof, survived the fire.

THE JEWEL TOWER

The three-storey tower was built in 1365–6, probably by master mason Henry Yevele, to store the king's jewels, furs and other valuables. At the extreme southern edge of the palace complex, it was partially surrounded by a moat.

Above: The Jewel Tower is built from Kentish ragstone. Today it houses a collection of local archaeological finds.

It continued to be used as a royal store for valuables until the reign of Henry VII (r.1485–1509).

WINCHESTER PALACE

Winchester Palace, the London home of the Bishop of Winchester, was built in Southwark in 1109. Like Westminster Palace, it was improved in the later medieval period but largely destroyed by fire in the 19th century. The marriage reception for James I of Scots and Joan Beaufort was held there in 1424. Tradition has it Henry VIII met his fifth wife Catherine Howard there in 1540.

Right: The west wall, with its magnificent rose window, c.1320, is the only part of the Great Hall to survive today.

THE HAMMERBEAM ROOF

The other surviving part of the palace is Westminster Hall, built by William Rufus in 1097. Significant alterations were made to the hall by Richard II from 1394 onward. Following designs by Henry Yevele, the walls were raised 2ft (0.6m) and refaced, and a magnificent hammerbeam roof, by Hugh Herland, was added. The roof, carved with angels and traceries, has a span of 69ft (21m), making it the largest timber roof in northern Europe, and soars to a height of 92ft (28m). Richard also built a gateway to the hall containing carved statues of English kings from Edward the Confessor onward.

EDINBURGH CASTLE
CASTLE ON A ROCK

During the reign of King David II of Scots (r.1329–71), major rebuilding work took place in Edinburgh Castle (see also page 358). The great volcanic rock on which the castle stands high above the city was a natural place for a fortified dwelling – and archaeologists have found evidence of settlement, as far back as the Bronze Age (2100–700BC). In the Norman era, Malcolm III (r.1058–93) built a stone castle on the rock. His queen, Margaret, died after hearing that Malcolm had been killed in an ambush in Northumbria; King David I (r.1125–53), her son, built the tiny Chapel of St Margaret in her honour in the castle precincts. This small, irregular chapel is the only part of the Norman castle that still survives today.

Below: Edinburgh Castle was a royal palace and military fortress until modern times.

DAVID'S TOWER

In the 14th century, Robert Stewart – grandson of Robert the Bruce, nephew of the reigning King David II, and himself the future King Robert II – built an L-shaped tower on the castle's northern side. Constructed in 1368–72 and almost 60ft (18m) high, the building, subsequently known as 'David's Tower', almost certainly contained royal apartments. Kitchens and offices were built alongside it in 1382–3. David's Tower is the first known example in Scotland of the tower house – a design pioneered by royalty that would become popular among the nobility. Historians cannot be sure of the exact layout of rooms within the tower, but above a vaulted ground floor they probably contained a first-floor suite for the king, comprising hall, private chamber and closet, with a similar suite for the queen on the floor above.

Above: St Margaret's Chapel is the oldest surviving building in Edinburgh. The tiny chapel holds only around 20 people.

The tower survived unscathed for around two centuries, but then its upper floors were destroyed in a 1573 siege during the reign of James VI of Scots, the future James I of England. The surviving part of the tower was then incorporated into the castle's Half Moon Battery, only to be rediscovered in the early 20th century.

IGHTHAM MOTE
A PICTURESQUE MANOR HOUSE

An idyllic manor house near Sevenoaks in Kent, Ightham Mote is arranged compactly around a courtyard and is enclosed by a stream-fed moat. The house retains a sturdy, well-worn and utilitarian beauty. The earliest buildings, including the massive Great Hall, date from the 14th century, but important additions, including a wonderfully decorated Tudor chapel, were made over the following 200–300 years.

IGHTHAM'S ORIGINS

The house's curious name comes from the nearby village of Ightham and that of the 'moot' (local council), which in medieval times met in the most prominent house in each locality. Its first named owner was Sir Thomas Cawne (d.1374),

Below: A stone urn stands on the lawn in the inner courtyard at Ightham Mote. The buildings behind are called the 'Elizabethan cottages' but in fact date to c.1475.

Right: The south-west front contains the central castellated gatehouse, accessed by a stone bridge across the moat.

who lived in the house from c.1340. The earliest surviving buildings are those on the east side of the courtyard: the Great Hall, the old chapel with crypt, a kitchen and two solars or private chambers. Timber dating indicates that these rooms were completed c.1330, although there is some evidence that the crypt is a survival from an earlier house on the site. The moat and bridge were also laid out in the first half of the 14th century.

In the years 1487–1519, the house's then owner, Edward Haut, added south and west sides to the courtyard. Facing the bridge over the moat, he built a battlemented three-storey entrance tower or gatehouse – the only fortification on the site. On either side of the tower, he built two-storey residential quarters and added a similar two-storey range on the south side of the yard.

TUDOR CHAPEL

In 1521–38, Sir Richard Clement, a notable figure at the court of Henry VIII, left his mark upon the house. Sir Richard added a new chapel on the north side of the courtyard in the form of an upper-floor timber room overhanging the moat with a cloister beneath. This beautiful Gothic chapel was fitted with a delicately carved tracery screen, six fine Dutch stained-glass windows, a hooded pulpit, linen-fold

BROUGHTON CASTLE

Built *c.*1300 by Sir John de Broughton, Broughton Castle, near Banbury in Oxfordshire, is another fine example of the 14th-century fortified manor house. The house, protected by a wide moat, can be reached only by a single bridge across the moat and through a gatehouse.

Sir John de Broughton's manor house was sufficiently splendid to catch the eye of William of Wykeham, Chancellor of England and Bishop of Winchester, who purchased the property in 1377. His great-nephew Sir Thomas Wykeham added battlements to the gatehouse under a licence 'to crenellate and embattle' granted in 1406.

The Fiennes family, later Lords Saye and Sele, acquired the manor through marriage to Sir Thomas Wykeham's

Right: Broughton Castle's moat covers 3 acres (1.2ha). The house has a medieval Great Hall and fine plaster ceilings.

grand-daughter, Margaret, in 1448. In the Tudor period Broughton Castle was substantially remodelled. During Charles I's reign, William, 8th Lord Saye and Sele, a leading Puritan and supporter of Parliament against the King, used Broughton as a meeting place for the King's opponents.

The family frittered away its wealth during the Regency period, but this had the unlooked-for and fortunate effect of subsequently saving Broughton from the

'improving' hand of Victorian architects. Building work was limited to repairs, begun in 1860 by Frederick, 16th Lord Saye and Sele, and continuing throughout the 20th century.

Broughton has won many admirers over the centuries: novelist Henry James called it 'the most delightful home in England' and it was used as the setting for *Shakespeare in Love* (1998) and *The Madness of King George* (1994).

wall panelling and an arched ceiling with panels brightly painted with the Tudor rose, the arrows of Aragon (birthplace of Queen Catherine), the Beaufort portcullis and other emblems.

Below: This carved stone head is from the courtyard at Ightham Mote.

When it was finished, the chapel was somewhat reminiscent of a tournament pavilion of the kind used at events such as the outdoor peace summit, at the Field of the Cloth of Gold in France, organized by Cardinal Wolsey in 1520. Sir Richard also added stained-glass windows to the Great Hall, and window barge boards, once again decorated with Tudor symbols, to the oriel room.

The essential elements that give Ightham Mote its great charm were now in place. In later years, notable owners included Sir William and Dame Dorothy Selby, who, in 1611–41, added the drawing room and the rooms alongside. After 1889, Sir Thomas Colyer-Fergusson carried out widespread repairs.

AMERICAN PHILANTHROPIST
In the second half of the 20th century, the house was saved from possible demolition by an enlightened American businessman, Charles Henry Robinson of Portland, Maine. He purchased

Ightham Mote and funded its renovation from afar, staying in the house during his visits to Europe. Upon his death in 1985, he left the house to the National Trust.

Below: There is a heraldic crest above the main entrance to Ightham Mote.

CHAPTER SIXTEEN

CASTLES AND MANOR HOUSES

1400–1485

Sir Edward Bedingfeld began building the fortified manor house of Oxburgh Hall, near King's Lynn in Norfolk, under a licence to crenellate granted by Edward IV in 1482. The house's elegant design and the superb brickwork of its imposing twin-towered gatehouse make a very grand impression. Auguste Pugin called the house 'one of the noblest expressions of the domestic architecture of the 15th century'. This was a period that saw the rise of the brick-built tower and fortified house. Brick began to replace stone at a time when 'castles' were, in fact, houses built in the style of fortresses, and did not have to be defensible against siege engines. The great appeal of bricks was that they made possible details of surface patterning that could not be produced in stone; they were also cheaper than dressed stone and could be made on site.

One of the pioneers of the brick-built tower was the soldier and courtier, Sir John Falstaff, who began the splendid Caister Castle, in Norfolk, in 1432. At around the same time, Sir John's old friend and companion-at-arms, Ralph, Lord Cromwell, Treasurer of England under King Henry VI, erected a superb brick tower at Tattershall Castle, Lincolnshire. A decade later, another prominent figure at King Henry VI's court, Sir Roger de Fiennes, also Treasurer of the King's Household, began work on the elegant brick-built country house of Herstmonceux Castle in East Sussex. Then, later in the century, Sir John Wenlock rebuilt in brick at Someries Castle in Bedfordshire in the 1460s, and Thomas Rotherham, Bishop of Lincoln, commissioned a fine brick palace at Buckden, Huntingdonshire, in the 1470s.

Left: Castle in brick. Henry VI's treasurer, Sir Roger de Fiennes, spared no expense on his country mansion of Herstmonceux Castle, spending £3,800 on its construction.

TATTERSHALL CASTLE
SPLENDID BRICKWORK

Tattershall Castle was, like Bodiam Castle in Sussex, purchased and renovated by Lord Curzon of Kedleston upon his return from service as Viceroy of India. In the case of Tattershall, Curzon's intervention was very timely because when he bought the property, in 1910, its four superb carved-stone fireplaces had been taken out of the brickwork tower and were packed in boxes in London, waiting to be shipped to the United States. Lord Curzon reinstalled the fireplaces and devotedly refurbished the castle, which he declared 'the most splendid piece of brickwork in England'.

THE GREAT TOWER
The magnificent surviving Great Tower at Tattershall was erected by Ralph, Lord Cromwell, in 1432–8, as part of improvements to an earlier castle built c.1231 by Robert of Tattershall.

Above: Putting elegance and comfort before defence, Tattershall Castle contains sizeable windows fitted with heraldic stained glass.

Left: Both inside and out at Tattershall, Cromwell's Flemish and French craftsmen produced brickwork of the highest quality.

A prominent figure at court, Cromwell served as an adviser to Henry V before he was appointed Treasurer of England by Henry VI in 1433. At Tattershall, he clearly set out to build a lordly dwelling that befitted his newly won eminence.

Cromwell spared no expense to make his mark: his tower, which rose 100ft (30m) above the flat Lincolnshire countryside, was built using costly small red bricks, which were becoming increasingly fashionable. In the tower and nearby buildings at the castle, Cromwell's builders used one million bricks made in his local kilns.

The tower was not a military stronghold: it had ornate traceried windows and no fewer than three doors at ground level, and the corner turrets at parapet level were not defensively functional, since they were covered by mini-spires. In fact, it was designed for grandeur and comfort. It contained a vaulted basement beneath four residential floors, each of which held a great central hall with additional rooms and garderobes in the thick walls and the corner towers. On the ground floor was a Courtroom or Parlour, its carved stone fireplace beautifully decorated with heraldic devices of Cromwell's family. The first floor contained a Great Hall; the second provided an Audience Chamber and ceremonial area with magnificent moulded brick vaulting; and the third was the Lord's Privy Chamber or bedchamber.

Throughout, the castle, brickwork and stone carving were exquisitely finished, and, thanks to Lord Curzon's initiative in renovating and refurbishing the castle, these features can be seen and appreciated today.

DEFENCES

Ralph Cromwell lavished money on the comfort and appearance of his show-piece tower, but he did not entirely neglect the castle's overall defences. He added an outer moat to the building complex and constructed no fewer than three gatehouses and three bridges to guard the approach to the castle from the north.

Cromwell probably repaired and strengthened the 13th-century inner curtain wall, which contained eight drum towers and enclosed in the inner ward a separate Great Hall, as well as kitchens and a chapel. Little remains today except the superb tower.

Above: From the cellars to the battlements, there are no fewer than six floors in the great Square Keep at Tattershall Castle.

CAISTER CASTLE, NORFOLK

Sir John Falstaff, a veteran of the Battle of Agincourt and Henry V's military campaigns in France, and subsequently Governor of Maine and Anjou, rebuilt his family home at Caister, in Norfolk, in some style in 1432–46. His 'castle' was a rectangular brick country house, as lavishly fitted and furnished as a palace. The English chronicler William Worcester described it as a 'ryche juelle' ('rich jewel'). But it was also fortified and surrounded by a moat. It originally had four corner towers, but only one remains, an impressive five storeys, 100ft (30m) in height. Although the tower has machicolations and gun-holes, its large windows would have made it difficult to defend against a besieging force.

Right: The builder of Caister Castle is thought to have been Shakespeare's model for the character of Sir John Falstaff.

RETURN TO THE SQUARE KEEP

Architectural historians note that the square keep was not commonly built in England at the time of Lord Cromwell – the great English square keeps at the Tower of London, at Colchester and Rochester had been constructed three centuries earlier. They suggest that Cromwell may have been inspired to build in this way by the contemporary square keeps he saw in France, when on campaign with the English Army. The quality and style of the workmanship suggests that he imported the finest craftsmen from Flanders and France to work on the building.

LINLITHGOW PALACE
HOME OF THE SCOTTISH KINGS

King James I of Scots began the extensive rebuilding of the royal palace at Linlithgow, between Edinburgh and Stirling, in 1424. In that year, James returned to Scotland, aged 30, at the end of a prolonged 18-year exile in England that had begun when he was captured by pirates, while travelling to France, and handed over to England's King Henry IV. Under the terms of his release treaty, signed in 1423 with England's new king, Henry VI, James had to pay a ransom of £40,000. Nevertheless, James still found the necessary funds to undertake the reconstruction of Linlithgow, where a terrible fire a year later had devastated the earlier fortified dwelling.

Above: The Renaissance-style north façade at Linlithgow was built by James VI and may have been based on the Chateau de Blois in the Loire Valley, France.

QUEENS AND KINGS AT LINLITHGOW

According to Scottish royal tradition, in June 1513 Queen Margaret (Tudor), English-born wife of James IV, waited at Linlithgow for her royal husband to return from the Battle of Flodden Field, unaware that he lay dead with 10,000 of his fellow countrymen. The castle's north-west tower, in which she is said to have waited, is named Queen Margaret's Bower in her honour.

Later, Mary, Queen of Scots, was born at Linlithgow in December 1542, and after she returned to the Scottish throne following her long French exile she often stayed at the palace. Subsequently, Linlithgow began to become neglected, although Charles I stayed there in 1617 and again in 1633.

In 1745, Bonnie Prince Charlie stayed at the palace prior to his unsuccessful attempt to march on London. Subsequently, the Duke of Cumberland (son of England's King George II) stayed there with his army. When these troops departed on 1 February 1746, a fire left unattended started a devastating blaze that severely damaged the palace. Significant repairs were carried out in the 19th century.

Left: Mary, Queen of Scots, spent the first seven months of her life at Linlithgow Palace and often returned afterwards.

FIRST ROYAL BUILDING

King David I of Scots was the earliest royal builder at Linlithgow, erecting a manor house of timber in the mid-12th century. When Edward I of England invaded in the late 13th century, he and his trusted castle architect, Master James of St Georges, fortified David's palace with earthworks, ditches and wooden palisades, but stopped short of building in stone. Edward garrisoned the castle with the English troops needed for his Scottish campaigns. Subsequently, David II carried out rebuilding in the 14th century, but his work was swept away by the fire of 1424.

JAMES I'S CONTRIBUTION

James built an impressive stone entrance block on the east side of the surviving palace building. The raised entranceway was accessed by a ramp and drawbridge from the outer barbican. Above the entrance was the royal coat of arms and on either side were niches, believed once to have held statues of St Andrew and St James. The block also contained a first-floor Great Hall, measuring 100 x 30ft (30 x 9m). At one end were the royal kitchens, while at the other, perhaps, was a great stone fireplace, although in James's time there may have been a great chimneyless central hearth, as in English medieval halls such as Penshurst Place and Stokesay Castle.

The finished palace at Linlithgow took the form of a courtyard house, with four 'wings' around a central garden containing a fountain. Only the eastern front and part of the southern range were finished by James I, but there is evidence that the palace's courtyard was part of the plans from the start. Scholars believe that James, who was an accomplished artist as well as a learned man, may have played a significant part in designing Linlithgow himself. His project

Below: The courtyard fountain of c. 1538. James V's queen, Mary of Guise, likened the palace to the best French chateaux.

was never finished, but it appears to have been conceived as a palace, a royal dwelling, rather than a castle. James changed the entrance from the south to the east, constructing a very grand raised but unfortified gateway that could be viewed advantageously from that direction, across the waters of the adjacent

Above: The palace stands beside Linlithgow Loch. This reconstruction shows the complex shortly after its completion by James V.

Loch Linlithgow. The palace may have been planned as the Scottish answer to England's Sheen Palace, which James must certainly have visited during his long exile in England.

THE PLAN COMPLETED

In the 15th and early 16th centuries, Kings James III and IV finished the work begun by James I, enclosing the courtyard by completing the southern range and then building on the north and finally the west sides. The west range contained some splendid royal apartments for James IV and his English queen, Margaret Tudor, daughter of Henry VII. James IV also made repairs and improvements to the Great Hall, to which he added a new roof, and built a new chapel.

In the time of James V, the main entrance was moved back to the southern range, and a new gatehouse built alongside it. James VI then made improvements to the northern range, including the addition of a fine Renaissance façade on the Long Gallery in 1618–24.

RAGLAN CASTLE
THE GRANDEST CASTLE IN WALES

The castle we see at Raglan was begun *c.*1430 by William ap Thomas, veteran of the Battle of Agincourt and later celebrated as 'the Blue Knight of Gwent', following his knighting by King Henry VI in 1449. William built the hexagonal keep known as the Yellow Tower of Gwent (*c.*1435–45), generally celebrated as being among the finest towers of the 15th century.

The Blue Knight was a follower of Richard, Duke of York, and his family's rise was accelerated by the success of the Yorkists, and in particular by Edward of York's coming to the throne as King Edward IV in 1461. By this time Sir William had died, but his son, another Sir William, was made Earl of Pembroke and Chief Justice first of South Wales, then of North Wales too. The younger Sir William completed the castle.

NORMAN CASTLE
Little remains of the early 12th-century motte-and-bailey castle that was built by followers of William FitzOsbern, Earl

Below: The Closet Tower stands to the right of the Great Gatehouse and contained a basement prison. The gatehouse, with its half-hexagonal towers, dates to the 1460s.

of Hereford, as the Normans pushed into Gwent. But it is likely that the Yellow Tower stands on what was the motte, or mound, of the Norman castle and that the castle's two enclosures, the Pitched Stone Court and the Fountain Court, occupy the land that was once the Norman castle's bailey.

YELLOW TOWER
The Yellow Tower of Gwent, so-called because it is made from a pale yellowish sandstone quarried locally at Redbrooke, has walls 10ft (3m) thick. It originally had four floors above the basement, but one level was lost when the castle was slighted in 1646 during the Civil War. Its ground-floor kitchen lay beneath a first-floor hall, which was surmounted by private and sleeping chambers on the levels above.

The tower was surrounded by an apron wall and a wide moat, and accessed only by a single drawbridge from the rest of the castle. It was a formidable stronghold in its own right, and certainly offered secure quarters to which the castle's defenders might retreat *in extremis*. Moreover, in an era of 'bastard feudalism', soldiers and retainers were bound to powerful lords by financial links rather than the ties of

Above: The Moat Walk at the foot of the Yellow Tower was added c.1600 by the Earl of Worcester. Niches in the wall once held statues of Roman emperors.

feudal loyalty, and the lords could not always be sure of the loyalty of the men they used to garrison them. As a result, they often fortified their own quarters within the castle, where they could, if the situation demanded, take refuge from their own garrison.

The younger Sir William was responsible for building the splendid Great Hall and accommodation ranged around the Fountain Court, which at one time contained a marble water fountain known

Below: At the top of the Great Gatehouse towers the machicolations can be seen. The windows are narrow for purposes of defence.

as 'the White Horse'. The retainers' area was in a second courtyard, the Pitched Stone Court, further north.

STRONG DEFENCES

Raglan is an exception to the general movement away from castles to fortified country houses, for it was designed as a fortress proper – one of the last genuine castles ever built. In addition to the Great Tower, it has a curtain wall containing hexagonal towers and a machicolated gatehouse, which was fortified with three heavy double doors, two portcullises and a drawbridge. Throughout the castle, circular gun-ports were provided in the towers to strengthen defences.

In the Elizabethan era, William Somerset, Earl of Worcester, improved the Great Hall. Building in fine red sandstone that makes an appealing contrast to the prevailing yellow stone, he and his descendants carried out significant rebuilding, adding a magnificent Tudor Long Gallery, now ruined.

Above: This aerial view shows the Yellow Tower (near left), the Fountain Court (top left), and the Pitched Stone Court (top right) behind the Great Gatehouse.

CIVIL WAR

Edward Somerset, Marquis of Worcester, was a staunch Royalist, and the castle was the first to be fortified for Charles I during the Civil War. It was a major royalist centre during the war and the last castle to be surrendered to the Parliamentary army. The worth of Raglan's defences was proved by the fact that the surrender took place, in the lavish Great Hall, on 19 August 1646, only after several weeks of heavy bombardment, at the end of one of the war's longest sieges. The victorious Parliamentarians looted and plundered the splendid castle, slighted its defences and partially demolished the Yellow Tower. Raglan Castle has never been restored, and today remains a handsome, evocative ruin.

ST GEORGE'S CHAPEL
AND WINDSOR CASTLE

The magnificent St George's Chapel at Windsor Castle in Berkshire was begun by Edward IV in 1477. By then, Windsor had been a royal stronghold for over 400 years (see pages 405 and 476).

King Edward the Confessor held his court in his palace of Kingsbury at Old Windsor nearby, but after the Conquest William I built the original Windsor

Below: The Choir in St George's Chapel. The banners of the knights of the garter hang above the garter stalls; beneath the banners are the knights' crests, helmets and swords.

Castle, a motte-and-bailey fortification in a strong position on an escarpment overlooking the River Thames. He raised a wooden keep where the Round Tower stands today, atop a 50ft (15m) motte, and enclosed a 13-acre (5ha) bailey with stakes in a boomerang shape.

A ROYAL FAVOURITE

William II chose the castle for his Easter celebrations in 1097; Henry I built a chapel and royal apartments there and married his second wife, Adeliza of Louvain, at Windsor in January 1121. In the 1170s, Henry II rebuilt William I's

Above: St George's Chapel is widely considered to be one of Europe's finest late medieval buildings.

original keep in stone, then reworked the defensive walls around the wards, adding square towers, and refashioned the royal apartments in the upper ward.

In 1216, the fortifications were fully tested when a baronial army besieged King John in the castle for three months. Although the castle held firm, Henry III added three round towers to the western wall. He also established St Edward's Chapel in the lower ward.

Edward III was born in Windsor Castle, in November 1312, and known as 'Edward Windsor'. In the 1360s, he extended and improved the castle, in particular building St George's Hall for the Knights of the Order of the Garter.

ST GEORGE'S CHAPEL

Edward IV began the construction of a vast new chapel dedicated to St George, situated to the west of the earlier one. Master mason Henry Janyns carried out the project, overseen by Richard Beauchamp, Bishop of Salisbury. It was to contain the King's funerary monument. The chapel was unfinished at Edward's death in 1483, and work soon stopped.

The chapel was completed in the reign of Henry VII and became a burial place for British monarchs. No fewer than ten kings and queens are buried there.

NORTON CONYERS

THE HOUSE THAT INSPIRED *JANE EYRE*

 Norton Conyers, a fine manor house near Ripon in Yorkshire, was developed by the Conyers, a Norman family granted land in the region after the Conquest of 1066. The house took its present form in the late 1400s, although the Dutch gables and carved doorway on the front are 17th century; the 15th-century brickwork is concealed by an 18th-century roughcast exterior. Norton Conyers appears to have been the inspiration for Thornfield Hall, Mr Rochester's house in Charlotte Brontë's novel *Jane Eyre*.

THE MAD WOMAN IN THE ATTIC

In 1839, when Charlotte Brontë was working as a governess for a family in Harrogate, she visited Norton Conyers and heard her host's account of how, in the 18th century, a mad woman had been locked away in the attic. In her novel *Jane Eyre*, published in 1847, Norton Conyers became Thornfield Hall and the mad woman the wife of the novel's Byronic hero, Mr Rochester.

Below: Charlotte Brontë. In 2004, just as described in Jane Eyre, *a blocked staircase was found at Norton Conyers.*

Norton Conyers stands in a landscaped garden enclosed by a grey stone boundary wall. Within, the impressive Great Hall dates from the 15th century, although its roof timbers have been hidden by a coved ceiling and the original wooden screens have been removed. Norton Conyers also boasts a magnificent 16th-century inlaid table in the hall.

CATHOLIC LORD DISPOSSESSED

The house takes the first part of its name from that of the Norton family, who came into ownership through marriage *c*.1370. However, Richard Norton cast his lot with the Catholic earls who plotted against Elizabeth I at Raby Castle, County Durham, in the doomed 1569 'Rebellion of the North'. As a traitor, Norton lost his property, which was forfeit to the Crown.

THE GRAHAMS TAKE OVER

Norton Conyers was later purchased by Sir Richard Graham, a member of the notable Scots Borders family, in 1624.

Right: The main oak staircase at Norton Conyers, built c.1630, showing some of the Graham portrait collection.

Above: Generations of prosperity. Tudor, Stuart and Georgian additions to the original 14th-century house take nothing away from the charm of Norton Conyers.

In 1644, family legend has it that a wounded Graham horseman rode back so fast from the Battle of Marston Moor that when he reached home his horse's hooves were red-hot. The animal carried its rider into the house because he was wounded, and left a hoof mark on the sweeping oak staircase of *c*.1630.

In 1679, the Grahams entertained the future King James II, then James, Duke of York, with his wife, Mary of Modena, on their way to Scotland. Sir Richard's descendants still own the house today.

OXBURGH HALL
A ROMANTIC MOATED MANOR

Oxburgh Hall has stylish defences — it lies within a square moat and has a gatehouse tower complete with battlements, arrow-slits and machicolations — but, as with many fortified manor houses, these features are more signs of status than effective elements of defence. For one thing, the moat is crossed by a fixed bridge rather than a drawbridge; for another, the arrow-slit arrangement means that defenders could not have provided effective cover fire from them. Moreover, the gate-tower has large windows. In addition, the Great Hall, even if sufficiently fortified to deter bands of marauders in the lawless late 15th century, would not repel well-equipped soldiers or withstand a siege.

The house, near King's Lynn in Norfolk, was begun in the 1480s by prominent nobleman, Sir Edward Bedingfeld, descendant of an originally Norman family. Sir Edward's ancestor, Sir Peter Bedingfeld, fought with honour alongside the Black Prince and King Edward III at the Battle of Crécy in 1346.

Below: In addition to its superb brickwork and royal connections, Oxburgh Hall is celebrated for its French parterre gardens.

The fixed bridge across the moat leads through the arched entranceway at the foot of the tower into a central courtyard. Originally, the Great Hall stood on the south side of the courtyard, directly across from the tower, with two-storey residential buildings on the other sides. The Great Hall was demolished by Sir Richard Bedingfeld in 1775 to open up the courtyard to the moat and countryside beyond. Subsequently, two squat towers were raised at the south-west and south-east corners of the courtyard, filling part of the south side.

Above: The fixed bridge across the moat and Oxburgh Hall's twin-towered gatehouse can be seen at the left side of the picture.

THE GATEHOUSE
The two towers of the gatehouse at Oxburgh Hall are topped with serrated battlements and decorated with horizontal brick mouldings. Within the gatehouse, a splendid brick-built spiral stairway rises from the ground-floor armoury to the roof. The first-floor chamber is known as the King's Room because it was occupied by King Henry VII when he visited Oxburgh in 1487. In a small side room on this floor are embroidered wall-hangings sewn by Mary, Queen of Scots, during her long captivity in England. She was assisted in this work by Bess of Hardwick (builder of Hardwick Hall). The second-floor chamber is named the Queen's Room.

During the reign of Mary I, Sir Henry Bedingfeld was in charge of keeping Princess Elizabeth, the future Elizabeth I, in custody, first in the Tower of London, and then under house arrest at Woodstock. However, Elizabeth showed that she bore no grudge to the family by visiting Oxburgh Hall in 1578.

HERSTMONCEUX CASTLE
FORMER HOME OF THE ROYAL OBSERVATORY

 Sir Roger de Fiennes, Treasurer of the King's Household under King Henry VI, began building the vast and magnificent fortified manor house of Herstmonceux Castle, in East Sussex, in 1441. Along with Lord Cromwell of Tattershall Castle and Sir John Falstaff of Caister Castle, de Fiennes was a pioneer of brick building in 15th-century England. At Herstmonceux, he used Flemish brick and probably Flemish craftsmen to erect a handsome moated country mansion.

The place took its name from 12th-century English noblewoman, Idonea de Herst, and her Norman lord, Ingelram de Monceux. Situated just a few miles from the site of the Battle of Hastings, Herstmonceux was a place of note many centuries before Sir Roger began building there.

Below: According to local legend, the lands besides the moat at Herstmonceux are haunted by a lady in white, who is said to have been seduced, then killed, by Sir Roger.

STYLISTIC DEFENCES

The castle is rectangular in shape, with a polygonal (many-sided) tower at each corner, plus smaller towers spaced out along the length of the walls, and an impressive twin-towered gatehouse, 84ft (25.5m) high, boasting a double row of battlements and heavy machicolation. The gatehouse towers are fitted with gun-holes at ground level and arrow-slits further up. However, the castle was built for comfort and elegance, not as a fortress: the brick walls were far too soft and thin to withstand bombardment, and the turrets, machicolation, moat and battlements are for style, not for defence.

FROM PRIVATE TO PUBLIC

Sir Richard de Fiennes, son of Sir Roger, became Baron Dacre in 1458. The house later passed to the Lennard family through marriage. Then, in the 17th century, Thomas Lennard, 15th Lord Dacre, was made Earl of Sussex by King Charles II and married Anne, Duchess of Cleveland. He frittered away the family money, and the castle was sold.

Above: Sir Roger de Fiennes' arms are carved in stone above the arch in the splendid 84ft (25.5m) gatehouse.

A later owner, Robert Hare, dismantled much of the castle's interior and used the bricks from it in rebuilding Herstmonceux Place, a nearby house. The castle was rescued and renovated by Lt-Col Claude Lowther in the early 20th century. He rebuilt the south front in 1911–12. In 1948–88, the castle was the base of the Royal Greenwich Observatory, but later it was turned into an international study centre by the Queen's University, Canada.

HADDON HALL
HOME TO THE 'KING OF THE PEAK'

The handsome medieval manor house of Haddon Hall, near Bakewell in Derbyshire, has a splendid late 15th-century Dining Room and Great Chamber, both with fine original ceiling paintings. In addition, the house and estate contain a 14th-century Banqueting Hall and largely unchanged adjacent kitchens, Jacobean Long Gallery and terraced Elizabethan gardens. Much of Haddon Hall's charm and interest lie in the fact that it was uninhabited – and so unchanged – for around 200 years after the early 1700s, when the owners (from the 16th century, the dukes of Rutland) removed to their other, grander, house at Belvoir Castle. Then, in 1924, the Marquis of Granby, subsequently the 9th Duke, began a sensitive and careful restoration of the house of his ancestors.

Below: Sparse furnishings, richly carved wood panelling and fine plasterwork ceilings typify the rooms at Haddon Hall.

Above: Henry VII celebrates his marriage to Elizabeth of York. The royal couple are carved in the panelling of the dining room.

Haddon Hall stands in the Peak District National Park, on a hill overlooking the River Wye, on land granted by William the Conqueror to an illegitimate son named William Peverel. The oldest parts of the house, including sections of the boundary wall, the lower part of Peverel's Tower and the font and

arches of the Chapel, date from the Norman period. The boundary wall was built under a licence of 1190, which forbade the use of crenellation and stated that the wall should be no more then 12ft (3.7m) high. The battlements on the walls and towers were added later.

BANQUETING HALL
This hall was built *c.*1370, and two windows and two gargoyles survive from the time of its construction. The oak screen and gallery are 15th century, and while the timber roof is a 20th-century one, it is a very skilful addition. Hanging in the hall is a tapestry of *c.*1470, of French *mille fleurs* design with the arms of England, which is believed to have been a gift from King Henry VIII. The kitchens alongside are fitted with well-used, centuries-old equipment, including a chopping block and a salting box.

MURALS AND MEDALLIONS
In the 15th century, fine murals were painted in the chapel: two of St Nicholas, one of St Anne and one of St Christopher carrying the Christ child across a river full of fish. These were

Below: The terraced gardens run down to the River Wye. They were restored in the 1920s to their appearance in Elizabethan times.

Above: A 15th-century mural in the chapel shows Saint Christopher's feet treading river waters as he carries the Christ child.

Right: Light floods into Haddon Hall's splendid Long Gallery through its expansive windows, creating a luminous promenade.

whitewashed by zealous Puritans in the 17th century, which protected the murals against decay. Also in the 15th century, a nine-panel alabaster reredos was built in the chapel and beautiful stained glass (dated 1427) installed.

At the end of the 15th century, Sir Henry Vernon built the Private Wing, including the Dining Room (originally known as the Parlour) and the Great Chamber above it. In the Dining Room, the painted ceiling (restored in 1926) includes black and red heraldic elements; in its wall panelling are carved medallions believed to represent Henry VII and his queen, Elizabeth of York.

'KING OF THE PEAK'

The celebrated oak-panelled Long Gallery, 110ft (34m) in length with beautiful oak panelling and carved walnut embellishments, was built by Sir George Vernon later in the 16th century. Sir George was celebrated for his hospitality and known as the 'King of the Peak'. Sir George's daughter, Dorothy, married John Manners, later Duke of Rutland. The house came to them, and the family lives there still.

GREAT HALL AT GREAT DIXTER

The cavernous Great Hall in the splendid timber-framed house of Great Dixter in East Sussex was built *c*.1440–54. Measuring 40 x 25ft (12 x 8m) and 31ft (9.5m) tall, it is one of England's largest surviving timber-framed halls. It has a splendid hammer-beam roof. Like Haddon Hall, Great Dixter was sensitively restored in the 20th century – in this case, by the architect Edwin Lutyens for owner Nathaniel Lloyd in 1910–11. Lutyens also designed a splendid topiary garden incorporating the manor's original farm buildings. Nathaniel Lloyd's sons, Quentin and Christopher, cared for the house and gardens respectively. Christopher, during whose period of care the gardens were internationally renowned and much visited, died on 27 January 2006.

Above: The porch at Great Dixter is 16th century or earlier.

PART FIVE

TUDOR AND STUART

1485–1714

The Tudor and Stuart monarchs were among the great royal builders, creating lavish palaces in England and Scotland. The reign of Elizabeth I was an extraordinarily rich period for architecture, with the construction of 'prodigy houses'. The establishment of the House of Stuart, under James I and Charles I, saw the introduction of classical architecture to England.

Left: James V's Renaissance-style building at Holyrood Palace was carried out for his first wife, Madeleine de Valois, but she died before she could enjoy it.

ENGLAND TIMELINE, 1485–1714

Above: Hampton Court Palace is the most magnificent Tudor palace surviving today.

Above: Burghley House, one of the 'prodigy houses' built in the reign of Elizabeth I.

Above: Marlborough House was the London home of the 1st Duke of Marlborough.

1485–1579

*c.*1485 Cardinal John Morton, Bishop of Ely, builds the episcopal palace of Hatfield House, Hertfordshire.

1514–19 Cardinal Wolsey, Lord Chancellor, builds a magnificent Renaissance residence at Hampton Court Palace.

1537–41 James V remodels Falkland Palace to create Scotland's first palace in the continental Renaissance style.

*c.*1540 Lawrence Washington, ancestor of the first US President, George Washington, builds Sulgrave Manor in Northamptonshire on the site of the dissolved Priory of St Andrew.

*c.*1540 Henry VIII builds Deal Castle in Kent.

1540–45 Henry VIII builds Pendennis Castle near Falmouth in Cornwall.

1547–52 Edward, Duke of Somerset, builds the splendid Syon House in Middlesex.

1555 Sir William Cecil begins building Burghley House in Northamptonshire.

*c.*1565–75 Robert Dudley, Earl of Leicester, carries out grand rebuilding at Kenilworth Castle in Warwickshire.

1562 Sir William More begins the transformation of Loseley House in Surrey into a 'prodigy house'.

1567 Sir John Thynne begins building his great 'prodigy house' of Longleat House in Wiltshire.

1580–1629

1580–88 Sir Francis Willoughby builds Wollaton Hall in Nottinghamshire.

*c.*1590 Sir Edward Phelips begins building Montacute House in Somerset.

1587 Work on Burghley House, Lincolnshire, completed, for Sir William Cecil, 1st Baron Burghley.

1591–97 Elizabeth, Countess of Shrewsbury – 'Bess of Hardwick' – builds Hardwick Hall in Derbyshire.

1603–08 Thomas Sackville, 1st Earl of Dorset, rebuilds the elegant country house of Knole in Kent.

1605–14 Thomas Howard, 1st Earl of Suffolk, builds Audley End in Essex.

1607–08 Robert Cecil, 1st Earl of Salisbury, rebuilds Hatfield House in Hertfordshire.

1612 The leading Elizabethan 'surveyor' (architect), Robert Smythson, begins work at Bolsover Castle in Chesterfield, his last major house.

1615 Inigo Jones begins work on the Queen's House, Greenwich, based on an Italian Medici villa at Poggio a Caiano.

1616–25 Robert Lyminge builds Blickling Hall in Norfolk for Sir Henry Hobart.

1619–22 Inigo Jones builds the Banqueting House in Whitehall Palace.

1623 Inigo Jones begins work on the Queen's Chapel in St James's Palace.

1630–1714

1636–40 Major work by Philip Herbert, 4th Earl of Pembroke, at his Wilton House in Wiltshire includes a new south front designed by Isaac de Caus and Inigo Jones.

*c.*1675 Charles II spends £130,000 at Windsor Castle, building new state apartments, and redecorating St George's Hall and the King's Chapel.

1687–1707 William Cavendish, 4th Earl of Devonshire, entirely rebuilds Chatsworth House in Derbyshire.

1688–96 Charles Seymour, 6th Duke of Somerset, builds Petworth House on the site of a 13th-century castle in West Sussex.

1689 Sir Christopher Wren begins rebuilding Hampton Court Palace for King William III and Queen Mary II. In the same year rebuilding begins to transform Nottingham House, Kensington, into Kensington Palace.

*c.*1690 Ford, Lord Grey of Werke, builds Uppark, West Sussex.

1696–1702 Nicholas Hawksmoor designs Easton Neston in Northamptonshire, regarded by some as the first country house in the Baroque style.

1709–11 Sir Christopher Wren builds Marlborough House in London for John Churchill, 1st Duke of Marlborough, and his wife, Sarah, Duchess of Marlborough.

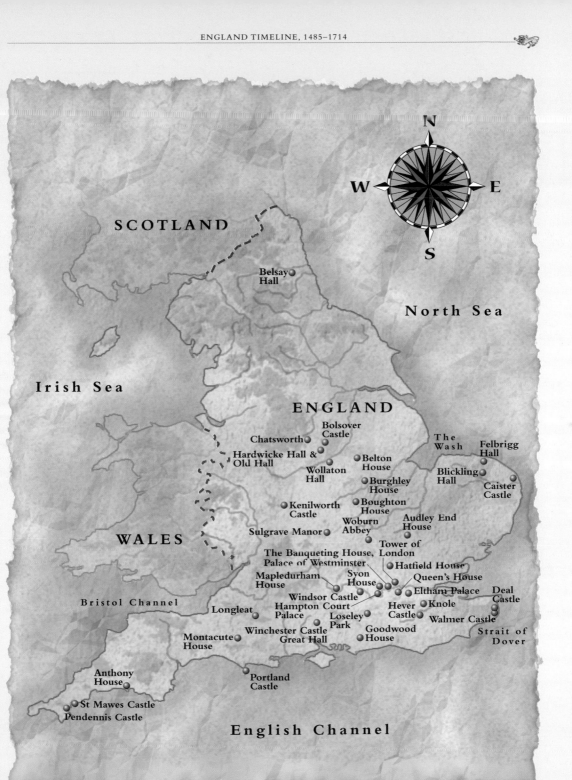

SCOTLAND, WALES
AND NORTHERN IRELAND TIMELINES, 1485–1714

Above: Holyrood Palace is the official residence in Scotland of the Queen.

SCOTLAND, 1485–1714

1512 James IV of Scots builds a Great Tower at Rothesay Castle, Isle of Bute.

*c.***1530** George Gordon, 4th Earl of Huntly, begins major rebuilding of Huntly Castle, Aberdeenshire.

1536 James V of Scots completes major rebuilding of Holyrood Palace.

1537–41 James V's rebuilding at Falkland Palace creates Scotland's first Renaissance palace.

1538–42 James V builds a palace within Stirling Castle.

*c.***1580** Lord Edzell builds a courtyard mansion at Edzell Castle, Angus.

*c.***1585** 5th Earl of Bothwell rebuilds Crichton Castle in the Renaissance style.

1594 The construction of Crathes Castle in Aberdeenshire is completed.

*c.***1595** 9th Lord Glamis embarks on a remodelling of Glamis Castle, Angus.

*c.***1600** King James VI of Scots builds Dunfermline Palace.

1626 William Forbes completes Craigievar Castle in Aberdeenshire.

*c.***1675** Charles II rebuilds Holyrood Palace in Edinburgh.

1628 John Erskine, 3rd Earl of Mar, builds Braemar Castle, Aberdeenshire.

1640 Threave Castle, Dumfries and Galloway, surrenders after a 13-week siege.

1699 The decay of Tantallon Castle, E Lothian, begins when the Douglas earls of Angus sell it.

N **W** **E** **S**

North Sea

Moray Firth

Huntly Castle
Castle Fraser
Crathes Castle
Braemar Castle
Glamis Castle
Edzell Castle

SCOTLAND

Stirling Castle
Falkland Palace
Dunfermline Abbey & Palace
Firth of Forth
Linlithgow Palace
Tantallon Castle
Crichton Castle
Edinburgh Castle, Holyroodhouse Palace

North Atlantic Ocean

Threave Castle

Solway Firth

ENGLAND

Irish Sea

Above: Carew Castle stands on the tidal creek of the Carew River in Wales.

WALES, 1485–1714

*c.*1560 Sir Richard Clough builds Bachecraig, Denbigh, celebrated as the first classical country house in Wales.

*c.*1575 Sir John Perrot rebuilds Carew Castle in Dyfed.

*c.*1580 Sir John also rebuilds Laugharne Castle in South Wales. He was given the castle by Queen Elizabeth I in 1575.

1587–92 Sir Edward Herbert builds a splendid Long Gallery as part of major rebuilding at Powis Castle.

Above: Killyleagh Castle is the oldest occupied castle in Ireland.

NORTHERN IRELAND 1485–1714

1611 Capt Willam Cole rebuilds Enniskillen Castle in Co Fermanagh.

1616 Rev Malcolm Hamilton builds Monea Castle in Co Fermanagh.

1620 Randall MacDonnell, 1st Earl of Antrim, builds a manor house within Dunluce Castle, Co Antrim.

1680 Springhill House, a 'Plantation' house, is built by William Conyngham in Co Londonderry.

CHAPTER SEVENTEEN

EARLY TUDOR PALACES AND COUNTRY HOUSES

1485–*c*.1550

At Hampton Court Palace in August 1546, Henry VIII made a bold statement of the glory of the youthful Tudor dynasty and his own regal largesse when he laid on feasts and entertainments for the French ambassador, a 200-strong body of French followers and 1,300 English courtiers. In the ten years *c*.1530–40, Henry had spent a massive £62,000 (around £18 million in today's money) on improving Hampton Court, already a glorious Renaissance-style palace built by Cardinal Thomas Wolsey in 1514–18.

At Hampton Court – and in a host of now ruined or demolished Tudor palaces – Henry's lavishly funded royal building expressed the magnificence of both Crown and state. Following his break with the Church of Rome and the establishment of the Church of England, the nation's greatest buildings were increasingly secular rather than sacred.

This new wave of secular building was funded in large part by the Dissolution of the Monasteries, when in the 1530s Henry suppressed England's great religious houses and seized their lands and wealth. The Crown's loyal servants and Henry's associates – such as Sir William Compton, builder of Compton Wynyates, and William Sandys, builder of The Vyne – were rewarded with grants of land and office that made them rich. In their service, English masons, woodworkers and glaziers who would once have worked for the Church exercised their skills in building the fine country houses of the early Tudor period.

Left: The Gateway in the Tudor West Front at Hampton Court Palace was begun by Cardinal Wolsey and finished by Henry VIII.

COMPTON WYNYATES
AND THE VYNE

The delightful red-brick manor house of Compton Wynyates, in Warwickshire, was begun by Edmund Compton in 1481, just prior to the accession of the House of Tudor. Edmund's sturdy but good-looking country house was given some elegant additions, including a porch and some towers, by his son, the prominent Tudor courtier, Sir William Compton, between 1493 and 1528.

EDMUND COMPTON'S MANOR
The house's name has an uncertain derivation: 'Compton' certainly means 'dwelling in the coombe (valley)'; but 'Wynyates' may refer either to the vineyards that once were planted in the area or to the nearby gap in the hills ('wind gate'?), where a windmill was built.

The Compton family had lived in the area since the early years of the 13th century and built an earlier manor house that Edmund Compton redeveloped. He kept little but the moat and its drawbridge from the earlier house when he built a new dwelling of four wings, enclosing a courtyard, with walls 4ft (1.2m) thick, and an impressive Big Hall with a linen-fold panelling screen and a gallery. Edmund used attractive raspberry-coloured bricks that give the

house an unforgettable glow against the greenery of the garden and the surrounding countryside. He dug a second, outer, moat – probably never filled with water – with its own drawbridge.

SIR WILLIAM COMPTON
Edmund Compton died in 1491 and his son, William, became a ward of the Crown. From the age of 11, William served at court as a page to Prince Henry, the future King Henry VIII, and in later life remained a great friend of

Above: In its idyllic setting, and with the soft glow of its bricks, Compton Wynyates is one of England's most attractive houses.

that charismatic king. William fought, jousted and banqueted alongside his royal master, as well as romancing the ladies of the court. Henry knighted William at the Battle of Tournai, in 1512, and, as a sign of special favour, allowed him to add the royal lion of England to the Compton coat of arms.

At Compton Wynyates, *c*.1515, Sir William built a grand entrance porch and chapel, while adding a tower at each of the four corners of the house. The entrance porch was carved with the royal arms alongside the Latin inscription *Dom Rex Henricus Octav* ('My Master King Henry VIII'). He also installed the Big Hall's timber ceiling and great bay window, fitted with heraldic glass; both these came from the ruins of Fulbrooke Castle, near

Left: Rich in tradition and history, Compton Wynyates has fine gardens and flowering plants climbing its red walls.

Warwick, which he had been given by
the King as a reward for his brave and
loyal service.

KING HENRY VIII'S ROOM

Among the rooms at Compton
Wynyates, King Henry VIII's Room is
of particular interest. Here, the monarch
stayed on several occasions, and the
stained-glass window features the royal
arms and those of Aragon (birthplace of
Queen Catherine). In later years, Queen
Elizabeth I slept in the same room in
1572, while King James I stayed there
in 1617. James made Sir William
Compton 1st Earl of Northampton.
Charles I, a close friend of Spencer
Compton, 2nd Earl of Northampton,
also stayed here. The ceiling (of 1625)
contains the monograms of all the
room's royal residents.

LATER DEVELOPMENTS

During the Civil War, the Comptons
remained staunch Royalists. The 2nd
Earl fought at the battle of Edgehill in
1642 and was killed at the Battle of

*Above: All who entered Sir William
Compton's home walked beneath the
motto "My Master King Henry VIII".*

Hopton Heath in 1643. In June 1644,
Compton Wynyates was besieged and
taken by the Parliamentarian army.
In 1645, the Comptons tried but failed
to retake the house and then fled into
exile, where they remained until the
Restoration. In line with their usual
policy of slighting royalist fortifications,
the Parliamentarians took the action of
filling in the house's moat.

In later years, Compton Wynyates
was uninhabited. The house decayed and
came close to complete ruin. Indeed, in
1768 Lord Northampton ordered its
demolition, but his agent fortunately did
not carry out his instructions. In the
later 19th century, Compton Wynyates
was restored and from 1884 was once
again inhabited, by the 5th Marquess of
Northampton and his wife.

THE VYNE, HAMPSHIRE

The prominent Tudor courtier, William
Sandys, built the manor house of The
Vyne, in Hampshire, c.1500–20. It was
built of attractive rose-coloured brick,
with corner towers and tall windows
across the main fronts, but had no moat
or internal courtyard. Sandys became
Lord Sandys in 1523 and was made Lord
Chamberlain in Henry VIII's household
in 1526. Henry visited The Vyne in
1510, 1531 and 1535, the third time with
his new wife, Anne Boleyn. Lord Sandys
died in 1540. Later owners of his house
included Chaloner Chute (a Speaker of
the House of Commons), who hired John
Webb to build a classical portico, the earliest
in an English country house, on The
Vyne's north front (see also page 408).

*Below: The placing of the original windows
was more haphazard than the symmetrical
arrangement of the later sash windows.*

HAMPTON COURT PALACE
AND THE COURT OF HENRY VIII

One of England's finest royal buildings, Hampton Court is forever associated with the magnificent court of Henry VIII, although major changes were made in the 17th century during the reign of William and Mary (see pages 412–13). The palace came into royal hands as a gift from the statesman, Cardinal Wolsey, to his royal master, Henry VIII.

WOLSEY'S PALACE
In 1514, Wolsey, Lord Chancellor and Archbishop of York, obtained the lease of the building from the religious order of the Knights Hospitaliers of St John of Jerusalem. In five years of lavishly funded redevelopment, he transformed the Knights' relatively modest country retreat into a splendid and extensive palace. The eastern part of the kitchen range and the nearby Base Court, a guest courtyard surrounded by private accommodation for 40 or so visitors, remain essentially as they were in Wolsey's time.

Below: The 19th-century artist Joseph Nash imagines Wolsey entertaining his lord and king at Hampton Court Palace.

Above: The turrets flanking the gatehouse in the Tudor West Front at Hampton Court hold roundels with the heads of Roman emperors.

Recent archaeological research has shown that Wolsey's palace was laid out in a great geometric design that formed two eight-pointed stars, one beside the other. The magnificent design followed very closely the instructions in an Italian book of 1510, Paolo Cortese's *de Cardinalatu*, which described the dimensions and features of a perfect Cardinal's residence. Wolsey's flamboyant house was therefore England's first Italian Renaissance palace.

Above: Wolsey laid out the first gardens at Hampton Court, then Henry VIII began a major redevelopment of them in 1529.

In 1528, Wolsey was falling swiftly out of royal favour because he was unable to provide Henry VIII with a divorce from Catherine of Aragon. He attempted to halt this alarming slide by making a gift of his precious palace to Henry VIII. The ploy did not work: Henry happily accepted the gift of Hampton Court and almost at once launched his own major building projects there, but Wolsey's reputation was not restored.

Henry built extravagant royal suites, a beautiful chapel, an enormous Great Hall and 36,000sq ft (3,300sq m) of kitchens. He provided a vast lavatory complex that could be used by 28 people at one time, with water piped through 3 miles (5km) of lead piping. He laid out 1,100 acres (445ha) of hunting grounds, a large pleasure garden, tennis courts and a bowling alley.

ELTHAM PALACE
Another of Henry VIII's favourite residences was Eltham Palace, once a manor house in the Kent countryside, now enveloped by south London. Given in 1295 by Anthony Bek, Bishop of Durham, to the future Edward II, Eltham became a much-frequented royal

LOST PALACES OF THE TUDOR KINGS

Several other major Tudor palaces have been lost to posterity. Nonsuch Palace, near Ewell in Surrey, was so called because it was beyond compare – there was 'none such' anywhere else.

The Tudor palace at Greenwich was knocked down in the 17th century and replaced by the Queen's House and what is now the National Maritime Museum, designed by Inigo Jones and Sir Christopher Wren. The once-magnificent

Below: A French chateau in Surrey. Henry VIII's Nonsuch Palace, near Ewell, was a magnificent sight in its Tudor prime.

Richmond Palace, beside the Thames on the site of the former Sheen Palace in Surrey, collapsed into ruins.

Nothing remains of Baynard's Castle, which once stood near Upper Thames Street in the City of London. It was extended in the reign of Edward VI and frequented by Elizabeth I, but it burnt down in the Great Fire of London of 1666. Little also remains of Henry VIII's Bridewell Palace (once south of Fleet Street in London), or of his Whitehall Palace, also in central London, or of his Oatlands Palace near Weybridge in Surrey, where he loved to go hunting.

Above: The cavernous Great Hall at Hampton Court, built by Henry VIII, has a magnificent hammer-beam roof.

new west front. But the palace began to fall into decline in the early 17th century, then was occupied and ransacked by Parliamentary soldiers during the Civil War. In the 1930s, the Great Hall was restored and incorporated into a splendid new Art Deco house built by Stephen and Virginia Courtauld (see page 488).

house in the 14th century. The French chronicler, Jean Froissart, described Eltham as 'a very magnificent palace', and the poet, Geoffrey Chaucer, as Clerk of the King's Works, was in charge of improvements carried out during Richard II's reign. In 1475–80, Edward IV built the magnificent Great Hall, with its splendid hammer-beam roof.

Henry VIII's reign saw the building of a new chapel and royal accommodation, and the laying out of gardens, an archery range and a bowling green. Elizabeth I gave the royal apartments a

Right: The Great Hall of King Edward IV (c. 1470) stands to the left of the Courtaulds' 1930s house at Eltham Palace.

HEVER CASTLE
THE HOME OF ANNE BOLEYN

The moated and fortified manor house of Hever Castle, near Edenbridge in Kent, was the childhood home of Anne Boleyn, mother of Elizabeth I. Henry VIII was a frequent visitor in the 1520s when he paid court to Anne.

THE BOLEYNS

The first fortified building at Hever was built *c.*1270: the outer defensive wall and forbidding three-storey gatehouse date from this time. A century later, Sir John de Cobham added battlements and a moat complete with drawbridge. In 1459, Sir Geoffrey Bullen, a former Lord Mayor of London, bought the castle. After Sir Geoffrey's grandson, Sir Thomas, married Lady Elizabeth Howard, daughter of the Earl of Surrey, the family (now calling itself Boleyn) rose to prominence. Thomas served Henry VIII as an ambassador and as Treasurer of the King's Household; he was made a Knight of the Garter in

Below: History breathes in the dining hall at Hever Castle, where Henry VIII paid court to the daughter of Sir Thomas Boleyn.

Above: In the early 16th century, Sir Thomas Boleyn, father of a future queen, built a Long Gallery at Hever Castle.

1523 and Earl of Wiltshire in 1529. His two beautiful daughters, Mary and Anne, both served as ladies-in-waiting to Queen Catherine (of Aragon) and both caught the King's eye. Mary was Henry's mistress for a while, before she was eclipsed by Anne, who was beheaded three years after she became queen.

CHANGES OF OWNERSHIP

Two years later, on Thomas's death, Hever Castle was taken over by the Crown. It was soon the possession of another royal, for Henry VIII gave it to Anne of Cleves on their divorce in

Above: In her youth, Anne served at court abroad. Margaret, Archduchess of Austria, praised Anne as "bright and pleasant".

1540, as he prepared to wed his fifth wife, Catherine Howard. After Anne's death in 1557, the castle reverted once more to the Crown until Mary Tudor made a gift of it to her courtier, Sir Edward Waldegrave. After many years of obscurity, the castle was bought in 1903 by the wealthy American financier William Waldorf Astor, who thoroughly renovated both house and estate.

MOCK TUDOR

As part of his restoration of Hever, Astor refashioned the adjacent farm buildings into a Tudor-style village, using 16th-century timber from the dismantled Tudor stables. He laid out the gardens in Italian style, complete with grottoes and marble pavements, and excavated a 35-acre (13ha) lake. He meticulously restored the interior of the castle. In the dining room, he fitted the door with a lock that Henry VIII had carried with him to secure his sleeping chamber when he travelled, and, alongside it, an almost identical modern replica.

LEEDS CASTLE
AND ITS TRANSFORMATION BY HENRY VIII

Henry VIII took a great liking to Leeds Castle in Kent, and carried out lavish improvements, transforming it from castle to fortified palace. The King was often in Kent, where he was entertained at Penshurst Place and visited Anne Boleyn at Hever Castle. Leeds Castle had well-established royal links, and had been favoured by kings and queens since Edward I honeymooned there in 1299 (see pages 316–17).

HENRY'S ALTERATIONS

Henry entrusted the work at Leeds Castle to Sir Henry Guildford, who became Comptroller of the Royal Household. He added a storey to the Gloriette Tower on the northern island, installing large windows in the royal apartments there. He erected the Maidens' Tower as space for the maids of honour and refashioned the 75ft (23m) Banqueting Hall, adding a large bow window. The hall now contains a portrait of Henry VIII, and a splendid tapestry of the Magi, c.1490.

Below: Henry VIII brought palatial luxury to Leeds Castle, in particular developing the Gloriette Tower and Banqueting Hall.

Above: The Queens' Bedroom was first used by Henry V's wife, Catherine de Valois. Anne Boleyn waited on Catherine of Aragon.

As well as investing heavily in the comfort of Leeds Castle, Henry VIII took care to maintain its defences, for he was always aware of the threat of foreign invasion. Towards the end of his reign, Henry gave Leeds Castle to Sir Anthony St Leger as a reward for his service as Ireland's Lord Deputy. The

TUDOR STYLE

By the 1530s and 1540s, memories of the Wars of the Roses were beginning to fade, and the new style in building celebrated the 'Tudor peace' by using increasing numbers of ever-larger windows. One feature particularly characteristic of Tudor houses is the oriel window, which projects out from an upper floor, supported from beneath by a bracket.

Tudor architectural style also moved away from the pointed Gothic arch to a flattened arch, subsequently known as the Tudor arch. Doors were smaller and more ornate, and houses were increasingly fitted with coal-burning fireplaces and chimneys. Within, many houses were fitted with wood panelling, often oak carved to resemble folded cloth, which was later known as 'linen-fold panelling'.

castle later belonged to John Culpeper, Chancellor of the Exchequer under King Charles I, and then to the Lords Fairfax. In the 20th century, the castle was restored by Lady Olive Baillie.

THE TOWER OF LONDON
A ROYAL PRISON AND PALACE

In the medieval era, one king after another dug deep into Treasury funds to strengthen fortifications at the Tower of London, while also developing the site as one of the capital city's royal palaces (see also page 278). Henry VIII enjoyed staying at the Tower, as well as despatching his enemies to the prison quarters there. He and his father, Henry VII, enlarged and improved royal accommodation in the Tower enclosure, but they were to be the last English monarchs to use it as a royal residence.

MEDIEVAL FORTIFICATIONS

William Longchamp, Bishop of Ely, serving as regent while King Richard I was on Crusade, enlarged the Tower complex *c*.1190–1200, improving ditch defences to the north and east, building new sections of the wall and erecting the Bell Tower in the south-west. However, these new fortifications did not save Bishop William when the King's brother John besieged him there; through lack of provisions, the bishop was forced to surrender.

Above: This 15th-century manuscript illumination is the earliest detailed image of the Tower. It depicts the imprisonment of Charles, Duke of Orléans.

MAJOR EVENTS AT THE TOWER

1381 Richard II takes refuge in the Tower during the Peasants' Revolt.

1399 Richard II renounces the crown in the White Tower and is succeeded by Henry IV.

1465 and **1470** Edward IV holds court at the Tower.

1471 Henry VI is imprisoned and probably murdered in the Wakefield Tower.

1483 Richard III celebrates his coronation at the Tower; the 'Princes in the Tower', Edward V and his brother Richard, probably meet their end in the White Tower.

1485 Henry VII holds his victory celebrations at the Tower after winning the crown at the Battle of Bosworth.

1535–42 Henry VIII has many notable figures – including Sir Thomas More, Anne Boleyn, Thomas Cromwell and Catherine Howard – imprisoned in the Tower and then executed there.

1554 Lady Jane Grey, queen for nine days, is executed on Tower Green on the orders of Mary I; Mary's half-sister, Princess Elizabeth (the future Elizabeth I), is imprisoned in the Tower.

1601 Elizabeth I's former favourite, Robert Devereux, Earl of Essex, is the last person to be executed on Tower Green, having fallen out of favour with the Queen.

DEFENSIVE TOWERS

In the early years of Henry III's reign, the Wakefield and Lanthorn towers were built on the riverfront, providing royal accommodation for king and queen respectively, while the Great Hall was extended and improved. In *c*.1238–41, Henry III built a new defensive wall along the east, north and west sides of the complex, with nine defensive towers (including the Devereux, Martin and Salt towers at the corners) and a moat on the outside filled from the Thames. Henry's improvements, which cost more

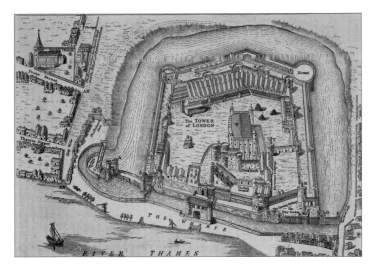

Right: This aerial view of the Tower was made in 1597, late in Elizabeth I's reign, by William Haiward and J. Gascoyne.

than £5,000, doubled the size of the Tower enclosure. He began regular use of the Tower as a prison and kept his extensive menagerie of animals there.

In 1275–85, Edward I further extended the enclosure, filling in his father's moat and building a second curtain wall to create concentric defences. Edward also built Beauchamp, Middle, Byward and St Thomas's towers, as well as a royal mint within the complex. Edward II did little further building work at the Tower, but he did move the royal accommodation from the Wakefield and St Thomas's towers to the Lanthorn Tower.

TUDOR IMPROVEMENTS

Henry VIII carried out extensive improvements to royal lodgings at the Tower. His father, Henry VII, had enlarged the royal accommodation in the Lanthorn Tower, providing a Tudor Long Gallery, a private room and a Library, as well as a garden. Henry VIII liked to stay in the improved Lanthorn Tower. He also built additional royal lodgings near the White Tower, erected the half-timbered King's House, which can still be seen today in the inner bailey's south-west corner, and rebuilt the Chapel Royal of St Peter ad Vincula (St Peter in Chains).

Meanwhile, Thomas Cromwell improved the defences of the fortified complex, and in the reign of Henry VIII the Tower saw many celebrated prisoners go to their deaths. In the space of just seven years, Sir Thomas More, Cardinal John Fisher, Anne Boleyn, Thomas Cromwell and Catherine Howard were all imprisoned in the Tower before their execution.

Above: Traitors' Gate – the riverbank water-gate at the foot of St Thomas's Tower – was built by Edward I in 1275–9.

Left: This view of the Tower from the river shows the Traitors' Gate in the centre foreground. All prisoners disembarked here and entered the Tower through this gate.

SULGRAVE MANOR
AND GEORGE WASHINGTON'S FAMILY

The sturdy, unpretentious manor house at Sulgrave, in Northamptonshire, was built in the early Tudor years by a direct ancestor of George Washington, the first President of the United States of America. Lawrence Washington, younger son of a prominent Lancashire family, was born *c*.1500. He became a wool merchant and bought the Priory of St Andrew, Northampton, from the Crown in 1539, following Henry VIII's Dissolution of the Monasteries.

Below: The compact south front of Sulgrave Manor, built of local limestone by Lawrence Washington, faces a pleasant garden.

THE ORIGINAL BUILDING

After his first wife, Elizabeth, died childless, Lawrence married Amy, daughter of landowner Robert Pargiter, and settled at Sulgrave, where he established Sulgrave Manor, which is a fine example of a smaller Tudor country house.

The house was built of local limestone, with a wide south frontage, a kitchen and buttery, a Great Hall, and above it a Great Chamber and two smaller private chambers. All these parts survive and can be seen today. Finds of what appear to have been Tudor-era foundation stones as much as 50ft (15m) west of the current house suggest that the original dwelling was considerably

Above: George Washington, first President of the United States, traced his family roots to a Northamptonshire manor house.

larger than the surviving house. The Great Hall has a stone floor, and its Tudor fireplace contains a salt cupboard carved with the initials of Lawrence Washington.

'ER' AND STARS AND STRIPES

Lawrence added an entrance porch to the house's south front after 1558. Over the doorway he set in plaster the royal arms of England and the letters 'ER', to indicate 'Elizabeth Regina' in honour of Henry VIII's daughter Elizabeth I, who had ascended to the throne. The doorway spandrels were decorated with the Washington family arms: two stripes and three stars. Some people have suggested that this design was one of the inspirations for the 'stars and stripes' of the American flag.

Lawrence's eldest son, Robert Washington, who was born in 1544, subsequently inherited Sulgrave Manor, along with 1,250 acres (506ha) of farmland. Robert was George Washington's great-great-great-great-grandfather.

HELLEN'S, MUCH MARCLE

The charming country house of Hellen's in the Herefordshire village of Much Marcle near Ledbury was once known as Hellion's Home or Hellinham Castle. It was owned by the lords Audley, earls of Gloucester in the 14th century; a certain Walter Helyon leased the estate and gave his name to the house.

Hellen's lower and older wing contains a venerable Great Hall, refurbished after an 18th-century fire, with a chimney hood decorated with the emblems of the 'Black Prince', son of Edward III. According to tradition, this was fitted in the 14th century by James Audley, companion of the 'Black Prince'. The larger wing is Tudor and contains a splendid oak chimney-piece.

In the 16th century, the then occupier, a Roman Catholic named Richard Walwyn, decorated an upstairs room in this wing with gold and red brocade in honour of Mary Tudor, later Queen Mary I, who was staying nearby in Ludlow Castle. The fireplace is decorated with Mary's initials and coat of arms.

Below: The Great Bedchamber is part of the original manor house rather than the 18th-century extension. This picture is c.1910.

Right: These stained-glass panels feature the Washington and Kitson arms and the Washington and Butler Arms, 1588.

LATER ALTERATIONS

A north wing, set at right angles to Lawrence Washington's manor, was added c.1700 by the then owner, John Hodges. It contains the Great Kitchen and the Oak Parlour, on the ground floor, beneath two sleeping chambers, now known as the White Bedroom and the Chintz Bedroom. Another extension, the west wing, was built in 1929 when the house was being restored.

WASHINGTON'S DESCENDANTS

Lawrence Washington's grandson, another Lawrence, became a rector at Purleigh in Essex. But during the English Civil War, the staunchly royalist Reverend Washington was evicted by Parliament from his living, and died in poverty. His son, John, sailed to the English colony of Virginia in 1656 and married Anne Pope from the Cliffs, a settlement in northern Virginia. They held an estate of 700 acres (385ha) at Mattox Creek Farm. Their eldest son, Lawrence, became a member of Virginia's House of Burgesses and had three children by Mildred Warner. The second, Augustine, was the father of George Washington, the first US President, born on 22 February 1732.

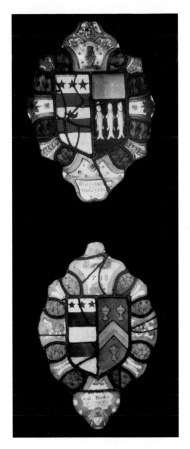

Below: Honouring the Queen. The royal arms of England and the initials 'ER' decorate the south porch, added c.1560.

EDINBURGH CASTLE
AND HOLYROODHOUSE

 Edinburgh Castle was a well-established stronghold and royal dwelling by the latter years of the 14th century, when the future Robert II built David's Tower, containing royal apartments (see page 323). In the mid-1430s, James I built a new Great Chamber, probably alongside the royal accommodation in the Tower. His successor, James II, brought the great siege gun of Mons Meg to the castle, which assumed an increasingly important role as a royal artillery.

GREAT CHAMBER, GREAT HALL
James IV extended the royal accommodation into the southern part of the rocky summit on which the castle stands, reconstructed James I's Great Chamber and built a Great Hall. These two buildings stand along the east and south sides of a courtyard (now Crown Square), with the 14th-century St Mary's Church along the north side (now the Scottish National War Memorial) and artillery buildings to the west. The extended

Below: James V built a Great Tower at the north-west corner of Holyroodhouse in 1528–32 and a new west front in 1535–6.

Left: Edinburgh Castle, on its rocky summit, proved too small for a sufficiently grand royal base, so Scotland's kings instead developed Holyrood Abbey into a palace.

Great Chamber had windows facing east, and must have provided fine views of the burgh below and the countryside beyond. The Great Hall was quite small, at 82 x 32ft (25 x 10m), because its size was limited by its location. It has large mullioned windows on the south side and a hammer-beam roof.

HOLYROODHOUSE
Holyrood Palace was originally part of a monastery. David I founded the Augustinian Priory of the Holy Rude in 1128, and after Edinburgh was made the capital of Scotland in the 15th century, the abbey guest house (Holyroodhouse) was increasingly used

by the royal family, eventually eclipsing the castle as the city's foremost royal residence (see page 404). Set among gardens and orchards, it provided more space and comfort than the cramped royal palace of Edinburgh Castle, perched on its rocky summit above the burgh.

James II was born in Holyroodhouse in October 1430, held his coronation and marriage in the abbey church and was buried there in 1460. James IV built a new palace at Holyrood in 1501–4, but little or nothing survives of this palace, which was extensively rebuilt by James V. In 1528–32, he built a great rectangular tower with round corner turrets as a royal lodging. This impressive building is still standing today in the palace front. Then, in 1535–6, he rebuilt the west wing of James IV's palace, and adapted the north and south wings.

Below: The royal arms of James V of Scots sit proudly on the wall at Holyroodhouse. James was buried in the abbey in 1543.

FALKLAND PALACE
AND STIRLING CASTLE

Falkland Palace began as a castle built by the Macduffs, earls of Fife, probably in the 13th century. James II extended the castle and frequently visited it to hunt deer and wild boar. After 1458, when he granted a charter, it was known as Falkland Palace. James IV built a new palace complex, to the south of the royal castle, in 1501–13; then James V remodelled and rebuilt it, using French and Italian craftsmen, in 1537–41, to create Scotland's first palace in the continental Renaissance style.

James IV's palace was laid out around a courtyard, with a Great Hall on the north side, royal apartments on the east side, and a chapel and vestry to the south; entry was from the west, providing access to the adjacent burgh. James V remodelled the eastern block, building a new front that led on to the courtyard, entirely reconstructing the southern (chapel) section and adding an impressive gatehouse at its west end, designed to function as a new entrance. He also built, in 1539, a real tennis court, to the north of the palace. This can still be seen today and is Scotland's oldest court. James V's daughter, Mary, Queen of Scots, was a frequent visitor to Falkland Palace after her return to Scotland from French exile in 1561.

Below: At Stirling, James V's craftsmen brought the elegance of Italian-French Renaissance architecture to Scotland.

STIRLING CASTLE

At Stirling, James V built a magnificent Renaissance-style palace as part of the royal castle. The original castle was 11th-century and, as at Falkland, was extensively rebuilt by James IV, who built a vast Great Hall c.1498–1503, which measured 128 x 36ft (39 x 11m) and 54ft (16.5m) high, with no fewer than five fireplaces.

In 1538–42, his son, James V, built a lavish three-storey palace within the castle complex, containing apartments for himself and his queen, Mary of Guise. This included an extraordinary Royal Presence Chamber with a ceiling that originally had 100 carved oak heads, some of which survive. The building's principal façade contains tall, elegant windows and niches holding sculptured figures.

Above: Elements of the design at Falkland derive from that of the chateau at Joinville, built by the Duke of Guise in c.1530–40.

RENAISSANCE STYLE

The courtyard façades of the eastern (royal accommodation) and southern (chapel) ranges at Falkland Palace feature bays with medallion heads, dormer windows and statuary. Together, these make an elegant exposition of the latest French-Italian Renaissance style that would have appealed to James V's French wives – first Madeleine of Valois and then Mary of Guise. Scholars compare the bay design to those of the chateaux of Fontainebleu and Villers-Cotterêts, owned by Madeleine's father, the French king, Francis I.

DEAL CASTLE
COASTAL DEFENCES

Henry VIII built the low-lying artillery fort of Deal Castle, in Kent, as one of a string of coastal fortifications built around England's south coast in the later 1530s and early 1540s. Following his break with the Church of Rome, he feared invasion by the armies of a Franco-Spanish Catholic alliance brokered by the Pope.

SOUTH-COAST FORTS

Henry built three forts at Sandown, Deal and Walmer to cover anchorage off the Downs coast. They were built in 18 months using press-ganged labour and stone from local religious houses suppressed by the Dissolution of the Monasteries, including the former Carmelite priory at Sandwich. Earth bulwarks linked the three forts into a single defensive system. Today, little remains of the Sandown fort, and the

Below: Tudor rose or double clover? The coastal fort at Deal in Kent has an impressive outline when viewed from the air.

Above: In the late 1530s, when he built these forts, Henry VIII was in his late 40s, less than a decade from his death (1547).

defences at Walmer were later transformed into a splendid coastal residence, the official dwelling of the Lord Warden of the Cinque Ports, and the place where the Duke of Wellington, holder of this position, died in 1852. But the fort of Deal stands almost exactly as

Henry VIII built it – with the exception of some battlements added in the mid-18th century.

THE TUDOR ROSE

Deal Castle is best viewed from the air. It was designed with a central circular tower and two tiers of semicircular bastions, giving the whole the shape of a double clover-leaf or Tudor rose. The circular walls had the advantage of deflecting cannon shot better than flat ones with vulnerable corners. The fort stood within a wide and deep moat, crossed by a drawbridge. Its entrance was formidable, with a portcullis, five murder-holes giving on to the entrance passageway from above, and an extremely thick oak door studded with iron.

The castle was a vast gun fortification with more than 200 cannon and gun ports, yet it was designed to be garrisoned by just 24 men plus a captain. They were equipped to withstand a siege: the basement contained a well and storage areas for food and drink, while the ground floor housed a bakery

Above: At Pendennis Castle in Cornwall, the gun tower rises above the two-storey block containing the castellan's rooms.

and kitchen. Also on the ground floor were living quarters for the garrison, with more spacious accommodation on the first floor for the captain and also his senior subordinates.

Deal Castle fulfilled its intended primary role as a deterrent and was not attacked in the 1530s. In fact, the only military action it has seen in its entire history was in the English Civil War, when, while originally garrisoned by Parliamentarians, it surrendered to Royalists, and then was besieged and recaptured with a loss of 80 Royalist lives in August 1648.

CORNISH STRONGHOLDS
Henry's coastal forts also included two handsome examples on Falmouth Bay in Cornwall: Pendennis Castle and St Mawes Castle, guarding the entrance to the River Fal estuary. Pendennis Castle was built in 1540–45: it was a keep within a curtain wall on Pendennis Head, with a smaller fortification, Little Dennis, on the rocks at the foot of the promontory. The keep combined a three-storey circular gun tower with a two-storey

rectangular block that contained the accommodation for the castle governor. These buildings were enclosed by a low but stoutly defended curtain wall, and the entrance to the castle was via a drawbridge across a dry moat and guarded by a portcullis.

The headland was enclosed by an outer curtain wall, creating a 4 acre (1.6ha) enclosure, in 1598. This followed Spanish sea raids on Cornwall in 1595 and was carried out amid fears that plans were afoot for a second Armada on the tenth anniversary of the first.

Across the bay, St Mawes Castle consisted of a circular gun tower with

three semicircular bastions around it so that, from above, the structure looked like a clover-leaf. Cannon were positioned on the roof of the tower and on the bastions, and also within the buildings to be fired through gun ports.

THE SIEGE OF PENDENNIS
Pendennis Castle was the last Royalist fort in England to surrender during the Civil War. Sir Thomas Fairfax and the Parliamentarian New Model Army arrived in Cornwall in early March 1646 and took St Mawes Castle without a fight on 12 March. But when he came to Pendennis Castle and demanded the surrender of the garrison, the 70-year-old castle commander, Colonel John Arundell, defiantly declared: 'The Castle was entrusted to my government by His Majesty… my age of 70 calls me hence shortly… I shall desire no other testimony to follow my departure than my… loyalty to His Majesty… I resolve that I will here bury myself before I deliver up this Castle to those who fight against His Majesty.' The siege began, and remarkably the castle, although blockaded by sea and land, survived for nearly five months before surrendering on 17 August. Two days later, Royalist Raglan Castle in Wales also surrendered.

Below: St Mawes Castle was vulnerable to a land attack, but was in an ideal position for defending against invasion by sea.

SYON HOUSE
AND SUDELEY CASTLE

The splendid Syon House, now surrounded by London's westward sprawl at Brentford in Middlesex, was built during the reign of Edward VI by his uncle Edward, Duke of Somerset, Lord Protector. Somerset built a three-storey building with battlements and angle turrets around a central courtyard. His house stood on the foundations of the abbey church that had belonged to the convent on the site.

The Lord Protector also established one of England's first botanical gardens at Syon House, in the care of his personal physician, Dr William Turner.

Below: The 'Wizard' Earl built this superb 136ft (41m) Long Gallery at Syon House in the late 1500s. The sumptuous décor was designed by Robert Adam in the 1760s.

While working on the garden at Syon House, Dr Turner wrote *The Names of Herbes*, published in 1548. Dr Turner is believed to have planted the mulberry trees, introduced to England from Persia (modern Iran) only half a century earlier, that still thrive at Syon House.

A COLOURFUL HISTORY

The land on which Syon House was built had originally belonged to a Bridgettine convent, founded at Twickenham by Henry V in 1415. In the 1530s, the nuns' father confessor, Richard Reynolds, refused to accept Henry VIII's new status as Supreme Head of the Church of England and was brutally executed, his body later placed on the gateway to the abbey. Henry dissolved the Syon convent – named in honour of Mount Zion – and took possession

of the building and lands in 1539. He incarcerated his fifth queen, Catherine Howard, at Syon House prior to her execution in 1542. After his death in 1547, Henry's coffin rested overnight at Syon *en route* from Westminster to Windsor. The next morning, the coffin was found to have burst open, and dogs were gnawing the royal corpse. Some people regarded this as divine retribution for Henry's desecration of the abbey.

Somerset was ousted as Lord Protector in 1549 and executed on trumped-up treason charges in 1552. His successor, John Dudley, Duke of Northumberland, took possession of Syon House. At Syon, Northumberland's daughter-in-law, Lady Jane Grey, agreed to the plan to make her queen on the death of Edward VI. When this scheme

SUDELEY CASTLE, GLOUCESTERSHIRE

The 15th-century Sudeley Castle in Gloucestershire was rebuilt in the late 1540s by Lord Thomas Seymour. Thomas was the brother of the Duke of Somerset, Lord Protector to Edward VI;

Below: Henry VIII, Elizabeth I and Charles I all paid visits to Sudeley. Charles's nephew Prince Rupert had his headquarters there in the Civil War.

their sister, Jane, had been Henry VIII's third wife, who had died giving birth to Edward in 1537, making the brothers the young king's uncles. In addition, Thomas married Henry VIII's sixth wife and widow, Catherine Parr, following the King's death.

Thomas and Catherine moved into Sudeley Castle, where they built a new set of rooms for Catherine's use. She gave birth at Sudeley to Lord Thomas's

Above: Sudeley Castle's 14 acres (6ha) of gardens have been lovingly redeveloped.

daughter, Mary, on 30 August 1548, but died of puerperal fever a week later and was buried in St Mary's Church near the castle.

After Lord Thomas Seymour's execution for treason in 1549, Sudeley Castle eventually passed into the hands of John Brydges, Lord Chandos, who entertained Elizabeth I at the castle three times.

failed, and Edward was succeeded by his sister, Queen Mary I, Northumberland, his son, Lord Guildford Dudley, and Lady Jane herself were all executed.

The Bridgettine nuns briefly came back from exile to live at Syon House under Mary I's rule, but in 1558 were banished once more. Then, in 1594, Syon House came into the possession of Henry Percy, 9th Earl of Northumberland, whose descendants still own the house today.

THE 'WIZARD' EARL

Henry redecorated Syon House internally, built new stables and erected a fine Tudor Long Gallery. Nicknamed 'the Wizard' because of his experiments with alchemy, he was a great scholar, friend of Sir Walter Raleigh and acquaintance of Shakespeare, Ben Jonson and Sir Edmund Spenser. However, on 4 November 1605, he entertained at Syon House a Roman

Catholic cousin, Thomas Percy, who was implicated in the following day's 'Gunpowder Plot' to blow up the Houses of Parliament. Considered guilty by association, Northumberland was thrown into the Tower of London by James I, where he remained for 15 years.

His son Algernon, 10th Earl of Northumberland, commissioned Inigo Jones to design and build an arcade on Syon House's east side. The 10th Earl served as governor of Charles I's son James, Duke of York (the future James II); in 1646, the King's children stayed at Syon House to escape the London plague. The 10th Earl was a great patron of the arts, notably of the artists Sir Anthony van Dyck and Sir Peter Lely.

A NEW LOOK

A little over a century later, in the 1760s, the 1st Duke of Northumberland commissioned Robert Adam to redesign the interior of Syon House (see page

448). He hired 'Capability' Brown to refashion the park. The Duke had inherited the estate through his marriage to the Percy heiress Elizabeth Seymour in 1750. He felt that Syon House, which he considered 'ruinous and inconvenient', needed thoroughly remodelling.

Below: Somerset built Syon House as a castle dwelling, with battlements and turrets. It sits in 40 acres (16ha) of gardens.

CHAPTER EIGHTEEN

'PRODIGY HOUSES': THE AGE OF GLORIANA

*c.*1550–1600

In 1555, leading Elizabethan statesman Sir William Cecil began building a country mansion sufficiently grand to receive and entertain his queen, Elizabeth I. He spared no effort and no expense in creating the magnificent Burghley House in Lincolnshire. At around the same time, his fellow courtier and friend Sir Christopher Hatton was building a similarly extravagant house at Holdenby in Northamptonshire.

Cecil and Hatton were not unusual. Several Elizabethan noblemen sank their wealth into the creation of 'prodigy houses' – country palaces fit for the Queen. Sir William More rebuilt his manor house of Loseley House in Surrey, reputedly on the instructions of Elizabeth herself; the Queen's great favourite, Robert Dudley, Earl of Leicester, lavished funds on Kenilworth Castle in Warwickshire in order to welcome his royal patron there; Sir John Thynne built the magnificent Longleat House in Wiltshire; and Sir Francis Willoughby sank his fortune into the extravagantly ornamented Wollaton Hall in Nottinghamshire. However, not all these houses achieved their objective. Sir William Cecil entertained Elizabeth and her court on 12 occasions at Burghley and his other houses. Elizabeth was entertained at Kenilworth Castle on several occasions, visited Longleat House even before it was finished and stayed at Loseley House at least twice. Yet, despite being a royal favourite, Sir Christopher Hatton – for all his devoted expenditure on Holdenby – was never honoured by a visit from the 'Virgin Queen'.

Left: A house, a prodigy – but not a home. Sir William Cecil was at court so much that he seldom lived at Burghley House.

BURGHLEY HOUSE
'E' FOR ELIZABETH

Sir William Cecil built his extravagant 'prodigy house' on the Burghley estate, which his father, Richard Cecil, had purchased after it had been seized from Peterborough Abbey on the Dissolution of the Monasteries under Henry VIII. Construction took 32 years, from 1555 to 1587.

During this period, Cecil proved an indispensable adviser to Elizabeth I, establishing himself as the leading politician of his day. Born in 1520, he had begun his career as secretary to the Protector, Edward Seymour, Duke of Somerset, during Edward VI's reign; on Elizabeth's accession in 1558, he was appointed Secretary of State, then made 1st Baron Burghley in 1571 and Lord High Treasurer in 1572.

A GIANT 'E'

Cecil was often absent from Burghley House, for his court and diplomatic responsibilities kept him very busy, but the building work was carried out largely according to his designs – with some assistance from a certain Henryk,

PATRONS AND BUILDERS

The great houses of the Elizabethan era did not have architects in the sense in which we use the word. The people responsible for the shape the houses took were the master masons, the surveyors and their patrons, who commissioned the building. The patrons – renowned figures such as Sir William Cecil, Sir Thomas Thynne of Longleat House and Bess of Hardwick, who built Hardwick Hall in Derbyshire – were intimately involved in the design and construction process. The houses were often the three-dimensional stone embodiment of a 'device' or conceit: Burghley House was a giant 'E' to honour Elizabeth, while Hardwick Hall was a Greek cross doubled with a square placed upon it. Such a 'device' would have been the idea of the patron, in a sense their signature, an expression of their character, a

Right: Statesman amd patron. Men such as William Cecil saw a great house as a lasting expression of their character and wit.

statement of their intellectual and artistic prowess. The surveyors and master masons were charged with bringing these ideas into three solid dimensions. Among the surveyors, the greatest was Robert Smythson, who oversaw the building of many of the finest 'prodigy houses', including Longleat House, Hardwick Hall and Wollaton Hall.

an Antwerp mason. In *c.*1555–65, Cecil raised the east side of the house, then proceeded in 1577–87 to lay out the remainder of the house in the shape of a long courtyard, with a Great Hall at one end and a grand gatehouse at the other. The unusually high Great Hall was built with a splendid double-hammer-beam roof and notably elongated windows. Overall, the house took the form of a giant letter 'E' in honour of Elizabeth, although this touch can no longer be appreciated because the north-west wing was demolished in the mid-18th century.

Left: Burghley's size and roofline inspired Daniel Defoe's 1722 remark that it was 'more like a town than a house'.

Few other alterations have been made to the exterior of Burghley House since the completion of Cecil's work. It has splendid façades of hard 'Barnack rag', a limestone quarried nearby in Northamptonshire, with great expanses of glass in its transomed and mullioned windows.

COMPLEX ROOFSCAPE

Burghley has a distinctive silhouette because its skyline is crowded with chimneys, cupolas and obelisks. Its lead roofing covers ¾ acre (over 3,000sq m). When English novelist, Daniel Defoe, visited Burghley House in 1722, he was particularly struck by the roof, which made Burghley look 'more like a town than a house…the towers and pinnacles, so high and placed at such a great distance from one another, look like so many distant parish churches in a town, and a large spire covered with lead, over the clock in the centre, looks like the Cathedral, or chief Church of that town'.

WEALTH OF ART

More than a century after its construction, Burghley's interior was transformed when Sir William Cecil's descendant, the 5th Earl of Exeter, embarked on a redecoration programme of the

public and most important private rooms in the Baroque style. Exquisite plaster ceilings, probably designed by Edward Martin, and delicate carved wood panelling by Thomas Young and Grinling Gibbons were installed. A series of ceiling and wall paintings by the Italian artist Antonio Verrio adorn the suite now known as the George Rooms. His most spectacular work is in the Heaven Room.

Above: The George Rooms (so called because they were decorated for a visit by the Prince Regent) contain paintings by the great Italian baroque artist Antonio Verrio.

The 5th and 9th Earls of Exeter, both great travellers and art collectors, amassed a remarkable collection of paintings now displayed in Burghley House. These include works by Pieter Brueghel, Rembrandt and Thomas Gainsborough, a portrait of Henry VIII by Joos van Cleve, portraits of the 5th Earl and of Antonio Verrio by Sir Godfrey Kneller, and a chapel altarpiece by Veronese.

GATES AND GROUNDS

In the late 17th century, Frenchman Jean Tijou added splendid wrought-iron gates to the principal gatehouse. In the mid-18th century, the 9th Earl of Exeter commissioned Lancelot 'Capability' Brown, both as an architect and to landscape the 300-acre (120ha) park. At this time, the house's north-west wing was demolished to allow better views of Brown's parkland from the south front.

Left: The vast kitchen at Burghley House dates back to Tudor times. It also contains 260 Georgian–Victorian copper utensils.

KENILWORTH CASTLE
ELIZABETH AND LEICESTER

In 1563, Elizabeth I granted Kenilworth Castle, a 12th-century Norman stronghold in Warwickshire, to her great favourite, Robert Dudley, Earl of Leicester. He built a gatehouse and elegant residential quarters to make the historic fortifications sufficiently grand for the Queen. She visited him at Kenilworth Castle in 1566, 1568, 1572 and 1575.

NORMAN ORIGINS
The original castle was built *c.*1122 by Geoffrey de Clinton, King Henry I's Chamberlain, on land granted to him by the King. Geoffrey built a simple motte-and-bailey castle, with a wooden tower enclosed by an earthwork bank. His works were remade in stone, probably by his son, Geoffrey de Clinton II, in the form of a two-storey stone keep with walls up to 20ft (6m) thick covering the original mound.

Above: This aerial view of the ruins of Kenilworth Castle shows the remains of the ornamental gardens laid out by Leicester.

Below: A reconstruction of the estate in the time of Elizabeth I. Leicester's Kenilworth was more country house than castle.

WATER DEFENCES
The castle passed into royal hands, and was greatly extended in 1210–15 by King John, who built an outer wall with defensive towers and a fortified dam that blocked several local streams to create a wide lake around the castle that covered 100 acres (40ha). The water defences played a key role in 1266, during the civil war between King Henry III and his son, Prince Edward, and rebel lords led by Simon de Montfort. The castle had been given to de Montfort by Henry, and when civil war broke out, de Montfort's supporters were besieged by a royalist force. The defenders held out for nine months, finally surrendering with honour. Castle-builders were impressed by the effectiveness of the lake in preventing attackers tunnelling into the castle or undermining its walls.

ONE HUNDRED KNIGHTS
In 1279, Kenilworth Castle was the scene of a famous jousting tournament held by Roger de Mortimer. In celebration of Arthurian chivalry, Roger established a 'Round Table' at the castle, and a company of 100 knights competed before an audience of 100 ladies on the lake dam.

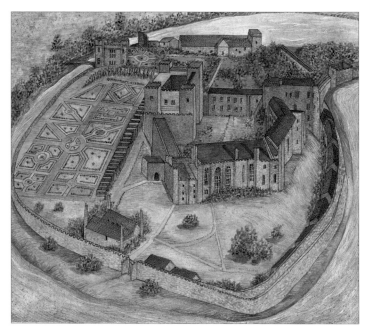

SHAKESPEARE AT KENILWORTH

According to popular tradition, an 11-year-old William Shakespeare travelled from Stratford-upon-Avon to nearby Kenilworth Castle to witness the extravagant theatrical pageantry laid on by the Earl of Leicester for Queen Elizabeth in July 1575.

As part of the extravaganza, Elizabeth watched, and apparently greatly enjoyed, a performance of a play, *The Slaughter of the Danes at Hock Tide*, by an acting troupe named 'The Men of Coventry';

Above: Leicester and Elizabeth — an earl courts a queen in a summer garden. The Arcadian romance that inspired Shakespeare touches the English soul.

there were 'Arcadian' pageants featuring figures from classical mythology and English folklore. Some writers suggest that the magic of Shakespeare's play *A Midsummer Night's Dream* derives in part from his treasured memories of the Queen's visit to Kenilworth Castle.

LEICESTER'S ALTERATIONS

After receiving the castle from Queen Elizabeth I, the Earl of Leicester created a grand entrance via a gatehouse to the north, added numerous windows to the keep, in the process of updating it to make it suitable for entertaining rather than siege defence, and built a residential suite (later known as Leicester's Buildings) to the south of the inner curtain wall. He also laid out a formal Elizabethan garden within the outer bailey.

In 1575, as part of her 'summer progress' around her kingdom, Elizabeth stayed at Kenilworth for 18 days, being entertained at Leicester's expense with pageants, jousting, dancing, theatrical shows, hunting and feasting. Leicester gave Elizabeth an entire wing and even had a garden laid out beneath her bedroom window when she complained of not being able to see the castle gardens from her private chambers. The visit reputedly cost Leicester £1,000 per day.

THE LOSS OF THE LAKE

During the Civil War, Parliamentary forces took the castle, and afterwards the north curtain wall and the keep's north wall were destroyed and the water defences drained. In later years, the castle crumbled into a romantic ruin, with only Leicester's gatehouse remaining habitable. The other major buildings, such as the keep and John of Gaunt's Great Hall, stood as evocative reminders of Kenilworth's importance in the Middle Ages and the Elizabethan age.

The earls of Lancaster came into possession of the castle, and in 1389–94 Edward III's son John of Gaunt, 1st

Below: John of Gaunt's Hall (left) and Leicester's Buildings (right) sandwich the Saintlowe Tower (part of the Great Hall).

Duke of Lancaster, built a magnificent Great Hall and luxurious accommodation in the castle's inner ward. His grandson, Henry V, built a banqueting house at the end of the lake, or Great Mere. Henry VIII later rebuilt this house within the castle precincts.

CRATHES CASTLE
AND THE SCOTTISH TOWER HOUSE

Built by the Burnett family in 1553–94, Crathes Castle in Aberdeenshire is a commanding example of the 16th-century Scottish tower house. In England, the long years of the 'Tudor peace' allowed wealthy merchants and landowners to concentrate on comfort and beauty rather than fortification, to build unfortified country houses rather than castles. But in Scotland, where times remained more turbulent, landowners built tower houses, which combined defensive capabilities with domestic comfort.

Crathes was begun by Alexander Burnett, descendant of the powerful, originally Anglo-Saxon, Burnard family, who were rewarded for service to King Robert I the Bruce with the barony of Leys and the position of Royal Forester in the Forest of Drum. Family legend has

Below: Generations of Burnetts poured their energies into building Crathes Castle. The family lived there until 1966.

it that the Horn of Leys, an ivory hunting horn encrusted with jewels and now displayed in the High Hall of Crathes Castle, was given to a Burnett ancestor, also called Alexander, by the Bruce himself and came with the Forester's office. Crathes Castle was completed by yet another Alexander, great-grandson of the original builder.

GRANITE TOWER

Crathes Castle is a great L-shaped granite tower, its rooms piled one on top of another. The lower parts of the granite walls are plain, and rise, tapering inwards slightly, to finish in a 'fairytale' explosion of gables, corbels and turrets at roof level.

The design of the tower house was dictated partly by defensive needs and partly by the shortage of wood in Scotland. Large roofs required a great deal of timber, so the tower house enclosed a large amount of living space beneath a small roof. At Crathes, the roof covers 1,800sq ft (548sq m); stone

SCOTTISH BARONIAL STYLE

The Scottish tower house was one of the key inspirations for the 'Baronial style' in Scottish architecture that was in vogue from the early 1800s until c.1920. The Baronial style, which also drew key elements from Gothic Revival buildings, used towers with small turrets, stepped gables and crenellations to create the appearance of a 'fairytale castle'. Important examples of the Scottish Baronial style include Balmoral Castle, Skibo Castle in the Highlands and, in a modernized form, Castle Drogo in Devon.

Below: The Baronial-style Castle Fraser near Aberdeen was built by Michael Fraser, 6th Laird, beginning in 1575.

vaulting rather than timber supports the whole of the first floor and most of the second. The High Hall, now floored with modern timber, originally had stone flags. Tower houses typically had a 'barmkin', or defensive wall, enclosing land at their base.

The tower at Crathes originally rose above a side wing erected to provide extra living space. This block was rebuilt as the Queen Anne Wing in the early 18th century by Thomas Burnett, who, as the father of 21 children, was in need of plentiful family accommodation. Thomas also removed the barmkin,

planting Irish yew hedges and an avenue of lime trees in its place. These plantings formed the basis of a beautiful garden developed by Sir James and Lady Burnett in the early 20th century. Unfortunately, Thomas's other legacy, the Queen Anne Wing, burned down in 1966. It was replaced by a modern two-storey range.

PAINTED CEILINGS

Crathes Castle is particularly notable for its original painted ceilings, seen to great advantage in the Chamber of the Muses, the Green Lady's Room and the Chamber of the Nine Worthies. The latter room, completed in 1602, features images of classical figures Julius Caesar, Alexander the Great and the ancient Greek hero, Hector; Old Testament figures Joshua, King David and Judas Maccabeus; and such legendary and historical figures as King Arthur, Charlemagne and Godfrey de Bouillon. An inscription translates as 'Good reader, tell me as you pass, which of these men the most valiant was?' The other ceilings are decorated with figures,

Right: The Chamber of the Nine Worthies at Crathes Castle has a thought-provoking decoration on its beautifully painted ceiling.

Below: The staircase at Craigievar Castle was too narrow for a coffin. So although William Forbes entered the castle by door, he finally had to leave by window.

abstract patterns, moral inscriptions and biblical and poetic quotations. Another fine ceiling, found in the Long Gallery, is panelled in oak and is unique in the whole of Scotland.

HAUNTED ROOM

The Green Lady's Room at Crathes Castle is so called because it is said to be haunted by the ghost of a young woman dressed in green and carrying a baby in her arms. Legend has it that she was a noble guest at the castle who was made pregnant by a servant. An unfortunate event involving the child may once have taken place in the room, for an infant's skeleton was found by workmen beneath the hearthstone.

CRAIGIEVAR CASTLE

Near to Crathes Castle, also in Aberdeenshire, stands the handsome six-storey, pink-granite Craigievar Castle. Finished in 1626, it was built in an L-shape by a prosperous merchant named William Forbes, brother of the Bishop of Aberdeen.

William, known as 'Danzig Willie' because he had made his fortune in trading with that port (now known as Gdansk), had purchased the land and half-finished castle in 1610 from the Mortimer family. He poured his wealth into this magnificent romantic castle, which survives virtually unchanged today as another superb example of the Scots tower house.

LONGLEAT HOUSE
AND THE CLASSICAL RENAISSANCE

Longleat House in Wiltshire, one of the greatest of the 'prodigy houses', was constructed by Sir John Thynne c.1567–80. In 1575, Elizabeth stayed there during her great summer progress.

Thynne, a Shropshire farmer's son, born c.1512, had made his name and fortune during the reigns of Henry VIII and Edward VI. He served Edward Seymour, Earl of Hertford, later Duke of Somerset and Lord Protector in Edward VI's boyhood. Thynne was knighted by Somerset on the battlefield at Pinkie, where the Duke's English troops routed a Scots army under the Earl of Arran on 10 September 1547. When Somerset was disgraced and executed, Thynne was cast in the Tower of London for two years and fined £6,000.

The house in which Elizabeth stayed was Thynne's second on the site. He bought the Augustinian Priory at Longleat for £55 in c.1540 and began building there in 1546. His first house burned to the ground in 1567, but with typical tenacity he began rebuilding it. The design is Thynne's own, although

Above: Tudor majesty. Longleat, celebrated as perhaps England's first classical country house, is largely unchanged externally.

to realize it he employed a number of surveyors, including Frenchman Allan Maynard and Englishman Robert Smythson – the latter subsequently responsible for Hardwick Hall.

Thynne created England's first house in the Italianate, or Renaissance, style. The layout was original: previously most English houses were built around a courtyard, with major rooms looking inwards on to this central space, or in the shape of an 'E', with two end wings

and an entrance porch creating the form of the letter. Thynne, however, built a great cube, with all the major rooms facing outwards towards the surrounding park, and the inner courtyards functioning only to admit light.

CLASSICAL FAÇADE
Longleat's square outline and decorative elements are derived from classical models. Its façade contains a large number of bay windows, a design inspired by French chateaux, and incorporates the first three classical 'orders'. Beneath the windows are round recesses to hold busts of Roman emperors. Cornices run between the floors, and at roof level there is a balustrade. On the roof are domed turrets intended to be used as intimate banqueting houses. Thynne used the best 'Bath stone' from a quarry at Box, which he bought for the purpose.

LATER ALTERATIONS
When Elizabeth visited in 1575, only eight years after Thynne had begun rebuilding following the fire, the house stood just two storeys tall. The third level, with Corinthian elements on the façade, was probably added after John Thynne's death, in May 1580, by his son, another John. Since then the exterior of Longleat House has survived largely unchanged, except for elements in the Baroque style that were added in the 1690s, when a doorway was built and four very fine statues were added to the balustrade.

Within the house, most of the rooms were altered in the 19th century; only the magnificent Great Hall survives largely as it was in Thynne's day. This cavernous room is 35ft (11m) high,

Left: Longleat's interior is much altered. The sweeping Grand Staircase is part of the early 19th-century alterations carried out by Sir Jeffry Wyatville.

Above: Beauty well maintained. In 1689, Henry Thynne, brother of Lord Weymouth, wrote that the house's condition was 'so excellent it makes my mouth water'.

with a vast hammer-beam roof. The elegant carved chimneypiece, Minstrels' Gallery and screen were added around 20 years after Thynne's death, *c*.1600. The Small Gallery dates to 1663, and was built for a visit by Charles II and Queen Catherine just three years after the Restoration. It was Charles II who granted the Thynne family the title of Lord Weymouth. In the years after 1806, most of the other rooms at Longleat were redecorated by Sir Jeffry Wyatville (see page 465). Further sumptuous redecoration and remodelling was carried out in the 1870s by J.D. Crace.

In the surrounding park, formal gardens were established in the 1690s by George London (d.1714), who also worked at Hampton Court Palace. These were removed by Lancelot 'Capability' Brown, hired in 1757 by the then current Lord Weymouth to landscape the grounds.

BISHOP KEN'S LIBRARY

Longleat is also famous for its libraries. The family's book and manuscript collection was begun by John Thynne's uncle, William, a clerk in Henry VIII's kitchens. Perhaps surprisingly for one so parsimonious, John Thynne himself greatly expanded it, and by 1577 the collection at Longleat numbered 85 books and manuscripts – a large number for that time. Today, there are eight libraries at Longleat, including the beautiful Bishop Ken's Library, which runs on the top floor along the entire east front of the house. It is named after Thomas Ken, Bishop of Bath and Wells, who was a friend of the Lord Weymouth of his day, and retired to Longleat in 1691 after he was deprived of his bishopric for refusing to swear the required oath of allegiance to William and Mary.

IN THE MODERN ERA

Longleat House made its mark in the 20th century by becoming, in a blaze of publicity in 1947, the first privately owned stately home to be opened to the paying public. Thereafter, it continued to pioneer new ways of funding its upkeep: in the 1960s, a safari park was opened in the grounds and the house's name became associated with the lions that roam there. Longleat also has a splendid, very challenging 1½ acre (0.6ha) maze, designed by Greg Bright.

THE THREE 'ORDERS' AT LONGLEAT

Longleat's façade incorporated the first three classical 'orders', or column styles, of ancient Greece and Rome: the Doric, the Ionic and the Corinthian. The house follows the style established by ancient Roman builders of using the columns as decorative features on a façade, running them upwards from ground to roof level: Doric at ground level, Ionic in the middle and Corinthian on the second storey. Longleat is hailed as the first English house to employ the classical orders conspicuously revived in Italy during the Renaissance and advocated in the architectural literature of the 16th century.

Right: Note the round recesses beneath the windows. These were intended to hold busts of Roman emperors.

HARDWICK HALL
'MORE GLASS THAN WALL'

Famously declared to be 'more glass than wall', Hardwick Hall is celebrated above all for its west front, with its glittering array of symmetrically marshalled windows. This bold and over-stated exterior conceals many subtle beauties within: its Long Gallery, at 166ft (50.5m) the second longest in Britain, and its elegant High Great Chamber, declared by Sir Sacherevell Sitwell to be 'the most beautiful room, not in England alone, but in the whole of Europe'.

BESS OF HARDWICK
Hardwick is an enduring monument to the pride and self-belief of its builder, Bess of Hardwick, who rose from fairly humble origins to a position of immense wealth and transcended the architectural fashions of the time to create a highly original house.

Bess, or Elizabeth, was born c.1520 to a squire of modest means. She made her first fortune through marriage at the age of 12 to Robert Barlow, a local man only two years older, who died within a few months of the wedding. Around 15 years later, she married Sir William Cavendish,

Above: Elizabeth's family portraits decorate the suitably grand Long Gallery in the East Front. It has an elegant plaster ceiling.

a very wealthy gentleman who served as Treasurer of the Chamber at the court of Henry VIII. Sir William bought a house at Chatsworth in Derbyshire and rebuilt it in a grand manner befitting his station. His death, in 1557, left Elizabeth hugely wealthy and in possession of several fine properties besides Chatsworth. In 1560, she married Sir William St Loe, Captain of the Queen's Guard, and when he too died, c.1565, Bess was wealthier still.

Her fourth and final marriage, to George Talbot, 6th Earl of Shrewsbury, was her grandest. He too predeceased her, on his death in 1590 leaving an immense inheritance that made Bess one of England's richest women. At the age of 70, Bess, rich enough to leave her mark in some style, set about building Hardwick Hall close to the site of the Old Hall at Hardwick in which she had been born.

This new building, designed to Bess's exacting demands by Robert Smythson, veteran of Longleat House, was built in just six years (1591–7). It was intended to demonstrate in stone and glass how far Bess had risen. Proud of her Shrewsbury title, she had the initials 'ES' ('Elizabeth Shrewsbury') cut beneath a countess's coronet on the house's skyline.

IMPORTANCE OF SYMMETRY
The house took the form of a three-storey rectangular block, with six four-storey towers arranged around it. It relies for its effect on glass: there is

EMBROIDERED DECORATION

Even the grandest Elizabethan houses generally had little furniture beyond a few tables, chairs, cupboards and chests for storage. These palaces of the nobility were decorated within using panelling, plasterwork, tapestry and needlework. Hardwick Hall is particularly known for its magnificent embroidery on curtains, wall hangings, cushion covers, upholstery and bedspreads. A fine example is on the bedhead in the State Bedroom.

Left: The monogram 'ES' for 'Elizabeth Shrewsbury' appears in this embroidered velvet hanging from Hardwick Hall.

little surface decoration on the house's exterior and the windows have no borders, while the mullions and transoms are kept thin, emphasizing the reflective expanses of window glass. Bess and Smythson put symmetry above all else in the design of the façades; in places, changes in floor level cut across the inside of the great windows.

Within, the two-storey hall is set at an angle of 90 degrees to the main front rather than parallel to it, as was usual with medieval halls. A magnificent, meandering, superbly wide stone staircase leads up to the High Great Chamber. This extraordinary reception room was built to hang eight vast Brussels tapestries, showing the story of wandering Greek hero, Ulysses, that Bess had bought in 1587. They hang beneath a painted plaster frieze representing Diana, the chaste Roman

Below: Hardwick Hall's famous West Front. Each of the six rooftop pavilions has 'ES' ('Elizabeth Shrewsbury') carved into it.

hunting goddess, surrounded by animals, nymphs and trees. We know from surviving documents that the beautiful frieze was created by an otherwise unknown craftsman named Charles Williams, who was identified by Bess as a 'cunning plasterer'.

VAST LONG GALLERY
By the time Bess was building Hardwick Hall, the Long Gallery was a Tudor innovation that had become an essential feature of any great house. It was a kind of indoor promenade, used for the display of portraits and tapestries hung along the gallery walls and for the gentle exercise of guests as they walked up and down the immensely elongated room. At Hardwick, the Long Gallery extends along the entire east front. Lit by 20 tall windows, it is hung with beautiful Flanders tapestries and portraits of Bess, her husbands and children, as well as of various entrepreneurs, including Elizabeth I, Mary, Queen of Scots, the Earl of Leicester and others.

Above: Hardwick's unusual shape – a long three-storey rectangle with six four-storey towers – can be seen in this aerial view. The house stands in 300 acres (120ha) of park.

MAPLEDURHAM HOUSE
THE REAL TOAD HALL

 This handsome Elizabethan country house is the heart of the tiny Oxfordshire village of Mapledurham. It lies near the River Thames and has a remarkably well-preserved working 15th-century water mill on the estate. The house was built in 1588, the year of the Spanish Armada, by Sir Michael Blount, Lieutenant of the Tower of London. It incorporated parts of a 12th-century timber-framed manor house. Sir Michael's grandfather, Richard Blount, had purchased the estate in 1490.

Sir Michael chose warm, rose-red bricks for his house, and his craftsmen achieved attractive patterns in the brickwork. In its essential aspects, the house's

exterior is unchanged since the Elizabethan era. The Blount family were Roman Catholics, and an interesting feature is the gable decorated with oyster shells at the back of the house – once an accepted signal that a house was a safe refuge for Catholics.

ALEXANDER POPE

In the early 18th century, poet Alexander Pope, a friend of the Blount sisters, Teresa and Martha, was a frequent visitor to Mapledurham House. Pope played a part in the redesign of the grounds there, introducing William Kent to the family for the commission, which included introducing a 'ha ha' (a sunken boundary, here in the form of a concealed ditch) to create an uninterrupted view of the eastern approach, and to plant a natural-looking 'Pleasure Ground' to the north.

After the Catholic Relief Act of 1791 lifted most of the sanctions against practising Catholics that had been in place since Henry VIII's time, the Blounts built a pretty family chapel in Mapledurham House in 1797. They used the then popular 'Strawberry Hill

Above: Mapledurham is a fine example of the lesser Elizabethan country house.

Gothic style', so called after Horace Walpole's house at Twickenham of 1753–78.

Mapledurham originally contained a splendid Great Hall, but this was refashioned as an entrance hall in 1828. By the fireplace are two remarkable wooden deer, carved from a single tree.

Below: The original 15th-century roof and wall timbers survive amid 17th-century additions in the Mapledurham water mill.

TOAD HALL?

Kenneth Grahame, author of children's classic *The Wind in the Willows* (1908), lived close to Mapledurham House at Pangbourne and loved the nearby stretch of the River Thames. E.H. Shepard, who provided the famous illustrations for Grahame's book, is believed to have used Mapledurham House as the model for Toad Hall.

Below: Kenneth Grahame first wrote parts of his book in letters to his partially sighted son, Alistair.

LOSELEY PARK
AND QUEEN ELIZABETH'S PROGRESS

In 1562, leading courtier and trusted royal adviser Sir William More began to rebuild his Surrey manor house at the request of Elizabeth I herself. Like many Tudor landowners, he profited from the Dissolution of the Monasteries, building his 'prodigy house' using blocks of worked stone from the suppressed Cistercian monastery at Waverley Abbey nearby. This stone had first been used 450 years earlier, and must have given his house an established and age-mellowed appearance even when it was newly built.

Sir William constructed a dignified and handsome country house that has survived largely unaltered to the present day. Above the doorway he carved the motto *Invidiae claudor, pateo sed semper amico* ('Envy is barred, but friendship always welcomed'). Elizabeth evidently appreciated Sir William's hospitality and his company, for she visited Loseley House four times. Nor was she the last royal to do so, for James I was a guest of

Below: Tradition comes to the fore in the handsome Great Hall at Loseley, with its family portraits, antlers and fine furniture.

Above: The Holbein fireplace and the gilded ceiling make grand companions in Loseley Park's remarkable Drawing Room.

Sir George More on two occasions, and many years later, in 1932, Queen Mary also visited Loseley.

INNER BEAUTIES

The high-ceilinged Great Hall has a splendid oriel window with heraldic glass and Tudor panelling believed to have been removed from Henry VIII's peerless Nonsuch Palace. In the beautiful wood-panelled library, Elizabeth's initials and arms are carved in the overmantel.

Above: Loseley Park's name is associated with the dairy products once made from the milk produced by its cows.

The Drawing Room has a breathtaking and unique fireplace cut from a single block of chalk to a design by Hans Holbein and a superb gilded ceiling that was installed for the visits of James I. In return, James gave the More family a portrait of himself and Queen Anne of Denmark, which can be seen in the Great Hall.

LATER ALTERATIONS

A new wing was added to Sir William's house *c.*1600, containing a gallery with extra rooms and a riding school. But this wing was demolished in 1820 after it had fallen into a poor condition. Then, in 1877, William More-Molyneux built a nursery wing on the house's south side.

The 21st-century occupants of the house, the More-Molyneuxs, are direct descendants of its 16th-century builder. Their estate of 1,400 acres (565ha) is partly occupied by a celebrated Jersey herd from whose milk the well-known Loseley Jersey ice cream was made. However, the Loseley dairy products are no longer made at the Loseley estate, the brand having been sold to Booker Plc in 1985.

CAREW CASTLE
AND THE WELSH COUNTRY HOUSE

The first stronghold on the site of Carew Castle, near Pembroke in South Wales, was an Iron Age Celtic fort. This was followed by a Norman timber and earthwork stronghold built in 1095 by Gerald de Windsor, a knight who held nearby Pembroke Castle from Henry I. Nothing remains of Gerald's fortress, but part of the east front probably dates from the 12th century. In the inner ward, the Old Tower was added in the early 13th century. A first-floor Great Hall, the Chapel Tower and the South-east Tower were erected in the late 13th century and the gatehouse was built in the early 14th century. This work was carried out by Sir Nicholas de Carew, who also raised a curtain wall to enclose the outer bailey.

Above: At Carew, the Elizabethan wing (with windows) is to the left; the rounded towers on the right are late 13th century.

SIR RHYS AP THOMAS

In the late 15th and early 16th centuries, Sir Rhys ap Thomas, an important Welsh ally of Henry VII who had acquired the castle in 1480 from a Carew lord, made

Below: The solid rooms at Carew Castle were visited by Tudor royalty. Henry VII attended Sir Rhys's grand 1507 celebration.

many further improvements, adding a second Great Hall, stairs and splendid accommodation. It was in Carew Castle that Henry Tudor stayed in 1485, while passing through Wales on his way to the Battle of Bosworth, where he won the crown. On the battlefield, Henry knighted Rhys and made him Governor of Wales. In 1507, Sir Rhys threw a lavish celebration at Carew to celebrate the early triumphs of the Tudor dynasty.

SIR JOHN PERROT

Tudor courtier and statesman 'Good Sir John' Perrot received the lordship and castle of Carew from Queen Mary in 1558, and in 1559, at Elizabeth I's coronation, he was one of the four bearers of her 'canopy of state'. He rose to high position under Elizabeth, who granted him governorship of Carew, serving the Queen first as Lord of Munster and then as Lord Deputy of Ireland. He added a

Below: This interior view of steep steps and low doorways at Carew gives a sense of what life was like within a medieval or Tudor castle.

Above: Laugharne Castle occupies a cliff, the site of a Norman ringwork, looking out across the estuary of the River Taf.

magnificent three-storey wing containing a majestic second-floor Long Gallery that ran for 130ft (40m). In its impressive, typically Elizabethan façade were two rows of big rectangular windows as well as two large oriel windows. Like the rest of this once-proud castle, it is now a sad ruin.

A man of fiery temper known for his 'majesty of personage', Perrot was rumoured at court to be an illegitimate son of Henry VIII, and, judging from his portraits, he certainly looked like the King. But his proud manner made him many enemies and he was convicted of high treason in 1591, before dying of natural causes the following year during imprisonment in the Tower of London.

LAUGHARNE AND POWIS

'Good Sir John' also refashioned and rebuilt the castle at Laugharne, in South Wales, into an Elizabethan country mansion after he was given the fortress by Elizabeth I in 1575. However, his work there apparently fell to ruin within a few years of his death in 1592, and most of what is visible today at Laugharne dates from the castle's earlier history.

A COUNTRY HOUSE CASTLE

Powis Castle in central Wales was another military stronghold upgraded to become a fine Elizabethan country house. This attractive battlemented building, celebrated above all for its magnificent terraced gardens, has seen many refurbishments, most recently in the early 20th century. In the Tudor era, Sir Edward Herbert, who gained ownership of Powis in 1578 and whose family still live there, undertook extensive rebuilding and modernization work in 1587–95. All that survives today is the Long Gallery, although the castle still has several rooms with Elizabethan furnishings.

Below: Powis Castle stands on a commanding hilltop, its steep south-east approaches today occupied by gardens.

MONTACUTE HOUSE
AND WOLLATON HALL

In the 1590s, Somerset landowner Sir Edward Phelips began building Montacute House from beautiful honey-coloured limestone quarried at nearby Ham Hill. He employed a gifted Somerset master mason, William Arnold, who must take a great deal of the credit for Montacute, and who later worked at Cranbourne Manor in Dorset for Robert Cecil, 1st Earl of Salisbury.

Below: The end of the east front at Montacute House, with its curved Flemish gables, slender chimneys and large windows.

Above: The salvaged archway from Clifton Maybank makes a grand entrance in the centre of the west front at Montacute House.

Sir Edward needed a house grand enough to match his position, for he was a leading lawyer and politician in London. An MP from 1584, he was elected Speaker of the House of Commons in 1604. As a lawyer, he made the opening speech for the prosecution at the trial of Guy Fawkes after the discovery of the 'Gunpowder Plot' to blow up the Houses of Parliament in 1605.

THE ENTRANCE FRONT

With William Arnold, Phelips created a remarkable east entrance front at Montacute. The façade, 90ft (27m) high and almost 200ft (60m) across, is another Elizabethan 'wall of glass': it contains 39 mullioned windows, arranged in three perfectly symmetrical tiers. These straight horizontal lines are brought to life by the curves of the Flemish gables, the vertical lines of the slender chimneys on the roof above and a wealth of carved detail in the façade itself, including curved cornices on some of the windows and circular recesses that probably once held terra-cotta medallions. A delightful touch is

Above: An oak bedstead at Montacute is carved with the arms of James I and of Frederick V, Elector Palatine of the Rhine.

WOLLATON HALL, NOTTINGHAMSHIRE

The great Elizabethan surveyor Robert Smythson, who worked at Longleat House as well as Hardwick Hall, built the ravishing Wollaton Hall in Nottinghamshire for Sir Francis Willoughby in 1580–88. He used Italian master masons and probably worked to the designs of celebrated artist John Thorpe, based on those of Sir Francis himself. This elegant 'prodigy house' is highly ornamented: the four large corner towers are topped with pinnacles and the façades incorporate niches filled with the busts of great philosophers. In the centre of the house, the hall is elevated above the surrounding wings. Wollaton Hall is reputed to have cost the astonishing sum of £80,000 to build.

Left: At Wollaton Hall the central hall rises above the rest of the house; its four square corner towers rise to pinnacles.

the inclusion between the windows of the top storey of statues representing the 'Nine Worthies', here in the guise of Roman centurions. All the detail is in the same rich-coloured Ham Hill limestone as the main house.

A grass forecourt with side flowerbeds extends before the east front and is enclosed by a low wall. Two delicate corner pavilions have domed roofs and oriel windows on all four sides. Originally, a grand gatehouse stood in the centre of the front wall between the two pavilions, but it has been demolished.

Montacute contains the longest of all Elizabethan Long Galleries: the top-floor 'promenade' runs 172ft (52m) along the entire length of the house, and is 20ft (6m) across. Groups of connected rooms lead off either end of the gallery. Today it houses a splendid selection of 100 Tudor and Jacobean portraits from the collection of the National Portrait Gallery in London.

Aside from the Long Gallery, Montacute's finest room is certainly the Library, originally the Great Chamber. The panes of heraldic glass in the windows, the chimney-piece of Portland stone, a fine plasterwork frieze and the beautiful 16th-century wood panelling on the walls are all original.

WEST FRONT AND GARDENS

In 1786–7, Edward Phelips changed the entrance front to the west side. He salvaged a beautiful stone porch from a Tudor house at Clifton Maybank in Somerset that was being pulled down, and had it fitted into the centre of the front. The porch is made from the same stone as Montacute, and although it was made around 50 years before Montacute, its detail fits its new setting perfectly.

Ornamental gardens with elegant lines of yew trees lie to the north and south ends of the house. In the fore court on the east front (the original entrance), are two flowerbeds planted in the 1950s to designs by Vita Sackville-West, poet, novelist and gardener.

Below: A late 19th-century watercolour shows one of the graceful domed pavilions in Montacute's formal east garden.

CHAPTER NINETEEN

THE JACOBEAN COUNTRY HOUSE

c.1600–c.1650

In 1616, Inigo Jones, recently appointed Surveyor of Works to King James I, began work on the Queen's House in Greenwich for James's wife, Anne of Denmark. Jones had recently returned from a visit to Rome, during which he had studied ancient Roman buildings and the work of Italian Renaissance architects, including Andrea Palladio and Vincenzo Scamozzi. Jones introduced 'classical' architectural design – inspired by Renaissance and ancient Roman buildings – into England.

As well as being England's first classical architect, he was a major influence on the 'Palladian' movement of the 18th century, in which architects returned to Palladio as a source of inspiration.

The elegant Queen's House was abandoned when Anne died in 1619 and only finished in 1635 for Charles II's queen, Henrietta Maria. In the mean time, Inigo Jones had designed and built the magnificent Banqueting House in the royal palace of Whitehall and the Queen's Chapel, St James's, and worked on or supervised country houses at New Hall, Essex, Stoke Bruerne, Northamptonshire, and Chevening, Kent. The career of Inigo Jones was a turning point in English architecture: the domestic tradition had come to a final flowering with acclaimed Jacobean houses such as Hatfield House, built in 1608–11; in contrast, the superb south front built in 1636–40 at Wilton House, Wiltshire, designed under Jones's supervision, showed a new way forward. It used a classical design, with devices such as the central window with carved figures that were taken directly from Jones's royal buildings in London, inspired in their turn by the designs of Scamozzi in Rome.

Left: Paintings by Sir Peter Paul Rubens were fitted in 1635 into the beamed ceiling of Inigo Jones's superb Banqueting House, Whitehall, completed in 1622.

KNOLE
HOME OF VITA SACKVILLE-WEST

The vast and historic country house of Knole, Sevenoaks, in Kent, was largely created by two men – Thomas Bourchier, a 15th-century Archbishop of Canterbury, and Thomas Sackville, 1st Earl of Dorset – in the early reign of King James I. This palatial house of grey Kentish ragstone with brown roof-tiles, so extensive that from a distance it resembles a village or small town, has remained largely unaltered since the sensitive external alterations and large-scale internal reworking carried out by Thomas Sackville around 400 years ago.

Sackville descendants have lived in Knole for over 400 years, and still inhabit part of the mansion today, although the house has been owned, managed and maintained by the National Trust since 1946.

Below: Knole's beautiful staircase, installed by Thomas Sackville, leads up to the equally grand Ballroom. Note the Sackville leopard atop the newel post (right).

HOUSE OF POETS

Thomas Sackville (1536–1608) was a poet and dramatist in his youth before settling into political life, and he co-wrote with Thomas Norton the first tragic play in English, *Gorboduc* or *Ferrex and Porrex*. The play, which describes conflicts among legendary rulers of ancient Britain, was performed on Twelfth Night 1561 in the Inner Temple Hall, London. Over the centuries, Sackville's house had many admirers. Edmund Burke declared it 'the most interesting thing in England'. Vita Sackville West (1892–1962) was born and lived there before her marriage to Harold Nicholson. Her sometime lover

Right: Vita Sackville West loved the colours of Knole. She wrote, "It is above all an English home ... It has the tone of England; it melts into the green of the garden turf."

and close friend Virginia Woolf used Knole as the setting for her novel *Orlando* (1928). Vita herself used the house as the setting for a novel, *The Edwardians* (1930), and wrote a book about the house, *Knole and the Sackvilles*, published in 1922.

MEDIEVAL AND TUDOR PALACE

Thomas Bourchier bought the estate at Knole with its 13th-century house in 1456 for £266. Over the next three decades, he reconstructed and extended it into a grand episcopal palace with seven interconnecting courtyards, including two extensive quadrangles – the Stone Court and the Green Court – which stand one in front of the other at the entrance. In line with 15th-century practice, his house made at least a show of fortification, with extensive battlements on walls and towers, as well as two gatehouses. On the inner gatehouse, known as 'Bourchier's Tower', there is decorative machicolation.

Knole was the palace of five archbishops of Canterbury, from Thomas Bourchier to Thomas Cranmer. After Cranmer it passed to King Henry VIII in 1538, and was a royal palace for 28 years until Elizabeth I gave it to

Thomas Sackville in 1566. The house was on lease until the year of Elizabeth's death, and so Sackville did not start his work on Knole until 1603, when he transformed the interior and made a series of well-judged alterations to the outer fabric that greatly accentuated its overall attractiveness.

SACKVILLE'S ALTERATIONS

To soften the house's fortress-like appearance, Thomas Sackville added mullioned windows and curved gables in the Flemish style, with decorative finials in the likeness of the leopards from the Sackville crest. In the Stone Court, he built a fine colonnade with a gallery above it.

Internally, he remodelled the Great Hall of 1460, adding a lower, plastered ceiling and a sumptuously carved oak screen. He added a beautiful timber Great Staircase, painted by artist Paul

Above: A great part of Knole's appeal lies in the fact that its exterior today looks largely as it did in the time of King James I.

Isaacson in yellows and greens, with a number of visual effects, including *trompe l'oeil* images of the balustrade on the walls, which were startlingly original at the time. The staircase, which has Sackville leopards above its newel posts, led to the Ballroom, where Sackville installed an extraordinary alabaster and marble chimney-piece and over-mantel made by Cornelius Cuer, royal master mason. This extravagantly grand room, which also features glorious painted oak panelling depicting mermaids and mermen, served as a reception chamber and dining room.

Sackville also built three grand galleries, including the Cartoon Gallery, with another splendid Jacobean ceiling and chimney-piece. The gallery takes it name from the copies of Raphael's cartoons (designs for paintings) made by artist Daniel Mytens, who was court painter to Charles I.

The cycles of time take solid form in this outstanding house. In addition to seven courtyards, for the days of the

Right: Thomas Sackville built the Cartoon Gallery in the 1600s, but the six copies of Raphael's cartoons were fitted in 1701.

week, there are said to be 52 staircases, for the weeks of the year, and 365 rooms, for the days of the year. Many have commented on Knole's very English beauty and atmosphere. The poet and novelist Vita Sackville West, who grew up there, said Knole had 'a deep inward gaiety' and likened the house to 'some very old woman who has always been beautiful, who has had many lovers and seen many generations come and go … and learnt an imperishable secret of tolerance and humour'.

LATER CHANGES

Since Thomas Sackville's changes, there have been some alterations to the house's furnishings and its decorative schemes, although the prevailing style remains Tudor and Jacobean. In the late 17th century, Thomas's great-great-grandson, Charles, 6th Earl of Dorset, added fine furniture and textiles. Then, around a century later, John Frederick, 3rd Duke of Dorset, installed many Old Masters that he had purchased during a Grand Tour of continental Europe.

HATFIELD HOUSE
HOME OF THE CECIL FAMILY

Robert Cecil, 1st Earl of Salisbury, had little choice when King James I 'suggested' that they swap houses. James would take for himself the beautiful Theobalds in Hertfordshire, built by Robert's father, William Cecil, Lord Burghley, and would give Robert the nearby royal palace of Hatfield.

The Tudor palace at Hatfield was built *c.*1485 by Cardinal John Morton, Bishop of Ely and later Archbishop of Canterbury under King Henry VII. Henry VIII seized it and used it mainly as a home, often effectively a prison, for his children. The future Elizabeth I spent most of her childhood at Hatfield, where she was told the news that her elder sister, Mary, had died, making her Queen of England. In her first act as Queen, Elizabeth appointed William Cecil her Principal Secretary, then held her first Council meeting in Hatfield's Great Hall.

The tower and Great Hall of the 15th-century palace are all that survive, for in 1607–08 Robert Cecil pulled

Below: A new direction? The tower, arcade, gables and forecourt point forward to the classical architecture of Inigo Jones – some say Jones himself designed the arcade.

down three sides of the original building as he set about constructing a new residence, devising his own floor plans and designs.

ROYAL VISITORS
Like Burghley House and the other great 'prodigy houses' of the Elizabethan reign, Hatfield was designed to be a fitting venue for entertaining the monarch. A central block contained the main staterooms used for receiving and entertaining guests: there was a Great Hall in the centre, with a Long Gallery and four great rooms on the upper floor; the chapel stood at the side. This central building was flanked by two wings containing apartments for royal visitors: the queen in the west wing and the king on the east side. Terraced gardens were laid out complete with a lake and fountains, and with rare plants and trees imported from continental Europe by the botanist John Tradescant.

The house was completed in four years (1607–11), but Robert Cecil died the following year. In later years, his house was often visited by kings and queens, including James I, Charles I, James, Duke of York (the future James II) and Queen Victoria and Prince Albert.

Above: Among the many treasures at Hatfield is this genealogical chart that purports to trace Elizabeth I's descent from Adam.

CONTRASTING STYLES
The north and south front are in contrasting styles. The north front, of red brick with symmetrical lines of wide windows, providing an essentially flat surface varied by shallow bays, appears to be in a familiar domestic 'Tudor' style. The south front, however, has two projecting wings forming a forecourt,

an elegant arcade in the Italian style, a delicate white tower and Flemish gables. Cecil's surveyor was Robert Lyminge and the master mason a certain Conn; Inigo Jones may have contributed to the stone forecourt on the south front. French, English and Flemish craftsmen were hired. They used bricks from the demolished wings of the Tudor palace, stone from Caen in Normandy and the finest marble from Carrara in Tuscany.

PORTRAITS OF A QUEEN
Hatfield House contains two of the most celebrated portraits of Elizabeth I. The first is the 'Ermine Portrait' by Nicholas Hilliard, so called because an ermine (an animal symbolic of royalty) is portrayed with the Queen; this hangs in the Marble Hall. The second is the 'Rainbow Portrait', probably by Hilliard's pupil, Isaac Oliver, but sometimes attributed to Marcus Gheeraerts the Younger. This is a veritable riot of symbolism, in which Elizabeth is shown wearing a gown embroidered with English wildflowers and holding a rainbow, symbolic of peace.

Below: The 'Rainbow Portrait' of Queen Elizabeth I.

Hatfield House contains two splendid examples of Jacobean style at its most flamboyant: the Grand Staircase, which is fitted with 'dog gates' to prevent animals going up, and is made of intricately carved oak, and the exuberantly decorated Marble Hall, which is often identified by architectural historians as the last great medieval hall in an English house. Also of note is the beautiful original stained glass, depicting Old Testament scenes, fitted in the chapel in 1609.

PROMINENT CECILS
Hatfield House has remained through the centuries in the hands of the Cecils, who, in the late 19th century, rose once again to great prominence – Robert Arthur Talbot Gascoyne-Cecil, 3rd Marquess of Salisbury, was leader of the Conservative Party and three times Prime Minister.

Below: The gardens at Hatfield House were restored in the Victorian era. They include herb gardens and orchards as well as terraces.

BOLSOVER CASTLE
SMYTHSON'S LAST HOUSE

Bolsover Castle, near Chesterfield in Derbyshire, was the last major house designed by the leading surveyor of the Elizabethan age, Robert Smythson. He began work at Bolsover for Sir Charles Cavendish in 1612.

The first castle on the site, a stone keep with a curtain wall, had been built by William Peverel (an illegitimate son of William the Conqueror) in the 12th century. But it was little more than a ruin by the mid-16th century, when it was bought by George Talbot, 6th Earl of Shrewsbury and fourth husband of Bess of Hardwick. He leased the castle in 1608 to his stepson, Sir Charles Cavendish. Sir Charles bought the house in 1613.

A FANTASY CASTLE

Sir Charles Cavendish and Robert Smythson built a delightful fantasy castle, an embodiment of Elizabethan-Jacobean ideals of chivalry. The tower keep,

Below: Bolsover Castle occupies a hilltop and commands fine views of the countryside – especially from the Terrace Range.

completed after Smythson's death in 1621, is today called 'the little castle'. It contains a series of elaborately decorated panelled rooms, with allegorical wall paintings and magnificent marble fireplaces. These rooms include the famous Star Chamber, Pillar Chamber, Elysium Chamber and Heaven Chamber. It gives on to a court with a central fountain (the Fountain Court). Tower and court occupy the site of William Peverel's original keep and inner bailey, and some parts of the walls of the Fountain Court are medieval originals.

The staterooms were in the Terrace Range, designed by Smythson and his son John, and included a Great Hall, very fine living quarters and a splendid 220ft (67m) Long Gallery. The Riding School range, designed by Robert Smythson's grandson, Huntingdon, has a superb timber roof of the early 1630s.

NEW OWNERS

In the Civil War, its owner, Sir William Cavendish, led the Royalist army at Marston Moor and following that defeat fled into exile. The castle was occupied by the Parliamentarians, but

ROBERT SMYTHSON

In a series of major building commissions between 1556 and his death in 1614, Robert Smythson achieved a creative blend of native English, Flemish and continental Renaissance architectural ideas. Although he was a figure of major significance for Elizabethan and Jacobean architecture, he lived before practitioners of his trade could claim great social standing. There is no surviving image of him, and we know little about him beyond the building projects on which he worked. His first house was Longleat for Sir John Thynne, begun when he was just 21. He was later surveyor on those jewels of the age, Hardwick Hall and Wollaton Hall.

Sir William returned after 1660. Subsequently, the castle passed through the hands of various owners and residents until it was given to the state in 1945 by William Cavendish-Bentinck, 7th Duke of Portland. English Heritage is currently responsible for the castle.

DUNFERMLINE PALACE
AND GLAMIS CASTLE

Before he became King of England, James Stuart, ruling as James VI of Scotland, established a fine royal palace at Dunfermline. The main part of the palace was originally a guesthouse in the Benedictine abbey founded by Queen Margaret and her son, David I; James also added a new building at Dunfermline, the Queen's House, for his wife, Anne of Denmark.

Royal connections to Dunfermline were well established. Queen (later Saint) Margaret was buried there, as was Robert I the Bruce, who had rebuilt the abbey's domestic buildings after they were ransacked by the army of Edward I of England. James I was born at the abbey, and James IV and James V stayed there.

James VI's palace was built around a courtyard, with the main range of royal apartments at the south-west, the new Queen's House to the north and the abbey buildings to the east. The main range incorporated parts of the medieval abbey guesthouse. The palace was the birthplace of Prince Charles (the future King Charles I, and the last monarch born in Scotland) in 1600. The palace is a ruin today, with only part of the outer shell of the south-west range surviving.

Below: The remains of the south-west range at Dunfermline Palace. It once contained a large hall, with a kitchen and chamber.

Above: Glamis Castle. The impressive main tower was constructed c.1435. The oldest part is the east wing, built c.1400.

GLAMIS CASTLE

The magnificent Banqueting Hall at Glamis Castle was built in the early 1600s as part of a substantial reworking of this largely 15th-century fortress by Patrick Lyon, the 9th Lord Glamis and 1st Earl of Kinghorne. The castle stands on the site of a building in which King Malcolm II was reputedly murdered; it was then a royal hunting lodge for many years and was the home of Janet Douglas, Lady Glamis, who was imprisoned and then burned at the stake as a witch. James V briefly seized the castle for four years. Mary, Queen of Scots, visited, and James VI came to stay often. In the 20th century, it was the childhood home of Queen Elizabeth, the Queen Mother; in 1930, she gave birth there to Princess Margaret, sister of Queen Elizabeth II.

AUDLEY END
A PALACE IN ALL BUT NAME

The country mansion of Audley End, near Saffron Walden, was built by Thomas Howard, 1st Earl of Suffolk, in 1605–14 to entertain King James I. Before its 18th-century alterations, it was more than twice the size it is today. Howard served as Lord Treasurer to the King and perhaps gave in to the temptation to divert funds towards the building of his house, for in 1619 he and his wife were imprisoned in the Tower of London, accused of embezzling thousands of pounds.

To create the grandest home in England of its day, Thomas Howard demolished an earlier house, Audley Inn, which had been erected by his grandfather, Sir Thomas Audley, in the middle of the 16th century. Sir Thomas himself had built on the site of a former Benedictine monastery, named Walden Abbey, given to him by Henry VIII in 1538 during the Dissolution of the Monasteries.

Below: The Great Hall. Note the Howard family crests in the plaster ceiling and the superb Jacobean carved wooden screen.

The new house, Audley End, built around two courtyards, has two porches on the front with separate entrances that led to separate suites of apartments for the king and queen. Within, the splendid Great Hall features a magnificent Jacobean carved oak screen, while the plaster panel ceiling is decorated with coloured crests of the Howard family.

Thomas Howard was rewarded with only one visit from James I, in 1614. James supposedly told his host: 'the building is too large for a King, but it might do for a Lord Treasurer'. In fact, Audley End became a royal palace between 1668 and 1701, when Charles II

Above: Audley End, built to impress James I, became a palace when Charles II bought it as a base from which to attend horse-racing at Newmarket.

purchased it for the sum of £50,000 (it was repurchased by the earls of Suffolk). He stayed there in style and comfort when attending horse-racing at nearby Newmarket.

FORMAL GARDENS

Thomas Howard created vast, elaborate gardens with extended avenues of trees, and geometric arrangements of alleys and rectangular ponds. These designs led the eye along a main vista from the house's principal front, with another, lesser, vista at right angles.

FASHIONABLE ALTERATIONS

In the 18th century, after many decades of neglect, Sir John Griffin Griffin, 1st Baron Braybrooke, and a descendant of the earls of Suffolk, abandoned these gardens and hired Lancelot 'Capability' Brown to remake the grounds in the then fashionable landscape style. He also engaged Robert Adam to create a fine set of eight rooms, squeezed into the lower ground floor, refit the saloon, create a picture gallery, redecorate the chapel and build a number of garden monuments, including the Tea House Bridge that crosses the River Cam.

BLICKLING HALL
A JACOBEAN MANSION

Robert Lyminge, surveyor-architect for Sir Robert Cecil at Hatfield House, built the Jacobean mansion of Blickling Hall in Norfolk in 1616–25 for Sir Henry Hobart, Lord Chief Justice under King James I. Blickling's delightful entrance front uses many of the features of Hatfield, including a large clock tower, a prominent and decorated porch and ogival cupolas at the corners.

The new house was built on the site of an older Blickling Hall that had once belonged to Sir Thomas Boleyn, father of Anne Boleyn, queen of Henry VIII and mother of Elizabeth I. Unlike Hatfield House, Blickling Hall was constrained by its setting – indeed the yew hedges and the former moat (now a flower garden) are a good deal older than the Jacobean house. Perhaps because of these constraints, Lyminge decided to build a conventional courtyard house rather than adopt the fashionable H-shape used at Hatfield.

Below: The Long Gallery has been used as a library since the 18th century. Today it houses a collection of rare books.

Above: This detail of a musician is from the plaster ceiling of the Long Gallery.

HALL AND LONG GALLERY

The main entrance hall contains the majestic original Jacobean oak staircase, which was moved and extended when the hall was rebuilt in 1767 by a local architect, Thomas Ivory. His staircase splits into two at the main landing, while the original had one flight only, but the reconstruction is a work of great skill.

Blickling Hall's Long Gallery was one of the last but also one of the finest long galleries built in an English country house.

BIRTHPLACE OF A QUEEN?

The Great Hall at Blickling contains statues of Anne Boleyn and Elizabeth I, the former marked with the legend *Anna Bolena hic nata 1507* ('Anne Boleyn was born in this place in 1507'). Scholars believe that the claim is false. Although Anne's father, Sir Thomas Boleyn, once owned Blickling, he moved to Hever Castle in Kent around 1505, so unless Anne was born before her generally accepted birth date of 1507, she was born at Hever, not Blickling.

It is 123ft (37m) long, and fills most of the house's east front. The room is a good deal wider than most long galleries, and has a magnificent plaster ceiling full of abstract and naturalistic designs, which was carved by Edward Stanyan in 1620. It houses a library of 12,000 volumes.

Below: The clock tower and ogival cupolas at the corners are among the features at Blickling Hall that recall Hatfield House.

THE QUEEN'S HOUSE, GREENWICH
'HOUSE OF DELIGHT'

Artist-turned-architect Inigo Jones's first major commission, after being appointed Surveyor of Works to King James I in 1615, was to design the Queen's House in Greenwich for James's wife, Anne of Denmark. Anne died in 1619, before the Queen's House was complete, but Jones returned to finish the work in 1635 at the request of King Charles I's wife, Henrietta Maria of France.

When Jones built the Queen's House it was part of the 15th-century royal palace of Placentia, birthplace both of Henry VIII (in 1491) and Elizabeth I (in 1533). This palace and its estate stood on the large riverside site now occupied by Greenwich Park, the National Maritime Museum and the Royal Naval College. Following the Restoration of the monarchy in 1660, Charles II set out to rebuild the Palace of Placentia to the designs of John Webb, an architect who, with Inigo Jones, pioneered the

classical style in England. The only part of Webb's work that survives today is the east range of the King Charles block; the rest has been demolished.

ITALIAN INSPIRATION

Jones's design for the Queen's House was based on that of an Italian villa at Poggio a Caiano, built for Florentine statesman Lorenzo de Medici and completed in 1485 by Giuliano da Sangallo. Like Poggio a Caiano, the Queen's House consists of two main parts: one part stood within Placentia Palace and the second was in Greenwich Park, and they were connected by a covered bridge over the public road (moved in 1699 by Lord Romney, Ranger of the Royal Park) linking Deptford and Woolwich. Other key elements of the design derived from Jones's Italian model are the curved steps, terrace and widely spaced windows on the palace side of the building (the north front) and the open colonnade of six Ionic pillars along the park face (the south front). From the colonnade, which Jones called 'a frontispiece in the midst', there is a splendid view of the parkland.

Above: An Italian villa in Greenwich. The south front, with its colonnade of Ionic pillars, commands superb views of the park.

FIRST OF JONES'S CUBES

Jones designed all the interiors. There were elaborate marble fireplaces and the rooms were adorned with carved wooden friezes. In the palace, or north, building he created a magnificent entrance hall, paved with black and white marble, its dimensions a perfect 40ft (12m) cube. This was the first of several cubes built by Jones – two side by side (a 'double cube') were used both in the Whitehall Palace Banqueting House and in the rebuilt south wing at Wilton House. In favouring these perfect dimensions, Jones was following one of the key tenets of Palladio, that houses should be designed in line with natural laws of symmetry, proportion and harmony. His entrance hall in the Queen's House was also the first instance in an English house of a hall designed for use as a reception room. Its ceiling was decorated with paintings by Orazio Gentileschi, representing the 'Arts of Peace'.

QUEEN'S CHAPEL, ST JAMES'S

Inigo Jones received the royal order to build the Queen's Chapel at St James's Palace in April 1623. It was planned as a Roman Catholic place of worship in which the intended wife of Charles, Prince of Wales, could hear Mass. Charles travelled to Spain with the Duke of Buckingham to woo the Infanta but failed in the mission, returning home empty-handed in October 1623. Instead, the chapel was used by Charles's eventual queen, Henrietta Maria of France, also a Roman Catholic. It is in the form of a double cube, with a gracefully curving coffered ceiling and at the east end an elegant arched three-light Venetian window – a much-used device in the Palladian revival.

Above: From the river side, the neat Queen's House is dwarfed by Sir Christopher Wren's Royal Naval Hospital.

THE 'HOUSE OF DELIGHT'

Jones also installed England's first open-well spiral staircase, the Tulip Staircase, bringing all his delicacy to bear when

Below: This ceiling of the Arts and Sciences (1636) was painted for the Queen's House but later moved to Marlborough House.

he designed a balustrade of wrought iron decorated with the fleur-de-lys device as a mark of respect for the French-born queen. In the Queen's Drawing Room there hung a fine tapestry of Cupid and Psyche by Jacob Jordaens, perhaps after which she called the building her 'House of Delight'.

After the Restoration, when Henrietta Maria, now the Queen Mother, returned to live there, the Queen's House was enlarged by John Webb as part of Charles II's large-scale plan to rebuild Placentia Palace. Nearby, Charles's new palace, the King's House, was begun on land beside the River Thames. It was never finished and later became the site of the Royal Naval Hospital, designed by Sir Christopher Wren.

STOKE PARK PAVILIONS

At Stoke Bruerne, Northamptonshire, Inigo Jones either designed or supervised the design of a country house for Sir Francis Crane. The house was never completed, and large parts were burned down in 1886, but two pavilions and colonnades have survived and can be seen today. The plan, with the

central house connected to two pavilions by a graceful curving colonnade, was based on that of the mid-16th-century Villa di Papa Giulio in Rome, built by Giacomo Barozzi da Vignola for Pope Julius II. At Stoke Bruerne, the west pavilion contained a library and the east pavilion a chapel.

Below: One of two graceful pavilions designed by Jones for Sir Francis Crane's country house at Stoke Bruerne, Northants.

THE BANQUETING HOUSE, WHITEHALL
A MASTERPIECE OF CLASSICAL ARCHITECTURE

When King James I's Banqueting Hall in Whitehall Palace burned down in 1619 he commanded his Surveyor of Works, Inigo Jones, to replace it. Jones's Banqueting House, completed in three years by 1622, is his masterpiece. One of England's first and greatest classical buildings, it is the only part of the once extensive royal palace of Whitehall to survive today above ground. Contemporaries, however, seem to have found Jones's conception too grand and rather at odds with the rest of the Tudor palace. One response, in 1621, was that the hall was 'too faire and nothing suitable to the rest of the house'.

IONIC AND CORINTHIAN
The Banqueting House was designed not for dining but principally as a setting for state occasions, plays and the masques that Inigo Jones continued to design for the royal court. Indeed, its completion was celebrated with the performance of *The Masque of Augurs*, by Jones and

Below: The Banqueting House survived in its original setting – as part of Whitehall Palace – for only 76 years, from completion in 1622 to the disastrous fire of 1698.

Ben Jonson, on Twelfth Night 1622. The building's interior was Jones's version of a Roman basilica (hall): it consists of a vast 50ft (15m) double cube, and is ornamented with Ionic columns beneath a cantilevered gallery and Corinthian pilasters above.

This formidable interior space originally had a beamed ceiling, but the celebrated painted panels by Sir Peter Paul Rubens were fitted in 1635. The paintings are allegorical representations of James I's reign as a time of

Above: Work of a master – Inigo Jones's Banqueting House façade facing Whitehall. Architects praise its vitality and harmony.

plenty and peace; Rubens had planned them at the time of building, but they were not finished until 1634.

Jones' façade for the Banqueting House also uses Ionic beneath Corinthian pilasters. Facing Whitehall, it was originally built using three colours of stone: brown for the basement, a dun colour for the upper walls and white Portland

INIGO JONES: CLASSICAL PIONEER

The son of a London cloth worker, Inigo Jones first found royal employment as a painter at the court of Christian IV of Denmark and Norway. His work there gained him an entrée at the royal court in London, where he served Queen Anne (Christian IV's sister) from 1605 onward as a designer of costumes, scenery and effects for royal entertainments, or 'masques'. His first architectural work, commissioned by Robert Cecil, 1st Earl of Salisbury, was a design for the New Exchange in the Strand, London (demolished in the 18th century). Jones was then appointed Surveyor of Works, first to Henry, Prince of Wales, in 1610–12, and in 1615–43 to Kings James I and Charles I.

Above: Jones was a superb theatrical designer and one of England's greatest architects.

An admirer of classical Roman and Italian Renaissance architecture, Jones pioneered 'classicism' in English architecture, basing his designs on those of the Roman architect Vitruvius and his Italian followers Andrea Palladio and Vincenzo Scamozzi, and on study of Vitruvius's and Palladio's writings on architecture.

In addition to his major royal buildings in London, Jones contributed to the design and interior decoration of a number of country houses. He also designed and laid out London's first integrated square at Covent Garden and restored the old St Paul's Cathedral, though his reputedly superb work there was entirely lost in the Great Fire of London in 1666.

stone for the columns and the elegant balustrade. But it was refaced with Portland stone throughout during restoration by Sir John Soane in 1829.

WHITEHALL PALACE

In the 15th century, the Archbishops of York built as their London base a palace named York Place, which stood on the site of Inigo Jones's Banqueting House. When Cardinal Thomas Wolsey became Archbishop of York in 1514, he extended the palace, which, like Hampton Court, another of Wolsey's splendid residences, attracted the covetous eye of Henry VIII. In the late 1520s, his reputation failing and desperately trying to retain the King's favour, Wolsey gave York Place to Henry. Renamed Whitehall Palace it became Henry VIII's principal royal residence.

The King further extended and improved it, rebuilding a fine Privy Gallery that he had taken from another of Wolsey's houses, at Esher. He built a

Right: Roman basilica updated – the great double cube of the Banqueting Hall. Note the Ionic columns beneath and the Corinthian pilasters above the gallery.

bowling alley, a tilt yard, a cockpit and real tennis courts and raised two great gateways over the roadway (from Charing Cross to Westminster) that ran through the palace complex. Within the many rooms of the palace, several walls and ceilings were painted by Hans Holbein, court painter from 1536.

The palace was later a favourite of Elizabeth I, although she made few alterations, and of Charles I. Most of this vast palace, which was said to contain 2,000 rooms, burned down in a single night in 1698 during the reign of William III and Mary II. Only Jones's Banqueting House was spared.

WILTON HOUSE
SEAT OF THE EARLS OF PEMBROKE

In the late 1630s, Philip Herbert, 4th Earl of Pembroke, built a magnificent new south front to his family's Tudor mansion at Wilton House in Wiltshire. Construction, carried out by the Frenchman Isaac de Caus, was supervised and directed by Inigo Jones, who designed seven magnificent state-rooms for the interior.

The original Wilton House was built by Sir William Herbert on land that formerly belonged to Wilton Abbey, which he was given by King Henry VIII in 1544. Sir William was related to the King by marriage, as his first wife, Anne, was the sister of Henry's sixth wife, Catherine Parr. In 1551, Henry made Sir William 1st Earl of Pembroke. At Wilton, Sir William built a fine courtyard house in the second half of the 1540s. The commanding tower in the centre of Wilton's east front is a survival from his splendid house.

WILTON'S SOUTH FRONT
The new south front of the 1630s was originally intended as the right half of a much longer façade, which was to have had a portico with six Corinthian

Below: In de Caus's original design, the south front as we see it was just the right half of a longer façade with a central portico.

columns at its centre; this was probably never carried through because the Civil War intervened. De Caus's original plan of this projected design, which still survives, was improved, perhaps by Jones, with the addition of towers at each end.

DOUBLE CUBE ROOM
While the building's facade has a classical, Italianate appearance, its extraordinary interior exhibits the influence of French style. The most celebrated

Above: The east front (right) and the south front (left) at Wilton. The sedate exterior gives no hint of the riches within.

of Jones's staterooms is the lavishly decorated Double Cube Room. This is not, in fact, the original room built in the 1630s, since a fire in 1647 or 1648 severely damaged the central part of the wing and the room was rebuilt and redecorated c.1648–53 by John Webb, under the direction of Jones, who was

A COLLEGE OF THE 'LEARNED AND INGENIOUS'
Wilton House was the scene of great events in the Elizabethan and Jacobean periods, when Mary, Countess of Pembroke (wife of Henry Herbert, 2nd Earl of Pembroke) was a great literary hostess. The writer John Aubrey declared: 'In her time, Wilton House was like a college, there were so many learned and ingenious persons'. Mary was herself a poet and her brother was Sir Philip Sidney, who often stayed with her and wrote the bulk of his prose romance *The Arcadia* there before 1581. Christopher Marlowe, Edmund Spenser, Ben Jonson and John Donne certainly visited Wilton; some writers believe Shakespeare himself was a guest of the Countess of Pembroke and that *As You Like It* had its first performance at Wilton House on 2 December 1603, with James I in the audience.

then over 70 years old. The room is called Double Cube because of its dimensions: 60ft (18m) long by 30ft (9m) wide and 30ft (9m) high. It is decorated with expanses of fruit and flowers carved in wood and then gilded and fixed to the white walls. The chimney-pieces are of intricately carved Italian marble; the coved ceilings are equally ornate. On the walls hang portraits by Sir Anthony van Dyck of the Herberts and the royal family. The room is today furnished with lavish gilt mirrors, and red velvet chairs and sofas designed in the 18th century by William Kent and Thomas Chippendale. Beside it is the similarly lavishly decorated Single Cube Room, a perfect 30ft (9m) cube. The latest thinking is that the fire did not reach this room, and therefore it appears today as it was decorated in the 1630s. The lower panels on its walls retell the story of Philip Sidney's *The Arcadia*. In World War II, remarkably, the Double Cube Room was a military operations centre in which the D-Day landings were planned.

Below: Wilton's Palladian bridge was the original of the three country-house bridges in this style. It was copied at Stowe (1738) and Prior Park, Bath (1756).

PALLADIAN BRIDGE

Wilton House is also celebrated for its Palladian-style bridge across the River Nadder, which flows through the grounds, built in 1737 by Henry Herbert, the 9th Earl of Pembroke. With its temple portico, it is one of three almost identical bridges of this period; others are to be found at Prior Park, Bath, and Stowe, Buckingham.

Above: The Double Cube Room. Credit for its decorative scheme should go to Jean Barbet and John Webb – especially Webb, who redecorated it after the 1647–8 fire.

In the 9th Earl's time, also, the gardens were landscaped in the 'picturesque style'; then, in 1779, Lancelot 'Capability' Brown was brought in to redesign them. At the start of the 19th century, Wyatt opened up the interior of the house by adding Gothic cloisters and building a new entrance via the north forecourt.

WILTON'S POPULARITY

Wilton House was a great favourite of James I, and across the centuries it remained close to the heart of national life, visited frequently by the reigning monarch. It so impressed Daniel Defoe that he wrote 'One cannot be said to have seen anything that a man of curiosity would think worth seeing in the country and not have been at Wilton House'.

More recently, the house and grounds have become a star of the screen. Major productions filmed at Wilton have included *The Madness of King George*, *Mrs Brown*, *Sense and Sensibility* and the 2005 version of *Pride and Prejudice*.

'PLANTATION CASTLES' IN ULSTER
BALFOUR, ENNISKILLEN, MONEA, TULLY AND KILLYLEAGH

In 1618, Scottish Protestant lord, Sir James Balfour, built Castle Balfour at Linaskea in County Fermanagh on the site of a fortress belonging to the Maguires, the leading family of Fermanagh since 1300. Sir James got the Maguire land as a beneficiary of James I's 'Plantation' of Ulster — the introduction of Protestant Englishmen and Scots into this rebellious and strongly Catholic part of northern Ireland.

Castle Balfour, now ruined, was built in the style of contemporary Scottish strong-houses, on a T-plan with stair turrets and parapets.

Another Maguire stronghold was rebuilt at nearby Enniskillen, County Fermanagh, by Captain William Cole – like Balfour, originally a man of Fife – in 1611. While living in a makeshift timber house, Cole reworked the ruined medieval fortress, adding a strong defensive wall and raising a new dwelling. He built a distinctively Scottish water-gate to guard the entrance from the adjacent Lough Erne. It has twin turrets with conical roofs. Stylistic similarities

suggest that Enniskillen and Balfour castles may have been rebuilt by the same Scottish masons.

SCOTTISH PROFILE AT MONEA
Castle Balfour and Enniskillen Castle are just two of several fortifications in Northern Ireland built or refashioned by Scottish or English incomers, who

Above: Enniskillen's substantial twin-turreted gate was built to guard against a waterborne attack across Lough Erne.

received their lands as part of the Plantation of Ulster. Near Enniskillen, the substantial Monea Castle was built *c*.1616 by Scottish churchman, Malcolm Hamilton, later Archbishop of Cashel. The rectangular three-storey stronghold, now ruined, was 50ft (15m) tall and 20ft (6m) wide, enclosed by a 300ft (91m) defensive circuit wall 9ft (2.7m) in height. On its west front stood two cylindrical towers with square rooms projecting diagonally at attic level – a distinctive profile probably copied from that of Claypotts Castle near Dundee in Scotland. The castle had a single entrance in the most northerly of these towers, with a spiral staircase leading to the well-lit main reception rooms, with big windows and window-seats, on the first floor and then to the bedrooms on the second floor.

Later, the castle was the residence of Gustavus Hamilton, Governor of Enniskillen and 1st Viscount Boyne. Hamilton was financially ruined during the Williamite Wars, during which he

---

DUNLUCE: A MANSION WITHIN A CASTLE

In *c*.1620, Randal McDonnell, 1st Earl of Antrim, constructed an elegant manor house with gables and large mullioned windows within the fortifications of a 13th-century castle at Dunluce, County Antrim, on a basalt rock above the sea. He was the son of Scottish adventurer, Sorley Boy McDonnell, who captured the castle in *c*.1560 from members of the locally powerful McQuillan clan and, after being evicted, retook it from an English garrison. In 1586, Sorley Boy was made Constable of the Castle by Elizabeth I, but his loyalty was not beyond question – two years later, he reputedly gave refuge to survivors from a Spanish Armada

galleon, which had foundered on Atlantic rocks below the castle; he also armed his castle with cannon taken from the ship.

Randal McDonnell married Lady Katharine Manners, the widow of great court favourite the Earl of Buckingham, and brought her to live at Dunluce. They equipped their mansion lavishly – with the finest tapestries and, it is said, a pair of curtains from Hampton Court Palace. Its remains can be seen today within the castle walls, alongside the columns of an extraordinary sandstone loggia that Sorley Boy erected, along the lines of one built by the Earl of Bothwell at Crichton Castle near Edinburgh.

Above: At Killyleagh, the original 17th-century towers are rather lost amid the mid-19th-century Scots Baronial reworking.

was Brigadier General of William III's army. After his death in 1691, his family remained in residence at Monea for some time, but eventually were forced by money difficulties to sell the castle.

TULLY CASTLE

Another Scottish planter, Sir John Hume of Berwick, built Tully Castle near Blaney village in County Fermanagh, overlooking Lower Lough Erne, in 1612–15. The village and area took the name Blaney from that of Sir Edward Blaney, who, as Lord Deputy in the service of King James I, had been despatched to Fermanagh to oversee and arrange the Plantation.

Tully Castle consisted of a defended enclosure or bawn, with four projecting rectangular corner towers, plus a two-and-half-storey fortified building. Today it is a substantial and picturesque ruin because it was captured and burned by Rory, scion of the Maguire family, during an attack on Christmas Day 1641 that was part of the bloody rebellion of that year by Irish Catholics. In the attack on Tully Castle, 16 men and 69 women and children were killed, although the Hume family survived.

ROUGHAN CASTLE

Near Newmills in County Tyrone, Andrew Stewart built Roughan Castle in 1618. His father was another Scottish nobleman and benificiary of the Plantation, Lord Castlestewart, who had founded Stewartstown, near Newmills. The three-storey castle has a 20ft (6m) central tower and four round corner towers. In the rebellion of 1641, the castle was held by Andrew Stewart's descendant Robert Stewart, who, after marrying into the O'Neill family, took the side of the rebels.

KILLYLEAGH CASTLE

Another beneficiary of the Plantation was Sir James Hamilton of Ayrshire, who was granted large territories in County Down that had previously belonged to the O'Neill clan. He built Killyleagh Castle, with a round tower and conical roof, on the site of a 12th century fortification raised by Norman adventurer-knight John de Courcy. The round tower survives on the south corner of the castle front; it is balanced by an identical tower on the north end of the front, added in the late 17th century following damage in the civil war. The castle was reworked in the Scottish Baronial style in the mid-19th century by Archibald Hamilton.

Above: The ruins of Monea Castle give a good indication of its former grandeur – and show off the distinctive design of the tower.

Right: Monea Castle in its prime, c. 1620. This view shows its distinctive round towers with square rooms projecting at attic level.

CHAPTER TWENTY

RESTORATION STYLE

c.1660–c.1714

During the years of the Commonwealth and Protectorate, many of England's leading Royalists were forced to abandon their country houses to live in exile in Europe. During these years, they were impressed by French, Italian and Dutch styles of architecture, decoration and garden design. When they returned with Charles II at the Restoration of the Monarchy in 1660, many brought with them continental tastes for elaborate decoration. Craftsmen such as the French metalworker Jean Tijou, the Dutch-born woodcarver Grinling Gibbons, and the Danish sculptor Caius Gabriel Cibber, worked on magnificent interiors for discerning patrons at houses such as Chatsworth, Petworth and Belton, for Charles II in his superb staterooms at Windsor Castle and, after the 'Glorious Revolution' of 1688, for William III and Mary II at Hampton Court Palace. Their work adorned Great Apartments – suites of grand reception rooms, which, in the 17th century, replaced the Great Hall as the principal feature of the great house and palace. These staterooms attempted to mirror the splendour of the chateaux and palaces of continental Europe, especially that of Louis XIV at Versailles. European taste and, in particular, Louis's great palace complex – a resounding expression of his absolute rule – also had an influence on the laying out of pleasure grounds around country houses and palaces in these years. At Hampton Court Palace, for example, both Charles II and, later, William and Mary created elaborate water and floral decorations in the French style.

Left: The originally Tudor Chatsworth House, completely rebuilt in grand style by the 4th Earl of Devonshire in 1687–1707, stands in a beautiful position beside the River Derwent.

PETWORTH HOUSE
AND GRINLING GIBBONS

Petworth House was built in 1688–96 by Charles Seymour, 6th Duke of Somerset, incorporating part of a 13th-century castle that belonged to the Percy earls of Northumberland. The Duke's great house, which stands on the edge of the West Sussex town of Petworth, is renowned particularly for its association with artists and contains a room of woodcarving generally agreed to be the masterpiece of the great craftsman Grinling Gibbons.

Petworth House is often cited as a rare example of direct French influence on the English great house. Horace Walpole declared it to be 'in the style of the Tuileries', the royal palace that once stood alongside the Louvre in central Paris. Petworth's original west entrance front is thought to have featured a

---

MASTER OF WOODCARVING: GRINLING GIBBONS

Born in Rotterdam, in 1648, to an English father, Gibbons had made his name in London as a wood carver by the early 1670s. He produced woodcarvings for Charles II at Windsor Castle and, in the 1680s–90s, made the carvings for Petworth House while also completing work at Hampton Court Palace and Kensington Palace, as commissioned by William III and Mary II. He was appointed Master Carver at the Royal Court in 1693. He also did exquisite work at St Paul's Cathedral, carving choir stalls and a fine organ screen, as well as working in stone on the exterior of Sir Christopher Wren's building (completed in 1710) and making a bronze statue of James II, now outside the National Gallery, London.

Above: Gibbons' delicate work had an enduring influence on country house decor.

Below: Grinling Gibbons' carving on the picture frames at Petworth House is marked by a breathtaking realism and delicacy.

central dome, with a series of elaborate urns around its cupola, while statues were arranged on the balustrade running across the entire front. This arrangement can be seen in a picture of the house *c.*1700, now at Belvoir Castle. However, the central dome was destroyed and the west front damaged in a fire of 1714. During restoration, the house was given a plainer appearance.

Even so, nine of the west front's 42 tall windows (three in the centre and three at each end) have busts and carving above them in a French style. The famous deer park at Petworth was landscaped by 'Capability' Brown in the 1750s.

ENTRANCE HALL

Within, the house contains nine interconnecting staterooms arranged along the front, facing the park, and behind them nine equally grand rooms along the east, or town, side of the house. In the centre of the west front is the Marble Hall, originally the entrance hall,

with a floor of white, green and black marble, a fireplace at its north and south ends and elaborate carving by John Selden around the doors and fireplaces and above the cornice. (Selden worked on the estate for the Duke, yet, despite the superb quality of his work, is little known aside from Petworth House.) In the 19th century, the entrance was moved from the park side to the house's other main front, on the east side facing the town.

GRINLING GIBBONS ROOM

Further along the front to the north is the Grinling Gibbons Room. In this large space, 20ft (6m) high, 24ft (7m) wide and 60ft (18m) long, Gibbons provided fantastically carved frames for seven portraits – including a large central one of Henry VIII, copied from the celebrated original of Hans Holbein. Gibbons' limewood-carving of flowers, fruit, leaves, musical instruments, birds, baskets and other intricate objects is wonderfully detailed and delicate.

CHAPEL

The chapel at Petworth House is a survivor from the 13th-century castle of the Percy earls. To this, in 1690–2, the 6th Duke added a plaster ceiling together with stalls, altar rail and gallery in gilded wood.

CAPTURED ON CANVAS

In the 1750s, Alicia Maria, Countess of Egremont, lavishly redecorated the sitting room now known as the White and Gold Room. This is probably the room painted by J.M.W. Turner in his celebrated picture *Drawing Room at Petworth*, now held by the National Gallery, London. This is one of a famous series of paintings by Turner, who visited several times in the 1830s as a friend of the 3rd Earl of Egremont.

FRENCH INFLUENCE AT BOUGHTON

At the same time that Petworth House was being built, the main north front at Boughton House, Northamptonshire, was constructed in a French style by the francophile Ralph, 3rd Lord Montagu, who had served as Charles II's ambassador to France in 1669, 1676 and 1677. The front has a protruding

Right: Gibbons' work in situ. Horace Walpole said the Gibbons Room at Petworth was 'the most superb monument of his skill'.

pavilion at each end and between these a ground-floor loggia (arcade) that Montagu called 'the cloisters'. Above the arcade was the five-room Great Apartment floored with parquet in the style of Versailles.

Lord Montagu was a colourful and notable character: Jonathan Swift declared him to be 'as arrant a knave as any in his time', while William Congreve dedicated his play *The Way of the World* to him in 1700. Lord Montagu received

Above: A regal French style in Sussex. The great west front at Petworth House faces the park and contains nine grand state rooms.

William III in the splendid surroundings of Boughton House in 1695. He also built a fine town house, Montagu House, in London, which subsequently became the first home of the British Museum. In 1705, Queen Anne made Lord Montagu Marquess of Monthermer and 1st Duke of Montagu.

HOLYROODHOUSE PALACE
SCOTTISH ROYAL RESIDENCE

In the 1530s, James V raised a conical-turreted rectangular tower at Holyroodhouse in Edinburgh containing royal apartments (see page 358). The palace served as the principal residence of Mary, Queen of Scots, and witnessed the murder of her secretary, David Rizzio, at the hands of men led by Mary's husband, Lord Darnley. In the reign of Mary's son, James VI of Scots and I of England, the palace fell into decline but was renovated in time for the Scottish coronation of James's son and successor, Charles I. During the Civil War, Parliamentarian forces were housed in the palace, which was badly damaged by fire.

CHARLES II'S RECONSTRUCTION WORK

During the 1670s, Charles II initiated a major reconstruction of the Palace of Holyroodhouse. Directed by Sir William Bruce, who was appointed Surveyor-General and Overseer of the King's

Below: Charles II's rebuilding at Holyroodhouse transformed the building into an elegant palace in the classical style.

Buildings in Scotland, and implemented by Robert Mylne, the King's Master Mason in Scotland, Charles's programme involved raising a southern tower on the entrance front to match the splendid northern one built by James V, and erecting a range between the towers with a fine Doric portico at the entrance. Fine classical façades were added to the inner quadrangle, with an elegant arcade at ground level.

The first floor contained the royal apartments, fitted with impressive plaster ceilings – especially in the West Drawing Room – and elegant wainscoting. In the Long Gallery, the Dutch artist Jacob de Wet painted 110 portraits of Scottish kings, both real and legendary, from Fergus I to Charles II, who commissioned the work. Charles also made the Holyrood Abbey Church the Chapel Royal for the palace. Charles, however, saw none of this fine work, as he did not once visit Holyroodhouse.

LATER DEVELOPMENTS

During the brief reign of Charles's successor, the Roman Catholic James VII of Scots and II of England, the King

Above: Charles II and James, Duke of York. James was deposed before he could enjoy the alterations he made at Holyroodhouse.

adapted the chapel so it could be used for Roman Catholic rites. In later years, his grandson 'Bonnie Prince Charlie' stayed at Holyroodhouse Palace for a few weeks in 1745, during his attempt to win the throne back for his father, but after the collapse of the '45 revolt no royal stayed there until Queen Victoria in the 19th century. Renovated in Victorian times and by George V, the Palace has regained its position as Scotland's foremost royal palace. It is Queen Elizabeth II's official residence when she visits Scotland each year.

WINDSOR CASTLE
AND CHARLES II

 Windsor Castle (see also page 334) was Charles II's favourite royal residence outside London, and he undertook a major rebuilding scheme there in the 1670s. Using Hugh May as architect, Antonio Verrio as principal artist and Grinling Gibbons for decorative carving, Charles built new state apartments and redecorated St George's Hall and the King's Chapel at an overall cost of £130,000. Much of this splendid work was remodelled in the 19th century by George IV and Sir Jeffry Wyatville (see page 476), but elements of the 1670s' alterations survive in the King's Dining Room, in the Queen's Presence and Audience Chambers and (outside) in the Long Walk, lined with elms for its 3 mile (4.5km) route from the south entrance of the castle to Windsor Great Park.

THE UPPER WARD
Externally, Hugh May rebuilt the castle's upper ward in a largely classical style. Its east front, for example, had four massive towers and a central *piano nobile* accessed by two staircases. Internally, the lavish state apartments attempted to replicate some of the magnificence of Versailles. They are identified by some architectural historians as the first English apartments in the Baroque style and were the inspiration for

Below: Charles II laid out the imposing Long Walk, lined with elms, approaching Windsor Castle across the Great Park.

Above: This reconstruction shows St George's Hall in the 1670s – as decorated by Verrio and Gibbons for Charles II.

sets of similarly magnificent staterooms at houses such as Burghley and Chatsworth. The king and queen had separate suites of apartments, including drawing rooms, audience chambers and bedchambers; the queen also had a ballroom. Gibbons' naturalistic carving of game birds, flowers, fruit and fish adorned the walls, which were also wainscoted; 13 ceiling paintings by Verrio represented the triumphs of the King and the Church of England.

ST GEORGE'S HALL
Charles's redecorated St George's Hall also featured grand historical-allegorical paintings by Verrio, depicting scenes from the history of the Order of the Garter, together with Charles II enthroned in grandeur. The hall was fitted with a gilt throne made by John van der Stein and Louis von Opstal.

GIBBONS' WORK IN EVIDENCE
Some of Gibbons' carving survives today in the Waterloo Chamber, which was created by George IV in the 1820s. In addition, the Royal Chapel contained wooden stalls carved in the shape of

laurel and palm by Gibbons; the walls were decorated with a set of Verrio murals depicting Christ's miracles, while the ceiling celebrated the Resurrection. Behind the altar was a version of the *Last Supper* and columns derived from Gian Lorenzo Bernini's Baroque-style *baldechino* (canopy) in St Peter's, Rome.

AN UNFINISHED PALACE
Charles II began a grand new royal residence at Winchester to replace the medieval castle and palace there. Building was begun in 1682 to designs by Sir Christopher Wren that aimed to replicate the glory of Versailles on English soil. At Charles's death in 1685, the shell of the building was complete. But thereafter work was stopped by James II, and Wren's building was never fitted out internally. The 'palace' was later used as a military barracks before burning down in 1894.

CHATSWORTH
'PALACE OF THE PEAK'

Chatsworth's superbly grand appearance, lavish interior, magnificent works of art and splendid gardens in a wonderful setting combine to make it one of the finest – and perhaps the most famous – of all England's stately homes. The house, which stands in the glorious countryside of the Derbyshire Peak District, is celebrated as 'the Palace of the Peak'. (See also page 477.)

The first major house at Chatsworth was built in the mid-16th century by Elizabeth Cavendish (later 'Bess of Hardwick', builder of Hardwick House) and her second husband, Sir William Cavendish, Treasurer of the Chamber at the court of King Henry VIII. This house was completely rebuilt in 1687–1707 by William Cavendish, the 4th Earl of Devonshire.

A long wing was built to the north of the 4th Earl's elegant house in the 19th century by yet another William Cavendish, 6th Duke of Devonshire, to the designs of architect Sir Jeffry Wyatville.

Below: Baroque aesthetics? This riot of figures is a detail from one of Laguerre's exuberant ceilings at Chatsworth.

Above: Garden diversion. The cascade installed in 1696 created interesting sound effects, as well as being a visual delight.

REBUILDING CHATSWORTH

The 16th-century house stood on the same site as the one we see today, on a terrace beside the River Derwent, and like its successor it was built around a central courtyard. In 1687, the 4th Earl began with the intention of rebuilding only the south front of this house, but when he found that this improvement showed up imperfections in the other parts of the house, he was persuaded to move on to another part, and then another. He intended each improvement

to be the last, but in the end, over the course of 20 years, he rebuilt Chatsworth entirely, one section at a time.

The new south and east wings were designed by William Talman, then an unknown architect. Talman grew increasingly frustrated by the Earl's autocratic behaviour, particularly his habit of changing his mind and tearing down

JEAN TIJOU

The supremely skilled metalworker, Jean Tijou, was a French Huguenot who came to England as a religious exile after 1685. He did exquisite work at Hampton Court Palace and its gardens and made screens and grilles for St Paul's Cathedral, as well as working at Chatsworth, Burghley House, Castle Howard and Easton Neston. The 'Golden Gates' he provided at Chatsworth are matched by his intricate gilded iron gates at Burghley House.

building work that had already been completed. The relationship was soured further by prolonged disputes over payment, which resulted in Sir Christopher Wren being despatched to Chatsworth in 1692 to make a judgement on how much the building had cost to that date: his arbitration was the sum of £9,025 16s 6¾d. As a result of this quarrel, Talman was not involved in the rebuilding of the west and north fronts. The west front was probably designed by Thomas Archer, while the north front may have been the work of the Earl himself (from 1694, the 1st Duke of Devonshire) or perhaps was created by John Fitch or even Wren.

LAVISH INTERIORS

The interior of the new house was lavishly decorated and fitted out by the finest craftsmen. Louis Laguerre painted the chapel frescoes (which have remained unaltered since 1694) and, together with Antonio Verrio and Ricard, decorated the ceilings of the staterooms and staircase. These rooms are arranged on the top floor of the three-storey house and

provide marvellous views of the park outside. The great stone staircase has a fine wrought-iron balustrade by Frenchman Jean Tijou; a second staircase rises beneath a coved ceiling by Sir James Thornhill, who also painted the illusionist decoration in the Sabine Room. In the State Music Room, the Dutch artist, Jan van der Vaart, painted another widely celebrated *trompe l'oeil*: an image of a very realistic violin hanging on a door.

THE GARDENS AND PARK

The extensive gardens and parkland we see today were largely created in the 18th century by 'Capability' Brown and in the 19th century by the 6th Duke, his architect Sir Jeffry Wyatville, and his gardener Joseph Paxton (later designer

of the Crystal Palace in London). However, the Great Cascade, the stepped waterfall that descends the slope behind the house, was designed in the 1st Duke's time by Thomas Archer in 1696. Waters from the moorland above feed into a 'Cascade House' and then run down the slope for around ¼ mile (0.4km) over steps varying in size and shape, which alter the sound made by the water as it falls. When the Great Cascade was built, Chatsworth's grounds contained formal terraces and parterres designed by the foremost landscape gardeners of their day: George London and Henry Wise.

Below: Chatsworth probably looks at its most beautiful when the rich hues of its stonework are set off by autumnal leaves.

FELBRIGG HALL
AN ARCHITECTURAL CURIOSITY

In the L-shaped country house of Felbrigg Hall, near Cromer in Norfolk, a Jacobean wing of 1621–4 meets at right angles with a classical wing of *c*.1680. Two architectural languages, the first native English, the second classical in origin, though only 60 years apart, meet here in curious juxtaposition.

LYMINGE'S JACOBEAN WING

The first Felbrigg Hall was medieval. Thomas Windham demolished all except the cellars when he commissioned Robert Lyminge to build a new house.

Lyminge's Jacobean wing has seven bays, including the central porch, and a homely rustic appearance, being built of a combination of flint, brick and stone. Within, the house originally contained a hall and kitchen on the ground floor, a bedchamber and private saloon on the second floor and a Long Gallery along the length of the third floor. Although these

Above: Two houses in one at Felbrigg. This view shows the Jacobean wing, with the classical wing just visible facing to the left.

rooms have been restructured in the intervening years, the actual façade remains largely untouched.

SAMWELL'S CLASSICAL WING

In 1675–86, Thomas Windham's son, William, built a contrasting classical wing, which was designed by gentleman architect William Samwell, with fine red brickwork, 16 tall windows and six small dormers in the roof. It connects with the Jacobean wing at the corner, but the two wings make no concessions to each other.

PAINE'S REMODELLED ROOMS

In 1749–56, William Windham's grandson, William Windham II, commissioned the architect James Paine to remodel the three main rooms on the ground floor of the 1680s wing. One, originally the entrance hall, he made the Dining Room; a second was the Drawing Room; the third, called 'the Cabinet', he fitted with red damask on the walls as a backing for a collection of paintings brought back by his patron from a continental Grand Tour.

In an upstairs room, Paine created a fine Gothic library to house William Windham II's large book collection. It is considered a splendid example of the early Gothic Revival style.

ENGLAND'S FIRST CLASSICAL PORTICO

The Vyne in Hampshire, built by Tudor courtier Lord Sandys, was owned during the Commonwealth period by Chaloner Chute, the Speaker of the House of Commons. In *c*.1654, he commissioned John Webb to build a classical portico on the house's north front, which was the first structure of its kind in the country.

Below: The first classical portico in an English country house looks out across the lake in the grounds of The Vyne.

NOTTINGHAM CASTLE
A DUCAL MANSION

William the Conqueror first established a timber fortress in Nottingham in the year after the Conquest. In 1170, Henry III built a stone castle on the same elevated site, establishing Nottingham Castle as the most important and formidable royal castle in the Midlands. Finally, William Cavendish, 1st Duke of Newcastle, and his son Henry, 2nd Duke, erected a ducal mansion on this historic site in 1674–9.

The castle witnessed numerous important events in the medieval period. In 1194, King Richard I the Lionheart used siege machinery to take the castle from his brother John (the future King John), who had seized power while Richard was on Crusade. Then, in 1330, Edward III broke into the castle through a 300ft (91m)- long subterranean passageway, surprising his mother, Queen Isabella, and her lover, Roger Mortimer, Earl of March, who together were the effective rulers of the country, although Edward wore the crown. Mortimer was executed in London. The passageway, known as Mortimer's Hole, can be seen in the

Below: Nottingham Castle – a ducal mansion rather than a fortress. Its elevated position gives it superb views of the city.

Right: An artwork reconstruction shows clearly the size of the original Nottingham Castle – and its imposing situation.

grounds. In 1485, Richard III rode out from Nottingham Castle to Bosworth Field, the battlefield on which he lost his crown to Henry Tudor, the future Henry VII and father of Henry VIII.

IN AND OUT OF ROYAL HANDS

In 1623, James I granted the castle and its adjacent parkland to Francis Manners, 6th Earl of Rutland. In the Civil War, Nottingham Castle was a rallying point for King Charles I, who raised the royal standard there in 1642. It was later garrisoned for Parliament under the command of Colonel John Hutchinson. His troops repulsed several royalist attempts to capture the castle. Then, after Charles I's execution in 1649, the stronghold was demolished on the orders of Parliament.

'PROSPECT HOUSE'

The mansion the 1st and 2nd Dukes built on the site of the original castle, was a 'prospect house': perched on its high rock, it had superb views over the town and parkland. The house had two wings. The staterooms for grand receptions were on the first floor. In the early

Hanoverian years, Thomas Pelham, the then Duke of Newcastle, was twice prime minister (1754–6 and 1757–62).

In the 19th century, the mansion was severely damaged when, in 1831, rioters protesting in favour of parliamentary reform broke into the house and started a great fire. (Its owner, Henry, 4th Duke of Newcastle, was a well-known opponent of reform.) The conflagration reduced the building to a shell, but it was restored and refurbished as an art gallery in 1878.

BELTON HOUSE
'A GLORIOUS HOUSE'

The elegant Belton House, near Grantham, was built in 1685–8 for Sir John Brownlow, High Sheriff of Lincolnshire. It is ranked as one of England's finest examples of a late 17th-century country house.

We know disappointingly little about Sir John Brownlow himself. He wed his cousin and fathered five lively daughters, and apart from being High Sheriff of Lincolnshire, he was twice MP for Grantham. Belton House was sufficiently grand for Sir John to entertain William III there in 1695, but two years later he took his own life.

Above: The south (right) and west fronts at Belton House. Note James Wyatt's elegant neoclassical doorway of 1777.

CHRISTOPHER WREN AS ROYAL ARCHITECT

Sir Christopher Wren is celebrated above all for his design of the rebuilt St Paul's Cathedral (and 52 other London churches). Yet he was also a significant royal architect, serving as the monarch's Surveyor of Works from 1669 to 1718, for Charles II, James II, William III and Mary II, Anne and George I. Wren was influenced not only by the classical architecture of Inigo Jones and John Webb in England, but also by the magnificent Louvre and Versailles palaces, which he saw on a trip to France in the 1660s. He was Professor of Astronomy at Oxford University and a founder and President of the Royal Society (an elite scientific body in London), and thus brought a vast intellect and a fresh outlook to his architectural work. He provided designs for rebuilding Whitehall Palace, designed a new palace (never finished) for Charles II at Winchester, made alterations to the Queen's Chapel, St James's, and added a small block of new staterooms there. Wren also designed the Royal Naval Hospital in Greenwich, in addition to substantial work at Hampton Court Palace and Kensington Palace. His range was wide: some claim him as an architect of the monumental Baroque (there are certainly elements of this style in some of his church designs), while others prefer to emphasize his more conventional work, which was carried out in a classical Renaissance style.

Left: Sir Christopher Wren, associated forever with the dome of St Paul's Cathedral, may have designed Belton House.

His architect is not known, although possible names mentioned by historians are William Winde, William Stanton and even Sir Christopher Wren. The design was closely based on that of Clarendon House on Piccadilly, London. This building, designed by Sir Roger Pratt for Edward Hyde, Earl of Clarendon, was highly regarded by contemporaries (Pepys called it 'the finest pile I ever saw in my life ... a glorious house'), but it was demolished in 1683 after the Earl's fall from favour and flight to France.

MELLOW STONE EXTERIOR

The H-shaped house at Belton has two near-identical façades: to the south is the main entrance and to the north the garden front. Thirteen large windows arrayed in two symmetrical lines of seven fill the main section of the front, between protruding end wings that are each two bays wide.

The north front has been unchanged since building, but on the entrance front James Wyatt added a neoclassical doorway with pilasters (flattened columns) and entablature (decorative carving above the columns) in 1777. The house is built of noble dressed stone from the quarry at nearby Ancaster, which has weathered delightfully over the years to give the house a mellow look.

INTERIOR GRANDEUR

The interior is lavishly decorated with woodcarving and stucco work. The Marble Hall and Saloon have exquisite limewood carving by the great Grinling Gibbons; the chapel has a wonderfully carved original reredos (ornamental screen) that may also be by Gibbons. The chapel is virtually unaltered and it and the Chapel Gallery also contain fine plaster ceilings modelled by Edward Goudge. The wall panelling in the Chapel Drawing Room is delicately painted to simulate marble.

ALTERATION AND RESTORATION

Upstairs, the Tyrconnel Room is a rare example of a late 18th-century painted floor: it features the arms of the Brownlow family amid decorative foliage. In *c*.1776–7, James Wyatt built the splendid library, which has a barrel-vaulted ceiling.

In the early 19th century, Sir Jeffry Wyatville added a fine staircase to Belton House and created the elegant

---

THE 'LADY ARCHITECT' OF WESTON PARK

Elizabeth, Lady Wilbrahim, rebuilt Weston Park in Shropshire in the 1670s. She designed in the classical idiom – visitors can see her copy of Palladio's *First Book of Architecture* annotated with notes for redesigning the house. But her house also exhibits French influence, in its semicircular pediments, and Dutch style in its combination of brick and stone. She inherited the medieval house that stood on the site, and then acquired wealth through marriage to Sir Thomas Wilbrahim in 1651. This remarkable woman also designed the parish church and stables at Weston Park.

Weston Park contains a magnificent art collection, including works by Holbein and van Dyck. It stands in an estate of 1000 acres (404ha), in parkland landscaped by 'Capability' Brown in 1765; in the 1770s, James Paine built a Temple of Diana in the grounds.

Above: Weston Park was designed by Elizabeth, Lady Wilbrahim, in the 1670s in the Palladian style.

In the 19th century, it was often visited by Prime Minister Benjamin Disraeli, who had an intense platonic relationship with Selina, Countess of Bradford, wife of the house's then owner, the 3rd Earl of Bradford. A collection of 1,100 letters from Disraeli to the Countess is displayed at the house. In modern times, the house was the venue for the G8 summit of world leaders in 1998.

Red Drawing Room, which has a wonderful *trompe l'oeil* frieze together with panels of crimson damask set in the wainscoting. The room is hung with a wealth of pictures, including a number of works by Van Dyck, Titian and Rembrandt.

Outside, Wyatville built an orangery and fountain and laid out an Italian garden. Later in the 19th century, the 3rd Earl of Brownlow sensitively restored Belton House, in particular rebuilding the balustrade and cupola on the roof.

ROYAL CONNECTIONS

Belton House sits in 36 acres (14ha) of fine formal and semi-formal gardens and a large landscaped park. The house remained in the hands of Sir John Brownlow's descendants until 1984, when it passed to the care of the National Trust. George III visited, as did Edward VIII before his abdication, at a time when the then Lord Brownlow was Lord-in-Waiting to the King. The library at Belton contains a display of objects associated with Edward VIII.

Left: Belton's 19th-century orangery, Italianate fountain and garden were designed by Sir Jeffry Wyatville.

HAMPTON COURT, KENSINGTON PALACE
AND THE WORK OF SIR CHRISTOPHER WREN

In 1689, William III and Mary II commissioned Sir Christopher Wren to rebuild Hampton Court Palace. Wren's intention was to sweep away the Tudor palace (see pages 350–1), retaining only the Great Hall, and to create a majestic Renaissance-style country residence grand enough to rival Louis XIV's palace at Versailles. In the event, due to lack of money and time (William and Mary were impatient to see results), Wren built only new sets of apartments for the King and Queen.

THE FOUNTAIN COURT
The apartments were around a new courtyard, the Fountain Court, which Wren raised on the site of the former royal lodgings. The building work also created a new east front for the palace. The King and Queen, who ruled as joint monarchs, were to have separate sets of rooms accessed by separate grand staircases.

Below: In red brick with Portland stone dressing, the east front at Hampton Court is a handsome example of Anglo-Dutch style.

Above: Detail of Wren's windows in the new east front at Hampton Court.

Work began in 1689 and was completed by 1694. The new buildings featured the finest stone carving by Grinling Gibbons and Caius Gabriel Cibber, as well as splendid ironwork by Jean Tijou. However, following Mary's death that year, William halted the work before the interiors were decorated. In 1698, after the destruction of Whitehall Palace in a vast fire, William

Above: William's and Mary's initials are intertwined on a Hampton Court façade.

ordered the resumption of work at Hampton Court. The interior decoration, under the supervision of William Talman and with the King's personal involvement, continued until 1702. The ceilings above the staircase and in the King's staterooms were painted by Antonio Verrio.

HAMPTON COURT GARDENS
Charles II had laid out a long 'canal' or elongated pond before the east front of the palace in 1668. William III filled in part of the 'canal' to create a parterre (a display of ornamental flowerbeds), designed by the Huguenot Daniel Marot. Working with the garden designer George London and with William Talman as architect, William also laid out a Privy Garden in the area between the palace and the River Thames and the Bushy Park Avenue to the north of the palace. The gardens contained splendid ironwork gates by Jean Tijou and architectural ornament by Cibber and Edward Pearce.

The Privy Garden was meticulously restored in 1991–5 with great concern for historical accuracy.

THE MOVE TO KENSINGTON

Asthma-sufferer William III was advised by his doctors to move away from the ᴍᵒʳᵉ ᵖᵒˡˡᵘᵗᵉᵈ ᵃᵗᵐᵒˢᵖʰᵉʳᵉ ᵖʳᵒᵈᵘᶜᵉᵈ ᵇy countless coal fires around Whitehall Palace. He found it easier to breathe the country air at Hampton Court, but in winter he suffered even there on account of the mists rising from the Thames. His search for a conveniently situated winter residence ended at Kensington, then well outside London.

THE NEW PALACE

William bought Nottingham House, a relatively modest Jacobean mansion built in about 1605 and owned by Daniel Finch, 2nd Earl of Nottingham, for around £20,000. Sir Christopher Wren enlarged it by adding a pavilion on each corner; he also moved the entrance to the west front, where he raised a two-storey portico and an entrance courtyard accessed through a clock-tower gateway.

The rebuilding began in July 1689 and was carried out very quickly, for William and Mary were in a great hurry to move in. In their haste, strict supervision of the site must have been lacking, for during that November part of the King's staterooms collapsed, killing eight labourers.

KENSINGTON GARDENS

Some 26 acres (10.5ha) of formal gardens at Kensington Palace were created by Queen Mary and Henry Wise. During Anne's reign, a big Baroque orangery was built by Sir John Vanbrugh. In about 1730, the Round Pond was created in Kensington Palace Gardens for Caroline, wife of George II, and the gardens were opened to the public c.1830.

Left: The Great Staircase at Kensington Palace was later painted by William Kent.

Right: No flourishes. John Evelyn thought Kensington Palace 'a very sweet villa'.

Above: Marot's formal east front gardens, which replaced Charles II's canal, remain one of the glories of Hampton Court.

EASTON NESTON
AND NICHOLAS HAWKSMOOR

Designed by Nicholas Hawksmoor, star pupil of Sir Christopher Wren, in 1696–1702, Easton Neston is often seen as a forerunner of the English Baroque style.

The patron, Sir William Fermor, 1st Lord Leominster, originally offered the job to Sir Christopher Wren, to whom he was related by marriage, around 1680. Then, or shortly afterwards, Sir Christopher designed two wings for the house, which were built, but the main house itself was not designed or constructed – probably because money was short. However, in 1692, after Fermor had made an advantageous marriage, he turned again to the project, and Wren recommended Hawksmoor, who designed and constructed Easton Neston unsupervised. Because the other major houses he was involved with (Castle Howard and Blenheim Palace) were undertaken in collaboration with Vanbrugh, Easton Neston is remembered as the only country house that this remarkable architect built alone.

PILASTERS AND COLUMNS

Hawksmoor's house is a small-scale palace. Built from the finest cream-coloured Helmdon stone (also used at Blenheim Palace and Stowe), Easton Neston is rectangular, with three storeys on the two main façades: first a ground floor, then two equal upper storeys each containing eight tall windows. At the four corners and between all the windows, pilasters (decorative features of attached pillars or columns) rise the entire height of the façade. On the entrance front, two rounded Corinthian columns, one

Above: In 1876, this engraving of Easton Neston and part of the grounds was printed in the Illustrated London News.

on either side of the door, rise to a round-topped pediment cut with the Fermor arms and motto *Hora e sempre* ('Now and forever'). Above the door, in line with the top-storey windows, is an arched 'Venetian window', while at roof level a balustrade is adorned with urns on top of each of the pilasters. The windows on the shorter sides of the house reveal the fact that it contains two 'mezzanine' floors for servants between the main floors of the house, making five storeys in all.

GRANDIOSE PLANS

Hawksmoor drew plans for a large and elaborate forecourt at Easton Neston. He suggested building two side wings to house stables on one side and servants' rooms on the other, and a splendid colonnade flanking the entrance. He did build the entrance piers (which are still standing) and the stable block (quickly demolished), but otherwise these grandiose plans did not come to fruition.

INTERIOR ALTERATIONS

The interior of Easton Neston has been changed somewhat since Hawksmoor built it – notably the Drawing Room was elaborately decorated with intricate

---

NICHOLAS HAWKSMOOR

Like his mentor, Sir Christopher Wren, Nicholas Hawksmoor is remembered above all as a church architect. Hawksmoor worked with Wren on the rebuilding of St Paul's Cathedral, built several superb London churches and designed the

towers on the west front of Westminster Abbey. He also played a major role in building Castle Howard and Blenheim Palace, in addition to Easton Neston.

Born around 1660 in Nottinghamshire, Hawksmoor began working for Wren by 1680. His career advanced swiftly: before his 40th birthday, he was working alongside Vanbrugh at Castle Howard. For many years his work was overshadowed by that of Vanbrugh and Wren, but today he is increasingly seen as a highly original and gifted architect who combined the classicism of Wren with the Baroque of Vanbrugh. Hawksmoor also designed a new quadrangle at All Souls College, Oxford University, combining a classical interior with a Gothic exterior. He died in London in 1736.

Left: The West Front at Westminster Abbey. The lower part was built in the 15th century, the towers added by Hawksmoor.

Above: Hawksmoor's design for Easton Neston exudes stately elegance. His grand plans for a dramatic Baroque-style use of space with a forecourt and side wings were, unfortunately, not brought to fruition.

plasterwork in the mid-18th century and his large hall divided in two in the late 19th century to make a dining room alongside a smaller hall. However, the other main rooms remain unchanged, and on a bright day are flooded with light through the tall windows that rise almost from floor to ceiling, as does the elegant staircase with Tijou-style balustrade in wrought iron.

CHANGE OF OWNERSHIP

Easton Neston remained in the hands of Sir William Fermor's descendants for a little over three centuries, always as a private home and never open to the public. But the costs of renovation following a fire in July 2002 severely

tested the family finances, and in 2005 Lord Hesketh sold the house and part of its 3,319-acre (1,343ha) estate to St Petersburg-born US-based fashion businessman, Leon Max.

A BAROQUE BUILDING?

In contrast with other leading architects of his day, Hawksmoor made no voyages to see Italian and French buildings at first hand, and his classical influences all came via the study of reproductions in books. Architectural historians see elements at Easton Neston derived from the mid-16th-century palaces built by Michelangelo in the Piazza del Campidoglio on the Capitoline Hill in Rome. But, especially in Hawskmoor's large-scale courtyard design that was never built, continental influences prevail. There are also traces of the Baroque – the dramatic and exuberant monumental style more fully expressed in later houses, such as Castle Howard and

Blenheim Palace, on which Hawksmoor worked with Sir John Vanbrugh. Easton Neston can be seen as a forerunner of these buildings, an early flowering of the English Baroque. It also anticipates the Petit Trianon at Versailles, built in 1762–8 by Ange-Jacques Gabriel for Louis XV's mistress, Madame de Pompadour.

Below: Easton Neston's owner in the 1930s, Thomas Fermor-Hesketh (1st Baron Hesketh), stands between his daughters.

MARLBOROUGH HOUSE
AND THE CHURCHILLS

Marlborough House, alongside St James's Palace in Pall Mall, London, was built in 1709–11 to plans by Sir Christopher Wren for John Churchill, 1st Duke of Marlborough, and his wife, Sarah, Duchess of Marlborough and close friend of Queen Anne. The Duchess was the driving force behind the project, arranging a lease on the land, selecting Wren as architect – rather than Sir John Vanbrugh, who was then engaged by the Duke on Blenheim Palace – and, indeed, overseeing the final stages of building herself.

The dignified, originally two-storey house was, as the Duchess requested of Wren, 'strong, plain and convenient'. The design may have been drawn by Wren's son, also called Christopher, with his father's guidance. Its red bricks came from Holland, and had been carried as ballast in ships returning from taking supplies to the Duke of Marlborough's armies in the Low Countries.

The house contains the grand two-storey Saloon with paintings by Louis Laguerre of the Duke's triumph at the Battle of Blenheim. The ceiling features a painting by Orazio Gentileschi,

originally in the entrance hall of the Queen's House, Greenwich, but removed to Marlborough House at the start of the 18th century with Queen Anne's approval. The magnificent Ramillies Staircase, with black marble steps, ascends beneath paintings by Laguerre of scenes from another of the Duke's great battles, Ramillies.

The Duke of Marlborough died in 1722 and his body lay in state in Marlborough House prior to his funeral in Westminster Abbey. The Duchess died

Above: 'Strong, plain and convenient' – and, with Hampton Court, another example of the Anglo-Dutch strain in Wren's output.

after a long widowhood at Marlborough House in 1744. Sir William Chambers extended the house in the 1770s, increasing it from the original two to three storeys.

A ROYAL PALACE

In 1817, the land and the house that stood on it reverted to the Crown. Marlborough House was the London residence of Edward, Prince of Wales (the future Edward VII), and his wife, Princess Alexandra of Denmark, from 1863 to 1901 and was immortalized in the popular name for the Prince's raffish friends, the 'Marlborough House set'. The future George V was born at Marlborough House, in 1865, and lived there while Prince of Wales in the 1900s.

Later, it was twice the home of widowed queens, first of Edward VII's widow, Alexandra, in 1910–25, and then of George V's widow, Mary, in 1936–53. In 1965, the house became home to the Commonwealth Secretariat and the Commonwealth Foundations and today is used for international conferences.

JOHN CHURCHILL, 1ST DUKE OF MARLBOROUGH

The 1st Duke of Marlborough is renowned as one of England's greatest generals. His reputation rests on the series of great victories he won over the army of Louis XIV of France, most famously at Blenheim (1704), Ramillies (1706) and Oudenarde (1708); the Baroque masterpiece of Blenheim Palace in Oxfordshire was begun as a gift from Queen Anne and country in gratitude for the first of these. Before these years of greatness, he had survived disgrace, including imprisonment in 1691, when he was suspected of plotting to restore James II to the throne.

Above: John Churchill by Christian Linke.

UPPARK
AN ELEGANT COUNTRY HOUSE

The delightful country house of Uppark near Petersfield in West Sussex commands a breathtaking view of the South Downs. It was built *c.*1690 for Ford, Lord Grey of Werke, who was created Earl of Tankerville in 1695. Some authorities identify the architect as William Talman, who was dismissed around this time by Sir William Cavendish, 1st Duke of Devonshire, from Chatsworth House.

AN ELEGANT DWELLING

Uppark was built on the site of an earlier house in a well-established country park belonging to the lords Grey. It has an elegant brick and stone south façade of nine bays, and the arms of a later owner, Sir Matthew Fetherstonhaugh, affixed to the pediment that rises over the central upper-floor

windows. Of particular interest are the highly decorated modillions, or brackets, that support the roof cornice and the pediment.

Uppark is also celebrated for its elegant 18th-century interiors, installed by Sir Matthew and his wife, Sarah. The principal rooms include a Saloon that recalls in its lavish decoration the Double Cube Room at Wilton House.

LADY HAMILTON

An Uppark resident of note in the late 18th century was Emma Hart, later better known as Lady Hamilton, wife of Sir William Hamilton and mistress of Horatio, Lord Nelson. In 1781, aged around 18, Emma lived at Uppark as the mistress of Sir Harry Fetherstonhaugh. The table in the dining room is the one on which Emma is said to have danced naked for Sir Harry and his friends.

Above: The splendid brick and stone south front at Uppark, with the Featherstonhaugh arms in the pediment.

A PHOENIX FROM THE ASHES

Following a disastrous fire, which gutted the house in 1989, Uppark became a virtual laboratory for the latest techniques in meticulous architectural restoration. As part of this restoration by the National Trust, the gardens were remade in line with the 18th-century designs of Humphry Repton.

Left: Gilded opulence. The lavish interiors of Uppark provided an arena for gracious living.

THE HOUSEKEEPER'S SON

The novelist H.G. Wells, author of *The Time Machine* and *The War of the Worlds*, spent some of his early years at Uppark, where his mother, Sarah Neal, was a ladies' maid and housekeeper in the 1870s–80s. At the time, Wells was trying to make his way in the world, and returned a number of times to Uppark after failed placements as a draper's apprentice, a chemist's assistant and a teacher. Wells wrote in his autobiography that 'the place had a great effect on me'; and he certainly took full advantage of Uppark's splendid library.

PART SIX

THE MODERN ERA

1714–TODAY

Many of the great houses of the 18th and 19th centuries served as magnets for the leading architects, designers, painters, sculptors and garden planners of the age. For much of this period, royal residences were overshadowed by the great country homes of the aristocracy, but later monarchs built on a much grander scale – notably at Buckingham Palace and Carlton House.

Left: Buckingham Palace. The Duke of Buckingham's town house became a royal residence in 1762 and was transformed into a palace by John Nash after 1826. Its east front was remodelled by Sir Aston Webb in 1913.

ENGLAND TIMELINE, 1714–TODAY

Above: Blenheim Palace is one of Sir John Vanbrugh's masterpieces.

Above: George IV and Wyatville rebuilt Windsor Castle in Gothic Revival style.

Above: Castle Drogo, Devon, Lutyens' extraordinary 20th-century castle.

ENGLAND, 1714–99

1715 Colen Campbell begins Wanstead House in Essex.

*c.***1720** Castle Howard nears completion.

1722 Blenheim Palace in Oxfordshire, close to completion.

1722 James Gibbs builds Ditchley Park, Oxfordshire, for the 2nd Earl of Lichfield.

1723 Campbell completes Mereworth Castle, Kent, based on a villa by Palladio.

1725 The 3rd Earl of Burlington builds Chiswick House (now in west London).

1734 William Kent begins building Holkham Hall, Norfolk.

1734 Kent builds the south portico, Stowe House, Buckinghamshire.

1747 Horace Walpole begins rebuilding his villa at Strawberry Hill, Middlesex.

1751–57 'Capability' Brown landscapes the park at Petworth House, Sussex.

1758 Robert Adam begins work at Kedleston Hall, Derbyshire.

1762 Robert Adam begins work on the interior of Syon House, Middlesex.

1762 George III buys the future Buckingham Palace as a family house.

1764–79 Robert Adam rebuilds Kenwood House in Hampstead.

1781 George III buys the Dutch House in Kew, south west London.

1783 The Prince of Wales begins refurbishment of Carlton House, London.

1788 James Wyatt completes work on Heveningham Hall, Suffolk.

ENGLAND, 1800–1899

1803 John Nash builds Cronkhill in Shropshire.

1805 Sandridge Park built in Devon, another Nash house.

1806–14 North front of Longleat House, Wiltshire, rebuilt by Jeffry Wyatt.

1810–20 Robert Smirke builds Eastnor Castle in the Norman Revival style.

1815–23 John Nash builds the Royal Pavilion, Brighton.

1823 onwards George IV and Jeffry Wyatville rebuild Windsor Castle in the Gothic Revival style.

1826 George IV begins the conversion of Buckingham House into a palace.

1837–45 Anthony Salvin builds Harlaxton Hall in Lincolnshire.

1845–51 Prince Albert builds Osborne House, Isle of Wight.

1847–50 An east front is added to Buckingham Palace.

*c.***1850** Anthony Salvin rebuilds Alnwick Castle, Northumberland.

1855 Paxton begins building Mentmore Towers, Buckinghamshire, for Baron Mayer Amschel de Rothschild.

1862 The future Edward VII buys the Sandringham estate in Norfolk.

1873–76 Pugin rebuilds Carlton Towers, Yorkshire, in the Victorian Gothic style.

1870 Buckler begins lavish rebuilding of Arundel Castle, West Sussex.

1874–79 Destailleur builds Waddesdon Manor, Buckinghamshire.

ENGLAND, 1900–TODAY

1900–03 At Elveden Hall, Suffolk, Lord Iveagh builds the marble Indian Hall.

1911 New east forecourt and Victoria Memorial at Buckingham Palace.

1912–30 Edwin Lutyens builds Castle Drogo, Devon, for Julius Charles Drewe.

1913 East front of Buckingham Palace refaced in Portland stone by Aston Webb.

1931–36 Courtaulds restore the 15th-century Great Hall at Eltham Palace, and build a superb Art Deco house.

1958–62 Phillimore builds Arundel Park for the Duke and Duchess of Norfolk.

1961–62 Patrick Gwynne builds an ultramodern country house at Witley Park, Surrey.

1963–65 The unusual country house of Stratton Park, Hampshire, incorporates the surviving Doric portico of a ruined 'Greek Revival' house.

1967–71 Raymond Erith and Quinlan Terry build Kings Walden Bury, Herts.

1971–73 John Dennys designs Eaton Hall, Cheshire, in the Modern style. In 1989 the house is refaced in a more traditional guise.

1976 Elizabeth II buys Gatcombe Park, Gloucestershire, for Princess Anne and Captain Mark Phillips.

1980 Duchy of Cornwall buys Highgrove in Gloucestershire, for Prince Charles.

2003 Quinlan Terry's Ferne Park, Dorset, wins acclaim.

N

W **E**

S

SCOTLAND

Banburgh Castle

Alnwick Castle

Seaton Delaval Hall

North Sea

Muncaster Castle

Castle Howard

Harewood House

Irish Sea

Brodsworth Hall

ENGLAND

Heaton Hall

Chatsworth

The Wash

Kedleston Hall

Nottingham Castle

Holkham Hall

Blickling

Sandringham

Houghton Hall

Rousham House

Weston Park

Upton House

Arbury Hall

Elveden Hall

Stoke Park Pavilions

Althorp

Woburn Abbey

WALES

Eastnor Castle

Ditchley Park

Stowe House

Hellens

Sudeley Castle

Waddesdon Manor

Knebworth House

Blenheim Palace

Hughenden Manor

Cliveden

Eltham Palace

Bristol Channel

Prior Park

Windsor Castle

Highclere Castle

Polesden Lacy

Port Lympne

Stourhead

Wilton House

Petworth House

Clandon Park

Strait of Dover

Beaulieu

Uppark

Arundel Castle

Castle Drogo

Osborne House

Carisbrooke Castle

Norris Castle

The Royal Pavilion

St Michael's Mount

English Channel

Kenwood House

Kensington Palace

Osterley Park

Chiswick House

Buckingham Palace

Westminster Palace

Syon House

Kew Palace

Marble Hill House

Strawberry Hill

LONDON

Hampton Court Palace

SCOTLAND, WALES

AND NORTHERN IRELAND TIMELINES, 1714–TODAY

Above: Balmoral Castle was Prince Albert's fantasy Highland castle.

SCOTLAND, 1714–TODAY

1746–89 Inveraray Castle, Argyll, rebuilt to the design of Robert Adam.

1777–92 Robert Adam works on the refurbishment of Culzean Castle, Ayrshire.

1815 William Wilkins's Dalmeny House, Lothian, is built in the Tudor Revival style.

*c.***1825** Architect William Burn's Carstairs House, Strathclyde, is built in the Elizabethan Revival style.

1855 Prince Albert completes Balmoral Castle, Grampian, in the Scottish Baronial style.

1891 A Scots Baronial east wing is added to Glamis Castle in Tayside.

1901–05 Manderston near Duns, Berwickshire, one of the finest of Edwardian country houses, is built by John Kinross for Sir James Miller.

1912 Lt-Col John MacRae-Gilstrap begins the restoration of 13th-century Eilean Donan Castle near Dornie.

1952 The Queen Mother buys and restores the Castle of Mey in Caithness.

*c.***1955** Edward Bruce, 10th Earl of Elgin, rebuilds the 17th-century Culross Abbey House in Fife.

1955 The Queen Mother adds a new wing to Birkhall near Balmoral.

1960 Claud Phillimore designs Abercairney at Crieff in Perthshire.

1938–70 Restoration of Kisimul Castle, Isle of Barra, by Robert MacNeil.

Irish Sea

Plass Newydd   Penrhyn
                Castle

Cardigan
  Bay

WALES

Picton
Castle
   Cresselly House

ENGLAND

Castell
Coch   Cardiff
        Castle

Bristol Channel

*Above: Castell Coch, Wales, was remodelled
by the 3rd Marquess of Bute and Burges.*

WALES, 1714–TODAY

1749–52 Picton Castle interior
remodelled by Sir John Philipps.
1770 Cresselly House built for
John Bartlett Allen.
*c.*1825 Thomas Hopper builds Penrhyn
Castle in the Norman Revival style.
1866 William Burges rebuilds Cardiff
Castle for the 3rd Marquess of Bute.
1875 Burges rebuilds Castell Coch, near
Cardiff, for Lord Bute.
1977 John Taylor builds Castle Gyrn in
Wales – a country house in castle form.

*Above: Castle Coole, a fine Irish neo-
classical house, was built by James Wyatt.*

NORTHERN IRELAND, 1714–TODAY

1790–98 James Wyatt builds
Castle Coole for the 1st Earl
of Belmore.
1819 Thomas Hopper begins
work on Gosford Castle, Co Armagh.
*c.*1835 Edward Blore rebuilds Narrow
Water Castle in the Tudor Revival style.
1867–70 Belfast Castle is built in the
Scots Baronial style.
1824 The Argory, Moy, a neoclassical
house, built for Walter McGeough.

Hezlett House   North
                  Channel

NORTHERN
IRELAND

Barons Court   Belfast
                  Castle

The Argory   Ballywater
                  Park
Florence   Castle   Mount
Court   Coole   Stewart
            Gosford
            Castle   Castle Ward

IRELAND   Narrow Water
                            Castle

                            Irish
                            Sea

CHAPTER TWENTY-ONE

THE BAROQUE AND PALLADIAN STYLES

c.1714–c.1760

Soldier, playwright and London socialite, John Vanbrugh, had no experience of building when, in 1699, in association with Nicholas Hawksmoor, he began to draw up designs for the grand and exuberant Castle Howard in Yorkshire. Starting from scratch as an architect, his revolutionary great house – a group of buildings full of energy and movement – was designed to be seen as a vast sculpture against garden structures and ornaments in a great landscape. It was the first major statement of the Baroque in English architecture.

The often sensuous and dramatic Baroque style in art and architecture had developed from *c.1600* in continental Europe, particularly in the strongly Roman Catholic countries of Italy and Spain. As it spread to Protestant countries, including England, it found expression in monumental and highly ornamented buildings set in grand, picturesque landscapes. Vanbrugh went on, with Hawksmoor, to design and build another great Baroque house, Blenheim Palace.

However, to some early 18th-century architects and patrons, the Baroque style seemed overblown. These men looked back to more sober classical buildings designed almost a century earlier by Inigo Jones, under the influence of the Italian Renaissance architect and theorist, Andrea Palladio. Led by Colen Campbell, Richard Boyle, 3rd Earl of Burlington, and William Kent, the Palladian movement resulted in the building of more restrained houses on the villa plan, such as Campbell's Mereworth Castle and Wanstead, Lord Burlington's Chiswick House and Kent's Holkham Hall.

Left: Castle Howard's crowning glory is its majestic dome and lantern. Vanbrugh and Hawksmoor added the feature to their design after building had begun in 1699.

CASTLE HOWARD
VANBRUGH'S MASTERPIECE

The immensely proud Charles Howard, 3rd Earl of Carlisle, had the opportunity to make a grand architectural statement when his centuries-old family mansion, Henderskelfe Castle in Yorkshire, was severely damaged by fire in 1693. He called on one of the leading architects of his day, William Talman, to draw up plans. But the men quarrelled over the architect's proposed charges, and Lord Carlisle dismissed Talman. Then he made an astonishing decision, entrusting the vast project to John Vanbrugh, a rising playwright and man-about-town in London. Vanbrugh had already proved himself a brilliant man, but there was clearly no way of knowing whether he could apply his abilities to architecture.

Vanbrugh turned to his friend, the architect Nicholas Hawksmoor, for help and also worked closely with Lord Carlisle himself on the house. Credit for the exuberant Baroque masterpiece they created is usually given to Vanbrugh but should really be shared by all three. The first designs were made in 1699, and building – using a delightful pale yellow local stone – began in 1700.

Below: Vanbrugh's Temple of the Four Winds was unfinished at his death in 1726. It was completed in 1738. Francesco Vassalli decorated the inside with scagliola.

ENGLAND'S FIRST DOME
The main entrance front faces north. Beneath an imposing dome, its grand central block is faced with Corinthian pilasters and contains elegant arched doorways and windows; statues and urns occupy niches and stand on the balustrade. The magnificent dome and lantern, the first in England, was completed by 1706, predating the dome of St Paul's Cathedral, London, by two years. However, the dome visible today is actually a meticulous 20th-century reconstruction, built after the original dome was destroyed in a fire of 1940.

EAST AND WEST WINGS
Wings to the west and east were intended to extend forward to create a grand forecourt. The east wing was built by Vanbrugh and Hawksmoor, and beyond it is a second service enclosure, the Laundry Court. The original design called for a similar structure on the west side, but the western wing was not built, because Lord Carlisle lost interest in the project. (The west wing we see today was added in 1759 in the Palladian style by Sir Thomas Robinson.)

Above: Beauty, energy, exuberance, drama. Thanks to renovation, Castle Howard still has the magnificent profile its creators envisaged. The Atlas Fountain (foreground) was added by the 7th Earl in the 1850s.

The south, or garden, front also makes dramatic use of Corinthian pilasters: here smaller ones on the single-storey wings echo the large and impressive ones on the two-storey main block. The whole front has a rusticated basement with square windows that contrast with the arched ones above them.

THE ESSENCE OF THE BAROQUE
Inside, the hugely impressive entrance hall is 52ft (16m) square and is lit from the lantern in the dome, which rises to a height of 70ft (21m) overhead. Two staircases and four stone corridors lead off, creating a sense of movement through a dramatic use of architectural space that exemplifies the finest qualities of the English Baroque.

The hall frescoes and the decoration within the dome were painted by the Italian artist Giovanni Pellegrini in 1709–12. The fireplace and Niche of

Bacchus were made of *scagliola* (a combination of marble and plaster) by Italian craftsmen Bagutti and Plura in 1711–12. It is one of the earliest examples in England of the craft, which became very popular later in the century.

The largest of the other rooms is now the Long Gallery in the west wing, though prior to a fire in 1940 some of the many staterooms on the south front were grander. Left unfinished for 50 years, the gallery was completed by Charles Tatham *c.*1810. This wing also contained the main bedrooms.

DESIGNING THE GROUNDS

In the early 1720s, with the house inhabitable but the west wing not started, Lord Carlisle became more interested in setting out the gardens and park with pavilions and 'rustic' buildings than in completing the house to the original designs. Vanbrugh and Hawksmoor continued to work on these projects at Castle Howard until their deaths, in 1726 and 1736 respectively.

In the grounds, Vanbrugh designed the domed Temple of the Four Winds, originally known as the Temple of Diana and partly based on Andrea Palladio's Villa Capra near Vicenza (the same house that inspired Colen Campbell's Mereworth Castle). The temple was built in 1723–38.

The cylindrical mausoleum for the burial of Lord Carlisle and his descendants, the grandest in Britain, was

originally designed by Hawksmoor in 1729, although his plan was significantly altered in the 1730s by others, including Sir Thomas Robinson and Lord Burlington. In addition to the vaults, it contains a chapel with a graceful domed ceiling. It was finished in the 1740s. Hawksmoor based his design on that of the 1502 Church of St Pietro in Montorio in Rome, designed by Donato Bramante for Pope Julius II.

The grounds also contain an obelisk, erected in 1714, at the head of the drive where the great lime avenues intersect; a pyramid designed by Hawksmoor in 1728; a gatehouse that was originally a freestanding 'pyramid arch' designed by

Above: Eighteenth-century promenaders admire Castle Howard's south front.

Vanbrugh in 1719, but which had wings added by Sir Thomas Robinson in 1756–8; and mock fortifications in the style of medieval town walls, erected near the gatehouse in the 1720s.

DRAMATIC SETTING

Building these structures in the grounds was part of the architects' original conception, for they wanted to create the most dramatic of settings for their imposing house. Horace Walpole, connoisseur and creator of Strawberry Hill at Twickenham, visited Castle Howard in 1772. His reaction would doubtless have delighted Hawksmoor, Vanbrugh and Lord Carlisle, for he enthused about its sublime environs as much as the house itself: 'Nobody…had informed me that I should at one view see a palace, a town, a fortified city, temples on high places, woods worthy of being each a metropolis of the Druids, vales connected to hills by other woods, the noblest lawn in the world fenced by half the horizon, and a mausoleum that would tempt one to be buried alive; in short I have seen gigantic palaces before but never a sublime one.'

THE ENGLISH BAROQUE

The word 'baroque' denoted works of art that ignored the accepted proportions or rules. Paintings, sculpture and architecture by great Baroque artists, such as the Italian Gian Lorenzo Bernini, were sensuous and dramatic, aiming to appeal to the soul by way of the senses. When the style was taken up in Protestant northern Europe, it tended to be more formal and restrained, appealing to viewers through its monumental size, surface ornamentation, the geometric arrangement of its constituent parts and its interaction with its setting, be it the streets around a London church or a picturesque country park around a stately house. Some historians see the English version of the Baroque as springing fully formed from Vanbrugh and Hawksmoor at Castle Howard; others argue that it had its antecedent a little earlier in Hawksmoor's Easton Neston.

BLENHEIM PALACE
AND THE MARLBOROUGHS

In 1705, Queen Anne gave the royal manor of Woodstock near Oxford to John Churchill, 1st Duke of Marlborough. The land was to be the setting for a great mansion, a lasting tribute from a grateful queen and country for Marlborough's victory over a French-Bavarian army in August 1704, at Blenheim, in southern Germany.

To build the great house that would become known as Blenheim Palace, the Duke chose John Vanbrugh. In doing so he overlooked the more obvious claim of Sir Christopher Wren, Surveyor of the Queen's Works and the choice of Marlborough's strong-willed and powerful wife, Sarah. As a result, Vanbrugh and the Duchess got off to a bad start, and they were at odds throughout the building, much of which took place while the Duke himself was away at war.

With Nicholas Hawksmoor, Vanbrugh set out to build a monument to the Duke's great victories and the age of

Queen Anne, a Baroque mansion that placed enormous emphasis on style and grandeur. The Duchess, however, wanted a country house designed for comfort.

ROYAL DISFAVOUR

Building began in 1705. The arguments between Vanbrugh and the Duchess were compounded by major problems in paying for materials and labour: costs were supposedly to be covered by the Queen and the state but money was often not forthcoming, particularly after the Marlboroughs lost favour with the Queen and retreated into continental exile in 1712. Work at Blenheim ceased that year, with the workforce owed £45,000. After Anne's death in 1714, the Duke and Duchess returned and work resumed on the house. But after a major row with the Duchess, Vanbrugh resigned in fury in 1717, and Hawksmoor worked on alone. The great house was largely completed by 1722, the year of the Duke's death, but this brought no

Above: Aristocratic breeding. Churchill (left), with wife, Lady Sarah, and five children.

end to the animosity between the Duchess and Vanbrugh. In 1725, he was even refused entrance by the Duchess when he attempted to visit with the Earl of Carlisle to view his work.

THE GREAT COURT

Everywhere at Blenheim, the scale is vast. The house's main entrance stands beneath a towering portico bearing the Duke's arms on the pediment, amid the extravagantly ornamented splendour of the Great Court. On either side of the portico are curved arcades; the four corners of the 480ft (145m) wide central block are topped with extraordinary towers bearing pinnacles 30ft (9m) high carved by Grinling Gibbons. Tuscan colonnades connect the house to the service and stable courts. Enclosed by these side wings, the Great Court is no less than 300ft (90m) deep.

A long straight drive leads directly into the Great Court, but modern visitors enter through the East Gate in the wall of the service court, and then through another fine gateway beneath the clock tower into the Great Court. The house's plainer, and perhaps more elegant, south front contains another great portico topped with a 30-ton marble bust of Louis XIV. This was a spoil of war that the Duke had taken from Tournai in 1709.

SIR JOHN VANBRUGH

Vanbrugh was born in 1664 and served as a soldier, 1686–98. He was imprisoned in the Bastille in Paris as a spy. He came to eminence as a playwright in London, with *The Relapse* and *The Provok'd Wife*, and mixed with great men of the day in the Kit Cat Club, where he met Lord Carlisle, who commissioned him to design his first house, Castle Howard in Yorkshire. Vanbrugh worked with Nicholas Hawksmoor on Castle Howard, Blenheim Palace, and Kimbolton Castle. Working alone, he built Kings Weston House in Gloucestershire, Eastbury in Dorset and Seaton Delaval Hall in Northumberland – the last regarded as another great masterpiece. His final work was the north front of Grimsthorpe Castle, Lincolnshire (1722–6). Vanbrugh

Above: Sir John Vanbrugh, engraved by artist John Simon (c.1675–1751).

served as Comptroller of Royal Works under Anne and George I. Until his death in 1726, he worked for Carlisle at Castle Howard, where his Temple of the Four Winds was completed after his death.

THE GREAT HALL

Blenheim's interior was designed on a correspondingly vast scale and decorated by the finest craftsmen. Behind the entrance portico stands the Great Hall – 67ft (20m) high, with vast Corinthian columns and tall arches, beneath a painted ceiling, by Sir James Thornhill, of Marlborough showing a map of Blenheim battlefield and being rewarded by Britannia with a laurel wreath. The hall leads into the Saloon, decorated with heroic murals and ceiling by Louis Laguerre and also featuring magnificent marble door frames by Hawksmoor. From the Saloon, a great room leads off on either side; these rooms were originally state apartments but were later turned into drawing rooms.

The last part of the house to be completed was the west wing. It contains the splendid Long Library, 180ft (55m) long, designed as a picture gallery but finished by Hawksmoor as a library, and the chapel, featuring a grand marble tomb designed by William Kent and carved by John Michael Rysbrack to hold the remains of the Duke and Duchess.

GARDEN AND PARKLAND

As at Castle Howard, Vanbrugh and Hawksmoor devoted as much attention to the setting of Blenheim as to its façades and interior. On the south side,

Right: In the Red Drawing Room hangs a portrait of the 9th Duke and his American heiress wife, Consuelo Vanderbilt.

a monumental parterre was laid out by Henry Wise, gardener at Hampton Court. A 134ft (41m) column of Victory, raised to celebrate the Duke's military triumphs, stands at the end of an avenue of elms planted to recall the arrangement of Marlborough's soldiers at the Battle of Blenheim. Vanbrugh channelled the River Glyme into three streams and built a vast bridge across them; the bridge was partly submerged when 'Capability' Brown landscaped the park in the 1760s and created a lake in place of the streams.

BAROQUE EMBODIMENT

The great house in its carefully orchestrated setting aims throughout for an impression of power, a celebration of great English victories and the military prowess of Marlborough himself: an embodiment that was, in Vanbrugh's words, a

Above: An aerial view allows the eye to take in the complete composition, with 300ft (90m)- deep enclosure and colonnades linking to the east and west courts.

creation of 'beauty, magnificence and duration'. Such an achievement is not to everyone's taste, however. Even when it was newly finished, the great palace was not universally approved. At a time when the classical Palladian movement was gathering force, Blenheim appeared to many as heavy, indulgent and overblown. But others have seen it as the highest and fullest expression of the English Baroque, an achievement, according to Sir John Soane, architect of the Bank of England in 1788, that proves Vanbrugh (and perhaps, in truth, also Hawksmoor) to have been no less than 'the Shakespeare of architects'.

MEREWORTH CASTLE
AND PALLADIAN HOUSES

The elegant Mereworth Castle in Kent, a domed rectangular block with a classical portico on each of its four sides, is a recreation of the mid-16th-century Villa Capra, or Rotonda, built by Andrea Palladio near Vicenza in Italy. Built by the Scottish architect Colen Campbell in 1720–3, Mereworth is one of the finest early examples of the Palladian movement in 18th-century English architecture (the first in England being Wilbury House in Wiltshire, built c.1710 by William Benson).

ROMAN STYLE

'Palladianism' takes its name from Andrea Palladio (1508–80), who, as well as being the architect and designer of elegant villas and churches, was an interpreter of classical building and, in particular, of the work of 1st-century BC Roman architect, Vitruvius. Palladio's illustrated volume, the *Four Books of Architecture*, first published in 1570, was reissued in a lavish English edition in London in 1715, at a time when – following the accession of King George I in 1714 – many of the wealthy elite of Georgian England, who had often travelled widely in Italy, were turning away from the prevailing taste for

Below: Palladio in England. This elevation of Mereworth Castle was published in Colen Campbell's Vitruvius Britannicus *(1724).*

extravagantly ornate houses and developing an enthusiasm for more restrained, classical buildings.

The 'Palladians' looked back to the buildings of Inigo Jones, who, almost a century earlier, had tried to put the principles of Palladio into practice in the Queen's House, Greenwich, and the Banqueting House, Whitehall. Following Palladio, they believed buildings should be constructed 'rationally' in line with the principles of proportion, symmetry and harmony found in the natural world.

One of the leading Palladians was the architect of Mereworth Castle, Colen Campbell, who, also in 1715, published his *Vitruvius Britannicus* – a survey of classical buildings in England. In the introduction he praised 'great Palladio' and dismissed the Baroque artist, Bernini, as 'affected and licentious'.

PALLADIANISM AT MEREWORTH

Mereworth Castle is a triumph of elegant design. Its dome is encased in lead and contains 24 chimneys that pass through its shell to exit via a single opening at the top. Beneath the dome is a delightful circular hall, called the Saloon by Campbell, measuring 35ft

Above: Campbell built Stourhead House, Wiltshire, in the 1720s. Note the statues above the pedimented portico. The side pavilions were added in the 1790s.

(11m) in diameter and 80ft (24m) high, and lit from above by windows in the base of the dome. It has terracotta walls decorated with stucco in the form of foliage and graceful reclining figures. An extremely refined drawing room fills the whole length of the south front. A spiral staircase leads to a circular gallery at first-floor level that looks over the hall.

Below: Stourhead gardens were designed by Henry Home II in 1741–80 and inspired by the landscapes of Poussin and Claude.

The villa stands on a mound in a broad valley and was, until the late 1800s, surrounded by a moat. The moat was a ⬚⬚⬚⬚⬚⬚ from the original castle on the site, inherited and redeveloped by Campbell's patron John Fane, after 1736 the 7th Earl of Westmorland. The two graceful pavilions that flank the entrance front of Campbell's villa were added in the late 1730s, probably by James Stuart.

OTHER PALLADIAN HOUSES

Before he began work at Mereworth Castle in 1720, Campbell had already designed and started building (c.1714) a

Below: The 3rd Earl of Burlington's Chiswick House (now in west London) was based on the same Palladian villa at Vicenza that Campbell recreated at Mereworth Castle.

big influential Palladian villa at Wanstead House in Essex, as well as creating, in 1717, the first Palladian façade in London for Burlington House, Piccadilly, home of Richard Boyle, 3rd Earl of Burlington, himself a key figure in the Palladian movement. In addition, he built Stourhead House, in Wiltshire (c.1717–25), for banker Henry Hoare and later worked alongside James Gibbs at Houghton Hall, in Norfolk, from c.1722.

Several Palladian houses were built at this time. The 3rd Earl of Burlington, Campbell's patron for Burlington House, built his own Palladian villa,

Above: The Palladian bridge at Prior Park was part of a landscape garden created by Bath entrepreneur Ralph Allen.

Chiswick House (now in west London), beginning in 1725. Burlington's protégé, the painter William Kent, turned architect in 1734 when he designed Holkham Hall in Norfolk with Lord Leicester, another influential figure in the Palladian revival. Finally, in 1735–48, John Wood the Elder built Prior Park, near Bath, with gardens created by Ralph Allen and advice from poet Alexander Pope and 'Capability' Brown.

WANSTEAD HOUSE

Colen Campbell began work in 1715 on Wanstead House in Essex for banker, Sir Richard Child, later Earl Tylney. Now demolished, the house was a Palladian villa of significant size, measuring 260 x 70ft (79 x 21m), and was graced by a classical portico with a pediment 60ft (18m) wide and six Corinthian columns. It was built on the site of an earlier mansion Sir Richard inherited from his half-brother, Sir Josiah Child. Leading gardener George London developed the grounds.

Right: Wanstead House had a lavish ballroom, which is seen at its finest in this 'conversation piece' by William Hogarth.

HOLKHAM HALL
AND WILLIAM KENT

The stately Holkham Hall, near Wells in Norfolk, built after 1734 by William Kent and Matthew Brettingham, with copious advice from Lord Burlington and especially Thomas Coke, the Earl of Leicester, is celebrated as the most distinguished of all the great Palladian houses in England. Its coolly magnificent Marble Hall, which Kent and Leicester designed along the lines of a Roman basilica and which contains tall Ionic columns of alabaster, makes an unforgettable impression on all who see it.

The house consists of a rectangular central block containing the Marble Hall and staterooms, and four 'wings', one attached to each corner of the rectangle, containing visitors' apartments, family rooms, a chapel and kitchens. The wing containing the family rooms, which included the elegant Long Library, could be used as a self-contained house when Leicester was not entertaining in style and did not need the staterooms.

AUSTERE SOUTH FRONT

Holkham Hall's principal south, or garden, front is much discussed, for it takes Palladian restraint and distaste for ornament to the point of austere plainness. It is 344ft (105m) across, including the south-west and south-east

wings at the sides. In the centre rises a portico with six tall columns; towers project at the corners of the main block, each containing an arched three-light Venetian window on the *piano nobile* (the first floor, containing the principal apartments). Above these – and above the four square windows that are aligned horizontally across the front – rises an expanse of plain yellow brickwork where the eye might normally expect to see further windows or architectural ornament.

Above: The wide south front at Holkham, with its six-column portico, looks across formal gardens (designed in the 1850s by Nesfield).

Beneath the *piano nobile* is a rusticated basement containing small, functional windows. The overall effect borders on the severe – a precise study in symmetry and proportion.

Below: Elegant proportions, beautiful symmetry. Kent and Leicester created a vast Palladian house at Holkham in windswept Norfolk.

ARCHITECT AS DESIGNER

The house's interior is comparatively lavish, but even its richest interiors are handled with a fine Palladian sense of restraint. The ravishingly elegant Marble Hall rises to a height of 50ft (15m) and contains a wide flight of marble steps. These climb to a peristyle forming a gallery, off which lead doorways to the state rooms. Classical influences abound: the gilded ceiling is taken from an Inigo Jones design that was copied from the Pantheon in Rome; the fluted columns of Derbyshire marble are derived from those in the Roman Temple of Fortuna Virilis.

The staterooms are grandly elegant and display paintings and statuary acquired by Coke during a famous and extended Grand Tour of 1712–18. Beyond the hall is the Saloon, with gilded ceiling and door surrounds and velvet-lined walls. The Statue Gallery, which leads across the house from south to north, houses Coke's fine classical statues in curved niches – including an ancient Greek bust of Athenian aristocrat and historian, Thucydides, dating to c.4BC. The rooms are furnished with velvet-covered chairs and sofas, as well as side tables, all designed by Kent (at Holkham, he pioneered a new role for the architect as designer of all aspects of the patron's living space). He also designed fine interiors for the family rooms in the south-west wing, especially in the Long Library.

HOLKHAM'S STYLE

Other men also had a significant input into the house's appearance. These were Thomas Coke himself and Kent's chief patron and the great promoter of the Palladian style, Lord Burlington, as well as the Norfolk architect Matthew Brettingham, who was Clerk of Works on the project and later a competent architect with a good practice.

Right: Badminton House, Gloucestershire, where Kent reworked an earlier house in the Palladian style. This view is by Canaletto.

WILLIAM KENT

William Kent excelled as an architect, and as an interior and garden designer. He began as a painter, and while studying painting in Rome in 1709–19 he met his great patrons Richard Boyle, 3rd Earl of Burlington, and Thomas Coke, later Earl of Leicester. In 1719, he formed a lifelong association with Burlington when he decorated Burlington House in Piccadilly, London. Burlington secured Kent the position of Master Carpenter in the Office of Works in 1725, and in this capacity he rebuilt the stable block of King's Mews, Charing Cross, in 1732. (Now demolished, it stood on the site of the National Gallery in Trafalgar Square.)

William Kent also designed the Treasury Buildings and built the Horse Guards Building, both in Whitehall. As well as designing Holkham Hall, he was also architect of Badminton House, Gloucestershire. He designed interiors for Ditchley Park, Oxfordshire, and furnishings for Hampton Court Palace. As a garden designer, his work at Rousham

Above: William Kent's ability as a garden designer and interior decorator probably outshone his skill as an architect.

Park and Stowe House led a movement away from formal French-style gardens into informal 'natural' landscapes of the kind that would be further developed later in the century by 'Capability' Brown. He died in 1748.

Plans for the house may have first been conceived by Coke, Burlington and Kent when they met in Rome in 1715. Holkham Hall was not begun until 1734, however, largely because Coke lost a fortune in the collapse of the South Sea Company in 1720. Building work then carried on for 30 years until 1764, after the deaths of Kent (1748), Burlington (1753) and Leicester himself (1759). The house was dutifully completed by the Earl's widow – Lady Margaret, Baroness Clifford.

The park at Holkham, among the largest in England, contains an obelisk designed by Kent and erected before the house was built, in 1729. Formal avenues were created, but the park was landscaped by 'Capability' Brown later in the 18th century.

DITCHLEY PARK
AND JAMES GIBBS

The country house of Ditchley Park, near Oxford, is celebrated less for its exterior of weathered Burford stone and beautiful parkland setting, than for its elegant and well-preserved interiors designed by William Kent and Henry Flitcroft in the 1720s. It is also well known for its role in World War II, when it served as the weekend HQ for Winston Churchill and his War Cabinet in 1940–2, at a time when the Prime Minister's country residence at Chequers, in Buckinghamshire, was under threat of being bombed.

INELEGANT ROOFLINE
The house was designed and built not by Kent but by James Gibbs in 1722. His patron was George Henry Lee, 2nd Earl of Lichfield and grandson of King Charles II, and his mistress Barbara Villiers, Duchess of Cleveland. It consists of a central block connected to two perfectly symmetrical wings by curved colonnades. The main block has a truncated appearance, for its two main

Below: Gibbs's design for Ditchley Park inspired that of Arundel Park, Sussex, in the 1950s, which in turn began a revival of Palladianism in the later 20th century.

JAMES GIBBS: FAVOURED ARCHITECT OF TORY LORDS

Born in Aberdeenshire in 1682, James Gibbs studied in Rome and in his early career was an Italian Baroque architect. In this style he designed the Church of St Mary-le-Strand in London in 1714–17. But he was influenced by the prevailing enthusiasm for 'Palladianism' and began to mix classical and Baroque elements as in his celebrated Church of St-Martin-in-the-Fields, London (1722–6), which has both classical portico and towering steeple and was copied for churches throughout Britain and North America.

He was also a successful and influential country-house architect. He designed or contributed to at least 50 houses. While Vanbrugh was a favourite of the Whig nobility, Gibbs was the leading architect employed by Tories. His *Book of Architecture* (1728) was widely used as a pattern book. He was also a favourite at England's leading universities, designing the Senate House at Cambridge University (1722–30) and the Radcliffe Camera for Oxford University (1737–49).

Right: A Baroque Palladian? Gibbs' designs for both country houses and churches were highly influential.

floors, equipped with gracefully tall windows, are topped with a squat third level and an unsuccessful roofline with poorly positioned statues of Fortune and Fame and inelegant chimneys. Architectural historians point out that

Gibbs' original designs proposed the use of either a pediment and cupolas or a columned portico, and speculate that the final design must have been the result of a sudden shortage of funds when building was underway. The two wings, however, are very attractive: each has ten windows in the façade, a hipped roof and a clock tower.

ELEGANT INTERIORS
Ditchley Park's interiors are superb examples of early Georgian elegance. The entrance leads into a central hall two storeys high: its walls carry busts of leading philosophers and writers; carved embodiments of the Arts and the Sciences recline above the doorway into the Saloon, the splendid fireplace and the alcove opposite it; the hall ceiling was painted by Kent; and the Saloon contains a riot of Italian stucco work.

Above: A decidedly Eastern influence is evident in the design of this furnishing silk of 1738, which is hung at Ditchley Park.

Furniture and works of art are of the highest quality: in the White Drawing Room are two very fine eagle tables designed by Kent, and portraits by Sir Peter Lely of Charles II and Barbara Villiers. The house's chimney-pieces – always the most expensive items in decorative schemes – are by Christopher Horsenail and Henry Cheere.

AMERICAN CONNECTIONS

The house passed from the 2nd Earl of Lichfield through many generations of Dillon-Lee descendants until 1932,

Left: Intricate beauty. This side table, elegantly designed by Kent, is part of the interior decor at Ditchley Park.

when the 17th Viscount Dillon sold it. One branch of the Oxfordshire Lees settled in Virginia, where their most famous son was Confederate commander, Robert E. Lee.

In 1932, another American came to the rescue of Ditchley Park. He was Ronald Tree, a former managing editor of *Forum Magazine* in New York, who later became MP for Harborough, Leicestershire. With his wife, Nancy, also an American, he modernized the house and restored the garden. He came to

Above: The entrance hall at Ditchley. Note the ceiling painting by Kent and the busts of thinkers and writers arrayed around the walls.

know Churchill and agreed to the Prime Minister's request that leading Cabinet members might use Ditchley Park as a weekend HQ.

In the 1950s, David Wills bought the house and presented it to the Anglo-American Ditchley Foundation, which holds international conferences for invited academics, politicians, business people, industrialists and civil servants to further international understanding. The house is periodically open to the general public, subject to booking.

HOUGHTON HALL
AND SIR ROBERT WALPOLE

England's first prime minister, Robert Walpole, used Colen Campbell, James Gibbs and Thomas Ripley as architects and William Kent as interior designer in building the sumptuous Houghton Hall, near King's Lynn, Norfolk, in 1722–35. Walpole eschewed the Norfolk brick later used by his near-neighbour at Holkham Hall, and built his country house of fine Aislaby sandstone from Yorkshire, expensively transported by sea from Whitby to King's Lynn.

Robert Walpole had inherited a relatively small Jacobean manor house and estate at Houghton in 1700, at the age of 24, on the death of his father. In the same year he began his political life, when he was elected Member of Parliament for his father's seat of Castle Rising, Norfolk. After making an enormous fortune as Minister at War, Walpole began the building of a grand new house on the estate in 1722, by which time the politician had become Chancellor of the Exchequer and First Lord of the Admiralty.

Above: The entrance front, Houghton Hall. Note the standing statues above the portico, the double staircase and the side colonnades.

RESTRAINED EXTERIOR

The house has a coolly elegant Palladian exterior. The original design, by Colen Campbell, was reproduced in his *Vitruvius Britannicus* and called for a rectangular block with a tower at each corner, although the towers were replaced on James Gibbs' advice with four domes. The garden front has a grand double staircase and four-column portico beneath a carved pediment topped with three standing statues. Fine curving colonnades lead off at the sides to the wings, which contain a kitchen on one side and the one-time Picture Gallery on the other. On the entrance front, statues of Britannia and Neptune, carved by the great John Michael Rysbrack, rest above the central window.

Below: Sir Robert Walpole. He was father of Horace Walpole, builder of Strawberry Hill.

Below: The rose garden at Houghton Hall contains 150 varieties of the species.

Above: Colen Campbell's design for Houghton was improved by James Gibbs's addition of domes on the four corner towers.

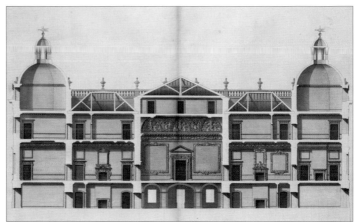

SUMPTUOUS INTERIORS

The interiors are far more richly decorated than the restrained façades. Everywhere, especially in the Great Staircase, there is a profusion of mahogany, at that time only recently and expensively introduced to England. The staircase climbs stylishly to the staterooms on the *piano nobile*; the walls above the stairs are painted by Kent. Chief among the staterooms is the sumptuous Stone Hall: an elegant 40ft (12m) cube, lined with ashlar, it has a superb fireplace by Rysbrack and an extravagant stucco ceiling by Artari. The hall contains a marble bust of Sir Robert, again by Rysbrack, and a portrait of the great man by John Wootton. It also contains a bronze carving of the ancient Greek seer-priest, Laocoon, by the Frenchman François Girardon, which was given to Sir Robert by the Pope. The elegant chairs designed by William Kent are covered in their original velvet.

This is only one of many magnificent rooms in the house, for everywhere the immense wealth of Sir Robert is displayed. The Green Velvet Bedchamber contains an elaborate bed, designed by Kent, with a cockleshell headboard and green velvet hangings. The Marble Parlour, which was used as a dining room, has both a Rysbrack fireplace and serving alcoves carved from mauve and white marble, as well as portraits of Sir Robert by Jean van Loo and Sir

Godfrey Kneller. The Saloon has walls lined with crimson velvet and a gold mosaic painting by Kent on its coved ceiling. It is extravagantly furnished with Kent's gilt furniture.

ARTWORKS FOR SALE

Above the chimney-piece in the Saloon hangs a portrait of Catherine the Great. In his long political career, Sir Robert amassed a magnificent collection of artworks: indeed, his group of paintings was of such size and quality that it later formed the basis of the collection of the State Hermitage Museum in St Petersburg, Russia. Sir Robert's grandson, the 3rd Earl of Orford, ran up such enormous debts that he was reduced to

Above: A cross-section shows Campbell's design for the cube-shaped Stone Hall, with state rooms either side on the piano nobile.

selling off the paintings in the late 1770s to Catherine the Great (Empress Catherine II of Russia).

The house stands in a 350-acre (142ha) park laid out by Charles Bridgeman, today occupied by a herd of white deer. The grounds contain a water tower built in 1731–3 to the designs of the 'Architect Earl', Henry Lord Herbert, subsequently 9th Earl of Pembroke. There is also a recently renovated 5 acre (2ha) walled garden with elaborate floral displays and a superb rose garden.

CHARLES BRIDGEMAN

Born in 1690, Charles Bridgeman first came to notice when working at Brompton Park Nursery in Kensington for Henry Wise. In 1726, Bridgeman was appointed joint Chief Gardener to George I with Wise, before filling the role alone on Wise's retirement the following year.

Bridgeman worked for the Prince of Wales and his mistress the Countess of Suffolk on the gardens at Marble Hill House, Twickenham. As well as laying out the grounds at Houghton Hall, he

also worked on the gardens at Rousham Park, Stowe House, Chiswick House, Cliveden and Claremont.

In his capacity as royal gardener, he cared for and in places designed the royal gardens of Hampton Court, St James's Park, Windsor Castle, Richmond and Hyde Park, where he laid out the lake known as the Serpentine by damming the River Westbourne. Bridgeman also designed the elegant Round Pond in Kensington Gardens, near Kensington Palace. He died in 1738.

ROUSHAM PARK
'THE PRETTIEST PLACE'

The beautiful grounds at Rousham Park near Steeple Aston, Oxfordshire, were laid out by royal gardener, Charles Bridgeman, in the 1720s and developed by William Kent from 1738 onward. They are one of England's first landscape gardens, and the only one in the country to survive essentially unchanged to the present.

The first house at Rousham Park was built in the Jacobean style by Sir Robert Dormer in the 1630s. It has since been much altered, but the original hall remains at the centre of the house. Sir Robert, a proud Royalist who was imprisoned during the Civil War, died in 1649. His grandson, Robert Dormer, inherited the house in 1719 and hired Bridgeman to set out the grounds.

'THE PRETTIEST PLACE'

When poet Alexander Pope, a friend of Robert Dormer, visited in 1728, he was impressed with Charles Bridgeman's work, writing that: 'Rousham is the

Above: Nature orchestrated in a vision of Arcadia at Rousham Park. A circular pond is one of the attractions in 'Venus's Vale'.

prettiest place for water-falls, jetts [sic], ponds inclosed with beautiful scenes of green and hanging wood, that ever I saw.'

Historians identify Charles Bridgeman as an early pioneer in the transition of the formal gardens of the later 17th and early 18th centuries into the 'landscape' gardens that were to be developed by William Kent and, subsequently, by 'Capability' Brown. It was Bridgeman who popularized the 'ha-ha', a concealed – usually sunken – boundary to garden or parkland that was used to make the country-house grounds appear to merge with the surrounding countryside.

THE PALLADIAN LANDSCAPE GARDEN

Palladian architects led a movement away from formal French- or Dutch-influenced gardens, with straight artificial plantings, to landscape gardens with meandering lines more like those found in nature. The landscape garden was no more natural than the formal parterres it replaced, but it was designed to look like nature – nature framed and perfected, like the vista reproduced (and perhaps slightly touched up) by a landscape artist such as Claude or Poussin. Kent and Burlington were the pioneers, creating at Chiswick House, in 1734 the first landscape garden, with wandering stream and pathways. For the Whig nobility, the straight lines of formal gardens symbolized the autocratic rule of the House of Stuart, from which England had been freed by the 'Glorious Revolution' of 1688, while the carefully produced natural appearance of the landscape garden was an image of freedom.

Left: A temple at Rousham. Roman temples and other romantic ruins appeared often in Palladian gardens.

Above: Kent designed the garden at Rousham so that a pedestrian on the winding paths would encounter a series of statues, ruins and other aesthetically pleasing 'classical' scenes.

KENT'S PICTURESQUE VISTA

Robert Dormer died in 1737 and was succeeded at Rousham by his ageing brother, James Dormer, who had served under the Duke of Marlborough and been wounded at the Battle of Blenheim in 1704. James Dormer called in William Kent in 1738 to develop the gardens further and to make alterations to the house. He set out to create visions of ancient Roman temples, statues and landscapes in the English countryside.

To the north of the house, Bridgeman's garden contained a bowling green and descending terraces that led down to the River Cherwell. Kent reworked the terraces as a smooth slope and set to work making the vista as picturesque as possible, incorporating an old mill beyond the Cherwell and a medieval bridge across the river and adding an eye-catching ruin of his own. In the woodland garden and Venus's Vale, he built temples in the style of ancient Rome, added statues and laid out circuitous paths and winding streams with ponds and artificial cascades.

The whole was intended to have the appeal of a landscape painting by the then highly popular 17th-century artists, Nicolas Poussin and Claude Lorrain.

The circuitous stream Kent channelled through the Watery Walk has been claimed as the first 'serpentine' feature in garden design, the precursor of those so frequently employed in the landscaped designs of 'Capability' Brown. Kent was able to visit Rousham only infrequently, and much of the work was carried out under his direction by the estate's head gardener, John McClary, and Clerk of the Works, William White.

Kent's garden soon became an attraction for visitors. The architect-gardener had created a separate entrance for this purpose, allowing tourists to enter and view the landscape without going near the house.

PALLADIAN INTERIORS

Kent also set to work on the house, adding a battlement, cupola and very fine octagonal-paned windows (later sadly, replaced) in the entrance front. He added two wings to the house, each containing a typically elegant 'William Kent' interior: the Painted Parlour and the Library (partially altered as the Great Parlour in 1764).

In the Painted Parlour, Kent built an elaborate marble chimney-piece and over-mantel, together with wall brackets for the display of Dormer's bronzes. He also painted the mythological scene that decorates the ceiling, fitted a number of dummy doorways to provide the required symmetry and proportion, and designed the exquisite parcel-gilt chairs and gilt-wood tables. Only one element of his design is lacking: the original colour scheme, probably in gold and white, was later repainted, most recently in green c.1910.

In the Library, Kent constructed a ribbed and vaulted ceiling and Gothic-style cornice. The room was once lined with books, but these were removed in 1764 when Thomas Roberts transformed the Library into the Great Parlour for Jane, Lady Cottrell-Dormer, adding rococo plasterwork around portraits on the walls. In one of these frames hangs Lady Jane's portrait, by Benjamin West; that of Lt-Gen James Dormer, Kent's patron, is displayed nearby in a more restrained gilt-wood frame.

Below: The cupola was one of Kent's additions to Rousham Park. He also added the castellation to the roof, as well as building two substantial wings.

STOWE HOUSE AND GARDENS
AND THE ENGLISH PALLADIAN MOVEMENT

A colonnaded mansion set within a great park, Stowe House is a veritable English arcadia. House and gardens together form, perhaps, the finest embodiment of the English Palladian movement's vision.

MANY ARCHITECTS

The core of the mansion was built on the site of a medieval manor house in 1676–83 by Sir Richard Temple, 3rd baronet, employing Sir Christopher Wren's master joiner, William Cleare. Stowe House was then developed in the first half of the 18th century by architects including Sir John Vanbrugh, William Kent and James Gibbs. In the same period, Stowe's original formal gardens were gradually transformed into a landscape park by the leading architect-gardeners of the day – who included Charles Bridgeman, Kent and Lancelot 'Capability' Brown. More than 30 temples and picturesque 'classical ruins' were put up in the parkland.

RENOWNED PARKLAND

Initially, the house had a parterre garden, but this was replaced in 1711–26 by a Baroque parkland designed by Vanbrugh and Bridgeman. During this period, Vanbrugh also built several structures in the park, including the Temple of Bacchus (1719), the

Above: The Marble Saloon, beneath a dome 56ft (17m) high, was built after 1775.

Doric Arch (1722) and the Egyptian Pyramid (1724–6), and he built the North Portico on the house.

Kent, Gibbs and Giacomo Leoni, publisher of Palladio's *Four Books of Architecture* in English, worked at Stowe in the 1730s-40s. Kent built the two-tiered South Portico on the house *c.*1734 and the Temple of Venus (*c.*1731), the Temple of British Worthies (*c.*1735) and the Temple of Ancient Virtue (*c.*1736); he laid out the 'Elysian Fields' and applied the 'natural' landscaping techniques developed at Rousham to the parkland.

Lancelot 'Capability' Brown was head gardener in 1741–50 and laid out the

Above: The Temple of Ancient Virtue is one of the classical buildings erected by Kent.

'Grecian Valley', building the Grecian Temple (later called the Temple of Concord and Victory) in 1747. He reworked Charles Bridgeman's more formal 'Eleven-Acre Lake' and 'Octagonal Pond' in an irregular shape. The very fine 'Palladian Bridge' is one of three near-identical bridges built at around the same period; the other two bridges are at Prior Park near Bath (see page 431) and Wilton House near Salisbury (see pages 396–7).

The parkland became renowned throughout the country and attracted many noble visitors. Brown's first employment at Stowe involved showing visitors around, and in this way probably made many valuable connections that later paid off in the form of commissions to improve the grounds of country houses. Stowe is said to be the first house and grounds for which a guide book was published. The house is, today, home to an English public (fee-paying) school, while the grounds are open to the public through the National Trust.

Left: The building of Stowe House's north front was completed by the 1780s.

PETWORTH HOUSE

AND 'CAPABILITY' BROWN

Lancelot 'Capability' Brown was one of England's leading garden designers when, in 1751, the 2nd Earl of Egremont hired him to redesign the grounds at his 17th-century mansion of Petworth House, West Sussex. Brown created a vast serpentine lake filled via a one-mile (1.6km)-long brick conduit. To do this he moved 47,000 tons of earth and lined the lake with 17,000 tons of clay. He did away with the formal gardens near the house and, by means of skilful plantings of trees, including limes, beeches, sycamores, oaks and horse chestnuts, created the impression that the Earl's parkland led away naturally into the surrounding countryside.

Today, the 700-acre (280 ha) park at Petworth House is celebrated as the finest surviving example of Brown's work. A great herd of fallow deer – the largest and oldest herd in England – graze the park, and come right up to the windows of the house.

'CAPABILITY' BROWN

Born in 1716, Lancelot Brown began life as a gardener's boy in his native Northumberland. His first big break came when he found employment in the gardens at Stowe House in

Buckinghamshire. There he contributed to the creation of one of the country's best-known informal landscape parks, initially working for William Kent but later working as head gardener in his own right.

Following Kent's death in 1748, he set to work independently as a garden designer. He got his nickname of 'Capability' because he was renowned for declaring that places always had 'capabilities of improvement'. In contrast to Kent, he seldom used statuary or classical buildings in his landscaped grounds, preferring to create natural-looking forms using – as at Petworth House – areas of grass, irregularly shaped lakes, the rising and falling of the terrain and trees planted singly and in groups.

Among 'Capability' Brown's many other commissions was his reworking of the park at Blenheim Palace, where he created the splendid lakes that partly submerged John Vanbrugh's majestic bridge. At Chatsworth House, he did away with formal parterres and planted the park, while rerouting the River

Above: More 'natural' than nature. At Petworth House, by moving trees and digging a great lake, 'Capability' Brown created an ideal piece of countryside.

Derwent in a serpentine course more pleasing to the eye. He also worked on the gardens and parks of a great many other prominent country houses, including Audley End, Burghley, Longleat and Syon House.

Below: A neoclassical Doric temple stands in the gardens of Petworth House.

Left: 'Capability' Brown. He learned from the architect and garden designer William Kent.

CHAPTER TWENTY-TWO

LATE GEORGIAN AND REGENCY HOUSES

*c.*1760–1830

In 1811, King George III began rebuilding the state apartments at Windsor Castle in the Gothic style, to the designs of James Wyatt. His reign had seen the rise of Robert Adam and the spread of his 'Adam style' in architecture and interior decoration, which brought a lighter touch, an increased knowledge of 'antique' decoration and a breadth of knowledge of French and Italian influences to the pure Palladianism of the early 18th century.

The Gothic transformation of Windsor Castle was completed by James Wyatt's nephew, Jeffry Wyatville, for George IV. This gradually developing taste for a revival of indigenous English styles in architecture, which can also be seen at Penrhyn Castle in Wales and Dalmeny House in Lothian, Scotland, was partly a reaction to the French Revolution of 1789, forming a desire to set aside continental influences, to emphasize the continuity of British-English traditions and to celebrate great British victories, from Trafalgar to Waterloo.

At around the same time, more exotic influences also made an appearance, as Chinese and 'Hindoo' (Indian–Turkish) styles were enthusiastically employed at Carlton House in London and the Royal Pavilion in Brighton. Then, as the 19th century advanced, these Gothic and Tudor Revivals were balanced by a renewed enthusiasm for classicism in the Greek Revival movement, which was seen in the design of country houses such as Meldon Park, Belsay Hall and The Grange.

Left: In the Great Hall at Syon House, London, the use of recesses and the effect of the black-and-white floor exemplify the 'movement' that was a key element of the 'Adam style'.

STRAWBERRY HILL
AND THE GOTHIC REVIVAL

 Writer and connoisseur Horace Walpole, youngest son of Prime Minister Robert Walpole, inspired an architectural movement with his villa at Twickenham, then a country village but now part of south-west London. Over 45 years, beginning in 1747, he added medieval-style towers, battlements, arches, fireplaces, stained-glass windows and other features to transform his villa, Strawberry Hill, beside the River Thames into a 'Gothick Castle'.

The Gothic Revival movement was born in the Georgian era among imitators of Walpole's light-hearted experiments. It then became a more serious and scholarly movement in the 19th century, when it gave rise to buildings such as Sir Charles Barry and A.W.N. Pugin's rebuilt Houses of Parliament at Westminster. The Victorian Gothic Revival continued as a popular style for churches and university buildings well into the 20th century.

Below: The Long Gallery's delicate ceiling at Strawberry Hill was based on that of the Henry VII Chapel in Westminster Abbey.

'COMMITTEE OF TASTE'

Walpole used medieval architectural elements for decorative effect and – because of their romantic associations with little concern for architectural integrity – for reproducing features in the way they would have been used in their original setting. He worked alongside his friends, some of whom he appointed to a 'Committee of Taste', instructed to adapt Gothic architectural details (seen in other buildings or in books of reproductions) for his use at Strawberry Hill. Friends who served on this committee included illustrator

Above: In creating a 'little Gothick Castle' at Strawberry Hill, Walpole indulged his taste for 'charming irregularities' in architecture.

Richard Bentley, John Chute, owner of The Vyne in Hampshire, and poet Thomas Gray.

GOTHIC *SHARAWAGGI*

Walpole chose the Gothic because he was attracted to its lack of symmetry. He was doubtless reacting against the Palladian orthodoxy in England, which called for ordered, harmonious and symmetrical design, and perhaps also

Above: Walpole wrote the first history of art in English, as well as the first Gothic novel.

against the first appearance around him of Neoclassical designs inspired by the temples of ancient Greece. In a letter to his friend Sir Horace Mann, Walpole declared that the trouble with classical-inspired buildings was that they lacked variety and 'charming irregularities'; he was instead attracted, he wrote, to *sharawaggi* or 'want of symmetry'.

Walpole began by 'Gothicizing' the outside of the villa, adding battlements, quatrefoil (four-leaf) windows and Tudor style chimneys. Subsequently, he built an extension containing a Long Gallery, with a fan-vaulted ceiling based on that of Henry VII's Chapel in Westminster Abbey, and erected two towers – the Beauclerc Tower and the Round Tower.

Strawberry Hill was extended in the mid-19th century by Frances, Countess Waldegrave, who added a new wing. Today the house belongs to St Mary's College, part of the University of Surrey.

Besides building Strawberry Hill and leaving a vast collection of letters that provide a wonderful picture of 18th-century aristocratic life, Walpole's other claim to fame is that he was the author of the first 'Gothic novel'. His *The Castle of Otranto* was first published anonymously in 1765, supposedly as a translation of an Italian book of 1529. Earlier in 1757, he had established a

private press at Strawberry Hill, in which he published several of his own books and Thomas Gray's *Odes*.

THE VYNE

In 1754, Walpole's friend John Chute inherited The Vyne in Hampshire – a Tudor mansion later given the first classical portico on an English country house. A member of Walpole's 'Committee of Taste' – which often met in The Vyne – Chute shared his friend's passion for the 'Gothic'; Walpole referred to him as 'my oracle in taste …

Above: Walpole's reinvention of the Gothic has had a wide influence. Strawberry Hill does not look as unusual today as it did when new.

the genius that presided over poor Strawberry!' Chute intended to Gothicize the entire interior of The Vyne (indeed, he had his portrait painted while holding a plan for a Gothicized interior at the house) but, in the event, applied the new style only to one room, the Antechapel. Elsewhere, he used a serene classical style to build a staircase and galleries in place of the Tudor Great Hall.

ARBURY HALL, WARWICKSHIRE

Sir Roger Newdigate, for 30 years from 1750 MP for Oxford University, was a pioneer of the Georgian Gothic Revival in his house at Arbury, Warwickshire. His exuberant and light-hearted alterations of an old house of monastic origins were, like those at Strawberry Hill, chiefly for decorative effect, having no structural function. In the Drawing Room (designed in 1762), he installed a fireplace inspired by the tomb of Aymer de Valence in Westminster Abbey. The Dining Room (designed by Henry Keene *c.*1772) has an elaborate fan vault and another extraordinary chimney-piece. The Saloon

(designed by Henry Couchman and Sir Roger in 1776–96) is probably the house's finest room and features delicate plaster tracery above its large bow window. The novelist, George Eliot, grew up on the estate and represented Sir Roger and his house in her *Scenes of Clerical Life* (1858). Sir Roger is also remembered as the founder of the Newdigate Poetry Prize for Oxford University students, won by poets such as Matthew Arnold and Andrew Motion.

Right: An extravaganza of delicate and beautifully finished plasterwork rises above the bow window in the Arbury Hall Saloon.

KEW PALACE
AND QUEEN CHARLOTTE'S COTTAGE

On the banks of the Thames in south-west London, Kew Palace, originally known as 'the Dutch House', was a significant royal residence between 1728 and 1818. Apart from Queen Charlotte's Cottage, the orangery and pagoda, the palace is the only surviving royal building of many that once stood at Kew.

Kew Palace is a fairly modest four-storey brick manor house, built in 1631 by Dutch merchant, Samuel Fortrey: his initials, those of his wife, and the date can be seen on a carved brick set above the south door. It is a villa, with symmetrical south and north façades featuring pediments and pilasters. Its chief room is the King's Dining Room, measuring 31 x 21ft (9.3 x 6.3m), with ceiling decoration featuring a Tudor rose.

The house was leased by Queen Caroline in 1728; William Kent added new stairs and sash windows at this time. It was principally used as a residence for the princesses Anne, Amelia and Caroline. Then, in the 1750s, Frederick, Prince of Wales, was

Below: This engraving shows Kew Palace as it was c.1815–20, around the time when Queen Charlotte lived there briefly.

living in the adjacent White House and used the Dutch House as a school for his eldest sons, George, Prince of Wales (the future George III), and Prince Edward. The house was again a princely school in the 1770s, this time for George III's sons George, Prince of Wales, and Frederick, Duke of York.

King George bought the house outright in 1781. In 1801–6, he lived there occasionally with Queen Charlotte; by this stage the King's health was poor following recurrent attacks of porphyria. He subsequently lived mainly at Windsor. Then Queen Charlotte, herself seriously ill, lived in Kew Palace for the

Above: Palace and formal garden. After a major restoration by Historic Royal Palaces, Kew Palace opened to the public in April 2006.

last few months of her life in 1818 – during which three royal weddings took place in the building. These were the marriages of Prince Adolphus to Princess Augusta of Hesse-Cassel, of William, Duke of Clarence (the future William IV), to Princess Adelaide of Saxe-Meiningen and of Edward, Duke of Kent, to Princess Victoire of Saxe-Coburg (the parents of Queen Victoria).

THE WHITE HOUSE, KEW

Kew Palace originally stood alongside a much larger royal residence: Kew House. This was used by George III's parents, Frederick, Prince of Wales, and his wife, Princess Augusta, from the 1730s onward. It was rebuilt by William Kent, who gave it a coolly elegant white stucco façade that earned the building its new name of 'the White House'. Kent also designed the lavish interiors.

Frederick died in 1751 and Augusta lived on in the White House as Dowager Princess of Wales. Several buildings and features in the gardens were built for her by Sir William Chambers, including an orangery and pagoda. The house was demolished in the early 19th century.

Right: White Lodge, Richmond Park. George II's queen, Caroline, loved this Palladian villa. The future Edward VIII was born here on 23 June 1894.

RICHMOND LODGE

Another riverside residence with delightful gardens was Richmond Lodge in Richmond Old Deer Park. It stood on the site of a ruined ancient royal palace, in a position where Charles II had considered building a new residence to designs by Sir Christopher Wren; William III subsequently built a hunting lodge on the ancient ruins. The future George II and Queen Caroline used William III's lodge as Prince and Princess of Wales from 1718 and, after coming to the throne, made it Queen Caroline's dower house. In the 1730s, Charles Bridgeman and William Kent redesigned the gardens, adding a temple, a dairy and even a 'Merlin's Cave'. (These grounds and those surrounding the Dutch House and the White House were joined together during George III's reign and became the Royal Botanic Gardens of Kew in 1841.)

George III and Queen Charlotte used Richmond Lodge as a country house for over a decade after 1761, but in 1772 they moved into the White House, following the death of his mother, and the lodge was demolished.

THE 'NEW PALACE'

King George III had grand plans for a new palace in the Old Deer Park, Richmond. Sir William Chambers drew up three sets of plans, the first of which was for a Palladian-style palace with a Corinthian portico like that of Holkham Hall, but these all came to nothing. Then, in 1800, James Wyatt designed a Gothic-style castle palace with a square central keep and four cylindrical towers. Building began in 1801 on the site of the demolished White House and continued for a decade at a cost of £500,000. But work was halted in 1811 because of the King's illness, at a stage when the castle was just a shell. George IV hated the new palace and had it destroyed with explosives in 1827.

THE WHITE LODGE

The New Park Lodge (or White Lodge) in Richmond Park was a hunting lodge in the form of a Palladian villa, designed by Roger Morris for George I in 1727. This building stands in the park we know today as Richmond Park, which was originally called the New Park. (The New Park is on the other side of Richmond from the older royal hunting grounds of the Old Deer Park.) George died before the lodge was finished and George II completed it for Queen Caroline. Today it is the junior section of the Royal Ballet School.

Below: William Chambers drew inspiration from a youthful visit to China when he designed the 163ft (50m)- tall Great Pagoda for the Dowager Princess Augusta in 1761.

THE QUEEN'S COTTAGE

Queen Charlotte's Cottage stands in a nature conservation area amid a wild bluebell wood in Kew Gardens. The cottage was given to Queen Charlotte, in September 1761, on her marriage to George III. The royals used the building as a summerhouse. In 1818 it was the venue for the tea, following the double wedding of her sons William, Duke of Clarence, and Edward, Duke of Kent.

Below: Queen Charlotte's Cottage was opened to visitors in 1959.

SYON HOUSE
AND ROBERT ADAM

Sir Hugh and Lady Betty Smithson, later Duke and Duchess of Northumberland, commissioned the rising architect-designer Robert Adam to remodel and redecorate the interior of Syon House, Middlesex, in 1762. The house, built in the mid-16th century by Edward Seymour, Duke of Somerset and Lord Protector of the Kingdom, already had a long and colourful history (see pages 362–3).

Adam was forced to work with the structure he inherited, for Sir Hugh and Lady Betty did not want him to rebuild the Tudor mansion and turned down his request to build a circular domed room in the central courtyard. Instead, he created a suite of five rooms running around the west, south and east sides of the courtyard house.

THE 'ADAM STYLE'

Adam's five rooms – the Great Hall, the Ante-room, the Dining Room, the Red Drawing Room and the Long Gallery

Below: The Red Drawing Room. The finest Spitalfields silk hangs on its walls.

– lead one into another. They are celebrated as the first fully realized statement of the 'Adam style', which deployed ancient Roman architectural elements with a new freedom and lightness of touch. The key element of the 'Adam style' is 'movement', which Robert and James defined in the Preface to *The Works in Architecture of Robert and James Adam* (two volumes, 1773 and 1779) as 'the rise and fall, the advance and recess, with other diversity of form, in the different parts of a building'.

Adam's use of recesses and steps in the cool black-and-white Great Hall at Syon House exemplifies this movement. In the gorgeously grand Ante-room he brought Rome to London in the form of a dozen green antique marble columns found on the bed of the River Tiber. The floor of muted yellow, red and blue makes a harmonious composition with the gold of the statues on top of the columns and the gilt stucco panels in the walls.

'GREAT VARIETY'

The Dining Room, a triple cube 63ft long by 21ft wide and high (19 x 6 x 6m), contains gilt and ivory decoration. The Red Drawing Room has sumptuous red silk wall coverings, an elegant coved ceiling beautifully painted by Angelica Kauffman and a fine carpet designed by Adam and woven by Thomas Moore in 1769. After this series of triumphs, Adam achieved perhaps his finest effect in redecorating the Jacobean-era Long Gallery. This room, 136ft long by 14ft wide and high (41 x 4 x 4m), was decorated and furnished in a colour scheme of pale green and gilt, with bookshelves and furniture of his own design. He achieved, in his own words, 'a style to afford great variety and amusement'.

Right: These designs, including folding doors, are from one of Adam's pattern books.

Above: Grandly transformed within, thanks to its Adam decorations, on the outside Syon House is a rather plain Tudor block.

AMERICAN CONNECTION

Robert Adam's patron at Syon House, Sir Hugh Smithson, had an illegitimate son named James Smithson, born in France to his mistress, Elizabeth Kate Hungerford Macie. James was a chemist and geologist, and on his death in 1829 he left $508,318 to found 'an establishment for the increase and diffusion of knowledge among men': the result was the Smithsonian Institution, established in Washington, D.C., in 1846.

HAREWOOD HOUSE
AND THE 'ADAM STYLE'

The stately Palladian mansion of Harewood House, near Leeds, was built in 1759–72 for the immensely wealthy Edwin Lascelles, 1st Lord Harewood. John Carr of York designed the main block, while Robert Adam was responsible for the side wings and interiors.

CHIPPENDALE AND ADAM

The 16 staterooms on the principal floor of the house are exquisitely decorated and furnished in the 'Adam style', with elegant chairs and other furniture by the leading 18th-century cabinetmaker Thomas Chippendale. Adam's grand

Entrance Hall has Doric half-columns painted to imitate red marble; they make a telling contrast with the elegant grey-blue walls. The room now called the China Room was originally the Study in Adam's plan; it contains a collection of superb Sèvres porcelain with pieces once owned by Louis XV and XVI and Queen Marie Antoinette.

The State Bedroom was intended for visiting members of the royal family: it contains magnificent Chippendale pieces including a spectacular state bed, fine wall mirrors and a satinwood commode and secretaire that many identify as Chippendale's finest work. The less

Above: Originally, Harewood House's south front gave on to the park, but a formal terrace garden was added in the mid-19th century.

grand East Bedroom was used by 1st Lord Harewood: it retains its Adam frieze and sunflower ceiling decoration.

The sumptuous Long Gallery is 77ft long, 24ft wide and 21ft high (23 x 7 x 6m). The ceiling was designed by Adam and painted by Biagio Rebecca. Of all the staterooms, the Music Room remains closest to Adam's original design: the colourful Adam carpet contains lyres and reflects the ceiling roundels painted by Angelica Kauffman; trumpets, lyres and pipes are carved in the marble chimney-piece; the chairs and sofas, and even the frame for the portrait of the 1st Earl's sister-in-law are by Chippendale.

ROBERT ADAM

The architect and designer Robert Adam was born in 1728 in Fife, son of the leading Scottish architect of his day, William Adam, who served as Master Mason to the North British Board of Ordnance. On his father's death in 1748, Robert and his brother James were appointed to the position and in 1748–54 undertook many architectural and decorating commissions, including Fort George, near Inverness, and Dumfries House in Ayrshire. After travelling in continental Europe in 1754–7, Robert settled in London and soon made his name with his 'Adam style'.

By 1761 he was already receiving major commissions to redecorate the interiors of grand houses both in London and in the country, such as Alnwick Castle (Northumberland), Kedleston Hall (Derbyshire) and Osterley Park (Middlesex – now the London Borough of Hounslow). In the same year he was appointed Architect to the King's Works. Both before and after his work on the interior at Syon House in 1762, Adam was architect on a number of houses, designing the south front at Kedleston Hall in 1757–9, then building Mersham-le-Hatch (Kent) in 1762–72 and Luton Hoo (Bedfordshire) in 1766–74; he remodelled Kenwood House in 1767–8. In later life he designed a number of Gothic Revival castles including Culzean in Ayrshire; he is particularly remembered in Scotland for his design of Edinburgh University and of Edinburgh's Charlotte Square. He died in 1792 and was buried in Westminster Abbey.

Left: Robert Adam closely studied the architecture of ancient Greece and Rome to create the 'Adam style'.

LATER ALTERATIONS

In 1772, Lancelot 'Capability' Brown began to redesign the park. In the 19th century, Sir Charles Barry removed Carr's classical portico on the south front, added a third storey to the house and swept away part of Brown's landscape to create a terrace garden. For part of the 20th century, Harewood House was home to George V's daughter, Mary, the Princess Royal, who married the 6th Earl of Harewood in 1922. The house, today, belongs to her son George, the 7th Earl, who is the Queen's first cousin.

KEDLESTON HALL
AND KENWOOD HOUSE

Robert Adam was initially commissioned at Kedleston Hall *c*.1758 to design classical temples and rustic buildings in the park, while Sir Nathaniel Curzon, subsequently 1st Baron Scarsdale, was rebuilding his family mansion. But Adam impressed Sir Nathaniel sufficiently to be granted control over the design of the house, ousting architects Matthew Brettingham and James Paine.

DRAMATIC FAÇADE
Adam's south front contains a four-column triumphal arch – based on the Arch of Constantine in Rome – beneath a domed roof and above a beautiful curving double staircase, which leads up to a large glass entrance door. To right and left of this central block are identical wings of three floors. The façade combines great drama with wonderful delicacy, and – perfectly embodying the Adam concept of 'movement' – is considered both a quintessential Robert Adam design and an architectural masterpiece.

Below: The Marble Hall at Kedleston, with its 20 pink alabaster columns, lies directly behind the vast portico on the north front.

Kedleston was the first building to make use of a triumphal arch in an English stately house.

The impressive north, or entrance, front, 350ft (107m) across, was begun by Brettingham. It consists of two substantial end pavilions linked to the main block by curving corridors. The east pavilion contains rooms for the use of Sir Nathaniel and family, the main block houses the staterooms and the west pavilion the service quarters. The main building has an imposing six-column

Above: The north front at Kedleston was largely as designed by Brettingham, but Adam emphasised the six-column portico.

portico; it was begun by Paine and completed by Adam in more dramatic style than originally planned.

MARBLE AND ALABASTER
The portico entrance leads into the grandly classical Great Hall, probably designed by Brettingham like a Roman basilica, along the lines of the equally magnificent Marble Hall he built with William Kent and Lord Leicester at Holkham Hall, Norfolk.

The Great Hall at Kedleston has an Italian marble floor and contains 20 fluted alabaster columns set before alcoves containing classical statues; the walls and doors are decorated with classical scenes; the hall fills the entire height of the house and the only sources of light are the skylights in the roof. The hall leads into the circular Saloon, which stands behind the arch of the south front and is lit from above through glass in the dome 62ft (19m) above. The room was designed as a sculpture gallery; it contains four sets of double doors, with surrounds of green *scagliola*.

The other staterooms include the Great Apartment – a formal bedroom with gilded chairs and a superb state bed – and the Drawing Room, which boasts a chimney-piece of the Derbyshire stone bluejohn and doorcases and window surrounds made from local alabaster. The other main rooms are the Dining Room, the Library and the Music Room. A magnificent staircase leads down from the principal rooms on the *piano nobile* to Caesar's Hall on the ground floor.

ADAM'S LANDSCAPED PARK
At Kedleston Hall, Adam also landscaped the 820-acre (332-ha) park with the help of the landscape gardener, William Emes. He created five serpentine lakes in the style of 'Capability' Brown from canals and ponds that had been laid out earlier by Charles Bridgeman. Adam also built a beautifully judged bridge, fishing house and boat house, as well as a number of classical buildings, such as the North Lodge – which was another triumphal arch.

KENWOOD HOUSE
In 1764–79, Robert Adam remodelled the early 17th-century Kenwood House in Hampstead for the Scottish Law politician and judge, William Murray, 1st Earl of Mansfield. Adam built an Ionic portico on the north, or entrance, front and created a celebrated library on the east side of the south front. The Library's widely admired interior has a curved ceiling with flat oval and rectangular panels for decoration, its shape described by Adam as 'much more perfect than that which is commonly called the cove ceiling'. The house originally stood close to the road from Hampstead to Highgate, but in the 1790s the 2nd Earl of Mansfield moved the road; the house now stands in a secluded position on Hampstead Heath, in gardens designed by Humphry Repton. The 1999 film *Notting Hill* was partly filmed at Kenwood House.

IVEAGH BEQUEST
In 1928, Kenwood House and a substantial collection of fine art was bequeathed to the nation by Edward Cecil Guinness, the 1st Earl of Iveagh, head of the Guinness brewing family from Ireland and the man responsible for the lavish rebuilding of Elveden Hall in Suffolk. Lord Iveagh built up the art collection in the late 19th century. It included some very important

Above: The highly colourful Library at Kenwood House is thought to be one of the finest of all Robert Adam interiors.

paintings, including a self-portrait of *c*.1665 by Rembrandt, the delicate *Guitar Player* by Vermeer and several fine works by Turner, Lawrence and Reynolds. Further paintings have been added to The Iveagh Bequest over the years. They are on display in the beautiful surroundings of Kenwood House.

Below: A modern touch at Kedleston Hall. In the recesses of the Saloon, the pedestals beneath the urns are actually stoves.

HEVENINGHAM HALL
AND JAMES WYATT

When James Wyatt returned to London from six years' study in Italy in 1768, he quickly won national renown for his theatre, The Pantheon, in Regent Street. The extraordinary domed building, which opened in 1772 but was later demolished, was based on the design of the Hagia Sophia ('Church of Sacred Wisdom') in Istanbul. Horace Walpole called it 'the most beautiful edifice in England'.

Wyatt began to work as a country-house architect in the Neoclassical style at Heaton Hall in Lancashire (1772); at Heveningham Hall, Suffolk, the Dutch merchant Sir Gerard Vanneck commissioned him in 1788 to complete the grand 25-bay remodelling (begun by Sir Robert Taylor) of an earlier house.

Wyatt was principally responsible for Heveningham Hall's interiors, which include the beautiful Vaulted Hall. The rooms are considered to be among Wyatt's finest work and have recently been restored and renovated.

Above: The great expanse of Heveningham Hall. Between them, Wyatt and Taylor created a most impressive house.

Heveningham Hall still stands in extensive parkland, which was originally set out by Lancelot 'Capability' Brown. This includes a stable block in the shape of a horseshoe, a temple and an ice-house. The recent restoration includes the addition of further Neoclassical buildings, including a bridge across the lake, a new temple, an orangery and a boat house.

Below: Inner beauty. Heveningham Hall – detail of James Wyatt's library.

JAMES WYATT

Born in 1746 in Staffordshire, James Wyatt was still in his twenties when he set out as a country-house architect with his work at Heaton Hall. He became Robert Adam's great rival in the Neoclassical style, but could work with equal success in the Gothic Revival mode. Wyatt enjoyed a long career that stretched into the second decade of the 19th century; from 1796 he served as Surveyor General to the Board of Works and was involved in the restoration of many great English cathedrals, including Durham, Salisbury and Hereford. His ventures into the Gothic were dismissed by more serious followers of the Gothic Revival in the mid-19th century. Wyatt built a number of Gothic Revival country houses, including Lee Priory in Kent

(1783–90) and Ashridge in Hertfordshire (1808 onward). But he is remembered, above all, as the designer of the extravagant and extraordinary Gothic country house of Fonthill Abbey in Wiltshire (now ruined), built in 1796–1807 for William Beckford, author of *Vathek* (1786).

Below: The design for Fonthill Abbey. Its steepled tower collapsed three times.

CASTLE COOLE
AND THE NEOCLASSICAL REVIVAL

James Wyatt was the leading architect of his day when he designed Castle Coole for the 1st Earl of Belmore in 1790–8. The palatial building, alongside the river that links the lower and upper lakes of Lough Erne in Co Fermanagh, Ulster, is celebrated as one of Northern Ireland's finest country houses.

The two-storey central block is nine bays in width. On the entrance front, a towering pedimented portico containing four plain Ionic columns 27ft (8m) tall stands in the centre of the main block; on either side, two wings each fronted by a colonnade of six Doric columns lead to an end pavilion. On the garden front, the central bow is curved on account of the Oval Saloon within. Wyatt used pale Portland stone brought at great expense from Dorset. The stone was taken by ship to Ballyshannon (Co Donegal), carried overland to Lough Erne, then shipped by barge across the water as far as Enniskillen, before being brought the final 2 miles (3km) by cart.

Below: The entrance hall, Castle Coole. The door leads to the Oval Saloon.

TOP-LIT LOBBY

Behind the entrance portico, the restrained Great Hall is of one storey only and contains a line of Doric columns, two plain chimney-pieces and a Doric frieze. The hall gives on to the Staircase Hall, which contains a double-return stone staircase up to a first-floor landing with four Doric columns of brown and yellow *scagliola*. The lobby, also on the first floor, is lit from above, in line with Irish country-house tradition, by glass domes hidden on the entrance front behind pediment and balustrade. The lobby contains an attic-level gallery, from which rooms lead off,

Above: The main front at Castle Coole. Note the elegant symmetry of the two Doric colonnades leading to twin end pavilions.

with a graceful colonnade said to be copied from the interiors of the temple of the sea god Poseidon at Paestum and the Parthenon in Athens.

Behind the curved centre of the garden front is the elegant Oval Saloon, which runs out to the Drawing Room and Dining Room on either side, with plasterwork to Wyatt's designs by Joseph Rose of London and *scagliola* work by Dominic Bartoli.

THE GREEK REVIVAL

In his use of more austere, less ornamented ancient Greek rather than Roman architectural elements, for example the baseless column used in the colonnades on the entrance front, Wyatt followed the fashion for Hellenism in Neoclassical architecture at the close of the century. Under the influence of James Stuart and Nicholas Revett's *The Antiquities of Athens* (published in three parts in 1762, 1789 and 1795), a growing interest in archaeology and the discovery of Greek antiquities, Neoclassicists held that ancient Greek architecture was purer and more rational than ancient Roman building. This enthusiasm fed into the Greek Revival movement of the 19th century.

ALTHORP
THE SPENCERS AND THE ROYALS

In *c*.1790 Henry Holland handsomely refaced the Spencer family's country house at Althorp, Northamptonshire, also adding pediments to the south and north fronts and corridors along the forecourt wings. By this date the Spencers were already well established at Althorp, having lived there since 1508, when Sir John Spencer bought the original moated medieval manor house, built of a local orange stone, with grounds of 300 acres (120ha). Today, Althorp is one of the most visited country houses in England,

Above: Classical good taste. Althorp is an Elizabethan house in 18th-century dress.

for its estate contains the burial place of Diana, Princess of Wales, whose father was the 8th Earl Spencer.

THE GROWTH OF ALTHORP

The first Sir John Spencer or his grandson, another Sir John, rebuilt the medieval house at Althorp to make a more substantial redbrick dwelling with an internal courtyard. Then, in 1575, the younger Sir John added two wings on the south side to create the entrance forecourt. In 1660–2, Dorothy, widow of Henry Spencer, 1st Earl of Sunderland, covered the internal courtyard and built the Grand Staircase. Her son, Robert Spencer, 2nd Earl of Sunderland, created a classical façade with columns and balustrade, and internally transformed the Great Hall on the upper floor of the west wing into a Long Gallery, while on the north side creating staterooms including the Saloon. He had formal gardens laid out to designs by the Frenchman André Le Nôtre, landscaper of the royal Palace of Versailles. The house in this era greatly impressed diarist John Evelyn, who called it a 'palace...a noble pile',

PRINCESS DIANA AND ALTHORP

Lady Diana Spencer was born at Park House on the Sandringham estate. Her parents divorced in 1969, when she was eight, and her father was awarded custody of the children. He inherited Althorp in 1975 when she was 13, and she spent her teenage years there, when she was not at boarding school or staying at her mother's home in London. Indeed, she first met her future husband, Prince Charles, at Althorp when he visited to shoot in November 1977.

Following her death in Paris in 1997, her body was brought in a cortege from the funeral at Westminster Abbey to Althorp, where she was interred on an island in the lake known as the Round Oval. An urn on the island, designed by Edward Bulmer and made by Dick Reid, celebrates her memory, which is also honoured by an exhibition of her life and work in Althorp's Italianate stables, built by Roger Morris *c*.1733. The summerhouse by the lake is set aside in her memory.

Below: The summerhouse at Althorp, now a memorial to Diana, once stood in the grounds of Admiralty House, London.

Below: Princess Diana in May 1997. As Lady Diana Spencer, she spent part of her childhood at Althorp.

and declared its rooms and furnishings to be 'such as may become a great prince', also noting that its gardens were both 'exquisitely planted and kept'.

The next stage of work was in the 18th century. First, Charles Spencer, the 5th Earl of Sunderland, refashioned the Entrance Hall following Palladian designs by Colen Campbell that were actually implemented by Roger Morris after Campbell's death (1729); Morris also built the stone stables with two classical porticoes, and artist John Wootton painted a series of Spencer hunting scenes. Then, George Spencer, the 2nd Earl Spencer, commissioned the fashionable architect Henry Holland – who was simultaneously working for the Prince of Wales on the Marine Pavilion in Brighton (later rebuilt as Brighton Pavilion) and redesigning Carlton House in London – literally to give the essentially Elizabethan house an 18th-century facelift.

A 'MATHEMATICAL' FAÇADE

Holland refaced the red brick with white brick rebate tiles, which were called 'mathematical tiles' by contemporaries because they fitted together so exactly. The view then current was that brick was not a suitable material for a grand house, despite the great and enduring beauty of Tudor brick houses such as Compton Wynyates; rebate tiles were popularized by Holland, who used them to face his own London house, Sloane Place.

In addition to adding pediments to the garden and entrance fronts, Holland filled in the medieval moat, and within the house moved the main reception rooms to the ground floor of the west wing, creating a fine progression of

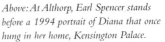

Above: At Althorp, Earl Spencer stands before a 1994 portrait of Diana that once hung in her home, Kensington Palace.

rooms through the Long Library, the Yellow Drawing Room and the Dining Room. Althorp has changed little over the 200-odd years since Holland's alterations were carried out: although a medieval and Elizabethan house at its core, its classical 18th-century facing dominates its appearance and gives it its essential character.

THE SPENCER 'FAMILY SILVER'

Althorp is also celebrated for the Spencer family's superb collection of sculpture, ceramics, furniture and paintings, including fine works by Rubens, van Dyck, Lely, Reynolds and Gainsborough. In addition, it contains widely admired doors, chimney-pieces and other fittings designed by John Vardy and James 'Athenian' Stuart for the family's London mansion, Spencer House, in the 18th century. The fittings were removed to Althorp when Spencer House was leased in 1924.

Left: Althorp is full of the finest furniture, paintings and other fittings – much of it brought there from Spencer House, London.

BRIGHTON PAVILION
AND THE PRINCE REGENT

The exotic domes and minarets of the Royal Pavilion in Brighton were built in 1815–23 by architect John Nash for George, the former Prince of Wales, who was Prince Regent in 1811–20 due to the illness of his father, George III, and King in 1820–30. Nash used the briefly fashionable 'Hindoo' style, derived mainly from that of Islamic temple architecture in India and a strain of the taste for the exotic that flowered in the Regency period, partly in reaction to the uncluttered, 'rational' designs of Palladian and Neoclassical architects. Nash built on and around the Prince's earlier house, the Marine Pavilion, which had itself been constructed on the site of a humble farmhouse by Henry Holland from 1787 onward.

GEORGE'S FIRST PAVILION

George, Prince of Wales, was very taken with Brighton – then a village called Brighthelmstone – when he first visited in 1783 to stay with his uncle, the Duke of Cumberland. George returned in 1784 and leased a farmhouse on the Steine, an area of grassy land to the east of the village, later setting up home there with his Roman Catholic wife, Maria Fitzherbert, whom he had secretly married in 1785. The house built on this site by Henry Holland was Neoclassical, with a domed saloon and wings extending to south and north.

In 1802–3, the Prince began to redevelop his Pavilion in an oriental style. Initially, the look was Chinese rather than 'Hindoo': he redecorated the interior of the house with bamboo panelling and with Chinese chimney-pieces,

Above: Oriental romance by the Sussex sea – the domes and minarets of the Pavilion suggest a temple more than a palace.

wallpaper, porcelain, statuary and furniture, and commissioned William Porden to refashion the exterior as a Chinese pagoda. But then the Prince's taste turned to Indian- and Turkish-inspired architecture, and in 1804–8 he had Porden build a splendid domed stable block and riding school in a 'Saracenic' style that most closely resembles a Turkish mosque.

NASH REPLACES REPTON

The prominent landscape gardener, Humphry Repton, was known to the Prince because he had worked on the gardens at Carlton House in London. He was invited to Brighton, where he acclaimed Porden's domed stable block as 'stupendous and magnificent…distinct from either Grecian or Gothic' and drew up a detailed plan to rebuild the entire Pavilion in a 'Hindoo' style. The Prince declared himself delighted and indicated that he would 'have every part

Left: The Court at Brighton à la Chinese. Cruikshank's cartoon satirizes George's lavishly indulged taste for the Oriental.

Above: It cost more than £500,000 to furnish the Banqueting Room, a setting for exotic dinners, in such brilliant luxury.

JOHN NASH

After training under Sir Robert Taylor, Nash began his career as a speculative builder in London. Declared bankrupt in 1783, he moved into country-house architecture to rebuild his reputation and worked with landscape gardener Humphry Repton. Nash returned to London in the 1790s and from 1798 was employed by the Prince of Wales, later working on redesigning the Brighton Pavilion and the rebuilding of Buckingham House in London, as well as developing Regent's Park and Regent's Street. Nash's own house, East Cowes Castle on the Isle of Wight, was an influence on the early 19th-century phase of the Gothic Revival. His country houses include the 'picturesque' Italianate Cronkhill in Shropshire (1802) and Sandridge Park in Devon (c.1805), and also the Gothic Revival-style Caerhays Castle in Cornwall (1808). He also built four Gothic castles in Ireland, including Killymoon Castle in County Tyrone (1803).

of it carried into immediate execution'. Due to financial difficulties, however, he did not actually begin the work until 1815, and then, to Repton's dismay, it was carried out to designs by John Nash.

Using a cast-iron framework over Holland's original house, Nash added the distinctive onion-shaped domes, minarets, cupolas and pinnacles that give the Pavilion such a distinctive look today. The interior was lavish, decorated and furnished with great Regency wit and an extravagant sense of the exotic. First, Nash built a new pink and green Entrance Hall and light green Long Gallery, decorated in the Chinese style with dragon panels. Then he planned the kitchen with four remarkable iron columns, made to look like palm trees with bronze leaves, to support the lantern roof, and equipped it with all the latest gadgets to enable the staff to get food to the Prince Regent's table piping hot.

PUBLIC ROOMS

Next, in 1812–20, he built new end wings containing the Pavilion's main apartments, the Music Room and the Banqueting Room, each measuring 40 x 60ft (12 x 18m). In the Banqueting Room, the 45ft (13.5m)-high domed ceiling was painted to resemble an eastern sky with a silver dragon holding a vast chandelier, lit by gas rather than candles, and almost a ton in weight and 30ft (9m) high. The Music Room also

had a domed ceiling and gas chandelier; here, the Prince entertained his guests with music performed by an orchestra dressed in Turkish costumes, sometimes himself singing as a baritone. On one occasion, he received the Italian composer Gioacchino Rossini there. In his private apartments, George had a bath 6ft deep, 10ft wide and 16ft long (1.2 x 3 x 4.8m), which was filled with salt water pumped directly from the sea.

AN ABANDONED PALACE

George apparently grew bored of all this splendour: after 1827 he did not return to the Pavilion, preferring Windsor Castle and Buckingham Palace. As Brighton grew, so the Pavilion was gradually surrounded by housing and the King felt the need for greater privacy. According to some accounts, he finally abandoned his Brighton house because his new mistress, Lady Conyngham, declared that she disliked it. Among his successors, William IV used the Pavilion, but Queen Victoria loathed it and was considering having it knocked down before she and Albert settled at Osborne. The building, owned by the Brighton local authority, has recently been restored.

Below: This contemporary aquatint indicates that the Pavilion may simply have been too grand for comfortable living.

PENRHYN CASTLE
AND THE NORMAN REVIVAL

The favoured royal architect, Thomas Hopper, built the Norman-style Penrhyn Castle near Bangor *c.*1825. This romantic building, complete with turrets and battlements, was one of a series of early 19th-century houses in the shape of Norman and Tudor castles – in what came to be known as the Norman and Tudor Revival styles.

Before building Penrhyn Castle, Hopper served the Prince of Wales by designing a glass-and-iron 'Gothick' conservatory at the Prince's lavish townhouse, Carlton House, in 1807. In 1819 he began Gosford Castle in Co Armagh, Northern Ireland, for Archibald Acheson, 2nd Earl of Gosford, who later served as Governor of Canada. Built of pale local Bessbrook granite with an angular keep, circular towers and bastions, Gosford was Ireland's largest country house when built.

Hopper's patrons at Penrhyn were the relations of a Liverpool merchant, Richard Pennant, who had built up a great fortune from Jamaican sugar and, after 1785, developed the local Penrhyn Quarry for mining slate. The castle at

Below: 'Prodigy house' revisited. Anthony Salvin's extravagant Harlaxton Hall used a hybrid Elizabethan-Jacobean Revival style.

Penrhyn incorporates a medieval hall dating to the time of Llywelyn ap Iorwerth ('Llywelyn the Great') and a later 'mock castle'. Hopper designed the castle interior and fittings using fine wallpapers, 'Norman' furniture, stained glass and delicate carvings. The building and fitting took 25 years (1820–45).

Penrhyn Castle also contains a splendid Grand Staircase, a bed made of local slate weighing one ton for a visit by Queen Victoria, and a magnificent art collection put together by the Pennant family. Its kitchens and servant quarters have

Above: Penrhyn Castle stands in 45 acres (18ha) of park. In spring, the daffodils and snowdrops are a glorious sight, with distant views of Snowdonia to further stir the spirit.

been restored to their condition in 1894, when they were prepared for a banquet in honour of a visit by the Prince of Wales (the future Edward VII). With magnificent views of Snowdonia and the Menai Straits, the castle stands in impressive grounds, which include a sheltered walled garden with many tropical plants such as palm trees and Chinese gooseberries.

REVIVAL STYLES

At the close of the 18th century and in the early 19th century, architectural styles for country houses became increasingly diverse. The general adherence to Palladian and Neoclassical designs was submerged in a return to a number of earlier styles, including the Gothic, Tudor (sometimes called Elizabethan), Jacobean and Greek Revivals.

THREE REVIVAL CASTLES

A precursor of the Norman Revival was the castellated Norris Castle on the Isle of Wight, built on the site of a 16th-century fortress by James Wyatt for Lord Henry Seymour in the 1790s. (Happy memories of childhood visits here led Queen Victoria to buy Osborne nearby.)

In 1810–20, Sir Robert Smirke then used the Norman Revival style at Eastnor Castle in the Malvern Hills for John Somers Cocks, the 1st Earl Somers. Within the castle, Sir George Gilbert Scott built a Great Hall measuring 55ft high, 30ft wide and 60ft long (17 x 9 x 18m) and A.M.W. Pugin used the Gothic Revival style in the Drawing Room.

In Northern Ireland, Edward Blore employed the Tudor Revival style – sometimes called 'Tudor-Gothic' or 'Elizabethan Revival' – at Narrow Water Castle in Co Down in the 1830s. His patron was Roger Hall, High Sheriff of Co Down. The elegant Revival house stands alongside a long house built in a loose Wren style in the 17th century and close to the original 13th-century Norman castle on the site. Blore's castle has a beautiful interior with exquisite panelling, plasterwork, wooden over-mantel and furniture.

OTHER REVIVAL BUILDINGS

A similar Tudor Revival style was used by the architect William Wilkins in 1815 for Dalmeny House in Lothian, Scotland, and the following year for his reworking of Tregothnan, near Truro, in Cornwall. Both have the elaborate profile of an Elizabethan 'prodigy house'. Jeffry Wyatville used Tudor

Revival elements at Lilleshall Hall in Shropshire in the 1820s–30s for George Granville Leveson-Gower, Marquis of Stafford and later 1st Duke of Sutherland. Around the same time William Burn built an Elizabethan Revival mansion, Carstairs House, Strathclyde, for Henry Montieth.

The extraordinary Harlaxton Hall at Harlaxton in Lincolnshire was slightly later, built in a Jacobethan style and combining elements of Elizabethan and Jacobean architecture and extraordinary

Above: Robert Smirke's Staircase Hall at Eastnor Castle has cast-iron bannisters, plus a wooden chandelier, dragon benches and hall chairs, all dating from the 17th century.

internal features in German Baroque. It was constructed in 1837–45 by Anthony Salvin, later a master of Norman Revival castle-building in the mid-19th century. Today the house, known as Harlaxton College, is the British campus of the University of Evansville, Indiana, USA.

BUCKINGHAM PALACE
AND ST JAMES'S PALACE

Buckingham Palace was originally a town house, built for the Duke of Buckingham in 1702 by William Talman and a gentleman architect by the name of William Winde, on the site of an earlier pre-Civil War residence named Arlington House. George III bought Buckingham House in 1762 as a family residence to which he and Queen Charlotte could escape from court life at St James's Palace. Renaming it the Queen's House, he built a large library. Fourteen of George and Charlotte's 15 children were born in the Queen's House – all except George IV, who was born in St James's Palace.

After his accession in 1820, George IV initially wanted to modernize Buckingham House and to continue using it as a private dwelling. However, in 1826 he decided to convert it into a palace, using designs by John Nash, who had recently completed work on the Royal Pavilion in Brighton.

THE MARBLE ARCH
Nash enlarged the main house, building a new set of rooms on the garden, or west, side and replacing the existing

Below: A view of Buckingham Palace and Marble Arch from St James's Park, c.1835. The arch was moved to Hyde Park in 1851.

north and south wings, thus creating a U-shaped house enclosing an east-facing courtyard on three sides. He designed the façades of Bath stone in a French Neoclassical style favoured by the King. To use the courtyard, iron railings and a grand Marble Arch, inspired by the Arch of Constantine in Rome, were constructed. The arch was intended partly as a war memorial to Britons killed at the battles of Trafalgar and Waterloo; it was also a tribute to the

Above: This view dates to c.1820, before George IV and John Nash set to work to transform Buckingham House into a palace.

King and was intended to support a statue of George IV by Sir Francis Chantrey. However, George died before the work was complete and the statue was finally erected in Trafalgar Square. The arch itself was built in 1827 and formed the eastern entrance to the palace forecourt for almost a quarter of a century, until it was moved in 1851 to its present position, at the north-east corner of Hyde Park.

THE NEW STATEROOMS
Internally, Nash laid out a splendid set of staterooms in Buckingham Palace. From the Grand Hall, the marble Grand Staircase rose to the Picture Gallery in the centre of the block and beyond it to new staterooms on the garden front, with its elegant bow: the Blue Drawing Room, the White Drawing Room and, in the domed bow, the Music Room.

ST JAMES'S PALACE

A stone's throw from Buckingham Palace, St James's Palace is today ranked as the 'senior palace of the sovereign' and is still officially a royal residence. It was largely constructed in red brick by Henry VIII in 1531–6 on the site of the Hospital of St James. Several parts of the original palace survive, including the Chapel Royal and the great Gate House, now at the southern end of St James's Street. For three centuries it was one of the principal royal residences in London, birthplace of Charles II, James II, Mary II, Queen Anne and George IV. After most of Whitehall Palace burned down in 1698, all monarchs spent part of the year at St James's Palace. It was badly damaged by fire in 1809, and George IV undertook a grand refurbishment of its staterooms in the 1820s. William IV was the last monarch to live at St James's; from the reign of Victoria, the ruling monarch has resided in Buckingham Palace when he or she is in London.

Right: The gatehouse of St James's Palace.

Above: Carlton House's Grand Staircase rose majestically beneath a great chandelier.

Below: The lavish surroundings of the Throne Room at Buckingham Palace. Queen Victoria would use it as a second ballroom.

On the east front, facing into the open courtyard, the apartments included the Throne Room and Green Drawing Room. Many of the fittings in these rooms had been salvaged from Carlton House when it was demolished in 1827.

PUBLIC OUTCRY

The designs, amid a clamour for parliamentary reform, were not popular. There was considerable public disquiet over the cost and Nash's perceived extravagance: George IV initially asked for £500,000, but his prime minister agreed to only £150,000 – a sum later increased to £200,000. But when George IV died in 1830, it emerged that the still unfinished work had cost £501,530. The dome on the garden side was ridiculed as 'a wretched inverted egg-cup'.

Following a government investigation, amid concerns that some of the work was not structurally sound, Nash was dismissed, having been judged to be guilty of 'inexcusable irregularity and great negligence'. George's successor, William IV, commissioned the more modest Edward Blore to complete the palace; the well-known east front facing the Mall, which contains the balcony, was added in 1850, then redesigned and refaced in Portland Stone in 1913 by Sir Aston Webb.

THE GRANGE AT NORTHINGTON
AND THE GREEK REVIVAL

The Greek Revival arose following the circulation in the late 18th and early 19th centuries of illustrations of Greek art and architecture and the arrival, in London in 1803, of the 'Elgin Marbles' – fragments of ancient Greek sculpture brought to London by Thomas Bruce, 7th Earl of Elgin, who had been British ambassador to the Ottoman Empire. The British upper classes became convinced of the superiority of ancient Greek sculpture and buildings in comparison with those of other ancient or more modern cultures. The Revival was principally an urban phenomenon – evidenced in town halls,

Above: This engraving shows The Grange in 1830, within a quarter-century of its building by William Wilkins in 1804–9.

Above: The original house looks out between columns at The Grange. Pevsner declared the Doric portico to have 'tremendous pathos'.

Below: The Grange's great portico of Doric columns faces east; note also the central block of four square piers and pilasters between the bays on the south side.

courts of justice, hospitals, colleges, theatres and other buildings decorated with Greek columns and loosely made to look like Greek temples. The Revival, which swept through Europe, was also particularly popular in the United States, where it became known as the 'National style'.

AN ARCADIAN VISION
A striking early example of Greek Revival style in country-house building was The Grange at Northington, near Winchester in Hampshire. In 1804–9, William Wilkins refashioned an existing 17th-century house in the image of a Greek temple, specifically in the likeness

of the Theseum in Athens. On the east side, overlooking a lake, Wilkins raised a portico consisting of two lines of six great Doric columns. On the north and south sides, each composed of nine bays, he added a central block containing four square piers.

The archaeologist and architect C.R. Cockerell had boundless admiration, writing of The Grange in the early 19th century: 'Nothing can be finer (or) more classical… there is nothing like it on this side of Arcadia.' Today, the house is partly ruined, but the extraordinary portico can still be seen.

JOHN DOBSON

The country house of Meldon Park in Northumberland was built in 1832 by the well-known Newcastle architect John Dobson for Isaac Cookson. Its Ionic entrance porch and clean lines make it a good example of the Greek Revival style.

Dobson was an accomplished town architect, and like Nash in London, the builder of delightful Regency-style townhouses. In Newcastle he built Grainger, Market and Grey Streets and, after completing Meldon Park, constructed the city's acclaimed railway station. At Meldon

Above: Doric columns surround the front door at Arlington Court in Devon. Visitors may try out one of the National Trust's large collection of horse-drawn carriages there.

he produced a studiedly plain exterior that is decorated only by the columns of the entrance porch; all its essential drainpipes and guttering are hidden from view.

MORE REVIVAL HOUSES

Other early examples of the Greek Revival country house include Longford Hall in Shropshire, designed in 1789 by Joseph Bonomi: its portico has four columns and its Great Hall a fine Grecian frieze. In 1803, at Stratton Park in Hampshire, George Dance the Younger built a two-storey portico with vast Doric columns; the house has been demolished but the portico remains as part of a 1960s mansion.

In 1808, Joseph Gandy, the highly talented assistant of Sir John Soane, who so imaginatively illustrated Soane's architectural schemes, built a fine Greek Revival house at Storrs Hall on the shores of Lake Windermere: it has a splendid Doric colonnade on its entrance front. Arlington Court near Barnstaple in Devon was designed with a Doric-columned entranceway and Doric entablature by local architect Thomas Lee for Colonel John Chichester in 1820.

BELSAY HALL, NORTHUMBERLAND

At Belsay Hall, in 1807–15, Sir Charles Monck built an austere square limestone house with a vast Doric portico and a Doric frieze running around the building. Sir Charles had returned in 1806 from a two-year trip to Greece, in which he was greatly impressed by ancient Greek temple architecture. With the help of John Dobson, designer of Meldon Park, Sir Charles set out to create a Greek Revival house for his recently inherited estate. Internally, he laid out the rooms around a central space lit from

above, in the style of a Greek or Roman dwelling. The Belsay Hall estate also contains a 14th-century tower house (called 'the Castle') and the ruins of one wing of a 17th-century house. There are magnificent gardens, partly laid out by Sir Charles himself, including one in the quarry from which his workmen cut out the limestone to build the Hall.

Below: The imposing Doric columns on the main front at Belsay Hall. Note also the Doric frieze running around the building.

RESTORATION AT WINDSOR
UNDER GEORGE IV

In the 1820s, George IV and his architect Jeffry Wyatville carried out a major restoration of the royal buildings at Windsor, which, combined with earlier work by James Wyatt in 1800–11, created the 'picturesque' Gothic castle we see today. Within the palace, George and Wyatville swept away many of the superb interiors created by Charles II (see page 405), but they were also responsible for a magnificent series of royal apartments and the creation of the remarkable Waterloo Chamber to house portraits of the military heroes who had defeated Napoleon at the Battle of Waterloo.

GEORGE III AT WINDSOR

In 1778–82, George III and Sir William Chambers rebuilt Queen Anne's Lodge, which stood to the south of the castle's upper ward. Renamed the Queen's Lodge, the building was George and Queen Charlotte's favoured residence at Windsor (it was demolished by George IV in 1823). Within the castle in the 1780s and 90s, he restored St George's Chapel (see also page 334) and made improvements to the staterooms, including the addition of historical paintings of scenes from the life of Edward III by the American artist, Benjamin West.

WYATT'S ADDITIONS

James Wyatt began work for the royal family at Windsor with the rebuilding of Queen Charlotte's House at Frogmore, adjoining Windsor Great Park. George III bought the Frogmore estate for the

Above: The Green Drawing Room is one of the splendid set of new rooms that was created by Wyatville in the castle's east front.

Queen in 1790 and Wyatt impressed both with his work there in the 1790s. In 1800–11, he was commissioned to rebuild the state apartments in the castle's upper ward in the Gothic style. He put in pointed Gothic windows to replace those inserted by Hugh May in the 17th century, constructed a cloister in Horn Court and raised a splendid entrance from the quadrangle. He also installed a Grand Staircase to replace the former 'King's Stair' and created a suite of private rooms on the ground floor of the north block. In these rooms, George III was confined in his final illness.

WINDSOR TRANSFORMED

The Prince Regent used John Nash to rebuild the Lower Lodge, situated about 3 miles (4.5km) south-east of the castle in the Great Park, as the Royal Lodge.

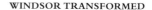

Left: The State Dining Room. Both this and the Green Drawing Room were restored after the damage caused by fire in 1992.

The Prince lived there while at Windsor, but following his father's death in 1820 he moved into the castle, and began a new round of rebuilding. Jeffry Wyatt, nephew of James Wyatt, won a competition in 1823, whose details had been drafted by Sir Charles Long, to take on the work. (Although now referred to as Jeffry Wyatville, the architect was known by his original name until 1824, when he changed his name to Wyatville in line with the taste for the Gothic; he was knighted in 1828.)

In the upper ward, Wyatville added a battlemented upper storey to the southeast and north sides of the quadrangle. He moved the private apartments from the north to the south and east sections. The north-side rooms were set aside for state occasions.

In the east front, he created a superb set of royal rooms, including the Dining Room and the White and Crimson Drawing Rooms, which are as grand as any of the interiors lost for posterity when Carlton House in London was demolished. Indeed, these rooms at Windsor, like the apartments in Buckingham Palace, contain several fittings and pieces of furniture salvaged

from Carlton House. Along the inner and south front of the quadrangle, he created the splendid Grand Corridor, more than 500ft (150m) in length. He raised the height of the Round Tower by around 30ft (9m), and remodelled the outer walls of the upper ward's south wing, creating a distinctive symmetrical façade for the castle.

WATERLOO CHAMBER

Wyatville created the Waterloo Chamber by roofing in the former Horn Court. Here, he placed some Grinling Gibbons' carving removed from the Charles II-era Royal Chapel, and hung specially commissioned portraits by Sir Thomas Lawrence of royal and military figures associated with Wellington's triumph at Waterloo – including Georges III and IV, the Duke of Wellington and Field Marshall von Blücher.

LONGER WALK

As part of Wyatville's rebuilding, the Long Walk created by King Charles II to link the castle to Windsor Great Park was lengthened in 1823 to run right up to a new entranceway,

Above: Windsor Castle from the Great Park. The 19th-century work at Windsor created a skyline in the Picturesque Gothic.

the George IV Gateway. This entailed knocking down King George III's Queen's Lodge. (See also page 476.)

Below: This 19th-century aquatint shows the castle's sweeping Grand Staircase shortly after its completion.

LONGLEAT HOUSE

Jeffry Wyatville is also remembered for his work at Longleat House – the 16th-century 'prodigy house' in Wiltshire built by the Elizabethan courtier Sir John Thynne. In 1806–14, Wyatville reconstructed the north front, built a magnificent Grand Staircase to connect the two inner courtyards and redecorated several rooms. Among other houses on which he worked were Chatsworth House, where he built an extension to the north wing in 1820–41, and Fort Belvedere in Windsor Great Park, famously the home of Edward, Prince of Wales, briefly Edward VIII and later Duke of Windsor, where he added extensions in 1827–30.

CHAPTER TWENTY-THREE

VICTORIAN STYLE AND REVIVALS

*c.*1830–1901

On 27 August 1839, the 13th Earl of Eglington held a medieval tournament complete with jousting in the lists at Eglington Castle in Ayrshire. A great crowd of spectators in medieval costume saw Lady Eglington – styled the 'Queen of Beauty' – receive the chivalrous offerings of mounted knights. Unfortunately, after these preliminaries, Scottish rain sweeping in from the west was the winner, for the competition was washed away by a great noon downpour that obscured visibility and reduced the lists to a mud bath. But the tournament at Eglington was a remarkable reflection of an aristocratic interest in the cult of chivalry and medieval life that resulted in the rebuilding of many country homes in the style of castles.

At Cardiff Castle and Castell Coch in Wales, John Crichton Stuart, the 3rd Marquess of Bute, and his architect William Burges produced exquisite romantic recreations of the medieval castle. Likewise, at Arundel in Sussex and at Alnwick in Northumberland, the dukes of Norfolk and Northumberland and their architects 'improved' the ruins of their ancient strongholds and castles to create picturesque turreted skylines and sumptuous interiors. Certainly not least among these ambitious essays in the revival castle was the rebuilding by Queen Victoria's husband, Prince Albert, at Balmoral, in which he turned a modest country house on the River Dee in Scotland into a turreted fairy-tale fortress in the Scottish Baronial style.

Left: Arundel Castle ranks below only Windsor and Alnwick as a supreme example of the Romantic recreation of the Middle Ages by Georgian and Victorian architects.

BUCKINGHAM PALACE
THE OFFICIAL LONDON RESIDENCE OF QUEEN VICTORIA

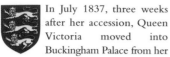

In July 1837, three weeks after her accession, Queen Victoria moved into Buckingham Palace from her childhood home at Kensington. She made the palace the monarch's official London residence. Shortly after moving in, she put in train a number of improvements to make her quarters more private; as part of these works Nash's unpopular dome (previously derided as 'a wretched inverted egg-cup') was removed (see pages 460–1).

A NEW EAST WING
On Victoria's marriage in 1840 to Prince Albert of Saxe-Coburg-Gotha, it became clear that the lack of nursery accommodation in the palace would be a problem; in addition, the state apartments of George IV were found to be too small to hold a court ball. In 1847–50, the famous London builder, Thomas Cubitt, constructed a new wing along the east side of the palace courtyard, facing the Mall. It was designed by Edward Blore, with nurseries on the top floor and apartments for prominent visitors on the first floor. The building work was

partly funded by the sale of Brighton Pavilion, and the interiors of the new wing also made use of furnishings and fittings from the Pavilion, notably in the Chinese decorations of the Luncheon Room and the East Room. To make room for the new wing, the Marble Arch was moved to its present position

Above: The palace Ballroom as it looked on completion in c.1855. It has since been redecorated in white with gold details.

at the north-east corner of Hyde Park, formerly the site of the Tyburn gallows. Blore used a soft French stone that proved vulnerable to the weather and London atmosphere, and the east wing of the palace was refaced with Portland stone just before World War I by Sir Aston Webb (see page 484).

A LAVISH BALLROOM
The required Ballroom was added, together with a State Supper Room and new galleries, on the west front of the palace. This work was designed by James Pennethorne, a pupil of the disgraced John Nash, and built in 1852–5 by Cubitt. The impressive Ballroom measured 123 x 60ft (37 x 18m). The interior was lavishly decorated, under the guidance of Prince Albert, as advised by his artistic designer, Professor Ludwig Grüner, with murals by Niccola Consoni and sculptures by William Theed.

THE ROYAL MEWS

The Royal Mews in Buckingham Palace Road, which house the Queen's carriages, horses and motor vehicles, were built in 1824–5 by John Nash, with two Doric arches and two sets of stables as well as grand coach-houses.

The Mews had been established in this location in 1760 by George III: Sir William Chambers built an indoor riding school there in 1763–6. In 1855, Victoria added a school on the site for the children of Royal Mews staff, and in 1859 constructed further accommodation there. Visitors to the Mews can see the gold state coach built for George III to designs by Sir William Chambers in 1762 and used for all coronations since.

Left: The gold state coach of George III, used for coronations and state occasions.

BALMORAL
AND THE SCOTTISH BARONIAL STYLE

Queen Victoria and Prince Albert bought the estate and modest manor house of Balmoral on the River Dee in the Grampian region of Scotland in 1852. Albert and architect William Smith at once demolished the existing house and in 1853–5 built a turreted castle in the Scottish Baronial style.

The Queen and her husband had fallen in love with Scotland during holidays at Taymouth and Blair Atholl in the early 1840s. They leased Balmoral and stayed there for the first time in the autumn of 1848. Their initial visit was a great success, although the original house – called 'a pretty little castle in the old Scotch style' by Victoria – was too small for their needs: members of the royal household had to stay in nearby

Below: Balmoral has been a favoured royal retreat since Prince Albert designed it and Victoria described it as 'this dear paradise'.

cottages and wait each morning for their breakfast to be delivered by wheelbarrow from the main house.

A COUNTRY HOUSE

Albert set out to design a holiday retreat rather than a grand royal residence, in his words a building 'not like a palace but like a country gentleman's house'. In contrast to Osborne House, Balmoral has no Audience Chamber or Council Room in which the Queen may receive ministers and other officials; there are only general-purpose rooms for significant visitors on the south side of the main block's ground floor. Otherwise, the main block contains the Dining Room, Drawing Room, Billiard Room and Library, with private rooms for the Queen and Prince on the floor above. Throughout, as at Osborne House, the most modern conveniences were provided, with hot-air heating, four bathrooms for the royal family and 14

BELFAST CASTLE

Above: The 19th-century Scots Baronial house stands on the site of a Norman fortification and a 17th-century castle.

Prince Albert's work at Balmoral set a fashion for the Scottish Baronial architectural style. In the light of this and as a way of underlining Ulster's connection to Scotland, the architect W.H. Lynn used the same romantic blend of gables and turrets for Belfast Castle, built in a beautiful position overlooking the city, for the 3rd Marquess of Donegall and his wealthy son-in-law, Lord Ashley, in 1867–70.

water-closets – at the time, a record for a British country house. There was also a servants' wing, stables and offices.

Victoria and Albert moved into the main house in September 1855, and returned each autumn until Albert's death in 1861. After that dark event, Victoria often visited twice a year: in June and from August to November. The place had special significance because of its association with her husband: it was, she wrote, 'Albert's own creation, own work, own building, own laying out', and she added 'my dearest Albert's … great taste and the impress of his dear hand have been stamped everywhere'.

OSBORNE HOUSE
VICTORIA'S FAVOURITE HOUSE

Queen Victoria's favourite royal residence was the palatial seaside villa of Osborne House on the Isle of Wight. At Osborne – designed and built by her beloved husband, Prince Albert, in collaboration with Thomas Cubitt – she spent many of her happiest hours of family life and here, at the end of a long and highly productive reign, she died on 22 January 1901 surrounded by her children and grandchildren.

Victoria wanted a seaside retreat but intensely disliked the Royal Pavilion in Brighton, with its associations with the extravagant and colourful private life of George IV and which had been engulfed by the growth of the resort and therefore lacked privacy. She decided to sell the Pavilion and to buy a house and estate on the Isle of Wight, which she knew from happy childhood visits to Norris Castle in 1831 and 1833.

With the help of her then prime minister, Sir Robert Peel, Victoria and Albert found Osborne House, overlooking the Solent on the north

side of the Isle of Wight, and, after a successful stay in 1843, the royal couple purchased the 1,000 acre (405 ha)-estate – which came with its own private beach as well as a substantial Georgian house – from Lady Isabella Blanchford in 1845. Victoria wrote of her pleasure at having 'a place of one's own, quiet and retired'.

Above: Palazzo style. The view from the Lower Terrace, with the Andromeda Fountain, back up to the Clock Tower.

AN ITALIANATE VILLA

The Queen and Prince Albert demolished the existing house, and, with Cubitt, who had made his reputation developing Highbury and Belgravia in London, Albert built a splendid Italianate villa in 1845–51. Osborne's design, with two *campanile* towers, was a tribute to the Italian Renaissance *palazzo* (palace) and influenced by a pair of villas built by Sir Charles Barry: Mount Felix at Walton-on-Thames, Surrey (1836), and Trentham Hall in north Staffordshire (1842). Its façades mixed Roman, Florentine and Palladian elements to charming effect. When he visited Osborne, the twice prime minister, Benjamin Disraeli, was enraptured, describing it as 'a Sicilian Palazzo with garden terraces, statues and vases shining in the sun, than which nothing can be conceived more captivating'.

The house was laid out, with the privacy of the royal family in mind, in two main parts: a rectangular Family Pavilion for the Queen, Albert and children

---

BRODSWORTH HALL

The Italianate *palazzo* style used by Prince Albert at Osborne House was widely influential. A particularly fine example is Brodsworth Hall in South Yorkshire, designed for Charles Thellusson by an unknown Italian architect, Chevalier Casentini, in 1861–3. Casentini replaced the original 18th-century hall with an elegant but very substantial villa containing more than 30 rooms.

The house has been maintained carefully since it was taken over from its last owner, a Thellusson descendant, by English Heritage in 1990 and is one of the least altered of all Victorian country houses. The estate has fine

Above: Casentini did not visit Yorkshire. His design for Brodsworth was implemented by English architect, Philip Wilkinson.

gardens with an Italian-style fountain and statue walks, summerhouse, woodland, ornamental flowerbeds and a quarry area – all restored since 1990 to their 1860s' condition and plan.

Above: At Osborne, where she had often retreated following the loss of Albert, Victoria lay in state after her own death.

linked by the grand Marble Corridor to a substantial and asymetrical east wing, intended for visitors and members of the royal household.

The Family Pavilion was built in 1845 and splendidly fitted out in 1846, and the royal family moved in during September of that year. On their first night of residence, Prince Albert led prayers seeking God's blessing on the house and recited sections of a Lutheran hymn.

The German art professor, Ludwig Grüner, acting as Prince Albert's artistic designer from 1845, was in charge of decorating the interior of the Family Pavilion. Its most splendid section was without doubt the Marble Corridor, which featured floor tiles designed by Prince Albert and polychrome stencilling on the walls in blue, umber, black and red. Along the walls were displayed Albert's collection of contemporary sculptures by artists including R.J. Wyatt and John Gibson.

Prince Albert believed that English country houses were generally too gloomy, so he designed the three main rooms on the ground floor of the Family Pavilion with large plate-glass windows. These rooms are the Dining Room, the Drawing Room and the

Right: Italian towers and terraces look down on formal gardens at Osborne House and have beautiful views of the Solent.

Billiard Room, the last two divided only by Corinthian columns in yellow marble, together essentially forming one sizeable L-shaped room. The Drawing Room contains a bow window giving fine views over the terraced gardens to the Solent.

On the first floor was a private suite designed for the Queen and Prince Albert, consisting of two bathrooms, two dressing rooms, a bedroom and a sitting room. Above that, on the second floor, were the nursery rooms. Albert and Cubitt also co-operated in the design of formal terraced gardens at Osborne in 1847. The grounds included a Swiss Cottage – a miniature dwelling designed as a playhouse for the royal children.

INDIAN HALL
Towards the end of Queen Victoria's reign, after she had become Empress of India in 1877 and was taking a significant interest in Indian affairs, a new wing was added at Osborne House in 1890–1. Its ground floor consisted of a large Reception Hall decorated in Indian style by imported craftsmen and designed by Bhai Ram Singh, an expert on Indian architecture, with advice from Rudyard Kipling's father, John Lockwood Kipling, who was director of Lahore Central Museum. Called the Durbar Hall, the new building featured elaborate Moghul-style plasterwork. Above the Reception Hall, on the second floor of the wing, were apartments for Victoria's youngest daughter, Princess Beatrice, and her family.

A MODERN HOUSE
Throughout Osborne House, Cubitt used the most up-to-date materials, providing the very latest plumbing and central-heating systems. Also in 1890, electric lights were fitted throughout Osborne House.

Victoria's son and successor Edward VII disliked Osborne House and donated it to the nation. Her apartments have been open to the public since 1954.

ALNWICK, EASTNOR AND ARUNDEL
GREAT VICTORIAN CASTLE REVIVALS

In the 1850s, the architect Anthony Salvin and Algernon Percy, 4th Duke of Northumberland, substantially rebuilt the great Percy stronghold of Alnwick Castle in Northumberland, adding both the imposing Prudhoe Tower and the North Terrace. Salvin's very impressive rebuilding, which swept away much of the Georgian Gothic remodelling carried out at Alnwick in the 18th century by Robert Adam, was one of the greatest of a swathe of Victorian castle revivals undertaken in the mid-19th century.

ALNWICK'S HISTORY

The first castle on the site was built in 1096 by Yves de Vescy, Baron of Alnwick. Strongly fortified in the next century, it twice repelled sieges by William I 'the Lion' of Scots; on the second occasion, in 1174, 'the Lion' was

Below: In the 1860s, Anthony Salvin converted the courtyard at Muncaster Castle into the barrel-vaulted Drawing Room.

taken prisoner in fog outside the castle and thrown into jail. The first Percy ancestor at Alnwick, Henry, 1st Lord Percy, bought the castle in 1309 and began its restoration.

Of this work, one semicircular tower survives today (of the seven that initially comprised the keep), as does much of the curtain wall, several other towers and the gateway that stands between the two baileys. Later Percys were to suffer for their Roman Catholic faith: Thomas Percy, 7th Earl of Northumberland, lost his head for his part in the 'Rising of the North' against Queen Elizabeth I.

In the 17th century, the castle fell into decay, but it was rebuilt and modernized by Sir Hugh Smithson and Percy heiress, Lady Betty Seymour, later the 1st Duke and Duchess of Northumberland, in the mid-18th century. At the same time they commissioned Robert Adam to redecorate Syon House in Middlesex. At Alnwick, they employed Adam alongside James Paine to work in the

Above: For all the rebuilding and restoration work, Alnwick Castle retains its original plan – of a motte and two baileys.

Georgian Gothic Revival style, remnants of which include the life-size stone figures on the battlements.

THE 4TH DUKE'S ADDITIONS

In 1847, and at the age of 55, Algernon Percy succeeded his brother Hugh as 4th Duke of Northumberland towards the end of a very busy and fruitful life in which he had served in the navy during the Napoleonic Wars and had, subsequently, been one of the first Englishmen to excavate the tombs of ancient Egypt. He displayed several of his archaeological finds in the Castle Museum at Alnwick, established in the Postern Tower and opened to the public as early as 1826.

In their rebuilding of Alnwick, Salvin and the 4th Duke constructed a new chapel, the Guest Hall, the Falconer's Tower and a riding school with stables, in addition to the great Prudhoe Tower. The Duke combined the castle's rugged Gothic Revival exterior with the most luxurious Italian Renaissance-style interiors, including widely admired coffered ceilings and superb scarlet damask and gold hangings in the Drawing Room. Within the Prudhoe Tower, he installed a fine Library and, in the place of the medieval Great Hall, created a Dining Hall with a wonderful carved, unpainted pine and cedar ceiling.

ANTHONY SALVIN

Salvin, architect of the extraordinary 'Jacobethan-Baroque' Harlaxton Manor in Lincolnshire in 1837–45, ably extended and rebuilt a large number of castles for Victorian patrons. These included Muncaster Castle, overlooking the River Esk near Ravenglass in Cumbria, where he worked for Gamel Augustus Pennington, 4th Lord Muncaster, from 1862 onward. Salvin converted the courtyard into the fine Drawing Room with barrel ceiling, built a north-west tower to match the 14th-century pele tower at the south-west of the site and added battlements and transomed and mullioned windows.

Another of Salvin's notable commissions was Peckforton Castle in Tarporley, west Cheshire. Peckforton was a new country house built in the style of a medieval castle for MP John Tollemache (subsequently Lord Tollemache) in 1844–51. Its centrepiece was the Great Hall, with stone vaulted ceiling, minstrels' gallery and intricately carved screen; the main reception rooms gave on to a splendid pentagonal stairwell.

EASTNOR CASTLE

In Herefordshire, John Somers Cocks, 1st Earl Somers, and the architect Robert Smirke built the vast Eastnor Castle in a Norman Revival style in 1810–20. At this time timber was in short supply because it was being used to build ships for the Royal Navy to

Below: Social unrest persuaded John Tollemache that Peckforton Castle should be fit to withstand a siege.

repel an expected Napoleonic invasion, so Smirke used cast iron for roof trusses and in place of large beams. The main building material was a handsome sandstone, brought from quarries in the Forest of Dean by canal and then mule. Smirke created a simple, medieval-style interior. The 1st Earl's descendants

Above: The great Gothic Revivalist A.W. Pugin created this magnificent 'medieval' Drawing Room at Eastnor Castle in 1849.

added to this, commissioning a superb Gothic drawing room in 1849 and lavish work in the Long Library and State Bedroom in the 1860–70s.

ARUNDEL CASTLE

Arundel Castle in West Sussex stands on a Norman motte (of 1068), and contains a medieval gatehouse and barbican, but it is primarily a Victorian recreation of the Middle Ages. This magnificent achievement is in small part the work of Charles Howard, the 11th Duke of Norfolk, and architect Francis Hiorne in 1791–1815, and in large part the creation of Henry Fitzalan-Howard, the 15th Duke, and architect CA Buckler in 1870–1900. The superb Gothic library, with its vaulted roof of mahogany, was built by Jonathan Ritson in 1802. Buckler's chapel is celebrated as one of the best Victorian Gothic interiors. The 15th Duke also equipped the castle with 'mod cons' – Arundel was one of the pioneers of fitting electricity and central heating in English country houses.

Above: Purists may dismiss many Victorian 'improvements' of England's medieval legacy, but it is impossible not to admire the Gothic chapel at Arundel.

CARDIFF CASTLE AND CASTELL COCH
WILLIAM BURGES AND CONJECTURAL RESTORATION

John Crichton Stuart, 3rd Marquess of Bute, was said to be the richest man in the world in the 1860s. He had inherited a vast fortune, derived partly from the export of Welsh coal from Cardiff, as an infant in 1848. In 1866, aged only 19, he commissioned architect William Burges to rebuild Cardiff Castle in an opulent Victorian Gothic style.

ROMAN AND NORMAN REMAINS
The castle stands in the centre of Cardiff, on the site of a Roman fort and a Norman stronghold. Remains from both these periods are incorporated into the building: approaching the main entrance, for example, Roman stonework is visible at the base of Norman walls, while within the enclosure the Norman shell keep still stands proudly on its motte. For centuries, the castle was an important fortress, passing from one powerful lord to another: the de Clare family in the 12–13th centuries; Hugh le Despenser in the reign of Edward II; Richard Neville, Earl of Warwick ('the Kingmaker'), and Richard, Duke of Gloucester (later Richard III), in the 15th century; and the Herbert

Below: The Gothic towers and crenellations of Bute and Burges combine with Roman and Norman stonework at Cardiff Castle.

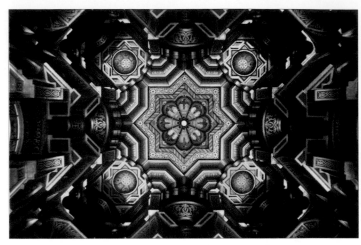

lords in the 16th century. It was finally passed by marriage into the hands of the Bute family in 1766.

THEMED ROOMS
Bute and Burges raised Gothic towers and created elaborate interiors with stained glass, murals, wood and stone carving and marble fireplaces. A number of the rooms were elaborately themed: the Winter Smoking Room, for example, has the theme of passing time, being decorated with images of the seasons and days of the week.

THREE GREAT TOWERS
The work on Cardiff Castle was complemented by Bute and Burges' equally lavish restoration of the Marquess's country retreat near Cardiff – the 13th-century castle of Castell Coch. Beginning in 1875, Burges built almost from scratch, for the original fortress had been reduced to ruins in the 15th century. He raised three great towers with conical roofs: the Keep Tower, next to the gatehouse, was linked to the Kitchen Tower by the Banqueting Hall; the curtain wall then followed an irregular circle around to the Well Tower.

Above: Kaleidoscope of colours – a detail of the fantastically elaborate decoration in the Arabian Room, Cardiff Castle.

The castle was compact, its three towers grouped around a courtyard only 55ft (17m) across. It stood within a dry moat and, with great attention to medieval detail, was fitted with a portcullis and a drawbridge, as well as murder-holes for pouring boiling water or oil on to intruders.

Below: Eastern promise. Beautiful blue-black floor tiles combine with delicate carving in this lavish interior at Cardiff Castle.

Left: The reddish sandstone used at Castell Coch, near Cardiff, gives the building its popular name of the 'Red Castle'.

of animals and birds and, above the splendid tiled fireplace, exquisitely carved figures of the Three Fates from ancient Greek mythology. A raised balcony runs around the second-storey level and a beautiful azure and gold vaulted ceiling painted with stars and birds rises above.

On the third and fourth floors of the tower, beneath a double dome ceiling, is the Lady's Bedroom, decorated with gilt and mirrors and containing a

remarkable 'Moorish' bed fitted with eight crystal balls and derived from the interiors of the Alhambra in Granada, Spain. Other rooms include the more austere Banqueting Hall, the Lord's Bedroom, the Servants' Hall and kitchen. All the work at Castell Coch was meticulously researched by Burges in the British Museum for historical accuracy, and he wrote extensive justifications of this 'conjectural restoration'.

Below: The two-storey Drawing Room at Castell Coch. Note the Three Fates above the fireplace, the painted panels and the balcony beneath the domed azure ceiling.

LAVISH DECORATION

As at Cardiff Castle, the interiors were lavishly finished; many were, in fact, not decorated under the architect's supervision, for he died in 1881, but were overseen by William Frame working from Burges' detailed plans for the decor. The Keep Tower contains a two-storey Drawing Room, decorated with scenes from Aesop's Fables: delicate painted panels depicting plants, mouldings

CARLTON TOWERS

Carlton Towers at Goole in North Yorkshire was twice 'Gothicized' in the Victorian era, creating one of the most celebrated of Victorian Gothic country houses. The original Jacobean house of 1614 was initially remodelled in 1840 by Miles, the 8th Lord Beaumont, before it was reworked more substantially, in 1873–6, by E.W. Pugin (son of Augustus Welby Pugin) for Henry, 9th Lord Beaumont. Then, after Lord Beaumont quarrelled with his architect, he commissioned John Francis Bentley, the Roman Catholic architect of Westminster Cathedral, to decorate the interior. The result was a superb suite of staterooms that incorporated the Armoury, Venetian Drawing Room, Card Room and Picture Gallery.

WINDSOR CASTLE AND FROGMORE
VICTORIA AND ALBERT

Queen Victoria and Prince Albert are particularly associated with Osborne House and Balmoral, but in fact they spent the majority of each year at Windsor, where Albert was a Ranger of the Great Park and carried out a number of improvements on the estate. He worked in the Home Park, encompassing the Frogmore estate and Shaw Farm to the north of the castle, as well as in the Great Park. In particular, he rebuilt the Home Farm in 1852 in a Tudor Revival style and in 1858 reconstructed George III's dairy building with an admired interior featuring Minton tiles and sculpture by John Thomas. See also pages 334, 405 and 464.

ALBERT MEMORIALS

However, the most significant building work at Windsor Castle during Victoria's reign was carried out in memory of Albert, who died of typhoid fever there on 14 December 1861. Victoria insisted that Albert's rooms were kept exactly as they had been on the day of his death, and rebuilt the chapel that stood above

Below: An aerial view of Windsor Castle shows the upper ward to the right and the lower ward to the left of the Round Tower.

PRIVATE BURIAL

Victoria broke with royal tradition in being buried in a mausoleum on private ground rather than in a cathedral or major church. The idea of a mausoleum had come from her Uncle Leopold, who built one at Claremont for his wife, Princess Charlotte – which in turn inspired Prince Albert to raise one at Coburgh for his father and Victoria to construct one for her mother, the Duchess of Kent, also at Frogmore. After Victoria's death, the former Edward VIII was buried at Frogmore following his death in 1972 and his wife, Wallis, the woman for whom he gave up the throne, was buried alongside him in 1986.

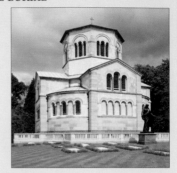

Above: Windsor's Albert Memorial. On her death in 1901, Victoria joined her late husband in the Frogmore Mausoleum.

the Tomb House (behind St George's Chapel) as the magnificent Albert Memorial Chapel. This work was carried out in 1863–73, principally by George Gilbert Scott, who installed fine stained-glass windows and marble reliefs by Jules Destréez on the walls.

At Frogmore, Victoria built a mausoleum for her husband and herself. Designed by Ludwig Grüner and built by A.J. Humbert in 1862–71, the

mausoleum has a granite and Portland stone exterior with gunmetal doors; the interior features frescoes by Italian and German painters in the style of Italian Renaissance master Raphael, whom Albert had considered the finest of all artists. The sarcophagus is of marble, granite and bronze and bears effigies of Albert and Victoria, both carved in the 1860s, although Victoria's was, of course, not put in place until her death in 1901.

CHATSWORTH
AND JOSEPH PAXTON

William, 6th Duke of Devonshire, began a 19-year programme of alterations at Chatsworth House, Derbyshire, in 1818 (see also pages 406–7). Sir Jeffry Wyatville began by remaking the Long Gallery as a Library, then added a new north wing to the house (in 1820–7), containing the Theatre, Sculpture Gallery, Dining Room and offices. He redecorated the staterooms in 1832–42 and proceeded to work on the Duke's private apartments in the west front. In October 1832, the first stage of Wyatville's redecoration was inspected by the future Queen Victoria, who, aged 13, was entertained to dinner in the new, lavish gold and white Dining Room with her mother, the Duchess of Kent.

GARDENS TRANSFORMED

The Duke appointed the 23-year-old Joseph Paxton – future designer of the Crystal Palace – as Head Gardener at Chatsworth House in 1826. He had met Paxton in Chiswick, where the Horticultural Society gardens the young man managed abutted the grounds of Chiswick House, which the Duke had inherited, along with the other Devonshire estates, in 1811. Paxton

Below: Chatsworth's Long Gallery, remade by Wyatville as a Long Library, offers exercise for both the body and the mind.

Above: The Emperor Fountain, installed by Paxton in 1844, can send its waters twice as high as the house behind.

transformed the gardens at Chatsworth, creating a vast rock garden, planting rare species from around the world and experimenting with glasshouses and heating apparatus to help them flourish in Derbyshire. His extraordinary Great Conservatory, built in 1840 (and demolished in 1920), was the forerunner of the Crystal Palace. Paxton also designed and installed the Emperor Fountain, capable of launching a water jet to a height of 298ft (90m), and so called because its installation was intended to

mark a visit to Chatsworth by Tsar Nicolas I of Russia, though in the event the visit did not take place.

The 6th Duke spent lavishly at Chatsworth and by his death in 1858 owed a massive £1,000,000. Yet debt did not detract from the great pleasure he received from the house and gardens: 'What happiness I have in Chatsworth, adorable Chatsworth, happiness beyond words.' He entertained continuously on a grand scale: notable visitors included Queen Victoria and Prince Albert.

Below: In addition to building glasshouses, Paxton also dug a coal tunnel in the gardens, which has recently been excavated.

KNEBWORTH HOUSE
AND HUGHENDEN MANOR

Edward Bulwer Lytton, author of best-selling historical novels and former Member of Parliament, inherited Knebworth House on the death of his mother, Elizabeth, in 1843. The original house was a quadrangular brick manor built by a distant ancestor, Sir Robert Lytton, in 1492; this had been reduced to a single wing rebuilt in the Regency Gothic style and covered in stucco by Mrs Bulwer Lytton in 1811–16. Employing the architect H.E. Kendall Junior and the decorator John G. Crace, Edward added pinnacles, towers, gargoyles and heraldic decorations. In the State Presence Room (now known as the State Drawing Room), Crace designed a Victorian Gothic chimney-piece and over-mantel, installed Tudor rose panelling and fine stained glass with a portrait of Henry VII, and fitted 44 coats of arms into the ceiling. This room survives and is, as Crace designed it to be, 'very Gothic'. The Tudor connection arose because some ancestral

Below: The main façade of Knebworth House, showing the towers and crenellation added by Edward Bulwer Lytton.

Above: Edward Bulwer Lytton's study at Knebworth House. He was a highly popular and influential writer in his day.

Left: Disraeli followed the fashion for rebuilding an old house in Gothic style.

research revealed that one of Bulwer Lytton's ancestors on his mother's side was an aunt of Henry VII.

HUGHENDEN MANOR

The country house of Hughenden Manor, in Buckinghamshire, was the home from 1848 to his death in 1881 of Benjamin Disraeli, a favourite of Queen Victoria and twice Conservative prime minister (1868 and 1874–80). Queen Victoria visited Hughenden Manor in 1877 – the year after Disraeli

had secured her the title she longed for, that of 'Empress of India' – and again in 1881, following his death, to lay a wreath on the vault containing his body in the local church. She later erected a memorial to Disraeli in the church.

Hughenden's main interest lies in its association with 'Dizzy'. The house, bought by the rising politician in 1848 for £35,000, was originally a modest farmhouse but was rebuilt in the Gothic style by John Norris in the 1840s. In 1862, the architect Edward Buckton Lamb made a number of alterations, in particular adding pinnacles to relieve the stark outline of the main façade. The gardens were laid out by Disraeli's beloved wife, Mary Anne, now carefully restored to their Victorian prime by the National Trust.

Within, the house is kept as a museum of Disraeli's life and times. It contains a wealth of mementoes of his career as statesman, including a fan signed by all the representatives at the Berlin Congress of 1878, and in the hall – which he called his 'Gallery of Friendship' – hang portraits of several leading political figures of the 19th century. His study remains substantially as he left it.

SANDRINGHAM
AND YORK COTTAGE

Albert Edward, Prince of Wales and the future Edward VII, bought the house and estate at Sandringham, in Norfolk, in 1862 for £220,000. The next spring he settled there with his new wife, Princess Alexandra of Denmark.

The idea of a country home for Albert Edward had begun with his father, Prince Albert, who thought that time spent in outdoor pursuits, such as shooting, would be a healthy change for the Prince of Wales, and that country life would help him keep away from the temptations of city delights, such as courtesans and gambling. However, following Prince Albert's death in December 1861, it was left to his son to complete the search for a house. He chose Sandringham after a single viewing on 3 February 1862.

Above: Sandringham sits in 60 acres of gardens. After a bomb from a German zeppelin made a crater in 1915, King George VI had it turned into a duck pond.

HUMBERT'S NEW HOUSE

After making do with minor amendments for a few years, the Prince of Wales decided in 1870 to knock down the existing house and start from scratch. He used one of his late father's favoured architects, A.J. Humbert, who, employing red brick with stone dressings, built a large and entirely uninspiring house in a Jacobean Revival style with gables, mullion windows and turrets.

Below: Jacobean style at Sandringham. Houses such as Blickling Hall were the model for A.J. Humbert's design here.

YORK COTTAGE

A second architect, R.W. Edis, made additions, including a bowling alley and the Ballroom in 1883 and in the next decade added a new top storey to the house following a fire that broke out during the Prince of Wales's 50th birthday party in 1891. Edis also built a villa, later called York Cottage, in the grounds.

Edward VII's second son, Prince George, Duke of York and the future King George V, moved into York Cottage in 1893 following his marriage to Princess Mary of Teck. It was George's favourite house, reputedly because its modest rooms reminded him of cabins aboard ship and recalled the enjoyable years he had spent in the Royal Navy. Indeed, after his accession he always stayed in York Cottage when visiting, and left the big house to his widowed mother until she died in 1925. George V also died at Sandringham in January 1936.

Born at York Cottage, George VI felt particularly at home on the estate. He wrote to his mother, Queen Mary,

'I have always been so happy here, and I love the place'. He too died at Sandringham House, on 6 February 1952. Elizabeth II made many visits to Sandringham during her childhood and continues to enjoy her Norfolk estate as a welcome country retreat.

CHRISTMAS AT SANDRINGHAM

By the 1930s, Sandringham had become established as the royals' Christmas and New Year retreat. George V made his first Christmas broadcast live by radio on Christmas Day 1932, while, 25 years later, Elizabeth II delivered the first televised Christmas message from the Library.

Below: In November 1902, a royal shooting party gathered at Sandringham during the visit of Germany's Kaiser Wilhelm II.

CHAPTER TWENTY-FOUR

THE COUNTRY HOUSE REVIVAL

1901–TODAY

On his death in 1940, Philip Henry Kerr, 11th Marquess of Lothian, bequeathed his handsome Jacobean mansion of Blickling Hall, Norfolk, to the National Trust. It was the first house to be passed to the Trust under the Country House Scheme of 1937, which Lothian had helped establish, and which enabled owners to leave their property to the Trust in lieu of death duties.

In the 20th century, although country houses continued to be built and lavishly remodelled, and although King Edward VII and his descendants continued to rework Buckingham Palace and other royal residences, many landed families struggled to maintain their houses and estates. Taxes mounted, depression in agriculture ran almost continuously from 1875 to the outbreak of World War II and rental income from land declined. As a result, art collections were broken up and rare library collections sold off to pay for repairs and meet demands for taxes and death duties. Eventually, in the interwar years, some people began to focus on ways to preserve the more historic houses and their collections. By the end of the 20th century, the National Trust carefully maintained and preserved around 350 stately homes, buildings and gardens.

Among new country houses built in these years, the fashion was predominantly neo-Georgian. Buildings such as Castle Drogo and Eaton Hall proved the exception, while neo-Palladian designs, such as Arundel Park, were generally considered more appropriate for a house expected to take its place at the heart of a country estate.

Left: Julius Charles Drewe, immensely wealthy founder of a chain of grocery shops, sought immortality in stone with Castle Drogo, Devon, built by Edwin Lutyens in 1912–30.

ELVEDEN HALL, POLESDEN LACEY
AND THE ROTHSCHILD MANSIONS

In the first years of the 20th century, the great Irish philanthropist and business-man, the 1st Earl of Iveagh, immensely wealthy head of the Guinness brewing dynasty of Dublin, lavishly rebuilt his recently acquired country house, Elveden Hall in Suffolk. It contained, in the Indian Hall (1900–3), perhaps the grandest of several great marble halls created in the Edwardian era. It was sufficiently magnificent for Edward VII to agree to spend every other New Year week there – in alternation with Chatsworth.

Lord Iveagh bought Elveden Hall in 1894 following the death of its previous owner, the former Indian maharajah, Prince Duleep Singh. Removed by the British from his throne following the annexation of the Punjab in 1849, the Prince had been granted a substantial government pension and settled in Suffolk, where he lived in great style and, after buying the original Elveden Hall in 1863, redeveloped it in Indian style. Lord Iveagh built a new wing in the same shape and style as the Prince's house and connected the two with a great copper-domed central block.

ROTHSCHILD MANSIONS

In the late 19th and early 20th centuries, leading members of the Rothschild banking dynasty entertained lavishly in magnificent English country houses. Among these was Exbury in Hampshire, where Lionel de Rothschild built a Neoclassical house in the 1920s and created a superb 200 acre (80 ha)–woodland garden. Other Rothschild houses are Waddesdon Manor, Buckinghamshire, built in the style of a French chateau for Baron Ferdinand de Rothschild by the French architect, Gabriel Hippolyte Destailleur, in 1874–89, and Mentmore Towers, also in Buckinghamshire, built in a neo-Elizabethan style for Baron Meyer Amschel de Rothschild by Sir Joseph Paxton (former Chatsworth head gardener and designer of the Crystal Palace). Another was Ascott House, 3 miles (4.5km) from Mentmore Towers, built by Leopold de Rothschild in the 1870s.

Right: Baron Ferdinand de Rothschild filled Waddesdon Manor with artworks.

THE INDIAN HALL

Within the domed block was the Indian Hall, built on the basis of Indian durbar halls to designs by William Young with the advice of Sir Caspar Purdon Clarke, who was in charge of the Indian collection at the Victoria and Albert Museum in South Kensington, London.

Lord Iveagh spent £70,000 on the marble for this vast, dazzlingly white and intricately carved hall, which fills the full height of the domed section of the house. A special branch railway line was created from the nearest station, at Barnham, to bring the marble, stone and other materials to the site.

Left: Imperial grandeur – the superb Marble Hall at Elveden. In creating it, Lord Iveagh doubled the size of the existing hall.

Below: At Elveden Hall, Lord Iveagh hosted the grandest guests. King George V arrives for a shooting party in 1910.

Above: Entrance front at Polesden Lacey. In summer, vegetables and fruit grown on the 1,000-acre (400 ha)-estate were sent to Mrs Greville's London home each day.

Grandeur, however, was clearly more important than comfort: the hall had only two fireplaces and, despite under-floor central heating, was described by Elizabeth, Countess of Fingall, as 'England's coldest room'.

ROYAL SHOOTING PARTIES

Elveden was especially renowned for its shooting; indeed, Lord Iveagh was first attracted to the estate because Prince Duleep Singh had developed it for game. Before Lord Iveagh's time, Edward VII, while still Prince of Wales, enjoyed shooting at Elveden in the company of Prince Duleep Singh; Lord Iveagh then hosted not only Edward VII but also George V and the future George VI for shooting parties on the estate.

POLESDEN LACEY

Another ostentatious Edwardian country house supported by brewing money was Polesden Lacey in Surrey: its owner, Margaret Greville, was the daughter of the Edinburgh brewer, Sir William McEwan. She entered English high society when, in 1901, she married Captain Ronald Greville, who through his friends the Keppels had access to

Edward VII. Margaret Greville became one of the leading hostesses of the day, welcoming politicians, ambassadors, foreign heads of state and the King himself to her lavish weekend parties.

The house at Polesden Lacey had once belonged to dramatist Richard Brinsley Sheridan in the 18th century, but became so dilapidated that it was entirely rebuilt by the great London builder Thomas Cubitt for Joseph Bonsor *c.*1835. The house was restructured and redecorated in 1902–5 by Ambrose Poynter for Sir Clinton Dawkins before it was bought by Sir William McEwan in 1906.

Employing the celebrated architects Charles Mewès and Arthur Davis (designers of the Ritz Hotel in London), Mrs Greville transformed the interior. Some of her rooms would have seemed overdone and even distasteful to a Victorian guest, but they were appreciated by the racy, sophisticated, 'modern' members of Edward VII's set. For example, she installed the reredos of a demolished Sir Christopher Wren church – St Matthew's, Friday Street, London – above the fireplace in her darkly panelled Hall; in her Drawing Room she fitted gilded panelling from an Italian palace and lines of tall mirrors. A second Drawing Room was provided for playing bridge.

A gentlemen's wing at Polesden Lacy included a Smoking Room, Billiard Room and Gun Room. There was also a Library and a fine Dining Room. The finest food was a necessary attraction when the gourmand Edward VII was among the guests, and Mrs Greville was famed for the quality of her 'table'and her French chef.

Below: The Drawing Room at Polesden Lacey had five pairs of French windows – when they were unshuttered, the room was a blaze of light on chandelier and gilding.

BUCKINGHAM PALACE
AND CLARENCE HOUSE: ROYAL REFURBISHMENT

Standing proudly at the end of The Mall in central London, Buckingham Palace is the Queen's official London residence and probably the most recognizable and celebrated royal building in Britain (see also page 468). Its balcony facing The Mall has been the setting for many iconic royal moments, such as the celebration of victory in 1945 by George VI and the royal family, including a teenage Princess Elizabeth (the future Queen Elizabeth II). However, before the start of the 20th century the palace was little used by the country's royals.

It was Queen Victoria who established Buckingham Palace, rather than St James's Palace nearby, as the monarch's official London residence. But she did not spend much time there, living with Prince Albert mainly at Windsor Castle when they were not in the country, and, after Albert's death, spending prolonged periods at Balmoral and Osborne House while dust sheets covered the fine furniture and lavishly decorated rooms at Buckingham Palace.

GLITTER AND GLAMOUR

Edward VII, however, had different ideas. He moved into the palace on his accession in 1901 from his previous London base, Marlborough House. He redecorated and refurnished the palace

Above: The base of the Victoria Memorial, which is at the east front of Buckingham Palace, contains 23,000 tons of marble.

in the year of his coronation, 1902, and restored glitter and glamour to court life. Unfortunately, his redecoration of the palace swept away many of the splendid Regency and early Victorian interiors, which were replaced by a rather uninspiring white and gold decorative scheme designed by C.H. Bessant.

IN MEMORY OF VICTORIA

The forecourt in front of the palace's east front was laid out at the beginning of George V's reign, in 1911. At the same time, the Victoria Memorial statue by Thomas Brock was set up before the palace on a great base of white marble, designed by Sir Aston Webb. The statue of Victoria faces towards The Mall, while

Left: While Edward VII certainly breathed new life into Buckingham Palace, historians regret that his redecoration (here of the King's private Sitting Room) was uninspiring.

on the other three sides are figures of the Angels of Justice and Truth and a personification of Charity. The golden figure on the pinnacle represents Victory.

The Admiralty Arch at the other end of The Mall, separating it from Trafalgar Square, was designed by Sir Aston Webb as part of the Victoria Memorial scheme and erected in 1910, a year earlier than the statue itself.

NEW EAST FRONT

In 1913, Sir Aston undertook the refacing of the east front of Buckingham Palace. When building the east front in 1847–50, Edward Blore had used a soft Caen stone, which had not weathered well in soot-laden London and so needed replacing; Sir Aston used a fine, grey Portland stone. His dignified east façade faces on to a gravelled forecourt enclosed by splendid ironwork gates and

railings, providing a suitably grand public face for the palace. Webb created new gateposts but reused a number of older stone piers between the lengths of railing: among these are some, with floral swags and regal lions' heads, made in 1800 by Edward Wyatt for George III. The forecourt is the setting for the Changing of the Guard ceremony.

'GEORGIAN' REFURBISHMENT

In George V's reign, Queen Mary carried out a substantial refurbishment at the palace. She used what was then considered a 'Georgian' colour scheme of Chinese yellow, buff and celadon green. In 1914, the Picture Gallery was remodelled, and a new glazed ceiling installed to replace the work of Nash. Charles Allom decorated it using Chinese wallpapers and silk hangings that had been found in storage (and were probably

Above: A bedroom in the royal suite at Buckingham Palace in the time of Edward VII, who redecorated the palace interior.

originally intended by George IV for the Brighton Pavilion) to redecorate the Yellow Drawing Room and the Centre Room. Allom's work was much acclaimed and rewarded with a knighthood.

CLARENCE HOUSE

An elegant stuccoed building in Stable Yard Road, beside St James's Palace, Clarence House is the London residence of the Prince of Wales and Duchess of Cornwall. It was built by John Nash in 1825–7 for William, Duke of Clarence (the future William IV), who continued to live there while reigning as King in 1830–7.

The house has had a varied history within the royal family, having been the London home of William IV's unmarried sister, Princess Augusta, in 1837–40, then of Victoria's mother, the Duchess of Kent, in 1840–61. Subsequently it served as the official residence of Prince Alfred, Duke of Edinburgh, in 1866–1900: during these years, a Russian Orthodox chapel was installed on the first floor for use by Alfred's wife, Marie Alexandrovna, Duchess of Edinburgh, who was the daughter of Tsar Alexander II of Russia. In 1900–42, Arthur, the Duke of Connaught and third son of Queen Victoria, lived in the house. For the last three years of World War II,

Clarence House was used on the headquarters of the Red Cross and the St John's Ambulance Brigade.

Clarence House became the London home of Princess Elizabeth (the future Elizabeth II) and the Duke of Edinburgh on their marriage in 1947. Following

Above: The Drawing Room at Clarence House in 1981, when it was the London residence of Elizabeth, the Queen Mother.

Elizabeth's accession, Clarence House was the London residence of Queen Elizabeth, the Queen Mother, from 1953–2002.

MANDERSTON AND SENNOWE PARK
THE EDWARDIAN COUNTRY HOUSE

The 18th-century country house of Manderston at Duns, in Berwickshire, was lavishly rebuilt in 1901–5 by the architect John Kinross for Sir James Miller. A wealthy trader's son, Sir James had entered the top drawer of the British aristocracy in 1893 by marrying the Honourable Eveline Curzon, daughter of Lord Scarsdale. Lady Miller had grown up amid the splendour of the Robert Adam interiors at Kedleston Hall in Derbyshire, and Sir James wanted to keep his bride in the style to which she was accustomed. He told Kinross that money was no object in the redevelopment of Manderston. In the event, the house combined the elegance of Kedleston Hall with the convenience of the latest 20th-century inventions.

Above: The garden front at Manderston. The house combined elegance and tradition with all the latest modern conveniences.

TRIBUTE TO KEDLESTON HALL

Kinross enlarged the main house, rebuilding the attic, as well as adding a basement, a service court and a new

Below: The Drawing Room at Manderston. The Millers' designers, Mellier and Co., used an opulent, French-influenced style.

west wing of gentlemen's rooms, including a gun room and bachelor bedrooms. He completely rebuilt the entrance front.

Much of the interior was a tribute to Kedleston Hall: in the Entrance Hall, the stuccoed fireplace and rounded patterning of inlaid floor marble are copies of those in the Marble Hall at Kedleston, while the Ballroom ceiling is derived from that of the Kedleston Dining Room. The lavish interior also

features a Louis XVI-style staircase with a silvered balustrade, based on that of the Petit Trianon palace at Versailles. Kinross also took account of the requirements of modern comfort and style, including electric lighting and a 'motor house' containing a basement engineer's area.

SENNOWE PARK

Sennowe Park, at Guist in Norfolk, was designed by the Norwich architect, George Skipper, for Thomas Cook, grandson of the founder of the travel firm of that name, beginning in 1905. Skipper created a flamboyant mansion with a curved bay on the entrance front topped with standing figures. Within, the highly decorated staircase beneath an oval cupola and the vast fireplace with Grinling Gibbons-style carving in the grand 50ft (15m)-long Saloon added to the highly individual mix of styles. Elaborate stone carving throughout was done by Italian masons.

CASTLE DROGO
SIR EDWIN LUTYEN'S 20TH-CENTURY CASTLE

Celebrated as the last castle built in Britain, this imposing granite pile occupies a crag overlooking the River Teign gorge in Devon, with breathtaking views of Dartmoor. It was built in 1912–30 by Edwin Lutyens for Julius Charles Drew, who had made a great fortune importing Indian tea and establishing a chain of grocer shops.

Armed with a genealogy that suggested he was descended from a Norman knight named Drogo via the Drewe family of Drewsteignton, in Devon, Drew was determined to create a stone memorial to his wealth and his family's descent. He added an 'e' to his surname by deed poll and bought an estate in Drewsteignton. He then engaged the leading architect, Edwin Lutyens.

Drewe demanded a genuine stronghold, not a pastiche castle. The site was chosen in 1910. Over the next two decades, architect and client had

many disagreements. Lutyens was often away setting out the new Indian capital of Delhi, and work proceeded under the supervision of Devon masons, Cleeve and Dewdney, and Clerk of Works, John Walker.

Below: Above the doorway is the Drewe lion and beneath it the family motto Drogo Nomen et Virtus Arma Dedit ('Drewe is the name and Valour gave it Arms').

Below: As well as laying out Delhi and building many country houses, Lutyens designed the Cenotaph (London) and the British Embassy in Washington, D.C.

Above: Like a castle of old, Lutyens' building occupies the high ground, overlooking steep banks and a river far below.

A FORMIDABLE CASTLE

In the end, Lutyens and Walker created a formidable structure, with solid granite walls in places 6ft (1.8m) thick, austere façades, a turreted entrance with genuine portcullis, and a medieval-style interior with great expanses of granite and oak. Above the entrance door is a bas-relief of the Drewe lion by Herbert Palliser.

Drewe died in 1931, only a year after Drogo was completed; his grandson gave the castle to the National Trust in 1974.

ATTENTION TO DETAIL

The house combines a principal two-storey wing containing staterooms with a three-storey wing housing rooms for family and servants, both connected by a grand staircase. The Drawing Room and Dining Room are wood-panelled; the first contains large mullion windows and the second has an elaborate plaster-work ceiling. There is Edwardian luxury in the bathrooms. Lutyens attended to every feature of the design, down to the billiard table in the Billiard Room.

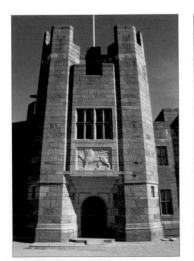

ELTHAM PALACE
THE COURTAULDS' ART DECO FANTASY

In 1931–6, Stephen and Virgina Courtauld built a splendid Art Deco house adjoining the historic remains of Eltham Palace in south-east London. At the same time, they undertook the restoration of the 15th-century Great Hall, built by Edward IV, and other parts of the palace, which was a boyhood haunt and great favourite of Henry VIII.

ART DECO STYLE

The Courtaulds commissioned John Seely and Paul Paget to build the new house and Peter Malacrida to decorate it. The sleek, elegant Art Deco style they used swept Europe and the United States in the wake of the 1925 Exposition Internationale des Arts Décoratifs et Industriels Modernes in Paris, from which it took its name. It used 'modern-looking', streamlined shapes often decorated with stylized or geometric ornament.

Below: The elegant Entrance Hall. After taking control of the house in the 1990s, English Heritage used period photos to restore the furnishings to their 1930s look.

Above: In the 1930s, Stephen and Virginia Courtauld remodelled the Tudor remains of Eltham Palace into an Art Deco house.

The Courtaulds' new house was built with all the most modern conveniences, such as underfloor heating and a sound system in all rooms. The interior was lavish: onyx and gold plate in the bathroom, an aluminium-foil ceiling in the Dining Room, veneered walls and elegant fitted furniture. The Entrance Hall was lit through a glazed concrete dome.

OLD-FASHIONED CLEANING

One way in which the new Eltham Palace was less than up-to-date was its use of a centralized vacuum cleaning system, which had been the latest thing at around the turn of the century, rather than the newest mobile vacuum cleaners. These centralized pumps had been used since *c.*1905, when one was fitted at Minterne Magna in Dorset.

NEW OWNERSHIP

The Courtaulds also redesigned the gardens at Eltham Palace, which contain the original moat and bridge. They lived

at Eltham until 1944, when they moved to Scotland, and the Royal Army Education Corps took on the lease. In 1995, the palace and Art Deco house passed into the care of English Heritage, who carried out a painstaking restoration.

Below: The bathroom is lined with gold mosaic. A statue of the goddess Psyche looks down on the bath and its gold-plated taps.

PLAS NEWYDD AND PORT LYMPNE
REX WHISTLER AND THE MODERN COUNTRY HOUSE

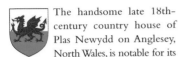

The handsome late 18th-century country house of Plas Newydd on Anglesey, North Wales, is notable for its architecture and situation as well as for its interior decoration. The house was built in 1793–9 by James Wyatt, architect of Heveningham Hall, Suffolk, and Fonthill Abbey, Wiltshire. It combines the Classical style with the Gothic for which Wyatt was celebrated. Situated overlooking the Menai Straits, the house has breathtaking views of Snowdonia.

REX WHISTLER

Whistler had made his name aged 22 in 1927, when still a student at the Slade School of Art in London, by creating a highly imaginative mural entitled *The Expedition in Pursuit of Rare Meats* in the Tea Rooms at the Tate Gallery. As well as painting society portraits and working in book illustration, theatre design and advertising, he continued throughout his short career to paint

Below: Whistler's extraordinary mural in the Dining Room at Plas Newydd is the largest of the artist's many wall paintings.

large-scale murals at country homes such as Plas Newydd, which is particularly celebrated for his 58ft (18m) mural of a romantic Italianate coastal landscape in the Dining Room, painted in 1936–7. It was commissioned by Plas Newydd's owner, Charles Paget, 6th Marquess of Anglesey, and while staying there Whistler fell in love with his daughter, Caroline, and made a number of rather whimsical references to his passion in the painting. In one part of the image,

Above: Herbert Baker drew on his experience building Cecil Rhodes's South African home in designing Port Lympne.

Lady Caroline (as Juliet) stands on a balcony while beneath stands the pining figure of Romeo (a self-portrait). Although apparently a mural, the painting is in fact a vast canvas.

Whistler's work inspired a vogue for ambitious country-house murals that lasted throughout the 20th century, but his career was cut short when he was killed, aged 39, during active service in World War II in July 1944. Earlier, at Mottisfont Abbey, a former priory turned country house in Hampshire, he painted, in 1938–9, an extraordinary *trompe l'oeil* Gothic Drawing Room that mimics intricate plasterwork in paint.

PORT LYMPNE

This handsome house in Kent was built for Sir Philip Sassoon, just before World War I, by the fashionable architect, Sir Herbert Baker, in the 'Dutch Colonial Style' used in South Africa. It was very highly regarded at the time, being described as 'the most remarkable modern house in England'. Here, Whistler created a widely admired 'tent room'.

THE 'GOLDEN TRIANGLE'
GATCOMBE, HIGHGROVE AND NETHER LYPIATT

Gloucestershire claims the name of 'the royal county' because there are three country houses owned by members of the Queen's family in the area. The three houses – Gatcombe Park near Minchinhampton, Highgrove House near Tetbury, and Nether Lypiatt Manor near Stroud – are known together as the royals' 'Golden Triangle'.

GATCOMBE PARK
The Queen bought Gatcombe Park, near Minchinhampton, for Princess Anne and her first husband, Captain Mark Phillips, as a belated wedding present in 1976.

Both keen riders, Princess Anne and Captain Phillips held the annual Gatcombe Park horse trials on the estate each August. After their marriage was dissolved in 1992, Princess Anne married Commander Timothy Laurence and the Princess and her family continued to hold the annual event.

Below: Highgrove House. The Prince of Wales's sheep graze on the lawn before the Georgian building. In the 1980s, the Prince added an open balustrade to the house.

Above: Gatcombe Park was built in the 1740s of Bath stone. The estate, venue for the horse trials, is of 730 acres (295ha).

Gatcombe Park was built in the 1740s by a local master mason, Francis Franklin, for Edward Sheppard; wings were added in the early 19th century by George Basevi, cousin of Disraeli and pupil of the architect, Sir John Soane. Later work included the addition of a conservatory in 1829. Its owners have included Samuel Courtauld and the Conservative minister 'RAB' Butler.

HIGHGROVE HOUSE
Purchased by the Duchy of Cornwall in 1980, Highgrove House was home to Prince Charles and Diana, Princess of

Wales, during the early years of their marriage. The three-storey five-bay Georgian building is rectangular with an originally columned portico (now glazed and enclosed) on the entrance front; within, there are four reception rooms. It was built in 1796–8 for a locally prominent Huguenot family named Paul. It originally stood in 350 acres (140ha), but the estate has been greatly enlarged by the Prince, who practises organic farming on the land. The Prince has also developed a fine walled garden on the Highgrove estate.

NETHER LYPIATT MANOR
Prince and Princess Michael of Kent bought Nether Lypiatt Manor in 1981. The house was built in 1698 by Judge Cox. It is said to be haunted by the ghost of the judge's son, who committed suicide in one of the rooms. Most of the main rooms are fitted with elegant beech, chestnut or oak panelling; there is a splendid original staircase. The house is faced in Cotswold stone.

Below: Nether Lypiatt. Apart from the fact that it has royal owners, the house is most celebrated for its 17th-century staircase.

BIRKHALL, MEY AND GLAMIS
SCOTLAND'S ROYAL RESIDENCES

The modern period has seen the restoration of several ancient buildings by members of the British royal family.

BIRKHALL

The relatively modest royal house of Birkhall stands on the edge of the Balmoral estate in Aberdeenshire, overlooking the River Muick. It is the Deeside residence of the Prince of Wales, where he spent a two-week honeymoon in 2005, following his marriage to the Duchess of Cornwall.

Birkhall was built in 1715. The house was bought by Queen Victoria and Prince Albert in 1849, the year after their first stay at Balmoral. It has been popular with many generations of their descendants, including the Duke and Duchess of York (the future George VI and Queen Elizabeth) in the 1930s; and by Princess Elizabeth (the future Queen Elizabeth II) and Prince Philip, the Duke of Edinburgh, in 1947–52; as well as Prince Charles. Queen Elizabeth, the Queen Mother, made it her Deeside residence in 1952–2002; she built a new wing containing six bedrooms in the 1950s and visited every spring. Prince Charles and the Duchess of Cornwall used the interior designer Robert Kine to redecorate the house.

Below: The Castle of Mey stands just 1,200ft (370m) from the sea, with views of Pentland Firth and the Orkney Islands.

THE CASTLE OF MEY

This castle in Caithness was restored by Queen Elizabeth, the Queen Mother, after she purchased it in 1952. The castle, a stone tower house built on a Z-plan by George, 4th Earl of Caithness, in 1566–72, was seriously dilapidated when the Queen saw and fell instantly in love with it in 1952, when she was mourning the death of her husband, King George VI. In a romantic position on the rugged Caithness coast, just 6 miles (9.5km) from John O'Groats and overlooking the Pentland Firth, it is Britain's most northerly castle. Its 2,000-acre (800 ha) estate includes celebrated gardens. When purchased by the Queen in 1952, it was known as Barrogill Castle, but has since reverted to its ancient name, the Castle of Mey.

GLAMIS CASTLE

Queen Elizabeth, the Queen Mother, always had a strong emotional attachment to Scotland, having spent many childhood summers at her family's ancestral home, Glamis Castle in Tayside. The castle, famous above all as the setting for William Shakespeare's play *Macbeth*, was originally a royal

Above: The Sitting Room used by Queen Elizabeth, the Queen Mother, at Glamis Castle. With two bedrooms, it is part of a suite set aside for royal visitors at Glamis.

hunting lodge. It was transformed into a castle with an L-shaped keep in the early 15th century by the Queen Mother's ancestor, Sir John Lyon. In the Victorian era, the castle was modernized, with the introduction of gas and electricity; the east wing, in the Scottish Baronial style, was added in 1891. In 1930, the future Queen Mother gave birth to Princess Margaret there.

Below: In the words of the late Queen Elizabeth, the Queen Mother, Birkhall is 'a small big house, or a big small house'.

EILEAN DONAN AND CLANDON PARK
MAGNIFICENT RESTORATION

 Beneath vast skies, on its own small island at the head of Loch Duich and looking towards Skye, Eilean Donan castle is perhaps the most spectacularly situated building in Britain. A castle has stood here since *c.*1220, but the building we see today is the product of a painstaking 20th-century rebuilding. For 20 years, beginning in 1912, Lt-Col. John MacRae-Gilstrap rebuilt the ruined castle that had been guarded by his MacRae ancestors in the 16th century.

EARLY BEGINNINGS

The original castle had a long and romantic history. Its name refers to Abbot Donan, an Irish missionary to Scotland from Iona who reputedly built his hermitage on this spot during the early 600s. The first castle was built around 600 years later, in the reign of Alexander II, to defend

this strategically important location against Danish and Norse incursions. Alexander III gave the fortress to Colin Fitzgerald, ancestor of clan MacKenzie, in 1263, as a reward for service at the Battle of

Above: Strategic position. Eilean Donan Castle commands the waters of Loch Duich. On clear days, the Isle of Skye is plainly visible in the distance.

Largs, in which the defeat of Norway won Scotland control of the Western Isles. Then, in 1306, Robert the Bruce was given refuge in the castle.

THE MACRAE PROTECTORS

In *c.*1360, the MacRaes entered the service of the MacKenzie clan as bodyguards, proving so effective that they became known as 'MacKenzies' Mail Shirt'. The MacRaes were appointed hereditary constables of Eilean Donan Castle in 1509, a position that brought with it significant rights of control and enforcement over the surrounding hotly contested region. They often came under attack – famously in 1539, when Donald MacRae and his garrison kept at bay an army of 400 under Donald Gorm, Lord of the Isles, and MacRae is said to have killed Gorm with his very last arrow.

NAVAL ONSLAUGHT

The castle was reduced to ruins by the might of the English Navy in 1719. William MacKenzie, 5th Earl of

---

HIDDEN GLORIES: RESTORING CLANDON PARK AND UPPARK

The National Trust has carried out a series of painstaking restorations of castles and country houses. Pride of place should, perhaps, go to its first major restoration project: Clandon Park, near Guildford in Surrey. The Palladian mansion – designed *c.*1730 by Italian architect Giacomo Leoni and set in 'Capability' Brown parkland – was given to the Trust in 1956. Over two years, the Trust spent around £200,000 restoring the house to its 18th-century prime.

Its magnificent Marble Hall features stucco work by the celebrated Italian craftsmen Arturi and Bagutti, which was skilfully finished to look like marble. Restorers discovered this delicate work beneath thick layers of whitewash.

The Trust's inspired and painstaking restoration of the 17th-century country house of Uppark, West Sussex, in the 1990s, combined the latest scientific techniques with a revival of a number of historic crafts. The project was made necessary by a devastating fire that struck on 30 August 1989. The Trust's craftsmen and women restored Uppark – which, prior to the fire, was celebrated as one of England's best-preserved houses – to quite superb condition.

Left: Clandon Park was given the kind of meticulous restoration appropriate for one of England's finest Palladian mansions.

Above: Eilean Donan Castle's colourful past and beautiful situation – and the romance associated with its restoration – explain its great appeal as a subject for photographs.

Seaforth, was a supporter of the Jacobite cause (the movement to restore the House of Stuart to the throne) and garrisoned Eilean Donan with a small group of Spanish troops sent to lead an uprising. Three English warships bombarded the fortress until it was a mere ruin. Meanwhile, because a Spanish support fleet failed to arrive, the 1719 uprising petered out in a low-key defeat of a small force of Spaniards and highlanders at Glenshiel by a royalist army from Inverness.

RETURN TO GLORY

Eilean Donan remained an evocative ruin for almost two centuries until a 20th-century MacRae set out to honour his ancestors' memory by restoring the castle to its former glory. Even the restoration has a romantic tale attached to it. Because the castle was so badly ruined, the restorers could not be sure what it had looked like, but a clan descendant named Farquhar MacRae had a vision in a dream of the castle as

it once was, and worked with the castle's new owner to make the vision a reality. Then, when restoration was nearing completion, plans of the castle dated to 1714 were found in Edinburgh; curiously, they matched the details of the vision in remarkable detail.

THE CASTLE TODAY

A stone causeway leads from the mainland across the loch to the island. A portcullis guards the entrance in the outer walls; above the entrance is a Gaelic inscription that translates: 'If a MacRae is inside, there will never be a Fraser outside.' This refers to an alliance between the clans that dates back to the 14th century, when the MacRaes fostered a young heiress who later married into the Frasers. On the gate of Beaufort Castle, she raised a similar inscription, in Gaelic: 'If a Fraser resides within, no MacRaes will be left without.'

Within, across a walled courtyard, stands the three-storey main tower of the castle. In its barrel-vaulted basement, which has walls 14ft (4m) thick, is the Billeting Room, hung with pictures of the MacRaes in battle, at Sheriffmuir in 1715 and Glenshiel in 1719. Above is the Banqueting Hall, with an oak-timbered

ceiling, a circular wrought-iron chandelier and splendid chimney-piece. The hall also contains a portrait of Lt.-Col. John MacRae-Gilstrap, the castle's rebuilder, and a broadsword connected to his ancestor John MacRae, dubbed 'the Bard of Kintail', who fought at the Battle of Culloden in 1746 and then in the American War of Independence. On the floors above are sleeping chambers, accessed via a staircase turret. From the battlements stretch magnificent views of three lochs: Alsh, Long and Duich.

Below: A stone roadway connects the castle on the 'Isle of Donan' to the mainland. It was added as part of the restoration work.

NEO-PALLADIAN COUNTRY HOUSES
ARUNDEL PARK, KINGS WALDEN BURY, WAVERTON AND NEWFIELD

Waverton House in Gloucestershire and Newfield in North Yorkshire are fine examples of the Neo-Palladian country house that has been widely popular since the mid-20th century. Both houses were designed by architect Quinlan Terry, the first in 1977 for Jocelyn Hambro of the Hambro banking family, and the second in 1980 for carpet magnate Michael Abrahams. Although some country house patrons have chosen to build in the Modern style (see below), most have chosen neo-Palladian or neo-Georgian architecture

for its emphasis on continuity and tradition – and perhaps also from a desire to celebrate England's heritage.

ARUNDEL PARK

The revival of Palladian designs began at Arundel Park, Sussex, in the 1950s. The Duchess of Norfolk became unhappy with the lack of privacy resulting from the opening of Arundel Castle to the public, and persuaded her husband to build a new house in a more secluded spot in the grounds. Architect Claud Phillimore built the house in 1958–62 on Neo-Palladian lines,

with a central block linked to two side pavilions. (This design was in fact the Duchess's own idea; she is said to have been inspired by a visit to Ditchley Park in Oxfordshire.)

Arundel Park's handsome main block contains a Dining Room and Drawing Room along the garden front and a grand, top-lit Staircase Hall filling the whole height of the house beneath a vaulted ceiling. The interior harmonizes with the 18th-century elegance of the exterior: Phillimore designed double doors that are a copy of those in the Double Cube Room at Wilton

---

THE MODERN STYLE IN COUNTRY HOUSES

Eaton Hall in Cheshire was once the most notable modern country house. It was built in 1971–3 for Robert Grosvenor, 5th Duke of Westminster, to designs by John Dennys on the site of an imposing but largely demolished Victorian house at Eaton. Dennys's angular design caused a major controversy and was likened by the Duke of Bedford to a factory office block on a bypass. But in 1989 work began to encase it in a more traditional facing believed to blend more happily with the countryside.

Stratton Park in Hampshire is among the most prominent of the country houses built in the later 20th century in the Modern style. Constructed in 1963–5 by Stephen Gardiner and Christopher Knight, it stands alongside a vast Doric

portico – all that remains of a 19th-century Greek Revival mansion built by George Dance the Younger. The L-shaped house contains the main family rooms in a wing (the long arm of the L) running parallel with the portico, while at right angles a conservatory and pond link to the

Left: John Dennys's angular design for Eaton Hall was the subject of controversy and the building was refaced in 1989.

Above: The white block of Eaton Hall stood a little incongruously at the centre of a very grand estate – with formal gardens on one side and an avenue on the other.

evocative classical remains of the portico. Another substantial Modern country house is Witley Park, Surrey, built by Patrick Gwynne in 1961–2. Its two wings are hexagonal, its interior filled with gadgetry.

House and imported antique marble chimney-pieces. Interior decorator, John Fowler, supervised the colours and decorative details.

KINGS WALDEN BURY

Arundel Park's three-part neo-Palladian design was highly influential, as was a house in a similar style – built by Quinlan Terry with his then partner, Raymond Erith, at Kings Walden Bury in Hertfordshire, in 1967–71. The patron, Sir Thomas Milburne-Swinnerton-Pilkington, wanted to replace the 1890s house on the site with a new and elegant mansion.

Erith and Terry, outspoken critics of the Modern movement in architecture and ardent promoters of Classicism, produced a handsome and substantial house in Italian-Palladian style, with a columned and pedimented entrance front with 'Venetian windows', leading into a large hall with a stone floor and a barrel-vaulted staircase. The four principal rooms are the Drawing Room, Sitting Room, Dining Room and Kitchen.

Below: Quinlan Terry used classic Palladian proportions at Waverton House. The doorcase on the entrance front has Ionic supports.

WAVERTON HOUSE

Kings Walden Bury proved to be a prototype for country houses in the last decades of the 20th century. At Waverton, Gloucestershire, Terry again used the design of a central block and side pavilions. The large, seven-bedroom main house has a grand Staircase Hall, featuring a central staircase lit from above. The Drawing Room, Kitchen, Study and Dining Room are on the ground floor. Staff quarters and service rooms are in the long side wings. Terry made good use of local materials (on the insistence of the local planners): the roof has flags of Cotswold stone, while the walls are faced in stone from demolished local barns.

Above: Newfield was designed as a working house at the centre of a farm. A substantial forecourt extends before it, just as in Palladio's villas in the Veneto.

NEWFIELD

At Newfield in North Yorkshire, Quinlan Terry reworked the designs of his patron, Michael Abrahams – who had himself studied Palladio. The house they produced between them consists of a handsome central block, containing the Drawing Room, Hall and Dining Room with kitchen, with small side wings for staff and necessary service spaces. As at Waverton House, it is built of local stone.

A CLASSICAL FUTURE?

The preference for Neo-Palladian and other English classical styles in country house architecture has remained strong in the early years of the 21st century. In 2001–3, Quinlan Terry worked with his son, Francis, in the creation of the country house of Ferne Park, Dorset: its entrance is adorned with four large columns and a pediment and leads into a square hall with Doric columns. It is built in Portland and Chilmark stone.

Another design by Quinlan Terry, at Juniper Hill in Buckinghamshire in 1999–2002, features a large Ionic portico on its main entrance that strongly recalls the first English Palladian houses, such as Colen Campbell's Stourhead House, Wiltshire.

PROPERTY LISTINGS

All information was accurate at the time of going to press.

ALNWICK CASTLE
Alnwick, Northumberland NE66 1NQ
01665 510777
www.alnwickcastle.com

ALTHORP
Althorp, Northampton NN7 4HQ
01604 770107
www.spencerofalthorp.com

ANTONY HOUSE
Torpoint, Cornwall PL11 2QA
01752 812191
www.nationaltrust.org.uk/antony

ARBURY HALL
Nuneaton, Warwickshire CV10 7PT
02476 382804
www.arburyestate.co.uk

ARUNDEL CASTLE
Arundel, West Sussex BN18 9AB
01903 882173
www.arundelcastle.org.uk

AUDLEY END HOUSE
Saffron Walden, Essex CB11 4JF
01799 522842
www.english-heritage.org.uk

BALMORAL CASTLE
Balmoral, Ballater, Aberdeenshire
AB35 5TB
013397 42534
www.balmoralcastle.com

BAMBURGH CASTLE
Bamburgh, Northumberland NE69 7DF
01668 214515   www.bamburghcastle.com

BANQUETING HOUSE, THE
Whitehall, London SW1A 2ER
0844 482 7777
www.hrp.org.uk/BanquetingHouse

BEAULIEU
Brockenhurst, Hampshire SO42 7ZN
01590 612345
www.beaulieu.co.uk

BEAUMARIS CASTLE
Beaumaris, Anglesey LL58 8AP
01248 810361
www.beaumaris.com

BELSAY HALL
Belsay, near Ponteland, Northumberland
NE20 0DX   01661 881636
www.english-heritage.org.uk

BELTON HOUSE
Grantham, Lincolnshire NG32 2LS
01476 566116   www.nationaltrust.org.uk

BELVOIR CASTLE
Grantham, Leicestershire NG32 1PE
01476 871002   www.belvoircastle.com

BERKELEY CASTLE
Gloucestershire GL13 9BQ
01453 810332
www.berkeley-castle.com

BERKHAMSTED CASTLE
Berkhamsted, St Albans, Hertfordshire
HP4 1LJ   01536 402840
www.berkhamsted-castle.org.uk

BIGNOR ROMAN VILLA
Bignor, Pulborough, West Sussex
RH20 1PH   01798 869259
www.bignorromanvilla.co.uk

Left: Marlborough House.

BLENHEIM PALACE
Woodstock Oxfordshire OX20 1PX
08700 602080
www.blenheimpalace.com

BLICKLING HALL
Blickling, Norwich, Norfolk NR11 6NF
01263 738030
www.nationaltrust.org.uk

BODIAM CASTLE
Bodiam, near Robertsbridge, East Sussex
TN32 5UA   01580 830436
www.nationaltrust.org.uk

BOLSOVER CASTLE
Castle Street, Bolsover, Chesterfield,
Derbyshire S44 6PR   01246 822844
www.english-heritage.org.uk

BOUGHTON HOUSE
Kettering, Northamptonshire NN14 1BJ
01536 515731
www.boughtonhouse.org.uk

BROCH OF GURNESS
Aikerness, Orkney   01856 751414
www.historic-scotland.gov.uk

BRODSWORTH HALL
Brodsworth, near Doncaster, South
Yorkshire DN5 7XJ   01302 722598
www.english-heritage.org.uk

BROUGHTON CASTLE
Broughton, near Banbury, Oxfordshire
OX15 5EB   01295 276070
www.broughtoncastle.com

BUCKINGHAM PALACE
London SW1A 1AA
020 7930 4832
www.royalcollection.org.uk

BURGHLEY HOUSE
Stamford, Lincolnshire PE9 3JY
01780 752451
www.burghley.co.uk

CAERLAVEROCK CASTLE
Glencaple, Dumfries DG1 4RU
01387 770244
www.historic-scotland.gov.uk

CAERLEON ROMAN FORT
High Street, Caerleon, Gwent NP18 1AE
01633 422518
cadw.wales.gov.uk

CAERNARVON CASTLE
Castle Ditch, Caernarvon LL55 2AY
01286 677617   cadw.wales.gov.uk

CAERPHILLY CASTLE
Caerphilly CF8 1JL
029 2088 3143
cadw.wales.gov.uk

CAISTER CASTLE
Caister-on-Sea, Great Yarmouth, Norfolk
NR30 5SN   01664 567707
www.caistercastle.co.uk

CAMBER CASTLE
Camber, near Rye, East Sussex TN31 7RS
01797 223862
www.english-heritage.org.uk

CARDIFF CASTLE
Castle Street, Cardiff CF10 3RB
029 2087 8100
www.cardiffcastle.com

CARISBROOKE CASTLE
Newport, Isle of Wight PO30 1XY
01983 522107
www.english-heritage.org.uk

CASTELL COCH
Tongwynlais, Cardiff CF4 7JS
029 2081 0101
cadw.wales.gov.uk

CASTLE COOLE
Enniskillen, Co Fermanagh BT74 6JY
028 6632 2690 www.nationaltrust.org.uk

CASTLE DROGO
Drewsteignton, Exeter EX6 6PB
01647 433306
www.nationaltrust.org.uk

CASTLE FRASER
Sauchen, Inverurie AB51 7LD
0844 4932164   www.nts.org.uk

CASTLE HOWARD
York, North Yorkshire YO60 7DA
01653 648333
www.castlehoward.co.uk

CASTLE OF MEY
Thurso, Caithness KW14 8XH
01847 851473
www.castleofmey.org.uk

CAWDOR CASTLE
Nairn IV12 5RD   01667 404401
www.cawdorcastle.com

CHATSWORTH
Bakewell, Derbyshire DE45 1PP
01246 565300
www.chatsworth.org

CHEPSTOW CASTLE
Chepstow, Gwent   01291 624065
cadw.wales.gov.uk

CHESTERS ROMAN FORT
Chollerford, near Hexham,
Northumberland NE46 4EU
01434 681379
www.english-heritage.org.uk

CHISWICK HOUSE
Burlington Lane, London W4 2RP
020 8995 0508
www.english-heritage.org.uk

CLANDON PARK
West Clandon, Guildford,
Surrey GU4 7RQ   01483 222482
www.nationaltrust.org.uk

CLIVEDEN
Taplow, Maidenhead, Buckinghamshire
SL6 0JA   01628 605069
www.nationaltrust.org.uk

CONWAY CASTLE
Conwy LL32 8AY
01492 592358
www.conwy.com

Above: Hampton Court Palace.

CRATHES CASTLE
Banchory AB31 5QJ   0844 4932166
www.nts.org.uk

CULZEAN CASTLE
Maybole KA19 8LE   0844 4932149
www.nts.org.uk

DEAL CASTLE
Victoria Road, Deal, Kent CT14 7BA
01304 372762
www.english-heritage.org.uk

DITCHLEY PARK
Enstone, Oxfordshire OX7 4ER
01608 677346
www.ditchley.co.uk

DOVER CASTLE
Dover, Kent CT16 1HU   01304 211067
www.english-heritage.org.uk

DUNFERMLINE ABBEY AND PALACE
Dunfermline, Fife KY12 7PE
01383 739026
www.historic-scotland.gov.uk

EASTNOR CASTLE
near Ledbury, Herefordshire HR8 1RL
01531 633160
www.eastnorcastle.com

EDINBURGH CASTLE
Castlehill, Edinburgh EH12NG
0131 225 9846
www.historic-scotland.gov.uk
or www.edinburghcastle.gov.uk

EILEAN DONAN CASTLE
Dornie, Kyle of Localsh, Wester Ross
IV40 8DX
01599 555202
www.eileandonancastle.com

ELTHAM PALACE
Court Yard, Eltham, London SE9 5QE
020 8294 2548
www.english-heritage.org.uk

FALKLAND PALACE
Falkland KY15 7BU
0844 4932186
www.nts.org.uk

FELBRIGG HALL
Felbrigg, Norwich, Norfolk NR11 8PR
01263 837444
www.nationaltrust.org.uk

FISHBOURNE ROMAN PALACE
Salthill Road, Fishbourne, Chichester,
West Sussex PO19 3QS
01243 785859
www.sussexpast.co.uk

FRAMLINGHAM CASTLE
Framlingham, Suffolk IP13 9BT
01728 724189
www.english-heritage.org.uk

GLAMIS CASTLE
Glamis by Forfar, Angus DD8 1RJ
01307 840393
www.glamis-castle.co.uk

GOODRICH CASTLE
Ross-on-Wye, Herefordshire
HR9 6HY
01600 890538
www.english-heritage.org.uk

GOODWOOD HOUSE
Goodwood, Chichester, West Sussex
PO18 0PX   01243 755000
www.goodwood.co.uk/house

GREAT DIXTER HOUSE
Northiam, Rye, East Sussex
TN31 6PH
01797 252878
www.greatdixter.co.uk

HADDON HALL
Bakewell, Derbyshire DE45 1LA
01629 812855
www.haddonhall.co.uk

HAMPTON COURT PALACE
Surrey KT8 9AU   0870 752 7777
www.hrp.org.uk

HARDWICK HALL
Doe Lea, Chesterfield, Derbyshire
S44 5QJ   01246 850430
www.nationaltrust.org.uk

HARDWICK OLD HALL
Doe Lea, Chesterfield, Derbyshire
S44 5QJ   01246 850431
www.english-heritage.org.uk

HAREWOOD HOUSE
Harewood, Leeds, West Yorkshire
LS17 9LG
0113 2181010
www.harewood.org

HARLECH CASTLE
Harlech LL46 2YH
01766 780552
www.harlech.com

HATFIELD HOUSE
Hatfield, Hertfordshire AL9 5NQ
01707 287010
www.hatfield-house.co.uk

HEATON HALL
Heaton Park, Manchester M25 5SW
0161 773 1231
www.heatonpark.org.uk

Left: Edinburgh Castle.

HELLENS
Much Marcle, Ledbury, Herefordshire
HR8 2LY
01531 660504
www.hellensmanor.com

HERSTMONCEUX CASTLE
Hailsham, Sussex BN27 1RN
01323 834457
www.herstmonceux-castle.com

HEVER CASTLE
Hever, Edenbridge Kent TN8 7NG
01732 865224
www.hevercastle.co.uk

HIGHCLERE CASTLE
Newbury, Berkshire RG20 9LP
01635 253210
www.highclerecastle.co.uk

HOLKHAM HALL
Wells-next-the-Sea, Norfolk NR23 1AB
01328 710227
www.holkham.co.uk

HOLYROODHOUSE PALACE
Canongate, The Royal Mile EH8 8DX
0131 556 5100
www.royalcollection.org.uk

HOUGHTON HALL
Houghton, King's Lynn, Norfolk PE31 6UE
01485 528569
www.houghtonhall.com

HOUSESTEADS ROMAN FORT
near Haydon Bridge, Northumberland
NE47 6NN
01434 344363
www.english-heritage.org.uk

HUGHENDEN MANOR
High Wycombe HP14 4LA
01494 755565
www.nationaltrust.org.uk

IGHTHAM MOTE
Mote Road, Ivy Hatch, Sevenoaks, Kent
TN15 0NT
01732 810378
www.nationaltrust.org.uk

JEWEL TOWER
Abingdon Street, Westminster, London
SW1P 3JX
020 7222 2219
www.english-heritage.or.uk

KEDLESTON HALL
Derby DE22 5JH
01332 842191
www.nationaltrust.org.uk

KENILWORTH CASTLE
Kenilworth, Warwickshire CV8 1NE
01926 852078
www.english-heritage.org.uk

KENSINGTON PALACE
London W8 4PX
0870 751 5170
www.hrp.org.uk

KENWOOD HOUSE
Hampstead Lane, London NW3 7JR
020 8348 1286
www.english-heritage.org.uk

KEW PALACE
Kew Gardens, Kew, Richmond, Surrey
TW9 3AB
0844 482 7777
www.hrp.org.uk

KIDWELLY CASTLE
Kidwelly, West Glamorgan SA17 5BG
01554 890104
cadw.wales.gov.uk

KILLYLEAGH CASTLE
Killyleagh, Downpatrick, Co Down
BT30 9QA
028 4482 8261
www.discovernorthernireland.com

KNEBWORTH HOUSE
Knebworth, Hertfordshire SG3 6PY
01438 812661
www.knebworthhouse.com

KNOLE
Knole, Seveoaks, Kent TN15 0RP
01732 462100
www.nationaltrust.org.uk

LAYER MARNEY TOWER
near Colchester, Essex CO5 9US
01206 330784
www.layermarneytower.co.uk

LEEDS CASTLE
Maidstone, Kent ME17 1PL
01622 765400
www.leeds-castle.com

LEWES CASTLE
169 High Street, Lewes, Sussex
BN7 1YE
01273 486290
www.sussexpast.co.uk

LINLITHGOW PALACE
Linlithgow, West Lothian EH49 7AL
01506 842896
www.historic-scotland.gov.uk

LONGLEAT HOUSE
Longleat, Warminster, Wiltshire
BA12 7NW
01985 844400
www.longleat.co.uk

LOSELEY PARK
Guildford, Surrey GU3 1HS
01483 304440
www.loseleypark.co.uk

LUDLOW CASTLE
Castle Square, Ludlow, Shropshire
SY8 1AY
01584 873355
www.ludlowcastle.com

LULLINGSTONE ROMAN VILLA
Lullingstone Lane, Eynsford, Kent DA4 0JA
01322 863467
www.english-heritage.org.uk

MANDERSTON
Duns, Berwickshire, Scotland TD11 3PP
01361 882636
www.manderston.co.uk

MAPLEDURHAM HOUSE
Mapledurham, Reading RG4 7TR
01189 723350
www.mapledurham.co.uk

Above: Windsor Castle.

MARBLE HILL HOUSE
Richmond Road, Twickenham TW1 2NL
020 8892 5115
www.english-heritage.org.uk

MIDDLEHAM CASTLE
Castle Hill, Middleham, Leyburn,
North Yorkshire DL8 4QR
01969 623899
www.english-heritage.org.uk

MONTACUTE HOUSE
Montacute, Somerset TA15 6XP
01935 823289
www.nationaltrust.org.uk

MUNCASTER CASTLE
Ravenglass, Cumbria CA18 1RQ
01229 717614
www.muncaster.co.uk

NORTON CONYERS
Near Ripon, North Yorkshire
HG4 5EQ
01765 640333
www.ripon.org/norton.php

NOTTINGHAM CASTLE
Nottingham NG1 6EL
0115 9153700
www.nottinghamcity.gov.uk

ORFORD CASTLE
Orford, Woodbridge, Suffolk
IP12 2ND
01394 450472
www.english-heritage.org.uk

Above: Arundel Castle.

OSBORNE HOUSE
Osborne House, Royal Apartments,
East Cowes, Isle of Wight PO32 6JY
01983 200022
www.english-heritage.org.uk

OSTERLEY PARK
Jersey Road, Isleworth, Middlesex
TW7 4RB   020 8232 5050
www.nationaltrust.org.uk

OXBURGH HALL
Oxborough, King's Lynn, Norfolk
PE33 9PS   01366 328258
www.nationaltrust.org.uk

PALACE OF WESTMINSTER
London SW1A 0AA
0844 847 1672
www.parliament.uk/about/
living-heritage/building/palace

PEMBROKE CASTLE
Pembroke SA71 4LA   01646 681510
www.pembroke-castle.co.uk

PENDENNIS CASTLE
Falmouth, Cornwall TR11 4LP
01326 316594
www.english-heritage.org.uk

PENRHYN CASTLE
Bangor LL57 4HN   01248 353084
www.nationaltrust.org.uk

PENSHURST PLACE
Penshurst, near Tonbridge, Kent
TN11 8DG   01892 870307
www.penshurstplace.com

PETWORTH HOUSE
Petworth, West Sussex GU28 0AE
01798 342207
www.nationaltrust.org.uk

PEVENSEY CASTLE
Pevensey, Sussex BN24 5LE
01323 762604
www.english-heritage.org.uk

PEVERIL CASTLE
Market Place, Castleton, Hope Valley
Derbyshire S33 8WQ
01433 620613
www.english-heritage.org.uk

POLESDEN LACEY
Great Bookham, near Dorking, Surrey
RH5 6BD
01372 452048
www.nationaltrust.org.uk

PORTCHESTER CASTLE
Portsmouth, Hampshire PO16 9QW
02392 378291
www.english-heritage.org.uk

PORTLAND CASTLE
Castletown, Portland, Weymouth, Dorset
DT5 1AZ
01305 820539
www.english-heritage.org.uk

POWIS CASTLE
near Welshpool SY21 8RF
01938 551929
www.nationaltrust.org.uk

PRIOR PARK LANDSCAPE GARDEN
Ralph Allen Drive, Bath BA2 5AH
01225 833422
www.nationaltrust.org.uk

QUEEN'S HOUSE, GREENWICH
Park Row, Greenwich, London SE10 9NF
020 8858 4422
www.rmg.co.uk/queens-house

RABY CASTLE
Staindrop, Darlington, Co Durham
DL2 3AH   01833 660202
www.rabycastle.com

RAGLAN CASTLE
Raglan NP5 2BT
01291 690228
cadw.wales.gov.uk

RHUDDLAN CASTLE
Castle Gate, Castle Street, Rhuddlan
LL18 5AD   01745 590777
cadw.wales.gov.uk

RICHMOND CASTLE
Tower Street, Richmond, North Yorkshire
DL10 4QW
01748 822493
www.english-heritage.org.uk

ROCHESTER CASTLE
The Lodge, Rochester-upon-Medway,
Medway ME1 1SW
0870 3331181
www.english-heritage.org.uk

ROUSHAM HOUSE
near Steeple Aston, Bicester, Oxfordshire
OX25 4QX
01869 347110
www.rousham.org

ROYAL PAVILION, THE
Brighton, East Sussex BN1 1EE
03000 290900
www.brighton-hove-rpml.org.uk

ST MAWES CASTLE
St Mawes, Cornwall TR2 3AA
01326 270526
www.english-heritage.org.uk

ST MICHAEL'S MOUNT
Marazion, near Penzance, Cornwall
TR17 0EF
01736 710265
www.stmichaelsmount.co.uk

SANDRINGHAM HOUSE
Sandringham, Norfolk PE35 6EN
01485 545408
www.sandringhamestate.co.uk

SCONE PALACE
Perth PH2 6BD   01738 552300
www.scone-palace.co.uk

SEATON DELAVAL HALL
Seaton Sluice, Whitley Bay,
Northumberland NE26 4QR
0191 237 9100
www.nationaltrust.org.uk

STIRLING CASTLE
Castle Wynd, Stirling FK8 1EJ
01786 450000
www.stirlingcastle.gov.uk

STOKE PARK PAVILIONS
Stoke Bruerne, Towcester,
Northamptonshire
NN12 7RZ
07967 730912
www.statelyhomes.com

STOKESAY CASTLE
near Craven Arms,
Shropshire SY7 9AH
01588 672544
www.english-heritage.org.uk

STOURHEAD
near Warminster BA12 6QD
01747 841152
www.nationaltrust.org.uk

STOWE HOUSE
Contact Visitor Services Manager,
Stowe School, Buckingham MK18 5EH
01280 818229
www.stowe.co.uk

**STOWE LANDSCAPE GARDENS
AND PARK**
near Buckingham MK18 5EH
01280 822850
www.nationaltrust.org.uk

STRAWBERRY HILL
268 Waldegrave Road, Twickenham
TW1 4ST
020 8744 1241
www.strawberryhillhouse.org.uk

SUDELEY CASTLE
Winchcombe, Gloucestershire
GL54 5JD
01242 604357
www.sudeleycastle.co.uk

SULGRAVE MANOR
Manor Road, Sulgrave, Banbury,
Oxfordshire OX17 2SD
01295 760205
www.sulgravemanor.org.uk

SYON HOUSE
Syon Park, Brentford TW8 8JF
020 8569 7497
www.syonpark.co.uk

TATTERSHALL CASTLE
Tattershall, Lincoln LN4 4LR
01526 342543
www.nationaltrust.org.uk

TINTAGEL CASTLE
Tintagel, Cornwall PL34 0HE
01840 770328
www.english-heritage.org.uk

TOWER OF LONDON
London EC3N 4AB   0844 482 7777
www.hrp.org.uk

UPPARK
South Harting, Petersfield GU31 5QR
01730 825415
www.nationaltrust.org.uk

UPTON HOUSE
Banbury, Warwickshire OX15 6HT
01295 670266
www.nationaltrust.org.uk

VYNE, THE
Sherborne St John, Basingstoke RG24 9HL
01256 883858
www.nationaltrust.org.uk

WADDESDON MANOR
Waddeson, near Aylesbury,
Buckinghamshire HP18 0JH
01296 653226
www.waddesdon.org.uk

WALMER CASTLE
Walmer, Deal, Kent CT14 7LJ
01304 364288
www.english-heritage.org.uk

Right: Stourhead.

WARWICK CASTLE
Warwick CV34 4QU
0870 442 2000
www.warwick-castle.com

WESTON PARK
Weston-under-Lizard, near Shifnal,
Shropshire TF11 8LE
01952 852100
www.weston-park.com

WILTON HOUSE
Wilton, Salisbury
SP2 0BJ
01722 746714
www.wiltonhouse.co.uk

**WINCHESTER CASTLE
GREAT HALL**
Winchester SO23 8PJ
01962 846476
www.hants.gov.uk/greathall

WINDSOR CASTLE
Windsor, Berkshire
SL4 1NJ
020 7766 7304
www.windsor.gov.uk or
www.royalcollection.org.uk

WOBURN ABBEY
Woburn, Bedfordshire
MK17 9WA
01525 290333
www.woburn.co.uk

WOLLATON HALL
Wollaton, Nottingham
NG8 2AE
0115 915 3900
www.nottinghamcity.gov.uk

GLOSSARY

architrave Part of the entablature (upper part) of a classical order. The architrave is the lintel (horizontal beam) directly above the top of the column and beneath the frieze. Also the moulded pane of a window or door.

bailey Area enclosed by the walls of a castle; also called 'ward'. Compare motte, the mound on which the keep was built. The most common early Norman castles consisted of a motte (with an, initially, wooden and, later, stone tower) and a bailey enclosed by an earthwork wall topped with a palisade.

barbican Heavily fortified defensive structure, often a double tower, usually built out from the castle gateway.

Baronial Style of Scottish architecture, employed only rarely in England, in vogue from the early 1800s until *c.*1920. The Baronial style used towers with small turrets, stepped gables and crenellations to create the appearance of a 'fairytale castle', such as Balmoral Castle.

Baroque Sensuous and dramatic style in art and architecture, originating in Rome around 1600, that found expression in highly ornamented, monumental buildings set in grand, landscaped parks. English Baroque buildings in *c.*1700–30 are characterized by their dramatic use of space and movement, surface ornamentation and dynamic interaction with their setting. Great examples include Castle Howard and Blenheim Palace.

basilica In ancient Roman buildings, a big public hall.

bastide Walled town built alongside a castle. Originally, a French term, but applied to castle-town developments, such as Conwy in Wales.

bastion Projecting fortification on the curtain wall of a castle.

battlements Low defensive wall or parapet on the top of a castle's curtain wall or its towers, with indented sections (*embrasures* or *crenelles*) and raised parts (*merlons* or *cops*). Battlements were later

Above: Buckingham Palace.

used for decoration to give homes the appearance of a castle.

bay Section of a house's outer wall, defined by vertical features, such as windows, columns and pilasters.

belvedere Raised building or room that commands a fine view.

burgh Anglo-Saxon fortified town.

chinoiserie Originally, French term for interior decoration that mimicked Chinese arts and colour schemes. Starting in the 17th century, chinoiserie remained in vogue until the 19th century.

classical Style in English architecture pioneered by Inigo Jones in the 17th century, inspired by buildings of ancient Greece and Rome and Italian Renaissance interpretations of them. Fine examples of Jones's classical architecture in England are the Queen's House, Greenwich, and the Banqueting Hall, Whitehall. *See also* Palladian.

corbel Projecting bracket in a wall supporting a vault or beam.

cornice Part of the entablature (upper part) of a classical order, consisting of a moulded decoration set horizontally above the frieze. Also (more generally) the moulding between wall and ceiling.

course Continuous line or layer of stones or bricks in a wall.

cupola Dome.

curtain wall A castle's outer wall, linking its towers.

drawbridge Movable bridge across the castle moat. Drawbridges could be moved horizontally or lifted vertically.

dressed stone Trimmed, smoothed and neatly cut stone.

eave Part of a sloping roof that projects over the top of the wall.

English bond In brickwork, the alternating use along a course of the brick ends ('headers') and the brick sides ('stretchers'). *See also* Flemish bond.

entablature The part of the classical order that is above a wall or column. Includes the architrave, the frieze and the cornice.

façade One of the main exteriors of a building, usually containing an entrance.

facing Layer of one material laid over another.

Flemish bond In brickwork, the use of the brick ends ('headers') throughout one course and then the brick sides ('stretchers') throughout the next. *See also* English bond.

fluting Vertical series of grooves cut on classical columns etc. *See also* orders.

frieze Part of the entablature of a classical order, found above the architrave and consisting of decorative sculpted or painted decoration. Also used more generally for a continuous strip of decoration around the upper walls of a room.

gable Triangular profile at the end of a gable-roof (one with two sloping sides). Sometimes, also, a triangular extension above a doorway.

garderobe In castles and medieval houses, a privy or toilet. Alternatively, a walk-in wardrobe.

Gothic Series of styles in medieval architecture *c.*1150–*c.*1500. In England, it applied principally to ecclesiastical architecture: there were no castles or fortified manor houses built in the Gothic style.

Great Hall Main room in the castle or medieval house, used up to Tudor times for dining and social occasions.

ha-ha Sunken ditch creating a hidden boundary between gardens and parkland in a country estate. Invented in the 18th century, it was invisible from the house and was reputedly named after the expression of surprise ('Ha! Ha!') uttered when a visitor chanced upon it. It kept grazing parkland animals out of the gardens.

hammer-beam roof One in which the roof arch is supported by short beams set into the wall at the base of the roof.

keep Most strongly fortified part of a castle, usually containing the lord's apartments and often called the *donjon* (French for 'lordship'). It functioned as a stronghold within the castle to which defenders could retreat if the outer bailey were captured by besiegers. The keep was usually a stone tower standing on the motte, when there was one.

linen-fold panelling Tudor decorative carving of wood, which was made to look like folded linen. An example is the linen-fold panelling screen in the Great Hall at Compton Wynyates.

Long Gallery Feature of Tudor and especially Elizabethan-Jacobean houses, a long room was used as a promenade in bad weather and to display portraits and sculptures. There are fine examples at Hardwick Hall and Montacute.

machicolation Section projecting from the outer face of a castle's curtain wall, with holes in the floor through which the defenders dropped missiles. Strictly, the machicolations were the actual holes.

mathematical tiles Tiles that resemble brick or stone. Used, for example, by Henry Holland to reface Althorp *c*.1790. Brick taxes around this time boosted the popularity of tiles as an alternative to bricks.

moat Man-made ditch surrounding a castle or town walls, usually full of water.

motte Mound on which the keep of a castle was built on an early type

mullion Vertical divider in a window containing more than one pane of glass (light). *See also* transom.

obelisk Tall square column tapering to a pyramidal tip. Obelisks were often raised among temples and other garden buildings in the carefully planned parklands of Baroque and Palladian houses.

orders Column types in ancient Greek and Roman architecture, used in classical, Palladian and Greek Revival English buildings. There are five types: the plain and unornamented Tuscan; Doric, which has triglyphs (channelled blocks) along the frieze; Ionic, which has decoration like a scroll of parchment in the capital (the head of the column); Corinthian, which has decoration representing acanthus leaves on the capital; and Composite, which combines scroll and leaf decoration.

oriel window Projecting window supported by stone brackets or corbels.

Palladian 18th-century development of the classical style in architecture, named after and inspired by the works of the great Italian Renaissance architect Andrea Palladio (1508–80). Holkham Hall and Mereworth Castle are good examples of Palladian country houses.

pediment Raised triangular feature above a portico, door or window. It derived from the triangular gable ends of Greek temples with pitched roofs.

piano nobile Derived from the Italian *palazzo*, the first-floor level containing the main rooms in a classical building.

pilaster Flattened column used for decorative effect on a façade. A pilaster follows the rules of the classical orders. It has no structural function.

portcullis Grill of wood or iron lowered for added defensive strength over a castle gateway.

portico Porch with roof and often pediment supported by columns.

Above: Balmoral Castle.

postern Small, secondary gate (often concealed) in castle or town walls. Members of the garrison could use the postern to make inconspicuous exits and entries or to launch a surprise attack on a besieging force.

revetment Retaining wall of masonry etc supporting the face of an earthen rampart or ditch.

Revival Use by patrons and architects of elements from an earlier architectural style. Examples include the late 18th-century/early 19th-century Greek Revival, and the several allied Victorian movements, such as the Norman, Tudor, Elizabethan and 'Jacobethan' Revivals.

rusticated Stone blocks that have been dressed roughly to suggest strength.

scroll Decorative moulding in the shape of an S.

shingles Wood pieces used in place of tiles.

solar Private chamber, usually on the first floor of a medieval–Tudor house, to which the lord's family could retreat from the public space of the Great Hall. The solar was so called because it was fitted with large windows to allow in as much sunlight as possible.

spandrel Triangular space between an arch and a wall or between two arches.

squints (hidden openings) in a wall.

strapwork Late 16th- and early 17th-century style in ornament, making use of interlaced leather-like bands.

transom Horizontal divider in a window containing more than one pane of glass (light). *See also* mullion.

Left: Conway Castle.

INDEX

ACKNOWLEDGEMENTS

METRO BOOKS
New York

An Imprint of Sterling Publishing
387 Park Avenue South
New York, NY 10016

METRO BOOKS and the distinctive Metro Books logo are trademarks of Sterling Publishing Co., Inc.

© 2014 by Anness Publishing Ltd

Publisher: Joanna Lorenz
Editor: Joy Wotton
Designer: Nigel Partridge
Illustrators: Vanessa Card, Anthony Duke and
   Rob Highton
Production Controller: Mai-Ling Collyer

ISBN: 978-1-4351-1835-5

For information about special sales, and premium and corporate purchases, please contact Sterling Special Sales at 800-805-5489 or specialsales@sterlingpublishing.com.

Manufactured in China

www.sterlingpublishing.com

10 9 8 7 6 5

NOTE
Although the advice and information in this book are believed to be accurate and true at the time of going to press, neither the authors nor the copyright holder can accept any legal responsibility or liability for any errors or omissions that may have been made.

page *1* Henry VIII by Hans Holbein the Younger; page *2* Castle Howard; page *3* The Imperial State Crown; page *511* Bodiam Castle; page *512 bottom left* Elizabeth I by Nicholas Hilliard; page *512 top* George VI and family on VE Day, 1945

PICTURE ACKNOWLEDGEMENTS

Alamy; AA World Travel Library. 325t, 462b; Keith Allan: 418–19; Arcaid: 393bc; Jon Arnold Images: 358br; Tim Ayers: 6; 270–1; Bill Bachmann 66br; Sandra Baker: 258b; Alastair Balderstone: 432b; Roger Bamber: 417tr; Quentin Bargate: 390t; Peter Barritt: 312b, 477br; Pat Behnk: 472bl; BEP 53t; Bildarchiv Monheim GmbH: 7, 49b, 8/b, 259t, 263b, 273t, 361b, 362, 439t, 442–3, 444t, 444bl, 445t, 445b; BL Images Ltd: 263t, 307b, 458t; Michael Booth: 6, 283t, 310–11, 322b, 382–3, 468b, 488bl; G P Bowater: 371b; Brinkstock: 473bl; David Cattanach: 333t; Adrian Chinery: 337t, 392; Gary Cook: 309b; David Copeman: 395b; CW Images: 345tr, 378t; Detail Nottingham: 381tc; Kathy deWitt 38t; Ros Drinkwater: 477t; Patrick Eden 223br; EDIFICE: 373b; Rod Edwards: 436bl; Guy Edwardes Photography: 258t, 321t; Elmtree Images 51tl, 340–1; Bernie Epstein: 281b; Robert Estall photo agency: 292b; Europhotos: 385t; Mary Evans Picture Library 5, 212–13, 222, 348b, 354, 370cr, 459b; eye35.com: 261t, 358bl, 404b, 458b; B E Eyley: 320bl; Paul Felix Photography: 305t, 376br; Joe Fox: 345c, 399t; Alan Gallery: 398t; gkphotography 73b; Chris Gloag: 312t, 313b, 313t; Tim Graham 413br, 464t, 464b; Greenshoots Communications: 475b; Duncan Hale-Sutton: 330t; Robert Harding Picture Library Ltd: 6, 346–7; Andrew Harris: 259b; Mike Haywood: 411tr; John Henshall: 470t; Jeremy Hoare: 290b, 393t; The Hoberman Collection: 413bl; Holmes Garden Photos: 436t; Doug Houghton: 272b; Iconotec 64b, 268, 323b; Image Source 223bl; Imagebroker: 424–5; ISP Photography: 489tr; iX Images: 283b; Michael Jenner: 286t, 322t, 359t, 397b; Hywel Jones: 321b; Justin Kase: 6, 342tc, 364–5, 373t; David Kilpatrick: 463b; Mike Kipling Photography: 294b, 295b, 318t; Ian Leonard: 420tr, 463t, 487tc; Nick Lewis Photography: 462tr; Pawel Libera: 351t; Liquid Light: 299t, 307t; Pedro Luz Cunha: 292t; David Lyons: 262b, 281t, 379b; Manor Photography: 291tr; The Marsden Archive: 478tr; Neil McAllister. 376t, 429b; David Millichope: 306b; Jeff Morgan: 379t, 474t; nagelstock.com 185bl, 359b, 372b, 375b; Eric Nathan 221b, 461tr; Frank Naylor: 388; David Newham: 332b, 329t, 479bl; North Wind Picture Archives: 409t; David Norton Photography: 405b; one-image photography: 302t; Pawel Libera 10b; Peter Packer: 367b, 367t; Derek Payne: 317t; PCL: 476b; John Peter Photography: 491bl; Photofrenetic: 355tl; The Photolibrary Wales: 304b; Pictorial Press Ltd: 417br; David Poole: 264–5; Popperfoto: 357bl, 415b, 482b; Powered by Light/Alan Spencer: 363c; Purestock: 389b; Ben Ramos: 438b; Rob Rayworth: 6, 288–9, 503; David Reed: 336t; Nigel Reed: 361t; Matthew Richardson: 328t; Rolf Richardson: 297, 369b, 456tr; David Robertson 66bl; David Rowland: 325br, 325bl; Ruleofthirds: 492t; Stephen Saks Photography: 331b; David Sanger Photography: 389t; Scottish Viewpoint: 491t; Brian Seed: 351c, 391t; Ian Shaw: 465t; ShelbyImages.com: 296t; Shenval 222t, 422; Simmons Aerofilms Ltd: 272c, 387t, 487b; Skyscan Photolibrary: 273bl, 277t, 286b, 298b, 306t, 360b, 368, 375t, 396t, 423t, 432t, 471t, 475tl; Nigel Stollery: 406t; Homer Sykes: 494bl; Howard Taylor: 278b; John Taylor: 472t; Travel Ink: 302b; Travelshots.com: 477bl; V&A Images: 435b; Darryl Webb: 269b, 293bl; www.white-windmill.co.uk: 324b; David Wootton: 479t; Worldwide Picture Library: 63t, 284t, 323t, 370bl

The Ancient Art & Architecture Collection: 4, 10t, 20–1, 22tl&tr, 23t&b, 24b, 25bl, 31br, 33cr, 50, 60, 61bl&br
The Art Archive: 16b, 34, 35bl, 37, 45t, 48, 55, 72, 86t, 87t, 102t, 115c, 123t, 141b, 148b, 150t&b, 152t, 155t, 159tr, 193bl, 216t, 279t, 279b, 301t, 338t, 396b, 430bl;

Army and Navy Club/Eileen Tweedy 161tr; Ashmolean Museum, Oxford 29b; Biblioteca Nazionale, Turin/Dagli Orti 24t; Bibliotheque des Arts Decoratifs, Paris/Dagli Orti 189b, 219t, 225b, 227b; Bibliotheque Municapale Dijon/Dagli Orti 25br; Bibliotheque Nationale, Paris: 54t, 85b; Birmingham City Art Gallery/Eileen Tweedy 201t; Bodleian Library, Oxford 16t, 27, 28t, 35br, 51b, 64t, 76b, 133t, 210bl; British Library 4, 8, 11tl&tr, 17bl, 26br, 30, 38b, 40–1, 42, 44t&b, 56, 57b, 71t, 90b; British Library/HarperCollins Publishers 17t, 46; British Library/Eileen Tweedy 26bl, 82bl, 205t; Chateau de Blerancourt/Dagli Orti 198t; Chateau de Blois/Dagli Orti 109b; Christ's Hospital/Eileen Tweedy 5, 156–7; Co of Merchants, City of Edinburgh 242; Cornelius de Vries 105t; Culver Pictures 141t, 189t, 193t; Dagli Orti 17br, 18–19, 43, 52t, 215b, 226t, 461tl; Doges' Palace, Venice/Dagli Orti 101bl; Galleria degli Uffizi, Florence/Dagli Orti 106b; Galleria Sabauda, Turin/Dagli Orti 147tr; Gripsholm Castle, Sweden/Dagli Orti 196; Guildhall Library/Eileen Tweedy 68t; Handel Museum, Halle/Dagli Orti 5, 178–9; Jarrold Publishing 11b, 28b, 47t, 52b, 105b, 109tl, 135b, 186, 256, 260b, 274t, 278t, 290t, 291d, 319t, 351b, 391br, 399bl, 423c, 423b, 439b, 453t, 476t, 492b; Mozarteum, Salzburg/Dagli Orti 203b; Musée Calvet, Avignon/Dagli Orti 100t; Musée de la Marine, Paris/Dagli Orti 128t; Musée de la Tapisserie, Bayeux/Dagli Orti 35t, 36, 275b; Musée de Louvre, Paris/Dagli Orti 92; Musée des Beaux Arts, Lausanne/Dagli Orti 124; Musée du Château de Versailles/Dagli Orti 50b, 78t, 96–7, 122bl, 132t, 182, 197br, 211b, 330b; Musée Saint Denis, Reims/Dagli Orti 62t; Musée Thomas Dobree, Nantes/Dagli Orti 86b, 88b; Museo Bibliografico Musicale, Bologna/Dagli Orti 193br; Museo del Prado, Madrid/Dagli Orti 13t, 115b; National Gallery/Eileen Tweedy 57t; Palazzo Barberini, Rome/Dagli Orti 102b, 360t; Palazzo Pitti, Florence/Dagli Orti 120, 144b, 154b; Plymouth Art Gallery/Eileen Tweedy 127b; Private Collection 222bl, 231tl, 232, 234t, 238b; Private Collection MD: 484b, 485t, 479br; Private Collection/Eileen Tweedy: 435tr; San Carlos Museum, Mexico City/Dagli Orti 75tr; Neil Setchfield 206b, 344; Society of Apothecaries/Eileen Tweedy 127t; Tate Gallery, London 171; Eileen Tweedy 185br, 190b; University Library, Geneva/Dagli Orti 139t; Victoria & Albert Museum, London/Sally Chappell 126t, 131b, 215t; Victoria & Albert Museum London/Eileen Tweedy: 350b; John Webb: 394t; Windsor Castle 1, 111
Courtesy of Berkeley Castle Charitable Trust: 320br
The Bridgeman Art Library: Apsley House, The Wellington Museum, London 209br; Archives Larousse, Paris, France 15tr, 233tr; © Ashmolean Museum, University of Oxford: 145t, 273br, 452c; Audley End, Essex 192b; John Bethell/Audley End, Essex: 390b; Bibliotheque Municipale, Arras, France 100b; Blenheim Palace, Oxfordshire: 428; Bolton Museum and Art Gallery, Lancs 166; © Bonhams, London/Private Collection: 444br; British Library, London 4, 31bl, 33b, 80–1, 83tl, 84, 89, 159b, 184tl, 218t; British Library, London/Giraudon 143t; British Museum, London 169t, 187b; © Bronte Parsonage Museum, Haworth, Yorkshire: 335bl; Burghley House Collection, Lincs 134t&b, 441bl;